Agricultural Law and Economics in Sub-Saharan Africa

Agricultural Law and Economics in Sub-Saharan Africa

Cases and Comments

Frederick O. Boadu

*Department of Agricultural Economics and Life Sciences,
Texas A&M University, College Station, TX, United States*

AMSTERDAM • BOSTON • HEIDELBERG • LONDON
NEW YORK • OXFORD • PARIS • SAN DIEGO
SAN FRANCISCO • SINGAPORE • SYDNEY • TOKYO
Academic Press is an imprint of Elsevier

Academic Press is an imprint of Elsevier
125 London Wall, London EC2Y 5AS, UK
525 B Street, Suite 1800, San Diego, CA 92101-4495, USA
50 Hampshire Street, 5th Floor, Cambridge, MA 02139, USA
The Boulevard, Langford Lane, Kidlington, Oxford OX5 1GB, UK

British Library Cataloguing-in-Publication Data
A catalogue record for this book is available from the British Library.

Library of Congress Cataloging-in-Publication Data
A catalog record for this book is available from the Library of Congress.

ISBN: 978-0-12-801771-5

For Information on all Academic Press publications
visit our website at https://www.elsevier.com/

Working together
to grow libraries in
developing countries

www.elsevier.com • www.bookaid.org

Publisher: Nikkie Levy
Acquisition Editor: Nancy Maragioglio
Editorial Project Manager: Billie Jean Fernandez
Production Project Manager: Melissa Read
Designer: Victoria Pearson

Typeset by MPS Limited, Chennai, India

Contents

Table of Cases

Chapter 1 — What Is Agricultural Law?

Chapter 2 — Contracts

Chapter 3 — Contract Farming

Chapter 4 — Agricultural Production and Share Contracts

Chapter 5 — Contracts Involving Illiterate Parties

Chapter 6 — Commercial Law

Chapter 7 — Trademarks and Patents

Chapter 8 — Cooperatives in Sub-Saharan Africa

Chapter 9 — Contracts Governed by International Conventions or Treaties

Chapter 10 — Tort Law

Chapter 11 — Eminent Domain

Chapter 12 — Forest Resources

Chapter 13 — Wildlife Resources

Chapter 14 — Water Resources

Chapter 15 — Environmental Law

Chapter 16 — Transboundary Water Resources and Wetlands

Chapter 18 — Food Safety Regulation

About the Author

Dr Boadu holds advanced degrees in Agricultural Economics and Law. He has taught a survey of Agricultural Law course for over 22 years in the Department of Agricultural Economics at Texas A&M University, College Station, Texas. He has also presented lectures on legal aspects of water resources, climate change, agricultural biosecurity, and bioenergy in the United States and sub-Saharan Africa. Dr Boadu is a member of the State Bar of Texas Committee on Continuing Legal Education in Agricultural Law. He has extensive international development experience and has worked with diverse stakeholders including governments, bilateral and multilateral development institutions, voluntary organizations, and private sector entities. He is a Diplomacy and Risk Policy Fellow of the American Association for the Advancement of Science, and the recipient of several teaching and research awards. He has published widely in law and agricultural economics journals.

Preface

Agricultural Law and Economics in Sub-Saharan Africa: Cases and Comments is the first textbook in the field of agricultural law and economics in sub-Saharan Africa (SSA). The book fills an important gap in the teaching and research on the role of law in improving agricultural performance in SSA. Agricultural law is a specialized area of law that addresses issues important to farmers, the agricultural value chain, and the organization of production, distribution, marketing, and consumption of agricultural goods and services.

The primary motivation for this book is the belief that agricultural law must be incorporated into the curriculum of institutions of higher education in SSA to enhance its role in poverty alleviation. Such incorporation will promote research and teaching innovation to enhance the contribution of the field to making agricultural laws and regulations. This is the approach followed by countries that have successfully incorporated agricultural law into the curriculum. The incorporation has expanded the market for legal services as lawyers have specialized in agricultural law to deliver services to the rural economy, the farm firm, agribusiness, and consumers. Such a market is missing in SSA. This void opens the door for enterprising lawyers to design and promote services to capture benefits from the latent agricultural law market.

The book may be used as a main text or reference source in a traditional economics, agricultural economics, law school, or an interdisciplinary social science course. Agricultural law researchers will find the extensive reference sources useful for international comparative law research and analysis.

About the Book

This book introduces the subject of agricultural law and economics to the higher education curriculum in common law countries in SSA. The book covers the general traditional law topics in contracts, torts, and property, but goes further to introduce cutting-edge and region-relevant topics, including contracts with illiterate parties, contract farming, climate change, and transboundary water issues. The book is supported by an extensive list of reference materials, study and enrichment exercises to deepen students' understanding of the principles discussed in the book.

Sources of Court Cases Used in the Book

Cases from the countries below were obtained from The Southern African Legal Information Institute, under open access in line with the objectives of the global Free Access to Law Movement. Permission to use these cases is on file with author. Permission to use cases from all other countries are on file with the author.

Botswana
Kenya
Lesotho
Malawi
Namibia
South Africa
Tanzania
Uganda
Zambia
Zimbabwe

Acknowledgments

I wish to express my sincerest thanks and appreciation to Hope Boadu, my wife, and to my children, Kwabena, Koko, and Amma who patiently tolerated the many hours of work on the book. Certainly writing the book would have been extraordinarily difficult if I did not have my two grandchildren, Austen and Lauren, to break the monotony and loneliness with their constant demand to play a game of "magic" with them.

CHAPTER 1

What Is Agricultural Law?

Keywords: Agricultural law; sources of law in your country; common law; written law; latent market; civil action; criminal action; court delay; court costs; plaintiff; defendant; evidence; parol evidence

1.1 Introduction

Agricultural law consists of the laws, regulations, decrees, treaties, and institutions (universities, financial and marketing systems, transportation) that govern the agricultural supply chain (production, marketing, and sales). The central focus is agriculture production (Kershen, 2008; Schneider, 2009). The growth of agricultural law in the United States and Europe has been influenced by the intellectual leadership made possible by the integration of agricultural law into the traditional law school curriculum, and by the participation of a knowledgeable industry/practitioner group that strengthens the industry- and client-based applied focus of agricultural law (Schneider, 2009). Some land grant institutions in the United States teach agricultural law at the undergraduate level in the department of agricultural economics. These schools also have lawyers working with the extension services serving farmers and the food industry. There is no law school in sub-Saharan Africa (SSA) with a formal agricultural law curriculum, and only a few lawyers in Africa list their practice areas to include agricultural law.

Law schools in SSA are currently not preparing lawyers to respond adequately to the needs of farmers, agricultural input suppliers, rural and urban communities, food processors, transporters, warehouses, and environmental groups. Consequently, legal and institutional issues related to contracting in agriculture, food safety and standards, agriculture lending, trade, land use, natural resources, and the environment are not being adequately addressed. A formal agricultural law curriculum in SSA law schools, economics, and agricultural economics departments will serve as a catalyst for the growing number of practitioners willing to explore markets for legal services focusing on agriculture and the food industry.

F.O. Boadu: Agricultural Law and Economics in Sub-Saharan Africa.
DOI: http://dx.doi.org/10.1016/B978-0-12-801771-5.00001-0

1.2 The Law and Economics Approach

This book introduces a law and economics approach to teaching agricultural law. This is the first application of this approach and is intended to emphasize the interconnectedness of law and economics and also the fact that agricultural law is today being taught in law schools, agricultural economics, and traditional economics departments. Economic analysis of law applies the tools of microeconomic theory to the analysis of legal rules and institutions (Posner, 2007). The Coase theorem is a central concept in law and economics and has spawned an extensive literature on the relationship between law and economics (Coase, 1961).[1] The theorem can be explained with a simple example.[2] Consider the following:

> A Fulani cattle herder is grazing cattle on open land and causing harm to five crop farmers. Each farmer suffers £75 worth of damage for total damage of £375.

The crop damage can be eliminated in one of two ways:

> Install a fence that costs £150.
> Buy each farmer a cattle trap that costs £50 each for a total of £250 (5 × £50).

Clearly the efficient solution is to install a screen for £150.

Consider the following two situations:

> If the farmers are entitled to safe crops, the cattle herder has three choices: (1) destroy the crops and pay damages equal to £375; (2) install a fence at cost of £150; or (3) buy cattle traps for the farmers costing £250. The efficient solution is to install a fence costing £150.
> If the cattle herder is entitled to graze anywhere, even if crops are destroyed in the process, the farmers have three choices: (1) suffer crop damages equal to £375; (2) purchase cattle traps at a cost of £250; or (3) install a fence for the cattle herder at a cost of £150. Again, the efficient solution is to install a fence costing £150 for the cattle herder.

The example shows that the efficient solution does not depend on the *initial allocation of entitlements*, that is, whether the cattle herder has a right to graze cattle anywhere or the farmers have a right to safe crops. This means, in the absence of factors that restrain the herders and the farmers from negotiating, the parties on their own would negotiate to an efficient outcome. The theory suggests that the main reason we do not observe widespread negotiations is due to the presence of *transaction costs*. Transaction costs consist of (1) information costs; (2) bargaining costs; and (3) policing (monitoring) costs (Johnson, 2005).[3]

Parties to a negotiation need information about each other and the subject matter of the negotiation. Obtaining such information could be quite costly. Bargaining is also costly, especially when one party engages in strategic behavior. For example, in a case where one party is entitled to safe crops, the party could engage in a *holdout* and insist that cattle herders be banned altogether even though the efficient result could be some type of compensation payment. Even after bargaining, one party may cheat. This imposes costs on the good party in terms of monitoring or policing the arrangement. What the Coase theorem teaches is that laws and regulations to promote the evolution of efficient markets should help to reduce the transaction costs so that parties on their own could negotiate to an efficient outcome in interaction with each other. As the reader goes through the decisions rendered by courts it is useful to ask how the courts are issuing decisions that promote, institution-building, justice, and efficiency to help society achieve maximum social benefits through private negotiations and interactions.

1.3 Sources of Law in SSA Common Law Countries

The sources of law in common law countries in SSA are uniformly based on a mixture of English common law and the customary law that existed in the country before of the introduction of English law. The sources of law in SSA common law countries include, the Constitution, laws passed by the legislature or Parliament of the country, customary law, and the common law.[4] Countries have defined their laws to reflect their diverse historical, ethnic, and religious backgrounds and experiences. For example, the sources of law in Kenya include Indian and Muslim sources given the significant non-African and Muslim groups in the country.[5] There is significant Roman-Dutch influence in the laws of Lesotho even though South African precedents are only persuasive (Dube). Nigerian sources of law also reflect the diverse cultural and religious background of the country. In addition to Islamic law, certain regions of the country also practice *Sharia Law*, "the principal feature being the introduction of religious based criminal offences, especially on matters of morality and the introduction of punishments sanctioned by the Koran" (Dina et al.).

The Ghana Constitution defines the common law as "the rules generally known as the common law, the rules generally known as the doctrines of equity and the rules of customary law including those determined by the Superior Court of Judicature."[6] The law did not completely replace the existing customary law and practices of the colony so long as such law or custom was not "repugnant to natural justice, equity or good conscience, nor incompatible either directly or by necessary implication with any enactment of the Colonial Legislature."[7]

Common law countries in SSA are gradually evolving their own "common law." For example, a "Ghanaian common law"[8] has emerged out of Ghanaian courts' interpretation of English law in the Ghanaian context. This trend is also observed in other SSA countries. The ability of courts to fashion a common law consistent with market-led growth raises two issues. First, jurisdictions in advanced countries that accepted the common law shared similar cultural and economic backgrounds with England. Countries in SSA, on the other hand, have a fundamentally different culture, and are only recently pursuing a market-led development approach. The customary rules under which individuals in SSA countries organized their affairs before the introduction of British rule may be inadequate to support the modernization of the country. As Professor Seidman points out, "excepting problems of land tenure, most of the claims made upon customary law are not claims of development" (Seidman, 1968). This is especially true today when the winds of globalization are moving countries towards new law and regulatory governance regimes that defy the institutional set-up of any single country.[9] One example of this evolving common legal regime is the United Nations Convention on Contracts for the International Sale of Goods (CISG), which "establishes a comprehensive code of legal rules governing the formation of contracts for the international sale of goods, the obligations of the buyer and seller, remedies for breach of contract and other aspects of the contract. The Convention entered into force on 1 January 1988."[10] Buscaglia considers the globalization phenomenon as a powerful force in legal transplantation.[11]

1.4 Written and Unwritten Law

In the common law tradition, decisions rendered by courts become a part of the law. Thus, law in Ghana consists of those made by the Parliament and those decisions made by courts in the country. These decisions by courts are sometimes referred to as "judge-made rules of law or precedents." These are laws because in the common law tradition, judges must follow the decisions from previous court rulings if the facts of a present case are the same as the facts that supported a previous ruling.[12]

1.5 Pressures on the Legal System

There is broad agreement that court costs, court delays, access, and complexity are the main challenges facing the court systems in countries in SSA.[13] The World Bank group has produced research and indices that help in assessing the empirical evidence on the extent to which these challenges impact the economic development goals of countries in SSA. Countries in SSA do poorly in terms of managing court delays, costs, and access compared to other countries around the world.[14]

1. *The Cost of Using the Legal System and Access to Courts*
    The cost of using the legal system may be viewed from both demand and supply perspectives. On the demand side, households and firms are unable to use the services of lawyers and the courts due to low household incomes. One legal expert has observed that, "in Ghana, there are whole regions where almost everyone qualifies for legal aid: 7 of 10, 8 of 10, and 9 of 10 in the Central and Northern Regions; the Upper East

Region, and the Upper West Region respectively" (Atuguba, 2007). Kenya's recent *Legal Aid Law* states, *inter alia*, "the objects and purposes of this Act are to establish a legal institutional framework to facilitate (a) provision of affordable, accessible, sustainable, credible and accountable legal aid services to indigent persons in Kenya at State expense in accordance with the Constitution" (Commission for the Implementation of the Constitution, 2013). The supply of legal services is constrained by both human and financial resources. Courts lack trained librarians and have poor technology infrastructure to support the processing of cases. Library resources are limited and lawyers and judges are unable to produce services at low cost.[15] Though not an exact measure, the cost of enforcing a contract gives some indication of the cost of using the legal system. According to the World Bank, the cost of enforcing a contract is 83.1% of the claim in Zimbabwe, 69.1% in Malawi, and 57.7% in Nigeria. Most countries have percentage costs above 30%. Ghana and Tanzania have lower percentage costs at 23% and 14.3%, respectively (World Bank, 2014).

2. *Court Delay*

A major problem facing the court system in SSA countries is delay in disposing of cases. Delays in case disposal lead to loss of confidence in using the system and encourage resort to costly non-judicial methods of dispute resolution. The delay problem has the potential to discourage investments and risk-taking, especially since it affects contract enforcement, an important component of a free market system. To put the discussion in perspective, consider the number of days and procedures one has to go through in enforcing a contract in an SSA country. In Singapore, ranked the most friendly country to do business, it takes an average of 150 days and 21 procedures to enforce a contract compared to, for example, 710 days and 38 procedures in Ghana, 611 days and 35 procedures in Zambia, and 509.8 days and 40.2 procedures in Nigeria (World Bank, n.d.).[16]

Several factors have combined to produce the backlog or delays in the courts. At one end of the spectrum are institutional rigidities, such as a failure on the part of an attorney to properly file an action and consequently having to refile if the period within which an action may be brought has not expired. In this context, stricter enforcement of court rules of procedure is needed to check unending adjournments and frustrations in using the courts (Kom, 1988). It is also important for investigating agencies to be diligent in investigations to avoid technical problems during trials (Agyemang, 1988). Court delays are also caused by the lack of court technology infrastructure and personnel. Most courts do not have recording equipment so judges have to record proceedings in longhand, a time-consuming process. The courts lack hardware such as typewriters, photocopy machines, telephones, shelf space, and cabinets, and the country's law libraries are poorly stocked. The effect of the poor infrastructure is that information processing is slow and consequently there are delays in case disposal. The delay problem has not been adequately addressed by policy makers.

3. *Jurisprudential Dissonance*

A society in which customary laws operate side-by-side with transplanted modern law faces what might best be described as "jurisprudential dissonance." Laws governing modern market practices are simply unknown to customary law (Seidman, 1968). In essence, the evolution of laws in SSA to support economic development may be described as a "work in progress," whereby the courts are struggling to fashion rules that promote efficient market interaction without sacrificing the rich cultural values that bind participants in the market place.

1.6 Court Process in Sub-Saharan Africa

While there may be slight modifications in procedure in the various SSA countries, civil litigation normally will proceed as follows, using Ghana as an example. Parties have several options for resolving disputes that arise between them. When a dispute arises, one party or both may choose litigation before a court, settle the dispute between them, or engage a third party as an arbitrator or mediator to settle the dispute.

If the parties decide to resolve the issue in court, one of the parties will file a *civil action*.[17] A civil action is an action brought to "enforce, redress, or protect private rights." An example of a civil action is an action to collect a debt or to stop another person from using your land without permission. A *criminal action* on the other hand is an action brought to establish the guilt or innocence of an individual for violation of a law. The party bringing a civil action is known as the *plaintiff* and the party against whom an action is brought is known as the *defendant*. The plaintiff in a civil action is another private individual while the state represented by the Attorney-General is the plaintiff in a criminal action. The penalty in a civil action is usually money damages against the loser, while a person may be imprisoned when found guilty in a criminal action. The constitution of Ghana makes it possible for citizens to participate in the production of justice through service on juries, participation in the public tribunal system, and assessor systems.

1.7 The Law and Economics of Evidence

Evidence has been defined as "any species of proof, or probative matter, legally presented at the trial of an issue, by the act of the parties and through the medium of witnesses, records, documents, exhibits, concrete objects, etc. for the purpose of inducing beliefs in the minds of the court or jury as to their contention" (Black, 1990). The definition found in most of the common law jurisdictions in Africa is consistent with the general dictionary definition. For example, Uganda's Evidence Act states, "evidence" denotes the means by which any alleged matter of fact, the truth of which is submitted to investigation, is proved or disproved and includes statements by accused persons, admissions, judicial notice, presumptions of law, and ocular observation by the court in its judicial capacity."[18] The rules of evidence are often detailed in a statute but sources of evidence are varied and depend on the nature of the issue at hand.[19]

The economic analysis of evidence law falls under the broader topic of the economics of procedural rules. Procedural rules in general are intended to maximize efficiency in the administration of justice by "minimization of the sum of two types of costs: 'error costs' (the social costs generated when a judicial system fails to carry out the allocative or other social functions assigned to it), and the 'direct costs' (such as lawyers,' judges,' and litigants' time of operating the legal dispute-resolution machinery. Evidence rules are focused primarily on the fact-finding aspect of the litigation process." One rule of evidence that helps to minimize "error costs" and direct costs is the commonly invoked *parol evidence rule*. The rules of evidence in Nigeria are found in the *Evidence Act* Chapter 112 of the Laws of the Federation of Nigeria 1990.[20] Part VI of the Nigeria Act references this rule, which states in part, "When any judgement of any court or any other judicial or official proceedings, or any contract, or any grant or other disposition of property has been reduced to the form of a document or series of documents, no evidence may be given of such judgement or proceedings, or of the terms of such contract, grant or disposition of property extents in cases in which secondary evidence is admissible under the provisions hereinbefore contained; nor may the contents of any such document be contradicted, altered, added to or varied by oral evidence."[21] What the rule means is that once intentions of a party are reduced to writing, no evidence may add, vary, or contradict the written terms. This rule has been uniformly applied in common law countries in SSA. The Zimbabwe Supreme Court case, *Sarudzayi Nhundu v (1) Phineas Chivazve Chiota (2) The Registrar of Deeds*, the Malawi High Court case, *Joseph Chidanti-Malunga v FINTEC Consultants* (1st Defendant) & *BUA Consulting Engineers* (2nd Defendant) (Malawi), and the Uganda case, *Akugoba Boda Boda Transport Development Services Ltd. v (1) Sun Auto Company Ltd and (2) Hajji Swaibu Kizito* define and apply the parol evidence rule.[22] The *Quist v Akuaba case* (Ghana) (footnote 23) discusses some of the exceptions to the parol evidence rule.

Sarudzayi Nhundu v (1) Phineas Chivazve Chiota; (2) The Registrar of Deeds

Supreme Court of Zimbabwe
Harare, March 5, 2007 & October 1, 2007
Cheda JA, Ziyambi JA & Malaba JA

ZIYAMBI JA

At the end of the hearing we dismissed this appeal with costs. The following are our reasons for so doing. The first respondent, to whom I shall refer as "the respondent", and the

(Continued)

(Continued)

appellant concluded an agreement of sale in respect of property known as 139 Rietfontein, Rietfontein Township, Harare ("the property"). Clause 2 of the agreement provided that the purchase price for the property was Z$28 billion and Clause 11 provided that:

> The parties acknowledge that this document constitutes the entire agreement between them and that no other terms, conditions, stipulations, warranties or representations whatsoever have been made by them or their agents other than those set out in this agreement and the parties agree that no variation of this agreement shall be binding on them unless first reduced to writing and signed by both parties.

The agreement was signed by the parties on 25 January 2006 at the offices of the Central African Building Society ("CABS"). Immediately upon signature by the parties, CABS gave instructions to its attorneys to attend to the registration of a bond which was to facilitate the registration of transfer and payment of the purchase price to the appellant.

On 30 January 2006, the appellant wrote a letter to CABS advising that she had cancelled the agreement of sale. The letter reads in relevant part:

> I write to inform you that I have cancelled sale of my house (Known as stand No 139 Rietfontein Township) to Mr Phineas Chivazve Chiota. I have informed him in writing. Cancelled is agreement of sale dated 25 January 2006. Thus done at your Platinum Office. Attached is a copy of my letter to him.

A similar letter was written to the respondent. It read:

> I hereby write to inform you that I have cancelled our agreement of sale of my house dated 25 January 2006. I have sent a copy of this letter to CABS. Also attached is a copy of a letter which I wrote to CABS.

The respondent was of the view that there was no basis for the cancellation since he had committed no breach of the agreement nor had any breach been cited in the letter. He therefore refused to accept the cancellation and sought redress in the High Court by way of an interim interdict restraining the appellant from disposing of the property to a third party. He obtained a provisional order granting the interim interdict sought and requiring the appellant to show cause why a final order compelling the transfer should not be issued in his favour.

The appellant opposed the confirmation of the provisional order. In her opposing affidavit, she claimed that the respondent had breached a condition precedent to the agreement, namely, that the respondent, who was then Deputy Minister of Industry and International Trade, orally agreed to make available to her two licences: one for the buying and selling of sugar; and the other for buying and selling of petroleum. For this reason, so she averred, the purchase price was pegged at the low price of 28 billion dollars as she would be able to trade with those licences and obtain, from so doing, such profits as would offset the low price at which the house was being sold. The agreement of sale, she stated, was reluctantly signed at CABS because the respondent had not, at the time of signature thereof, honoured the verbal

(Continued)

(Continued)

agreement by issuing the two licences to her. She did not give a date by which the alleged oral agreement was to be performed.

At the hearing for confirmation of the provisional order, the issues for determination by the trial court were whether the appellant had established that there was an oral agreement amounting to a condition precedent governing the written agreement signed by the parties and if so was the respondent in breach of that agreement; and, whether the cancellation by the appellant was valid. The learned Judge decided the issues in favour of the respondent and granted the final order against which the appellant now appeals to this Court.

The appellant submitted in this Court that the written contract is not a true representation of what the parties agreed and therefore evidence ought to be admitted to establish the "real and genuine agreement", which is, that the sale was subject to the oral condition precedent. It was contended on behalf of the respondent that the entire agreement between the parties is contained in the written contract and that the parol evidence rule prohibits the leading of extrinsic evidence to prove the existence of the alleged oral condition precedent.

The parol evidence rule was stated by WATERMEYER JA in *Union Government v Vianini Ferro-Concrete Pipes (Pvt) Ltd* [1941] AD 43 at P 47, where he said:

Now this Court has accepted the rule that when a contract has been reduced to writing, the writing is, in general, regarded as the exclusive memorial of the transaction and in a suit between the parties no evidence to prove its terms may be given save the document or secondary evidence of its contents, nor may the contents of such document be contradicted, altered, added to or varied by parole evidence.

See also *The law of Contract in South Africa 3* ed by R H Christie at p 212.

However, the learned JUDGE OF APPEAL went on to say further at the same page:

Whatever may be the correct view as to the precise nature of the rules, it is clear that they do not prevent a party from setting up the case that the contract is not a presently enforceable contract inasmuch as it is conditional upon the happening of some event which has not occurred.

Thus the parol evidence rule does not preclude extrinsic evidence that the contract is conditional upon the happening of an event which has not occurred. However, if the object of leading such extrinsic evidence is not only to prove the alleged oral condition precedent but to incorporate it into the agreement of sale and then to enforce the said condition by relying on the respondent's failure to comply therewith then the extrinsic evidence would be inadmissible. See *Philmatt (Pvt) Ltd v Masselbank Development CC* [1996] (2) SA 15 (A) at p 23. See also *Johnston v Leal* [1980] (3) SA 927 (A) at 943 where CORBETT JA remarked:

Dealing first with the integration rule, it is clear to me that the aim and effect of this rule is to prevent a party to a contract which has been integrated into a single and complete written memorial from seeking to contradict, add to or modify the writing by reference to extrinsic evidence and in that way to redefine the terms of the contract. The object of the party seeking to adduce such extrinsic

(Continued)

(Continued)

evidence is usually to enforce the contract as redefined or, at any rate, to rely upon the contractual force of the additional or varied terms, as established by the extrinsic evidence. . ..

And later on the same page:

To sum up, therefore, the integration rule prevents a party from altering, by the production of extrinsic evidence, the recorded terms of an integrated contract in order to rely upon the contract as altered.

The appellant herein seeks, firstly, to prove that, contrary to the provisions of clause 11 *supra*, there was a condition precedent governing the contract and, secondly, to enforce that condition so proved. In so doing, the appellant was seeking to redefine the terms of the contract. The parol evidence rule precludes her from leading extrinsic evidence with that objective. See also *Philmatt (Pvt) Ltd v Masselbank Development supra*.

In any event, even assuming for an instant that the court had been persuaded to allow parol evidence of the oral condition precedent, the evidence on record does not support the existence of such an oral agreement as the learned Judge correctly found. It was common cause at the hearing that the appellant's friend and confidante, Biata Nyamupinga ("Biata"), was actively involved in the negotiations preceding the conclusion and signature of the agreement. Biata averred in her supporting affidavit that no such condition precedent was ever discussed during the negotiations or at any time before the signature of the agreement by the parties. She relates the events following the offer of 28 billion dollars by the first respondent for the property as follows:

The applicant [the respondent] and [the appellant] shook hands and hugged each other after signing the agreement. All the dealings between the applicant [the respondent] and [the appellant] involved me as I was in essence the link between the two. At no stage during the negotiations for the sale of this property was there any discussion of the licenses that [the appellant] has referred to. This is the first time that I have heard of these licences. Such an issue never formed the basis of the agreement. The [appellant] was selling because of mounting debts. She owed me and several other people in town huge sums of money. The purchase price would have enabled her to pay off all debts and then acquire a smaller property.

Further, the respondent averred, and this was not contradicted, that neither of the two licences allegedly offered by him to the appellant fell within the mandate of his Ministry. In any event, since the alleged condition precedent had not been fulfilled there is no reason given in the papers as to why the appellant signed the agreement of sale and why, when she later cancelled the agreement, no reason was given for such cancellation.

In view of the above, we were satisfied that the judgment of the court *a quo* was unassailable and that the appeal was accordingly devoid of merit.

Joseph Chidanti-Malunga v FINTEC Consultants (1st Defendant) & BUA Consulting Engineers (2nd Defendant)

High Court of Malawi, Blantyre Registry
Commercial Case No. 6 of 2008 (June 25th 2008)
Hon. Justice Dr. M.C. Mtambo

Facts

FINTEC is an Egyptian firm that won an irrigation contract with the Government of Malawi. FINTEC was working with a local consulting firm, BUA, that in turn had hired the Plaintiff Malunga. All Egyptian personnel fell under the first Defendant while all Malawian personnel fell under the second Defendant. When FINTEC was ready to start the project, the plaintiff was out of the country and was removed from the contract. Plaintiff has brought this action claiming that there is a collateral contract between him and BUA to the effect that he would serve as Site/Resident Engineer. Plaintiff has filed this action for breach of contract and asking for damages to the tune of US$62,370.00.

The court addressed the following several issues including below on parol evidence:

i. Whether the Plaintiff can adduce parol evidence to show that the agreement for the provision of irrigation services was infact between the Malawi Government and both Defendants when the agreement clearly states that it is between the Malawi Government and the first Defendant.

Parol evidence

Parol evidence will not be allowed to add or alter the terms of a contract. This includes an allegation that some other party other than the party in fact appearing in the contract ought to have been the actual party. In the *Zeyaur Rahman Hashmi v DHL Express case*, the Plaintiff attempted to adduce parol evidence to show that even though it was Finance Bank Limited that appeared to be a party to the contract, the actual party was him only that he was a top official at Finance Bank Limited. Kapanda, J stated:

The question then becomes whether oral evidence can be adduced to add to the express written stipulations in a contract. Put differently, can the Plaintiff be allowed to adduce oral evidence to dispute the fact that the circumstances appearing in the express written contract herein were different from what they in fact prima- facie appear to be. Indeed, can the Plaintiff at this late lay evidence that the parties to the contract were not Finance Bank of Malawi Limited and the Defendant as is clearly shown on "PF1" but that it was himself and the Defendant.

The learned judge concluded:

It is obvious from the foregoing authorities that oral or extrinsic evidence cannot be tendered to vary or add to the terms of an express contract. The contract hence remains as it is expressly appearing i.e. that it is between Finance Bank of Malawi Limited and the Defendant.

(Continued)

(Continued)

And in *K.S. Kamwendo v Bata Shoe Company Malawi Limited*, Civil Cause Number 2380 of 2003, Mkandawire, J stated:

> *Rules on documentary evidence are very clear that a document speaks for itself. One cannot introduce parol evidence to contradict a document.*

As such, learned Counsel for the Defendant argues that as the main contract the subject matter of this action clearly spelt that the parties thereto are the Malawi Government and the first Defendant, the Plaintiff cannot bring parol evidence to show that in fact the second Defendant was also a party to the contract.

Ruling

The parties to the main contract are clearly stated to be the Malawi Government and the first Defendant. The Plaintiff cannot therefore bring extrinsic evidence to show otherwise that it is in fact between the Malawi Government and both Defendants.

I accordingly dismiss the Plaintiff's claim.

Akugoba Boda Boda Transport Development Services Ltd v Sun Auto Company Ltd v Hajji Swaibu Kizito

The Republic of Uganda
In the High Court of Uganda at Kampala
(Commercial Court Division)
HCT-00-CC-CS-0501-2006 AND HCT-00-CC-CS-0759-2006

The Honorable Mr. Justice Yorokamu Bamwine

Facts

Akugoba Boda Boda Transport Development Services Ltd, herein after conveniently referred to as 'Akugoba' where the context allows, is a Limited Liability company. It sued the defendant, Sun Auto Company Ltd, also a Limited liability company, for specific performance by way of delivery of registration number plates for 20 motorcycles, recovery of a certificate of title for land, recovery of one motor vehicle, general damages, interest and costs of the suit.

In its written statement of defence, Sun Auto Company denied dealing with Akugoba. It claimed that it had dealt with a one Hajji Swaibu Kizito in his individual capacity, which Hajji Kizito executed the sale agreement and offered his own property as security for the debt.

As the hearing came to a close, it transpired that Sun Auto Company had indeed instituted a separate suit against Hajji Swaibu Kizito which suit was founded on the same facts. In that suit, HCCS No. 759/2006, Sun Auto Company claims a sum of Shs.26,160,000 = being the balance due to it out of the sale of 20 motorcycles, the subject matter also in HCCS No. 501

(Continued)

(Continued)

of 2006. In order to save Court's time and because the issues in both cases revolve around who the correct parties to the contract were, both counsel proposed, and Court accepted the proposal, that the two suits be consolidated. Hence this judgment.

No point of agreement was generated at the Scheduling Conference. Three issues were framed for Court's determination in HCCS No. 501/2006:

1. Whether the plaintiff and the defendant entered into any contract.
2. The terms of the contract, if any.
3. Whether the plaintiff is entitled to the reliefs sought.

I will answer the same in the context of both suits.

Opinion

First, whether the plaintiff (AKUGOBA) and the defendant (Sun Auto Company Ltd) entered into any contract.

A contract is simply an agreement enforceable at law. An essential feature of a contract is a promise by one party to another to do or forbear from doing certain specified acts. One party has to make an offer to the other, who in turn must accept the offer, thus formulating an agreement. The agreement may be oral or written. Where complaints of breach are raised, as herein, and it so happens that the parties had reduced their agreement to writing, Courts resort to the said written agreements as an embodiment of the conditions and terms of the contract. And this brings me now to the parol evidence rule.

The parol evidence rule is to the effect that evidence cannot be admitted (or that even if admitted, it cannot be used) to add to, vary or contradict a written instrument. In relation to written contracts, the rule means that where a contract has been reduced to writing, neither party, can rely on evidence of terms alleged to have been agreed, which is extrinsic document, i.e. not contained in it. This rule is fundamental in interpretation of contracts.

In the instant case, the basis of the relationship between the parties is a Sale Agreement, D. Exh. 1. The opening paragraph runs as follows:

> *On behalf of M/S Sun Auto Company, I have transacted (sold) the above mentioned motor vehicle/ cycle to Mr/Mrs/Miss Hajji Swaibu Kizito c/o Akugoba boda boda Transport Ltd.*

In law a company and its Managing Director are totally different and distinct persons. It is settled law that a company is a distinct legal entity, separate from such persons as may be members of it, and having legal rights and duties. It may enter into contracts in its own right, own property, pay taxes, employ people and be liable for torts and crimes. These are fundamental attributes of corporate personality recognized long ago in *Solomon v Solomon & Co. Ltd* [1897] AC 22.

From the agreements, the company, Akugoba, was used merely as the address of Hajji Swaibu Kizito. As such, the presumption is that it had no interest in the transaction. It cannot incur liability under it or take advantage of it. The reason is simple: no stranger to the

(Continued)

(Continued)

consideration can take advantage of a contract although made for his benefit. Only a person who is a party to the contract can sue on it.

At the hearing, DW1 Mulinde testified that the person his company transacted business with was Hajji Swaibu Kizito. He did not know him or his company before the incident. He asked for motorcycles on credit and he gave him 20 of them. As security for the payment, Kizito surrendered to the seller his own certificate of title in respect of land described as Block 205 Plot 78 Kyaggwe. On top of that he surrendered to the seller his own vehicle, a Pajero Reg. No. UAF 238 D. The two documents are indeed in the names of Hajji Swaibu Kizito.

From the evidence, Court is satisfied that the transaction was between Sun Auto Company Ltd and Hajji Swaibu Kizito. Akugoba was used as Kizito's contact address. In all these circumstances, Court makes a finding that the contract was between those two persons, Sun Auto Company Ltd and Hajji Swaibu Kizito.

I now turn to the terms of the contract.

Both parties agree that the contract document is what was tendered in evidence, D. Exh.1. It is a standard form agreement, with terms and conditions printed in clear green ink. They are:

1. The buyer shall gain full ownership after paying the outstanding balance and the interest thereof B (iii) and meet the transfer costs in his names.
2. In the event of not fulfilling the outstanding balance the company shall repossess the above mentioned vehicle/cycle i.e. after the elapse of the agreed period and sell it to off set the balance and interest; plus the costs incurred in recovery and the balance shall be given to the buyer.
3. In case of motor cars, ..."

The balance stated in the document is Shs.31, 600,000; the date of delivery is 18/7/2005; and the agreed period 5 months only. It is argued for the plaintiff in HCCS No. 501/2006 that the terms were already written, favouring the defendant company. For as long as the terms were clear, not ambiguous, and were duly discussed, I do not see any problem with them to write home about.

It is further argued that the parties agreed that the defendant would deliver the number plates of the motor cycles within a period of 14 days. No such promise appears in the Sale Agreement. It is trite that where the contract is in writing, its terms can be ascertained by means of documentary evidence. Where they are clear, a Court must give them effect. It is therefore not the duty of the Court to re-write an expressly stated contract for the parties. As long as both parties address themselves to the terms of the contract and agree to be bound by them, the duty of the Court is to construe the agreement as it was when it was executed.

From the evidence of DW1 Mulinde and the Sale Agreement itself, the parties agreed that the buyer would gain full ownership of the cycles after paying the outstanding balance. Evidence about the purported giving out of the number plates within 14 days is extrinsic document. It is inadmissible, and even if admitted, it cannot be used to add to, vary or contradict a written instrument, D. Exh. 1.

(Continued)

(Continued)

I now turn to remedies.

From the evidence of DW1 Mulinde, which I found truthful, after the negotiations, Hajji Swaibu Kizito agreed to take the motor cycles on credit. DW1 agreed. Hajji Kizito issued his company's post-dated cheques to the seller and on top of the cheques pledged his own land and vehicle as security for payment. The goods were specific, ascertained and in a deliverable state. They were for a stated price.

Section 19 of the Sale of Goods Act provides that where there is an unconditional contract for the sale of specific goods in a deliverable state, the property in the goods passes to the buyer when the contract is made, and it is immaterial whether the time of payment or the time of delivery or both are postponed. This is subject to the intention of the parties. In view of this Court's finding that the agreement of the parties was that the buyer gains full ownership after paying the outstanding balance, their intention was that property in them would not pass till then. In cases of this nature, certain factors must be considered before damages can be calculated. One of these factors is the role of the injured party following the breach: he is expected to do what he can to look after his own interest. He must in other words mitigate his loss.

From the evidence, while Hajji Kizito claims that he had agreed with Mulinde that number plates would be given to him within 14 days, which he didn't, he (Kizito) went ahead and in turn sold them to third parties without the said number plates. The unpaid for cycles could not therefore be recovered from Hajji Kizito after the contract period of 5 months. In my view, by giving Sun Auto Company Ltd the post-dated cheques which in the end bounced and by surrendering to the company his own personal property (the land title and vehicle), Hajji Kizito committed himself to pay for the cycles on demand. The company has prayed in HCCS No. 759/2006 that it be paid a sum of Shs.26, 160,000 = being the balance on the purchase price. In his evidence, DW1 Mulinde admitted receipt of some payment. He gave the outstanding balance as Shs.24, 600,000 = although, as stated above, the amount claimed in HCCS No. 759/2006 is Shs.26, 160,000 = . PW1 Nabisalu put the figure at Shs.22, 750,000 = and Hajji Kizito himself at Shs.24, 000,000 = . I take the outstanding amount to be the figure admitted by Hajji Kizito. Accordingly, the sum of Shs.24, 000,000 = is decreed to M/S Sun Auto Company Ltd as against Hajji Swaibu Kizito. The decretal sum shall attract interest at the commercial rate of 25% per annum from the date of judgment till payment in full. Given that Hajji Swaibu Kizito has himself parted with custody of the suit cycles, M/S Sun Auto Company Ltd shall maintain custody of Hajji Swaibu Kizito's certificate of title and the vehicle pending payment. In default, the same shall be sold in execution to recover the amount due and the balance, if any, shall be given to the judgment-debtor.

Ruling

In the final result, judgment is entered for the plaintiff in HCCS No. 0759-2006 against the defendant therein on the terms stated herein above with costs as prayed. HCCS No. 0501-2006 is dismissed with no order as to costs. Upon being paid the decretal amount and costs, M/S Sun Auto Company Ltd shall release the 20 number plates to the judgment debtor.

I so order.

Notes

1. For an excellent review of the history of Law and Economics, see Kornhauser (2001).
2. This example is adapted from Mitchell Polinski (1983).
3. Johnson also says: "The costs other than the money price that are incurred in trading goods or services. Before a particular mutually beneficial trade can take place, at least one party must figure out that there may be someone with whom such a trade is potentially possible, search out one or more such possible trade partners, inform him/them of the opportunity, and negotiate the terms of the exchange. All of these activities involve opportunity costs in terms of time, energy and money. After a trade has been agreed upon, there may also be significant costs involved in monitoring or policing the other party to make sure he is honoring the terms of the agreement (and, if he is not, to take appropriate legal or other actions to make him do so). These are the main sorts of transaction costs, then: search and information costs, bargaining and decision costs, policing and enforcement costs. ...Indeed, many otherwise mutually advantageous trades do not take place because of the very high transaction costs that would be involved."
4. For example, in Ghana, According to Article 11 of the 1992 Constitution of Ghana, "Law" in Ghana consists of: (1) the Constitution; (2) Parliamentary enactments or legislation; (3) Orders, Rules, and Regulations; (4) the existing law; and (5) the common law.
5. In Kenya, Section 3 of the Judicature Act (Chapter 8 Laws of Kenya), enumerates the laws of Kenya to include: (1) The Constitution; (2) Acts of Parliament; (3) Specific Acts of Parliament of the United Kingdom; (4) Certain Acts of Parliament of India; (5) English Statutes of General Application in Force in England 12th August 1897; (6) The Substance of Common Law and Doctrines of Equity; (7) African Customary Law; (8) Islamic Law; (9) International Instruments (not listed in the Judicature Act). See Ojienda and Aloo (2006).
6. Ghana, formerly the Gold Coast, became a Crown Colony of the British in 1874. The basic law was established under the Gold Coast Supreme Court Ordinance of 1876, "the common law, the doctrine of equity, and the statutes of general application which were in force in England on the date when the Colony obtained a local legislature, that is to say, 24th July 1874, shall be in force within the jurisdiction of this court." The Reception date for English Law in Tanzania is July 22, 1920. See Nyanduga and Manning (2006). The Reception date for Kenya is August 12, 1897. See Ojienda and Aloo (2006).
7. Courts Ordinance, 1876, § 19 (Gold Coast).
8. The suggestion of an emerging 'Ghanaian common law' is valid. As Wabwile explains, "Section 17(1) of the Interpretation Act 1960 (Ghana) defines the common law as follows: "The common law" as comprised in the laws of Ghana consists in addition to the rules of law generally known as the common law, of customary law included in the common law under any enactment providing for the assimilation of such rules of customary law as are suitable for general application." This definition has national elements of native customary law. The courts of Ghana thus have a mandate to assimilate the received common law and blend it with the customs of the local communities." In Wabwile (2003), Wabwile compares the Ghana provisions with Kenya's Interpretation and General Provisions Act 1956 (Kenya) chapter 2, and writes, "notice that in this sense, reference is specifically made to English Law. It is not therefore entirely accurate to say that Kenyan courts have the competence to develop a 'Kenyan common law,'" p. 79.
9. "If customary law is deficient in the area of commercial and business law, it is completely empty in the area of modern public law. There simply is not even the germ of such institutions as planning, state enterprises, import control, central banking, exchange controls, limitations on the repatriation of profits, income taxation, trade unions and labor law, and a host of others. To search the interstices of customary law for aid in formulating the response to questions posed by the demand for institutions of this sort is to search in vain." See Hutchison (1968), p. 32−33.
10. Adopted 11 April 1980.
11. See Buscaglia, at 572, "In order to enhance trade openness abroad and at the same time attract foreign investment to their domestic markets, they [developing countries] provide a more stable environment in which to do business. Therefore, competitive pressures arise on LDCs to harmonize their legal systems with

those in countries exporting capital by incorporating foreign legal frameworks that developed-country firms perceive to enhance their productive efficiency."

12. See also Chuks Maduka (2010): "In Nigeria legal system judicial precedent is a decision establishing a principle of law that any other judicial body must or may follow when called upon to decide a case with similar issues". Also, "Zambia is a common law jurisdiction and a former British colony. It has adopted many English court practices. These practices include the doctrines of precedent and *stare decisis*," (Comfort Mulenga, n.d.). In Uganda, "The Supreme Court is the highest Court in Uganda, and is the final court of Appeal. The Supreme Court only decides cases on appeal from lower courts save for presidential election petitions, where the Supreme Court has original jurisdiction, which means that any aggrieved candidate in a presidential election has to petition the Supreme Court directly. The decisions of the Supreme Court form *precedents* which all lower courts are required to follow (Brenda Mahoro, 2006).

13. Amadi writes of the Nigerian court system, "Obstacles to access to justice in Nigerian civil justice system are challenging. These obstacles include: delays, cost of litigation, complex legal rules and procedure, lack of awareness and legal knowledge. The average duration of a trial, from the time of issue of summons to the point in time when a final judgment is delivered by the court is eight years, in many instances, beyond ten years." See Amadi (2009). For similar observations about other common law countries in SSA, see UN Economic Commission for Africa (2003).

14. The World Bank Group's *The Doing Business project* "provides objective measures of business regulations and their enforcement across 183 economies and selected cities at the subnational and regional level." One of the measures is "Enforcing contracts," which deals with procedures, time, and cost to resolve a commercial dispute. In the 2010 edition of the publication, the law enforcement index was based on the process used by litigants and courts to evict a tenant for non-payment of rent and to collect a bounced check. Of the 183 countries ranked in the publication, Ghana ranked highest (47) among the SSA common law countries. Most SSA countries were near the lower one-third of countries – Botswana (79); Zambia (87); Kenya (126); Uganda (116); Nigeria (94); Malawi (142); Sierra Leone (144); and Zimbabwe (78). See International Finance Corporation (IFC) (2009). The "Doing Business" website contains extensive literature on the theory and empirical approaches to measuring the challenges facing countries in SSA.

15. For details of the challenges facing governments in sub-Saharan Africa in expanding access to courts and dealing with financial constraints, see, United Nations Office for Drugs and Crime (Vienna) (2011).

16. Other countries in days and procedures are Sierra Leone (515, 39); Uganda (490, 38); Tanzania (515, 38); Gambia (407, 33); Zimbabwe (410, 38). Botswana has the best environment in SSA with 62.5 days (lower than Singapore) and 28 procedures.

17. From an economist's perspective, a party will file an action if the amount in controversy multiplied by the probability of winning is greater than the cost. This is an efficiency rule.

18. Government of Uganda, "Evidence Act 1909" (Cap 6). See also Chapter 6 "The Evidence Act of Tanzania, [G.N. No. 225 of 1967, 'evidence' denotes the means by which an alleged matter of fact, the truth of which if submitted to investigation, is proved or disproved; and without prejudice to the preceding generality, includes statements and admissions by accused persons; 'fact' includes − (a) anything, state of things, or relation of things, capable of being perceived by the senses; (b) any mental condition of which any person is conscious."

19. See, for example, South Africa's evidence note, "There is no all-embracing statute governing the South African law of evidence: Various statutes govern various aspects of it, but the common law is the main source." The Constitution also features prominently. All types of legal procedure look to the law of evidence to govern which facts they may receive, and how: civil and criminal trials, inquests, extraditions, commissions of inquiry, etc. See Note 1.

20. For an excellent discussion of how technology is changing evidence rules in sub-Saharan African countries, see Proshare (2012). See also, in the case of Kenya, "With increased computerization and technology as well as the rise of the digital office, courts have been forced to allow for the admittance of digital evidence," Mputhia (2008). The importance of the information age on the law of evidence is

succinctly stated in The Republic of South Africa's Electronic Communications and Transactions Act, 2002 (No. 25 of 2002), "The objects of this Act are to enable and facilitate electronic Communications and transactions in the public interest, and for that purpose to − (a) recognize the importance of the information economy for the economic and social prosperity of the Republic" (Parliament of South Africa, 2002).

21. Evidence Act, Laws of the Federation of Nigeria, 1990, Chapter 112, Section VI, 132 (1).
22. *K. Michael Quist v Akuaba Estates Limited*, High Court of Justice (Commercial Division), Accra, Ghana Suit No. BDC/93/06, July 9, 2007, "And yet another exception to the parol evidence rule is that in addition to express verbal incorporation, terms may be incorporated by the conduct of the parties. Such conduct may consist in one party drawing to the attention of the other, the terms on which he is willing to contract before the contract is concluded; or it may be inferred from a previous course of dealing between the parties or from their common understanding."

Questions

1. What is the relevance of agricultural law in a developing country?
2. What are the main sources of law in your country? What changes in these sources do you foresee?
3. What is the difference between "written" and "unwritten" law?
4. What is the difference between a civil action and a criminal action?
5. What is evidence? Under what circumstances may a court exclude the introduction of evidence in a case?
6. Define maximizing efficiency.
7. What is a "latent market"?
8. What can be done to alleviate pressures on the legal system in sub-Saharan Africa? Explain.
9. Why does it make sense for decisions of previous court rulings to be upheld if the facts presented in a new case are the same?

Problems

1. Conflict between livestock owners and crop growers is common in sub-Saharan African countries. What ideas from the Coase theorem may be applied to resolve these conflicts? What role may government and private entities play in finding a solution to these conflicts?
2. It has been suggested in this book that there exists a "latent market" for legal services in sub-Saharan Africa. In what ways may the modern agricultural lawyer take advantage of this latent market? What role if any does government have to play in exploiting this market? What opportunities are made available to economists and lawyers to effectively grow this market?

References

Agyemang, J.K., June 1988. Delays in the courts. Ghana Bar Bull. 1 (1), 20–23.

Amadi, J., 2009. Enhancing Access to Justice in Nigeria with Judicial Case Management: An Evolving Norm in Common Law Countries. Center for African Law and Development, SSRN. <http://ssrn.com/abstract=1366943> (accessed 05.09.10).

Atuguba, R.A., Dr. 2007. Legal aid in Africa: conceptual and practical peculiarities of legal aid in Africa and where should we be going. In: Paper Presented at the Regional Conference on Legal Aid and Access to Justice in West Africa organized by the Open Society Initiative for West Africa, 1–3 April 2007, M-Plaza.

Black, H.C., 1990. Black's Law Dictionary. sixth ed. West Publishing Company, St Paul, Minnesota, USA.

Buscaglia, E., 1999. Law and economics of development. In: Bouckaert, B., De Geest, G. (Eds.), Encyclopedia of Law and Economics. Edward Elgar Publishing, Washington University in St. Louis, USA.

Chuks Maduka, A. 2010. Understanding the Concept of Judicial Precedent and the Doctrine of Stare Decisis Under the Nigerian Legal System. <http://nigerialaw.blogspot.com/2010/08/understanding-concept-of-judicial_20.html> (accessed 10.09.14).

Coase, R., 1961. The problem of social cost. J. Law Econ. 3, 1.

Comfort Mulenga, n.d. Judicial Precedent in Zambia. Institutional Depository, University of Zambia. <http://dspace.unza.zm:8080/xmlui/handle/123456789/2818> (accessed 10.09.14).

Commission for the Implementation of the Constitution, 2013. The Legal Aid Bill.

Dina, Y., Akintayo, J., Ekundayo, F. Guide to Nigerian Legal Information, February 2005. <http://www.nyulawglobal.org/globalex/nigeria.htm#_LEGAL_SYSTEM> (accessed 02.12.16).

Dube, B.A. The Law and Legal Research in Lesotho. February 2008. <http://www.nyulawglobal.org/globalex/lesotho.htm> (accessed 02.12.16).

Hutchison, T.W. (Ed.), 1968. Africa and Law: Developing Legal Systems in African Commonwealth Nations. The University of Wisconsin Press, Madison, Wisconsin.

International Finance Corporation (IFC), 2009. Doing Business: Measuring Business Regulations. <http://www.doingbusiness.org/economyrankings/>.

Johnson, P.M., 2005. A Glossary of Political Economy Terms. <http://www.auburn.edu/~johnspm/gloss/transaction_costs> (accessed 21.03.15).

Kenya Law Reports, 2007. Laws of Kenya: The Judicature Act. National Council for Law Reporting, Kenya, Africa. <http://www.kenyalaw.org/Downloads/GreyBook/3.%20Judicature%20Act.pdf>.

Kershen, D., 2008. What is agricultural law? Proposing production agriculture as the core. Agric Law Update. 25 (12).

Kom, E.D., June 1988. Delays in the courts. Ghana Bar Bull. 1 (1), 20–23.

Kornhauser, L., 2001. The economic analysis of law. Stanford Encyclopedia of Philosophy. <http://plato.stanford.edu/entries/legal-econanalysis/> (accessed 26.02.10).

Mahoro, B., 2006. Uganda's Legal System and Legal Sector, *Global Lex*. <http://www.nyulawglobal.org/globalex/uganda.htm>.

Mitchell Polinski, A., 1983. An Introduction to Law and Economics. Little, Brown & Company, Canada.

Mputhia, C. 2008. Kenya: When Digital Evidence Is Admissible in Court. *Business Daily* (Nairobi, 24 June 2008. <http://allafrica.com/stories/200806241212.html>.

Nyanduga, B.T., Manning, C. Guide to Tanzanian Legal System and Legal Research. November 2006. <http://www.nyulawglobal.org/globalex/tanzania.htm> (accessed 02.12.16).

Ojienda, T., Aloo, L.O., 2006. Researching Kenyan Law. GLOBALEX. <http://www.nyulawglobal.org/globalex/Kenya.htm#_Sources_of_Kenyan_Law>.

Parliament of South Africa, 2002. Electronic Communications and Transactions Act, 2002. <http://www.internet.org.za/ect_act.html>.

Posner, R.A., 2007. Economic Analysis of Law, seventh ed. Aspen Publishers.

Proshare, 2012. Legal Alert – May 2012 – Admissibility of Electronic Evidence under Nigeria's Evidence Act 2011, Chapter 112, Laws of the Federation of Nigeria. <http://www.proshareng.com/articles/2437/Legal-Alert--May-2012--Admissibility-of-Electronic-Evidence>.

Schneider, S.A., 2009. What is agriculture law? Paper Presented at the Association of American Law Schools 2009 Annual Meeting (Agricultural Law Section Program, January 6–10, 2009).

Seidman, R.B., 1968. Law and economic development in independent, English-speaking, sub-Saharan Africa. In: Hutchison, T.W. (Ed.), Africa and Law: Developing Legal Systems in African Commonwealth Nations. The University of Wisconsin Press, Madison, Wisconsin.

UN Economic Commission for Africa. Judicial Reform for Improving Governance in Anglophone Africa A Distance Learning Program for Ethiopia, Ghana, Kenya, Nigeria, Tanzania and Uganda October–November, 2003. <http://www.uneca.org/itca/governance/Documents/Judicial_Reform_for_Good_Governance_tanzania.pdf>.

United Nations Office for Drugs and Crime (Vienna). Access to Legal Aid in Criminal Justice Systems in Africa: Survey Report, 2011. Viewed online on 10.13.14. at <http://www.unodc.org/pdf/criminal_justice/Survey_Report_on_Access_to_Legal_Aid_in_Africa.pdf>.

Wabwile, M.N., 2003. The place of English law in Kenya. Oxford University Commonwealth Law J. 3, 79, 1 (note 91).

World Bank (n.d.). Doing Business 2015: Going Beyond Efficiency (Country Tables) (published October 29, 2014), viewed at <http://www.doingbusiness.org/reports/global-reports/ ~ /media/GIAWB/Doing%20Business/Documents/Annual-Reports/English/DB15-Chapters/DB15-Country-Tables.pdf> (accessed 18.03.15).

CHAPTER 2

Contracts

Keywords: Contract; competent parties; proper subject matter; offer; acceptance; consideration; Statute of Frauds; parol evidence rule; impossibility of performance; frustration of purpose; damages; special and general damages; liquidated damages; specific performance; rescission; Sale of Goods Act, common law contract; meeting of the minds

2.1 The Law and Economics of Agricultural Contracts

A contract has been defined as "a legally binding exchange of promises or agreement between parties that the law will enforce" (USLaw.Com). There must be a *meeting of the minds*. Contract law is a classic example of the framework suggested by the Coase theorem because parties engage in bargaining that move resources to their most-valued uses. The allocation of resources is maximized when there is a meeting of the minds and the welfare-maximizing goal of society is realized. Contract law and courts help to achieve the welfare-maximizing goal of society by resolving conflicts that arise because parties cannot negotiate a complete contract that covers all possible contingencies. As explained under the Coase theorem, it is the presence of *transaction costs* that prevents the negotiation of complete contracts. The role of contract law and the courts is to reduce the presence of transaction costs.

This chapter explains how courts in sub-Saharan Africa (SSA) have applied general contract principles in resolving issues relevant to agriculture. Historically, issues involving land have been emphasized by economists and lawyers when discussing the relevance of law to agriculture. Today, the relevance of law to agriculture reaches beyond land and law is emerging as the critical bridge to tie production to markets to improve incomes. For economists and lawyers, there is a need to understand laws relevant to contract farming, forward contracting, input markets, especially seeds, fertilizer and equipment markets, agricultural credit availability, the value chain, water resources, and the environment. The list of issues is not exhaustive and is intended to draw attention to the fact that agricultural contract law is a legitimate subject to discuss under the general rules of contract law.

F.O. Boadu: Agricultural Law and Economics in Sub-Saharan Africa.
DOI: http://dx.doi.org/10.1016/B978-0-12-801771-5.00002-2

2.2 Elements of a Valid Contract—Competent Parties, Proper Subject Matter, Offer, Acceptance, Consideration, Counter-Offers, Writing Requirement

Courts do not write contracts for individuals; rather courts ensure that the individual performs the promises made to the other party in a contract.[1] Generally a valid contract must have the following elements: (1) legally competent parties, (2) proper subject matter, (3) offer, (4) acceptance, and (5) consideration. A court may intervene in a contract between parties if one of the parties is considered not *competent* under the law to enter into a contract. Children, the mentally ill, or a drunk are considered not competent to enter into a contract. A court may also intervene if the *subject matter* of a contract is not proper or illegal. An example is a contract to buy and sell an expired or banned pesticide. A contract is usually initiated with some form of an *offer*, that is, some manifestation of intent by a party to enter into a contract. The manner in which an offer is made could be problematic. For example, in a contract concerning the sale of land, a court may find the offer to sell to be vague if the conditions of sale (size of land, location, price, and other key terms) are not stated in the offer. A court may also intervene if the *acceptance*, that is, a manifestation of agreement to the terms of an offer is not proper. For example, an offer that specifically requires acceptance in writing may not bind a contract if the acceptance was oral. Generally, courts are involved in every aspect of a contract—formation, performance, excuses for nonperformance, and determination of remedies should a party fail to perform what is promised in a contract.

The determination of whether parties in a contract actually agreed to the terms in the contract is not an exact science. Courts in all SSA countries have engaged in "a balance of probabilities" of the evidence to determine whether an offer, acceptance, and a meeting of the mind were present to bind a contract. The *RESINEX AFRICA S.A* case from Ghana employs a "balance of probabilities" analysis to determine the presence of an offer and an acceptance to bind a contract.[2] The *Galaunia Farms Ltd v National Milling Company Ltd.* case from Zambia is an example of how the lack of specificity in making an offer and absence of a "meeting of the minds" to validate changes made in an offer could invalidate a contract.[3] The case also explained the nature of counter-offers and how an attempt was made to use the doctrine of *estoppel* to rescue a poorly defined contract. As the *Galaunia* case shows, the doctrine is narrowly applied and it failed in this case. The Tanzanian case of *Hotel Travertine Limited, J.D. Lamba and Eva Lamba v National Bank of Commerce Limited*,[4] explains the importance of accepting an offer consistent with the procedure for acceptance stated in the offer.

Resinex Africa S.A. v Prestige Chemicals Limited

High Court of Justice (Commercial Division)
Suit No. RPC/221/06
July 11, 2007
Her Lordship BARBARA ACKAH-YENSU (J)

FACTS

Resinex Africa S.A. (Plaintiff herein), a company based in Belgium supplied on credit to Prestige Chemicals Limited, a Ghanaian company (Defendant herein), three (3) containers of raw materials for production. As a result of a fire outbreak in Defendant's factory, which affected her capacity to utilize the materials and pay for same, Plaintiff's representatives in Ghana agreed to take back some of the materials which had not been used and sell to other interested customers. Plaintiff is saying that the agreement was that the proceeds of the sale would be used to defray the cost of one container of goods; Defendant is saying that the agreement was with regard to a different container.

It is Plaintiff's claim that Defendant had only paid US$1,000 of the total value of the goods that Defendant had already used. Plaintiff thus commenced the instant action in which she was claiming the following:

1. Payment of Euro12,376.16 or its Cedi equivalent, being the outstanding balance of goods supplied on credit by the Plaintiff to the Defendant.
2. Interest on the said Euro12,376.16 from 23/02/05 up to date of final payment at the prevailing Bank rate.
3. Costs.

At the Pre-trial Conference, Defendant submitted to judgment for US$11,703 together with interest and costs. It is therefore the difference of US$1,455 together with interest thereon which is the subject of this trial.

By her pleadings, Plaintiff claimed that Defendant was indebted to her in the sum of Euro 12,376.16, being the outstanding balance on goods supplied to her by Plaintiff. Defendant in her Statement of Defence, denied entering into any transaction with Plaintiff denominated in Euros, in which there was an outstanding balance of Euros12,373.16. In her Reply, Plaintiff contended that even though the invoices covering the goods were issued in US Dollars, the parties understood clearly that payment would be made in Euros. That Defendant's account with Plaintiff was denominated in Euros and that Defendant had in the past made payments in Euros to Plaintiff to cover supplies made to her.

The issues set out for determination at the Pre-Trial conference are as follows:

1. Whether or not the Plaintiff supplied goods to the Defendant.
2. Whether or not there was an outstanding balance to be paid by the Defendant to the Plaintiff.
3. And if so, how much?

From the pleadings there is no denying that the parties had done business together before, and that Plaintiff had supplied goods to Defendant in previous business transactions. Indeed by the

(Continued)

(Continued)

fact that Defendants submitted to judgment for part of Plaintiff's claim, it appears that Defendant had admitted that goods were supplied for which he owed. The real issue therefore is the quantum of the debt owed to Plaintiff. The evidence led on behalf of Plaintiff by Patrick Luclere (Managing Director of Resinex (Gh) Limited (P.W.1)), was that there was an outstanding invoice covering goods supplied to Defendant for which Defendant had not paid. He tendered in evidence (Exhibit 'A'), an invoice covering a total of US\$14,160 worth of goods. It was P.W.1's evidence that Defendant had paid \$1,000 out of this amount. P.W.1 also tendered in evidence, a Statement of Account (Exhibit 'B'), from Plaintiff which showed the value of the invoice submitted to Defendant and the payment made by Defendant.

It was P.W.1's further evidence that after the supply of three (3) containers of goods, Defendant's factory caught fire. At the time, Defendant had used only one container of goods or a part thereof. He said that Defendant gave back to Plaintiff the documents covering the remaining two (2) containers; one had the value of about \$12,000, and the other, about \$14,000.

The Agreement, he said, was that Plaintiff's representatives in Ghana would clear the goods from the bonded warehouse, sell them and pay Plaintiff company; which he says they did. It was P.W.1's contention that Defendant has to pay the balance outstanding on the first invoice (Exhibit 'A'), which amount is \$13,160 plus interest and cost. P.W.1 also testified that all transactions with Defendant were registered in Euros because Plaintiff's accounting systems was in Euros, so the US dollar invoice would be accounted for in Euros. The invoices covering the 2nd and 3rd containers were also tendered in evidence by Defendant through P.W.1. (Exhibits 1 series and 2 series).

RULING

In my view, the bone of contention between the parties is whether the amount payable by Defendant is with regard to Exhibit 'A' or Exhibit '1'? Plaintiff is saying that after the fire outbreak she agreed to collect the goods which had not been used, being the goods covered by Exhibit's '1' and '2' and sell them to other buyers. Defendant on the other hand is saying that the agreement reached by the parties was that Plaintiff would sell the unused goods, and give the proceeds to Defendant to pay for the goods covered by Exhibit 'A' which had been used but not paid for. So which is which; is it the Plaintiff's version or Defendant's version that was proved?

Plaintiff has the burden of proof and so I will examine Plaintiff's claim and the evidence adduced in support of her claim. The evidence of P.W.1 who represented Plaintiff in these transactions and dealt with Defendant Company, was that there was the agreement that Plaintiff would clear all the goods from the bonded warehouse and sell them. As at the time of the fire outbreak i.e. September 2003, Plaintiff had already used the goods covered by Exhibit 'A' and even though payment was due, had not paid for them. To prove this assertion, P.W.1 tendered in evidence, a Statement of claim, Exhibit 'B' sent by Plaintiff. D.W.1 admitted that the goods covered by Exhibit 'A' had been used but not paid for. Exhibit 'C' which is a letter covering the document pertaining to the goods in Exhibit '1' and '2' was tendered in evidence to prove that the agreement was that Plaintiff should clear the said goods and sell them. It is this same Exhibit 'C' that Defendant is claiming refers to the agreement between the parties

(Continued)

(Continued)

that the proceeds of the sale of the goods covered by Exhibit '1' should be sent back to Defendants. This is what the said Exhibit says:

Resinex Ghana Ltd,

36 Palace Street

North Industrial Area,

P.O. Box 903, Achimota

Accra.

Dear Sir/Madam 11/9/2003

We hereby enclose the following original documents pertaining to the shipment of 660 bags of PP Raffia H511-03 as per order number 03-06-RG-1399PL as agreed on phone.

They include:

1) *Invoice*
2) *Bill of Lading*
3) *Packing List*
4) *IDF, &*
5) *FCVR*

Yours faithfully

Prestige Chemicals

Received By. . . . . Dated. . . . .

I do not see how the interpretation being put to this by Defendant can be made from this letter. The phrase "as agreed on phone" could as well refer to the agreement Plaintiff says the parties reached.

Since this matter hinges on a purported agreement and the interpretation of the said agreement, I would like to delve a little into Contract, as basic as it may be.

In *Dormenyor v. Johnson Motors Ltd* (1989-90) GLRD 175, Ampiah JA, sitting as a High Court Judge, observed that *"in all contracts there must be an offer and an acceptance of some sort"*. The parties must be of the same mind concerning all the terms of the offer and acceptance. Where there is agreement on contractual terms, there is said to be *consensus ad idem* (i.e. a meeting of the minds). If there is no consensus, there is no contract. This principle was emphasized by Anin JA (dissenting) in *Addison v. A/S Norway Cement Export Ltd* (1973) GLR 151 at 162; SA Turqui & Bros v. Lamptey (1961) I GLR 190 (HC). Therefore, in SA Turqui & Bros v. Lamptey, Ollennu J observed that *"the minds of the parties were not ad idem. . . there is therefore no binding contract between the parties"*.

There must be certainty as to the terms offered and accepted. As Anin J.A. explained in his dissenting judgment in *Addison v. A/S Norway Cement Export Ltd.,*

(*Continued*)

(Continued)

The law is quite settled that if the terms of an agreement are so vague

or indefinite that it cannot be ascertained with reasonable certainty what

is the intention of the parties, there is no contract enforceable at all . . .

the parties must make their own contracts; and the Courts will not make

a contract for them out of terms that are indefinite or illusory.

And so if there is some uncertainty in that it is meaningless, and the circumstances are not such that one or other party to the contract may elect between meanings; or where the Court is unable to discern the concept which the parties had in mind; or where the terms of the contract require further agreement between the parties in order to implement them there is no contract. Therefore uncertainty may prevent a contract from arising at all. And I will find that the uncertainty in the said agreement between the parties herein is such as to prevent any binding agreement from coming into existence; and hence there is no enforceable contract.

The issue to be determined is therefore a question of fact; i.e. the Plaintiff's word against Defendant's; whose version of the story is to be preferred on the balance of probabilities, based on the evidence adduced.

Defendant is saying that the business practice is to deal with only the goods that are already due but not paid for, therefore the giving of the documents covering the goods covered by Exhibit 'A' frees him from liability for those goods. To me, this is neither here nor there. To a layman like me, who is not in the business of the parties, it sounds rather strange that goods that have been used by Defendant but not paid for can be deemed to have been paid for by selling other goods particularly when the values are not the same. I am wondering what Plaintiffs representatives could have sold when P.W.1 collected the documents for the goods covered by Exhibit 'A' since the goods had already been used by Defendant.

In any case, the evidence placed before the Court is that another invoice (Exhibit '2') was also due and not paid for; irrespective of the fact that the goods were not used, payment was due and the evidence is that because those goods were not used, Plaintiff's representative was able to sell those to settle Exhibit '2'. For me, the fact that Plaintiff has not made any demand on Defendant for the goods supplied under Exhibits '1' and '2', lends further credence to Plaintiff's Claim. It can only be because the goods covered by Exhibits '1' and '2' were collected and sold and the proceeds paid to Plaintiff. The only outstanding payment therefore is Exhibit 'A'.

RULING

I will therefore prefer P.W.1's evidence that the agreement was that Plaintiff's representative sells the goods covered by Exhibit '1' to defray the bill for those goods.

So, on the balance of probabilities, I will find that Plaintiff's Claim is to be preferred and hold that Defendant is liable to pay the difference between the amount outstanding on Exhibit 'A', US$13,160 and the amount of US$11,705 Defendant conceded to owing Plaintiff.

I will accordingly order that Defendant pays to Plaintiff the balance outstanding of US$1,455 together with interest at the prevailing Bank rate, from 23/02/05 till date of final payment. I will award Costs of ¢10,000,000.00 (Ten Million Cedis) against Defendant.

Galaunia Farms Ltd v National Milling Company Ltd

High Court of Zambia, 5th April, 2002
Justice S.S. Silomba

By a writ of summons filed in the principal registry on 23rd February, 1999, the plaintiff, Galaunia Farms Limited, is seeking an order for damages and consequential loss arising from the 1st defendant's breach of the agreement to purchase wheat from it. In support of the claim, the plaintiff called two witnesses whose evidence is on record. The evidence was that sometime in May, 1998, various companies were requested to submit tenders to buy wheat from the plaintiff. In response, the National Milling Company Limited, the 1st defendant in these proceedings, submitted its offer and after a thorough market survey, the plaintiff accepted the offer because it was the best available offer on the market.

The invitation to tender for the purchase of wheat was in form of a letter (see the document at page 1 in the plaintiff's bundle of documents). According to Mr. Michael Galaun (PW1, the managing director of the plaintiff, this was the document that the plaintiff and the 1st defendant signed into a binding contract under which the plaintiff was to supply wheat for purchase by the 1st defendant. The signatories were Mr. Michael Galaun himself, for the plaintiff, and Mr. Ron Darby, for the 1st defendant. With regard to the hand-written amendments appearing in the document, the evidence of Mr. Galaun was that these were inserted by Mr. Darby and accepted by him. Mr. Galaun later communicated the acceptance of the amendments to Mr. Darby by letter.

Later Mr. Galaunia went to see Mr. Darby to find out if the 1st defendant was in a position to buy the extra 500 tons of wheat over and above the 2000 tons already contracted for. Apparently, the 2,500 tons of wheat was the approximate amount of wheat Mr. Galaun was expecting to harvest that season. According to Mr. Galaun the meeting with Mr. Darby was cordial as he appreciated why the plaintiff wanted to sell the whole yield to one buyer, that is, the 1st defendant. After the meeting Mr. Galaun sent Mr. Darby what he considered to be a "clean contract", that is, a contract devoid of any alterations or amendments, now found at page 6 in the plaintiff's bundle of documents.

The evidence of the plaintiff's witness was that the contract on page 6 had incorporated more tonnage of wheat to be sold than what was in earlier contract at page 1 and besides the payment period was seven days, an improvement in the earlier contract at page 1. While the contract at page 6 was said to have been agreed upon at a meeting between Mr. Galaun and Mr. Darby the latter did not sign it. When Mr. Galaun later visited the 1st defendant's premises for the purpose of having the contract signed by the 1st defendant he did not find Mr. Darby, apparently, because he was out of the country. He, however met Mr. Eran Wilson, an employee of the 1st defendant, who told him that his employer was having financial problems and that it was in the process of being sold.

According to the witness Mr. Wilson later told him to send the "clean contract" immediately for confirmation by the 1st defendant's board, which the witness did on behalf of the plaintiff. When the promised "immediate response" was not forthcoming from the 1st defendant the witness reminded the 1st defendant to return the "cleaned up" version of the

(Continued)

(Continued)

contract as soon as it had been signed. In his reminder Mr. Galaun told the managing director of the 1st defendant that as far as he was concerned the plaintiff had a signed contract with the 1st defendant upon which they were relying. Despite the reminder the silence continued, a fact the led Mr. Galaun to think that all was well since they had not disputed the contract.

With regard to the allegation that the fact that the clean contract at page 6 of the plaintiff's bundle of documents was not signed meant the contract was not binding between the parties. Mr. Galaun thought there was no truth in the allegation. As far as he was concerned the clean contract was simply a version of the signed contract at page 1 of the plaintiff's bundle of documents, which the plaintiff had accepted following the 1st defendant's offer, by way of tender; that subsequent to the said contract at page 1, the 1st defendant agreed to negotiate the quantity of wheat to be supplied as well as reduce the terms of payment, which the plaintiff accepted – hence the clean contract.

The further evidence of PW1 was that Eran Wilson in fact told him to rely on the cleaned up contract. With this assurance, Mr. Galaun, in the company of his farm general manager, went to the 1st defendant's premises to go and inspect the space the 1st defendant had set aside for the storage of the wheat, the witness sent the 1st defendant a sample of the wheat, which they examined and found the moisture content in the crop to be within specification. On the 20th September, 1998, Mr. Galaun accompanied by his advocate and farm manager, attended a meeting at the 1st defendant's premises. Those who attended the meeting on the side of the 1st defendant were Mr. Fourie, the managing director and Mr. Hachipuka, the director. Also present was Mr. Peter Cook, a shareholder, from the management services.

According to the plaintiff's witness the meeting was about whether to deliver the wheat or not; the 1st defendant's delegation did not hide the fact that the 1st defendant was in financial difficulties and that if the wheat was delivered it might not be paid for as the 1st defendant company was about to be liquidated. As far as the witness was concerned there was no suggestion that the contract was in dispute; in fact the 1st defendant's representatives were happy with the price of the wheat as it was the cheapest on the market. Accordingly, Mr. Galaun was advised at the very meeting to immediately sell the wheat elsewhere in view of the financial difficulties the company was facing.

On 26th September, 1998, another meeting was held with the 1st defendant's delegation. At that meeting the 1st defendant produced a letter in which the plaintiff was released from the contract and given a free hand to sell the wheat elsewhere. Consequently, the entire crop of wheat was sold to Amanita Milling Company but on terms less favourable than those agreed upon with the 1st defendant. For example the payment terms under the contract with the 1st defendant provided for payment within 7 days from the date of delivery, while the terms with Amanita was that the payment for the total crop would be in four installments over a period of well over 90 days from the date of sale.

With regard to the price, the plaintiff's evidence was that he sold close to 2,500 tons of wheat to Amanita at US$ 30 per ton, which was less than what the plaintiff would have

(Continued)

(Continued)

fetched if it had sold to the 1st defendant. Instead of being paid within 7 days from the date of delivery as was to be the case had the wheat being delivered to the 1st defendant, the plaintiff was still being paid by Amanita in installments as at the date of trial, thereby attracting interest charges on the amount it had borrowed from Barclays Bank to finance the crop.

During cross-examination, Mr. Galaun admitted that he prepared the contract at page 1 of the plaintiff's bundle of documents one month before he called for the tenders on the 11th May, 1998. With regard to the alleged clean contract at page 6 of the plaintiff's bundle of documents, Mr. Galaun said that the document was the same as the document at page 1, only difference being that the document at page 6 provided for quantity of wheat under sale, the buyer's option as well as the option on the payments.

According to the witness the changes or clarification included in the document at page 6 were discussed with the 1st defendant and consensus reached on their inclusion but that the 1st defendant's agents never appended their signatures to the clean contract. In trying to secure the signatories to the contract, the witness dealt with various officials of the 1st defendant. These officials were, according to Mr. Galaun, people in authority who were expected to honour their word.

As to whether there was any letter of commitment from the 1st defendant stating whether or not they were bound by the terms of the contract Mr. Galaun stated that 1st defendant's letter of 11th September, 1998, implied that the contract had been approved (see page 11 of the plaintiff's bundle of documents). The further evidence in chief was that the plaintiff had borrowed US$550,000.00, as short-term seasonal loan from Barclays Bank Zambia Limited. The evidence of Mr. Majdra (PW2), an accountant of the plaintiff, was that the loan was to be repaid from the proceeds of sale of the wheat to the 1st defendant. However, when the 1st defendant failed to buy the wheat, the plaintiff sold the bulk of it to Amanita while the rest was sold to Kanele Milling and Seba Feeds.

According to the witness the sale of the wheat to buyers, other than the 1st defendant, resulted in a loss of US$74,804.45. The 1st defendant's projection was that if the sell to the 1st defendant had been fulfilled it would have netted US$ 604,707.60 as against the US $529,903.15 that was realized from the alternative buyers. Mr. Majdra's evidence was that the money realized from the sale of wheat was inadequate to fully cover the short term seasonal loan with Barclays Bank; that a balance of US$ 105,777.86 was incurred, which continues to attract interest.

There was no oral evidence from the defence to contradict the plaintiff's evidence. According or the 1st defendant's Counsel it was not possible to call the only witness from abroad because of lack of financial resources. Besides, it was the view of the Counsel that the evidence on record, as adduced by the plaintiff, only raised legal issues, the issues of offer and counter offer, which were well settled in law. On the basis of the counsel's submission the court called for written submissions and adjourned for judgment. To a greater extent I agree with the 1st defendant's Counsel that the evidence does raise issues of law.

(*Continued*)

(Continued)

The written submission has been duly considered. I will not summarize them in this judgment, but I intend to make references to them in the course of my judgment. The evidence on record and the submissions show that the plaintiff prepared a tender document in form of a letter and circulated it to all its potential clients, including the 1st defendant, inviting them to tender for the purchase of wheat that was to be harvested that year. The document can be found at pages 1 to 4 of the plaintiff's bundle of documents and it's dated 11th April, 1998.

The evidence also shows that after the tender document had been circulated the 1st defendant responded with an offer to purchase that year's wheat. The document was extensively amended by the 1st defendant and all the amendments were initialed for. One of the amendments worthy of mention was the insertion of 2000 metric tones of wheat to be purchased under the agreement. On receipt of the amended tender document, the plaintiff accepted the offer as amended and counter-signed it. In view of the amendments the plaintiff thought it necessary to produce a "cleaned up document" by re-engrossing in fresh document in order to eliminate alterations.

The acceptance of the offer was communicated to the 1st defendant in a letter dated 12th August, 1998 (see document No. 5 in the plaintiff's bundle of documents). It was under this same letter that the cleaned up contract was forwarded to the 1st defendant for it to sign. Up to the time of trial the cleaned up contract had not been signed. The plaintiff is insisting that although the cleaned up contract was not signed, the 1st defendant was still bound because of the verbal agreement between PW1 and Mr. Darby, a senior employee of the 1st defendant with authority to sign the contract. In saying so the plaintiff is relying on the alleged assurances and commitments the officials of the 1st defendant made.

It is, however, acknowledged by the plaintiff that at the time the cleaned up contract was sent for signing Mr. Darby had left the 1st defendant. According to the plaintiff's witness (PW1) Mr. Eran Wilson, who was now in charge of procurement, also agreed to the terms of the cleaned up contract but due to internal restructuring problems the contract could not be signed.

The validity of the contract has been vigorously contested by Counsel for the 1st defendant. It is contended that by making substantial and material amendments to the offer, the plaintiff was guilty of making a counter offer. The 1st defendant's Counsel has also contended that the cleaned up contract contained provisions or terms, which were different from the offer made (see amendments) by the 1st defendant. For example, in the amended tender document the 1st defendant offered 2000 metric tonnes of wheat, while the cleaned up contract provided for 2,500 metric tones.

The fact that the cleaned up contract contains terms that are different from the offer proposed by the 1st defendant is not disputed. That being the position the 1st defendant's counsel has argued that the inclusion of 2,500 tonnes of wheat in the cleaned up contract as opposed to the 2000 tones the 1st defendant offered to buy, constituted a counter offer. If his stand is acceptable to the court his prayer is for an order to have the contract nullified for lack of consensus.

(*Continued*)

(Continued)

As I have already pointed out the position of the plaintiff is that the cleaned up contract, found at pages 6 and 8 of the plaintiff's bundle, is valid for all intents and purposes because it was consented to by Mr. Darby and Mr. Eran Wilson of the 1st defendant. In this kind of scenario I would say that the arguments and counter arguments raise the issue and the issue is: whether or not the cleaned up contract amounted to a counter offer.

The learned authors of *Charlesworth's Mercantile Law*, 13th Edition, (London, Stevens and Sons, 1977), assert at page 14, that "if the acceptance varies the terms of the offer it is a counter offer and not acceptance of the original offer". The foregoing proposition is further illustrated in the case of *Neale v Merret* (1), a case quoted with approval by the learned authors of *Charlesworth's Mercantile Law*.

In that case Merret offered land to Meale at 280 pounds sterling. Neale replied accepting the offer and enclosing 80 pounds sterling with a promise to pay the balance by monthly installments of 50 pounds sterling each. On the basis of *Neale*'s response, the court held that there was no unqualified acceptance. In the present case, the 1st defendant offered to buy 2,000 tones of wheat by way of tender. The plaintiff purportedly accepted the offer but in communicating its acceptance decided to increase the tonnage of wheat to be bought by the 1st defendant to 2,500.

Looking at the present case it can be successfully argued that the acceptance was at variance with the terms of the offer. What is obvious is that the plaintiff did not accept all the terms contained in the offer. At this stage I find the quotation given by the 1st defendant's counsel the case of *Jones v Daniel* (2) very pertinent indeed. I have had occasion to look at the case and am satisfied with the quotation. Thus:-

> *A counter offer may come upon a scene not bearing its badge on its sleeve but dressed as an acceptance. In principle to be effective an acceptance must accept all the terms contained in the offer. In practice, however, many so called acceptances while purporting to accept also attempt to introduce new terms, such an acceptance is in fact a counter offer.*

Without doubt the issue of quantity was a fundamental term of the offer and for it to have been altered without the occurrence of the 1st defendant amounted to a counter offer. The argument that the 1st defendant was consulted and agreement obtained is not supported by the evidence on record. The letter at page 13 of the plaintiff's bundle of documents, to which the plaintiff's counsel has had occasion to refer the court to, is not conclusive that the 1st defendant had agreed to be bound by the cleaned up contract. In the said letter the 1st defendant is referring to 2000 tones of wheat and not 2,500 tones. At that stage the evidence would seem to suggest, and very strongly too, that the 1st defendant was not aware that the fundamental term as to quantity had been altered.

On 1st October, 1998, the plaintiff's counsel wrote a letter, now at page 14 of the plaintiff's bundle, purporting to convey the impression that the 1st defendant had, at previous meetings, accepted the counter-offer to buy 2500 tones and other terms as contained in the cleaned up contract. In his response thereto the 1st defendant's managing director (see his letter at page 16 of the plaintiff's bundle) vigorously spurned any suggestions that they had agreed to buy

(Continued)

(Continued)

2500 tones of wheat from the plaintiff. As far as he was concerned the cleaned up contract was a counter offer, which had never been accepted by the 1st dependent. With regard to the argument that the 1st defendant had, by its conduct and silence, accepted the terms of the counter offer and that as such it were estopped from asserting otherwise, the decision of Lord Denning, M.R in *Panchaud Frerers S.A. v Etablissements General Grain Co.* (3) is relevant. The Master of the Rolls, as he then was, espoused that the basis of estopped by conduct arose when "a man has so conducted himself that it would be unfair or unjust to allow him to depart from a particular state of affairs, another has taken to be settled or correct."

In order to succeed under the doctrine of estoppel, there must be a representation of fact intended to be acted upon by the person to whom it is made; the person to whom it is made must actually act on the representation; and by so acting it must be to his detriment. In the case of *Silver v Ocean Steamship Co.* (4) two parcels of cans of frozen eggs were shipped on the respondent's ship under a bill of lading, signed by the master, stating that they were shipped "in apparent good condition."

They were delivered damaged. The court held, as against the consignee of the eggs that the respondent was estopped from proving that the parcels were already damaged when they were shipped and consequently the respondent was liable in damages. The learned authors of Chatsworth Mercantile Law assert at page 85 by way of amplification, that:-

> ...the cause of action was that the respondent had damaged the eggs during transit, but the statement that they were in good order on shipment was an essential fact to be proved. Had there been no statement in the bill of lading the consignee would not have paid for the eggs. It was because the statement (which may have been false) was made that damages were payable.

The evidence will show that at no time did the 1st defendant conduct itself so as to give the impression that the counter-offer was in force. True to this the counter offer had not been signed at the time of trial despite the personal efforts PW1 made to secure the signatories of Mr. Darby or Mr. Fourie. Surely, had the two employees of the 1st defendant agreed to the cleaned up contract they would have signed the counter offer on the first day of their meeting with PW1. The fact that the 1st defendant sampled the wheat of the plaintiff in readiness for the delivery of the commodity is not proved as the facts on the ground tend to show that the sampling was done before the 1st defendant became aware that the plaintiff had made a counter offer. This explains, as I have already said above, why Mr. Fourie, the 1st defendant's managing director, made reference to 2000 tons of wheat at page 13 of the plaintiff's bundle.

It is contended that even though there was a counter offer the 1st defendant had, by its silence, accepted to be bound by the counter offer. In support of this position Mr. Dudhia has referred this court to a passage from Halsbury's Laws of England, Vol. 9, 4th Edition at paragraph 251 (3), which says:-

> Mere silence on the part of the original offer or on receipt of a counter offer will not usually operate as an acceptance but it might do so in the case of a late acceptance of an offer without definite time limit or where the original offer or only objects to some of the additional terms contained in the counter offer.

(Continued)

(Continued)

I have had occasion to visit paragraph 251; the above quotation in fact appears under sub-paragraph (2) and not sub-paragraph (3). The general rule is that mere silence on the part of the offeree does not constitute an acceptance of a counter offer. However, there may be other facts, which, if taken together with the offeree's silence, may constitute acceptance. In the case before me, the above quotation is given to highlight a situation in which may be taken to mean acceptance.

The learned authors assert that it might amount to acceptance where the offeree accepts a counter offer late or where the offeree objects to some of the additional terms in the counter offer. As I have already indicated above, the issue of the late acceptance does not arise in this case as there has been no acceptance at any one time. Similarly, there has been no objection to certain terms of the counter offer as such. At page 16 of the plaintiff's bundle, the 1st defendant is simply saying that the counter offer has never been accepted at all. In others words they are not saying that the counter offer is accepted *except for such and such terms*, but are rejecting the entire counter offer on the basis that it is a counter offer.

On the basis of what I have said in this judgment and on a balance of probabilities, the plaintiff's claim must fail on the ground that the counter offer as evidenced by the cleaned up contract did not constitute an acceptance of the offer. This meant that there was no contract at all. I will give cost to the 1st defendant to be taxed if default of agreement.

Hotel Travertine Limited, J.D. Lamba and Eva Lamba v National Bank of Commerce Limited

Court of Appeal, Dar es Salaam, Tanzania
Civil Appeal No. 82 of 2002, April 16th 2002
CORAM: Lubuva, J.A., Nsekela J.A., and Msoffe J.A.

Nsekela, J.A.:

The facts leading to this appeal may be briefly stated as follows. The first appellant, Hotel Travertine Limited, is a limited liability company; the second and third appellants are Directors of the first appellant. The respondent bank, National Bank of Commerce Limited, purportedly granted to the first appellant an overdraft facility amounting to Shs. 400,000,000. The agreement was secured by a joint and several guarantee of the Directors. The first appellant allegedly defaulted in the repayment of the overdraft facility and this triggered the respondent bank to institute a suit against the first appellant for the recovery of monies advanced. The High Court (Dr. S. J. Bwana, J.) entered judgment against the first appellant as principal debtor and against the Directors as guarantors of the overdraft facility. In addition the court below ordered that in default of the repayment of the decretal sum, Hotel Travertine should be attached. Aggrieved by this decision, the appellants have lodged this appeal.

Although the learned advocates for the appellants had preferred thirteen grounds of appeal against the judgment of the court below, we propose to deal only with the fourth ground of

(*Continued*)

(Continued)

appeal because, in our considered view, the resolution of that ground is sufficient to dispose of the appeal. The fourth ground of appeal was framed in the following manner -

The learned trial Judge erred in law in holding that exh. P6 constituted acceptance by the first appellant of the terms and conditions contained in the respondent's letter, exh. P3.

Exh. P3 is a letter from the respondent bank dated the 2.12.98 to the first appellant. This letter signified willingness on the part of the respondent bank to extend to the first appellant overdraft facilities on the terms and conditions enumerated therein. The concluding sentence was in the following terms -

Kindly acknowledge acceptance of the terms and conditions on the duplicate hereof.

Section 2 (1) of the Law of Contract Act Cap. 345 R.E. 2002 provides as follows -

2 (1) In this Act, unless the context otherwise requires -

(a) when one person signifies to another his willingness to do or to abstain from doing anything, with a view to obtaining the assent of that other to such act or abstinence, he is said to make a proposal.
(b) When the person to whom the proposal is made signifies his assent thereto, the proposal is said to be accepted, and a proposal when accepted, becomes a promise;

The real question for decision in this appeal is whether or not the first appellant's letter, exhibit P6 dated the 7.12.98 constituted acceptance. This takes us to Section 7 of the Law of Contract Act which provides -

7. In order to convert a proposal into a promise, the acceptance must —
(a) be absolute and unqualified;
(b) be expressed in some usual and reasonable manner, unless the proposal prescribes the manner in which it is to be accepted. If the proposal provides a manner in which it is to be accepted, and the acceptance is not made in such manner, the proposer may, within a reasonable time after the acceptance is communicated to him, insist that his proposal shall be accepted in the prescribed manner, and not otherwise; but if he fails to do so he accepts the acceptance.

Exhibit P6 is a letter from the first appellant to the respondent bank dated the 7.12.98. This letter is central to the resolution of this appeal. It reads in part as follows -

Please refer to your letter Ref. No. NBC "(1997)/FB/adv/C50/I of 2nd December, 1998 which I received on 5th December, 1998 regarding granting of T.Shs. 400,000,000 with the terms and conditions attached. The main work now being undertaken is to complete valuation of Hotel Travertine building which will be ready during this week. A reply to your above quoted letter will also be ready during the same variation period."

In the meantime, when valuation is being done at the same time a reply to your letter is being prepared, we request the service of the loan to continue being provided so as to enable us to make orders for the purchase of essential articles such as three lifts and others.

(Continued)

(Continued)

This letter was a reply to exhibit P3, a letter from the respondent bank to the first appellant which was rightly referred to by the learned trial Judge as "an offer". The learned trial Judge was of the view that exhibits P3 and P6 read together constituted an offer from the respondent bank and an acceptance by the first appellant respectively, thereby constituting a concluded agreement whose terms and conditions were embodied in exhibit P3.

As rightly pointed out by the learned trial Judge, exhibit P3 was the offer from the respondent bank. As stated before, the letter contained thirteen terms and conditions and concluded -

> *"Kindly acknowledge acceptance of the terms and conditions on the duplicate hereof."*

The thrust of Mr. Nyangarika's submission on this point is that the first appellant did not accept these terms and conditions. The first appellant did not sign the duplicate of exhibit P3 thus signifying the acceptance of its terms and conditions. On his part Mr. Mujulizi countered by submitting that the learned trial Judge considered the existence of the loan agreement and his answer was in the affirmative. The learned advocate referred to section 7 (b) and 8 of the Law of Contract Act and submitted that the subsequent conduct of the first appellant showed that the first appellant utilized the overdraft facility in terms of the contract.

The learned trial Judge after considering exhibits P3 and P6 came to the following settled conclusion -

> *I consider the contents of exh. P3 as being the offer and those of exh. P6 as the acceptance. Therefore in brief, there was a loan agreement between the parties and governed by the terms and conditions acknowledged by J.D. Lamba in exhibit P6.*

In exhibit P3, the respondent bank had prescribed an express method by which the terms and conditions of exhibit P3 were to be accepted, namely on the duplicate of that letter. This was not done. Instead, the first appellant wrote a letter exhibit P6 quoted earlier on.

DW1 John Lamba, the second appellant, in his examination in chief also stated so:

> *Concerning clause 2, to deposit some money. I can't tell where I would get the money to deposit even before the hotel opened. I didn't sign the letter because there was confusion regarding clause 2 as shown earlier. (emphasis added)*

In the case of *Brogden v. Metropolitan Railway Co.* (1877) 2 App. Cas. 666 (HL) Lord Blackburn observed as under -

> *I have always believed the law to be this, that when an offer is made to another party, and in that offer there is a request express or implied that he must signify his acceptance by doing some particular thing, then as soon as he does the thing, he is bound.*

The respondent bank had prescribed the mode of acceptance and the first appellant did not comply with the full knowledge of the respondent bank. How did the learned trial Judge handle this issue? He stated as follows -

> *The next key issue is whether there was a loan agreement inter parties. My considered view is in the affirmative. The defence case seems to suggest that there was none, as the defendants never*

(Continued)

(Continued)

countersigned any document accepting the same. This line of reasoning seems to be shortsighted. Exh. P3, which advises the defendants of the facility, authorizing a revolving overdraft of Shs. 400 million, was made in the form of a letter. **Therefore it was up to the defendants to countersign it and send back a copy to the plaintiff or to adopt a different approach. It seems the defendants opted for the latter.** *(emphasis added)*

With respect, we do not read anything in exhibit P3 which provides for an alternative route of accepting the offer — exhibit P3. The only method was to countersign the duplicate letter and the learned trial Judge clearly said so in his judgment. There is no provision for a different approach' in exhibit P3.

There is another aspect to exhibit P6. In this letter, the first appellant stated, inter alia -

A reply to your above quoted letter will also be ready during the same valuation period.

The learned trial Judge quoted this letter in his judgment but he inadvertently omitted this sentence. It is abundantly clear to us that this letter was not an acceptance of the letter dated 2.12.98 (exhibit P3). In the first place, this was not the prescribed mode of acceptance. Secondly, assuming it was, it was not a mirror image of exhibit P3. The import of exhibit P6 was to inform the respondent bank that a letter of reply was not ready as yet. In addition there was a request that the respondent bank do provide funds to enable the first appellant to purchase "essential articles such as lifts and others." In the case of *Gibson v. Manchester City Council* (1979) 1 WLR 294 (HL) Lord Dipiock at page 297 made the following pertinent observations -

"My Lords, there may be certain types of contract, though I think they are exceptional, which do not fit easily into the normal analysis of a contract as being constituted by offer and acceptance; but a contract alleged to have been made by an exchange of correspondence between the parties in which the successive communications other than the first are in reply to one another, is not one of these". I can see no reason in the instant case for departing from the conventional approach of looking at the handful of documents relied upon as constituting the contract sued upon the seeing whether upon their construction there is to be found in them a contractual offer by the corporation to sell the house to Mr. Gibson and an acceptance of that offer by Mr. Gibson.

With the greatest respect to the learned trial Judge, if we adopt the conventional approach as outlined above, as we do, the first appellant in his letter, exhibit P6, did not in law, accept the offer, exhibit P3. The parties it would appear were still locked up in negotiations. There is no evidence on the record that the first appellant had accepted exhibit P3 at any time. A reply to exhibit P3 was not ready and in any case the notification of acceptance was supposed to be on the duplicate letter of exhibit P3 and not a different letter from the first appellant.

Mr. Mujulizi, learned advocate for the respondent, like a good "soldier" he is, had also submitted that there was acceptance of the offer by conduct. The anchor of this submission was the alleged disbursement of Shs. 373,378,200/= to the first appellant. On the face of it, this is an attractive argument. However, acceptance by conduct was not pleaded. It should

(Continued)

(Continued)

have been pleaded in the alternative instead of the respondent bank relying solely on exhibits P3 and P6. Not surprisingly, the court below did not frame an issue along these lines and the learned trial Judge did not address his mind to this issue as well. His decision on the liability of the appellants was squarely based on the purported breach of agreement contained in exhibits P3 and P6. The issue of acceptance by conduct, if at all available, should have been pleaded and argued before the learned trial Judge. As a matter of general principle, an appellate court cannot allow matters not taken or pleaded in the court below, to be raised on appeal (see: *Gandy v. Gaspar Air Charters Ltd.* (1956) 23 EACA 139; *James Funke Gwagilo v. Attorney General* (CAT) Civil Appeal No. 67 of 2001 (unreported).

On a full consideration of the available evidence and the law on the issue we are of the settled view that the learned trial Judge was wrong to conclude that there was an agreement based on exhibits P3 and P6. It will be recalled that the first appellant had filed a counterclaim, claiming damages for the purported premature termination of the overdraft facility by the respondent bank. This was ground No. 12 in the memorandum of appeal. In view of the conclusion we have reached, the counter-claim has equally no leg upon which to stand.

In the result, we allow the appeal with costs and set aside the Judgment and order of the High Court. The appeal on the counterclaim is also dismissed.

2.3 The Writing Requirement—Statute of Frauds

One very important principle in contract law is the *Statute of Frauds* which requires that certain promises must be in writing to be enforced. The statute is an old Act of the Parliament of England that was enacted in 1677. The statute does not say that oral promises are invalid; it requires only that *certain* promises must be in writing to be enforced. The following promises must be in writing to be enforced:

1. Promise made in exchange of marriage;
2. Promise to pay for the debt of another;
3. Promise concerning an interest, transfer, or sale of land;
4. Promise that cannot be performed within one year from the date of the promise;
5. Promise for the sale of goods above a statutorily determined value.

One expert has stated that the traditional rationale for the Statute of Frauds is to prevent dishonest conduct. The literature identifies the following as the economic basis for the statute of frauds. First, the statute serves a "signaling" purpose, that is, to let it be known that they may initiate a legal action should a party not comply with the terms of a contract. Second, the statute serves an "evidentiary" purpose, that is, it provides a basis for the judiciary to determine cases, and third, the statute serves a "cautionary" purpose, that is, it forces parties to think carefully about the contracts they enter into.[5] The writing requirement fits neatly into a simple benefit−cost framework used by economists, that is, a contract will be reduced to writing if parties consider the benefits of a writing to be greater than the cost. In the case of *Akwei v. Agyapong and Another*, the court explained the application of the statute of frauds to the sale of land under common law and under customary law. The Uganda case of *Kagwa v. Turizm and others* applies the writing requirement to contracts exceeding a certain monetary amount, while the Zambia case of *Banda v. Mwanza* applied the statute to the sale of land under Zambia law.

Akwei v Agyapong and Another

HIGH COURT, Accra Ghana
1 GLR 277-279
1962-04-13

OLLENNU J.

JUDGEMENT

ACTION for declaration of title to land and recovery of possession.

The plaintiff claims declaration of title, an order for recovery of possession, damages for trespass and injunction in respect of a piece of land situated north of the Mental Hospital, Accra. The said piece of land is demarcated on the plan exhibit 1 and thereon edged pink.

The plaintiff's title to the land has been expressly admitted but the trespass is denied. It was pleaded for the first defendant that a binding agreement for sale of the said parcel of land exists between the plaintiff and first defendant, and that the entry of the first defendant upon the land was in pursuance of the said contract for sale, or upon leave and licence granted to him by the plaintiff.

The law of Ghana recognises two forms of contract for the sale of land. These are: (1) contract for the sale of land under the common law as defined in section 17 of the Interpretation Act, 1960 (C.A. 4), and (2) contract for the sale of land under customary law. [p. 278]

By section 4 of the Statute of Frauds, 1677, a statute of general application, applicable to Ghana by virtue of section 154 (4) of the Courts Act, 1960, a contract for the sale of land under the Ghana common law, with certain special exceptions, has to be evidenced by a note or memorandum in writing to make it enforceable. There is no such note or memorandum in writing in this case, and no circumstances have been shown which take this case out of the statute.

Contract for the sale of land by customary law is concluded by the offer of drink made by the prospective purchaser and acceptance of it by the prospective vendor. No negotiations in connection with the transfer of land or grant of an interest in land under customary law

(Continued)

(Continued)

can be concluded without drink given and received to seal it. As D.W.1 properly admitted, since no drink was offered and received, it means that the negotiations between the parties, whatever they were, did not reach a stage of conclusion. This is further borne out by the evidence of D.W.2 the surveyor, who, explaining why he did not sign the plan exhibit 1 drawn by him said that the said plan is not complete, and that the defendants simply wanted to know by the plan whether or not the land the defendants had started to build upon included the portion of the land of the plaintiff, and that after he had drawn the plan and the people had seen that the area included the plaintiff's land, they said they were going to negotiate with the plaintiff for the sale of his portion to them, adding that if the plaintiff agreed to sell, they would return to him and instruct him to prepare the final plan. He said the defendants had not gone back to him since he prepared exhibit 1. Thus apart altogether from the law on the point, this evidence of D.W.2 leads to a definite conclusion that the plaintiff never at any time agreed to sell the land, subject-matter of the suit, to the defendants or any of them, and he did not grant them or any of them leave and licence to go upon the land to put pegs on it, or to carry out building operations of any sort.

The evidence that both the first and second defendants went on the land without prior consent of the plaintiff and that they went for the purpose of carrying out building operations thereon and were met there by the plaintiff, has been admitted though there is a dispute as to the particular day and time when the plaintiff so met them. The initial entry by the defendants upon the land is trespass in each of them. The defendants aggravated the injury to the plaintiff by commencing to build thereon against opposition by the plaintiff, and persisting to rush through with it in defiance of the court's order for interim injunction.

The defendants have not claimed protection under the Land Development (Protection of Purchasers) Act, 1960. But I am bound to direct myself on the provisions of that Act. Having given the Act due consideration I have come to the conclusion that it does not apply to this case because, among other things, the defendants had not at the date of the institution of the action, erected a building on the land in terms of erection of a building as defined in section 4 (2) of the Act; whatever structures they now have on it were constructed during the pendency of the suit and in contempt of the court's order for interim injunction; their act is therefore not bona fide, and so this case does not come within the purview of the Act.

There will be judgment for the plaintiff against the defendants jointly and severally for: (1) declaration of his title to the land subject-matter of the suit; (2) an order for recovery of possession of the said land; (3) G50 damages for trespass to the said land; and (4) injunction. The plaintiff will have his costs fixed at 70 guineas inclusive.

DECISION

Judgment for plaintiff.

John Kagwa v Kolin Insaat Turzim Sanayi Ve Ticaret A.S. Nassur Bruhan

The Republic of Uganda
In the High Court of Uganda at Kampala
Commercial Court Division
HCT-00-CC-CS-0318-2012

BEFORE HON. MR. JUSTICE MASALU W. MUSENE

RULING

The plaintiff John Kagwa sued the two Defendants, Kolin Insaat Turzim Sanayi Ve ticaret A.S. and Nassur Bruhan, jointly and severally for breach of an oral contract for payment of commission. The alleged commission was a sum of US$500,000.00 (five hundred thousand United States Dollars). The plaintiff under paragraph (4) of the plaint also seeks to recover interest at the rate of 12% per annum, General damages, Punitive damages and costs.

Furthermore and according to paragraphs (2) and (3) of the plaint, the 1st Defendant is a body corporate operating in Uganda and having its registered office at Malcolm X Avenue, Kololo, Kampala, while the 2nd Defendant, Nassur Bruhan is the Country Director of the 1st Defendant.

The facts giving rise to the cause of action as alleged by the plaintiff are variously described under paragraph (5) of the plaint, but briefly that:

i. The plaintiff introduced the 2nd defendant to the personal assistant to the Minister of Roads in Kenya, and a contract to the then Rtd. Hon. Prime Minister of Kenya where upon he was entitled to a fees to be paid by the Defendants.
ii. That the plaintiff influenced the process and informed the Defendants of the opportunity to get a contract and construct Hoima Kaiso Tonya Road.
iii. That the Plaintiff arranged a meeting of the Defendants with the president of Uganda.
iv. The plaintiff engaged the then Mayor of Kampala, Hajji Sebaggala to sell out Plot 1 Sezibwa Road opposite Kampala Club to the defendants for construction of Commercial Centre, later consisted by Kampala Capital City Authority.
v. The Plaintiff organized a meeting in Nairobi between the 2nd Defendant on behalf of 1st. Defendant with Mr. Fidel Castro Odinga and Mr. Maliko Gichana, whereby extensive business opportunities and proposals were availed to the Defendants.

Under paragraph (1) of the written statement of defence, the 1st and 2nd Defendants stated that at the hearing, they would raise a preliminary objection to the effect that the suit is not maintainable in law and that the same is frivolous, vexatious, misconceived and does not disclose a cause of action.

Counsel for the Defendants raised the preliminary objection on a point of law under O. 6 rules 28, 29. And 30 of the Civil Procedure rules on grounds that the alleged oral contract upon which the plaintiff based his claim does not exist, and that notwithstanding, it contains elements that would render such contract unenforceable.

(Continued)

(Continued)

Learned Counsel for the Defendant cited the contract Act notably section 2 which defines *a contract as an agreement enforceable by law under S. 20 of the said Act.* Learned Counsel particularly stressed S. 10 (I) which provides that a contract is an agreement made with the **free consent** of the parties **with capacity to contract**, and for a **lawful consideration** and with the **lawful object**, to be legally **bound**. The same section 10 (2) also provides that a contract may be oral or written or partly written or may be implied from the conduct of the parties.

It was further submitted for the defendants that the plaintiff and the 2nd Defendant had no contractual relationship, as there was no written evidence to support plaintiff's claim and there was not agreement for commission at any point. They asserted that it was a personal relationship, whereby they introduced each other to their respective families, otherwise that the purported contract was voidable under sections 19(I), (2) and (3) of the contracts Act, 2010, and therefore void.

Counsel for Defendants cited the case of Makula International Ltd. Vs His Eminence Cardinal Nsubuga & Another (1982) HCB 11 and Broadways Construction Co. Vs Musa Kasule *Kagwa* & Others (1971) E.A. 16, where it was held that courts of law cannot sanction an illegality. And that once an illegality is brought to the attention of court, it overrides all questions of pleadings, including any admissions thereto.

It was further submitted that all acts that the plaintiff is claiming to have done are marred with inferences of corruption and influence peddling which are illegal under sections 2, 3, 4, and 8 of the Anticorruption Act No 6 of 2009. They added that even the principles of procurement under the Public Procurement and Disposal of Assets (PPDA) Act and the regulations there under would be violated. Counsel for the Defendants submitted that the alleged facts by the plaintiff also contravened Article 4 (f) of the African Union Convention on Prevention and combating corruption to which Uganda is a signatory. Otherwise the defendants denied the plaintiffs alleged contribution to the award of the contract and that the Defendants distanced themselves from any such dealings and commitments marred with corrupt tendencies and influence peddling.

Counsel for the plaintiff on the other hand, maintained that the plaint discloses a cause of action. He submitted that the courts should look at the plaint ordinarily and assume that the facts are correct in determining whether a cause of action is disclosed or not. He cited the case Attorney General Vs Olwoch (1972) E.A. 392 to support his argument. It was also submitted that O. 6 r. 28 of the Civil Procedure rules gives court a wide discretion as to whether to dispose of the preliminary point at or after hearing. Counsel for the plaintiff further submitted that the suit required evidence to be led first, before the issue of cause of action is determined.

On whether the said contract is enforceable or not counsel for the plaintiff referred to the case of J. K. Patel Vs Spear Motors Ltd. SCCA No. 4 of 1991, where it was held that if there has been an offer to enter into a legal relations on definite terms, and that after is accepted, the law considers that a contract has been made.

(Continued)

(Continued)

He added that since the above law is applicable, on oral contract is enforceable. Counsel for the plaintiff referred to the emails exhibits P4 and P5, which he submitted was a form of Data message for purposes of s. 10 (3) of the Contract Act. Otherwise, they added that the plaint shows that the plaintiff enjoyed a contractual right to be paid for his services by the defendants and that the defendants breached the contract and are liable.

It was further submitted that as far as section 10 (4) of the contract Act which provides for a contract exceeding twenty five currency points to be in writing, that the word "shall" in the above provisions is not **mandatory** but merely **directory**. Counsel for the plaintiff concluded that his role commenced after the award of a contract and he denied any allegations of corruption, bribery or influence peddling.

The court has considered the summarised submissions on both sides as far as the preliminary objection is concerned. The gist of the objection is that the contract alleged to have been breached by the Defendants should have been in writing. Section 10 (4) of the contracts Act provides:-

Section 10: agreement that amounts to a contract

"**10(4) a contract the subject matter of which exceeds twenty five currency points shall be in writing**"

According to the schedule to the Contracts Act, a currency point is equivalent to twenty thousand shillings, so twenty five currency points meant five hundred thousand (500,000) Uganda shillings.

It follows therefore that any contract exceeding Shs,500,000 like the present one, allegedly a commission of U.S. $500,000.00 should have been in writing.

Counsel for the plaintiffs reply was that the suit contract was partly oral and written in the Emails attached as exhibits P3, P4 an P5 respectively. I have looked at the said emails. P3 was an email from John Kagwa to Bruhan (the Plaintiff to 2nd Defendant). In summary it was a message of congratulations from the plaintiff to the 2nd Defendant upon the signing of the contract. And it goes on to lament that the plaintiff had forgotten him and cut off communications but that he was ready for one to one meeting at the convenience of the defendant. Then the Email, P4 was from B. N. (presumably 2nd Defendant), to John Kagwa, the plaintiff. It states that he was glad they were back to one on one relationship and that no one else could do better than the two of them. The 2nd Defendant then assures the plaintiff that he had no intentions to cheat him.

Lastly we emailed P5 which was from the plaintiff to the 2nd Defendant. It is to the effect that the plaintiff was apologising to the Defendant for whatever went wrong. He adds that **"we all learn through experience and that was an eye opener**." And that if there is another opportunity, then they all know their latitudes.

A close analysis of those emails by this court shows that there is nowhere in the said emails P3, P4 and P5 where the alleged commission of US$500,000.00 is mentioned. And as correctly submitted by counsel for the defendant In my view, the plaintiffs submissions with

(Continued)

(Continued)

regard to the emails is an attempt to deviate from his original claim of enforcing an oral contract of US$500,000.00, as set out in the pleadings. The emails exchanged and alleged data messages between plaintiff and 2nd Defendant confirm a social and private relationship between the plaintiff and the 2nd Defendant only.

There are not terms of any binding contract between the plaintiff and 2nd Defendant in those data messages, let alone the 1st Defendant which is a company. Nowhere in those data messages it is stated that the 2nd Defendant was acting on behalf of the 1st Defendant. And even then those emails fall short of containing elements of a valid contract as set out under S. 10 (1) of the Contracts Act.

It was an apparent attempt by the plaintiff to trap the 2nd Defendant and nothing completely to do with 1st Defendant which is a company. Needless to emphasise, parties are bound by their pleadings. That is the law practice. And as was held in the case of *Libyan Arab Uganda Bank Vs Messers Interpo Limited (1988) HCB 73*, in considering applications under O. 6 r 29, the court has to look at the pleadings alone and any annextures thereto, and not any subsequent affidavit.

This court therefore finds and holds that there was nothing at all in those emails to do with the alleged commissions of US$500,000.00 (over 1 billion Uganda shillings). And the Courts of Law cannot act on guesswork, particularly where it is in black and white that such contracts must be in writing. Counsel for the Plaintiff quoted the case of *Sitenda Sebalu Vs Sam Njuba*, Supreme Court Civil Appeal No 26. Of 2001 to support his submission that the word "shall" in S 10 (4) of the Contract Act is not mandatory but merely directory. I do not agree with those submissions because their Lordships in the Supreme Court were dealing with an issue of extension of time for service to Notice together with the petition on the Respondent within 7 days after presentation of the petition. And that was under the Parliamentary Elections Act of 2005 and Rules there under. It had nothing to do with the exercise of the court's discretion regarding contracts, the subject matter of which exceeds 25 currency points to be in writing. The Supreme court case was quoted completely out of context, In the case *of Steel Vs Sirs* (1980) All ER 529 Lord Diplock held:-

> *Where the meaning of the words is plain and unambiguous, it is not then for the Judges to invent fancied ambiguities as an effect to its plain meaning because they consider the consequences for doing so would be in expedient or even unjust or immoral.*

And in conformity with the above highly persuasive decision, I hold that the word "shall" under S. 10 (4) of the Contracts Act is mandatory. The provisions that such a contract shall be in writing is in plain English which can be understood by anyone who has gone to school. There is therefore no need for this court to bring in any other interpretations to suit the circumstances of the plaintiff's case. And the relationale behind that legislation under S. 10 (4) of the Contracts Act was to prevent persons or groups of persons from conspiring to claim huge sums of money from others under dubious deals. So in cases like the present one where hundreds of millions of Uganda shillings (after converting US$ 500,000.00) is being claimed this court cannot admit nothing less than a written contract.

(Continued)

(Continued)

And as was held in the case of *David May Vs Busitema Mining CIE Ltd.* HCT-00-CV-CS-0086-2008 quoted by counsel for the Defendants *noncompliance with the law rendered the contract invalid and unenforceable.*

That is the position as far as the plaintiff's case is concerned. I am further fortified in my findings by another highly persuasive case of *Olympic Holding Co L.L.C. Vs ACE Ltd* Slip Opinion No 209 — Ohio — 2057, cited by counsels for Defendant. In 2009, the Supreme Court of Ohio ruled that a party's breach of an alleged promise to sign an agreement does not eliminate the requirement under Ohio Statute of Frauds that such a contract is enforceable only if it is in writing and has been signed by the parties on which enforcement is sought. Justice Stratton noted:-

"Courts have long recognized that signed contract constitutes a party's final expression of his agreement. Thus the Statute of Frauds is necessary because a signed writing provides a greater assurance that the parties and the public can reliably known when such transaction occurs." I have no doubt whatsoever, that that was the similar intention under S.10 (4) of the contracts Act 2010 in this republic of Uganda.

In the circumstances a suit to enforce a contract of US$500,000.00 (over 1 billion Uganda Shillings) which is not in writing cannot be sustained and that is sufficient to dispose of the whole case.

I accordingly do hereby uphold the preliminary objection by the Defendants and dismiss the plaintiff's suit with costs under O. 6 rules 28, 29, and 30 of the Civil Procedure Rules.

Enesi Banda v Abigail Mwanza
In the High Court of Zambia at the Principal Registry Holden at Lusaka

(Civil Jurisdiction)
(2006/HP/A002) [2011] ZMHC 72 (3 August 2011);

JUDGMENT

The respondent in this matter will be referred to as the plaintiff, and the appellant as the defendant; the designations they were referred to in the Court below. This matter was commenced on 8th March, 2005, in the Subordinate Court of the First Class, by way of writ of summons. The plaintiff's claims were for the following:

1. Vacant possession of house number 18, Block 371, Chipata compound, which house was sold by the defendant's husband to the plaintiff;
2. Further, or in the alternative the return of K 8, 000, 000, being the purchase price of the said house;
3. Interest on the said sum; and
4. Costs.

(Continued)

(Continued)

During the trial, the plaintiff testified that her husband bought the property in issue from Kazumalo Bendicto Petrol, the husband to the defendant at a purchase price of K 8, 000, 000 = 00. The purchase price was paid in installments to the defendant's husband. And the last installment was paid sometime in July, 2004. During cross-examination, the plaintiff testified that she was not present when her husband transacted with the plaintiff. She also testified that she was not aware whether or not her husband also dealt with the defendant in the purchase of the property in issue. After the purchase price was paid in full, an occupancy license was issued to the plaintiff by the Lusaka City Council. The testimony of the plaintiff was supported by one witness; Mr. Humphrey Maliti. Mr. Maliti is the husband of the plaintiff. In essence Mr. Maliti confirmed that he bought the house in issue for the plaintiff. Mr. Maliti also confirmed that at the time the last installment was paid, a quarrel erupted between the defendant and her husband. Mr. Matili also testified that when differences arose between the plaintiff, and the defendant, the police advised them that the defendant should refund the plaintiff, else the title to the property would be registered in the name of the plaintiff.

In defence, the defendant contended in the Court below as follows: that she was not aware that her husband sold the house in issue to the plaintiff. The defendant maintained that when the plaintiff showed her the occupancy licence attesting to the fact that the plaintiff had bought the house, she refused to vacate the house because her husband was not the owner of the house in issue. During cross-examination, the defendant maintained that the house in issue was for her uncle, whose whereabouts, she did not know. And she further maintained that she did not know the whereabouts of her husband as well. To support her testimony, the defendant called her 16 year old son; Christopher Kazumiro as her only witness. Christopher testified that the house belonged to his grandfather who lives in George compound. He also confirmed that when the dispute arose, the police advised his father to refund the purchase price to the plaintiff.

On 28th December, 2005, the judgment was delivered in the Court below. In the course of delivery of the judgment appealed against, Mr. Hampande observed that the plaintiff claims vacant possession of a house she bought from the defendant's husband. He however noted that the defendant has refused to vacate the house on the ground that she was not consulted by her husband when he sold the house to the plaintiff. Mr. Hampande noted that when the defendant became aware that her husband had sold the house, the police advised the defendant's husband to refund the plaintiff the purchase price. Mr. Hampande went on to observe that the defendant's husband failed to refund the plaintiff the purchase price, hence the adjudication of the dispute in the Court below.

After evaluating the evidence, Mr. Hampande found that the assertion by the defendant that she did not know the whereabouts of her uncle was disputed by Christopher when he testified that the defendant's uncle lives in George compound. Mr. Hampande went on to hold that after the defendant discovered that the house had been sold, she should either have sued her husband, or in the alternative, she should have called her husband as a witness. Mr. Hampande opined that this was not done because the house belonged to the defendant's

(Continued)

(Continued)

husband. Mr. Hampande held that the only mistake the defendant's husband made was that he did not consult the defendant when selling the house. Mr. Hampande further held that he could not consult the defendant, because the two were at the material time at logger heads.

In view of the foregoing, Mr. Hampande held ultimately that he was satisfied that on a balance of probabilities, the plaintiff had proved the claim against the defendant. Thus, Mr. Hampande, entered judgment in favour of the plaintiff. And ordered that vacant possession be granted within fourteen days from the date of the judgment. Wit the 28th December, 2005. The defendant was dissatisfied with the judgment of the Court below. Consequently, on 10th January, 2006, she filed a Notice of Appeal. The Notice of Appeal was followed with the filing of the grounds of appeal pursuant to Order 44, rule 5, of the Subordinate Court Act. The grounds of appeal were stated as follows:

1. The Court below erred in law in accepting the evidence of the plaintiff that she bought the house from the defendant. The defendant's husband had no authority, express or implied, to do so, nor did he own it either alone or jointly with the plaintiff;
2. The Registration and Agreement Form for House Owners in existing areas; (DD Form 5/79), shows that the house was originally owned by one Siwalunda John Chibungo who sold it to the defendant contrary to the evidence of the plaintiff;
3. The evidence of the plaintiff shows (in cross examination) that the defendant was not there when the defendant's husband went to the plaintiff's house. The defendant could not possibly have consented to the sale of the house;
4. The Court also relied on the evidence of one Humphrey Maliti who stated that the husband was selling the house. His evidence that title changed in favour of the plaintiff is not supported by any documentary evidence. The evidence was relied upon in the absence of any evidence which suggested that the husband had express or implied authority to sell the house. Indeed, the quarrel alluded to between the husband, and the defendant should have put the purchaser on constructive notice that the purported vendor had no authority whatsoever to deal with the property.

On 3rd December, 2010, Mr. Banda filed heads of arguments on behalf of the defendant. After recapitulating the grounds of appeal, Mr. Banda contends that the plaintiff did not acquire good title to the property because the purported vendor; the defendant's husband, did not have express or implied authority, or indeed the defendant's consent, to sell the property in issue to the plaintiff. Mr. Banda further contends that the defendant has lived in the property since 1985, having acquired the same from her uncle; one Siwalunda John Chibungo.

In addition, Mr. Banda contends that in terms of section 4 of the Statute of Frauds, 1677, transactions, or dealings in land must be evidenced in writing. And such writing must meet the threshold, of a *"note or memorandum"*. The learned authors of Cheshire and Fifoots Law of Contract, 10th edition, 1981, state at page 185 that:

> *The agreement itself need not be in writing. A note or memorandum of it is sufficient, provided that it contains all material terms of the contract. Such facts as the names, or adequate identification of*

(Continued)

(Continued)

the parties, the description of the subject matter, the nature of the consideration, comprise what may be called the minimum requirements. But the circumstances of each case need to be examined, to discover if any individual term has been deemed material by the parties, and if so, it must be included in the memorandum.

Mr. Banda submitted that the pieces of writing on record, clearly do not qualify to meet the minimum requirements for a conveyance of land as required by law, because the defendant never executed any of the documents purporting to sell the property to the plaintiff. Thus, Mr. Banda argued that on that basis alone, the transaction should be set aside for being void, and the property reinstated to the defendant.

On 3rd December, 2010, Mr. Phiri filed the respondent's heads of arguments. First, Mr. Phiri submitted that there is no evidence to prove that the property in issue was jointly owned to justify the contention that the defendant's husband unilaterally dealt with the property without the consent of the defendant. Second, Mr. Phiri submitted that SS Form 5/79, referred to in the second ground of appeal, is not part of the record of appeal. Be that as it may, Mr. Phiri submitted that the Form is part of the *"ADDITIONAL DOCUMENTS TO BE USED AT TRIAL"*, which was filed on 24th September, 2009. Mr. Phiri argued that the Form clearly shows that the initial owner was Siwalunda John Chibunga. Further, he submitted that in the same documents, there is a contract of sale between Chibungo and B.P. Kazumalo. Kazumulo, Mr. Phiri submitted, Mr. Kazumulo is the husband to the defendant.

On 3rd December, 2010, both counsel for the plaintiff, and the defendant supplemented their written submissions, with oral arguments. Mr. Banda argued on behalf of the defendant that the property in issue was a matrimonial property to which the defendant was entitled to. He argued further that at no time did the defendant's husband procure in his name an occupancy licence in respect of the property in issue. Mr. Banda maintained that what the evidence suggests is that the defendant's husband had no legal capacity to own land because he hails from Mozambique. He submitted that this assertion has not been challenged by the plaintiff. Thus he argued that if the plaintiff had conducted a proper inquiry before he entered into the purported contract of sale, she would have discovered that the defendant's husband was a foreigner who had no capacity to own land.

In turn, Mr. Phiri submitted on behalf of the plaintiff that the only way in which title to property can be cancelled is if there is proof of fraud in obtaining title. In this case, he argued that the defendant has not adduced any evidence to show that title to the property was fraudulently acquired. Mr. Phiri maintained that the only evidence that has been adduced is that the defendant was the wife to the vendor. Mr. Phiri contends that there is no legal requirement that in order to lawfully dispose of a matrimonial property, parties to a marriage must both consent to the transaction.

(Continued)

(Continued)

I am indebted to counsel for the spirited arguments, and submissions. In my opinion the questions that fall to be determined in this appeal are as follows:

----

1. -----------
2. -----------
3. ----------
4. Whether or not the contract between the plaintiff and the defendant's husband complied with the Statute of Frauds of 1677.

Did the contract of sale comply with the Statute of Frauds?

The last question that falls to be considered is whether, or not the contract of sale complied with the Statute of Frauds. A contract to sell or make any other disposition of any interest in land differs from other contracts in at least three main respects. First, such a contract can only be made in writing in accordance with the formalities laid down by section 4 of the Statute of Frauds, 1677. Second, the usual remedy for the enforcement of such contract is specific performance rather than the normal award of damages. (See *Mundanda v Mulwani and Others (1987) Z.R. 29*). Third, as a consequence of this, a purchaser even before conveyance acquires an immediate equitable interest.

Section 4 of the Statute of Frauds, 1677, provides that:

> *No action shall be brought upon any contract for the sale of other disposition of land or interest in land unless the agreement upon which such action shall be brought, or some memorandum or note thereof shall be in writing and signed by the party to be charged therewith, or some other person there unto by him lawfully authorized.*

The agreement itself need not be in writing. A note or memorandum of it is sufficient, provided that it contains all the material terms of the contract. The material terms include the names, or adequate identification of the parties; the description of the subject matter of the contract, and the nature of the consideration. These constitute what may be called the minimum requirements. On the facts of this case the purported contract between the plaintiff and the defendant's husband does satisfy the requirements of section 4 of the Statute of Frauds 1677, because the note or memorandum contained in the *"Additional Documents to be used at Trial,"* adequately identifies the parties; the description of the property; and the manner in which the purchase price was settled. I therefore find and hold that section 4 of the Statute of Frauds was complied with.

In the final result, I however allow the appeal, because the defendant was not the legal owner of the house: he did not have the power to sell the house; and the plaintiff had constructive notice of the defendant's interest in the house.

For avoidance of doubt, the lawful owner of the house in dispute is the defendant, and the Lusaka City Council, is accordingly ordered to amend the records. Costs follow the event. And leave to appeal is hereby granted.

2.4 Breach of Contract and Excuses for Nonperformance

Under common law, a party has the choice to perform a contract as promised and avoid damages, or breach the contract and pay damages. Thus there has emerged an extensive literature on what is known as "efficient breach" in the law and economics literature. As succinctly stated, "in economic analysis, a breach of contract is efficient when the breaching promisor internalizes the costs of her decision by compensating the promise for losses caused by the breach. A promisor might breach by simply failing to perform on the date when performance is due. Alternatively, she may repudiate her contract before the time for performance by indicating to the promisee that she cannot or will not perform. Modern contract law treats the promisor's repudiation as a breach" (Triantis and Triantis, 1998).

Under certain circumstances, a court may excuse performance and not hold the breaching party liable to pay compensation. One such situation is where the breaching party raises the defense of *impossibility*. Impossibility means that the person or thing involved in the contract is no longer available. For example, suppose the parties enter into a contract to buy a particular pesticide supplied by the only licensed importer in the country. If the importer closes its business thereby making the pesticide unavailable, a court may relieve the supplier because performance has become impossible. But suppose the importer did not close the business but at the time to perform the contract, the price of the pesticide had doubled. The higher price will not support a defense of impossibility because the pesticide is available.

One court has defined the doctrine of impossibility using language that better reveals the economic rationale supporting the doctrine, "It is now recognized that a thing is impossible in legal contemplation when it is not practicable; and a thing is impracticable when it can only be done at an excessive and unreasonable *cost*."[6] A court engages in a three-step assessment to determine whether to allow the defense of impossibility of performance: (1) a contingency (something unexpected) must have occurred; (2) the risk of the unexpected occurrence must not have been allocated either by agreement or by custom; and (3) occurrence of the contingency must have rendered performance commercially impracticable.[7] *Agriculture Bank of Zimbabwe Ltd T/A AGRIBANK v. DATANET Technology Zimbabwe.*[8]

Another situation where a court might excuse performance is where the defendant raises the doctrine of *frustration of purpose*. The principle applies in a post-contract situation where the fulfillment of the contract by one party has no value to the other party.[9] The party invoking this principle to support their defense, carries the burden for showing that (1) a supervening event occurred that should excuse performance, (2) it did not bear the risk of the event, and (3) the event rendered the value of the performance worthless to him or her. For example, a party purchases a ticket to attend a music festival in an enclosed auditorium to better enjoy the sound effect. The party may rely on the principle of frustration of purpose if the festival was moved 45 miles away to an open stadium. In *Soboyejo v. Onidepe*[10] the High Court of Lagos explained the conditions under which a party may be excused from performance of a contract based on the doctrine of frustration of purpose.

Agriculture Bank of Zimbabwe Ltd T/A AGRIBANK v DATANET Technology Zimbabwe

High Court of Zimbabwe, Harare, 11 June 2008
Mtshiya J.

MTSHIYA J: The cause of action in this case arises out of an alleged breach of contract by the defendant for the supply of 20 IBM A50 desktop computers (computers) to the plaintiff.

The plaintiff is suing the defendant for specific performance or payment of damages in lieu thereof.

At the commencement of the trial the plaintiff applied to amend the damages figure or the summons to read $9 792 245 000 000-00 instead of $7 800 000 000-00. The amendment was meant to address the effect of inflation on the original figure. Counsel for the defendant did not oppose the application for amendment. I granted the application for amendment and consequently the plaintiff's claim herein is for:

(a) An order that the defendant supply and deliver to the plaintiff a total of twenty (20) IBM A50 desktop computers forthwith alternatively an order that defendant pays to plaintiff a total of $9 792 245 000 000-00 representing the current value of the said computers.
(b) Interest on the amount representing the value of the computers from the date of summons to the date of payment; and
(c) Costs of suit.

It is common cause that on 23 February 2005 the plaintiff ordered from the defendant a total of thirty (30) computers. Each computer was quoted at a price of $9 860 400-00, bringing the total cost, including V.A.T. payment, to $340 183 800-00. This amount was then paid in full on 28 February 2008. The defendant, however, only managed to deliver ten (10) computers on 2 March 2005. This left a balance of 20 computers. It is the non-delivery of these 20 computers that has led to this court action.

The defendant explains non-delivery by citing the failure to obtain the requisite foreign currency allocation from the Reserve Bank of Zimbabwe through the auction system which was then in operation. It is the defendant's position that both parties were fully aware that the amount paid by the plaintiff would be utilised for the purchase of foreign currency in order to meet the requirements of the defendant's foreign supplier, namely a company called 'Tri-Continental Limited' (Tri-Continental). However, plaintiff's position is that delivery was to be effected soon after payment and the total amount paid represented the full payment for the 30 computers ordered.

(Continued)

(Continued)

In view of the different positions taken by the parties, it was agreed that the issues for determination in this trial would be:-

(1) What were the terms of the Agreement between the parties?
(2) Whether it was agreed as between the parties that defendant would supply the computers upon receiving foreign currency allocation by the Reserve Bank of Zimbabwe.
(3) Whether the plaintiff is entitled to the order sought.
(4) Whether the defendant is liable to the plaintiff in damages.

The plaintiff called two witnesses to support its case and through the witnesses it submitted a total of nine (9) exhibits.

The first witness called by the plaintiff was Mr Patrick Gwara ("Mr Gwara") who said he is currently employed by the plaintiff as a Stores Supervisor with the main responsibility of taking care of the plaintiff's stocks. Mr Gwara testified that upon an evaluation of quotations the defendant was awarded the contract/tender to supply the plaintiff with thirty (30) computers. He said upon being paid the sum of $340 180 800-00 to cover the total cost of the computers, the defendant delivered ten (10) computers. The ten (10) computers were received by the plaintiff on 2 March 2005. That left a balance of 20 computers already paid for.

It was Mr Gwara's evidence that at the time of placing the order with it, the defendant had indicated that it had twenty-five (25) computers in stock and 'it would get the other five (5)'. He said, apart from paying the requisite purchase price for the computers, the plaintiff was not aware of the financial arrangements between the defendant and its suppliers. He went further to say if the plaintiff had known that the defendant would face supply problems, it (plaintiff) would not have placed the order with the defendant. This was so because the computers were needed urgently for its Harare and Bulawayo offices.

Under cross-examination Mr Gwara said he was not aware that his seniors had moved the delivery date to 1 July 2005 as indicated in the replication. He, however, maintained that as far as he was concerned delivery was to be made soon after payment. He said that although the plaintiff had in the past accepted long delivery periods with respect to other contracts, this was not the case with respect to the thirty (30) computers because they were needed urgently. The contract/tender, had been awarded to the defendant on the basis that it had the computers in stock. Mr Gwara denied knowledge of the offer by the defendant to refund the plaintiff. He said as far as he was concerned the plaintiff wanted delivery of the 20 computers.

The second witness called by the plaintiff was Mr Mischeck Chigatse ("Mr Chigatse"). He said he is employed by the plaintiff as a Procurement Officer. Mr Chigatse was, in that capacity, responsible for the procurement of goods and services for the plaintiff. He was, however, not aware of the issue of the thirty (30) computers since the contract had been entered into before he was employed by the plaintiff. The witness, however, gave evidence on current prices of computers such as those forming the subject of the dispute herein. He said the prices ranged from $300 billion to $700 billion. His evidence was based on three

(Continued)

(Continued)

(3) quotations obtained by the plaintiff. He said based on the quotations, the current price of a similar computer to the one that had been ordered by the plaintiff would be $489 billion.

The defendant called only one witness to support its case. It called Mrs Doreen Nyamusara ("Mrs Nyamusara"). She said she joined the employ of the defendant in April 2005 as a Finance Manager but was, as from January 2008 promoted to the position of General Manager. She told the court that she was unaware of the details of the contract in issue since she joined the employ of the defendant when the contract had already been concluded. She was, however, involved in negotiations with the defendant's suppliers for the delivery of the remaining twenty (20) computers.

Mrs Nyamusara testified that at one stage the defendant had asked the plaintiff to participate in the auctions(s) for foreign currency. The plaintiff had refused to do so. She said after all efforts to obtain foreign currency had failed to produce results, the defendant had offered to refund the plaintiff. The plaintiff had, however, declined the offer, insisting that it wanted delivery of the computers.

Mrs Nyamusara also stated that the parties failed to resolve the matter amicably largely due to differences in the calculation(s) of interest. As a result of the differences the matter was never resolved amicably. This was notwithstanding the fact that the defendant made a payment of $1 392 000-00 through the plaintiff's legal practitioners – which payment was still being held by the plaintiff's legal practitioners. Under cross-examination, she agreed that the sum of $1 392 000-00 was too little to pay for the twenty (20) computers.

Also admitting that the type of computers originally ordered by the plaintiff had been phased out, Mrs Nyamusara said a similar computer (ie A55 Lenovo) would, as per exhibit 24, cost $143 750 000 000-00.

Mr *Dondo* for the plaintiff submitted that there was no doubt that delivery was to be effected immediately upon payment of the full purchase price. He said the issue of foreign exchange was only brought up in an effort to justify a clear breach of contract by the defendant. He said that in concluding the contract the issue of foreign exchange was never raised. He said the quotations which resulted in the award of the contract were in local currency – with the foreign exchange element having been taken into account. It was his view that if indeed the issue of foreign exchange had been a factor, the parties would have said so upon executing the contract. He urged the court to dismiss the defendant's defence based on the shortage of foreign currency because it came as an afterthought. Relying on RH Christie's The Law of Contract in South Africa 3 ed, Mr *Dondo* submitted that 'an impossibility to perform must be absolute'. He argued that *in casu*, that defence was not available and as such the defendant was clearly in breach and was liable for the prejudice suffered by the plaintiff. To that end Mr *Dondo* prayed either for the delivery of the twenty (20) computers or payment of damages representing the current market value of the computers.

Mr *Dondo* submitted that if payment of damages were to be ordered, the sum of $9 792 245 000 000-00 would be reasonable because it would enable the plaintiff to procure the computers on its own. That value, he argued, had not been challenged. The primary aim in

(Continued)

(Continued)

asking for damages was to put the plaintiff to where it should have been were it not for the breach of contract by the defendant.

Mr Dondo further submitted that the issue of money paid to the plaintiff's legal practitioners should not be allowed to cloud the issues before the court. That money could still be recovered.

Ms *Shongedza* for the defendant submitted that the dispute was mainly on the issue of the delivery dates. She said that the parties were not agreed on what was the delivery date. She, however, agreed that the defendant's only witness could not testify to the terms of the contract since it was concluded before she joined the defendant's employ.

Ms *Shongedza* submitted that as per the plaintiff's replication, the delivery date in terms of the contract should have been 1 July 2005. That, according to her, meant there was no question of immediate delivery in line with the parties' conduct on previous supply contracts. She went further to suggest that the failure by Mr Gwara to explain the averment in the replication referring to 1 July 2005 supported the defendant's case in the sense that a delay of some four months after payment meant that the computers would be delivered only after the defendant had paid its supplier, namely Tri-Continental. Payment involved foreign currency.

It was therefore Ms *Shongedza's* submission that the plaintiff, despite denial, was aware from inception that delivery of the computers would only be effected after the procurement of foreign exchange by the defendant. Accordingly, when that became impossible, it meant the defendant could no longer deliver as had been agreed. The failure to obtain foreign currency was, in her view, a supervening impossibility which served to extinguish the defendant's obligations under the contract. She said according to Joubert's General Principles of the Law of Contract, the defence of a supervening impossibility was available to the defendant. To that end she quoted Joubert at page 293 where he states:-

> *Performance may become either absolutely or relatively impossible after the conclusion of the contract. In the case of absolute or objective impossibility of performance the rule is undoubtedly that the duty of the debtor to perform is extinguished ...*

On the basis of the above, Ms *Shongedza* submitted that it was improper for the plaintiff to insist on specific performance. In so doing, she argued, the plaintiff had contributed to its own loss. She said the loss would have been mitigated if the plaintiff had accepted the refund offered in May 2005. The defendant had, all the same, gone ahead to refund the plaintiff with a sum of $1 362 980-32. That money was still being held in trust by the plaintiff's legal practitioners. The amount, it was argued, had been calculated properly and therefore the defendant's view was that the plaintiff had been refunded in full. There was therefore no basis for this action.

On the possibility of the court finding in favour of the plaintiff and ordering payment of damages, Ms *Shongedza* submitted that the figures quoted by the plaintiff were excessive and did not accurately reflect the current prices for the originally ordered computers. She said although there was no case for damages, the defendant's own quotation of $143 750 000-00,

(Continued)

(Continued)

would represent a reasonable figure. The fact that the plaintiff's loss would have been mitigated if it had participated in foreign currency auctions or had accepted the refund as offered in May 2005 could not be ignored. Accordingly damages payable, if any, should be reduced, she argued.

Ms *Shongedza* also urged the court to be cautious when evaluating Mr Gwara's evidence. She said this was so because Mr Gwara had denied knowledge of the refund issue yet there was evidence that correspondence on the issue was copied to him.

I shall, taking into account evidence from both parties' witnesses and submissions by their legal practitioners, now deal with the agreed issues for determination. The issues are enumerated in the second paragraph at page 2 herein.

In dealing with this matter, I believe that a finding of whether or not delivery of the computers was subject to the availability of foreign currency to meet the defendant's suppliers' financial requirements will greatly narrow issues for consideration. In order for that argument to succeed the court has to be convinced that in paying the sum of $340 183 800-00 the plaintiff was fully aware that this was merely <u>part payment</u> which would go towards the purchase of foreign currency. There must be evidence that the defendant made it clear to the plaintiff that delivery would be dictated by the availability of foreign currency to meet the requirement of Tri-Continental, its supplier. This is clearly so because apart from quotations and payment confirmations, the contract terms were not reduced to writing.

In *casu* the evidence from papers and that lead in court leads me to the conclusion that the defendant cannot avail itself to the defence of a supervening impossibility. This is so because it is clear to me that the plaintiff gave the contract/tender to the defendant on the understanding that the computers were in stock and readily available. All what the plaintiff was required to do was to effect full payment and then delivery would follow immediately. The defendant had indeed indicated to the plaintiff that it had the computers in stock, at least 25 of them. The plaintiff effected full payment on 28 February 2008. Payment was in accordance with the defendant's quotation for the delivery of 30 computers.

Contrary to the defendant's legal practitioner's perception of Mr Gwara, I found him to be a credible witness who knew exactly what took place when the contract was entered into between the two parties. His failure to know subsequent details of discussions between the plaintiff's senior management and the defendant's representatives on the issue of delivery times and the refund, should not be allowed to carve a dent into his evidence.

The witness, Mr Gwara, was adamant that the issue of foreign currency was never raised when the contract was granted to the defendant. He pointed out that if at all the plaintiff knew there would be problems of foreign currency the contract would not have been granted to the defendant. The plaintiff needed the computers urgently and the defendant had indicated that it had twenty-five (25) in stock and would look for the other five (5). That evidence was never satisfactorily challenged in court. All the defendant could say was that the computers were in stock at Tri-Continental. Clearly, if that detail was necessary the defendant could have revealed it to the plaintiff at the time of concluding the contract. That was not

(Continued)

(Continued)

done and as submitted by the plaintiff's legal practitioner, I hold the view that the price quoted in Zimbabwean dollars included the foreign exchange component. Indeed, even upon the speedy delivery of ten (10) computers, there was no mention of a possible top up to cater for the foreign currency element required for the remaining twenty (20) computers. It is also significant to note that full payment was made on 28 February 2005 and within a few days (ie. 2 March 2005) ten (10) computers were delivered. That reinforces the issue of immediate delivery upon full payment and the availability of computers in stock in Zimbabwe.

As already indicated the defendant has also argued that failure to procure foreign currency rendered performance impossible and hence the defence of a supervening impossibility. As correctly argued by the plaintiff's legal practitioner, that defence is not available to the defendant. Right from the inception of the contract the defendant made the plaintiff believe the computers were in stock in Zimbabwe. That is why within 3 days the defendant was able to deliver 10 computers. The issue of foreign currency only came up as an excuse for failure to deliver.

I am therefore, on a balance of probabilities, satisfied that upon making full payment on 28 February 2005 the plaintiff had fully discharged its obligation under the contract. That means the issue of foreign currency was never raised when the contract was concluded and did not therefore form part of the contract terms.

Upon failure to reach an out of court settlement, the plaintiff remained ready to accept delivery. This remained the plaintiff's position up to the hearing of this matter. To that end I would reject the defence of a supervening impossibility because my finding is that when the contract was made the defendant assured the plaintiff of immediate delivery upon payment, as evidenced by the delivery of the first ten (10) computers. There was no basis for the plaintiff to ever think or imagine that the remaining twenty (20) computers were not in stock. The contract was not subject to the defendant being availed foreign currency by the Reserve Bank of Zimbabwe. If indeed that were the case, the contract would have said so. As was submitted by the plaintiff's legal practitioner, the issue of an agreement becoming impossible of performance is fully covered by R.H. Christie in his book 'The Law of Contract In South Africa 3 ed,' at pages 101-102 where he writes:-

> *The Roman law principle that a contract is a nullity if at the time it was made it was impossible of performance forms part of our law.*
>
> *By the Civil Law a contract is void if at the time of its inception its performance is impossible:* impossiblium nulla obligation (D50.17.185).
>
> *But the principle thus stated may easily be misunderstood and requires immediate qualification in four respects. First, the impossibility must be absolute as opposed to probable. The mere likelihood that performance will prove impossible is not sufficient to destroy the contract. Second, the impossibility must be absolute as opposed to relative. If I promise to do something which, in general, can be done, but which I cannot do, I am liable on the contract. Third, the impossibility must not be the fault of either party. A party who has caused the impossibility cannot take advantage of it and so will be liable on the contract. Fourth, the principle must give way to the contrary common*

(Continued)

(Continued)

intention of the parties. This intention may be expressed, as when a seller expressly represents or promises that the merx *exists. If it is found not to have been in existence at the time the contract was made, he will be liable for damages for breach of his promises or for his false representation if fraudulent or negligent. Or the common intention of the parties may be implied, as in the case of the sale or lease of a* res aliena. *The seller or lessor impliedly undertakes to deliver the property or to pay damages if he is unable to do so.*

In *casu*, there is nothing to suggest impossibility at the time of contracting or to suggest any conditionalities. There is also nothing to suggest that the issue of foreign currency led to a complete paralysis of the defendant's business. To date it is still in the business of selling computers.

As already stated, it is my finding that the defendant clearly represented to the plaintiff that he had the computers in stock and since the plaintiff needed them urgently he gave the contract/tender to the defendant. In breach of contract and without any fault on the part of the plaintiff the defendant delivered ten (10) computers only, leaving a balance of twenty (20) computers. Clearly therefore and in line with the principles of law enunciated by R.H. Christie in the above quoted passage, the defendant is liable for specific performance or damages. (See *Lupu v Lupu* 2000(1) ZLR 120 (S)).

The plaintiff still insists on specific performance or payments of damages to cover the cost of similar computers at today's prices. I also did not hear the defendant to say it cannot perform. The defendant is still in the business of selling computers. Quotations were produced to indicate current prices for similar computers. The defendant produced one quotation and argued that the plaintiff's prices were for superior machines. The defendant said that a computer similar to the one originally ordered would cost $143 750 000 000-00.

The plaintiff, however, believes that, in order for it to be put back to where it would have been had the twenty computers been delivered, a sum of $9 792 245 000 000-00 should be payable in the event of failure by the defendant to deliver. That amount is based on quotations for each similar computer on exhibits 8 ($382 455 561 600-00), 9 ($489 622 500 000-00) and 10 ($776 250 000-00). Given the effects of inflation the plaintiff recommended the midway price of $489 622 500 000-00. The defendant, on its part and despite denying liability, insisted that it was possible to procure similar computers at the price it quoted (ie. $143 750 000 000-00).

Counsel for the plaintiff submitted that the matter of a refund should not be allowed to cloud the real issues before the court. I agree. I believe the payment of $1 392 000-00 through the plaintiff legal practitioners only serves to confirm a failed attempt to settle the matter out court. In any case Mrs Nyamusara who testified for the defendant agreed that the money was too little to cover the cost of twenty (20) computers.

I hold the view that a party that is in clear breach should not be allowed to dictate the amount of damages that should be paid to the party that is not at fault and more so an innocent party that will have fully met its obligations under a contract. To allow that would be to encourage parties to pull out of contracts on the strength of their capacity to pay damages.

(Continued)

(Continued)

In *International Trading (Pvt) Ltd v Nestle Zimbabwe (Pvt) Ltd*,1993(1) ZLR 21 (H), addressing the issue of specific performance, the late ROBINSON J, as he then was, had this to say:

> *I would wind up by saying that if the right of specific performance is to be shown to have real meaning to businessmen, then the loud and clear message to go out from the courts is: businessmen beware. If you fail to honour your contracts, then don't start crying if because of your failure, the other party comes to court and obtains an order compelling you to perform what you undertook to do under your contract. In other words, businessmen who wrongfully break their contracts must not think they can count on the courts, when the matter eventually comes before them, simply to make an award of damages in money, the value of which has probably fallen drastically compared to its value at the time of breach. Businessmen at fault will therefore, in the absence of good grounds showing why specific performance should not be decreed, find themselves ordered to perform their side of the bargain, no matter how costly that may turn out to be for them...*

I fully endorse the above sentiments.

In view of the foregoing and having determined all the issues raised at page 2 in favour of the plaintiff, I believe that, *in casu* the circumstances demand that the relief prayed for by the wronged party, the plaintiff should be given favour by this court.

Accordingly, I order as follows:-

1. That the defendant be and is hereby ordered to supply and deliver to the Plaintiff twenty (20) IBM A55 (Lenovo) desktop computers forthwith.
2. That in the event of failure to deliver as indicated in 1 above, the defendant be and is hereby ordered to pay the plaintiff damages in the sum of $9 792 245 000 000-00 forthwith.
3. That the amount referred to in 2 above shall be payable with interest at the prescribed rate from the date of summons to the date of payment; and that the defendant shall bear the costs of this suit.

Soboyejo (Trading as Soboyejo Associates) v Onidepe (Trading as Megida Printers & Publishers)

High Court of the Lagos State of Nigeria
May 2nd, 1973
Adefarasin, J.

At the trial of the action and before evidence was led counsel believe that the defendant gave instructions for the detailed drawings on the understanding that they would be paid for and that the plaintiff did not know that he had inadequate funds until the drawings were already prepared. His idea was that since the financing of the project fell through he was absolved from any liability to pay. It was contended on behalf of the defendant that the doctrine of

(Continued)

(Continued)

frustration applied and the defendant is not liable since the arrangements for the financing of the project did not succeed. I take a contrary view. In the context of building and engineering contracts, frustration will normally arise by reason of some supervening event such as the destruction of the entire site or the passage of legislation rendering the work illegal. The basis of the doctrine is that the supervening event must be so unexpected and beyond the contemplation of the parties that neither party can be said to have accepted the risk of the event taking place when contract: see *Hudson's Building and Engineering Contracts*, 10th ed., at 348-350 (1970). There is no element of frustration whatsoever in the present case. In *Davis Contrs. Ltd. V. Fareham U.D.C. (1)* Lord Radcliffe, discussing the elements in frustration, said ([1956] A.C. at 729; [1956] 2 All E.R. at 160):

> ...*[F]rustration occurs whenever the law recognizes that without default of either party a contractual obligation has become incapable of being performed because the circumstances in which performance is called for would render it a thing radically different from that which was undertaken by the contract. Non haec in foedera veni. It was not this that I promised to do.*

> *There is, however, no uncertainty as to the materials upon which the court must proceed. 'The data for decision are, on the one hand, the terms and construction of the contract, read in the light of the then existing circumstances, and on the other hand the events which have occurred.'* (Denny, Mott & Dickson, Ltd. v. James B. Fraser & Co. Ltd. *([1944] A.C. 265, 274-275) per Lord Wright).*

The elements of frustration are absent in the instant case. Even if it was true that the arrangement for the National Bank to finance the actual construction of the project failed it was, in my judgment, the defendant who did not pursue it with any vigour. He cooled off and, as he explained in his later evidence, he abandoned the project for the Isolo area and embarked on a yet more elaborate complex at a cost of £140,000 with a far larger area of land elsewhere. The instruction Exhibit 1 which formed the basis of the contract between the parties did not make the relationship between them dependent on a loan. In fact it said nothing of a loan.

The defendant, having instructed the plaintiff to produce the drawings in the language used in Exhibit 1, would be liable to a *quantum meruit*. *Quantum meruit* is a right to be paid a reasonable remuneration for work done in a case where work is done at the request of the defendant and the price is not fixed by agreement. In such a case the law implies a term of payment of a reasonable remuneration. I am fortified in the views I have formed in this case by a statement of the law in *Hudson's Building and Engineering Contracts*, 10th ed., at 179. On the matter of remuneration it says:

> *Even if there is no express reference by the parties to the question of remuneration, the normal inference, except in cases of work done on approval, will be that an architect or engineer, like other professional men, does not intend and cannot be expected to give his services for nothing, and the employer will be held, by the fact of employment, to have bound himself to pay a reasonable reward for the services to be rendered.*

That brings me to the crux of the matter in this case: how much is the plaintiff entitled to by way of remuneration? The plaintiff charges at the rate of 4% of the cost of the building which is £15,000. He gave evidence of considerable skill. He is a Doctor of Philosophy in Mechanics

(Continued)

(Continued)

and holds a first degree in Civil Engineering and a Master's degree in Engineering Structures. He has a string of other qualifications. It was contended on behalf of the plaintiff that he is entitled to charge a fee of 4% of the total cost of the project. The schedule of fees of the Association of Consulting Engineers, Exhibit 7, shows the fees chargeable by a consulting engineer for a job between £10,000 and £30,000 to be £200 plus 8% of the cost of the works. In the instant case the plaintiff did not perform the duties of the work such as supervising and further advising because the defendant did not go ahead with the actual construction. Nowhere in Exhibit 7 is it stated that 4% is the appropriate fee to change in such a case. The court has a duty to consider what sum is reasonable for the amount of work done by the plaintiff, bearing in mind his degree of skill. I consider 3% of the total cost to be reasonable. By this a sum of £450 or N900 will become payable. Accordingly I enter judgment against the defendant for N900 with costs which I assess at N84.

Judgment for the plaintiff.

2.5 Remedies for Breach of Contract

Courts have fashioned several monetary and non-monetary damage measures for breach of contract.[11] Generally, an injured party must be put in the same position they would have been in had the contract being performed. Countries in SSA use a mix of statutory and common law principles in determining the remedies when a breach occurs. All the countries have a Sales Act that governs commercial transactions involving goods. The *Salongo v. Peggy Garments* case (Uganda) discusses the remedy rules under the Uganda Sales Act. The case also discusses the distinction between "special" and "general" damages, concepts that are elaborated on in the case of *Pearl Fish Processors Ltd. v. The Attorney-General*. There are also the common law rules that apply where the transaction does not involve goods. Generally, a court will give money awards for breach of contract but in certain situations the court will order *specific performance* and ask the breaching party to perform what was promised in the contract. Another common non-monetary award is *rescission and restitution*, whereby the contract is cancelled (rescinded) so that neither party is held for breach and any monies advanced by one party to the other is returned. The South African case of *Zithulele and 20 Others v. Mthokozisi* and the Nigerian Supreme Court case *Ezenwa v. Oko* explain that specific performance is an equity concept and courts carefully scrutinize the conditions under which such relief shall be granted. This remedy will be granted where the value of the item in dispute is difficult to ascertain, for example, land.

The payment of money damages (compensatory damages) takes different forms. One form of payment is *liquidated damages*, whereby the parties wrote the damages that a breaching will pay should a breach occur. Liquidated damages are placed in a contract by the parties themselves. *Punitive damages* are not available in contract cases. Another consideration in monetary damage awards is the distinction between *general damages special damages*. Courts in SSA rely on statutory guidelines in awarding general damages, for example, in a situation where the seller fails to deliver grain as promised in a contract and the seller keeps the grain, the buyer will be entitled to the difference between the market price at the time of the breach and the contract price. On the other hand consider the situation where the buyer fails to accept the grain and the seller has the grain, the seller will be entitled to the difference between the retail price and the contract price. The rationale is simple. A seller may refuse deliver only when the price at the time to deliver is higher than the contracted price. The buyer must be made whole by money damages enough to enable him to purchase grain elsewhere at a higher price. Likewise, a buyer will refuse to accept grain contracted for only if the price of grain at the time of contract performance is lower than the contract price. The seller must be made whole by a damage award that enables him to discount the grain in order to sell.

General damages on the other hand are referring to the other losses a party might have incurred as a result of the breach. A good example is a claim for "lost profits." General damages are essentially consequential damages. While following the statutory guidelines makes the determination of general damages less burdensome, the determination of specific damages is based on the evidence supplied by a claimant. It is for this reason that all common law jurisdictions in SSA have emphasized that a claim for special damages must be proven by credible evidence.

Fred Kitayimbwa Salongo v Peggy Garments Limited

THE REPUBLIC OF UGANDA
IN THE HIGH COURT OF UGANDA AT KAMPALA
COMMERCIAL COURT DIVISION
HCT-00-CC-CS-0345-2003

BEFORE: HON. MR. JUSTICE LAMECK N. MUKASA

JUDGMENT

The plaintiff, Fred Kitayimbwa Salongo, filed this suit against the defendant, Peggy Garment Ltd, claiming for special damages of Ugshs 7,774,000/= , general damages for breach of contract, interest and costs. The plaintiff's case is briefly, that on 9th February 2004, he sub-contracted the Defendant company to carry out automatic screen printing and heat pressing services on an assortment of Ndere Troupe Foundation Garments and Caps.

The contract was for designing and printing Ndere Troupe Foundation Logo, at a consideration of Ugshs 1,754,500/= on 50 caps, 20 polo T/Shirts and 315 round neck T/Shirts provided by the plaintiff. The Plaintiff contends that he worked together with the defendant to create the logo and agreed on a master sample which was approved by Ndere Troupe Foundation.

(Continued)

(Continued)

The defendant produced for the plaintiff's approval samples of the garments and caps printed with the logo. Having approved the samples the plaintiff delivered to the defendant the garments and caps to be worked on. That when the garments and caps were delivered by the defendant it was found that the logo printed on the round neck T-shirts did not match the approved logo and the logo was unproportionately placed thereon. The round neck T-shirts were rejected. The plaintiff accepted the 50 caps and 20 Polo T/shirts and made a total payment of shs360,000. The plaintiff contends that in breach of the contract the defendant has failed to produce the 315 round neck T/shirts conforming to the approved sample and generally to produce a professionally done job.

The defendant contends that the plaintiff was shown samples of the work to be printed prior to the final printing as per their custom and usage. That it was only after the plaintiff had approved the master/prototype samples that the garments were produced. That the plaintiff failed to raise money and pay for all the T-shirts and caps. The defendant counter-claims Shs1,343,500/= being unpaid money for work done. The defendant also counter-claims for general damages interest and costs.

At the scheduling conference the following facts were agreed upon:-

1. The plaintiff contracted the defendant company to carry out services of embroidering, heat pressing and screen printing on an assortment of garments.
2. The parties agreed on the samples of the works that were to be carried out.
3. The plaintiff delivered to the defendant 50 caps, 20 polo T/shirts and 315 round necked T-shirts.
4. The parties agreed to a cost of Shs1,754,500 out of which the plaintiff made an initial cash payment of Shs225,000/= and later another payment of Shs135,000/ = totaling to Shs360,000/= .
5. The plaintiff undertook to pay the balance upon delivery of the products.
6. The parties agreed on a master sample prior to the commencement of the work.
7. The defendant is still in possession of some of the garments and the plaintiff has not paid the balance of the contract sum in the total sum of Shs1,343,500/ = .

The parties agreed on the following issues:

1. Whether any of the parties was in the circumstances in breach of the contract.
2. Remedies available to either of the parties.

ISSUE NO: 1—WHETHER ANY OF THE PARTIES WAS, IN THE CIRCUMSTANCES, IN BREACH OF THE CONTRACT.

This issue can be broken down into the following:-

(i) -----------
(ii) -----------
(iii) -----------
(iv) Which party breached the contract.
(v) Whether or not the plaintiff rescinded the contract.

(Continued)

(Continued)

The fourth issue is **which of the parties breached the contract**? In contracts of sale of goods by sample section 16 of the Sale of the Good Act provides:-

1. A contract of sale is a contract for sale by sample where there is a term in the contract, express or implied, to that effect.
2. In the case of a contract for sale by sample there is ---
   a. an implied condition that the bulk shall correspond with the sample in quality.
   b. an implied condition that the buyer shall have a reasonable opportunity of comparing the bulk with the sample.
   c. an implied condition that the goods shall be free from any defect, rendering them unmerchantable, which would not be apparent on reasonable examination of the sample.

Section 15 of the Act provides that where the buyer expressly or by implication makes known to the seller the particular purpose for which the goods are required, so as to show that the buyer relies on the sender's skill or judgment and the goods are of the description which is in the course of the seller's business of supply, whether the seller is the manufacturer or not, there is an implied condition that the goods shall be reasonably fit for the purpose, expect that in the case of a contract for the sale of the specified article under its patent or other trade name, there is no implied condition as to its fitness for any particular purpose. While subsection (b) provides that where goods are bought by description from the seller who deals in goods of that description whether the seller is the manufacturer or not, there is an implied condition that the good shall be of merchantable quality except that if the buyer has examined the goods there shall be no implied condition as regards defects which the examination ought to have revealed.

I appreciate that the contract before me was not a contract for the sale of goods. It was a contract for the provision of services resulting into the production of specified end products by the services provider, the defendant. So the provisions of the Sale of Goods Act will only provide good guidance to me.

On a balance of probabilities I find that the plaintiff has proved that the defendant breached the agreement when they produced round neck T-shirts with logos which did not match the sample.

Despite the defects in the logo it is the defendant's case that the plaintiff took delivery of the round neck T-shirts but refused to pay for them fully. This brings me to the next question whether the plaintiff rescinded the contract. In the context of this case my view is that the issue regards whether the plaintiff had rescinded the contract for breach thereof. A contract can be rescinded by bringing legal proceedings. Rescission could also be by notice to the other party. It could also be by conduct of the party, say where he takes the goods back to the supplier. However, the right to rescind is barred by the impossibility of restitution. Recession involves restoration as far as possible the state of things which existed before the contract. Therefore the buyer who rescinds in order to recover the price must give back the goods to the supplier.

(Continued)

(Continued)

The Plaintiff's testimony is that the round neck T shirts, hereafter referred to as T-shirts, were delivered to him in two consignments, the first on 12th February 2004 and some on 14th February 2004. He testified that on 12th February, 2004 he sought delivery of the entire order he had made with the defendant. That Mrs. Odaka, DW1, refused to release the goods without payment. The plaintiff paid shs225,000/= and Mrs. Odaka cleared 60 T-shirts to be released to the plaintiff. The 60 T-shirts already wrapped were given to the plaintiff and he rushed to deliver the same to his client. When delivered to Ndere Troupe and unwrapped the T-shirts were found wanting and were rejected by his clients. It is the plaintiff's contention that he had not had a chance to look at the T-shirts until while at Ndere Troupe because he was in a rush to effect delivery and they had been handed over to him when already wrapped. He stated that he contacted the defendant's employees and informed them of the mistake. They promised to rectify the error. He therefore took back the 60 T-shirts to the defendant but the defendant refused to receive them back claiming that the plaintiff had already paid for them. He was stuck with the 60 T-shirts. Unlike exhibit P10, the 60 T-shirts did not have participants' names at the back. The plaintiff has since sold the 60 T-shirts to various people.

The plaintiff further testified that on 14th February 2004 the defendant gave him the rest of the items on the order that is the 20 Polo T-shirts, 50 caps and the balance of 255 T-shirts. The goods were released to him upon issuing a cheque in the sum of shs1,529,500/= payable to the defendant drawn on Nile Bank and dated 14th February 2004, Exhibit D7. The plaintiff contends that he had issued the cheque with a condition that it should not be cashed until he had finally approved the work.

The plaintiff testified further that when he returned the 225 T-shirts the defendant again worked on them in a bid to make them acceptable. After working on them the defendant gave him two of the T-shirts, one of which is exhibit P10, claiming that they were now okay. He stated in cross examination:-

The above evidence shows the plaintiff's inability to reinstate the 60 T-shirts. Restoration is impossible in circumstances which bar the plaintiff's right to rescind the contract. The law on rejection is that a party rejecting cannot do anything contrary to the supplier's interest in the goods. Section 35 of the Sale of Goods Act provides:

> *The buyer is deemed to have accepted the goods when he or she intimates to the seller that he or she accepted them or when the goods have been delivered to him or her and he or she does any act in relation to them which is inconsistent with ownership of the seller or when after the lapse of a reasonable time, the buyer retains the goods without intimating to the seller that he or she rejects them---* (underlining is mine)

In *Mohamed Anwar Vs Manjarid & another Civil Appeal No 5 of 1973*, (cited in Law of Contract in East Africa by R. W Hoddgin at page 180) the Appellant had purchased eleven second hand tractors and spares from the Respondent. When the appellant went to collect the tractors two were missing and others had been stripped of their spare parts. Nevertheless the Appellant removed the tractors on an understanding that what was missing would be

(Continued)

(Continued)

replaced. This was not done and the appellant stopped the payment. When sued for the price he alleged that he had repudiated the contract and that the consideration had totally failed. The Court of Appeal upheld the decision of the High Court that the Appellant's behaviour showed that the property in the goods had passed to him and therefore could not repudiate the contract but only availed with damages.

I therefore agree with the submission of Counsel for the defendant that if the plaintiff had rejected the 60 T-shirts he should not have kept them since he had an intention to claim for them. By his conduct he made restitution of the 60 T-shirts impossible.

As regards the balance of 225 T-shirt, counsel for the plaintiff submitted that before the plaintiff received them he raised his objection to the erratic logo. That he was, however, prepared to receive the T-shirts and taken them to Ndere so his rejection thereof would be confirmed by Ndere Troupe as the end user. That DW3 had accompanied him to Ndere Troupe premises for confirmation of the rejection by Ndere Troupe and not to collect payment.

In the plaintiff's Counsel's letter, exhibit D1, dated 24th February 2004 and addressed to the defendant it is stated:

--- That the products which you gave him were rejected by his clients — on account of the fact that there was a mix up of the colours in the final "logo" on the T-shirts, thereby constituting a fundamental breach of contract on your part. The purpose hereof is to draw to your attention the fact that our client demands a refund of the total purchase price he paid for the said T-shirts and compensation for loss of income (profits which would otherwise have accrued if the deal had not aborted.

Counsel for the defendant argued that it was clearly put in this letter that it was Ndere Troupe that rejected the goods and not the plaintiff.

This letter was written on 24th February 2004, after the plaintiff had on Monday, 16th February 2004, come back to the defendant, paid cash for and only picked the Polo t-shirts and caps. It is the evidence of both parties that delivery was always upon payment. It is the defendant's evidence that when there was failed payment the goods were returned to them by their employee.

Both parties' evidence is that the cheque was issued as security only for payment to be done on 16th February 2004. Though the cheque issued was in the sum of Shs1,529,500/= which covered the Polo T-shirts, caps and the remaining 255 T-shirts, the cash payment on 16th February 2004 only covered the Polo shirts and caps and delivery of which the plaintiff took. The 255 T-shirts remained and are still in possession of the defendant. Instead of collecting the T-shirts the plaintiff on that day, 16th February 2004, stopped payment of the cheque and on 24th February 2004 wrote the letter exhibit D1 notifying the defendant of the breach and seeking compensation for the breach.

(Continued)

(Continued)

Right from the time the defendant was contracted by the plaintiff the defendant was made aware that the end user was Ndere Troupe. This is evidenced in the Invoices and Receipts issued by the defendant which were made in favour of Ndere Troupe. That is exhibits D5, D6, P1, P3 and P4.

Even at the level of samples the plaintiff would always, before final approval, seek the approval of his client and the defendant's staff were aware. So it was not out of practice which had been adopted in the execution of this agreement that the plaintiff had to resort to his client before making a final decision, whether to accept or reject the products. It is in light of that that the plaintiff communicated the rejection by his client as clarification of the reasons for his rejection of the products. Further to the written notice, on 31st May 2004 the plaintiff filled this suit whereby he claims that the defendant was in breach of the contract for failing to produce a consignment that conformed to the approved sample and generally to produce a professional job. The plaintiff claims damages for the breach. All in all the plaintiff had thereby rescinded the contract and I so find.

REMEDIES

The last issue is that of remedies are available to the parties. The plaintiff prayed for special damages in the sum of shs7.774,000/=, general damages, costs of the suit and interest on all aforementioned at the court rate from date of filing until payment in full.

The defendant counter claimed and prayed for a declaration that the plaintiff is in breach of the contract, order for special damages in the sum of shs 1,343,500/=, general damages and interest at the Commercial rate from the date of breach till full payment.

I have already held that the defendant had breached the agreement. By taking delivery and retaining part of the defective products the plaintiff thereby treated the defendant's breach of the agreement as not of a fundamental nature. Section 52 of the Sale Goods Act provides.

(1) Where there is a breach of warranty by the seller, or where the buyer elects or is compelled to treat any breach of a condition on the part of the seller as a warranty, the buyer is not by reason only of the breach of warranty entitled to reject the goods but he or she may —
(a) set up against the seller a breach of warranty in diminution or extinction of the price; or
(b) maintain an action against the seller for damages for the breach of warranty.
(2) The measure of damages for breach of warranty is the estimated loss directly and naturally resulting in the ordinary course of events, from the breach of warranty.
(3) In the case of breach of warranty of quality such loss is prima facie the difference between the value of the goods at the time of delivery to the buyer and the value they would have had if they had answered to the warranty.
(4) The fact that the buyer has set up the breach of warranty in diminution or extinction of the price does not prevent him or her from maintaining an action for the same breach of warranty if he or she has suffered further damages.

(Continued)

(Continued)

The general rule is that whenever there is a breach of contract by the party the other is entitled to bring an action for damages. The basic principle is that the injured party should be placed in the same financial position as if the contract had been performed. Even a party who rescinds for breach can also claim damages for breach of contract. In *Surrey County Council & Anor Vs Bredero Homes Ltd (1993) 3 All ER 705* Steyn LJ held that an award of compensation serves three interests, that is compensation for the loss of expectation interest to put the aggrieved part in the same financial position as if the contract had been fully performed, the party is also compensated in respect of his losses due to reliance on the contract and lastly to deprive the defendant of the benefit gained by breach of contract.

By way of special damages the plaintiff claims:-

1. Cost of 315 T-shirts—shs 1,632,000/=
2. Printing charges (less caps and polo shirts)—Shs 1,619,500/=
3. Loss of earnings/profits on the main contract—Shs 4,532,000/=

It is trite law that special damages must not only be specifically pleaded but also strictly proved.

It is an agreed fact that the 315 T-shirts were provided by the Plaintiff. The Plaintiff testified that he had brought the 315 T-shirts from Sun – apparels (U) Ltd. He tendered in evidence Receipt No 71 dated 6th February 2004, exhibit P12. The receipt shows that he paid shs1,632,500/= and remained with a balance of Shs100,000/=. The Plaintiff had not yet paid that balance. Of the 315 T-shirts the plaintiff had taken delivery of 60 T-shirts on 12th February 2004 and another 2 T-shirts on 14th February 2004. The plaintiff was to earn back the cost of the T-shirts when paid by his client for the order. As a result of the defendant's breach the plaintiff's client rejected the T-shirts. The plaintiff must have paid Shs5182/50 for each of the T-shirts. The plaintiff was not challenged on the cost of the T-shirts. The plaintiff did not inform court how much he got from the sale of the 60 T-shirts. So court cannot establish whether the proceeds from the sale covered the cost for the 60 T-shirts. If it did not the onus was on the plaintiff to adduce evidence to that effect which he did not do. The plaintiff has not earned any money from the two T-shirts which he still has and from the 253 T-shirts which are still with the defendant. He has therefore not recovered the cost of the 255 T-shirts. At shs5182/50 each for the 255 T-shirts the plaintiff has lost a total of shs 1,321,537/50. There is no evidence adduced of a claim for the balance of shs100,000 by the plaintiff's supplier of the T-shirts.

While giving his testimony the plaintiff dropped the claim for shs 1,619,500/= for the printing charges and instead claimed shs 225,000 which he had paid as printing cost for the 60 T-shirts. The plaintiff testified that he had paid the sum of shs225,000/= on 12th February 2004 when he claims to have taken delivery of the 60 T-shirts. For all cash payment the plaintiff was issued with a receipt. The receipt dated 12th February 2004, exhibit P3, is for a payment of Shs 186,000/=. When pressed in cross examination the plaintiff stated that the sum of shs 225,000/= was made up of receipts exhibits P2 and P3. The sum of

(Continued)

(Continued)

shs 186,000/= paid vide exhibit P3 plus the sum of shs 39,000/= paid vide exhibit P2 make a total sum of Shs 255,500/=. However, exhibit P2 dated 12th February 2004 is a receipt not issued by the defendant but by Ms Jescar Enterprises Ltd. The plaintiff did not explain how receipt of payment to the defendant was acknowledged by a third party. Further the 60 T-shirts which the plaintiff claims to have paid for were retained and sold by him. He does not adduce any evidence to show that the proceeds from the sale did not cover his printing expenses in respect of the T-shirts. Unless he adduces evidence to show that he had sold the 60 T-shirts at less than the price agreed with his client which he did not do; the plaintiff cannot be permitted to make double earnings. He had not paid for the 255 T-shirts. Therefore this claim fails.

The plaintiff claims shs4,452,000 in loss of earning or profits from the main contract. The plaintiff testified that the contract for the supply of 315 T-shirts for the 6th UDTA harvest festival was to earn him a sum of shs6,142,500/=, that is at shs 19,500 each. He tendered in evidence an invoice dated 6th February 2004 in the above sum. As a result of the defendant's breach all the T-shirts were rejected by the plaintiff's client. Therefore the plaintiff did not earn the anticipated income from the supply of the T-shirts to his client in the sum of shs6,142,500/=. The Plaintiff received and sold off 60 T-shirts to alternative buyers. As stated in the *Mukisa Biscuits and Manufacturing Co Ltd Vs West End Distributors Ltd (No 2) 1970 EA 469* the burden of proving loss suffered is on the plaintiff. He did not earn any money from the 255 T-shirts. At shs 19500/= he lost the anticipated income of shs4,972,500/=. The sum was inclusive of the cost he had incurred on the purchase of the T-shirts. That is a sum of shs1,321,573,50 which has already been awarded to the plaintiff. Therefore the sum of shs4,972,500/= is scaled down by the sum of shs1,321,537/50 to come to shs3,650,962/50. It is his testimony that he did not pay the printing charges for 255 in the sum of shs1,343,500/=. So the plaintiff's claim is scaled further by that sum to come to shs2,307,462/50.

The damages recoverable must be for loss which is connected to the breach. Under the famous rule of *Hadley Vs Baxendale (1854) 9 Exch 43*, reiterated in *Victoria Laundry Ltd Vs Newman Industries Ltd (1949) 2 K. B. 528* the defendant is only liable for such loss as may fairly and reasonably be considered as arising naturally, that is, according to the usual course of things, so that any plaintiff would be likely to suffer the loss in question.

Clearly the defendant was not a party to the agreement between the plaintiff and Ndere Troupe. However, the plaintiff made it clear to the defendant that the end user of the products was Ndere Troupe and communicated to the defendant the specifications of the contract as given to him by Ndere Troupe. The specifications as to the products agreed upon between the plaintiff and Ndere Troupe were transmitted into the sub contract, now between the plaintiff and the defendant. The breach of the contract between the plaintiff and the defendant, resulted into the plaintiff's breach of the contract between him and his client. Thus entitling the plaintiff's client to reject the goods and the plaintiff to suffer the above

(Continued)

(Continued)

damages. The damages suffered followed directly from the defendant's breach. So the plaintiff is awarded special damages in the total sum of Ugshs3,629,000/= .

The plaintiff also claimed for general damages. General damages for breach of contract are compensatory for the loss suffered and inconveniences caused to the aggrieved party. The plaintiff testified that his money was held up as a result of the breach. His reputation had been affected and he had lost his big client. From the inconveniences and loss of business the plaintiff is awarded general damages in the sum of Ugshs 2,000,000/=

With regard to the defendant's counter-claim I have already found that it was the defendant who had breached the agreement. Breach of a contract entitles an aggrieved party to rescind an agreement. When the plaintiff's client rejected the T-shirts the plaintiff collected only the caps and the round neck T-shirts, which the defendant had produced in conformity to the sample, and paid cash for them.

Section 48 of the Sale of Goods Act provides.

(i) Where, under a contract of sale, the property in the goods has passed to the buyer, and the buyer wrongfully neglects or refuses to pay for the goods according to the terms of the contract, the seller may maintain an action against him or her for the price of the goods.

(I) Where, under a contract of sale, the price is payable on a day certain irrespective of delivery and the buyer wrongfully neglects or refuses to pay the price, the seller may maintain an action for the price, although the property in the goods has not passed and the goods have not been appropriated to the contract

In the present case evidence shows that the delivery of the goods would be upon payment for the goods. The plaintiff did not pick the remaining 223 T-shirts. He rejected the T-shirts and the defendant admits that it still has possession of these T-shirts. The plaintiff instead stopped payment of the cheque. He had issued and filed this suit. The defendant had failed to substantially perform its part of the contract. There was partial performance for which the defendant was paid. The defendant cannot recover payment for the goods that were defective and not taken by the plaintiff. Non fulfillment by the defendant of the obligation to which the duty of payment arises entitles the plaintiff to suspend payment until the obligation has been performed. The evidence available is that the defendant tried to collect the error but still failed and the 2 T-shirts given to the plaintiff after the attempt to put them right were also rejected and the plaintiff is still stuck with them. The defendant cannot recover payment for failed performance of its part of the contract. The defendant's counter claim fails and it is accordingly dismissed.

In the final result judgment is entered in favour of the plaintiff in the following terms:-

(a) Special damages in the sum of Ugshs3,629,000/=
(b) General damages in the sum of Ugshs2,000,000/=
(c) Interest on (a) and (b) above at the court rate from the date of judgment until payment in full.
(d) Cost of this suit.

Pearl Fish Processors Ltd v The Attorney-General & The Commissioner for Fisheries

The Republic of Uganda
IN THE HIGH COURT OF UGANDA AT KAMPALA
(CIVIL DIVISION)
HCT-00-CV-MC-0103-2007
(Arising from Miscellaneous Cause No. 92 of 2007)

THE HONOURABLE MR. JUSTICE YOROKAMU BAMWINE

RULING

This application by Notice of Motion was filed on 11th July, 2007. The applicant sought orders by way of judicial review. The reliefs sought included orders of mandamus, injunctions and declarations. The grounds upon which the reliefs were sought were that the Commissioner of Fisheries and Officers under his direct supervision and control closed the applicant's Factory, recommended particular changes to be made to the applicant's working procedures which was done. That the Commissioner and his officers thereafter notified the applicant that the fish it was exporting contained benzo (a) pyrene which was high and unacceptable to the European Community. That instead of educating the applicant of what remedial steps to take the respondents simply prejudicially closed the applicant's factory and withdrew use of its export number (EAN). It is averred in the statement in support of the claim that the applicant sought audience with the respondents but to no avail and response hence the application. In the reply thereto the respondents denied the claims and pleaded that the withdrawal of EAN was precipitated by the introduction of new control measures on smoked products in the European Union.

The controls related to benzo (a) pyrene, a chemical secreted during the combustion of any food product. The applicant's factory, according to the Department of Fisheries, deals and at the material time dealt specifically in smoked fish products.

From the records, the parties appeared before my colleague Stella Arach Amoko, J. on 22/08/07 and indicated to her their desire to explore a settlement. They were ordered to make a report to court on 19/09/07. Come that date, Counsel for the applicant, then Mr. Peter Katutsi, informed court that the parties had met as ordered by court. He reported that the applicant wanted the 2nd respondent for inspection of the premises; that the 2nd respondent requested for samples of fish to carry out compliance tests; that inspection was done on two occasions; and, that they were awaiting a report on the matter.

After a lengthy discussion, the parties agreed on the following plan of action:

1. The applicant to provide three (3) more samples.
2. The applicant to produce for samples only (not full production).
3. Respondent to review the results of earlier samples given as well.
4. The applicants shall use 10 kgs of fish per sample.
5. The samples will be ready on:
   1st . . . . 21st September, 2007
   2nd . . . . 24th September, 2007
   3rd . . . . 26th September, 2007
   All at 2.00 p.m. on each day.

(Continued)

(Continued)

6. The respondents shall select the samples on each day in the presence of the applicants. The samples shall be packed securely and the applicants shall escort the samples to the laboratory in Kampala.
7. The payments will be made when the results are out.
8. Other issues of the technical team and manual must also be resolved.
9. The respondents have agreed to write to EU Delegation after they have got positive results attaching copies of the inspection report and the recommendations. This will be done as soon as the results are out and payments made.
10. It is agreed that the communication to EU shall be copied to the court as well as counsel for the applicant, among others.
11. This exercise should be completed by 15th October, 2007.

From the records, the parties left court on 19/09/2007 fully convinced that due compliance with the above arrangement would resolve the dispute. The matter was accordingly adjourned till 18/10/07 at noon for mention.

The record is silent as to what transpired thereafter but when Mr. Wilfred Niwagaba for the applicant appeared before me on 09/03/2009, he confirmed to court that other aspects of the case had been handled except the issue of damages. Upon the parties failing to appear before me for purposes of addressing court on damages, I directed that they file written submissions. Hence this ruling.

As regards special damages, the rule has long been established that special damages must be specifically pleaded and strictly moved. In this case there has been an attempt by the applicant to state its loss in special damages in paragraph 8 of the Notice of Motion and paragraph 17 of Ms Horvath Maria affidavit in support of the claim. In one of the leading cases on pleading and proof of damages, namely, *Ratcliffe vs Evans [1892] 2 QB. 524*, Bowden L. J. stated (at pages 532–533):

> *The character of the acts themselves which produce the damage, and the circumstances under which these acts are done must regulate the degree of certainty and particularity with which the damage ought to be proved. As such, certainty must be insisted on in proof of damage as is reasonable, having regard to the circumstances and the nature of the acts themselves by which the damage is done. To insist upon less would be to relax the old and intelligible principles. To insist upon more would be the vainest pedantry.*

I agree.

Relating the above principle to the instant case, court is unable to hold that the applicant has sufficiently proved its claim for special damages, loss of profit and general damages for unlawful closure of its premises, all put together totaling to Shs.2,500,000,000/= .

The reasons for failure to do so are in my view two fold: the procedure adopted by the applicant and the two respondents' incessant failure to attend court. As regards the

(Continued)

(Continued)

procedure, P. G. Osborn in 'A Concise Law Dictionary, 5th Edn.', at p. 214, defines Motion as an application to court or a judge for an order directing something to be done in the applicant's favour. By implication, it is a simple procedure of enforcing one's rights. It presupposes existence of a right in the first instance. Black's Law Dictionary, 7th Edn., at p. 1031 defines it as a *"written or oral application requesting a court to make a specified ruling of order."*

By its very nature a notice of motion entails evidence at the trial to be by affidavit and yet affidavit evidence is rather unsatisfactory in some cases. I am of the view that this case is one of them. While it may have been suitable for the prerogative writs sought in the application, which remedies the parties have by consent sorted out outside court, it was not suitable for proof of special damages as claimed in paragraph 8 of the Notice of Motion and paragraph 17 of Horvath Maria's affidavit. Having said so, I have come to the conclusion that the claim for special damages has not been proved.

I accordingly grant the applicant no special damages.

As for general damages, the general principle is that they are pecuniary compensation given on proof of loss or breach. In this regard the claimant must be able to prove some loss.

Learned Counsel for the applicant has submitted that the pleadings clearly indicate how the respondents' action made the applicant suffer loss, which losses are particularized under group annexture A9, and that other than a general denial, the respondents declined to exercise their right to challenge the applicant on its specific losses. I have already indicated how the pleadings did not bring out the claim as to special damages and declined to make the award prayed herein. Having decided so, I have also directed my mind to the evidence of the applicant's witness, Ms Horvath Maria. It is undisputed that the suit arose out of the withdrawal of an EAN (Establishment Approval Number) from the applicant. This withdrawal was in March 2006 (annexture A1 to applicant's application). The closure resulted from the EU setting new standards relating to benzo (a) pyrene, a chemical secreted during combustion of any food product. While the withdrawal was in March 2006, the notification to the applicant of the need to comply and fit into the new regime of controls set by the European Union was in August 2006 (Annexture A6 to the applicant's application). Annexture A10 specifically outlines the effect of the new changes in the European Union. The issue as I see it is whether the 2nd respondent was justified to withdraw the EAN before a dialogue with the applicants on the matter. I am of the considered view that in a substantial investment of this magnitude, it was imperative that the management of the applicant be given notice of any deficiency and a chance to correct it, and that a reasonable notice of withdrawal of EAN be given. What we have on record is the withdrawal of EAN and then the subsequent acrimony between the parties over the withdrawal. Given the measures put in place at the instance of court, which measures ended the stand off between the applicant and the

(Continued)

(Continued)

respondents, I am of the considered view that the action of the Commissioner, though perhaps well intended and in the interests of the applicant's business, went against the rules of natural justice, the rule to be heard before action is taken. It is trite that the chief rules of natural justice are to act fairly, in good faith, without bias and in a judicial temper; to give each party the opportunity to adequately state his case, and correcting or contradicting any relevant statement or position prejudicial to his case, and not to hear one side behind the back of the other. In short, not only should justice be done, but it should be seen to be done.

From the applicant's pleadings, following the EAN withdrawal they contacted the Foods Standards Agency in U.K., which responded as per annexture A10. The said correspondence did clarify that presence of benzo (a) pyrene was a natural phenomenon brought about by past and current combustion processes. The correspondence clarified on what would be required by the applicant to meet the limits set by EU. It is argued for the applicant that the information contained in this correspondence is the sort of directory and supervisory information that the Commissioner should have passed on to them rather than rush to withdraw the EAN. I agree. I think all this information should have been available to the Commissioner before acting as he did. His action was in my view unresearched and it resulted in loss to the applicant, notwithstanding the positive side of it like the improvements mentioned in annexture C, to the respondents' affidavit in reply dated 4/09/06. In this correspondence, the applicant indicated that it had appointed a new quality Manager and Production Manager and that it was committed to ensuring that every batch of its exports is monitored from the beginning to the end.

It is trite that general damages are those which are not easily quantifiable in money terms. They are not specified in the claim, instead, the court decides how much the injured party deserves in compensation for his pain and suffering, which the court assumes the plaintiff did sustain. I don't hesitate to say that from the evidence before me, the applicant suffered some loss as a result of the 2nd respondent's act. I accordingly find that while the applicant has not been able to prove the loss specifically pleaded in the Notice of Motion and Ms. Horvath Maria's affidavit, it has made out a case for an award of general damages. Doing the best I can and taking into account the applicant's disallowed claim for special damages in the sum of Shs.2.5 billion, I consider an award in the sum of Shs.50,000,000 (fifty million only) adequate compensation to the applicant against the respondents for the loss caused to them. It is awarded to them.

The award shall attract interest at the commercial rate of 24% per annum from the date of this ruling till payment in full. In the final result, the application is allowed in part on the terms stated herein above.

The applicant shall also have the costs of the application.

Orders accordingly.

Mpange, Zithulele and 20 Others v Sithole, Mthokozisi

In the High Court of South Africa
(Witwatersrand Local Division)
Date of Judgment—22 June 2007
Case No: 07/7063

SATCHWELL J:

INTRODUCTION

Specific performance

(5) This judgment arises from issues attendant upon the legal dilemma faced by desperate tenants who find themselves at the mercy of an unscrupulous landlord. The vexed question concerns the remedies available to such tenants who are confronted with two equally unpalatable alternatives: on the one hand, homelessness and on the other hand, residence in an unsafe and inadequate building for which they are paying rental.

(6) There are a number of possible remedies available to the court where a slum landlord has failed to maintain premises in a safe or proper condition. One such remedy is an order for specific performance that the landlord render the building fit for the accommodation purpose for which he has rented it out to a number of tenants. Another remedy is an order that the rentals payable by the tenants to the landlord are reduced proportional to the reduction in use and enjoyment of the accommodation. Earlier decisions of our courts tended towards a refusal to grant such orders.

(7) This judgment first considers judicial and academic criticism of these decisions. Thereafter this judgment examines these remedies in the light of the obligation on this court to develop the common law in a manner that promotes the spirit, purport and objects of the Bill of Rights and the rights to adequate housing, dignity and privacy provided for in the Constitution. It against that background that this judgment determines both the remedies of specific performance and reduction of rental to be permissible in the present case.

(8) The applicant tenants were initially unrepresented in these proceedings. The court approached the Johannesburg Bar for assistance and is greatly indebted to Advocates Steven Budlender and Kate Hofmeyr who appeared as *amici* and, in that capacity, prepared comprehensive and thoughtful heads of argument and assisted this court with careful and creative submissions[12].

FACTUAL BACKGROUND

(9) It is common cause that, since January 2005, the respondent has been renting out rooms or portions of rooms in a building to at least 113 occupants and their families in Leyland House. These 113 occupants, including the applicants, currently pay the sum of R 420 per room per month into a bank account in the respondent's name. Access to the building is controlled by respondent's agents who require applicants and other occupiers to hand over their bank deposit slips. Applicants complain that proof of payment of rental monies is thereby destroyed but the respondent avers that the slips are returned.

(*Continued*)

(Continued)

(10) The building was apparently previously a three story warehouse or factory consisting of open workshops. Applicants aver that they each provided funds ranging from R 450 to R 900 to the respondent for the erection of brick walls so as to create rooms. It is not in dispute that there are only board partitions between rooms.

(11) The applicants complain of the conditions of the building and have attached photographs to their pleadings supporting certain of these complaints. The allegations include lack of privacy between rooms, illegal and unsafe electrical connections, insufficient and unhygienic sanitation facilities, accumulation of refuse, broken walls and windows, general decay and disrepair. Many of the problems are occasioned by the unsuitability of the building for its current, ie accommodation, purpose. It is also alleged by the applicants that the some problems are a result of alleged non payment of municipal charges and levies.

(12) The respondent contends that the conditions within and without the building are either exaggerated or will be attended to while certain of the problems are caused by or occasioned by the applicants. He also states that the alleged failure to pay municipal charges is not the concern of the applicants.

(13) Applicants aver that complaints or requests to the respondent concerning occupation, rental or the building are met with threats by the respondent or his agents who enter the building at night carrying firearms. It is common cause that one such agent is a group of men or a business entity known as 'Bad Boys'. It is claimed that the respondent has also advised the applicants that his position as a High Court advocate will protect him and the 'Bad Boys'. These threats and such behaviour are denied by the respondent.

RELIEF SOUGHT

(14) Applicants are all residents in Leyland House. They prepared their own pleadings and represented themselves in this application. The respondent, who is an advocate of the High Court, was legally represented throughout. The application was initially heard on an urgent basis and a number of interim orders were made pending finalization.

(15) The applicants placed the ownership of Leyland House and the administration thereof in issue. The applicants complain that the respondent is not the registered owner of this property and that even if he was, he rents out rental accommodation in contravention of certain Statute and regulations both by operating in the absence of required permits and by the appalling conditions to which he subjects the residents of the building. They plead, in some detail, that various of their Constitutional rights have been infringed by the behaviour of the landlord respondent.

(16) It was on this basis that the applicants sought orders that the respondent be prohibited from collecting rentals from them in respect of their occupancy of Leyland House; that the respondent be ordered to refund to the applicants monies unlawfully received by him from the applicants as rentals; that the respondent be prohibited from contacting the applicants or other occupiers of Leyland House or from entering into the property. Their notice of motion contained the catch-all prayer for "further or alternative relief".

(17) In the course of argument, counsel for the respondent pointed out that the applicants had primarily formulated their case on the basis of the alleged non-ownership of the property

(Continued)

(Continued)

by the respondent and that the relief sought by them did not amount to a claim for specific performance that the respondent render the building fit for the purpose for which it has been leased. However, this objection was subsequently abandoned.

(18) The applicants are quite obviously not persons of education or means. If they were, they would certainly not be living in these appalling conditions. They would not have had to rely on their own ingenuity to prepare this application to court. If they had been able to obtain legal representation the legal issues arising from the facts which they have set out in their papers might have been correctly identified and the relief sought might have been formulated accordingly.

(19) It has been long accepted that the court should make allowance for the inexperience of lay litigants who "cannot be expected to display the same ability of draughtsmanship and precision of language as is expected by a legally trained and experienced pleader"[13] This approach was restated by the Constitutional Court in Xinwa and others v Volkswagen of South Africa (Pty) ltd 2003 (4) SA 390 CC, where was said

Pleadings prepared by laypersons must be construed generously and in the light most favourable to the litigant. Lay litigants should not be held to the same standard of accuracy, skill and precision in the presentation of their case required of lawyers. In construing such pleadings, regard must be had to the purpose of the pleading as gathered not only from the content of the pleadings but also from the context in which the pleading is prepared. Form must give way to substance. [at paragraph 13][14]

(20) In the present case, the applicants have set out all relevant facts and the context to those facts. Over the course of four court appearances, the true legal issues and remedies possibly available have been discussed and argued in great detail notwithstanding that they were not all identified by the applicants in their Notice of Motion and supporting affidavits. There has been no prejudice to the respondent. Indeed, respondent's counsel submitted in the Heads of Argument which he prepared that the remedy of specific performance should be ordered and, in argument, presented certain proposals as to how this could be implemented.

REMEDIES

(21) Where the lessor fails to deliver or maintain the property in a condition fit for the purpose for which it is let there are a number of remedies available to the lessee. These include cancellation of the contract or a claim for specific performance from the lessor. Damages may be claimed in addition or in the alternative.[15] A reduction in rental is also permissible.

SPECIFIC PERFORMANCE BY THE LANDLORD – THE GENERAL RULE

The general rule

(22) A contracting party is, in principle, entitled to enforce specific performance of his or her contract. However, the granting of an order for specific performance is in the discretion of the court. In the context of lease agreements where the lessor has failed to deliver or

(Continued)

maintain the thing let in a proper condition, the courts have tended to refuse to order the lessor to effect the necessary repairs.[16]

(23) It has generally been accepted that a lessee who is unable to persuade a court to make an order requiring the lessor to effect the necessary repairs will be able to achieve the same result by effecting the repairs him- or herself and then recovering the costs thereof from the lessor. This may take the form of either a set-off against rental paid or a claim against the lessor for the amount of the repairs.[17] Such an option is apparently not easily available or at all to the applicants in the present case. They are without the finances and perhaps the skills themselves to effect the renovations needed to render the premises habitable. There are many occupants who are lessees and each would have different personal and financial circumstances as well as different needs and priorities for safe habitation. There are presumably a multiplicity of relationships between the tenants in the building and nothing to suggest that they have anything in common other than such residence or share either the desire or ability to work together on a project to renovate this building.

(24) In general courts have tended to exercise their discretion against awarding specific performance where damages would provide adequate compensation to a tenant, where it would be difficult for the court to enforce it's decree, where it would operate "unreasonably hardly" against the landlord, where the lease agreement is unreasonable, such an order would produce injustice or would be inequitable under all the circumstances (see Haynes v King Williamstown Municipality 1951 (2) SA 371 (A) at 378H).

(25) The basis for the courts' reluctance to grant specific performance where a lessor has failed to maintain the property let in a proper condition was described by de Villiers J in the case of Nissenbaum and Nissenbaum v Express Buildings 1953 (1) SA 246 (W) as follows:

as a general rule in disputes between landlord and tenant as to repair of buildings, or neglect to repair or failure to carry out some structural alterations, the Court will not order specific performance because it is a difficult matter for the Court to supervise and see that its order is carried out, and as the question whether there has been specific performance of the Court's order was difficult to determine, it would be difficult to enforce it. (At 249G-H)

The general rule is not inviolate

(26) As noted in Nissenbaum supra, specific performance is a discretionary remedy. It would follow that, although the cases may establish a general tendency on the part of the courts not to order specific performance in the context of a lessor's failure to maintain the property let, such tendency ought not to be elevated to an absolute rule.

these two cases, however do not show that that general rule is an absolute rule and that there cannot be exceptions, and it seems to me that where a landlord acts in a high-handed manner, ... the Court might very well, in a case which savours much more of spoliation than the present one, actually order the landlord to restore the buildings, and the Court would put a very high standard on such performances as a mark of disapproval of the high-handed action of the landlord (per De Villiers J in Nissenbaum supra at 249H−250A)[18]

(Continued)

(Continued)

(27) The Appellate Division has criticized the courts' general reluctance to order specific performance in such cases. In <u>ISEP Structural Engineering and Plating (Pty) Ltd v Inland Exploration Co (Pty) Ltd 1981 (4) SA 1 (A)</u>, Jansen JA commented that our courts had been "somewhat reluctant" to order specific performance "where it would be difficult for the Court to enforce it's decree" but went on to describe this as a "limitation developed from the English practice and not consonant without law" (at 5G).

(28) Jansen JA went on to point out that "even in England this limitation appears to have fallen in disfavour" (5C).[19] In <u>Tito v Waddell (No 2) 1977 Ch 306</u> Lord Megarry commented

The real question is whether there is a sufficient definition of what has to be done in order to comply with the order of the Court. That definition may be provided by the contract itself, or it may be supplied by the terms of the order, in which case there is the further question whether the Court considers that the terms of the contract sufficiently support, by implication or otherwise, the terms of the proposed order. (at 322B)

(29) This reluctance to order specific performance to compel a recalcitrant lessor to effect the necessary repairs to the property let has also attracted academic criticism See Kerr A J Principles of the Law of Sale and Lease (1998) 56; Cooper, The South African Law of Landlord and Tenant (1973) 81.

(30) It would seem that South African and English courts as well as academic writers have provided well founded criticism of the justification for refusing to grant an order of specific performance against a lessor to effect repairs so as to maintain the premises in a condition reasonably fit for the purpose for which they were let. The notion that such an order would be difficult to enforce would arise only when the person in whose favour it was granted alleges that the defendant has failed to comply therewith. Any factual disputes as to the question of compliance can be dealt with, at such a stage, by invoking the usual principles applicable to factual disputes (see Cooper, 1973). As Lord Megarry succinctly put it "The real question is whether there is a sufficient definition of what has to be done in order to comply with the order of the Court."

(31) After all, it is not unknown in the South African experience for our courts to craft supervision of orders and enforcement to be implemented pursuant to default.[20]

(32) On the facts of the present case, it is unlikely that the applicants have the means to effect the necessary repairs to the premises themselves. Without such an option available to them, and in the absence of an order for specific performance, the applicants will continue to occupy premises that present a danger to their health and safety, limit their privacy and impair their dignity. Continued occupation of the premises under such conditions therefore implicates the applicants' rights under sections 10, 14 and 26(1) of the Constitution.

(33) To suggest that the applicants could decline to rent these premises and seek accommodation elsewhere ignores the realities of the shortage of accommodation for poor people in Gauteng and the plight of inner city residents at the mercy of slum landlords. The applicants could report the respondent to the municipal authorities and have the building declared a health hazard and unfit for human habitation. This approach also ignores the desperation of the homeless and the plight of the applicants who do not wish to become homeless.

(Continued)

(Continued)
CONCLUSION

Specific Performance

(34) I have no doubt that the facts of this case should persuade this court to exercise it's discretion in favour of an order for specific performance against the respondent that he, as landlord, do those things specified by the court to render the accommodation at Leyland House fit for the purpose for which it has been leased.

(35) At common law, the courts have already acknowledged a need for flexibility in this area. Moreover, the constitutional injunction to consider the applicants' rights of access to adequate housing, dignity and privacy in the exercise of a court's discretion to grant an order of specific performance points towards the appropriateness of such a remedy in a case such as this.

(36) However, details as to the priorities for renovation and repair, expertise with regard to such endeavours, the costs thereof, the time periods involved, the disruption to current inhabitants in their occupation whilst such renovations endure, possible alternative accommodation for the duration of such renovation and numerous other issues have not been canvassed by any of the parties to this litigation. For appropriate design and successful implementation of such a structural interdict a specific plan of action to render Leyland House fit for human habitation would have to be carefully prepared and presented. Notwithstanding that the respondent has already indicated in his papers that he has such a plan in mind and that architectural plans have already been submitted to the municipal authorities, he has given no details thereof. Absent details of renovation and regeneration of the building it is not possible to grant either an order for specific performance or a declarator that there will be a reduction of rental until necessary and specified repairs are effected to the building.

(37) In addition I am mindful that the respondent is not the owner of the building and that the registered owner has neither been joined in nor notified of these proceedings. This failure does implicate the appropriate remedy in this case.

(38) Any order requiring a non-owner lessor to effect repairs to the property will necessarily impact on the owner's rights in respect of the property. In addition to this, it is unclear what recourse the owner may have against a lessor who effects repairs with which the owner is dissatisfied. Of particular significance in this regard is the fact that an owner who is dissatisfied with the repairs done to the property pursuant to a court order is unlikely to have a claim for damages against the lessor given that the requirement of unlawfulness for such a claim to succeed will not be satisfied. Since the repairs would have been carried out pursuant to court order, they would not have been unlawfully effected.

(39) The direct and substantial interest of the registered owner in any order of specific performance granted by this Court, suggests that it's non-joinder or non-notification in this case must militate against the appropriateness of a specific performance remedy.

(40) I have considered a variety of possible orders involving a postponement of the application or an interim order for reduction of rental pending service on or joinder of the registered owner. The purpose thereof would be to allow to the registered owner the opportunity to engage with this dispute and express views as to any order for specific performance in regard to the owner's building. Again, the stumbling block remains the absence of particularity as to such specific performance.

(Continued)

(Continued)

(41) I have concluded that it is inappropriate for this court to be overly interventionist and creative in resolution of this dispute. In due course, the applicants may themselves seek the relief of specific performance having joined the registered owner (or Liquidator) in such an application. It may also be open to the respondent to approach this court for variation of the order for reduction in rental on presentation of a plan or scheme to render Leyland House safe for human habitation, with due regard to the interests of the registered owner.

ORDER

(42) It is ordered as follows:

4. The Respondent and/or his agents are interdicted from demanding or soliciting or receiving from any tenant or occupant or family group in and of the building known as Leyland House situate at 15 Jannie Street, Jeppestown, Johannesburg (Erf 1111 Registration Division IR Tvl) a rental for occupation of a unit or room in such building in excess of R 170 per unit or room (one hundred and seventy rand) per month.

5. The Respondent shall continue to provide such services, such as caretaking and cleaning, as were provided by him at date of launching of this application.

6. There is no order as to costs.

Benjamin Onwughamba Ezenwa v Okpara Oko, Michael Oko Okpara & Eze O. Eze

In The Supreme Court of Nigeria
On Friday, the 25th day of January 2008
S.C. 426/2001

Walter Samuel Nkanu Onnoghen. J.S.C

This is an appeal against the judgment of the Court of Appeal, holden at Enugu in appeal No.CA/E/102/79 delivered on the 11th day of November, 1999 in which the court dismissed the appeal of the appellant against the judgment of the High Court of Imo State Holden at Afikpo Division in suit No.HAF/13/78 delivered by that court on the 18th day of June, 1979 in which it dismissed the appellant's claim for statutory right of occupancy, trespass, injunction and specific performance, but awarded the sum of ₦500.00 (Five Hundred naira) damages in lieu of specific performance.

On the 26th day of May, 1978 the appellant, as plaintiff, caused a writ of summons to be issued against the respondents, as defendants, claiming the following reliefs:-

(i) A declaration that plaintiff is the person entitled to a statutory right of occupancy to a parcel of land near Eke Market, Afikpo and which is part of a larger area of land situate at Amachi Village, Afikpo in Afikpo Local Government Area of Imo State within Judicial Division, the annual value which is ₦10.00 (Ten Naira).

(ii) ₦500.00 (Five Hundred Naira) being general damages for trespass upon the said land.

(Continued)

(Continued)

(iii) Injunction perpetually restraining the defendants, their servants, agents and workmen from further entry upon or interference with the land.

(iv) Specific performance against the defendants in respect of the contract and for lease agreement made on the 26th day of January, 1965 in connection with the renewal of the lease.

The facts of this case are very simple and straight forward just as they remain undisputed. The original 1st defendant granted a lease of the property in dispute to the appellant on the 26th day of January, 1965 for 10 years as evidenced in Exhibit A. Exhibit A was therefore to expire on 26th day of January, 1975 with an option for renewal. In 1966 appellant took possession of the land and laid foundation for a concrete building thereon up to the floor level before the Nigerian Civil War forced him to flee Afikpo to his home town, Achina from where he returned in 1971 to find motor mechanics in occupation of the property who atoned tenancy to him as appellant continued with the leasehold.

Sometime in February, 1975 the appellant approached the original 1st defendant/respondent for the renewal of the lease who refused to allow appellant exercise the option and refused to collect further rents from the appellant on the ground that the original 1st defendant/respondent has made a gift of the land in dispute to the 3rd respondent.

On his part, the 3rd defendant/respondent knew of the lease to the appellant and the fact that the mechanics on the land were the sub-tenants of the appellant. In 1978, the 3rd respondent peacefully quitted the mechanics from the land and surveyed same after which the land was formally conveyed to the 3rd respondent by the 1st respondent and he commenced building thereon in April, 1978. In May, 1978 when it finally dawned on the appellant that the 1st respondent had no intention of changing his mind on the option of renewal of the lease, the appellant instituted this action claiming the relief's earlier reproduced herein.

Learned counsel for the appellant, Chief H. B Onyekwelu in the appellant's brief filed on 30th day of September, 2007 and adopted and relied upon at the hearing of the appeal on the 29th day of October, 2007, formulated the following issues for the determination of the appeal, to wit:-

3.1 Whether specific performance of the appellant's equities cannot be enforced against the 3rd respondent whose ostensible interest over the land is that of a mere volunteer, but is the alleged successor in-title of the 1st respondents;

3.2 Whether on the facts of the case, the appellant was guilty of delay at all or such delay as in the circumstances could deprive the appellant, enforcement of specific performance against the 1st respondent or the 3rd respondent or their successors-in-title;

3.3 ------

3.4 ------

3.5 ------

3.6 ------

3.7 Whether the provisions of the Land Use Act 1978, made it impossible for an order of specific performance to be entered against the 1st and 3rd respondent.

(Continued)

(Continued)

On the other hand, learned counsel for the respondent, Chief Ebele Nwokoye identified the following issues for determination in the respondent's brief filed on 18th day of October, 2005:

3.1 Whether specific performance of this appellant's equitable interest could not have been ordered by the court below in the circumstances of this case;

3.2 As opposed to appellant's 2nd issue, whether the appellant has pleaded argued and satisfied the court that the special reasons to interfere with the concurrent findings that appellant did not come to court promptly to claim the equitable relief of specific performance;

3.3 -----

3.4 -----

3.5 -----

3.6 -----

3.7 -----

3.8 -----

In arguing issue 1, learned counsel for the appellant submitted that the 3rd respondent, having stepped into the shoes of the 1st respondent in respect of the land, was bound by any equities attached to the land in that before he acquired his supposed interest, the 3rd respondent was a volunteer with full knowledge of the appellant's equities in the land; that it is trite law that where a purchaser of land or a lessee is in possession of the land and has paid the purchase money to the vendor or has paid the rent to the lessor as the case may be, then in either case, the purchaser or the lessee has acquired an equitable interest in the land which is as good as a legal estate and this equitable interest can only be defeated by a purchaser of the land, for value without notice of the prior equity, relying on the case of *Obijuru vs Ozims (1985) 2 NWLR (Pt. 6) 167 at 179*. Learned counsel also cited and relied on Vol.36, *Halsbury's Laws of England* (3rd Eel.330 Para. 482) which states that

where there is a contract for the sale or demise of property and the property is thereafter transferred to a third party, the general practice is that specific performance may be had against the transferee;

i. If he is a volunteer, or
ii. Takes with notice of the prior contract, or
iii. Acquired only an equitable title and has no better equity than the purchaser or intended lessee

Learned counsel for the appellant argued that the 3rd respondent being a volunteer who also took the land with notice is liable to specifically perform the contract of renewal attached to the land by virtue of Exhibit A, that the lower court was in error when it held that specific performance cannot be ordered against the 3rd respondent because he was not privy to the agreement to renew the lease particularly as that court had earlier held that the 3rd respondent stepped into the shoes of the 1st respondent in relation to the land in dispute; that it is not correct, as held by the lower court, that the original lease had expired before appellant started to ask for renewal as there is evidence to show that appellant started to

(Continued)

(Continued)

demand for renewal before 25 January, 1975 when the lease expired; that even if the lease had expired, appellant continued in possession and was collecting rents from his sub-tenants until April, 1978 thereby being led to believe that the 1st respondent was ready or could be persuaded to renew the lease.

On his part, learned counsel for the respondents referred to the holding of the lower court at page 202 of the record to the effect that:

> *I have already held that at the time appellant went to court, the basis of his claim had lawfully ceased to exist. It was the continued existence of his status of a tenant at sufferance that would have made the 1st respondent compellable*

meaning that the appellant lost the status of tenant at sufferance or the relationship of tenant and landlord which must exist to qualify him to seek specific performance to compel 1st respondent and that since appellant cannot compel performance against 1st respondent he cannot also do so against the 3rd respondent; that the lower court did find that the appellant's option for renewal had ceased to be and there was not, for that reason, a cause of action, sealed the fate of the appellant; that appellant did not appeal against this specific finding and should not now be allowed to impugn same; that the issue of privity of contract does not really arise nor have effect on the conclusion judging from the above findings of the lower court which completely took care of the appellant's case, that the court should refuse the grant of specific performance on the following grounds:-

(a) the trial court refused to exercise its discretion in favour of the appellant and the appellant did not appeal against that refusal;

(b) the Court of Appeal did not interfere with the exercise of the discretion not to grant specific performance and, indeed, affirmed what the trial court did as appellant has shown no special circumstances to warrant the interference of this court;

(c) the lower courts finding that the appellant's option to renew had ceased to be and there was not for that reason a cause of action even though complained against in ground 11 of the grounds of appeal before the lower court, the same was abandoned when no issue was raised therefrom;

(d) the appellant who covenanted to build on the land could not do so after possessing the land for over 13 years and contented himself with a mere concrete foundation up to floor level;

(e) appellant brought action for declaration of title against his former landlord;

(f) that the claim on specific performance is an after thought as the same was not claimed in the writ of summon; that the claim for specific performance as claimed on the statement of claim was never paid for.

Having taken care of the preliminary matter, the issue is whether this is a proper case for the court to exercise its equitable jurisdiction by ordering specific performance.

In cases where there is a subsisting contract or agreement for the sale or lease of land, the court, being also a court of equity is always inclined to grant specific performance because the land being sold or leased may have a peculiar value or significance to the purchaser or

(Continued)

(Continued)

lessee particularly where it is a choice land in a busy commercial centre of the town, as in the instant case.

Since the grant of an order of specific performance is at the discretion of the court, it is always advisable that the party claiming same should call evidence on damages claimed or suffered in the event that the court, for some reason is unable to grant specific performance.

It is also settled law that the onus is on the person who seeks to enforce his right under a contract to show that he has fulfilled all the conditions precedent, and that he has performed all those terms which ought to have been performed by him. Where the plaintiff fails or defaults in the discharge of his own obligations under the contract, the action must fail—*See Balogun vs Alt -Owe (2000) 3 NWLR (Pt.649) 477 Ezenwa vs Ekong (1999) 11 NWLR(Pt.625)55.*

From the above stated principles, it is very clear that a decree or an order of specific performance is a form of relief that is purely equitable in origin and the fundamental rule is that specific performance will not be decreed or ordered if there is an absolute remedy at law in answer to the plaintiffs claim, for instance, where the plaintiff would be adequately compensated by the common law remedy of damages. The jurisdiction in specific performance is therefore anchored on the inadequacy of the remedy of damages at law—*See Afrotec Tech. Serv. (Nig) Ltd vs MIA & Sons Ltd (2000) 15NWLR (Pt. 692) 730 at 790.* The question then is, how do the facts of this case fit into the principles guiding the order of specific performance?

It is not disputed that appellant entered into a lease with the 1st respondent in respect of the land in dispute for a term of 10 years which was to expire on 25th January, 1975 with an option to renew same for a further term of years.

The lease duly came to an end by efflux of time though appellant had meanwhile put up a foundation on the land up to the floor level before abandoning same following the outbreak of the Nigerian Civil War. It is important to note that the lease ended without the 1st respondent agreeing to renew the lease nor, to accept further rents from the appellant. The lower courts therefore came to the right conclusion when they held that the lease was duly terminated by efflux of time.

However, the action for specific performance appears to be founded on the option to renew contained in the lease between the appellant and 1st respondent.

Learned counsel for the appellant has submitted that the 3rd respondent can be ordered to specifically perform the contract of option to renew particularly as he stepped into the shoes of the 1st respondent and was a volunteer and did take with notice of appellant's equities— option to renew. By "a volunteer" the law means a person who enters into any transaction of his own free will or a person to which property is transferred without valuable consideration. It is the second meaning that is more relevant to the facts of this case.

We have to bear in mind that the principles of specific performance relate to enforcement of contract entered into between the parties and that a contract involves offer and acceptance of the offer coupled with provision of consideration. One may ask in relation to this case,

(Continued)

(Continued)

what is the contract that appellant wants the court to specifically enforce? There is only one lease agreement between the parties which lease expired by effluxion of time. With that expiration any rights arising therefrom became spent or non-existent and consequently unenforceable or is the appellant talking of the option to renew as constituting the contract he wants specifically enforced? If so is an option to renew a lease a contract enforceable by specific performance particularly where there is no provision in the lease to the effect that the lease is renewable in perpetuity or that the landlord or lessor shall not withhold consent to renew the lease? Even where there is a provision that the lessor shall not unreasonably withhold consent to renew the lease, it still leaves the lessor with the discretion either to renew or not to renew the lease how much more where there is no such provision and the lessor refuses, as in the instant case, to renew the lease. Is he bound to renew the lease?

If the option to renew is considered the contract to be enforced, where is the acceptance of that offer by the lessor 1st respondent, and what, if one may ask, is the consideration so as to make the alleged contract binding and enforceable? I am unable to see the basic constituents of a valid contract existing between appellant and 1st respondent and by extension 3rd respondent which can be said to be amenable to specific performance having regard to the fact that the only valid contract between them had expired without renewal. It is on the above basis that one has to agree with the lower court that the appellant's option to renewal had ceased to be and there was not, for that reason, a cause of action.

It should be noted that the facts of this case are different from the usual factual situations where specific performance is obtainable. Learned counsel for the appellant has cited and relied on the decision in *Obijuru vs Ozims (1985) 2 NWLR (Pt.6) 167 at 179* where it was held thus:-

"It is trite law that where a purchaser of land or a lessee is in possession of the land and has paid the purchased money to the vendor or has paid the rent to the lessor as the case may be, then in either case, the purchaser or the lessee has acquired an equitable interest in the land which is as good as a legal estate and his equitable interest can only be defeated by a purchaser of the land for value without notice of the prior equity" and also *Halsbury's Laws of England* (3rd Ed) 330 Para. 482 where it is stated thus:-

> *Where there is a contract for the sale or demise of property and the property is thereafter transferred to a third party, the general principle is that specific performance may be had against the transferee,*

(i) If he is a volunteer, or
(ii) Takes with notice of the prior contract, or
(iii) Acquired only an equitable title and has no better equity than the purchaser or intended lessee.

Though the above statements represent the law applicable to the situations described therein, the principles do not apply to the facts of the instant case because primarily, and this is the

(Continued)

(Continued)

most important consideration for its applicability, there is no existing valid contract of lease or purchase of land between the parties, the earlier one having expired by effluxion of time so the 3rd respondent cannot be said to have taken the property *"with notice of the prior contract"* between the appellant and 1st respondent neither has he acquired any further interest in the property in issue by payment of rents particularly as 1st respondent refused to renew the lease or collect further rents from the appellant. I hold the considered view that an option to renew a lease is an offer made to the landlord, the acceptance of which would constitute a valid contract enforceable by specific performance; it remains an offer until accepted. In the instant case, it was never accepted by the 1st respondent so no enforceable contract exists. I therefore resolve the issue against the appellant.

Appeal dismissed.

Nangunga Livestock Co-Operative Society Ltd v M/S Energo Project Corporation

THE REPUBLIC OF UGANDA
IN THE HIGH COURT OF UGANDA AT KAMPALA
CIVIL SUIT NO.207 OF 1993

BEFORE: THE HONOURABLE MR. JUSTICE I. MUKANZA.

JUDGMENT

The plaintiff which is Co-operative Society incorporated under the co-operative Act 1963 filed this action against defendant Energo Construction Company incorporated and carrying on business in Uganda claiming payment of shillings 7.000.000/= plus general damages for breach of contract plus interest and costs.

According to the plaint on 15th day of November 1991 the plaintiff delivered 30.767 tons of beans each one being at the cost of shillings 150.000/= to the defendant's site at Kiganda Mityana Mubende District. The total cost of the aforesaid 30.767 tons was shillings 4,500,000/=. The relevant photostat copy of the delivery note was attached and marked "A". The plaint further showed that on the 22nd day of November 1991 they delivered 20.559 tons of maize each one being at the cost of shillings 125.000/= to the defendant's site at Kiganda Mityana, Mubende District. The total cost of the aforesaid 20.559 tons was shillings 2,500,000/= and the relevant photocopy of the delivery note was annexed and marked "B".

The plaint further showed that despite numerous demands for payment the defendant had neglected and/or refused to pay them and that the whole purchase price is still unpaid. The defendant's refusal to pay them constituted breach of contract as a result of which they had suffered great loss of business profit and financial embarrassment and business inconvenience.

(Continued)

(Continued)

In its written statement of defence the defendant pleaded that it has no knowledge of and does not admit the plaintiff's claim. It will be put to strict proof thereof. And the defendant would seek for further and better particulars of the claim such as order for the supply of the said beans and maize because the defendant company does not deal in the said produce and was not supplying its workers with the same.

At the commencement of the trial of this case the following issues were framed and agreed upon by parties namely:

(1) Whether there was request for supply of goods mentioned in the plaint by the plaintiff or alternatively whether the plaintiff applied to the defendants to supply the goods.
(2) Whether the said application to supply was accepted by the defendants.
(3) Whether the goods were actually supplied and finally.
(4) What remedies are available to the plaintiff?

On the side of the plaintiff two witnesses testified in support of the plaintiff's case George William Kigozi (PW1) was the treasurer of the plaintiff's society, while Mbabali Steven PW2 was a former employee of the defendant company. He was a mechanic.

On the part of the defence also two witnesses were called in support of the defence version. Bradislav Govannovic DWI was the project manager of the defendant company whereas Charles Olulu DW2 was an investigation officer from the Immigration Department Headquarters Kampala.

PWI testified that the society used to buy maize and beans and sometime they used to buy soya beans. They used to sell crops to companies. In the course of their duties they used to deal with the defendants. He was working in conjunction with the chairman of the society who passed away in 1992. There was a tender for the supply of the produce as per exhibit P1. They supplied 30 tons of maize. They supplied on 22nd November 1991. The deliveries were made at the defendant's site at Kiganda and according to PW1 two trips were made. They were selling maize at 150 shillings per kilogram and that would realise about 4.5 million shillings. Beans cost Shs. 125/= per kilogram and this culminated into the figure of shillings 2.5 million and thus bringing the total cost to Shs. 7 million. They issued delivery notes acknowledging receipts of the said commodities. The delivery note was tendered in Evidence and marked as exhibit P. 2. The defendant was supposed to pay for the produce within 14 days but they failed and/or neglected to pay them. They told them to hang on because they had some financial constraints. Despite repeated demands for payment the defendant did not respond and they decided to institute an action against the defendants and that the money they used in purchasing that produce delivered to the defendant was a loan from the bank and the bankers were on their necks.

The evidence of PW2 was simply that he was employed by the defendant company as a mechanic at Kiganda site. He joined the company on 2nd February 1990. He used to service motor vehicles and tractors. He left the company on 15th October 1992. He left the company when it stopped operating. He left honorably as shown in exhibit P3. He knew the names of some officers of the company. Among them he knew a personnel manager called

(Continued)

(Continued)

George and there was another one called Dragon. The latter was an employee of the company. He was in the company in *1991* and left the company in the year 1992. His immediate boss was called Datishi and by the time he left the personnel manager was stable and that was the very officer who signed exhibit P3. At Kiganda they (the workers) used to get amenities like clothes, shoes and food. Money for food, clothes and shoes used to be deducted from their salaries. They used to get food like maize flour, beans and maize uncrushed. They used to get food from the atc.es in Kiganda and that was a company stores. During his stay there they used to see lorries deliver food to the company. He used to see PW1 and Senyonga in 1991. They used to sell maize and beans to the company. They did that by motor vehicles. He saw 5 vehicles which used to deliver maize and beans. Two lorries brought in maize and the rest were for beans. The store food was manned by two men, a European called Nicholas and an African by the name Kasule. The latter used to sign for commodities and by the time he left Nicholas was still there.

For the defence DWI testified that he was the project manager and by his duties he was overall in charge of administration, financial, technical and general welfare. All those departments would report to him. His company was involved in road construction from Mityana to Mubende. In 1991 he employed local labour force of 200 people and about 30 Yugoslav experts. The Yugoslavs had a restaurant and for the Ugandan, they were provided with allowance to purchase their food. There was no time when his company bought maize and beans and supplied them to the workers. At his place there was no place where he used to keep maize and beans. He continued to work as project manager up to the end of 1992 after which he came to Kampala but still remained as the project manager.

When in Kiganda there was a man called Dragon Minjlovic. He came in January 1992. He was employed by the company. He came direct from Belgrade. He had never been in Uganda before actually not during his time. He was a personnel manager and as such he could not take decisions without his knowledge. The former personnel manager came to Uganda in 1991 and was a lady called Mirjana Jouvanovic. The headed paper (Exp 1) looks like from his company. In November 1991 Dragon was not in Uganda. The letter dated 5th November 1991 talks about food supply. He was the project manager and never ordered for such beans and maize. Dragon could have signed that letter because he was in Uganda by then. He was familiar with Dragon's signature. The letter bears their stamp. He is of the view that somebody from their office misused their stamp and the head paper but was certain that was not Dragon's signature.

He had never seen PWI before and the latter had never supplied him with beans and maize. And that when a man works in the basement of the mechanical shop he could not see what takes place in the office. The workshop was ten metres below the ground level. And the workshop was not open there were buildings surrounding it. They never received commodities shown in the delivery notes exhibit P2. The company does not owe the plaintiff anything.

On the other hand the evidence of DW2 showed that he had been in the Department for 2 years. The Immigration Department deals with monitoring and controlling aliens in the

(Continued)

(Continued)

country. It also issues work permits to anybody who is an alien. They maintain individual files for every applicant. That when one seeks a work permit the following documents may be required.

(a) The formal written application by the firm one intends to work in established in the country.
(b) They require registration of such firms in the country already registered here.
(c) They also require photostat copies of one's passport, the particular pages of the passport which contain personnel detail and the arrival visa where one arrived in the country. He came with file No. IM 129/92 exhibit DI which contains an application for work permit in the name of Dragon Mihaljovic.

The application was made by the Ministry of Works Transport and Communication on behalf of Energo project. The date of the application is 28th January 1992. The application for work permit was granted on 30th April 1992. It was for 2 years. He arrived on 15.1.1992 through Entebbe International Airport. DW1 continued that from the pages they have, they do not have any entry visas to Uganda. If he had worked here before he could not have had one file. They maintain one file at a time. The whole file was tendered in evidence as Exh.D1.

On issue No. 1. There is a letter from the defendant company dated 5th November 1991, addressed to chairman Nangunga Cooperative Society P.O.BOX 30754, Kampala allowing tender of the commodities.

Dear Sir,

Re: Tender to supply 30 tons of beans and 20 tons of maize.

With reference to your application for supply of food stuffs, we are grateful to inform you that you are granted a tender to supply the following:-

(1) 30 tons of beans at shillings 150/= per kilogram.
(2) 20 tons of maize at shillings 125/= per kilogram.

If the prices as quoted above will match with your calculations, please start to supply with immediate effect.

The stuff must reach our stores not later than three months from the date of the tender

Yours faithfully,

Energo Project

Mityana

Fort Portal Road

Project

"Dragon Mihajlovic Manager"

PWI was consistent that as a result of Exh.P1 they PWI and the deceased chairman Ssenyonga proceeded and delivered the commodities on two occasions as shown in the delivery notes

(Continued)

(Continued)

exhibit P2. PW2 who was employed by the defendant company at the time those commodities were supplied, he witnessed the deliveries.

DWI denied knowledge of the delivery of the said commodities. He averred that his company did not engage in such commodities. At the time the produce was delivered one Dragon was not in the country. He admitted however that the head notes of Exhibit P1 was from the defendant company and the stamp there on also was from the company but was of the view that someone might have misused the same. Equally DW2 who produced EXH.DI was consistent that Dragon came to Uganda on 15.1.1992 and that he had never been in this country before and that he was issued with a work permit but never collected the same.

As could be deduced from the evidence on record Dragon was a central figure in this dispute more so as far as the defence was concerned. The defence chose not to summon him as their witness pleading that it would cost millions of shillings by way of transport to bring him to Uganda. Since they were affirming the fact that Dragon was not in Uganda in November 1991 and that he never signed exhibit P1 the burden shifted on them to prove what they were affirming. See Evidence by Rupert cross DCL, 2nd Ed. London Butterworth page 72 (B). "The shifting of the Burden." In fact professor Nokces when dealing with the shifting of burden of proof in an introduction to Evidence 3rd Edition p. 472 had this to say.

> *The prosecutor or plaintiff has one burden/obligation that is to prove one set of facts. While the accused or the defendant may have another burden. This is an obligation to adduce evidence of different facts, such as payment of debt or other matter in disproof of the opposing evidence. The shifting of evidence means that "A" lays down his load and 'B" picks another load. But "A" never tosses his load and B never tosses it back to A. What shifts is the obligation, but it is an obligation to prove different facts.*

In the instant case the plaintiff testified that they supplied commodities to the defendant and that one Dragon signed Exhibit P1 and Exh.P2 showed that the commodities were received. The burden of proof shifted the defendant to affirm that Dragon was not in the country at the time. They would have done this by calling him as witness. Thy failed to do so thus failed to discharge the aforesaid burden of proof.

In fact in my humble opinion this was a contract for sale of goods whereby the plaintiff transferred or agreed to transfer the property in the goods to the defendant for money consideration. See Section 3 of the Sale of Goods Act Cap 79. If the defendant wrongly, neglects or refuses to pay for the goods in accordance with the terms of the contract as appears to be the case here the plaintiff may maintain an action against him for the price of the goods. See Section 49 of the Sale of Goods Act.

Infact of the two versions I would prefer the plaintiff's case to that of the defence. DW1 and DW2 did not impress me as truthful witnesses. DW1 tried as much as possible to exonerate the company from payment and DW2 seemed not to be well versed with the issuance of work permits, entry permits visas and extra. He was a mere investigating officer. And from all that has transpired above issue No.1 is in affirmative in that there was a request for the supply of goods by the defendant.

(Continued)

(Continued)

On Issue No. 2. There is evidence from PW1 to the effect that the defendant accepted the supply of the commodities. That was reflected in the delivery notes EXP P2 and EXP I the tender for supply. As stated earlier DW1 merely denied knowledge of the receipt of such commodities. He said their company had nothing to do with the receipt of beans and maize but I believed PW2 that he at least witnessed PW1 and Ssenyuga deliver beans and maize at the site at Kiganda. It was submitted on behalf of the defendant that the mechanical workshop being in the basement PW2 could not see when deliveries were made outside in the open. But there was evidence that being interested in the commodities PW2 together with other workers assisted in offloading the lorries. Because of what I have stated above it may not be true that he never saw what went on outside. It is true the plaintiff did not call the drivers of the two lorries UPF 816 and UPG 416 as shown in the delivery not EXP 2. I do not think that failure to do so was fatal to their case since I found that they delivered the commodities. There were some contradictions between the testimonies of PW1 and PW2 as to the number of lorries involved in the deliveries of the said commodities. There were also some contradictions and inconsistency in the number of trips made.

It has been held that only grave inconsistencies if not explained satisfactorily will usually result in the evidence of a witness being rejected, minor inconsistency will not usually have that effect unless they point to deliberate untruthfulness. See Leonard Anisath v. R 1963 EA 206, Tajar's case EACA Cr. Application No. 167/1969 unreported.

I am of the view that the contradictions and/or inconsistency in the evidence as given by PW1 and PW2 were minor and did not amount to deliberate untruthfulness. Their testimonies should not be rejected. They appeared to be telling nothing but the truth, I believed them.

Mr. Nshimye submitted that the plaintiff's company had collapsed and was bankrupt as of now and no bank could have advanced money to such society. That could possibly be correct but that would not exonerate the defendant company from paying for the commodities. The plaintiff company had not collapsed when it instituted the instant case. From what has been explained above issue No.2 is in the affirmative.

Issue No. 3 should also be in the affirmative in that the goods were actually supplied.

As regards Issue No. 4, the plaintiff had proved that the defendant had not paid for the price of goods supplied to them and according to paragraph 7 of the plaint they had bank loans and interest accumulated. Mr. Lutakome submitted that they be awarded 10 million shillings.

The position is that there was a breach of contract. It has been held that:-

> *where two parties have made a contract which one of them had broken, the damages which the other party ought to receive in respect of such breach of contract should be such as may fairly and reasonably be considered arising naturally in according to the usual course of things, from such breach of contract itself, or such as may reasonably be supposed to have been in the contemplation of both parties, at the time they made the contract, as the probable result of the breach of it. See Hadley vs. Boxendade 1854 9 Exch 341 at P. 354. See also Law of contract sixth Edition Cheshire and Fifoot p. 515.*

(Continued)

(Continued)

In the instant case at the time both parties entered into the contract of supplying the commodities they never thought that if there was a breach there would be payment of such colossal damages to the tune of 10 million shillings. The defendant did not at least have that in mind. The defendant did not know at the time that the plaintiff had got a loan from the bank with which he purchased the commodities he supplied to the defendant company. I am of the view that the damages ought to be received by the plaintiff in respect of such breach of contract should be such as may fairly and reasonably be considered as arising naturally from the said transaction. Because of what has transpired above the interest of 40% claimed by the plaintiff on the decretal sum is rather on the wrong side of the coin.

The sum total of all this however is that the plaintiff has proved his case on a balance of probabilities. I therefore enter judgment in his favour as follows:

(a) Payment for the price of commodities supplied to the defendant to the tune of Shs. 7 million.
(b) General damages for breach of contract fixed at shillings 2 million. Interest on (a) and (b) supra, at court rates with effect from delivery of this judgment.
(c) The plaintiff is awarded costs of this suit.

Notes

1. "What the Learned Trial Judge did was, in effect, to purport to revise the parties' contract and conclude a new amended contract for them. This is anathema to orthodox common law contract doctrine." See *City & Country Waste Ltd. v. Accra Metropolitan Assembly* (2007−2008) 1 SCGLR 409 at 424. In this case, a trial judge exercised his discretion by changing the fee to be paid under a contract that he had declared illegal by ordering the payment of what he considered fair.
2. A High Court in Botswana (Lobatse) (Walla, AG. J.) used a "balance of probabilities" approach in determining whether there was an offer and an acceptance of a rental agreement in the case of *Shripinda and Company v. Kalahari Ranches (PTY) Ltd.* Misca. No. 41 of 2002, September 26, 2002.
3. High Court of Zambia (Justice S.S. Silomba), 5th April, 2002.
4. Court of Appeal, Dar es Salaam (CORAM: Lubuva, J.A., Nsekela J.A., and Msoffe J.A.), Civil Appeal No. 82 of 2002, April 16, 2002.
5. These explanations have been vigorously challenged by Posner. See Posner (1996).
6. *Transatlantic Financing Corp. v. United States*, 363 F.2d 312 (D.C. Cir. 1966).
7. *Id.*
8. *Agriculture Bank of Zimbabwe Ltd T/A AGRIBANK v. DATANET Technology Zimbabwe*, High Court of Zimbabwe, Harare (Mtshiya, J.), 11 June 2008.
9. The distinction between impossibility of performance and frustration of purpose has been explained as follows, "Under frustration analysis the court is concerned with the impact of the event upon the failure of consideration, while under impracticability, the concern is more with the nature of the event and its effect upon performance."
10. *Soboyejo (trading as Soboyejo Associates v. Onidepe (trading as Megida Printers & Publishers)* High Court of the Lagos State of Nigeria (Adefarasin, J.), May 2, 1973.
11. An excellent review of damage measures may be found in Shavell (1980). For a more recent survey of damage measures, see Coloma (2008).

12. Michael van Kerckhoven first alerted me to the need to reconsider the remedies available to a tenant where the landlord is in breach of his obligations.
13. *Viljoen v Federated Trust Ltd* [1971] (1) SA 750 (O) at 757 B-C.
14. In *Xinwa* there is reference to the approach in the United States that pleadings prepared by laypersons are held to "less stringent standards than formal pleadings drafted by lawyers" (*Haines v Kerner et al* [1971] 404 US 519 at 520) and that "where a plaintiff pleads pro se in a suit for the protection of civil rights the court should endeavour to construe the plaintiff's pleading without regard for technicalities" (*Picking et al v Pennsylvania R Co et al* 151 F 2nd 240 at 244).
15. *Woods v Walters* [1921] AD 303.
16. *Marais v Cloete* [1945] EDL. 238 at 243; *Barker v Beckett & Co Ltd* [1911] TPD 151 at 164; *Hunter v Cumnor Investments* [1952] (1) SA 735 (C) at 740D.
17. *Poynton v Cran* [1910] AD 205 at 227; *Lester Investments (Pty) Ltd v Narshi* [1951] (2) SA 464 (C) at 468C; *Harlin Properties (Pty) Ltd & another v Los Angeles Hotel (Pty) Ltd* [1962] (3) SA 143 (A) at 150H-151H.
18. In this case de Villiers J ordered the lessor to reinstate the water supply.
19. In the case of *Shiloh Spinners Ltd v Harding* [1973] AC 691 at 724, Lord Wilberforce held that it was time to move away from certain 19th-century authorities which posited as the basis for not granting orders of specific performance, "the impossibility for the courts to supervise the doing of the work." According to Megarry VC, in the case of *Tito v Waddell* [1977] (No 2) Ch 306, it was at one time said that an order for the specific performance of the contract would not be made if there would be difficulty in the court supervising its execution. The Vice Chancellor expressed himself "unable to see the force of this objection" and commented that, after it had been discussed and questioned in *C H Giles & Co Ltd v Morris* [1972] 1 W.L.R. 307, 308 the House of Lords "disposed of it" in Shiloh Spinners *supra*.
20. See *Pretoria City Council v Walker* [1998] (2) SA 363 CC; *Dawood v Minister of Home Affairs* [2000] (3) SA 935 CC; *August v Electoral Commission* [1999] (3) SA 1 CC; *Willy Aaron Sibiya v Director of Public Prosecutions*, Johannesburg (3) CCT 45/04; *Minister of Health v TAC* [2002] (5) SA 721 CC.

Questions

1. What is a contract?
2. Under what circumstance may a party be declared incompetent to enter into a contract?
3. Give examples of subject matters that may be considered improper to support a contract.
4. What is an offer?
5. What constitutes proper acceptance of an offer?
6. What constitutes consideration in support of a contract?
7. Why do courts focus on enforcing contracts as opposed to writing contracts?
8. What is the social and economic importance of contracts?
9. Define "meeting of the minds" in your own terms.
10. Give some examples of contracts that you have used in your life and explain how these contracts impacted your life.

Problems

Mr Olu leased his land to Mr Sigi for an unspecified period of time. Mr Sigi planted some palm trees and soon began to harvest and sell palm kernels for the market, and also produced some palm oil. Mr Sigi's reputation for growing good palm kernels grew and his sales skyrocketed. Mr Sigi's success attracted Olu's attention and he approached Mr Sigi with a business proposition. Olu proposed that he will fell the old palm trees and start a palm wine enterprise. He also proposed to establish a distillery and produce Apio, liquor (the "hot stuff") for the export market. Mr. Sigi turned the proposal down so he could focus on the production of kernels and palm oil.

One day Mr Olu went to the farm to discover that some palm trees had been felled and a full-blown palm wine production operation was ongoing. He went to talk to Mr Olu about the operation. Mr Olu admitted felling the palm trees and insisted that as owner of the land he has all the rights of ownership of the trees and Mr Sigi was entitled to the palm kernels so long as he remained a tenant.

Mr Sigi sues Mr Olu for trespass, an injunction, and accounting for the profits from the sale of the palm wine. What results?

References

Coloma, G., 2008. Damages for breach of contract, impossibility of performance and legal enforceability. Rev. Law Econ. 4 (1), Article 5.

Cooper, W.E., 1973. South African Law of Landlord and Tenant, 81. Juta and Company, Durban, South Africa.

Posner, E., 1996. Norms, formalities, and the statute of frauds: a comment. Univ. Penn. Law Rev. 1971.

Shavell, S., 1980. Damage measure for breach of contract. Bell J. Econ. 11, 466−490.

Triantis, A.J., Triantis, G.G., April 1998. Timing problems in contract breach decisions. J. Law Econ. XLI, 162−207.

USLaw.Com, Free U.S. Law Dictionary. <http://www.uslaw.com/us_law_dictionary/c/Contract + Law>.

CHAPTER 3

Contract Farming

Keywords: Contract farming; transaction cost; market specification contracts; resource-providing contracts; production management contracts

3.1 Introduction

An agricultural processing firm may buy all its inputs from spot markets to produce outputs. In this case, the firm is completely non-integrated. Alternatively, the firm may establish its own input farms and supply its processing units with inputs from its own farm. In this case, the processing firm is described as completely integrated. A third option is for the firm to contract-out the input production component of its processes. This is what is known as "contract farming." Contract farming has been defined as a "contract between Producer ('grower') and a Contractor (processor) to (1) sell or deliver all of a designated crop raised in a manner set forth in the agreement and is paid according formula established in the contract; or (2) agrees to feed and care for livestock or poultry owned by the contractor until such time as the animals are removed, in exchange for a payment based on a formula typically tied to the performance of the animals" (Kunkel et al., 2009). There is an extensive literature on whether the institution of contract farming could contribute to raising incomes in developing countries.[1] It is likely that contract farming will increase in number and complexity as processors demand more raw products from growers to support expanded production in response to food security, bioenergy production needs, and the need to increase rural income generation.

Contract farming provides several benefits to the producer and the processor. The producer gets steady income, technical knowledge, and guaranteed markets. The contractor on the other hand is assured of a reliable supply of inputs, gains better control of risk, and promotes capacity utilization (Wu, 2003). There are also costs associated with contract farming. The producer loses bargaining power since sometimes these contracts are offered on a "take it, or leave it" basis. The producer may also be subject to retaliation should they refuse the contract terms offered by a processor. The processor faces problems of sunk costs, potential hostage-taking, and opportunism.[2]

F.O. Boadu: Agricultural Law and Economics in Sub-Saharan Africa.
DOI: http://dx.doi.org/10.1016/B978-0-12-801771-5.00003-4

The three main types of contract farming schemes commonly discussed in the literature are "(1) market-specification, (2) resource-providing, and (3) production management. Market specification contracts are pre-harvest agreements that bind the firm and grower to a particular set of conditions governing the sale of the crop. These conditions often specify price, quality, and timing. Resource-providing contracts oblige the processor to supply crop inputs, extension, or credit, in exchange for a marketing agreement. Production management contracts bind the farmer to follow a particular production method or input regimen, usually in exchange for a marketing agreement or resource provision" (Kunkel et al., 2009). The choice of contract scheme depends on the specific needs and risk considerations by contracting parties.

3.2 The Law and Economics of Contract Farming

Contract farming is one way to address the problem of market failure. Specifically, it has been suggested that contract farming is in response to the "need to minimize transaction costs in light of increasing uncertainty, asset specificity and market failures associated with changes in agri-food systems" (da Silva, 2005). Transaction costs refer to the information, bargaining, and policing costs associated with a contract. The processor that may be a major agri-business firm has more information than the producers who are mostly rural dwellers. This information asymmetry raises the cost to the producers. There are also costs in bargaining, especially where a processor has to bargain with a large number of producers. Some producers may "hold-out" and raise bargaining costs. Form contracts are often used to reduce the bargaining costs. Probably the major source of transaction costs is the policing costs incurred to ensure compliance with the agreed terms of the contract. The uncertainties associated with agricultural production may lead to output price fluctuations and encourage a party to breach the contract. Box 3.1 discusses some of the challenges facing tomato growers and a processor in Ghana.

The cases presented highlight some of the major issues associated with contract farming. The Zimbabwe case of *Webster Mandikonza and Jack Mandikonza v Cutnal Trading (Pvt) Ltd. and David E.G. Long and Deputy Sheriff* (Nyanga) points to the need for proper contract specification to avoid costly litigation. One aspect of the contract in issue is prohibited by law/public policy. While the court did not reach the issue of whether that aspect of the contract prohibited by law is enforceable, the case still points to the need to abide strictly by the terms in a contract. The Zambia case, *National Milling Company Limited v Vashee* (suing as Chairman of Zambia National Farmers Union)[3] is a classic example of how sudden changes in market price at the time of contract performance would encourage breach by a disadvantaged party. The case also raises the important issue of *capacity* to sue, that is, who has capacity to sue where a large number of outgrower farmers seek to bring an action against the purchaser of their product. There can also be problems

---

BOX 3.1 Pwalugu factory shut down

www.ghanaweb.com
Business News of Thursday, 13 March 2008

It was recommissioned last year

The Northern Star Tomato Processing Factory, at Pwalugu in the Upper East Region, has been closed down due to lack of raw materials.

The factory, which was recommissioned last year, cannot get its supply of tomatoes from tomato farmers in the region following the failure of the management and the farmers to agree on a number of issues. These include the type of tomato species to be planted, and how much the farmers should sell to the factory.

Mr Philip Abayori, president of the Award Winners of Farmers and Fishermen's Association, when contacted by the Ghanaian Times on the issue gave assurance of the farmers' readiness to do business with the company based on negotiations that are of mutual benefit to both sides.

He said that the farmers failed to sell their products to the company because of its failure to assist them following the losses suffered as a result of the recent floods.

Mr Abayori explained that under the circumstances, the association on behalf of the farmers, approached the Agricultural Development Bank (ADB) which granted them a GHA¢564,000.00 loan which included provision of inputs and tractor service.

He said as a result of the low funding, the farmers could not produce much to feed the factory.

Mr Abayori said following a misunderstanding between tomato farmers in the Upper East Region and the Ghana Tomato Traders and Transporters of Ghana, which controls and distributes tomato nationwide, the farmers entered into an agreement with the latter.

The agreement, he explained, was to ensure that farmers produced quality tomatoes to prevent the traders from travelling to Burkina Faso to purchase tomatoes and also to ensure realistic prices for the local tomato farmers.

Mr Abayori said the farmers in the region cultivated about 1,465 hectares of tomatoes from which 700 hectares had already been harvested and sold out.

He gave the assurance that the remaining 765 hectares would be enough to feed the nation when harvested in April.

Meanwhile, Mr. Kwame Bonsu, factory manager, has confirmed that the farmers have failed to sell their produce to them because of a disagreement over pricing.

While the factory is buying a crate of tomato at GHA¢15.00, traders buy it at GHA¢45.00.

Source: Ghanaian Times.

associated with the determination of quantities of output in an outgrower contract. The Ugandan case, *Namazi Grace v Kinyara Sugar Works, Ltd.* presents issues associated with the determination of output quantities in a poorly specified contract.

Webster Mandikonza and Jack Mandikonza v Cutnal Trading (Pvt) Ltd and David E.G. Long and Deputy Sheriff (Nyanga)

High Court of Zimbabwe, Harare
Uchena J.
19 November and 15 December 2004

UCHENA J: The first and second applicants are farmers in Nyanga. In August 2003 they entered into a contract with the first respondent who financed their potato crop for the 2003 to 2004 season. The contract had as part of its terms provisions requiring the applicants to grow a certain hectarage of potatoes and to sell the table and seed potatoes they were to grow to the first respondent.

It is common cause that the hectarage the applicants were to grow is more than the sizes of the farms allocated to them. The sale of seed potato to the first respondent is prohibited by law. The agreed sale price for the table potatoes was too low compared to the market price.

The first respondent alleges they entered into another agreement in terms of which the applicants were to sale their crop to the open market and the respondent would get 50% of the proceeds.

The applicants deny that there was a subsequent agreement. A term of the agreement provided for the referral of disputes between the parties to arbitration. In terms of that clause the parties' disputes were referred to the 2nd respondent who I will hereinafter refer to as the arbitrator.

The arbitrator made his determination and awarded the first respondent certain sums payable by the first and second applicants.

The applicants did not pay. The first respondent registered the award with this court and a warrant of execution was issued.

The third respondent attached the applicant's farm equipment. The applicants have now made this urgent application to stop the third respondent from selling their equipment in execution pending their application to set aside the arbitral award.

Mr *Colgrave* for the applicants submitted that there is no order by a Judge of this court recognizing the award granted after the first respondent's application for recognition and enforcement.

Mr *Colgrave* also submitted that the registration of the award was irregular as no notice was given to the applicants. He further submitted that the application for registration of the award should be on notice to the other party and be in the form of a court application made in terms of the rules of this court.

(Continued)

(Continued)

He submitted that the basis for setting aside the arbitral award is that the agreement is contrary to public policy and that the applicants have prospects of success in that application as the agreement of the sale of seed potato to the 1st respondent is prohibited by law.

Mr *Ranchhod* for the respondents submitted that the arbitral award was properly registered as there is no need to make a formal application. He said the application is made to the Registrar of the High Court who registers it and can then enforce it. He submitted that there is no need to give notice of such an application to the other party.

The issues to be decided are:

1. Is the application for recognition and enforcement of an arbitral award to the Judge or to the Registrar?
2. Is notice to the other party a requirement when such an application is made?
3. Is the award likely to be set aside for being contrary to public policy?

In my view the determination of the first two issues is capable of resolving the dispute between the parties. If the award was irregularly recognised then there is nothing to enforce as there is no High Court Order authorising enforcement. The irregularity could be due to the incorrect procedure having been used or due to failure to give the applicants notice of the application to recognise the award.

The first two issues can be resolved by interpreting Articles 35 and 36 of the Arbitration Act No. 6 of 1996.

"Article 35 provides as follows:

1. An arbitral award irrespective of the country in which it was made, shall be recognized as binding and upon application in writing to the High Court, shall be enforced subject to the provisions of this article and Article 36.
2. The party relying on an award or applying for its enforcement shall supply the duly authenticated original award or a duly certified copy thereof and the original arbitration agreement referred to in Article 7 or a duly certified copy thereof. If the award or agreement is not made in the English language, the party shall supply a duly certified translation into the English language." (emphasis added)

My understanding of article 35 is that:

1. An arbitral award can only be recognized and be enforced if the party seeking to enforce it makes an application to the High Court.
2. The application shall be subject to articles 35 and 36.
3. The requirements under article 35 are that the application shall be in writing and be accompanied by the following documents:
   (a) A duly authenticated original award or certified copy thereof and
   (b) The original arbitration agreement or a certified copy thereof and
   (c) If the award or agreement is not in English a duly certified translation thereof into the English language.

(Continued)

(Continued)

It seems to me whoever has to recognize and order the enforcement of the award must be someone qualified to understand the application, the arbitral award, and arbitration agreement.

A combination of what has to be considered and the need for an application to the High Court suggests that the application should be to a Judge and not the Registrar. If the application is to a judge then it should be in terms of the High Court rules and notice to the other part would be a requirement.

This issue cannot be resolved without considering the meaning of article 36 as the application for enforcement has to be in terms of articles 35 and 36.

"Article 36 provides as follows:

(1) Recognition or enforcement of an arbitral award, irrespective of the country in which it was made, may be refused only -

(a) at the request of the party against whom it is envoked, if that party furnishes to the court where recognition or enforcement is sought proof that:-

(i) a party to the arbitration agreement referred to in article 7 was under some incapacity; or the said agreement is not valid under the law to which the parties have subjected it or, failing any indication thereon, under the law of the country where the award was made; or

(ii) the party against whom the award is invoked was not given proper notice of appointment of an arbitrator or the arbitral proceedings or was otherwise unable to present his case; or

(iii) the award deals with disputes not contemplated by or not falling within the terms of the submission to arbitration, or it contains decisions on matters beyond the scope of the submission to arbitration, provided that, if the decisions on matters submitted to arbitration can be separated from those not submitted that part of the award which contains decisions on matters submitted to arbitration may be recognized and enforced or

(iv) the composition of the arbitral tribunal or the arbitral procedure was not in accordance with the agreement of the parties or, failing such agreement, was not in accordance with the law of the country where the arbitration took place; or

(v) the award has not yet become binding on the parties or has been set aside or suspended by the court of the country in which or under the law of which, that award was made; or

(b) If the court finds that-

(i) The subject matter of the dispute is not capable of settlement by arbitration under the law of Zimbabwe; or

(ii) The recognition or enforcement of the award would be contrary to the public policy of Zimbabwe.

(2) If an application for setting aside or suspension of an award has been made to a court referred to in paragraph 1(a)(v) of this article, the court where recognition or enforcement is sought may; if it considers it proper, adjourn its decision and may also, on the application of the party claiming recognition or enforcement of the award, order the other party to provide appropriate security."

(Continued)

(Continued)

A reading of article 36 (1) and (2) clearly indicates that in considering the application referred to in article 35 the application of a judicial mind is called for. In Article 36(1)(a)(i) the capacity of the party against whom the award is to be invoked and the validity of the law under which the award was made has to be considered. The legislature could not have intended that issues such as these be dealt with by a person who is not a judge as was urged upon me by the respondent's counsel. The court also has to consider the validity of the agreement under the law of a foreign country. That obviously requires the attention of a Judge and certainly not that of the Registrar.

In terms of Article 36(1)(a)(iii), the court has to consider whether the award is within the terms of the referral to arbitration. This in my view calls for a proper application which should be considered by a Judge.

In terms of Article 36(1)(a)(iv) the court has to consider the composition of the arbitral tribunal and the propriety of the arbitral procedure. This in my view is not a task for administrative officers in the Registrar's office. It is clearly a task for a Judge of this court.

In terms of Article 36(1)(b)(i) the court has to determine whether or not the subject matter of the dispute is capable of settlement by arbitration under Zimbabwean law. In terms of Article 36(1)(b)(ii) the court has to consider whether or not the arbitration award is contrary to the public policy of Zimbabwe.

These again point to the hearing having to be before the court and not the Registrar.

Article 36(2) refers to the court hearing the recognition or enforcement application adjourning its decision if the other party has applied for the setting aside of the award. The adjourning of the court's decision suggests a proper court application before a Judge. In fact both Articles 35 and 36 make reference to the application being made to the High Court or the court.

In Order 1 Rule 3 of the High Court Rules the word "court" is defined as meaning "the High Court".

The words "court application" mean an application to the court in terms of paragraph (a) of subrule (1) of rule 226."

The word "registrar" means

(a) the registrar of court;
(b) the deputy registrar and an assistant registrar who has been designated as a registrar of the court but does not include a deputy registrar or assistant registrar who has been designated as a registrar of the Supreme Court while acting in his capacity as registrar of the Supreme Court.

In view of these clear definitions of the words "court" and "registrar" I do not see how the words "High Court" and "court" used in Articles 35 and 36 can ever be taken to mean the registrar. The High Court is presided over by judges therefore the applications referred to in Articles 35 and 36 should be applications before a judge and not the registrar. I would therefore accept Mr *Colgrave's* submissions and reject Mr *Ranchhod's*.

(*Continued*)

(Continued)

Article 36(1)(a) of the Act provides for the party against whom an award is to be invoked requesting the court to refuse to recognize and enforce the award. This suggests the party against whom the award is made must be notified of the application to recognize and enforce the award. When this is considered together with the provisions of Article 35(1) which provides that the award "shall be recognized as binding upon application in writing to the High Court" there can be no doubt that a proper application in terms of rule 226(1) of the High Court Rules 1971 has to be made by the party seeking to register the award. Failure to comply with that procedure is fatal to the recognition and enforcement of the award. It simply means the award has not yet been recognized. It therefore is not yet enforceable.

In the present case it is common cause that the purported recognition was by the registrar. That there is no court order authorising the recognition and enforcement of the award. The warrants of execution which were used to attach the applicant's equipment were therefore invalidly granted.

In view of the conclusion I have arrived at as regards the recognition and enforcement of the award I need not consider whether or not the applicant's application for the setting aside of the award has prospects of success to warrant the stay of execution applied for by the applicant.

At the end of the hearing counsel for both parties agreed that I grant or dismiss the application in terms of the final order sought as they had exhaustively argued the matter before me and there was no need for the application to be confined to the granting or dismissing of the provisional order.

I will therefore grant the applicant a final order as follows:-

(1) That the warrant of execution of property issued by this court on the 3rd of November 2004 under case no. HC 11698/04 be and is hereby set aside.
(2) That the 3rd respondent be and is hereby ordered to return to the applicants all the property that was attached and removed by him from the custody and possession of the applicants pursuant to the writ of execution that was issued by the court on the 3rd November 2004.
(3) That the respondent be and is hereby ordered to pay the applicant's costs.

National Milling Company Limited v A. Vashee (Suing as Chairman of Zambia National Farmers Union)

Supreme Court of Zambia
Ngulube, CJ, Lewanika and Chibesakunda, JJS
10th February, 2000 and 18th February, 2000, and 1st June, 2000
(SCZ Judgment No. 23 of 2000)

NGULUBE CJ, delivered the Judgment of the Court.

(Continued)

(Continued)

The basic facts of this case were fairly common cause. As was the practice and custom which had evolved over the years in those days, representatives of the Zambia National Farmers Union would meet the top officials of the appellant company to negotiate and to agree on a basic price for wheat to be grown and sold in an ensuing marketing season. The appellants were then the only buyers for the crop worth talking about. And so it was that at a meeting held on 15th April 1993, an agreement was concluded and signed between the union and the company fixing the 1993 season factory delivered price of wheat per metric tonne at USD302.00. The union was represented by Mr Hudson, its Chairman at the time and another member while the company was represented by the General Manager and two other top officials. The agreement clearly showed that it was to benefit the wheat-growing farmers. Forty-two such farmers grew wheat, obviously acting upon the agreement and the knowledge that there was an assured basic price.

In the meantime, government adopted a liberalized market policy in consequence of which the doors were flung wide open for the importation by whosoever of very cheap sometimes duty-free wheat flour from South Africa and elsewhere. The appellant company found that it would not have a market for its own wheat flour if it stuck to the previously agreed price with the farmers. Efforts were made jointly by the parties to persuade the government to ban the importation of wheat-flour and otherwise to protect the local wheat farming, all without success. The company resorted to offering to buy wheat from the farmers at much reduced prices ranging from K140,000 to K232,000 per tonne which the farmers felt constrained to accept, at considerable loss to themselves. Aggrieved by this turn of events, the farmers sued. At first, their union was named as plaintiff. Objection was raised. It was conceded that as an unincorporated association, it lacked legal capacity to sue or to be sued. The incumbent Chairman, Mr Ben Kapita who had since succeeded Mr Hudson, was then named as plaintiff in his capacity as Chairman and to represent originally forty-one farmers which number was later amended to forty-two affected farmers details of whom are on the record. When Mr Vashee became Chairman, the action was once again amended to name him as the representative plaintiff. The defence denied that there was any agreement with the plaintiff, averring that the company had entered into separate agreements with each farmer and that if there had been a collective agreement, the same had been varied with new conditions negotiated with the farmers. The company also pleaded that in the absence of government funding, the agreement with the union had become impossible of performance. The learned trial judge rejected an argument that the agreement was some kind of memorandum of understanding only, holding that there was a clear and binding agreement intended to create legal relations. The judge also rejected the contention that there was variation of the agreement or that there was frustration because the government did not fund the purchases. The learned trial judge was satisfied that the company was fully aware that the action had been brought in a representative capacity on behalf of named and identified farmers who would receive damages to be assessed by the Deputy Registrar.

We heard a number of arguments and submissions based on a variety of grounds of appeal. There was a ground and related submissions that the union, as an unincorporated society lacked the necessary legal capacity to contract and could therefore not sue or be sued. That

(*Continued*)

(Continued)

being the case, it was submitted that the contract could simply not be entered into and there was thus no valid contract between the parties; only an agreement binding in honour. With regard to the naming of successive chairmen of the union as the plaintiff representing the farmers, it was argued that these were strangers to the agreement so that only the original signatories could sue. It was further submitted that as the office bearers lacked perpetual succession, they could not enter into a contract to benefit the members from time to time nor could they pass on the benefits. It was said that Mr Vashee was not an eligible plaintiff himself so as to be able to bring himself within the provisions of Order 14 of the High Court Rules regarding representative actions.

In response to the grounds concerning the capacity of the union to enter into a contract, Mr. Chonta while conceding to the basic proposition contended that the individuals representing the union had capacity as such individuals to contract as agents for the other farmers. He submitted that the action ought not to be declared a nullity merely for misjoinder or non-joinder especially that contracts entered into with an unincorporated association are not nullities. We were referred to the learned authors of Chitty On Contracts in the passages (at paragraphs 675 and 676 of the 26th edition) under the subheading "Liability of unincorporated associations" and "Representative action" which read −675 liability of unincorporated associations. An unincorporated association is not a legal person and therefore cannot sue or be sued unless such a course is authorized by express or implied statutory provisions as in the case of a trade union and a trustee savings bank. Nor can a contract be made so as to bind all persons who from time to time become members of such an association. But a contract purportedly made by or with an incorporated association is not necessarily a nullity.

If the person or persons who actually made the contract had no authority to contract on behalf of the members they may be held to have contracted personally. On the other hand, if they had the authority, express or implied, of all or some of the members of the association to contract on their behalf, the contract can be enforced by or against those members as co-principals to the contract by the ordinary rules of agency 676 representative action. By the rules of agency, therefore, a large number of members of an association may find themselves parties to a contract. In practice it would be impossible in such a case to join all the members as plaintiffs or defendants, and therefore recourse must be had to the device of a representative action. Order 15, r. 12, of the Rules of the Supreme Court provides that where there are numerous persons having the same interest in any proceedings, the proceedings may be begun and, unless the court otherwise orders, continued by or against any one or more of them as representing all or as representing all except one or more of them.

The attitude of the courts is to interpret the open textured language of Order 15, r. 12, in a liberal manner. Its language, according to Megarry V.-C., is wide and permissive and the rule should be used as *"a flexible tool of convenience in the administration of justice."*

(Continued)

(Continued)

We respectfully agree with the observations by the learned authors both as to the question of capacity or lack thereof of the association and on the issue of a representative action. The agreement in the instant case was not a nullity and the persons who represented the union could properly be regarded as representing themselves and the other wheat-growing members. The propositions founded in the Rules of the Supreme Court, Order 15, coincide with the principles in our own High Court Rules, Order 14. It follows that the criticism that the Chairmen were not qualified and competent representative plaintiffs was a valid one since they were not themselves eligible plaintiffs personally having any community of interest in the outcome. The question arose what should be the result of this. Counsel for the company submitted that the whole of the action be dismissed so that any competent plaintiffs should start a fresh action while Counsel for the farmers argued that a retrial could be ordered in these same proceedings. As we see it, a fresh trial would appear to be justified by the line of defence adopted, the thrust of which was to deny the competence of the union and of the Chairmen and to argue that there had been variation and separate contracts with the farmers.

Indeed, the whole of the appeal has been argued along those same lines, including the argument that there was no intention to create legal relations when clearly the representation comprised in the agreement was intended to be published and to be acted upon by the wheat-growing farmers, as they in fact did. The question of misjoinder and/or non-joinder of the correct parties has predominated and it has relegated the issues on the merits to the background. Yet, our Order 14 of the High Court Rules provides the necessary answers. For instance, Rule 5(3) specifically prohibits the defeasance of suits for misjoinder or non-joinder which would be the effect of acceding to the arguments by Mr Matibini and Mr Nchito.

A perusal through the reported cases shows that the courts have consistently upheld the principle underlying Order 14 Rule 5(3). Even in this case, the learned trial judge would have been perfectly entitled to have exercised her powers to allow substitution of correct parties: For an example of a case dealing with misjoinder or non-joinder we need cite only the case of *Mugala And Another v The Attorney-General* (1). We accept that, arising from any substitution of plaintiffs, both sides may wish to reformulate their respective cases; certainly, we can imagine the defendants wishing to put forward against each represented plaintiff the subsequent bargain under which wheat was purchased at reduced prices.

It follows from what we have been saying that the appeal is allowed to the extent that the judgment below is set aside and a retrial ordered before another judge of the High Court. We direct that the Court below should allow amendments by way of substitution of plaintiffs and any consequential amendments to the pleadings on either side as may seem fit. The costs hereof will abide the outcome of the retrial.

Appeal allowed

Namazi Grace v Kinyara Sugar Works, Ltd

High Court of Uganda, Kampala HCCS NO. 50 of 2000, September 29th 2003
Hon. Lady Justice M.S. Arach-Amoko

Judgment

The Plaintiff is a sugar cane farmer of Kabahara, Bujenje County, and Masindi District. The Defendant is a sugar milling factory in the same district. The facts of this case are briefly that the Plaintiff and the Defendant entered into a contract dated 24/7/96 under the Kinyara Sugar Works Outgrowers Scheme whereby the Plaintiff agreed to grow sugar cane in her field specified in the contract, and the Defendant undertook to harvest and purchase the said sugar cane from the Plaintiff. In March 1998, the Defendants servants entered into the said field and harvested the sugar cane pursuant to the said contract. The Defendant then transported the sugar cane to its factory, where at the same was weighed and found to be 402.5 tons; for which the Defendant paid.

The Plaintiff is dissatisfied with the result, and contends that her field yielded approximately 753 tons out of which the Defendant transported only 402.5 tons, leaving approximately 350 tons of cut sugar cane lying to waste all over the field. The Plaintiff alleges the failure by the Defendant to collect the 350 tons amounted to breach of contract by the Defendant. That she was also further denied any income from sugar cane for that season as the sugar cane purchased was only just enough to pay off her loan from the Defendant. She contended further that the Defendant's failure to collect the 350 tons of cut sugar cane from her field also led to her incurring expenses in clearing the field in preparation for the next seasons planting and also led to the next season's diminished harvest, thereby occasioning her further financial loss and damage. Therefore the Plaintiff prays for Judgment against the Defendant for:

a. Specific damages in the sum of Shs.7, 780,500/.
b. General damages for breach of contract.
c. Costs.
d. Interest on (a) (b) and (c) at a rate of 20% p.a. from date of the cause of action till payment in full.

The Defendant denied the Plaintiff's claim and averred that:

a. It harvested, transported, weighed and purchased 402.5 tons of sugar cane from the Plaintiff's field valued at Shs.8,077,374/ only.
b. It was a term of the loan transaction that the Defendant offsets the loan advanced to the Plaintiff, with interest at the time of buying the Plaintiff's sugar cane; which it did. The outstanding loan was Shs.8,133,222/. The balance due from the Plaintiff is Shs 5,848.
c. The cane was weighed after transportation to the Defendant's factory and the Plaintiff was notified of the total harvest.
d. The Plaintiff was fully paid for the 402.5 tons of cane by offsetting her loan advances. She is therefore not entitled to any relief claimed.

The following facts were agreed at the commencement of the hearing:

1. That there was a contract between the parties
2. 402.5 tons of cane was harvested, collected and paid for.

(Continued)

(Continued)

3. The Defendant was to ferry the cane to the factory and deduct the cost from the Plaintiff.
4. The particular field was 5 hectares.
5. The Defendant was under obligation to purchase all the cane grown by the Plaintiff.

The agreed issues were:

1. Whether the Plaintiffs field was capable of yielding 753 tons.
2. Whether the Defendant harvested *753* tons.
3. If so, whether the Defendant left 350 tons of cane in the field.
4. Remedies available if any.
5. I have also added another issue under the Courts powers under 0.13 r 5 to include the issue:
6. Whether or not the Defendant breached the contract at all.

The first issue is whether the plaintiff's field was capable of yielding 753 tons of sugar cane; Counsel for the plaintiff submitted that it was. He relied on the testimony of the plaintiff's four witnesses to support his argument. Learned counsel for the defendant on this part submitted that the plaintiff has failed to adduce sufficient evidence to prove that her field was capable of yielding 753 tons of sugar. Her claim was not supported by evidence. She only said that she was told in a seminar that a model field could yield 150 tons per hectare. She did not support this proposition by scientific evidence. Her evidence was just general, that hers was a model garden.

I have carefully perused the evidence of the Plaintiff on this issue, starting with the Plaintiff's testimony.

As can be gathered from her testimony, the Plaintiff honestly believed that her field was capable of yielding 750 tons of sugar cane because:

— It was a model garden in the area used by Kinyara Sugar Works as a model to train other outgrowers.
— She is able to estimate that the cane left was 350 because they were trained during seminars by Kinyara Sugar Works Superintendent called George Batuusa, who conducted seminars for outgrowers two months after planting that one hectare would yield 150 tons. Her field was 5 hectares.
— The sugar cane she is complaining about was from the first harvest.
— The second harvest was 450 tons. The first harvest is usually greater than the second. According to PW2, a fellow farmer, and Chairman of the Kinyara Sugar Cane Growers Association, who went to the Plaintiff's field after receiving her complaint, he saw a lot of cane in the field. Grace had maintained her field so well that they sometimes used it as a model field at training workshops. According to how the cane looked, and the way it was looked after, one would expect to harvest 140 tons of cane per hectare — that is about 700 tons. Under cross examination, PW2 stated that his first harvest yielded 136 tons per hectare on average. His field is however 53 km away from the Plaintiff's in the Western zone. He got 98 tons per hectare in 2000. In 1998, there was El Nino and the best farmer scored 198 tons per hectare and 152 per hectare in 1999.
PW4 is also a sugar cane cultivator and chairman of the Association in the same area. He estimated the cane left in the Plaintiff's field to be 300–400 tons. He had also

(Continued)

(Continued)

attended the seminars where they learnt from the Defendant's officials that a farmer can get 150 tons of sugar cane out of every hectare from a properly looked after field. The Plaintiff's field was one of those fields which had been properly looked after. Her field was one of those the Defendant brought visitors to learn from.

It is clear from the foregoing evidence that the Plaintiff has not produced any scientific evidence that her field was capable of yielding the 753 tons of sugar cane alleged. Her evidence is general; that hers was a model garden. On this issue, I agree therefore with the Defence Counsel and therefore answer it in the negative. The second and 3rd issues are whether the Defendant harvested 753 tons of sugar cane and whether they left 350 tons in the field. The Plaintiff testified that she was physically present when the Defendant's workers were cutting sugar cane from her field. They did not cut all the sugar cane from the field. Some were cut, others were not cut. Some of the sugar cane was taken and the rest were left behind. Apart from estimating the cane left behind as 350 tons, she has not adduced any evidence to support the contention that the Defendant harvested 753 tons. If, as stated, a model field like hers was capable of yielding 753 tons, and yet according to her, some of the sugar cane was not cut, it is inconceivable then that the cane which was harvested amounted to 753 tons.

PW2 informed Court that he could not tell how much sugar cane he saw in the field. PW3 did not take the photograph of the whole field. PW4 said he saw about 300—400 tons of sugar cane left in the field. He based his estimate on the seminar conducted by the Defendant's officials who had told them that a well tendered field would yield about 150 tons per hectare.

All in all, I find that the Plaintiff has also failed to establish to the satisfaction of this Court that Defendant harvested 753 tons of sugar cane from her field. The Plaintiff has however established that the Defendant did leave sugar cane on her field which was over and above the accepted loss of 3 tons per hectare. That she was dissatisfied with the way her sugar cane was harvested by the Defendant's workers. This was her first harvest and she had looked after it very well to the extent that it was regarded as a model field in the area. She therefore expected more sugar cane from her field than the 402 tons. She was expecting at least 150 tons per hectare, making a total of 750 tons. 402 tons was therefore a bit too low in the circumstance. She was even able to harvest more sugar cane in the second harvest and yet the evidence of the other witnesses including the Defence witnesses is to the effect that the yield reduces with the subsequent harvest. She stated that she got 450 tons of sugar cane during the second harvest. This was because the heap of cane which was left in the field affected the growth of the later sugar cane. PW2 visited her field and said he saw a lot of cane in the field, some cut and some not cut; and covered with trash. PW2 stated that he inspected the field with the extension officer of the Defendant called Mr. Awilia. He then reported to Mr. George McIntyre, the Defendant's Manager; who advised that the Plaintiff should plant the cane that had remained in the field. In my view, Mr. McIntyre could not give this advice unless he was also aware that a lot of sugar cane had been left in the Plaintiff's field. He said the Defendant also refused to send back the harvesting team and equipment to transport the cane on the ground that it was too expensive. PW2 estimated about 300 tons of cane

(Continued)

(Continued)

left in the field. His first harvest was 136 tons per hectare and yet his was not a model field.

I have also seen the photographs in Exhibit D2. It shows that a lot of sugar cane was left on the field under trash although some of it has now been heaped together. I find the evidence of the Defence witnesses merely calculated to support the case for their employer and to save their jobs. They are not independent witnesses. I have therefore placed very little value on their evidence. DW4 who said he participated in transportation of the sugar cane from the Plaintiff's field for instance stated in cross-examination that no cane was left in the Plaintiff's field, and in the same breath, admitted that some cane was left in the field. He also stated that he never checked under the trash for any cane before leaving the field. DW2, stated that he was the Defendant's harvesting supervisor at the material time. He described how sugar cane was supposed to be harvested. That it was harvested green and not burnt. He stated that he controlled the harvesting operation throughout until it was over. In cross-examination however, he stated that he could not tell how many cutters or field assistants they used in the Plaintiff's field.

That it was impossible for him to supervise each cutter. He admitted that sometimes cane can be mixed with trash during harvesting; when a worker has not detrashed the cane properly or when he has not cleared the ground where to pile the cane or when cane drops on the trash at the time of loading. In the case of the Plaintiff, as the photos showed, some cane remained in the field, although he could not tell how much. DW1's testimony was full of contradictions and outright lies. He testified that he was asked by the Senior Superintendent Mr. Batuse to investigate the Plaintiff's case. He went to the field in the company of the Plaintiff. This was after 2 weeks. He saw some stalks of sugar cane in some few heaps. He deliberately underestimated the cane in the photographs (Exhibit P2) to be only 40 kg, 20 kg, and 4 kgs only with a lot of trash.

He then contradicted himself when he said:

"I reported to my supervisor that I had seen a few sugar cane stalks in the field. I informed him that it was 0.2 tons that is 200 kgs. It is normal to find such sugar cane after harvest. There is acceptable loss of 3 tons per hectare." and where he stated: "I was there at the time of harvest and loading... I made sure that all the cane had been properly cut and loaded. I found everything properly harvested. There was nothing left." and then where he stated:

"When sugar cane is harvested green, there is a possibility that some cane falls under the trash. Some may be under the trash because the trash is thick....You cannot see any cane buried under the trash even when the toppings wither unless the farmer re-arranges when I visited the field, the trash was not re-arranged. I saw the sugar cane when the trash was not re-arranged."

He insisted that the Plaintiff's farm was not properly looked after and was never visited during seminars. During cross examination he stated that: "I went to the field, the trash was not cleared. I raised the trash myself to see whether there was cane under the trash. I did not raise the trash all over the 5 hectares. I made spot checks at some points. I was alone." He admitted that the photos in Exhibit P2 reflect what he saw in the Plaintiff's field. He stated

(Continued)

(Continued)

that there was too much trash at the time of cutting, so some sugar cane was left under the trash; all over the field which could not be detected at the time of harvest.

I have also not placed much weight on the evidence of DW 3, the Agronomist firstly because the report (Exhibit D2) he sought to rely on is not signed by him. An unsigned report has no evidentiary value. The sketch map of Kabahara does not also help much. It is not related to any official map of the area. It could have been drawn anywhere. The Agronomist carried out his study in March 2000 that is two years after the fact. The study was actually carried out after the filing of this suit. He did not carry out any tests on the soil before planting. He took photos in Exhibit D3 during dry season to show how unproductive and unimpressive the Plaintiff's garden was. The season complained of was in 1998 where he also acknowledged that there was El Nino; so the garden was nice and green. I do find his report and his testimony full of theories and biased in favour of the Defendant, his employer. It is l9ts in the category of expert evidence referred to by J.D Heydon in his text book entitled 'Evidence – Cases and Materials' at page 384 on Opinion evidence where he states that:

"There is a general feeling also that expert witnesses are selected to prove a case and are often close to being professional liars: 'it is often quite surprising to see with what facility, and to what an extent, their view can be made to correspond with the wishes or the interests of the parties who call them. They do not, indeed, willfully misrepresent what they think, but their judgments become so warped by regarding the subject in one point of view, that, even when conscientiously disposed, they are incapable of forming an independent opinion. Being zealous partisans, their Belief becomes synonymous with faith as defined by the Apostle, and it too often is but "substance of things hoped for, the evidence of things not seen" (Taylor, P 59). Lord Campbell put it more harshly: 'hardly any weight is to be given to the evidence of what are called scientific witnesses; they come with a bias on their minds to support the cause in which they are embarked' (Tray Peerage Claim (1843) 10 Cl & Fin 154 at 191). And Best says: "there can be no doubt that testimony is daily received in our Courts as 'scientific evidence' to which it is almost profanation to apply the term; as being revolting to common sense and inconsistent with the commonest honesty on the part of those by whom it is given (P491)."

Counsel for the Plaintiff pointed out that the study was carried out to manufacture evidence for the suit. I am inclined to agree with him.

In conclusion under these two issues, I rule that the Plaintiff has not established that the Defendant harvested 753 tons of sugar cane from her field at the material time, and that the Defendant left 350 tons of sugar cane in the field. The Plaintiff has however, established that the Defendant left a large part of the sugar cane it had harvested under trash in the field, which is over and above the accepted loss, which brings me to the issue whether the Defendant breached the contract or not. Section 5 provided that:

"The Miller shall:

5.1. Undertake to purchase all sugar cane that is cultivated on the land between the age 15 & 27 months, and shall become the owner of the sugar cane once it has issued to the farmer a certificate of its weight as delivered to the buying station."

(Continued)

(Continued)

> The section obliged the Defendant to purchase all sugar cane harvested on the Plaintiff's field. The evidence shows that the Defendant left a lot of sugar cane on the Plaintiff's field and hence did not pay for it in accordance with the contract. This amounted to breach of contract. Under the law, a breach of contract exists where one party to contract fails to carry out a term, promise or condition of the contract. See: Blacks Law Dictionary 5th Edn at 171.
>
> The last issue is remedies available. The Plaintiff prayed for:
>
> a. Special damages in the sum of Shs.7, 780,500/. It is trite law that special damages must not only be pleaded, but must be strictly proved, although they need not be proved by documentary evidence in all cases. See: *Kyambadde v Mpigi District Administration* [1983] HCB 44.

In the case before me, I have ruled that Plaintiff has failed to establish that her field was capable of yielding 753 tons and that the cane left on her field was 350 tons; which was the basis for the Shs.7, 780,500/ claim. This prayer is therefore not proved and it is disallowed accordingly.

Prayer (b) is for general damages for breach of contract. I have ruled that the Plaintiff has established that the Defendant left a substantial amount of sugar cane in her field, which was over and above the accepted loss. This was breach of contract. The evidence on record shows that the Plaintiff went through a lot of inconvenience as a result of the Defendant's action. As soon as she noticed that some cane had been left on her field, she went to their Chairman and reported the matter. She even went to the extent of hiring a freelance photographer (PW2) to take the photograph of the field (Exhibits P2). She could not use the sugar cane left in the field for gapping because they were too old. The second harvest was also affected because of the heap, which was left in the field. She got only 450 tons as a result. In the second planting, her garden was no longer a model garden. She could not get the highest output. PW2 corroborated her testimony, when he stated: "I did not agree with the advice. In the first place, the said cane had outgrown, it could not be used as a planting seed. Secondly, her field was not ready for planting. Thirdly, it involved a lot of labour because some of it was not out."

Learned counsel for the Plaintiff has not proposed any sum under this head. Doing the best I can and taking all the circumstances of the case, I am of the view that the sum of Shs.5m would adequately compensate the Plaintiff and I award it to her. She is also entitled to the costs of this suit. In the result, I enter Judgment in favour of the Plaintiff as follows:

1. Shs.5m general damages for breach of contract.
2. Costs of the suit.
3. Interest on 1 and 2 at Court rate from date of Judgment till payment in full.

Notes

1. See, for example, Porter and Phillips-Howard (1997). The United Nations Food and Agriculture Organization (FAO) maintains a useful website on the institution of contract farming. See FAO (n.d.).
2. For details on the benefits and costs, see Kunkel et al. (2009); Wu (2003). For an analysis of hostage-taking in contractual interaction, see Williamson (1983). Opportunism occurs when "a performing party behaves

contrary to the other party's understanding of their contract, but not necessarily contrary to the agreement's explicit terms, leading to a transfer of wealth from the other party to the performer." See Muris (1980). Muris' paper contains an extensive list of literature on opportunism.
3. Supreme Court (Ngulube, CJ, Lewanika and Chibesakunda, JJS (SCZ Judgment No. 23 of 2000)).

Questions

1. Provide a definition of "sunk costs."
2. Compare and contrast integrated and non-integrated firms.
3. What are risk considerations that contracting parties have to consider?
4. Perform an internet search of "information asymmetry." Provide a definition and cite your source.
5. What is a way that information asymmetry can be reduced in contract farming?
6. What role, if any, should courts play to promote contract farming in sub-Saharan African countries?
7. The *Namazi* case (Uganda) addresses problems associated with the common agricultural practice of outgrower arrangement and holding the firm to its commitment to deal with unequal bargaining power of parties. Discuss the issues of policing output and problems of monitoring. Contrast this case with the tomato farmers in Ghana and the problem of perishable products.

Challenge Question

Consider Box 3.1 regarding the plight of tomato farmers in the Northern region of Ghana. Would you recommend government intervention in the tomato market, and if so, what form of intervention would you recommend? Should Government be "buyer of last resort" in the tomato sector? What do you think of the following economics argument?

The idea of government as buyer of last resort is based on the following economic argument. Profit-maximizing firms will not purchase tomatoes from areas and regions where the marginal cost of operation is greater than the marginal revenue. What emerges in Ghana is a situation where farmers and producers of perishable products are constantly complaining about difficulties in finding markets for their produce.

References

FAO, n.d. Contract Farming Resource Center. <http://www.fao.org/ag/ags/contract-farming/en/> (accessed 11.09.10.).
Kunkel, P.L., Peterson, J.A., Mitchell, J.A., 2009. Agricultural Production Contracts. University of Minnesota Extension Service, <http://www.extension.umn.edu/distribution/businessmanagement/DF7302.html>.
Muris, T.J., 1980. Opportunistic behavior and the law of contracts. Minn. Law Rev. 65, 521

Porter, G., Phillips-Howard, K., 1997. Comparing contracts: an evaluation of contract farming schemes in Africa. World Dev. 25 (2), 227–238.

da Silva, C.A., 2005. The Growing Role of Contract Farming in Agri-Food Systems Development: Drivers, Theory and Practice. FAO, Rome.

Williamson, O.E., 1983. Credible commitments: using hostages to support exchange. Am. Econ. Rev. 73 (4), 519–540.

Wu, S., 2003. Regulating Agricultural Contracts: What Are the Tradeoffs? Choices, First Quarter.

CHAPTER 4

Agricultural Production and Share Contracts

Keywords: Sharecropping; tenancy; risk and transaction costs; cash rents; bargaining power, information asymmetry

4.1 Introduction

Sharecropping is one of the most common agricultural institutions in sub-Saharan Africa. According to one estimate about 20% and 15% of agricultural production in Ghana and Malawi, respectively, is subject to sharecropping (Zezza et al., undated). In a study of the cocoa sector in southwest Nigeria, the author found that tenant sharecropping was the most common labor type used overall and was reported by 70% of producers.[1] Sharecropping has been described as "an agreement to produce agricultural products, where the landowner provides the land (and sometimes the other inputs) and the sharecropper provides the labour (and occasionally inputs such as seeds). At the end of the agricultural cycle the harvest is divided between the parties on a pre-agreed basis" (FAO, 2001).[2] As suggested by the FAO, the underlying driver for the research and policy on sharecropping is the belief that "it is possible to devise suitable arrangements which balance the interests of the landowner and the tenant and which can improve access to farms and lead to better agricultural production and improved stewardship of the land" (Zezza et al., n.d.).

4.2 Law and Economics of Sharecropping

Earlier economists did not favor share tenancy because it was considered inefficient and wasteful of resources. The view was that a tenant is unlikely to give maximum effort if part of the produce will be paid to a landowner who committed no labor to the production. This view is known as the "Marshallian" view after the notable eighteenth century economist (Cheung, 1969). Over time this view has changed in recognition of the role of risk and transaction cost in shaping contracts (Allen and Lueck, 1992, 1993; Boadu, 1992; Murrell, 1983; Shaban, 1987). The idea is that parties to a contract weigh the risk they face and

F.O. Boadu: Agricultural Law and Economics in Sub-Saharan Africa.
DOI: http://dx.doi.org/10.1016/B978-0-12-801771-5.00004-6

other considerations when negotiating a contract. Thus, terms in a contract reflect the natural risk and transaction costs as perceived by the individual.

Natural risk is the contribution by nature or state of the world to the variance (or standard deviation) of the product value (Cheung, 1969). In agriculture, weather, pests, and rainfall influence output variation. Transaction costs refer to the information, bargaining, and policing costs associated with a contract. In sharecropping, parties need information about each other, determine the distribution of responsibility under the contract, and policing effort and the level of output. Since parties cannot negotiate a complete contingent cropshare contract, law is used to fill the gaps in the contract.

The cases on share contracts reflect efforts by the courts in sub-Saharan Africa to bring the customary share contract regime to reflect modern realities. In the case of *Attah and Others v Esson*, the court interprets the customary share tenancy arrangement in the context of modern realities and rejects a time-honored practice that the court found to be repugnant to development in a modern society. In the second case, *Manu v Ainoo and Another*, the Court of Appeal strengthened the bargaining power of the tenant by approving of their right to sue for accounting even though a tenant does not own the land. These cases reflect efforts by courts to participate in the progressive development of the customary law system to meet the needs of modern society. The South African case, *Department of Land Affairs and Popela Community and ors. v Goedgelegen Tropical Fruits (PTY) Ltd.* is not strictly a cropsharing case but has been included to show how the relationship between tenant and land owner is changing in response to the demands of social and political forces.

ATTAH and Others v ESSON

Court of Appeal, Ghana
5 December 1975

Facts: The plaintiff was the tenants in perpetuity of the defendant in respect of a large piece of land. The defendants entered the land and felled over 400 palm trees admittedly cultivated by the plaintiff. The value of a palm tree was at least £G2. The plaintiff sued for damages for trespass and perpetual injunction. The counsel for the defendants contended that under the customary law rule as stated by Sarbah and which had not as yet been declared unreasonable by any court, the first defendant's family were entitled (as the landlords) to enter the land at any time to fell the palm trees — being economic trees — and enjoy the fruits thereof whether or not the palm trees were already on the land before the tenancy or were planted by the tenant after the creation of the tenancy. The trial judge held that the defendants were not entitled to cut down the palm trees. General damages for trespass were subsequently assessed

(Continued)

(Continued)

at ¢200.00 and an order for perpetual injunction was also made against the defendants. The defendants are appealing this adverse ruling.

Opinion: *Per curiam*. No proposition would be more out of accord with the hopes and aspirations of Ghanaians today than that a landlord who has spent no effort whatsoever towards that end should enter and collect at will the fruits of the labour of his tenant. Who amongst us would today be prepared to take land to cultivate on that basis? We cannot imagine an arrangement more ruinous of agricultural enterprise, subversive of expansion and consequently prejudicial to national development than that... At the trial, counsel informed the court that they had agreed that a point of law which would dispose of the whole case be taken first. That preliminary point which was taken, arises out of the following pleadings of the parties. By paragraph (10) of the statement of claim, the plaintiff pleaded:

> That in spite of all these consent judgments, awards and orders the defendants have unlawfully entered the said land without the plaintiff's consent and permission felled over 400 palm trees which the plaintiff's family has cultivated on the land in dispute. The value of one palm tree is at least £G2.

In answer to this pleading, the defendants stated in paragraph (6) of their defence:

> The defendants say that in view of customary law which empowers a landowner to enter upon his land in the possession of another as tenant to collect palm nuts or enjoy the palm and other indigenous edible trees on the land, the defendants can exercise the right to enter the said land for that purpose and are therefore not liable to the plaintiff as claimed in any amount or at all and thereon join issue with the plaintiff.

The defendants in agreeing that a decision on the legal point raised by these pleadings would dispose of the case before the court, admitted that the plaintiff and his family were their tenants and further that they, the defendants, had entered on to the land occupied by the plaintiff's family and cut down the palm trees as alleged. Moreover, the defendants' concern was not with distinctions between palm trees already on the land before the tenancy was created on the one hand and palm trees planted by the tenant after the creation of the tenancy. To the defendants, in either case the landlord was entitled to the palm trees on the land. Therefore they did [Page 131] not in their pleadings specifically deny the claim of the plaintiff that his family had planted the palm trees. In view of the pleadings quoted above and of counsel's agreement that a decision on the legal point arising therefrom disposes of the whole case we are bound to accept that the palm trees in this case were planted by the plaintiff's family as claimed.

Did the defendants have this right they claimed or not? No less an authority than Sarbah supports their contention. In his *Fanti Customary Laws* first published in 1897 he said (and I quote from the third edition (1968) at pp. 69−70):

> The original owner or his successor can at any time go upon and retake possession of the land as soon as the tenant asserts an adverse claim to it. In the absence of such adverse claim he cannot

(Continued)

(Continued)

disturb the quiet enjoyment of the tenant, without prior notice to the tenant that he requires the land. Where, however, there are palm-trees on the land, whether planted by the owner of the land or by the tenant, the landowner has full right, at any time he pleases, to cut trees or gather any nuts there from. Custom does not permit any person to be improved out of his land, and palm-trees not only improve, but also enhance the value of lands.

Where nuts from a palm land are manufactured into oil, the owner of the land receives half of the oil, and the oil manufacturer the other half, and the expenses of preparing the oil is equally shared by them. If, instead of oil manufacture, there is extracted from the palm-trees palm-wine, then the owner of the palm-trees is entitled to one-fourth of the proceeds of such palm-wine, the person who fells the trees and prepares the wine is entitled to one-fourth of such proceeds, and the person who sells such palm-wine is entitled to half of such proceeds. According to a well-known practice of the Law Courts, each palm-tree is valued at twenty shillings.

This statement of the law seems to have obtained in more recent times some endorsement from Bentsi-Enchill. At p. 398 of his *Ghana Land Law* he said: "income-yielding shrubs and trees already on the land, such as palm-trees, kola, and timber generally, are understood to belong exclusively to the landlord." Bentsi-Enchill, it appears, was not prepared to go the lengths which Sarbah did because he limited the landlord's rights to economic shrubs and trees "already on the land." And his statement was made when discussing the arrangement "where the tenant is given virgin land to bring into cultivation." On the proposition that the land-lord was entitled to the fruits of economic trees planted by the tenant on the land, Bentsi-Enchill expressed no view. Sarbah's proposition cannot, therefore, be said to have got the unqualified approval of as modern a writer as Bentsi-Enchill.

The pith of the learned trial judge's argument in rejecting the opinion of Sarbah is contained in the one sentence which said that: "It sounds unreasonable indeed that where a tenant has by his own labours planted palm trees his landlord should indiscriminately enter the land and cut the palm trees at any time as he pleases." Like Archer J., we do not wish to cast doubt on the distinction and learning of Sarbah. Indeed the learned judge accepted that what Sarbah wrote might have represented the customary law of the nineteenth century. So do we. But even if this was so, customary law embodies the rules of conduct of the people at a particular time. These rules represent what is reasonable in any given situation in the society. Customary law, therefore, must develop and change with the changing times. What was reasonable in the social conditions of the nineteenth century would not necessarily be reasonable today. A contrary theory would ensure that the customary law becomes ossified and incapable of growth to meet new challenges and demands. No proposition would be more out of accord with the hopes and aspirations of Ghanaians today than that a landlord who has spent no effort whatsoever towards that end should enter and collect at will the fruits of the labour of his tenant. Who amongst us would today be prepared to take land to cultivate on that basis? We cannot imagine an arrangement more ruinous of agricultural enterprise, subversive of expansion and consequently prejudicial to national development than that.

(Continued)

(Continued)

One point taken by Mr. Short, counsel for the defendants, was that the decision of Archer J. was given per incuriam inasmuch as the court failed to consider the case of *Egyin v Aye* [1962] 2 G.L.R. 187, which, being a decision of the former Supreme Court of Ghana, was binding on it. van Lare J.S.C. giving the judgment of the court in that case had said at p. 194, "It must be pointed out that the felling of palm trees is by customary law an exercise of unequivocal acts of ownership reserved only to an owner of land, or a pledgee holding of the owner." Mr. Short relied on this statement in support of the argument in favour of the landlord's right to economic trees. But that statement has to be considered in the context in which it was made. *Ashon v Barng* [1897] Sar.F.C.L. (3rd ed.) 153 was a case to determine the right as between an owner of land and his pledgee to cut palm trees on the land pledged. Redwar Ag. J. at p. 156 found by a preponderance of evidence that "the custom of cutting down the palm-trees by a pledgee until the debt is repaid is clearly and satisfactorily proved ..." The owner's claim for damages in trespass against the pledgee failed because the pledgee "had a legal right to do what he had done ..." Far from the case showing the owner's invariable right to fell palm-trees whoever had possession of the land and whatever the terms of possession it shows that as between the owner and his pledgee, the customary law then recognised the right of the pledgee to cut the palm-trees. *Egyin v Aye* (supra) on the other hand was a case in which two persons, one of whom had no title, disputed the title to land. The fact that [Page 133] one of the disputants had pledged the land and that his pledgee felled the palm-trees was used as evidence determining the issue of ownership in favour of that particular pledgor. In neither case was there an issue as to whose was the right as between an owner and his tenant to fell palm-trees on the land. The decision in *Egyin v Aye* did not, therefore, bar Archer J. from taking the view that he did.

We have no doubt that customary law today would not permit a landlord to enter onto agricultural land granted to his tenant to gather the fruits of economic trees planted on it by the tenant. We would understand a principle which forbids the tenant from committing such waste on the land as would destroy or reduce the value of the reversionary interest of the landlord. But the maxim, if maxim it be, that "custom does not permit any person to be improved out of his land" used to justify what in modern eyes looks no less than a landlord's charter for plunder, appears to us, however beautiful it may sound and whether representative of the values of Ghanaians in the nineteenth century, totally indefensible today. We accordingly agree with the conclusion of Archer J. that the landlord is not entitled to the fruits of economic trees planted by the tenant. In so far as the defendants' contention is that they, as landlords, are entitled to palm trees on the land whether planted by them or by the plaintiff's family, we hold that this appeal must fail.

Learned counsel for the defendants has argued that if Sarbah's proposition was wrong no court has so declared before, and, therefore, presumably persons were entitled to act in accordance with Sarbah until a court declared to the contrary. We do not think so. We think that the customary law as stated by Sarbah became outdated and ceased to be law as soon as conditions in society changed so as to make it unreasonable for persons to conduct

(Continued)

(Continued)

themselves by it. It is, therefore, not necessary for the society to await a court's ruling before deciding to act in a manner contrary to a rule of conduct which has become unreasonable.

But what of the part of the customary law as stated by Sarbah which gives the right to economic trees already on the land to the landlord? The objection, in those cases, to that leg of Sarbah's rule on the ground that it acts as a disincentive to economic progress is not as strong. And there are considerations why we cannot say that that aspect of the rule has been or must be discarded. Archer J. in holding that the enjoyment of economic trees like the palm belonged to the tenant unless expressly reserved by agreement between the parties to the landlord relied on a passage in Ollennu's book on the *Principles of Customary Land Law in Ghana*. That passage which appears at p. 59 of the book reads as follows:

> *Another important incident of the determinable title is the right to palm and cola nut and other economic trees of the land. In all parts of Ghana where the oil palm tree and other species of palm grow, it is the owner of the determinable title in the land, and he alone who is vested with the right to harvest the fruits, to fell the palm trees or to tap wine from them. Neither the owner of the absolute title nor the owner of the sub-absolute title can go upon [Page 134] land to harvest cola nuts, palm nuts or fell palm trees for palm wine. They may request the owner of the determinable title to supply so many pots of palm wine, or a quantity of palm nuts or cola nuts as customary services, but they are not permitted by custom to go upon land in possession of a subject to take any of these things.*

The learned judge seems to have equated the expression "the owner of the absolute title" used by Ollennu in this passage to "the landlord" in our present classification, and the expression "the owner of the determinable title in the land" appearing in the quotation to our "tenant." With all due deference, we do not think that Ollennu was here discussing the ordinary relationship of the landlord and tenant. His concern for the moment was with the various degrees of ownership recognised by the customary law and their incidents. Thus he spoke of "the owner of the absolute title" who would be the allodial owner of the land like the stool and "the owner of the determinable title" who would be a subject or family member properly on the land. The passage referred to therefore, does not contemplate incidents attached to the rights of a tenant under an ordinary tenancy. That aspect of the matter is dealt with by Ollennu in chapter 6 of his book on tenancies. At p. 87 of the book, the learned author says:

> *Except by special agreement, palm trees, kola nuts and such like fruits are generally excluded from the operation of* abusa *or* abunu *tenancy, and that is so even though in the process of the cultivation and maintenance of the* abusa *or* abunu *farm, the tenant must do work which must improve such trees growing in the farm, e.g., he must trim palm trees from time to time, or clear the bush round such trees. These trees are the special prerogative of the owner of the determinable title. It is he alone who has the right to the fruits. The tenant may pick a few fruits for his personal consumption, but he should not harvest them for sale, and he should not without the express authority of the landlord fell any oil palm tree, agor palm, dawadawa tree or shea butter tree.*

(Continued)

(Continued)

The distinction in Ollennu's terminology between "the owner of the determinable title" and "the tenant" is brought out clearly in this passage. And as between these two it is not the tenant who has the right to the fruits of economic trees on the land.

In the present case, the relationship between the plaintiff's and the defendants' families is such as may well justify the finding that the plaintiff's family were the owners of the determinable title in the land. They certainly were not ordinary tenants. They were tenants in perpetuity. The consideration for their right to occupation was the payment of 27 shillings, that is two cedis 70 pesewas, yearly.

Arbitrators have held that the plaintiff's family should join the defendants together "in sharing debts, performing funeral obsequies, and any other family transactions together as their ancestors were doing." And in that case, the adoption of the statement of Ollennu which gives the [Page 135] enjoyment of economic trees on the land to the owner of the determinable title in order to vest such enjoyment of trees already on the land in the plaintiff's family cannot be objected to. We believe it was on the basis that the present plaintiff's family had such title to the land as would warrant their being designated as owners of the determinable title according to custom that the learned judge drew his general conclusion that "a tenant in perpetuity is entitled to the palm trees on his tenancy and that the landlord has no right whatsoever to enter the land and cut palm trees or to collect palm nuts unless such rights have been expressly reserved to him by agreement between the parties."

We are, however, anxious that the generality of that holding should not be considered as applying to the ordinary customary tenancy agreement over land on which already existed economic trees like the palm or kola tree. The customary rule in that respect, allocating the fruits not to the tenant but to his landlord has not been shown to be unreasonable. Ollennu whose statement of the law impressed the learned judge as the modern exposition of the law, confirms, as we have seen, the view that except by special agreement, the enjoyment of the fruits of these trees continues with the landlord. We have no cause to differ from that view. That rule must, therefore, be accepted as still governing the relationship of landlord and tenant.

Ruling

The court per Baidoo J. awarded ¢400.00 for the palm trees felled and ¢200.00 as general damages for trespass. He also granted the perpetual injunction against the defendants asked for. The defendants' argument against the damages awarded was not so much a complaint of excessiveness of amount; it was that as no court had previously declared the principle under which they acted as illegal, the award of damages in the circumstances was unreasonable. Taking the view we do about the unreasonableness of the principle under which they acted, we remain unpersuaded by their argument on this point. But they have argued further that as the landlords, the grant of a perpetual injunction against them from entering their own land was wrong. We agree that the grant of the perpetual injunction was wrong. In the circumstances we would allow this appeal to the extent of cancelling the order for a perpetual injunction otherwise we would dismiss the appeal.

MANU v AINOO and Another

Court of Appeal, Accra, Ghana
24 February 1976

Facts: The appellant was first employed as a head labourer by J.A. Winney, on Winney's farms and subsequently as an abunu tenant and they executed a customary tenancy agreement. J.A. Winney died in 1963 and the appellant continued his tenancy undisturbed until 1966 when Winneys' successor, J.K. Arthur, attempted to dispossess him of the farm he was cultivating. J.K. Arthur sued the appellant in the Wassaw-Fiasi District Court Grade II, Mpohor and won. The victory was short-lived as the decision was soon set aside on appeal to the High Court, Sekondi, which ordered a retrial. Meanwhile J.K. Arthur had died and the suit apparently abated with his death. In 1970 the head of J.A. Winney's family reinstated the appellant and advanced him some money to rehabilitate the farms. However the appellant was arrested soon thereafter and before he could harvest, and between 1970 and 1973, the new successor to J.A. Winney gave the farms to some other people to harvest.

The appellant thereupon sued the respondent, the new successor, and a member of J.A. Winney's family, for inter alia an order for accounts of the proceeds of the farms for the period he had been deprived of them. In their defence the respondents contended that there was lack of fiduciary privity between them and the appellant because since the appellant had not rendered accounts for the period he was in charge of the farms he had abrogated the fiduciary relationship that might have existed and justified the call for accounts. The trial circuit judge dismissed the appellant's claim on the grounds that since the appellant had no possessory right over the farms he could not sue for accounts and injunction and, furthermore, that the appellant could not sue for breach of contract because he had not recognised the respondents as contracting parties. The appellant appealed.

Opinion: The issue for determination in this appeal may be simply stated. It is whether an abunu or abusa tenant farmer can sue for accounts. The answer can equally readily be given, and it is in the affirmative. But since the circuit judge who heard the matter and the respondents herein take a different view of the law, it is necessary to examine the matter in a little more detail. But first, the facts. By his writ filed on 11 July 1972, the plaintiff-appellant (hereinafter referred to as the appellant) sought an:

> "(1) Order for accounts of the proceeds of the cocoa and coconut collected from the farm of the late Winney by the defendant.
> (2) Injunction restraining the defendant from interfering with the plaintiff's rights in respect of late Winney's farm. Alternatively the plaintiff claims damages for breach of contract of employment."

Questions of accounts can always be legitimately raised where a fiduciary relationship exists between parties together with a correlative obligation to settle the differences that arise from the state of their finances. So long as the contractual relationship of an abunu tenant existed, and the appellant had introduced himself to the successors of Winney as custom demanded and the evidence affirmed, he was entitled to call for an investigation of accounts.

(Continued)

(Continued)

The learned circuit judge's rejection of the appellant's claim for an order for accounts is based on two main grounds, which I recapitulate from his judgment:

> "(1) The claims for account and injunction in the instant case to my mind will enure for one who has possessory rights and not one in the position of a head labourer, as the plaintiff, who claims on his own behalf.
>
> (2) The action for breach of contract, which is one of the reliefs, even though it can properly be maintained by the plaintiff, must be on stated conditions recognising the co-defendant and his agent, the defendant, as contracting parties which unfortunately the plaintiff refused to accept…".

Accordingly he held that the appellant's claim was sufficiently misconceived to be dismissed. I propose now to examine these formulations on which the circuit judge propped his judgment. The first that the appellant's claim could only subsist if he had possessory title is clearly a misconception of the law. Customary tenancies like abunu and abusa do not derive their validity from a possessory title. Indeed abunu and abusa tenancies are created in respect of the share of proceeds only. The ownership of the land remains always in the landlord. It is trite learning that being merely physically on land, does not create a possessory title. In *Kweku Sasu v Kwame Asomani* [1949] D.C. (Land) '48-'51, 133 at p. 136 *Quashie-Idun J.* (as he then was) said:

> *'abusa' custom does not imply a right in an owner of the land to divide a farm cultivated by another person into three and himself collect the proceeds of the third share. 'Abusa' implies that the owner of the land is entitled to be paid a third share of the proceeds accruing from the whole farm cultivated by another.*

Ollennu in his *Principles of Customary Land Law* in Ghana says at p. 83:

> *that the tenant is not entitled to have the farm shared. The real legal position is that title to the farm is vested in the owner, subject to the tenant's right to occupy and his obligation to pay a third share of the proceeds of the yield of the land to the owner.*

> *The same legal position applies to the abunu tenancy. The tenant does not get a moiety of the farm, he occupies the farm and gives a moiety of the proceeds of the crops of the farm to the owner.*

The learned author quotes in support of the principle an unreported judgment of his, *R. A. Darko v Kwasi Abore*, High Court, Accra, 12 April 1961.

The interest of the abusa or abunu tenant is the right to cultivate the land and to partake of the proceeds. He does not acquire title or estate in or a share of the farm. The tenant's interest however is protected and can be defended by the courts. That a tenant cannot be molested at will… It would follow that the appellant had a cause of action available to him to protect his interests by calling for accounts. The matter is put beyond controversy in the case of *Akofi v Wiresi and Abagya* [1957] which established the right of a tenant farmer to sue for a declaration as to his equitable share vis-a-vis his landlord's on such a tenancy. Coussey P. said at p. 259 that though the tenant farmer

(Continued)

(Continued)

> *has no ownership in the soil, [he] has a very real interest in the usufruct of the land. The arrangement may be carried on indefinitely, even by the original grantee's successor, so long as the original terms of the holding are observed.*

The circuit judge's second ground is a clear misreading of the evidence. It cannot be said in truth that the appellant challenged his landlord. The late Winney's family, like many a Ghanaian family, indulged in the usual petty squabbles about succession. One Aka Akua was first appointed to succeed J.K. Arthur. It was only after Aka Akua had renounced the successorship that the co-respondent, J.K. Ackom, was appointed. There is no title of evidence to suggest that the appellant regarded himself as owner (except of an indisputed farm). Nor is there evidence of any challenge by the appellant of the title of his overlords. The appellant was only concerned that the status quo ante existing in Winney's time should not be summarily disrupted by his successors. The appellant had the law on his side. For a successor cannot unilaterally vary or abrogate a customary grant.

Judgment: It was not the respondent's case that the circuit court should hold the appellant's abunu share forfeited. No such claim was made. Indeed as has been shown above, no counterclaim was urged against the appellant. On the facts and on the law therefore, there was no lawful warrant for the circuit judge's refusal of the appellant's claim for an order of accounts. His error must be redressed. In my view this can satisfactorily be done by allowing the appeal, and setting aside the judgment of the circuit court, and ordering that the accounts between the parties be investigated by a competent authority.

Department of Land Affairs and Popela Community and Ors. v Goedgelegen Tropical Fruits (PTY) Ltd

Constitutional Court of South Africa
Case CCT 69/06, June 6, 2007

MOSENEKE DCJ:

This case raises complex legal issues related to restitution of land rights to people who were labour tenants in a painful period of our history. The social injustice of the termination of their rights as labour tenants is not in question. What the case turns on is whether the termination of labour tenancies by private farmers entitles labour tenants to redress under the Restitution of Land Rights Act[3] (the Restitution Act).

The Popela Community (second applicant), alternatively the third to the eleventh applicants (individual applicants), claim restitution of rights in land under the Restitution Act. The Popela Community is a community or group of people acting in concert in claiming restitution of land rights. To this end, they have organised themselves into a voluntary association known as the Communal Property Association (CPA). The third to the eleventh applicants are men and women who claim restitution of land rights as individuals. They share much in common. They have the

(*Continued*)

(Continued)

same ethnic lineage and all bear the Maake surname barring one claimant. They originate from the same rural neighbourhood and they are all former labour tenants on the farm Boomplaats. As members of the CPA, they seek to enforce their claims with its assistance.

A party in its own class is the first applicant, the Department of Land Affairs (the Department). It bears certain statutory obligations to facilitate the achievement of the constitutional aims of land restitution and land reform.[4] It seeks to appeal to this Court in its own name but clearly acts in the interests of the applicants.[5] It asks for no material relief other than to have the decision of the Supreme Court of Appeal substituted with the order sought by the applicants. It must be added that the Department seeks to have the costs order of the Supreme Court of Appeal reversed. The order requires it to pay the costs of the appeal jointly and severally with the other applicants.

The land in issue forms part of the erstwhile farm Boomplaats 408 LT in the Mooketsi area of the Limpopo province. The farm Boomplaats is now consolidated into the farm Goedgelegen 566 LT and its registered owner is Goedgelegen Tropical Fruits (Pty) Ltd (respondent). The respondent opposes the claims.

The Land Claims Court dismissed the claims of the community and of the individual claimants. An appeal to the Supreme Court of Appeal faltered. It was dismissed with costs. Aggrieved by the decision of the Supreme Court of Appeal, the applicants ask for leave of this Court to contest the decision.

History of dispossession

At the very outset, certain mainly uncontested background facts loom large and cast a wide shadow over this tale of dispossession of rights to land. The narrative has all the hallmarks of forcible dispossession of indigenous ownership of land, which in time, has degenerated into dispossession of mere labour tenancy.

On all accounts, the ancestors of the individual applicants originally settled on the farm Boomplaats in the 1800s. The individual applicants, most of whom bear the family name Maake, trace their uninterrupted family settlement on the Boomplaats land back to the mid-19th century. According to the individual applicants, their forebears enjoyed undisturbed indigenous rights to the land and exercised all the rights that came with it. These rights included living on the land as families; bringing up their children on it; tending the elderly; paying spiritual tribute to their ancestors; and burying the dead. They were entitled to cultivate the land and to use it for livestock.

They did in fact exercise these rights. They lived on the land; they built families and inevitably a community; they buried their dead on it; and the graves are still there. On the same land, they paid homage to their ancestors. They tilled the land and reared livestock on it. The land provided subsistence necessary for the families without them being beholden to anyone. The applicants say these land rights were capable of being passed on to direct descendants and that their ancestors did transmit them to successive generations. However, this seemingly idyllic and rustic mode of living was not to last forever.

(Continued)

(Continued)

Initially, the Land Claims Court judgment records the colonial shift of land ownership patterns in terse terms:

> According to a research report submitted by the Regional Commissioner, the ancestors of the claimants were already living on the farms during the middle of the 19th century. When the whites came to settle on the farms, they found them there. The white settlers required them to render services for a certain period every year in return for being allowed to stay on and use the farms.[6]

Later, in the course of deciding whether the dispossession of indigenous title of the claimants to land occurred prior to 1913, the judgment had the following to say:

> It might be that the claimants are part of an indigenous community which occupied Boomplaats before the Zuid Afrikaanse Republiek granted the land to white owners during 1889, thereby depriving the community of their communal ownership and forcing their members into labour tenancy. The white owners took possession of the land, and compelled the inhabitants to become labour tenants[7]

This conclusion of the Land Claims Court on the forcible dispossession of indigenous ownership of land is well warranted by the facts. The research report of the Regional Commissioners[8] reveals that the farm Boomplaats was registered in the deeds registry for the first time in 1889 in the name of Mr PDA Hattingh.[9] On 22 February 1887, the land was transferred by title deed to Mr J de Villiers de Vaal and was further transferred to Mr JB de Vaal on 10 December 1897.

It is beyond question that, throughout the tenure of successive registered landowners, the applicants, as their ancestors did, continued to live on the land but as no more than labour tenants. They had to work for the registered owner or his appointee in order to live there. The inexorable result was that, by 1969, the title of the applicants, the very descendants of the Maake people, had been whittled down to a vulnerable labour tenancy in relation to their ancestral land. Then, as I intimated earlier, Mr August Altenroxel together with his brother, Mr Bernard Altenroxel, leased the farm from their father on Boomplaats and farmed there in partnership. As we already know, they became registered owners of the farm, but only several years later.

In the trial before the Land Claims Court, Mr August Altenroxel was the first and main witness for the respondent. It fell on him to relate how the applicants were deprived of their land rights to the Boomplaats land. He was born in 1934 and worked on the farm from the age of seventeen years. He still lives on it. He is now retired. He has no interest in the corporation that now owns the farm. He narrates that when he and his brother started farming there, the Maake people, including the individual applicants and their families, lived there. The brothers as well as their father had found the Maake people there as labour tenants on Boomplaats.

He testified that the labour tenants were allowed to build homes for themselves and their families and were entitled to plant crops and to graze their livestock. In his words, the white farmer showed them the fields that they were permitted to plough. The labour tenants were not allowed more than ten head of cattle per family and a specified number of goats and sheep. In return, the labour tenants and their respective family members had to work for the Altenroxels for two days a week.

(Continued)

(Continued)

During 1969, Mr August Altenroxel and his brother decided to terminate the labour tenancy of the individual applicants, which they did. It is common cause that the applicants did not receive any compensation for the loss of their rights to land in Boomplaats.

Mr Altenroxel explained what the dispossession of the cropping and grazing rights meant to the erstwhile labour tenants. They were stopped from ploughing. Within two years, they had to dispose of all of their livestock. Thereafter, they were not allowed to keep livestock. They all became full time wage earners on the farm. They were paid what the surrounding farmers were paying their farm labourers. Those who did not accept the new employment regime left Boomplaats for the nearby "homeland" reserved for black people. However, he says, the erstwhile labour tenants were not compelled to leave the farm. In fact, nine applicants became permanent farm workers and continued residing on the Boomplaats farm. By 2001, there were six applicants living on the farm. Three applicant families still live on the farm although they are not wage earners. The remaining applicants will not be compelled to leave the farm. The owner of the farm, the respondent, has given an informal assurance to that effect during the hearing before the Supreme Court of Appeal.

Mr Altenroxel says that they terminated the labour tenancy because it did not work well for them. In their commercial farming environment, they needed a regular, adaptable and well-controlled workforce. The labour tenancy system did not fulfil that business need. He elaborated that, at times, the services of labour tenants were simply not available or adequate when needed. He insisted that the labour tenancy of the applicants was terminated for business purposes and not at the behest of any government official or pursuant to any law or regulation.

Mr Altenroxel conceded under cross-examination that he was aware that other farmers in their area were terminating the labour tenancy relationships as between their black labour tenants and that the trend on other farms spurred them on to do the same. He rejected the suggestion that he must have been aware of legislation by government aimed at abolishing the labour tenancy system for black people. In his time, he says, "we never saw or heard about, about that legislation …." He knew of the apartheid government's policy to establish homelands for blacks. He read about it in the Star newspaper and in the Farmers Weekly. But he had never heard of the 1913 Natives Land Act,[10] the Native Trust and Land Act of 1936,[11] the Bantu Laws Amendment Act of 1964[12] or of the Government Notice 2761 of 1970[13] proclaiming the government's intention to eradicate labour tenancy completely. He nonetheless admitted that he was a regular reader of the journal Farmers Weekly and that, during 1960 to 1968, he occasionally attended meetings of the local farmers association, during which the subject of the termination of labour tenancy had never been discussed.

The claims

Given the background that I have sketched, it is vital, at the outset, to characterise the claims for restitution of land rights accurately. In this Court, particularly in relation to remedy, applicants vacillated over the nature of their claims. On occasion, they tended to invoke the

(Continued)

(Continued)

loss of their indigenous land rights rather than dispossession of labour tenancy rights. It is indeed plain that the forebears of the applicants were deprived of their indigenous rights to the Boomplaats land during the second half of the 1800s. For better, for worse and perhaps for reasons better left unexplored, our Constitution has chosen not to provide for restitution of or equitable redress for property dispossessed prior to 19 June 1913. Since the dispossession of the indigenous title occurred before 1913, it seems self-evident that it is outside the restitutionary beneficence of section 25(7)[14] of the Constitution.

This, of course, means that ordinarily, even if the applicants were to establish dispossession of indigenous communal ownership that occurred before the constitutional cut-off date of 19 June 1913, they would not be entitled to exact restitution or redress.[15] In the words of this Court in *Alexkor Ltd and Another v Richtersveld Community and Others*, dispossessions that took effect before 19 June 1913 are not actionable.[16]

By this I do not mean to convey that registered ownership of land always enjoys primacy over indigenous title. To do that would be to elevate ownership notions of the common law to the detriment of indigenous law ownership for purposes of restitution of land rights. Rights acquired under indigenous law must be determined with reference to that law subject only to the Constitution.[17] In appropriate cases, under the jurisdiction crafted by the Restitution Act, registered ownership in land will not be held to have extinguished rights in land recognised under indigenous law. One such case is *Prinsloo and Another v Ndebele-Ndzundza Community and Others*[18] where Cameron JA correctly observes that:

> *The Act recognises complexities of this kind and attempts to create practical solutions for them in its pursuit of equitable redress. The statute also recognises the significance of registered title. But it does not afford it unblemished primacy. I consider that, in this case, the farm's residents established rights in the land that registered ownership neither extinguished nor precluded from arising.*[19]

The facts in the present matter are different. The applicants themselves, so too the Regional Land Claims Commissioner, locate in time their dispossession of indigenous title to Boomplaats before 1913. Documentary and other evidence warrant this stance. Further, in their claim forms and in pleadings in the Land Claims Court, the claimants restrict their claims for restitution or equitable redress to dispossession of labour tenancy rights in 1969. Here the applicants have chosen not to seek, as the claimants did in *In Re Kranspoort Community*,[20] an order restoring their rights in the original farm along with an order in terms of section 35(4)[21] of the Restitution Act, adjusting those rights to full ownership. The individual claimants have even curtailed the extent of the land sought to be restored to accord with their labour tenancy claims:

> *The land claimed is the land formerly known as the remaining extent of the farm Boomplaats No. 408 LT. Vide diagram S.G. NO. A 1639/08 and Deed Grant No. 3343/1889. (DB357/23), which has now been consolidated into the farm Goedgelegen 566LT.*
>
> *The land claimed excludes the land, which was used by the landowner as marked in the map, attached herewith marked 'LC2' and the map attached to the notice of amendment dated 6 May 2002.*

(Continued)

(Continued)

The individual claimants are each claiming the land where their homesteads are or used to be and the land immediately around it comprising approximately 800 m^2 and the whole land which they used jointly for ploughing and for grazing[22]

However, this does not mean as the respondent will have us accept, that the history of dispossession of property preceding the retroactive cut-off point of 19 June 1913 is of mere passing interest. The correct approach towards the historical context before the cut-off date is set out by this Court in *Richtersveld*:

This did not mean that regard may not be had to racially discriminatory laws and practices that were in existence or took place before that date. Regard may indeed be had to them if the purpose is to throw light on the nature of a dispossession that took place thereafter or to show that when it so took place it was the result of racially discriminatory laws or practices that were still operative at the time of the dispossession.[23]

I revert to this matter later in the contextual analysis related to whether the dispossession of rights in land, if any, suffered by the applicants is as a result of racially discriminatory laws or practices.

For now, it should suffice to characterise the claims of the applicants accurately. The claims are in two parts. First, the applicants seek, individually or as a community, an order that they have been dispossessed of their labour tenant rights in 1969 as a result of racially discriminatory laws or practices and that they are therefore entitled to restitution or equitable redress under the Restitution Act. Second, as restitution or equitable redress, the individual applicants are each claiming the restitution of the land where their homesteads are or used to be and the land immediately around it, comprising approximately 800m^2, and the whole land that had been used jointly for ploughing and for grazing.

Litigation

As required by the provisions of section 14(1)(b) and (d)[24] of the Restitution Act, the regional land claims commissioner referred the contested claims for restitution to the Land Claims Court. At the trial, the Court heard evidence and, in the end, dismissed the collective claim of the Popela Community and the claims of the eleven individual claimants. The Court took the view that there is no clear evidence whether the individual claimants in this case voluntarily accepted the new system or whether they were forced into it. For that reason, it preferred to assume without deciding that during 1969, the Altenroxels dispossessed the individual claimants of cropping and grazing rights. However, the dispossession, it held, was not from a community of labour tenants but from individual labour tenants. The Court concluded that, whatever the case may be, the dispossession was not the result of a past racially discriminatory law or practice. It accordingly found no merit in any of the claims.

With leave of the Land Claims Court, the Supreme Court of Appeal heard the appeal of the claimants and dismissed it with costs. It found that the claimants, whether as individuals or as a community, had not shown that their dispossession of labour tenants rights in 1969 was the result of a past racially discriminatory law or practice.

(Continued)

(Continued)

Issues

A claim for restitution of a right in land under section 2 of the Restitution Act may succeed only if: (a) the claimant is a person or community or part of a community; (b) that had a right in land; (c) which was dispossessed; (d) after 19 June 1913; (e) as a result of past racially discriminatory laws or practices; (f) where the claim for restitution was lodged not later than 31 December 1998; and (g) no just and equitable compensation was received for the dispossession.[25]

In this Court, besides one jurisdictional issue and remedy, if any, only two elements of the claim remain in contention. This means that the issues that fall to be decided are: (a) whether leave to appeal should be granted; (b) whether the Popela Community is a "community" dispossessed of a right in land for purposes of section 2(1)(d)[26] of the Restitution Act; (c) whether the individual claimants were dispossessed of their right in land as a result of past discriminatory laws or practices as required by section 2(1)(a) of the Restitution Act; and (d) what the appropriate remedy should be, should the appeal succeed. I examine each issue in turn.

Leave to appeal

There is no gainsaying that the substantive issues for determination are constitutional matters. The claims are made under section 2(1) of the Restitution Act. This legislation provides for the restitution of rights in land to persons or communities dispossessed of such rights after 19 June 1913 as a result of past discriminatory laws or practices. Although, at first, the Act was passed under the interim Constitution,[27] section 2(1) has been amended several times[28] in order to give effect to the provisions of section 25(7) of the Constitution.

Is the Popela Community a "community" dispossessed of a right in land?

Section 25(7) of the Constitution and section 2(1)(d) of the Restitution Act entitle a community dispossessed of a right in land after 19 June 1913 to claim restitution or other equitable redress. A community, unless the context otherwise indicates, is any group of persons whose rights in land are derived from shared rules determining access to land held in common by such group.[29]

At the heart of this enquiry is whether the occupational rights in the land were derived from shared rules determining access to land held in common. At its core, the question is whether the labour tenants, through shared rules, held the land rights jointly. The community and individual applicants contend that they did.

However, what is clear on all the evidence is that the indigenous ownership of land in the original Boomplaats farm was lost before 1913. Once they had lost ownership, they were compelled to work for the owner. Their relationship with the owner was coercive. The Land Claims Court found, correctly in my view, that "the white owners took possession of the land, and compelled the inhabitants to become labour tenants,"[30]

(Continued)

(Continued)

There is no justification for seeking to limit the meaning of the word "community" in section 2(1)(d) by inferring a requirement that the group concerned must show an accepted tribal identity and hierarchy. Where it is appropriate, as was the case in *Ndebele-Ndzundza*, the "bonds of custom, culture and hierarchical loyalty"[31] may be helpful to establish that the group's shared rules related to access and use of the land. The "bonds" may also demonstrate the cohesiveness of the group and its commonality with the group at the point of dispossession.

However, what must be kept in mind is that the legislation has set a low threshold as to what constitutes a "community" or any "part of a community." It does not set any pre-ordained qualities of the group of persons or any part of the group in order to qualify as a community. This generous notion of what constitutes a community fits well with the wide scope of the "rights in land" that are capable of restoration. These rights, as defined,[32] go well beyond the orthodox common law notions of rights in land. They include any right in land, whether registered or not; the interests of labour tenants and sharecroppers; customary law interests; interests of a beneficiary under a trust; and a beneficial occupation for a continuous period of not less than ten years before the dispossession. The legislative scheme points to a purpose to make good the ample hurt, indignity and injustice of racial dispossession of rights or interests in land that continued to take place after 19 June 1913.

In my view, the Land Claims Court was wrong to hold that the applicants were not a community because they did not prove an accepted tribal identity, or that they did not live under the authority of a chief designated by tribal hierarchy or that they did not occupy the land in accordance with ancient customs and traditions. None of these attributes are requirements in themselves or collectively.

In my view, it is clear from the evidence that the Maake people were a community at the time they were dispossessed of their indigenous ownership of the Boomplaats land in 1889 and eighty years later, in 1969, when they lost the remnants of their original rights in land in the form of labour tenancy. Even when they submitted the current claim for restitution, they were a community with sufficient communality with their Maake forebears. They have retained much of their identity and cohesion as part of the erstwhile Maake or Popela clan.

This however is not the end of the enquiry. The acid test remains whether the members of the Popela Community derived their possession and use of the land from common rules in 1969. The answer must be in the negative. By then, each of the families within the community had been compelled to have its own separate relationship with the Altenroxels. They pointed out the land for use by each family. They ordered them to dispense with their livestock. They required them singularly, and often also their children as young as ten years, to toil on the farm if they were to live there. The registered owner made it clear that he did not heed any rules of the community on land occupation. They made the rules and the labour tenant had to obey. The 1969 unilateral and summary termination of the land interests of the labour tenants makes the point loudly. Some erstwhile labour tenants stayed and accepted the prevailing labour wage while others went into the "diaspora" at Ga-Sekgopo in the nearby so-called black homeland.[33]

(Continued)

(Continued)

In any event, at its very core, labour tenancy under the common law arises from a so-called innominate contract between the landowner and the labour tenant, requiring the tenant to render services to the owner in return for the right to occupy a piece of land, graze cattle and raise crops.[34] In name, it is an individualised transaction that requires specific performance from the contracting parties. This means that labour tenancy does not sit well with commonly held occupancy rights.[35] It is a transaction between two individuals rather than one between the landlord and a community of labour tenants. It must however be recognised that despite the fiction of the common law in regard to the consensual nature of labour tenancy, on all accounts, the labour tenancy relationships in apartheid South Africa were coercive and amounted to a thinly veiled artifice to garner free labour.[36]

I conclude that by 1969, no rights in land remained vested in the labour tenants as a community. It has not been shown that, at the point of dispossession in 1969, the community of tenants on Boomplaats held the land in common under shared rules that they could enforce effectively in the face of an individualised system of labour tenancy. I need not assume. On the contrary, the evidence shows clearly that the individual applicants, who were labour tenants on the farm Boomplaats in 1969, were dispossessed of occupation,[37] ploughing and grazing rights in that land as envisaged in the Restitution Act.

The phrase "as a result of"

The entitlement to claim equitable redress or restitution of dispossessed property derives from the Constitution itself. Section 25(7) of the Constitution provides:

> *A person or community dispossessed of property after 19 June 1913* as a result of *past racially discriminatory laws or practices is entitled, to the extent provided by an Act of Parliament, either to restitution of that property or to equitable redress. (Emphasis added)*

Section 2 of the Restitution Act echoes this injunction from the Bill of Rights by providing that a person shall be entitled to restitution of a right in land if he or she has been dispossessed of a right in land *as a result of* a past racially discriminatory law or practice.

I draw attention to the phrase "as a result of" because much in this case turns on the meaning that we accord to it. The pivotal question relates to the meaning of the phrase in the context of the constitutional and legislative provisions within which it occurs. Important to that interpretive task are two definitions in section 1 of the Restitution Act. Racially discriminatory laws include "laws made by any sphere of government and subordinate legislation". Racially discriminatory practices are:

> . . . *acts or omissions, direct or indirect, by—*

(a) any department of state or administration in the national, provincial or local sphere of government;

(b) any other functionary or institution which exercised a public power or performed a public function in terms of any legislation"

(Continued)

(Continued)

The Supreme Court of Appeal endorsed the approach of the Land Claims Court that the words "as a result of" connote a causal connection[38] but that, in this case, there was no discernible causal connection. For this conclusion, both courts relied on the "but for" test which asks whether, but for the act or omission labelled as the possible cause, the result would have occurred. In applying this test, these courts have asked whether, but for the discriminatory laws and practices, the Altenroxels would have terminated the claimants' labour tenancies. They concluded that, regardless of the legal and social context, the farm owners would have dispossessed the applicants of their rights in the land. Thus, past discriminatory laws and practices did not cause the dispossession.[39] They held that the dispossession was as a result of a private decision of the farmers concerned.

In summary, from the 1920s and 1930s with greater momentum towards the 1950s and 1960s, the minority apartheid government with the support of the South African Agricultural Union, chose to control, limit and eventually eliminate labour tenancy on South African farms.

Entitlement to redress under the Restitution Act does not hinge on any form of blameworthy conduct such as intention or negligence or a duty of care. Equally important is that the operative legislation does not hold liable any party for historical dispossession, whatever the motive of the dispossessor. It merely sets conditions that entitle a claimant to restitution. What section 2 of the Restitution Act does is to set its own limitations. In this context, it requires that only conduct or omissions that are causally connected to discriminatory laws or practices of the state or of a public functionary will entitle a dispossessed claimant to restitution.

The claim is against the state. It has a reparative and restitutionary character. It is neither punitive in the criminal law sense nor compensatory in the civil law sense. Rather, it advances a major public purpose and uses public resources in a manifestly equitable way to deal with egregious and identifiable forms of historic hurt.

I conclude that the term "as a result of" in the context of the Restitution Act is intended to be less restrictive and should be interpreted to mean no more than "as a consequence of" and not "solely as a consequence of". It is fair to add that, on this construction, the consequence should not be remote, which means that there should be a reasonable connection between the discriminatory laws and practices of the state, on the one hand, and the dispossession, on the other. For that determination, a context-sensitive appraisal of all relevant factors should be embarked upon. It is to that appraisal that I now briefly focus.

Was the dispossession as a result of past discriminatory laws and practices?

I think that the applicants are correct in submitting that all these features constituted a grid of integrated repressive laws that were aimed at furthering the government's policy of racial discrimination. It created both spatial apartheid and a cheap labour force that was perceived to be malleable and was based upon an inequality between those classified as blacks and those classified as whites.

(Continued)

(Continued)

It must be borne in mind that labour tenancy, by its nature, presupposes a legally recognised relationship of a private nature. Accordingly, ending labour tenancy could not be accomplished by state-forced removals, with notices from the state to get out by a date, followed by state bulldozers and trucks with a police presence. It would be the farmers themselves who would have to take the steps to extinguish the rights on a farm-by-farm basis. The racist state policy and practice was clear: the farmers were encouraged to get on with the job as rapidly as possible, and the proclamation was introduced as an ultimate form of coercion to deal with recalcitrant farmers who were slow or reluctant to move. In this sense, the farmers were expected to be the direct agency for the achievement of racist state objectives. Looked at as a whole, the destruction of the limited rights of the labour tenants by the Altenroxels was consequent upon and facilitated by state laws and practices and furthered avowedly racist state objectives.

It must be added that the government policy of abolishing labour tenancy was not simply driven by callous economic motives to create more cheap black labour. Nor was it merely a push to replace feudal forms of productive relationships with market-based ones. It was part of the grand apartheid design. Its notorious objective was to eliminate any vestiges of black land rights in what was designated as white South Africa. The goal was to cut any residual legal ties that identifiable black families and communities had to identifiable pieces of land. The Restitution Act acknowledges this by expressly including recognition of labour tenancy rights as a basis for restitution.

In my view, the causal connection under section 2 of the Restitution Act should not be understood to require that the state or a public functionary should itself perform the dispossession of rights in land. It is sufficient if the termination of rights in land is permitted, aided and supported by racially discriminatory laws or practices of the state or other functionaries exercising public power. The question is not whether the dispossession is effected by the state or a public functionary, but rather whether the dispossession was as a consequence of laws or practices put in place by the state or other public functionary.

I conclude that the individual applicants were dispossessed of rights in land after 19 June 1913 as a result of past racially discriminatory laws or practices as contemplated in section 2 of the Restitution Act.

Remedy

In this Court, the applicants did not press for a remedy beyond a declarator that the individual claimants are entitled to restitution of or equitable redress for being dispossessed of a right in the Boomplaats land after 1913. More significantly, the Department, which is charged with the duty to implement the Restitution Act, did not seek relief beyond a declarator. As I understood counsel for the Department, with a declarator of this Court in hand, the Department will facilitate the final resolution of the nature and extent of restitution or equitable redress envisaged by the operative legislation.

(Continued)

(Continued)

However, it is appropriate to record that in the claims to the Regional Land Claims Commissioner, the claimants sought more. They asked that land formerly known as the remaining extent of the farm Boomplaats 408 LT, which has now been consolidated into the farm Goedgelegen 566 LT, be restored to them. They each claim the land where their homesteads are or used to be and the land immediately around it, comprising approximately 800 square metres, and the whole land which they used jointly for ploughing and for grazing. However, the difficulty is that, from the record of proceedings, the cadastral dimensions of the portion of the farm Goedgelegen 566 LT, which the third to the eleventh applicants claim are by no means clear.

The sensible course available to this Court is to make a declarator only. At the hearing, the claimants urged us not to remit the matter to the Land Claims Court and assured us that the Department would decide, in conjunction with the claimants, on the finalisation of this claim. The respondent did not object to the attitude of the applicants that the matter should not be remitted. We do not remit this matter to the Land Claims Court on the clear understanding that, should no agreement be reached on the terms of the restitution or other equitable redress, any affected party may approach the Land Claims Court for an appropriate order on remedy as envisaged in section 35 of the Restitution Act.

Finally, it is appropriate to observe that rights of the individual applicants were not merely economic rights to graze and cultivate in a particular area. They were rights of family connection with certain pieces of land, where the aged were buried and children were born and where modest homesteads passed from generation to generation. And they were not simply there by grace and favour. The paternalistic and feudal-type relationship involved contributions by the family, who worked the lands of the farmer. However unfair the relationship was, as a relic of past conquests of land dispossession, it formalised a minimal degree of respect by the farm owners for the connection of the indigenous families to the land. It had a cultural and spiritual dimension that rendered the destruction of the rights more than just economic loss. These are factors that might require appropriate consideration by the Department or the Land Claims Court when an appropriate remedy is fashioned.

Before I turn to costs, I must mention that the second to the eleventh applicants filed their application for leave to appeal one day late. They seek an order condoning their late filing of the application. The relief they ask for is not opposed and, in any event, it is justified. Secondly, Mr Abram Maake, the ninth applicant, and Mr Maselaelo Mosibudi Maake, the tenth applicant, have since passed away. The respective executors of their deceased estates ask for leave to be substituted for the deceased applicants. This application is not challenged and it is well grounded. An order to this effect will be made. Should any of the individual applicants pass away before the finalisation of this claim, his or her lawful heir or executor may be substituted for the deceased.

Costs

The Land Claims Court did not make any order as to costs at the end of the trial but directed that costs of the subsequent application for leave to appeal shall be costs in the appeal.

(Continued)

(Continued)

However, the Supreme Court of Appeal ordered the claimants and the Department to pay costs jointly and severally including costs attendant upon the use of two counsels. The applicants have raised an important matter of land restitution and have succeeded in this Court. I can find no reason why this Court should not set aside the costs order of the Supreme Court of Appeal.

What remains is to consider which costs order to make in this Court. In this judgment, I have emphasised that a claim for restoration of rights in land under the Restitution Act is a claim against the state. The owner of the land, which is the object of the claim, is entitled to resist the claim but that does not alter the core character of the statutorily devised claim as one against the state. The claim is not retributive but restorative in purpose. Nothing in the manner in which the respondent has conducted its case justifies an order of costs against it.

On the other hand, I keep in mind that the individual applicants have incurred substantial costs in the Supreme Court of Appeal and in this Court. However, it seems that their cause was made possible by the worthy and selfless support of the Nkuzi Land Rights Legal Unit, a public interest law firm. On the other hand, the individual claimants enjoyed the support of the Department which has made common cause with them in the Supreme Court of Appeal and in this Court. I consider it just and equitable that this Court makes no order as to costs.

Order

The following order is made:

1. The application for the condonation of the late filing of the application for leave to appeal is granted.
2. The executor in the deceased estate of the late Abram Maake, who was the eighth appellant in the Supreme Court of Appeal, is substituted in these proceedings as the ninth applicant.
3. The executor in the deceased estate of the late Maselaelo Mosibudi Maake, who was the ninth appellant in the Supreme Court of Appeal, is substituted in these proceedings as the tenth applicant.
4. The application for leave to appeal is granted.
5. The appeal of the second applicant, the Popela Community, is dismissed but the costs order of the Supreme Court of Appeal against the second applicant is set aside.
6. The appeals of the first applicant and of the third to the eleventh applicants against the decision of the Supreme Court of Appeal are upheld.
7. The orders of the Land Claims Court and of the Supreme Court of Appeal relating to the first applicant and to the third to the eleventh applicants are set aside in their entirety.
8. It is declared that the third to the eleventh applicants were each dispossessed of a right in land after 19 June 1913 as a result of past racially discriminatory laws and practices and that they are accordingly entitled to restitution under section 2 and the other relevant provisions of the Restitution of Land Rights Act 22 of 1994.
9. No order as to costs is made.

Notes

1. See Gockowski and Oduwole (2001). The study was based on a survey of 1080 cocoa-producing households in Southwest Nigeria.
2. Additionally, Wikipedia (n.d.) tells us that "Sharecropping is a system of agriculture in which a landowner allows a tenant to use the land in return for a share of the crop produced on the land (e.g., 50% of the crop). This should not be confused with a crop fixed rent contract, in which a landowner allows a tenant to use the land in return for a fixed amount of crop per unit of land (eg, 1 T/ha)." In Ghana, for example, Polly Hill identified six main types of labor contracts. The most popular are the "abusa" contract where the farm tenant receives two-thirds of the produce, and the land owner receives a third; "abunu" where the tenant and landowner share equally; and the "nkotokuano" contract where the tenant is paid a fixed sum for each load of produce harvested. See Polly Hill (1963).
3. Act 22 of 1994.
4. Section 25(5) of the Constitution states:

   The state must take reasonable legislative and other measures, within its available resources, to foster conditions which enable citizens to gain access to land on an equitable basis.

5. Section 38 of the Constitution states:

   Anyone listed in this section has the right to approach a competent court, alleging that a right in the Bill of Rights has been infringed or threatened, and the court may grant appropriate relief, including a declaration of rights. The persons who may approach a court are—

   . . .
   (c) anyone acting as a member of, or in the interest of, a group or class of persons;
   (d) anyone acting in the public interest . . ."

6. *Popela Community v Department of Land Affairs and Another* LCC 52/00, 3 June 2005, unreported at para 4.
7. Id at para 61. However, in footnote 68 of the judgment, the Land Claims Court held that it was "not established that the claimants are part of, or members of, such a community."
8. Section 4(3) of the Restitution Act provides for the appointment of Regional Land Claims Commissioners who serve in designated regions under the Chief Land Claims Commissioner. Their powers and duties are set out in section 6 of the Restitution Act. These include receiving claims for the restitution of rights in land; assisting claimants in preparing and submitting claims; investigating the merits of the claims; mediating and settling disputes arising from such claims; drawing reports on unsettled claims for submission as evidence to the Court; and presenting any other relevant evidence to the Court.
9. By deed of transfer T3343/1889.
10. Act 27 of 1913.
11. Act 18 of 1936.
12. Act 42 of 1964.
13. Government Gazette 2761 GN R1224, 31 July 1970.
14. The full text of section 25(7) appears in para 48 below.
15. This is distinguishable from the case of *Alexkor Ltd and Another v Richtersveld Community and Others* 2004 (5) SA 460 (CC); 2003 (12) BCLR 1301 (CC) at para 81 in which this Court found that the indigenous law ownership possessed by the Richtersveld Community in the subject land had not been effectively extinguished prior to 19 June 1913, with the result that it survived beyond the constitutional cut-off date.
16. Id at para 40.
17. Id at paras 50–51.

18. 2005 (6) SA 144 (SCA); [2005] 3 All SA 528 (SCA).
19. Id at para 38. Reference to the "Act" and "statute" in the quotation is made in relation to the Restitution Act.
20. 2000 (2) SA 124 (LCC) at para 83.
21. Section 35(4) of the Restitution Act provides:

> The Court's power to order the restitution of a right in land or to grant a right in alternative state-owned land shall include the power to adjust the nature of the right previously held by the claimant, and to determine the form of title under which the right may be held in future.

22. Amended description of the land claimed filed by the claimants with the Land Claims Court on 31 March 2003 ahead of the trial proceedings.
23. Above n 16 at para 40.
24. Section 14 of the Restitution Act states:

> (1) If upon completion of an investigation by the Commission in respect of specific claim—
>
> . . .
>
> (b) the regional land claims commissioner certifies that it is not feasible to resolve any dispute arising from such claim by mediation and negotiation; or
>
> . . .
>
> (d) the regional land claims commissioner is of the opinion that the claim is ready for hearing by the Court,
>
> the regional land claims commissioner having jurisdiction shall certify accordingly and refer the matter to the Court.

25. For a similar tabulation of the legislative requirements of section 2 of the Restitution Act see *Richtersveld* above n 16 at para 19; *In re Kranspoort Community* above n 21 at para 21.
26. Section 2 of the Restitution Act states:

> (1) A person shall be entitled to restitution of a right in land if—
>
> . . .
>
> (d) it is a community or part of a community dispossessed of a right in land after 19 June 1913 as a result of past racially discriminatory laws or practices . . . .

27. Section 121(2) of the interim Constitution, 1993, provided that:

> A person or a community shall be entitled to claim restitution of a right in land from the state if—
>
> (a) such person or community was dispossessed of such right at any time after a date to be fixed by the Act referred to in subsection (1); and
> (b) such dispossession was effected under or for the purpose of furthering the object of a law which would have been inconsistent with the prohibition of racial discrimination contained in section 8(2), had that section been in operation at the time of such dispossession.

28. Section 2 of the Restitution Act was amended by section 2(1) of Act 78 of 1996, substituted by section 3(1) of Act 63 of 1997 and by section 2 of Act 18 of 1999.
29. Section 1 of the Restitution Act defines a community as:

> . . . any group of persons whose rights in land are derived from shared rules determining access to land held in common by such group, and includes part of any such group.

30. Above n 4 at para 61.
31. Above n 19 at para 30.

32. Section 1 of the Restitution Act defines a right in land as:

    ... any right in land whether registered or unregistered, and may include the interest of a labour tenant and sharecropper, a customary law interest, the interest of a beneficiary under a trust arrangement and beneficial occupation for a continuous period of not less than 10 years prior to the dispossession in question.

33. This term is used evocatively by Dodson J in *In Re Kranspoort Community* above n 21 at paras 44 and 48, when referring to forced removals that resulted in harrowing displacement and homelessness.

34. *De Jager v Sisana* [1930] AD 71 at 81 and 83. See also Hathorn and Hutchison (1990).

35. Section 1 of The Land Reform (Labour Tenants) Act 3 of 1996 defines a labour tenant as a person:

    (a) who is residing or has the right to reside on a farm;
    (b) who has or has had the right to use cropping or grazing land on the farm, referred to in paragraph *(a)*, or another farm of the owner, and in consideration of such right provides or has provided labour to the owner or lessee; and
    (c) whose parent or grandparent resided or resides on a farm and had the use of cropping or grazing land on such farm or another farm of the owner, and in consideration of such right provided or provides labour to the owner or lessee of such or such other farm,
    including a person who has been appointed a successor to a labour tenant in accordance with the provisions of section 3(4) and (5), but excluding a farmworker ...

36. See Hathorn and Hutchison (1990) for a discussion on the obligations of labour tenants in labour tenancy relationships.

37. See the definition of a "right in land" above n 37. It is not contested and, if anything, it is clear from the evidence that the individual claimants lived on the farm Boomplaats for an uninterrupted period of at least ten years before the dispossession of land rights in 1969.

38. For this finding, the Land Claims Court relied on *Minister of Land Affairs and Another v Slamdien and Others* 1999 (4) BCLR 413 (LCC); [1999] 1 All SA 608 (LCC) at paras 37–38; *Boltman v Kotze Community Trust* [1999] JOL 5230 (LCC); *In Re Former Highlands Residents: Naidoo v Department of Land Affairs* 2000 (2) SA 365 (LCC) at 368G-369C.

39. The causation enquiry has two parts to it: "factual causation" and "legal causation". The first stage, or "factual causation" enquiry, applies the *conditio sine qua non* or "but for" test. The test asks whether, but for the act or omission labelled as the possible cause, the result would have occurred. If the test does not identify the act or omission as a necessary condition for the result to occur, the enquiry ends. However, if the act or omission is a necessary condition, the second enquiry into legal causation must be conducted. The second enquiry seeks to ascertain whether the cause identified is a legally recognised cause or whether there is a sufficiently close relationship between the two events so that the former constitutes the legal cause of the latter. At this stage, one adopts a flexible approach that draws on reasonableness, common sense, other relevant policy considerations and the facts of the case. See *Slamdien* above n 44 at para 38.

Questions

1. What are the most common forms of share contract arrangements and what economic rationale supports the choice of share contract structure? See for example, FAO, "Contract Farming: Partnership for Growth," FAO Agricultural Services Bulletin 145, p. 58. http://www.fao.org/docrep/014/y0937e/y0937e00.pdf.

2. Some have suggested that farmers, especially small farmers have weak bargaining power and so are at a disadvantage in negotiating the terms of a share contract

arrangement. Would you recommend a law stipulating how landowners and tenants negotiate share contract arrangements? Why or why not?

3. What needs to be taken into consideration while developing a contract between a landowner and tenant in a sharecropping circumstance?
4. Under sharecropping, what risks does the tenant face?
5. What is the definition of natural risk? Provide two examples not listed in the book.
6. What do you think happens to the tenant if a crop fails in a sharecropping situation?
7. List three countries in sub-Saharan Africa where sharecropping is practiced and discuss the legal basis supporting the practice. What differences if any, do you see in these systems?

References

Allen, D.W., Lueck, D., 1992. Contract choice in modern agriculture: cash rent versus cropshare. J. Law Econ. 35, 397–426.

Allen, D.W., Lueck, D., 1993. Transaction costs and the design of cropshare contracts. RAND J. Econ. The RAND Corporation. 24 (1), 78–100.

Boadu, F., 1992. The efficiency of share contracts in Ghana's cocoa industry. J. Dev. Stud. 29, 108–120.

Cheung, S.N.S., 1969. Transaction costs, risk aversion, and the choice of contractual arrangements. J. Law Econ. 12 (1), 23–42.

FAO, 2001. Good Practice Guidelines for Agricultural Leasing Arrangements . . . FAO Land Tenure Studies – 2, Y2560/E. <http://www.fao.org/docrep/004/Y2560E/y2560e03.htm#bm3.2.5/>.

Gockowski, J., Oduwole, S., 2001. Labor Practices in the Cocoa Sector of Southwest Nigeria with a Focus on the Role of Children: Findings From a 2001 Survey of Cocoa Producing Households. International Institute of Tropical Agriculture (IITA), Ibadan, Nigeria. <https://books.google.com/books?id=E2x5hlVlaUUC&dq=gockowski+and+oduwole&source=gbs_navlinks_s>.

Hathorn M., Hutchison D., 1990. Labour tenants and the law. Murray C., O'Regan, C. (eds) (1990). No Place to Rest - Forced Removals and the Law in South Africa. Oxford University Press, Cape Town, South Africa, pp. 198–201.

Hill, P., 1963. The Migrant Cocoa-Farmers of Southern Ghana: A Study in Rural Capitalism. Cambridge University Press, Cambridge, England.

Murrell, P., 1983. The economics of sharing: a transactions cost analysis of contractual choice in farming. Bell J Econ. 14 (1), 283–293.

Shaban, R.A., 1987. Testing between competing models of sharecropping. J. Polit. Econ. 95 (5), 893–920.

Wikipedia, n.d. Entry for Sharecropping. <http://en.wikipedia.org/wiki/Sharecropping> (accessed 09.12.10).

Zezza, A. et al., n.d. Rural Household Heterogeneity in Access to Assets, Inputs and Markets: A Cross Country Comparison. <http://www.oecd.org/dataoecd/8/59/41688539.pdf> (accessed 09.12.10).

CHAPTER 5

Contracts Involving Illiterate Parties

Keywords: Information asymmetry; illiterate party; adverse selection; moral hazard; Illiterate Protection Act

5.1 Introduction

Sub-Sahara Africa (SSA) had the lowest adult literacy rate (63%) in the world in 2008 (Huebler, 2008). There is also significant gender disparity with a gender parity index (GPI) of 0.75.[1] However, there was an 8% improvement in the GPI parity between 1990 and 2008. The relationship between a literate society and economic development is well known (eg, Jogwu, 2010). The ability of market participants to engage in effective and informed interaction in the market place is critical since countries in SSA are transitioning to market-led development.

5.1.1 The Law and Economics of Contracts Involving Illiterates

A properly functioning contract market facilitates the movement of economic resources to their most highly valued uses. Contract law requires that parties engaged in contracting to do so freely, and that there is a "meeting of the minds." This basic premise of contract law raises questions for countries in SSA where a large percentage of the population is classified as illiterate, that is, cannot read or write. Illiterates interact with literates in the market place. The literate–illiterate interaction may engender "information asymmetry" in contracting, that is, a situation where one of the parties to a contract, the literate party has information that is not available to the illiterate party.

Two common problems associated with information asymmetry are *adverse selection* and *moral hazard*. In adverse selection, the illiterate party may negotiate a contract that actually hurts their interest, for example, paying a lower price for a product thinking they got a good deal when in fact the product is of low quality. With moral hazard, the illiterate party lacks the ability to enforce the terms of the contract.[2] Contracts that face these problems cannot be value-maximizing, and courts step in to fill the gaps. The challenge is to define contract rules that do not destroy incentives on the part of literate parties to interact with illiterate parties in the market place.

F.O. Boadu: Agricultural Law and Economics in Sub-Saharan Africa.
DOI: http://dx.doi.org/10.1016/B978-0-12-801771-5.00005-8
141

The cases that follow discuss some of the difficulties that courts have faced in interpreting contracts between illiterate and literate parties. An example of the basic principle guiding contract interpretation in cases involving an illiterate party is the Ghanaian case of *Kwamin v Kuffour* (1914) 2 Ren. 808, P.C., where the Privy Council stated: "Where an illiterate executes a document, any other party to the document who relies upon it must prove that it was read over, and, if necessary, interpreted to the illiterate." This principle is captured in the common law plea of *Non est Factum* (it is not my deed),[3] and has been applied widely in common law jurisdictions in sub-Saharan Africa. In *Tatiyia v Waithaka & K-Rep Bank Limited* (Kenya), the Court explains that in a contract involving an illiterate party, it is not the satisfaction of technical requirements to consummate the contract that matters but rather the question of whether the illiterate party understood the contract they had entered into.[4] The Nigerian Supreme Court case of *Paterson Zochonis S & Co. Ltd. v 1. Mallam Momo Gusau; 2. Mallum Baby Dan Kantoma* defines an "illiterate" under the Nigeria Illiterates Protection Act. The *Kormor v Coosah* case (Sierra Leone) presents a situation where two illiterates along with a literate party were involved in a contract. The Supreme Court of Sierra Leone explained that in such cases, native law and statute must both be employed to resolve the conflict. The principle of *Non est Factum* applies also to illiterate witnesses, and there is a suggestion that the evidentiary requirement may even be higher in the case of witnesses.[5] The case of *Zabrama v Segbedzi* cautions that while courts have been steadfast in protecting the rights of illiterates in contractual interaction with literates, the *Kwamin* principle may not be used to protect illiterates in validly negotiated contracts even though there may be some defects in following statutory requirements, or used to protect against criminal enterprises.[6]

In cases involving illiterates, all the statutes in the various countries require that a document must be explained to the illiterate "in a language that he understands."[7] The Zambia High Court interpreted the meaning of this phrase in the case of *Geofrey Chakota, Benda Makondo, Johnson Makoti and Morris Kapepa v Attorney-General*. The Uganda case of *Kenya Airways Limited v Ronald Katumba* examines the applicability of the common *Illiterates Protection Act* to the information on airline tickets. In this case the court was called upon to decide whether a Plaintiff could rely on the Uganda Illiterates Protection Act to deny the applicability of the Warsaw Convention on airline liability.[8]

Atta Kwamin v Kobina Kufuor

Privy Council Appeal No. 94 of 1912
FROM
THE SUPREME COURT OF THE GOLD COAST COLONY
JUDGMENT OF THE LORDS OF THE JUDICIAL COMMITTEE OF THE PRIVY COUNCIL,
DELIVERED THE 21ST JULY 1914.

(Continued)

(Continued)

Present at the Hearing:

LORD KINNEAR.

LORD SHAW.

LORD PARMOOR.

[*Delivered by* LORD KINNEAR.]

Their Lordships have seen no sufficient reason for disturbing the judgment in this case. It raises some questions of considerable difficulty. But the difficulties are occasioned by the obscurity of the facts; and the learned Judges below, from their familiarity with the customs and sentiment of the natives, have an advantage for dealing with the evidence which is wanting to this committee. In such a case, it would not be consistent with an approved rule to reverse the concurrent judgments of two Courts, unless it be shown with absolute "clearness," to use the language of Lord Herschell, "that some blunder or error is apparent in the way in which the learned Judges below have dealt with the facts."[9] It is true that Lord Herschell's rule applies in terms to those cases only in which the judges have been unanimous; and one of the Judges of the Court of Appeal has dissented in the present case. But this ought not to detract from the weight which is due to the opinion of the majority on the matter of fact, since the dissent is not based on a different view of the evidence, which indeed the learned Judge has hardly considered, but upon grounds of law which their Lordships are unable to adopt.

The controversy relates to certain lands called Bibianiha in the Western Frontier district of the Gold Coast Colony; and the question to be decided is whether the respondent Chief of Enkawie, who was plaintiff in the action, is bound by an agreement alleged to have been made in 1899 in the name of his predecessor Ntwiegye the younger, who was then chief, to surrender in favour of a chief style Kwasie Tinney, of Pataboso, in the district of Sefwhi, all right and title in the lessor's part of a lease of gold mines, and in the property of Bibianiha comprised in it. Chief Ntwiegye was not himself a party to this agreement, nor was he present when it was made, but he is said to be sufficiently described as the Chief Aichil Aigay, which is supposed to be an alias of Ntwiegye, and to have been represented by his linguist Kojo Badu, who signed the memorandum of agreement, by making his mark, or touching the pen with which the mark had been made. The memorandum recites that a lease for 99 years had been made in 1891 by Chief Kwasie Tinney of certain gold mines within the lands of Bibianiha in Sefwhi to Dr. Arthur Mather Kavanagh, since deceased, and purports to record an agreement whereby "in consideration of the sum of 300*l.* to be paid on or before the 10th day of May 1899 by the Chief Kwasie Tinney to Kojo Badu, for and on behalf of Chief Aichil Aigay, the latter Chief recognizes the lease and withdraws all claims, demands, rights, titles, privileges, advantages, benefits to and arising from the afore-mentioned lease and the Bibianiha property comprised therein." This is badly expressed, but if the agreement be valid there seems to be little room for question as to its meaning and effect in law. It assumes a right or at least the assertion of a right on the part of the Chief of Enkawie to give or withhold a lease of Bibianiha property, which is exercised by recognizing a lease already

(*Continued*)

(Continued)

granted by Tinney, and thereupon it makes him surrender absolutely and completely in Tinney's favour, not only the lessor's interest in the lease just confirmed, but all right and title whatever in allege agreement, the respondent has no fault to find with it in so far as it recognizes this lease of 1891.

On the contrary his case is that the lease was originally granted with the authority of his predecessor Ntwiegye who never disputed its validity, but consistently maintained his right as the true lessor to the rents payable by the lessee. But he maintains that in so far as it surrenders the rights of Enkawie it is invalid and ineffectual, and this on two grounds, first, that Kojo Badu had no authority to surrender his chief's rights or to dispose of property belonging to his stool of Enkawie, and secondly, that he did not understand the memorandum of agreement and did not know what he was doing when he was made to sign it. These are separate and distinct grounds in law, but they are both resolvable into questions of fact, and before considering either separately, it will be convenient to examine the circumstances out of which the transaction arose, and the conditions under which the memorandum was executed.

The lands of Bibianiha are at some distance from Enkawie, and since the delimitation of the frontier in 1906, they have been placed within the Gold Coast Colony, whereas Enkawie is in Ashanti. The origin and early history of the Enkawie right are not clearly brought out in evidence. But it is proved that for a considerable, if indefinite, period before 1891, when the lease to Kavanagh was granted, the respondent's predecessors as Chiefs of Enkawie held the lands as part of the possessions of their family stool, and exercised their right of ownerships by levying rents or tribute from members of other tribes whom they permitted to occupy them. Among these were natives of a tribe called Appolonians, who came upon the land to mine for gold. They explained their object to the people of Sefwhi, whose territory is immediately adjacent to Bibianiha; Eduampon, the Chief of Sefwhi, reported the matter to the Chief of Enkawie, who gave permission to the Appolonians to work the gold upon the Bibianiha lands. In return they paid a certain proportion of the gold extracted to the Sefwhi Chief, who paid over one half as tribute to the Chief of Enkawie. But, the actual collection for this purpose seems to have been generally made by a Sefwhi tribesman named Kwasie Tinney as representing his chief. Matters were in this position when, in 1890, Dr. Kavanagh appeared on the land in search of a mining concession.

This was reported by Tinney to Ntwiegye of Enkawie, who consented to a lease being given to Kavanagh for mining purposes. The lease referred to in the minute of agreement above mentioned was accordingly granted for 99 years at a rent of 300/ a year. It is made in favour of Kavanagh and his assigns, and before the date of the alleged agreement it had passes into the hands of an English Limited Company, the Bibiani Goldfield Company, who still hold it by a title which is not disputed by either of the parties to this litigation. On the fact of it Tinney appears as lessor, but there can be no question that it did not in reality proceed upon any exclusive title in him, but was granted by him, with the authority of the Chief of Enkawie and also of his own immediate chief, Yaw Gebill, of Sefwhi, who had by that time succeeded Eduampon. Tinney's name as lesser of course implies an assertion of a right and title to grant

(Continued)

(Continued)

the lease, but not necessarily of an independent right of property in the lands comprised in it. If they belonged to Enkawie, the owner was Ntwiegye; if they belonged to Sefwhi, as the appellant maintains, the owner was Yaw Gebill; and both of these chiefs authorized the lease. Yaw Gebill did so by countersigning the lease by his mark; and Ntwiegye did so orally before the lease was executed. This difference implies an admission of conflicting claims on the part of an Ashanti Chief, who knew anything of the practice of creating or transferring rights by written documents. It must be admitted that in the abstract of written title the nature and extent of the rights possessed by the Sefwhi chiefs are left in considerable obscurity. The learned Chief Justice is of opinion that neither Tinney nor the Sefwhi Chief can properly be called tenants, and they were caretakers for Enkawie. But however their right of occupation might be legally defined, the material point is that before the agreement of 1899 it was not an exclusive right of property.

Nothing was done to relieve them of their liability to pay tribute to the Chief of Enkawie, or to derogate from his paramount right.[10] The Court below has accordingly taken it as well established in evidence that at that date the ownership was still, as it had been for generations, in Ntwiegye of Enkawie, and that the only question for consideration was whether it had been effectually surrendered by the alleged agreement. This, indeed, is the assumed basis of the agreement itself, which must be altogether ineffectual if Ntwiegye had no good title to confirm or reject the lease. From this point of view, the first question to be decided is whether the memorandum was, in fact, authenticated by Kojo Badu touching the pen. This is not in substance or effect the signature of a written contract, but a symbol of assent which must be proved by oral testimony, and the testimony is conflicting. The Court, however, has held it to be sufficiently proved that Kojo Badu touched pen after his mark had been made by a witness named Duncan, who Captain Way, a manager of the British Company, appears to have called in for the purpose of attesting the execution of the document. This point, therefore, must be taken as decided in the appellant's favour. But it does not go far to solve the more important questions, whether Kojo Badu was empowered to make any such contract for his chief, and whether he knew the meaning of the paper which he was supposed to sign.

As to the first of these points, there is no evidence to prove that Kojo Badu had any antecedent authority to make a new contract with Tinney. At that time there was no dispute between Ntwiegye and Tinney. But the rents due by the English Company had been unpaid for several years, and according to the respondent's evidence, which the learned Judges have believed, the sole purpose for which Kojo Badu and certain elders of the tribe were sent to Cape Coast was to get the Enkawie share of these rents. It was argued that the respondent's own evidence shows that a contract of sale was intended, because he says that Badu was "told to go with Tinney to Cape Coast for the purchase of money of the Bibiani lands"; and it is said that purchase implies sale. But the respondent was speaking in Fanti, and without questioning the general accuracy of the Court interpreter, it can hardly be assumed that the native witness was using the words of his own language with exact reference to the conceptions of English law. It is evident indeed, from another passage in his evidence, that the distinction between a sale and a lease for 99 years, if he understood it at all, was not

(Continued)

(Continued)

present to his mind, because he says that "when the land was leased to the white 'man,' Tinney did not go to Enkawie about the sale, but he sent messages," and my ancestor "permitted him to sell."

No stress therefore can fairly be laid upon the mere use of such terms as purchase and sale in the mouths of native witnesses; and whatever may have been the respondent's understanding of their legal import, it is certain that he did not intend to suggest the notion that Ntwiegye had authorized a sale to Tinney. He makes it perfectly plain that his chief's instructions to Badu and his companions were that they should go along with Tinney to Cape Coast where they and Tinney together were to collect 1,000*l.* from the white man, and to divide the money. Tinney was not expected to purchase the land and pay the price, but to collect overdue rents from the white man who was already in possession. For much the same reasons the statement of the appellant's witness Kwesie Barku that Ntwiegye's messengers were told "to sell the lands to Tinney" may be disregarded. This witness is discredited by the comment of the learned Judges on his testimony as to the execution of the memorandum, and on this point he is thrown over by the appellant himself. On the other hand Mr. Justice Gough who saw and heard the witnesses, states expressly that he was favourably impressed by the evidence of the respondent. But assuming Barku's evidence to be perfectly honest, it is confused and self-contradictory. He agrees with the respondent that the 1,000*l.* for which Badu was sent to be collected from the white man; and the notion of a sale to Tinney was probably a mere blunder.

At most, this is an ambiguous phrase which cannot be set up against the great weight of evidence tending to prove that when Ntwiegye gave his instructions to Badu there was no dispute with Tinney, and that "beyond telling Badu to go and get the money, Ntwiegye gave them no other instructions." This is entirely in accordance with all the probabilities. The Chief Justice points out with great force that there was "no reason why Kojo Badu should have been deputed to give away the rights to Tinney." They were in agreement as to the white man's lease, and they were also agreed that his rents in which they were to share were in arrear. It was perfectly natural that they should join in a demand on the white man; but it is not intelligible that Ntwiegye should desire to sell his right to Tinney, in consideration of something less than the share of rent which he would be entitled to recover, if he kept his land unsold. It is said that Badu would not have touched pen if he had not been authorized to consent to the agreement. But it is proved that Ntwiegye knew nothing of the agreement either before or after it was signed; and the evidence as to its execution by Tinney, and Badu is loose and unsatisfactory to the last degree. The best evidence has been lost by the death of both of these men.

But the Courts below had to decide on the evidence actually adduced; and there is nothing in that to suggest that any negotiation took place between them, or that there was any reason for negotiation before the memorandum was put before them as a completed document, and the marks set upon it, which were to stand for their signatures. It was a document in the English language, and it was presented to them for signature by Captain Way, the manager of the English Company, in his house at Cape Coast, it was interpreted by a native clerk in his employment, and when it had been signed, neither the document itself, nor any copy of it was delivered to either of them. It was retained by Captain Way as his own document, and when

(Continued)

(Continued)

the trial took place, it was still in possession of the English Company. It was obtained by Captain Way in return for payment of 900*l.* of arrears of rent, and it is manifest that it's true purpose was to confirm his Company's right to the concession. Nevertheless, it purports to be a contract between Kojo Badu and Tinney; and that is said, not unnaturally, to be a singular form of instrument to adopt if the mutual rights of the two chiefs were not to be adjusted.

But the learned Chief Justice observes, and this is a point on which his experience gives weight to his observation, that owing to the terms of the Concession Ordinance, Captain Way had a material interest to hold under a concession, dated before 1895. He thinks it "fair, therefore, to assume that Captain Way was anxious to retain the advantage given by the lease of 1891 rather than have a new joint lease from Ntwiegye and Tinney, dated in 1899." He considers that the rents were withheld until the agreement had been signed, and he adds, "there can be no doubt that the agreement was made by the European concessionaires for them and in their interest."[11] It would have served that purpose if it had been no more than an explicit recognition of the lease that had been granted by Tinney; and in that case, it might have been within Badu's authority to sign it as representing his chief. But the question is whether he signed it in the full knowledge that it went beyond this purpose and made over to Tinney of Sefwhi, the Enkawie Chief's whole right, title, and interest in the Bibiani lands.

It is very possible that the superfluous words may have been inserted by an unskillful English draftsman with the notion that they would somehow make the confirmation of the lease more explicit or more effectual. But however this may be, there is not a shadow of evidence that they were inserted because of a new bargain between Badu and Tinney, or that their meaning and legal effect was explained to either of the natives. The only evidence tending to show that they understood the agreement at all is that it was read over to them in the Fanti language by a native of the Gold Coast named Kraku in the employment of Captain Way; and this is plainly not enough to show that they assented to it with an intelligent appreciation of its contents. Kraku, who is still alive, was not examined, as he ought to have been, and even if it be assumed that the Fanti language possesses an exact equivalent for each of the English legal terms which are brought together in the Memorandum, it cannot be supposed that Badu could appreciate the legal effect of a multiplicity of words expressing unfamiliar conceptions on their being once read to him. He had no legal adviser, and no English adviser of any kind to explain the document.

It is very probable that he understood that the paper was asked by the lessee to sign related only to the lease or to the rents which he had been sent to collect. It is not, however, proved that he acted under that impression. But the possibilities of misunderstanding are so obvious as to render it imperative on the appellant who alleges his intelligent consent to a contract expressed in a language which he did not understand, to prove that it was clearly explained to him. For this purpose it was indispensable to examine Kraku, and the appellant's failure to put him in the witness box is equivalent to an admission of his inability to prove his case by the best attainable evidence.

In these circumstances the learned Judges have rightly thought it material to consider how far the agreement has been acted upon, because a subsequent acceptance by Ntwiegye would have bound him as effectually as an antecedent mandate. The appellant relies upon a receipt

(Continued)

(Continued)

appended to the agreement. But the value of the receipt depends on the same consideration as the validity of the contract. There is no other evidence that the sum of 300*l*. was paid to Ntwiegye as "the consideration" mentioned in the agreement. It is proved that he received a larger sum, but to account of the rent to which he claimed to be entitled. All the other evidence of subsequent conduct shows that neither Ntwiegye nor Tinney knew anything of an agreement by which the former had abandoned his rights in Bibiani. No copy of the agreement was given to either; and when Badu returned from his mission he told his Chief nothing about any such contract. He brought back with him 420*l*. as the Enkawie share of the 900*l*. of arrears paid by Captain Way, after certain deductions which it is immaterial to examine. Ntwiegye would therefore be left under the belief that his mission had been exactly accomplished.

But a more material fact is that Tinney continued to recognize the Chief of Enkawie's right in the lands by paying over to him a share of the rents received from the lessees; and a number of letters have been produced in which he distinctly admits the right of Enkawie. The Judges also attached considerable importance to an event which occurred after the respondents' accession to the chiefship. The respondent had heard that a paper lease had been granted, and also that a cane or rod had been present to Tinney by the European lessees inscribed with the words "Bibiani Gold Fields, Limited, to King Quesi Tinney, 1902." "By the native mind," says the Chief Justice, "this would be regarded as the evidence that Tinney was owner of the land." But on the respondent's demand, Tinney sent the cane to him, and agreed to send him the lease when he should obtain it from his lawyer, and the learned Judge says that "to anyone acquainted with the native mind this would indicate that Tinney knew that the respondent was the real owner of the land."

Notwithstanding these considerations, it is said to be a mere assumption that Kojo Badu did not know the terms of the contract. But this is inaccurate. The question is whether his knowledge is proved, and the respondent cannot be required to prove a negative. The learned Judges say in effect that the assertion that he signed the agreement in knowledge of its contents is so improbable that they refuse to believe it, on the evidence adduced. This is a perfectly legitimate method of reasoning; and it is impossible for their Lordships to say that they are so clearly wrong that their judgement must be reversed. But the respondent's case does not depend upon Badu's state of knowledge. It may be that this would afford no sufficient ground for setting aside a contract which Badu had been duly empowered to make, since in that case the Chief might well have been held to have taken the risk of his own agent's intelligence. But its true importance lies in the valuable light which it throws on the fundamental question of his power to bind the Chief of Enkawie. The learned Chief Justice says he is satisfied that Badu would not have signed away his chief's lands without orders to that effect; and that observation would have afforded a very strong argument to the appellant, if it had not been accompanied by a clear opinion that Badu did not understand what the agreement meant. It is material on the other hand to observe that if Badu's authority to contract is not proved by direct testimony, it is just as little to be inferred from any assertion implied in his consent to sign.

(Continued)

(Continued)

The dissent of Mr. Justice Earnshaw is, as he explains, based entirely on the contract. But the learned Judge assumes that the contract is binding which, with great respect, is the very question in dispute. The contract itself does not prove that one of the parties was empowered to bind a third person, nor that a native of Africa understood a legal instrument in the English language. These are matters of fact which must be proved by the party who avers them. The respondent's case is not that a contract binding upon him should be set aside on the ground of fraud or misrepresentation, but that no contract was ever made which could bind him or his predecessor. So far as this rests on want of authority in the person professing to bind him, the law is perfectly clear. But in so far as it rests on mistake or ignorance it is by no means to be governed, as the learned Judge seems to assume, by the same considerations as a purely English contract.

The principle of law is the same in both cases, but the presumptions of fact are widely different if a contract is subscribed, without negligence, in the honest belief that it is a document of a total different nature, it is not binding upon the subscriber, not by reason of fraud or misrepresentation but because the mind of the signer did not accompany his name or mark is appended.[12] But then when a person of full age signs a contract in his own language his own signature raises a presumption of liability so strong that it requires very distinct and explicit averments indeed in order to subvert it. But there is no presumption that a native of Ashanti, who does not understand English, and cannot read or write, has appreciated the meaning and effect of an English legal instrument, because he is alleged to have set his mark to it by way of signature. That raises a question of fact, to be decided like other such questions upon evidence.

For these reasons their Lordships will humbly advise His Majesty that this appeal should be dismissed with costs.

Pariken Ole Tatiyia v Samuel Kamau Waithaka (1st Defendant) & K-Rep Bank Limited (2nd Defendant)

In the High Court of Kenya at Nairobi
Commercial & Admiralty Division, Milimani Law Courts
Civil Case No 315 of 2013

J. KAMAU, Judge

Ruling

1. The Plaintiff's application dated 17th July 2013 and filed on 23rd July 2013 was brought under the provisions of Section 3A & 63(c) & (e) of the Civil Procedure Act and Order 40 Rule 2 of Civil Procedure Rules. Prayer (1) and (2) were spent. It sought the following orders:-
    1. . . . .
    2. . . . .
    3. That pending the hearing of this suit the Defendants be restrained from selling, transferring or otherwise disposing of the suit property.
    4. Costs of this application be provided for.

(Continued)

(Continued)

2. The grounds under which the Plaintiff relied upon were generally that:-

i. The Plaintiff who was illiterate had entered into an agreement with the 1st Defendant in which he had agreed to sell and the 1st Defendant had agreed to purchase fifty (50) acres of the subject property namely Keromyokie/11 Kisumet/138 for the sum of Kshs 4,000,000/= .

ii. Instead the 1st Defendant charged the property to the 2nd Defendant, without the consent of the Plaintiff and the charge was thus tainted by fraud. The Plaintiff averred that there was no relationship between him and the 1st Defendant that would have warranted the said charge to secure the debts of the 1st Defendant to the 2nd Defendant.

iii. The 2nd Defendant did not caution the Plaintiff as was required in Section 74 of the Registered Land Act and that the prerequisites and requirements at the Land Control Board were absent.

iv. The lending to the 1st Defendant by the 2nd was reckless and fraudulent.

Affidavit Evidence

3. In his Supporting Affidavit sworn on 17th July 2013, the Plaintiff deponed that he could not read and write and that he only spoke the Maasai language. He averred that after the burial of his wife around December 2011, he scouted for buyers to purchase a portion of his fifty (50) acres to offset debts that had been incurred during the hospitalisation of his wife.

4. He further stated that he was introduced to the 1st Defendant by a Moses Mosoi Konte who also did all the translations between him and the 1st Defendant. He said that he released his title deed to the 1st Defendant who was to sub-divide the suit property and excise fifty (50) acres therefrom for a consideration of Kshs 4,000,000/= , being Kshs 80,000/= per acre.

5. He, however, admitted signing some documents at Rewans Bar in Kiserian and at the offices of M/S Gitonga, Kamiti & Kairaria Advocates but that thereafter the 1st Defendant stopped picking his calls. Upon conducting a search on the property, he found that the same was not sub-divided as he had agreed with the 1st Defendant but that rather the same had been charged to the 2nd Defendant. The Plaintiff said that he later came to find out that the 1st Defendant took a loan of Kshs 9,000,000/= from the 2nd Defendant and that a person the 1st Defendant had sent to demarcate the land was actually a valuer and not a surveyor.

6. The Plaintiff contended that the documents submitted to the 2nd Defendant by the 1st Defendant were fraudulent and that he never signed the consent forms required by the Land Control Board which he noted were signed by the 1st and 2nd Defendants. He contended that the Defendants and their advocates concealed from him the exact nature of documents that he signed and that having failed to conduct due diligence on the 1st Defendant, the 2nd Defendant had been negligent. He said this was borne in the Statutory Notice dated 4th July 2012 where the 2nd Defendant had pointed out that the statements used by the 1st Defendant to obtain the loan were fake.

(Continued)

(Continued)

7. He further stated that he managed to trace the 1st Defendant who paid him a sum of Kshs 2,500,000/= leaving a balance of Kshs 1,500,000/= . It was his contention that the whole transaction between the 1st and 2nd Defendants was fraudulent and that he would suffer grave injury if the suit property where he stayed with his family was disposed of as had been threatened in the Statutory Notice of Sale.

8. The Plaintiff tendered in evidence copies of the Title Deed, Permit for Burial, Charge, Letter of Consent dated 13th March 2012, Application for consent of Land Control Board, Bank Statement from Equity Bank, Statutory Notice and a Demand letter from Plaintiff's Advocates dated 25th April 2013 which were all marked as "POT 1–POT 8".

9. In response thereto, Gitonga Kamiti, and advocate in the firm of M/S Gitonga, Kamiti & Kairaria Advocates swore a Replying Affidavit on 5th September 2013. He said that his firm received instructions from the 2nd Defendant to charge the suit property to secure a sum of Kshs 9,000,000/= and that the Plaintiff and the 1st Defendant duly went to his office where they both executed the Charge. He was emphatic that he had explained to them the consequences of borrowing monies from the 2nd Defendant as was required under Section 74 of the Registered Land Act Cap 300 (Laws of Kenya) (now repealed.) He said that the Plaintiff informed him that he was a good friend to the 1st Defendant and that they used to assist each other in business. He stated that they spoke in Kiswahili throughout and that the issue of purchase of land was not brought to his attention.

10. George Muema, a Legal Assistant of the 2nd Defendant also swore a Replying Affidavit. It was sworn and filed on 9th September 2013. He stated that credit appraisal in respect of the 1st Defendant was done but that in any event there was no regulation requiring them to obtain the 1st Defendant's and Plaintiff's credit appraisal. He said that the Plaintiff's role was limited to consenting to the loan while it was the 1st Defendant's role to repay the money.

11. The 2nd Defendant tendered in evidence a copy of a letter dated 3rd September 2013 from Kajiado North Sub-County confirming that the consent to charge the suit property herein was sought and regularly issued by the said office. He said that the application form for consent was properly signed and any errors of dates therein were not material. In addition, he averred that the statutory power of sale had crystallised and the Statutory Notices had been sent to the Plaintiff's and 1st Defendant's to their last known addresses as could be seen from the certificate of postage which he had attached to his Replying Affidavit at pp 22-24 therein.

12. It was the 2nd Defendant's case that the Plaintiff was paid a sum of Kshs 2,500,000/= by the 1st Defendant and that he should not be allowed to misuse the court to pursue a debt through the 2nd Defendant. The said advocate was categorical that the Plaintiff had demonstrated selective memory in the facts that he disclosed to the court on 16th September 2013.

13. The Plaintiff swore a Supplementary Affidavit in response to the 2nd Defendant's Replying Affidavit on 5th September 2013. It was filed on the same date.

14. He reiterated that his photos were taken at the said Advocates' offices, a fact that Gitonga Kamiti Advocate denied. He also said that he did not take his original title deed

(Continued)

(Continued)

to the said advocates' offices as he had earlier on surrendered the same to the 1st Defendant for purposes of sub-division of the suit property. He also denied being able to speak Kiswahili as had been alleged by the said advocate or that the allegations about his relationship with the 1st Defendant were true.

15. He denied ever attending the Land Control Board and annexed a copy of a letter dated 30th May 2013 to the Oloo Laiser Land Control Board marked "PO 1-1" asking for the minutes of the Land Control Board that sat on 13th March 2012 but that the same had not been availed to him or his advocates.

16. In response to the Replying Affidavit of George Muema sworn on 9th September 2013, the Plaintiff admitted executing documents which he believed were for transfer of land to the 1st Defendant and that it was doubtful that the Land Control Board meeting was held on 13th March 2012.

Legal Submission by the Plaintiff

17. The Plaintiff's written submissions were dated and filed on 17th October 2013. He submitted that the whole transaction was tainted by fraud as the 2nd Defendant did not take a debenture over the assets of the supermarket for which the 1st Defendant and his wife had taken the loan to finance but had instead taken a person guarantee from him without ascertaining the relationship between him and the 1st Defendant.

18. It was his submission that the negligence by the 2nd Defendant was deliberate to draw the sum of Kshs 9,000,000. Further, the Plaintiff argued that in normal borrowing a bank would insist on a guarantee from the actual shareholders of the business being advanced money and that it was curious the 1st Defendant and the wife were not asked to execute the said guarantees. His argument is borne by the fact that Exhibit "MM1" annexed to the affidavit of George Muema shows that the 2nd Defendant conducted a background management and business history for a supermarket whose directors were the 1st Defendant holding 60% shareholding while his wife held 40% shareholding.

19. It was his case that he was not aware of the nature of the transaction when he signed the Charge and the Guarantee and that his consent was not valid and informed as it was obtained by fraudulent misrepresentation of facts by the 1st Defendant.

20. It was also his contention that he was not advised to take independent legal advise. He referred the court to Sarkar's Law of Evidence 16th Edition 2007 Vol 2 at page 1735 where it was stated that "...*the Courts of Chancery in England always extend to the weak, ignorant and infirm....*" He argued that the Defendants took advantage of his weakness and relied on the case of *Barclays Bank PLC vs Obrien & Another (1993) 4 All ER 417* which addressed the issue of conflict of interest by the advocate who acted for both the Guarantor and the Bank, as with the Plaintiff 2nd Defendant herein. He also relied on the case of *Graham vs Attorney General of Fiji [1936] 2 All ER 992* which made it clear that there was great necessity for advocates to maintain the highest standard of professional duty where clients were illiterate. He maintained that the explanation under Section 74 of Registered Land Act was in a language he could not understand.

(Continued)

(Continued)

21. The Plaintiff also pointed that the Charge was lodged on 28th March 2013 yet the Charge was lodged on 26th March 2012. He questioned the hurry to register the charge even before the stamp duty was assessed and paid.

22. It was his argument that merely reading a document to an illiterate person in a language he understands is not sufficient but that it had to be proved that the document was explained to the illiterate person and that he clearly understood the nature and effect of the transaction. He relied on the case of *Omanhene Vs O, A 1937 PC 274* cited in Sarkar's Law of Evidence (Supra) on page 1736–1937.

23. The Plaintiff therefore argued that he had established a *prima facie* case that he was illiterate and did not understand the nature of the transaction when he executed the charge. It was his submission that he and his family would suffer irreparable loss if this ancestral home was sold and urged the court to grant the orders sought to preserve the suit property pending trial of the court.

Legal Submission by the Defendant

24. In its submissions dated 5th November 2013 and filed on 6th November 2013, the 2nd Defendant argued that it appraised the 1st Defendant and that in any event, the Plaintiff's contention that it did not conduct credit appraisal on the 1st Defendant was irrelevant since the Plaintiff was attempting to usurp its role in credit appraisal and approval.

25. The 2nd Defendant referred the court to the case of *John Mwenja Ngumba and 2 others vs National Industrial Credit Bank Ltd and Another (2013)* in this regard.

26. The 2nd Defendant was emphatic that the advocate explained the implications of Section 74 of the Registered Land Act (now repealed) and that the certificate was duly executed. It was its argument that the Plaintiff did not deny ever having visited the advocates' offices and that there was no proof of any fraudulent actions. It relied on the case of *Wangari Ndegwa vs Housing Finance Co Ltd [2007]* where the court refused to find that there was any fraudulent misrepresentation on the part of the Plaintiff therein when she executed the charge.

27. It was the 2nd Defendant's averment that the letter issued by the Deputy County Commissioner Kajiado North Sub-County was in line with the new government structure and the same confirmed that the consent had emanated from its offices.

28. It was also its contention that the stamp duty was assessed and paid on 26th March 2013 and that the submission advanced by the Plaintiff in this regard was incorrect. The property was properly valued by M/S Metrocosmo Ltd and that the statutory Notices of Sale and Notification by the auctioneer were proper and in accordance with the law following the default by the 1st Defendant. It referred the court to the cases of *CA 148/95 Nyangilo Ochieng & Another vs Fanuel B Ochieng & Another* (unreported), *Eliazer Kiprugut Kosgei vs Barclays Bank of Kenya & Another [2013]*.

29. The 2nd Defendant therefore submitted that the Plaintiff had not met the test in *Geilla vs Cassman Brown case* and asked this court to find that the charge had properly crystallised, that the statutory power of sale had been regular and properly exercised and that the creation, perfection and registration of the charge was done in strict compliance with the law.

(Continued)

(Continued)
Legal Analysis

30. Although as the 2nd Defendant has correctly stated that credit appraisal of the 1st Defendant was an internal mechanism and the Plaintiff could therefore not purport to scrutinise the same, it has not escaped the attention of the court that the 2nd Defendant's letter dated 4th July 2012 to the Plaintiff and the 1st Defendant stated as follows:-

    ... it has come to our attention that your statements which we relied on in approving your loan facility were not authentic. We also note that you have failed to honour your monthly instalments
    ...

31. Perusal of the minutes marked as "MM 1" page 1 (b) in the 2nd Defendant's Replying Affidavit shows that the approval was made without conditions compared to other borrowers shown in the said minutes. Whereas the 2nd Defendant had concerns about the collateral that the 1st Defendant had been given as security and recommended that a Professional valuation be done within the bank's panel, the loan application was approved upfront.

32. This was unlike the cases of Anne Wamuyu Kamau and Boaz Ndunge Atenya shown in the said minutes, the requests for money were approved by the committee subject to the following conditions:-
    i. ....
    ii. Legal charge over property pledged as collateral.
    iii. Professional valuation over the property to be undertaken by a valuer within the bank's panel.
    iv. Insurance cover over the property against fire and burglary with bank's interest noted on the policy.

33. The procedure in approving loans by the 2nd Defendant is a relevant and pertinent issue that needs to be interrogated further in view of the fact that the 1st Defendant appeared to have duped the 2nd Defendant by using fake bank statements when obtaining the loan of Kshs 9,000,000/= . The Plaintiff was categorical that he was under the impression that he had been executing documents for the sub-division and transfer of fifty (50) acres to the 1st Defendant.

34. While the court appreciates the 2nd Defendant's position that the charge was created, perfected and registered strictly in accordance with the law and that the statutory power of sale crystallised, the court cannot ignore the principle of *non est factum* in arriving at a just resolution of this matter. The Plaintiff may have executed the Charge but the question that arises is whether or not his intention was to execute a Charge or a transfer to the 1st Defendant. The Plaintiff's receipt of Kshs 2,500,000/= from the 1st Defendant would require to be looked into to establish the circumstances under which the same was paid. The 1st Defendant's non-attendance all the times this matter has come up in court can only lead the court to inquire as to what his real intentions with the Plaintiff were. The court cannot purport to know what these facts were until it hears all the parties to the dispute herein.

(Continued)

(Continued)

35. This is a case of the Plaintiff's word against the 2nd Defendant's advocate who said he met and explained to the Plaintiff the implications and consequences of Section 74 of the Registered Land Act (now repealed). The issue of the language and literacy of the Plaintiff is also one that has been hotly contested by the 2nd Defendant and needs to be resolved as well as whether the Plaintiff and his family members attended the Land Control Board.

36. Having carefully considered the affidavit evidence, the oral and written submissions by counsel for the Plaintiff and the 2nd Defendant, this court is satisfied that it would be in the interests of justice to preserve the suit property pending the hearing and determination of the suit herein. This is because the Plaintiff has established a *prima facie* case with a probability of success. He has demonstrated that he will suffer irreparable loss which cannot be adequately compensated by damages and the conditions for granting an injunction on a balance of convenience are present. This court is satisfied that the Plaintiff has met the criteria set out in *Geilla vs Cassman Brown & Co Ltd [1973] EA 358* and an injunction ought to be granted in his favour pending the hearing and determination of the suit herein.

Ruling

37. The upshot of this court's ruling is that prayer No 3 of the Plaintiff's Notice of Motion dated 17th July 2013 and filed on 23rd July 2013 is hereby allowed. Costs in the cause.

38. Orders accordingly.

Paterson Zochonis S & Co. Ltd v 1. Mallam Momo Gusau; 2. Mallum Baby Dan Kantoma

In re: Mallam Baba Kantoma
Federal Supreme Court of Nigeria
ADEMOLA, C.J.F., UNSWORTH, TAYLOR, F.J.J., 28TH April, 1962]

Taylor, F.J.: The plaintiffs sued the defendants in the High Court of the Kano Judicial Division for the sum of £512-10s-7d being the amount alleged to be due and owing by the 1st defendant to the plaintiffs on his produce account and guaranteed by the 2nd defendant to the plaintiffs on his produce account and guaranteed by the 2nd defendant as per contract of guarantee dated the 27th day of October, 1958. The 1st defendant admitted this claim at the hearing and judgment was accordingly entered against him. The case proceeded to proof against the 2nd defendant, who denied liability and after evidence was heard, judgment was similarly entered against him in the same sum.

The 2nd defendant has appealed against this judgment and the grounds of appeal argued in his favour urge that: —

(1) The trial Judge erred in holding that the guarantee was written by the Manager of the respondent company when the typist was the writer.

(Continued)

(Continued)

(2) The trial Judge erred in holding that s. 3 of the Illiterates Protection Act was complied with.

At the trial in the High Court and during the arguments before us, the point was argued as to whether the appellant was, in fact, an illiterate within the meaning of the Illiterates Protection Act. It will, I think, be convenient to deal with this point at the outset, for if the appellant is not a person protected by this Act then it serves little purpose dealing with the two grounds of appeal which are based on the provisions of s.3 of the said Act. The learned trial Judge has this to say on this point:

> *I conclude from the evidence that the 2nd defendant is not literate in English. The Illiterate Protection Ordinance does not supply any definition of the expression "illiterate person" in s. 3 but I take it to mean a person who is unable to read the document in question in the language in which it is written, subject to the provision that the expression includes a person who, tho' not totally illiterate, is not sufficiently literate to read and understand the contents of the document. The provision follows from the decision of the Federal Supreme Court in* S.C.O.A. v. Okon *(FSC. 147/1959—unreported)...*

In this case on appeal before us, there was evidence on record to show that though the appellant could not read English, the language in which the guarantee was couched, yet he was able to read and write in Arabic. The word "illiterate" is defined in the Oxford Dictionary as meaning "Ignorant of letters or literature, without education, unable to read," *i.e.* totally illiterate in the sense that he is unable to read or write in any language. To hold a person is illiterate or not literate because he is unable to read or write in a particular language is in my view to stretch the meaning of the word to an absurdity. A Frenchman enters into a contract with a Nigerian. The contract is written in English, which only the Nigerian can understand though interpreted to the Frenchman. By that interpretation the Frenchman would not be regarded as literate. In the case of *S.C.O.A v. Okon* (FSC. 147/1959) to which the learned trial Judge made reference, the guarantor could only write his name. There is nothing in the Judgment to indicate that he was able to read or write in any language, and even as to his ability to sign his name this is what was said by this Court in the judgment delivered by *Quashie-Idun, Ag. F.J.* (as he then was):

> *The waybills which were signed by the defendant and upon which the plaintiffs rely in support of the contention that the defendant is not illiterate, have been seen by this Court. It is clear to me that the signatures of the defendant on them are not those of a person who could be regarded as literate in the sense that he can read and understand the meaning of Exhibit 'A'....*

When the case was heard in the High Court, this is what the learned Chief Justice said in his judgment:

> *It seems to me that a man may be sufficiently literate to sign his name and read figures, but not sufficiently literate to understand the meaning and effect of a document such as a bond. The evidence of Mr. Briggs is to the effect that the contents of this document were not explained to the defendant in the plaintiffs' office. That, in my opinion, is important.*

(Continued)

(Continued)

With the greatest respect, I agree with this view of the learned Chief Justice. The Illiterates Protection Act refers to an "Illiterate person" and "illiterate" is defined in the Concise Oxford Dictionary as "ignorant of letters, unlearned, or unable to read". I think that "illiterate" in the Act should be construed in its ordinary meaning as thus defined. In my view, on the evidence on record, the appellant was not illiterate in this sense and did not come within the purview of this Act. Further, it must be borne in mind that there is no challenge to the following findings of fact by the trial Judge which read as follows:

> *I am satisfied that the guarantee was read over and explained to the 2nd defendant and that he subsequently signed it; I am satisfied that the 2nd defendant said that he understood the guarantee and I reject his evidence the plaintiffs' clerk misinformed him with regard to his liability. I am satisfied that the 2nd defendant raised no objection when the guarantee was read over to him and I conclude that the guarantee correctly represents his instructions.*

These findings of fact further differentiate the facts of this case from those of *S.C.O.A. v. Okon* and further go to show that the applicant was not a person envisaged by the provisions of the Illiterates Protection Act, for apart from being able to read and write in Arabic, he also understood the Hausa language, the medium of interpretation used by the 2nd plaintiff witness. The Illiterates Protection Act was designed to protect illiterates from being taken advantage of by being made to sign or acknowledge a writing or document which does not bear out their real intention. In the case on appeal before us the trial Judge has found as a fact, and it has not been challenged, that this document truly represents the intention of the appellant; that it was interpreted to him; that he understood it and agreed to it before appending his signature.

As for the contention that the typist was the writer of the guarantee and not the Manager of the respondent company, there is no substance in this point and I need say no more than that the fact that the typist who typed the guarantee was working in the office of the respondent company of which P.W.I. was the Manager, coupled with the fact that on the evidence of P.W.I. the latter made manuscript insertions on the document, brings him within the definition of a "writer" as contained in s.7 of the Act.

Appeal dismissed.

KORMOR v COOSAH

(1961), 1 S.L.L.R. 66
Supreme Court of Sierra Leone
(Cole, J,):

COLE, J.:

(Continued)

(Continued)

The plaintiff claims from the defendant's possession of certain premises at Morfindor Road, Kailahun; damages for trespass and mesne profits.

The plaintiff, an old and illiterate man, was the owner of a building at Morfindor Road, Kailahun. This building consisted of a house and shop. About August of 1952, soon after the election of the present Paramount Chief Ngobeh as paramount chief of the Luawa Chiefdom, Kailahun, the chiefdom people decided to make a gift to the newly elected Paramount Chief of a house then occupied by the second defendant Asinu K. Lamin. As a result of this decision Asinu Lamin, the second defendant, was turned out of that house. The plaintiff, who had known Asinu Lamin before that date, since Lamin's mother had been previously plaintiff's sweetheart, agreed in the circumstances to take Lamin into his house. The plaintiff offered Lamin a room in the house and also the shop premises. Lamin was to stay in the room and use the shop free of rent. It should be noted that before the election the plaintiff was the chiefdom speaker holding a position next to that of the Paramount Chief; but after the election he was deposed. The plaintiff said that he made the arrangement I have already referred to at the request of the new Paramount Chief Ngobeh.

According to the plaintiff the second defendant Lamin lived in his house and used his shop. He said that about 2 months after Lamin took possession he (the plaintiff) was called into the Paramount Chief's bedroom where he met the Paramount Chief and Lamin. There he was shown a paper and was told by the Paramount Chief that he had previously asked him (the plaintiff) to give the shop portion of his building and a room in the house to second defendant Lamin. If he (the plaintiff) thought it was perfectly all right, and so he signed the paper by putting his thumbprint on the paper. I should here note that, like the plaintiff, the Paramount Chief is illiterate, but the second defendant Lamin was and is a highly educated gentleman, having attended the Bo Government Secondary School. This paper in question turned out to be Exhibit A dated August 22, 1952, which purported to transfer to the second defendant Lamin all the plaintiff's right and interest in the plaintiff's house at Morfinder Road. This document, as it came out in evidence, was drafted by the second defendant Lamin and typed by the then Luawa N.A. Clerk Vandi Kallon, now a Regent Chief of Jawi Chiefdom. This gentleman gave evidence for the defence and was third defence witness.

On the strength of Exhibit A, the second defendant Lamin entered into an agreement on November 4, 1959, with the first defendant Coosah (Exhibit B) whereby Lamin let to Coosah the house and shop in question for a period of 3 years at a rent of £150 per annum. The plaintiff was at that time living in the premises and when Coosah took possession he tried to evict the plaintiff forcibly from the house. These proceedings are the result of the first defendant's attempt at eviction.

It is clear that the second defendant Lamin bases his title on Exhibit A and the first defendant on Exhibit B. For the second defendant to succeed, I must be satisfied not only that the title on which he relies is valid but also that the plaintiff fully appreciated what he did, and voluntarily and without any misrepresentation did what it is alleged he did. The parties to Exhibit A are both natives and I have no evidence before me that the transaction contained in Exhibit A was to be regulated exclusively by English law. I am therefore bound by the

(Continued)

(Continued)

provisions of s.39 of the Courts Ordinance (cap. 50) to take into consideration and apply native law and custom in the determination of matters arising between natives in the provinces.

Evidence was led for the plaintiff that according to native law and custom the prior consent of all the relatives of a native was required before there could be an out-and-out transfer of a house built on family land. This is the uncontradicted evidence that I have before me. I have also evidence before me that the land in question on which the plaintiff's house was built was family land. I also have evidence before me given by one of the witnesses for the defence, Moriwa Nyele, fourth defence witness, who claims to be a relation of the plaintiff, that neither his own personal consent nor that of the other relatives at Borbordu was obtained before Exhibit A was a prerequisite. On this ground alone, the document becomes invalid, even if it was voluntarily entered into by the plaintiff with full knowledge of its effect.

But after careful scrutiny of the evidence as a whole I am far from being satisfied that at the time it was thumb-printed by the plaintiff he knew that document was an out and out transfer of all his interest in his house and shop to the second defendant. Although the evidence for the defence was to the effect that Exhibit A was carefully explained by the third defence witness, Vanid Kallon, in the presence of all the signatories to that document there is evidence before me by at least two of those signatories, Sinneh Borbor, the Chiefdom speaker (second plaintiff's witness) and Sampha Ngainda, the Section Chief (third plaintiff's witness) that he was not present when it was executed. One of them further said that they were merely told that the paper related to the room and shop that the plaintiff had allowed Lamin to use. It is most significant that there is no mention on Exhibit A that it was explained and interpreted to the plaintiff before he thumb-printed it, particularly as it was a document drawn up by the second defendant and typed by the witness Vanid Kallon at the request of the second defendant. Furthermore, the witness Lamin Ngobeh—educated and the brother of the Paramount Chief, who swore he was present at the execution of Exhibit A—did not sign the document.

Furthermore, the document does not comply with the Illiterates Protection Ordinance (*cap.* 105) which has been applicable to the Provinces since April 7, 1898. This Ordinance, which was passed for the protection of illiterate persons, provided, *inter alia*, that a document written at the request, or on behalf or in the name of any illiterate person should bear the name of the writer thereof and his full and true address. The evidence here is that the second defendant drafted the document, Vandi Kallon typed it and he (Vandi Kallon) signed as a witness. In these circumstances, I am inclined to the view that Exhibit A was never truly presented nor properly explained to the plaintiff and he did not appreciate its full effect before executing it and this I so find.

I am strengthened in this view by the conduct of the plaintiff. No sooner had he found the first defendant in his premises than he started making trouble to such an extent that the second defendant had to offer him the sum of £20 as a beg bone. This sum the plaintiff refused and straightway consulted a solicitor. In view of this finding the second defendant cannot rely on Exhibit A as his title. Up to the date of Exhibit B, ie, November 4, 1959, the

(Continued)

(Continued)

second defendant remained a tenant at will of the room and shop. In these circumstances the plaintiff is entitled to recover possession of the room and shop from the second defendant.

As regards the first defendant it is clear from Exhibit B that the second defendant let the premises in question to the first defendant on the strength that he (the second defendant) was owner of those premises. In view of my finding that the second defendant was not owner but merely tenant at will he could not give what he did not have. A tenancy at will is a tenancy which may continue indefinitely or may be determined by either party at any time. The tenant has nothing which he can alienate. In the circumstances the first defendant when he took possession of the house and shop in question had no valid estate or interest and committed an act of trespass by attempting forcibly to evict the plaintiff. I accept the plaintiff's evidence and that of Sinneh Borbor and Sampha Ngainda that the first defendant attempted forcibly to evict the plaintiff. The second defendant, having assigned his interest in the house and shop to the first defendant, thereby determined his tenancy at will and should pay a reasonable sum for the period he held over November 4, 1959, the date of the tenancy agreement, Exhibit B.

Order accordingly.

ZABRAMA v SEGBEDZI

COURT OF APPEAL, ACCRA
27 June 1991

FACTS

The plaintiff, an illiterate, brought an action against the defendant to redeem a house he alleged he had pledged to the defendant nine years earlier for the sum of ¢200. The defendant however denied that claim. His defence was that the plaintiff sold the house to him for the stated amount. In support of his case, he tendered exhibit A, the document they had executed to evidence the sale. The defendant's evidence was corroborated by the letter-writer who wrote exhibit A for the parties. He testified that he interpreted the document in the Twi language to the plaintiff before the parties executed it. The Odikro of the town also testified that when the parties, in accordance with the practice in their traditional area, sought his consent to their transaction he had the document interpreted to them and their witnesses and it was only after the plaintiff had affirmed the sale to him and his elders that he gave his consent to the transaction. The trial judge accordingly dismissed the plaintiff's action. Aggrieved by that decision, the plaintiff appealed on the grounds, inter alia, that "the judge misdirected himself and gave an erroneous decision." Furthermore, he failed to consider the fact that since exhibit A contained no interpretation clause showing that the contents were read over and interpreted to him in a language he understood and he appreciated what was read before he made his mark on it, the document offended the Illiterates' Protection Ordinance, Cap 262 (1951 Rev).

(Continued)

(Continued)
OPINION

Kpegah JA. On 24 July 1990, this court dismissed the plaintiff's appeal and reserved its reasons. I now proceed to give reasons why my vote was cast for its dismissal. This is an appeal against the judgment of his Honour Judge Aryeetey sitting at the Circuit Court, Akim Oda dismissing the claim of the plaintiff. The plaintiff's claim as endorsed on the writ of summons is for "the redemption of his house No A/76, situate lying and being at Bawdua." The defendant produced a document he said evidenced the sale of the house by the plaintiff to him. The plaintiff therefore decided to bring an action in the courts to redeem his property from the pledge.

At the trial, the plaintiff claimed the document executed by him and relied upon by the defendant was never read and explained to him before he made his mark. In support of his case, the plaintiff called one Dandekwei Zabrama who accompanied him to the letter-writer and was one of the attesting witnesses. This witness supported the plaintiff's claim that the document was not read over and interpreted to them. I will say that the evidence of the plaintiff in court is markedly different from his pleaded case which was that he pledged the house [Page 225] to the defendant for ¢200; not ¢60 as stated by him in his evidence in court. The evidence in court would have brought the total amount involved and covered by the document to ¢220.

The defendant's case was that the house in question was sold to him by the plaintiff for a consideration of ¢200 and that a document evidencing the sale was executed in his favour by the plaintiff. Before the execution of the document, it was read over and interpreted to the plaintiff in the Twi language by the letter-writer who also signed as an attesting witness. In accordance with the practice prevailing in the traditional area that any document evidencing the sale of land had to be attested to by the Odikro of the town, he and the plaintiff went to the Odikro who invited some of his elders and counsellors. The document was again read and interpreted to all present, including the plaintiff and his witness. The plaintiff was then asked if indeed he was selling the house to the defendant and he replied in the affirmative. Both were then asked to pay sixteen cedis each to the Odikro and his elders before the chief would consent and attest to the document. They paid the amount demanded by the chief and the document was accordingly attested to.

(a) ....
(b) The finding of the learned trial judge that the transaction was a sale rather than a pledge was not supported by the evidence.
(c) That the document relied upon by the defendant as evidencing the sale contains no *jurat* indicating that it was read over and interpreted to the plaintiff in a language he understands before making his mark, contrary to section 4(1) of the Illiterates' Protection Ordinance, Cap 262 (1951 Rev) and therefore not binding on the plaintiff.

Mr Tsegah's contention on behalf of the defendant may also be summarised as follows:

(a) The trial court disbelieved the story of the plaintiff and accepted that of the defendant as the truth. The implication is that the court has found as a fact that the transaction was a sale and not a pledge.

(Continued)

(Continued)

(b) There is enough evidence on record to justify the finding of the trial court that the transaction was a sale and not a pledge as alleged by the plaintiff.

(c) That the document, exhibit A, to which exception is being taken was only one of the pieces of evidence adduced by the defendant to show that the transaction was a sale rather than a pledge.

Mr Apatu-Plange's next assault was directed at exhibit A, the document relied upon by the defendant as embodying the sale transaction between him and the plaintiff. The complaint is that exhibit A has no interpretation clause or declaration to show that it has been read over and interpreted to the plaintiff in a language he understood before he made his mark. Taken to its logical conclusion, the argument is that the document, exhibit A, violates Cap 262 and is therefore not binding on the plaintiff. The basis for this argument, of course, is the fact that the plaintiff is illiterate and neither reads nor writes English, the language in which the document is recorded.

I think our courts have always recognised the need that in the orderly conduct of human affairs touching on contractual rights and responsibilities, it is of the utmost importance that men should be kept to their bargains when properly and fairly entered into. The rationale is that much confusion and uncertainty would result in the field of contract if a party to a contract were allowed to disclaim his signature simply by asserting he did not understand that which he had signed. In the case of *Kwamin v Kufuor* (1914) 2 Ren 808 at 814, Lord Kinnear reading the advice of the Privy Council said:

> . . .*when a person of full age signs a contract in his own language his own signature raises a presumption of liability so strong that it requires very distinct and explicit averments indeed in order to subvert it.*

While agreeing with the general concept of Lord Kinnear's proposition, my only reservation is that it fails to take into account the fact that a person signing a contract in "his own language" may be unable to read or write the said language. For example, Yaw Esenam Dela, an Ewe, may sign a contract written in Ewe without being able to read or write the said language. If the purport is to be sure that the signatory really understood the document before making his mark, then the issue should not be whether it is written in "his own language" or not. Before the signature can raise the level of presumption against a person, the question, to my mind, should be whether he can read and write the said language and not whether the document is in a language he can only speak. Despite any claims to development, I am sure there are people in the British society who can speak English very well but can neither read nor write it, just as in this country there are citizens who can speak either Ewe, Twi, Ga or Dagbani perfectly without being able to read and write same. In [Page 231] my view, they are illiterates so far as these languages are concerned.

Who then is an illiterate as Cap 262 does not offer a definition? In the case of *Brown v Ansah*, High Court, Cape Coast, 10 April 1989, unreported, I had to decide whether a testator, who could read Fanti and spoke some English but could neither read nor write English, was an

(Continued)

(Continued)

illiterate within the context of section 2(6) of the Wills Act, 1971 (Act 360). This is what I said in that case:

> *It is necessary here to repeat that there is no dispute that the will in question has no declaration of the interpreter to the effect that the will has been read and explained to the testator who perfectly understood the contents before executing same. To meet this factual deficiency of the will, learned counsel for the defendants, Mr E F Short, submitted that there is evidence that the deceased could read some Fanti and understand some English so he is not an illiterate but semi-illiterate and therefore section 2(6) of Act 360 does not apply in this case since it is relevant only to cases where the testator can be said to be a complete illiterate. It is true the Act does not define who an illiterate is. But I think whether a person is to be considered as literate or illiterate in this context, it must be related to the language in which the document is prepared, that is the ability to read and write the said language. In this case it is English. A person who can perfectly read and write the Ewe or Fanti language may be an illiterate within this context if the will is written in English which he can neither read nor write. It is the ability to read and write the language in which the document is written which to me is relevant and not whether the fellow can be classified as semi-literate or demi-semi-literate. The evidence is that the testator cannot read and write English. He is to me an illiterate within the context of the law.*

I will offer the same definition under Cap 262. This definition should make it possible for even a professor emeritus in the English language from Oxford to seek protection under the law if he should come to this country and sign a contract written in Dagbani. I will therefore re-state the principle in *Kwamin v Kuffuor* (supra) to be: *that when a person of full contracting capacity signs a document in a language he can read and write his own signature raises against him a presumption of liability so strong that it requires very distinct and explicit averments in order to subvert the document.*

To every rule, they say, there is an exception. So the general proposition I have just stated implies the counter-proposition that *where a person of full contracting capacity signs a document written in a language he can neither read nor write, or cannot understand, it is imperative on the proponent of the document to prove that it was clearly read and explained to the person against whom the document has been cited.* This situation was also recognised long ago. In *Kwamin v Kufuor* (supra), Lord Kinnear continued his statement of the law thus:

> *. . .there is no presumption that a native of Ashanti, who does not understand English, and cannot read or write, has appreciated the meaning and effect of an English legal instrument, because he is alleged to have set his mark to it by way of signature. That raises a question of fact, to be decided like other such questions upon evidence.*

The rationale, as pointed out by Lord Kinnear in *Kwamin v Kufuor* (supra), is that the possibilities of misunderstanding are so obvious. It therefore behoves the person relying on the document, and who alleges the illiterate person's intelligent consent to a contract expressed in a language he can neither read nor write, to prove that the document was clearly explained to him and he appreciated same. The case of *Waya v Byrouthy* (1958) 3 W.A.L.R. 413 was a case in which an illiterate signed a hire-purchase agreement by affixing his thumbprint. It was held that where an illiterate executes a document, any other party to the

(Continued)

(Continued)

document who relies on it must prove that it was read over, and, if necessary, interpreted to the illiterate, and that it was apparently understood by him.

In *Dadzie v Kokofu* [1961] G.L.R. 90, SC, the plaintiff, claiming as a successor to one Kwame Adufo, said that in or about 1942 his predecessor had pledged his cocoa farm to the defendant in return for a loan of £7. The defendant contended that the transaction was a sale and relied on a document which was executed by Kwame Adufo. Both the defendant and Kwame Adufo were illiterates. At the trial the defendant made no attempt to prove the document. The court, relying on the case of *Graves v Ampimah* (1905) 1 Ren 318, held that the document of sale was executed by an illiterate person, and in the absence of evidence that it had been interpreted to him no claim based on it could be sustained. See also the case of *Goodman Moshie v Kwaku* [1965] G.L.R. 566. This was a case in which the plaintiff was injured in the course of his employment. The plaintiff brought an action against the defendant for breach of his statutory duties and his duty of care at common law. The plaintiff had earlier been paid some compensation under the Workmen's Compensation Act, 1963 (Act 174), after which he signed certain documents relieving the defendant of any further claims. The defendant relied on these [Page 233] documents and pleaded estoppel. The plaintiff was a Moshie who spoke the Moshie language. The document was said to have been interpreted to him in Twi by one Quartey, a Ga man. He was not called to testify. It was held that even though the plaintiff had received compensation under Act 174 and had signed certain documents, this did not create an estoppel barring him from taking action at common law because the documents not having been read and interpreted to the plaintiff in a language that he understood, the plaintiff could not be said to have had knowledge of their contents. I will refer to this case again when I come to consider the standard of proof required in such cases.

The other submission of Mr Apatu-Plange is that the absence of a declaration on exhibit A that it was read over and interpreted to the plaintiff is fatal and therefore renders the document void and not binding on the plaintiff. This submission is made obviously with section 4(1) of Cap 262 in mind. Section 4 specified conditions to be fulfilled by whoever writes a letter or document for an illiterate. One of the requirements is that the writer of the said letter or document should clearly and correctly read and explain to the illiterate the contents of the document. This particular requirement is contained in section 4(1) which states:

> *4.(1) Every person writing a letter or other document for or at the request of an illiterate person, whether gratuitously or for a reward shall -*
>
> *(1) Clearly and correctly read over and explain such letter or document or cause the same to be read over and explained to the illiterate person.*

If I understand the submission of learned counsel for the plaintiff, a document to be binding on an illiterate signatory, must show, *on its own face*, that it had been read and interpreted to the party in a language he understands. If the document, *on the face of it*, does not indicate it had been so read and interpreted, an illiterate can successfully resist it. He may appear to have some support in the case of *Goodman Moshie v Kwaku* (supra) where one of the

(Continued)

(Continued)

documents being relied on was said to have been silent whether it was read and interpreted to the plaintiff. This is what Attoh J said at 571:

> As to exhibit 1 this is also a document that does not show *that it has been read and interpreted to the plaintiff in his own language by the letter writer or any other person.* The omission *[Page 234]* to do this is definitely against section 4(1) and (2) of the Illiterates Protection Ordinance *[Cap. 262 (1951 Rev.)]. For the above reasons, I therefore hold that exhibits 1 and 2, not having been read and interpreted to the plaintiff in a language which he understands, the plaintiff had no knowledge of the contents of exhibits 1 and 2. Exhibits 1 and 2 are therefore not legally binding on the plaintiff.*

(The emphasis is mine.) I do not think the court would have arrived at the same conclusion in respect of exhibit 1 if there were available evidence from other sources to the contrary. The question then is, what is the evidential value of a jurat or interpretation clause on a document signed by an illiterate person? Does its presence create any presumption, either rebuttable or irrebuttable, against the illiterate signatory? And also does its non-appearance on the face of the document, irrespective of credible evidence to the contrary, mean that the illiterate cannot be held to his bargain?

I think the principle is firmly established by a stream of decided cases, some of which I have reviewed in this judgment, that where an illiterate executes a document which compromises his interest and this document is being cited against him by a party to it or his privy, there is no presumption in favour of the proponent of the document, and against the illiterate person, that the latter appreciated and had an intelligent knowledge of the contents of the document. The party seeking to rely on the document must lead evidence in proof that the document was actually read and interpreted to the illiterate who understood before signing same.

What then is the standard of proof on a party relying on a document to which an illiterate is a party? Does the presence of a declaration on the document that it had been read and interpreted to him and that he appeared to have understood before signing same satisfy this requirement of proof or there is need for some corroborative evidence outside the document? In *Goodman Moshie v Kwaku* (supra), as has been seen, Attoh J in holding that the document had not been proved appeared to suggest that he was of that view because the "document…does *not show* it has been read and interpreted to the plaintiff in his own language by the letter writer or any other person." (The emphasis is mine.) And again in the case of *Youhana v Abboud* [1973] 1 G.L.R. 258 at 262, Abban J (as he then was) said:

> The defendant is a university graduate, while the plaintiff is a completely illiterate woman. She cannot read or write English. Neither can she read nor write Arabic. The agreement…was written in Arabic and there is nothing on the face of it to *[Page 235]* show that it was interpreted to the plaintiff. *The agreement merely states that it was 'read to the parties.' But it does not indicate that it was also interpreted to the plaintiff in the language which the plaintiff speaks or understands and that the plaintiff understood the contents thereof before she made her alleged mark.*

(Continued)

(Continued)

(The emphasis is mine.)

It does appear to me that if the document had had an interpretation clause to the effect that it had been read and clearly interpreted to the plaintiff in a language she understood and that she appreciated the contents of the document before making her mark, Abban J (as he then was) might have held that the presence of the said declaration would have been conclusive against the illiterate party. In arriving at his decision, Abban J (as he then was) quoted with approval the headnote in the case of *Boakyem v Ansah* [1963] 2 G.L.R. 223, SC where the illiterate persons against whom the document was being proffered were attesting witnesses only and not parties to the document. The Supreme Court speaking through Akufo-Addo JSC (as he then was) considered the issue of the standard of proof in such a case and rightly held on the facts at 225–226 as follows:

> It would be observed that in Kwamin v Kufuor *and in the more recent case of* Waya v Byrouthy *[(1958) 3 W.A.L.R. 413] in which the principle in* Kwamin v Kuffuor *was applied, the illiterate person affected in each case was actually a party to the contract written in the English language. In this case the illiterate persons concerned. . .were not parties to the deed; they were attesting witnesses only.* The evidential requirements necessary therefore to affect them with an intelligent knowledge of the precise and relevant contents of the deed are far greater than those enunciated in Kwamin v. Kufuor.

(The emphasis is mine.) The court then proceeded to deliver itself that when an illiterate attests to the execution of a document as a witness by making his mark on it, there is no presumption that he has any knowledge of the contents of the document. The presumption, the court held, is rather the other way round, and a heavier onus rests upon any person claiming that an illiterate who has attested to a document is aware of the contents of such document to prove it. The standard of proof required, I agree, is proper since the risks of an attesting witness not concerning himself with the actual contents of the document is higher.

In my humble opinion, it was unnecessary for Abban J to have adopted the standard of proof enunciated by the Supreme Court in *Boakyem v Ansah* (supra) when the case before him fell squarely within the principle enunciated in *Kwamin v Kuffuor* (supra). I must not be taken to mean Abban J (as he then was) was wrong in his decision. Indeed, there was *no evidence* in that case that the plaintiff who was a complete illiterate understood the document which was written in Arabic. As had been pointed out, in *Kwamin v Kuffuor* (supra), the issue whether an illiterate fully understood the contents of a document before making his mark or not "raises a question of fact, to be decided like other such questions upon evidence." Being a question of fact, I think the presence or otherwise of an interpretation clause on a document is one of the factors a court should take into account in determining whether the document in question was fully understood by the illiterate. In my view, an interpretation clause is only an aid to the court in satisfying itself that the illiterate against whom the document is being used appreciated the contents before its execution. The presence of an interpretation clause in a document is not, in my humble view, conclusive of that fact, neither is it a sine qua non. It should still be possible for an illiterate to lead evidence outside the document to show that despite the said interpretation clause he was not made fully aware of the contents of the

(Continued)

(Continued)

document to which he made his mark. While its presence may lighten the burden of proof on its proponent, its absence on the other hand should not be fatal to his case either. It is still open to him to lead other credible evidence in proof that, actually, the document was clearly read and correctly interpreted to the illiterate who appreciated the contents before executing same.

I hold this view because the standard of proof required in law to affect an illiterate person with the knowledge of complete appreciation of the contents and import of a document, written in a language he can neither read nor write, and to which he is a signatory, cannot be achieved by merely saying:

> *Look at the document. There is an interpretation clause on it to the effect that it had been clearly read and interpreted to him and he understood it fully before executing it so he is bound by it.*

I will recommend that type of proof which settles for preponderance of evidence in a civil case. If a court after assessing all the available evidence is *satisfied*, upon the preponderance of evidence, that the document was read and interpreted to the illiterate person, and that he fully understood the contents before making his mark, then the burden of proof would have been discharged by the person relying on the document. This is because just as it is bad to hold an illiterate to a bargain he would otherwise not have entered into if fully appreciated, so also is it equally bad to permit a person to avoid a bargain properly and voluntarily entered into by him under the guise of illiteracy. In the case of *State v Boahene* [1963] 2 G.L.R. 554 at 568, Sowah J (as he then was) put it nicely:

> *I agree that there is no presumption that an illiterate person appreciates the meaning and effect of a legal instrument or for that matter of any instrument or letter just because he has signed it; this is sound principle for the protection of an illiterate person against an unprincipled opponent, but this principle is not to be stretched to make illiteracy a cloak for fraud or criminal activities.*

I adopt these words as my own and will only add that illiteracy is not a privilege but rather a misfortune. Cap 262 is therefore a shield and not a sword. Although there is no interpretation clause on exhibit A in this case, there is sufficient evidence on record to justify a finding of fact that the document was read over and dutifully interpreted to the plaintiff before he made his mark.

JUDGMENT

Held, dismissing the appeal: (1) to state in a notice of appeal, as did the appellant's counsel, that "the trial judge misdirected himself and gave an erroneous decision" without specifying how he misdirected himself, was against the rules and rendered such a ground of [Page 222] appeal inadmissible. The implications of rule 8(2) and (4) of the Court of Appeal Rules, 1962 (LI 218) was that an appellant after specifying the part of a judgment or order complained of, must state what he alleged ought to have been found by the trial judge, or what error he had made in point of law. It did not meet the requirement of those rules to simply allege "misdirection" on the part of the trial judge. The requirement was that the ground stated in the notice of appeal must clearly and concisely indicate in what manner the trial judge

(Continued)

(Continued)

misdirected himself either on the law or on the facts. The rationale was that a person who was brought to an appellate forum to maintain or defend a verdict or decision which he had got in his favour should understand on what ground it was being impugned. Therefore as the ground of appeal alleging the misdirection failed to meet the required standard, it was clearly inadmissible.

(2) The principle was firmly established by a stream of decided cases that where an illiterate executed a document which compromised his interest and that document was being cited against him by a party to it or his privy, there was no presumption in favour of the proponent of the document, and against the illiterate person, that the latter appreciated and had an intelligent knowledge of the contents of the document. The party seeking to rely on the document must lead evidence in proof that the document was actually read and interpreted to the illiterate who understood it before signing same. Being a question of fact, the presence or otherwise of an interpretation clause on a document was one of the factors a court should take into account in determining whether the document in question was fully understood by the illiterate.

The presence of an interpretation clause in a document was not conclusive of that fact, neither was it a sine qua non. It was still possible for an illiterate to lead evidence outside the document to show that despite the said interpretation clause, he was not made fully aware of the contents of the document to which he made his mark. If a court, after assessing all the available evidence was *satisfied*, upon the preponderance of the evidence, that the document was read and interpreted to the illiterate person, then the burden of proof would have been discharged by the person relying on the document. That was because just as it was bad to hold an illiterate to a bargain he would otherwise not have entered into if he fully appreciated it, so also was it equally bad to permit a person to avoid a bargain properly and voluntarily entered into by him under the guise of illiteracy. In the instant case, although there was no interpretation clause on exhibit A, there was sufficient evidence on record to justify a finding of fact that the document was read over and dutifully interpreted to the plaintiff before he made his mark. *State v Boahene* [1963] G.L.R. 554 applied. *Kwamin v Kufuor* (1914) PC '74-'28, 28 explained.

Geofrey Chakota, Benda Makondo, Johnson Makoti and Morris Kapepa v Attorney-General

(1980) Z.R. 10 (H.C.), 1979/HP/D/1482
HIGH COURT, ZAMBIA 1ST FEBRUARY, 1980
Judgment

KAKAD, COMMISSIONER:

The four applicants, Geofrey Chakota, Benda Makondo, Johnson Makoti and Morris Kapepa (for easy reference I will hereinafter refer to them as first, second, third and fourth applicant)

(Continued)

(Continued)

applied separately for issue of a writ of habeas corpus *ad subjiciendum.* This is therefore an application of the first, second, third and fourth applicant for the issue of a writ of habeas corpus *ad subjiciendum.*

Each of the applicants was detained under reg. 33 (1) of the Preservation of the Public Security Regulations and the grounds of detention were duly served on each as required under Art. 27 (1) (a) of the Constitution of Zambia, Cap. 1.

The first and the second applicants were detained on 23rd October, 1976, and the grounds of detention were served on each on 5th November, 1976.

The third and fourth applicants were detained on 23rd February, 1977, and it appears that both were duly served with the grounds of detention on 7th March, 1977.

The common issue raised in each case is that the grounds of detention furnished to the applicants were in a language which each of the applicants did not understand and consequently it did not comply with the provision of Art. 27 (1) (a) of the Constitution of Zambia, Cap. 1.

The legal issues raised in these applications are common and will be dealt with together. Material parts of the facts are also common. I therefore propose to deal with the common part of law and facts together.

At the conclusion of the case 1979/HP/1482, the learned counsels made their respective submissions; and at the conclusion of the remaining three cases, ie. 1979/HP/1483, 1979/HP/1484 and 1979/HP/1485, the learned counsel urged this court to rely and adopt the submission made in 1979/HP/1482. In the circumstances I consider it proper to write a single judgment and this judgment for the purpose of "judgment in each case" will be the judgment in each of these four cases I have heard.

Article 27 (1) (a) reads as under:

(1) where a person's freedom of movement is restricted, or he is detained, under the authority of any such law as is referred to in Article 24 or 26, as the case may be, the following provisions shall apply:

(a) he shall, as soon as is reasonably practicable and in any case not more than fourteen days after the commencement of his detention or restriction, be furnished with a statement in writing in a language that he understands specifying in detail the grounds upon which he is restricted or detained.

Article 27 (c) and (d) permits a detainee to make representation to a detaining authority and/or to the Tribunal.

All the applicants, it is apparent from their respective grounds of application, had made representations to the Tribunal and had appeared before the Tribunal. The first applicant appeared in June, 1978. The second applicant appeared in July, 1978. The third and fourth applicants appeared in August, 1978. The first applicant in his evidence testified that prior to

(Continued)

(Continued)

his detention he was a miner. He admitted that the grounds of detention were served on him after he was detained. He deposed that he spoke and understood Kachokwe language. According to him the grounds were written in English which he did not understand; and the said grounds were not explained to him in Kachokwe. He said that he could neither write nor read. In re-examination he admitted that later on the grounds were explained to him in the language he understood.

The second applicant in his evidence deposed that he knew a bit of English. He said that at the time the grounds of detention were served on him they were explained to him in Kaonde language which he understood. He agreed that the document containing the grounds though in English were explained to him, but he refused to sign the statement as he did not agree with the alleged allegations.

The third applicant testified that he was a carpenter before he was detained. He deposed that the document containing grounds of detention and which was served on him was in English. He said that he did not understand English and the grounds were not explained to him in Lunda, the language he spoke and understood. In cross-examination he admitted that he knew why he was detained. He deposed that he could neither write nor read. He admitted that the grounds were explained to him later by a detainee.

The fourth applicant in his evidence said that he was a labourer at a farm and spoke and understood Lunda. He deposed that the grounds of detention served on him were in English which he did not understand. According to him the grounds were explained to him by his fellow prisoners. He said he could neither read nor write.

It is therefore common cause that each of the applicants in these cases, was detained under reg. 33 (1) and each was duly served with written grounds of detention as required under Art. 27 (1) (a). All the statements containing the grounds undoubtedly were written in English. It is not controverted that the first, third and fourth applicant were illiterate and could not understand, read or write English. The second applicant knew a bit of English but spoke and understood Kaonde. The first applicant spoke and understood Kachokwe. The third and fourth applicants spoke and understood Lunda. Article 27 (1) (a) provides that a detainee within fourteen days of his detention should be furnished with a statement in writing in a language that he understands specifying the grounds upon which he is restricted or detained. The learned counsel for the applicants submitted that the ground raised in the supplementary affidavit was based on the construction of Art. 27 (1) (a) of the Constitution of Zambia, Cap. 1. The common ground raised in the supplementary affidavit in each of the cases reads:

> *That the grounds of detention furnished to the applicant were in a language which the applicant does not or did not understand and did not comply with Article 27 (1) (a) of the Constitution of Zambia Act, No. 27 of 1973.*

The applicants' counsel went on to say that on decided cases in Zambia the provision of Art. 27 (1) (a) had to be strictly complied with otherwise the detention was unlawful. He referred to the case of *A-G. v Chipango* (2) and stated that in that case the Court of Appeal had held that the compliance of the provisions of Art. 26 (1) (a) which is now Art. 27 (1) (a), was

(Continued)

(Continued)

mandatory and the detaining authority was bound to comply with the said provisions. He contended that the legislature in imposing mandatory provisions under Art. 27 (1) (a) provided a protection for an individual.

He submitted that the question in these cases was that the written grounds furnished to each of the applicants should have been in a language understood by each of the applicants. In short the learned counsel contends that the grounds of detention served on the firm applicant should have been in Kachokwe, on the second applicant should have been in Kaonde and on the third and fourth applicants should have been in Lunda.

The learned counsel argued that the fact that the grounds (written) furnished to the applicants were in English, denied the applicants their right to know why they were detained and that amounted to a fundamental breach of the constitutional provisions. He contended that the fact that the grounds were explained to the applicant by others did not amount to compliance with Art. 27 (1) (a). He submitted that it was irrelevant that English was the official language in Zambia, and contended that if that was the intention of the legislature it would have stated so in Art. 27 (1) (a).

The learned State Advocate in reply submitted that it was clear from the evidence that each of the applicants was made aware of the grounds of detention. She did not agree that the rights of the applicants in Art. 27 (1) (a) were infringed. She contended that all the applicants being illiterate, all that was required was to bring to the understanding of the applicants the grounds of detention. According to the State Advocate in these cases it would have made no difference in which language the grounds were written. She said that the applicants being not able to read and write would not have been in a position to read them and would have had to rely on what was explained. She contended that had the legislature intended that the statement had to be stated or written in the mother tongue of a detainee it would have stated so. According to her in these cases the use of English language was relevant as English was the official language of Zambia.

The applicants' counsel submitted that the provisions of Art. 27 (1) (a) of the Constitution of Zambia, Cap. 1, were mandatory and had to be strictly complied with by the detaining authority. I agree with this. This issue has been firmly established by our final courts in the following cases: In the High Court case *Chipango v A-G.* (1) Magnus, J., delivering the judgment said:

> He describes these as *'constitutional conditions subsequent to arrest'* and I prefer this description as applied to paragraphs (a) and (b) of Section 26 A (1) of our constitution rather than Mr Baron's bold description of them as *'condition subsequent'*. As I held that these are constitutional conditions subsequent to arrest, they are all mandatory and fundamental rights of the individual, and if they are not followed, I can only conclude that such non-compliance must render further detention unconstitutional and unlawful.

On appeal of the above quoted case to the Court of Appeal, the High Court decision on the point in issue was upheld. The learned Chief Justice delivering the judgment of the Court of

(Continued)

(Continued)

Appeal in *A-G. v Chipango* (2), in dealing with the question of Constitution of Zambia, at p. 64 said:

> *I consider that the condition is not a mere procedural step in the furtherance of consideration of a detainee's case, but it goes vitally to the fact of detention. In my opinion the provision must be adhered to strictly, and failure to do so causes further imprisonment under the detention order to be invalid. It is not strictly necessary for me to determine whether the same considerations apply to a failure to comply with paragraph (a). The argument is not so strong. The provision does however appear to be in some order of descending importance. A person is entitled to know within a short period why he is detained. I would be prepared to hold that failure to comply with this paragraph also has the same result.*

In *Sharma v A.-G.* (3), the learned Deputy Chief Justice delivering the judgment in the Supreme Court at p. 167, pronounced:

> *I am satisfied therefore that when a person is detained pursuant to reg. 33 (6), the provisions of Art. 27 of the Constitution must be complied with.*

Coming to the common law point raised in the applications before this Court, the learned counsel for the applicants contended that the detaining authority by serving a written statement in English language on each of the applicants who did not understand English and who only understood their mother tongue, had infringed the provisions of Art. 27 (1) (a), and therefore further detention of the applicants was unconstitutional and unlawful.

Article 27 (1) (a) reads: "He shall as soon...restriction, be furnished with *a statement in writing in a language that he understands* specifying in detail the grounds upon which he is restricted or detained."

The phrase "a statement in writing in a language he understands" on the face of it sounds and appears to be simple. I have gone through most of the authorities in our courts dealing with applications of this nature, and it appears to me, that this is the first time this point has been raised. In my view this is a relevant point and well taken.

The quiz in the phrase "a statement in writing in a language he understands", as I see it, appears in the wording "in a language that he understands". It is common knowledge that English is the official language of the Republic of Zambia. Equally it is common knowledge that there are many other vernacular languages spoken and understood in Zambia. Though English is the official language in Zambia, it does not necessarily follow that every Zambian or a resident in Zambia, understands, reads or writes English. There are I believe a number of people in Zambia who are not literate in English. Amongst them are the applicants. According to the learned counsel for the applicants, where a detainee is an illiterate in English, it was, under Art. 27 (1) (a) mandatory for the detaining authority to serve on the detainee a statement in writing specifying the grounds of detention in the language that he understands and not in English, and it was in such a case irrelevant that English was the official language of Zambia. He argued that if the legislature had intended the statement to be in the official language it would have said so. The learned State Advocate on the other

(Continued)

(Continued)

hand contended that the legislature did not intend that a statement under Art. 27 (1) (a) should be written in the mother tongue and if it had so intended it would have been so specified. Both these arguments in my view have some force in them.

On this point the observation of the learned Magnus, J., in *Chipango v A.-G.* (1) (*supra*) are, in my view, befitting. At p. 6 of the judgment he said:

> It would, of course, be desirable in all cases, and more especially in cases where the liberty of the subject is concerned, if the legislature were more specific in what it intended to do. I suppose, however, that this would be a counsel of perfection which, although it would lighten the work of the courts, would be achieving some thing which no legislature appears to have achieved so far. It therefore falls upon the courts, as it so often does, to construe what Parliament in its wisdom intended should be the law.

The objects of serving on a detainee a written statement specifying grounds of his detention in a language that he understands as provided under Art. 27 (1) (a), I believe, are (1) that the detainee should within the stipulated period be made aware of the reasons as to why he is detained; and (2) that the detainee could at the earliest opportunity make a meaningful representation to a detaining authority or to the Tribunal. In my view it is in this light that it is provided under Art. 27 (1) (a) that a detainee should strictly be served with a statement specifying the grounds of detention in a language that he understands. There certainly would be no problem where a detainee is literate in English.

On the common law point raised in the applications before this court, the counsel for the applicants quoted the Indian Supreme Court case—*H. Das v The Magistrate, Cuttack* (4). In that case it was found that the detained person did not have the grounds served upon him within five days as by law prescribed, and the grounds, which ran into fourteen, typed pages, and referred to his activities over a period of thirteen years, were given to him in a language he did not understand and without any attempt at explanation. The court in that case held that the failure to serve the grounds within the five days required made the order invalid. It should be noted that in that case the main reason to find the order invalid was on account of failure to serve the grounds within a stipulated period and not because the grounds were in a language that the detainee did not understand.

In another Indian case *Harikisan v The State of Maharashtra & Others* (5) at p. 918, the detainee was served with the order of detention and the grounds in English. He did not know English and asked for a translation of these in Hindi. This request was refused on the grounds that the order and the grounds had been orally translated to him at the time they were served upon him and that English still being the official language, communication of the order and grounds in English was in accordance with the law and constitution. The Supreme Court of India on appeal from High Court in that case held:

> That the provisions of Art. 22 (5) of the Constitution were not complied with and the detention was illegal. Article 22 (5) required that the grounds should be communicated to the detainee as soon as may be and that he should be afforded the earliest opportunity of making representation against the order. Communication in this context meant bringing home to the detainee effective knowledge of the facts and

(Continued)

(Continued)

grounds on which the order was based. To a person who was not conversant with English language, the detainee must be given grounds in a language which he can understand and in a script which he can read, if he is a literate person. Mere oral translation at the time of service was not enough.

In that case the learned Chief Justice delivering the judgment of the Indian Supreme Court, at p. 925, observed:

We do not agree with the High Court in its conclusion that in every case communication of the grounds of detention in English, so long as it continues to be official language of the State, is enough compliance with the requirements of the constitution.

If the detained person is conversant with English language, he will naturally be in a position to understand this gravamen of the charge against him and the facts and circumstances on which the order of detention is based. But to a person who is not so conversant with the English language, in order to satisfy the requirements of the constitution, the detainee must be given the grounds in a language which he can understand, and in a script which he can read, if he is a literate person.

The provisions of our Constitution dealing with detention and the provisions of the Indian Preventive Detention Act, 1950, were closely examined and compared in the High Court case of *M.W. Chipango v The Attorney-General* (*supra*) and I find it not necessary to deal with them in these cases. However, under Art. 27 (1) (a) of the Constitution of Zambia it is provided that the written statement specifying grounds of detention must be in a language that a detainee understands whereas that provision is silent in the Indian Preventive Detention Act, 1950. Under the Indian Detention Act all that is required is that the grounds should be communicated within the prescribed period to a detainee.

The vernacular languages in Zambia and in India have their own script and dialect. The only minor distinction, I believe, is that each of the Indian vernacular languages has its own alphabet whereas the vernacular languages in Zambia are written in most of the English alphabet. However, this distinction is immaterial in so far as the distinct nature of a vernacular language is concerned. Therefore, a person in Zambia could well be literate in a Zambian vernacular language though not necessarily literate in English language.

All the applications before this court are based on the ground that each off the applicants was an illiterate person, in that he could speak and understand a vernacular language but could not write or read any languages. In my considered view where a detained person is illiterate, the detaining authority should, at the time of serving a written statement of grounds under Art. 27 (1) (a), make certain that the grounds are fully explained and translated in a language that the detainee understands; and a certificate of such explanation stating the language in which it was explained should be attested by the officer who explained the grounds to the detainee. Where a detainee is illiterate in English, the detaining authority following the above procedure would in my view be considered as having strictly complied with the provision "a statement in writing in a language that he understands" under Act. 27 (1) (a). The interpretation and explanation of the grounds to a detainee illiterate in English, in a vernacular language that he understands, I consider, affords a constitutional protection and places him in a position to be able to make representation as provided under Art. 27 (1) (*d*).

(Continued)

(Continued)

I have observed that in two written statements of grounds exhibited in the cases before this court, a certificate of explanation has been attested. However in those certificates the language in which the grounds were explained is not stated. I am not dealing with a case where a detainee is literate in a vernacular language but not in English. In my opinion the wording "in a statement in writing in a language that he understands" under Art. 27 (1) (a) being mandatory, may have significant implications where the detainee is literate in a vernacular language and who is served with grounds of detention in English. The decision in the Indian case of *Harikisan v The State of Maharashtra & Others* (5) (*supra*) though not binding on our courts is highly persuasive.

The first applicant claims to be totally illiterate. According to him he cannot read or write and could only understand and speak Kachokwe. He admitted that the grounds of detention were some time later explained to him in the language he understood. However, looking at the statement containing the grounds which was served on the applicant (attached to the supplementary affidavit), it is apparently clear that the serving officer had explained the grounds to him. There is a certificate to that effect on the statement. Secondly, looking at the grounds in the written statement and the grounds sworn by the applicant in this application, it is clear that the applicant was fully aware of the grounds of his detention. Thirdly, the applicant had appeared before the Tribunal where his case appears to have been comprehensively renewed by the Tribunal. I am therefore satisfied that the grounds of detention were explained and communicated to the applicant in the language he understood. The applicant being unable to read and write, it would, I consider, have made no difference in what language the statement containing the grounds were written. I am therefore satisfied that in the circumstances of the case, the detaining authority had fully complied with Art. 27 (1) (a) of the Constitution of Zambia, Cap. 1. The detention of the applicant therefore was neither unconstitutional nor unlawful. In the result the applicant's application is dismissed.

The second applicant in his evidence admitted that he knew a bit of English. According to him he spoke and understood Kaonde. In his evidence he said that he was explained the grounds by the officer, but he refused to sign the statement containing the grounds because he did not agree with the alleged grounds of detention. The applicant therefore was fully conversant with the grounds which I find were fully explained to him by the serving officer. On the facts and in the circumstances the detaining authority I find had complied with Art. 27 (1) (a) of the Constitution. The applicant's detention therefore was constitutional and lawful. The application is therefore dismissed.

In the case of the third applicant there is no doubt that he is illiterate and can only speak and understand Lunda. He admitted that the grounds of detention were explained to him by a fellow detainee. The applicant had in fact appeared before a Tribunal and his application was heard by the Tribunal. This is evident from the grounds he submitted in his application. The grounds of detention in his application before this court are more or less what they are in the written statement that was served on him. In the circumstances of the case and on facts the applicant I find was fully made aware and was fully explained the grounds of detention in the language he understood and because of that he was able to make a representation to the

(Continued)

(Continued)

Tribunal. He being illiterate it would have made no difference in which language the grounds were written. I therefore find that the detaining authority had not breached the provisions of Art. 27 (1) (a) of the Constitution. The applicant's detention I find was neither unconstitutional nor unlawful. The application is therefore dismissed.

The fourth applicant claimed to speak and understand Lunda. There is no dispute that he is illiterate, i.e. he cannot read or write. The written statement of the grounds written in English was duly served on him. He admits that the grounds in the statement were explained to him by a fellow prisoner in a language he understood before he made a representation to the Tribunal. The applicant therefore knew what the grounds were, otherwise he, I believe, would not have been in a position to make representation to the Tribunal. I am satisfied that in the circumstances it would have made no difference in which language the statement and the grounds were written. I consider that the detaining authority had not infringed Art. 27 (1) (a) of the Constitution, Cap. 1. The applicant's detention therefore was neither unlawful nor unconstitutional. The application, in the result, is dismissed.

As the applicants are represented by the Legal Aid Department, it would, I consider, be proper that in all these four cases, each party bears his own costs.

Application dismissed

Kenya Airways Limited v Ronald Katumba

The Court of Appeal of Uganda, Kampala
Coram: Hon. Justice L.E.M. Mukasa Kikonyogo, DCJ
Hon. Justice A.E.N. Mpagi-Bahigeine, JA
Hon. Justice S.B.K. Kavuma, JA
Civil Appeal No. 43 of 2005
(Appeal from the judgement and decree of the High Court of Uganda at Kampala before Honourable Mr. Justice R. O Okumu Wengi, dated the 28th day of February 2005 in civil Case No. 75 of 2005)

Judgement of Hon. Justice A.E.N. Mpagi-Bahigeine, JA

This appeal arises from the judgement and orders of Okumu Wengi, J, dated 28-02-05.

The respondent sued the appellant seeking special and general damages arising out of breach of contract and negligence. The appellant denied the allegations, relying on the terms of the said contract. The learned Judge preferred the respondent's story. Hence this appeal.

The facts, briefly, are that the respondent was a frequent passenger on the appellant's airline from Dubai to Entebbe and vice versa. On 30-01-2003, armed with a return air ticket to Dubai, the respondent checked in his luggage weighing 56 kilograms, on flight No. KQ413H and KQ310H. He, however, did not declare any special value for the baggage, nor did he pay

(Continued)

(Continued)

any sums over and above that indicated on the ticket for the said special value of the baggage.

On arrival back at Entebbe, the respondent's baggage was found to be missing. At the request of the appellant, the respondent filled in a property irregularity form, informing the appellant that he had not retrieved his luggage; it was missing. The appellant took steps to try and locate the missing luggage. Arrangements were made to fly him to Nairobi in an effort to trace the missing luggage. It was, however, irretrievably lost. The appellant thus offered to compensate the respondent in the sum of US. $ 1120, in accordance with the terms and conditions stated on the Air ticket, under the Warsaw Convention, which is US $ 20 per kilogram lost, for the 56 kgs.

The respondent declined the offer and opted to file a suit seeking U$ 17963 as the value of the goods lost together with U$ 150 additional cost for the flight to Nairobi, with general damages and costs.

The appellant denied liability beyond the limit of US $ 1120. The learned Judge held that the appellant's liability was not limited as claimed and ordered it to pay US $ 17,963 to the respondent as prayed.

The memorandum of appeal is dated 30-06-05 and comprises the following grounds:

1. The learned trial Judge erred in law in finding that the appellant's liability was not limited under the Warsaw Convention.
2. The learned trial Judge erred in law and in fact in finding that notice of the limitation of the appellant's liability was not brought to the attention of the respondent.
3. The learned trial Judge erred in law in holding that the Illiterates Protection Act cap 78 applies to airline tickets.
4. The learned trial Judge erred in fact in holding that the respondent was illiterate.
5. The learned trial Judge erred in law and in fact in holding that there was an element of wilful misconduct on the part of the appellant.
6. The learned trial Judge misdirected himself on the law governing the award of special damages and erred in awarding the sum of US$ 150 to the plaintiff as special damages.
7. The learned trial Judge misdirected himself in evaluating the evidence on record and arrived at a wrong decision.

At the conferencing, three issues emerged for determination by the court:-

1. Whether the appellant's liability is limited. (This issue covers grounds 1, 2, 3, 4, 5 and 7 of the Memorandum of Appeal).
2. Whether the trial Judge properly directed himself on the remedies available to the respondent. (This issue covers grounds 6 and 7 of the Memorandum of Appeal).
3. What remedies are available to the parties.

Regarding issue No.1, Mr. Sim Katende, learned counsel for the appellant, citing Article 22 (2) of the Warsaw Convention, pointed out that its wording limiting the appellant's liability was replicated on the airline ticket issued to the respondent and that the respondent was

(Continued)

(Continued)

aware of it. In support of this submission learned counsel relied on *Ethiopian Airlines v Olowu Motunrola Court of Appeal Civil Appeal No. 30 of 2005*, where this court held that in the absence of any special declaration of excess baggage, the airline's liability for lost baggage was limited to US$ 20 per kg under the Warsaw Convention. Similarly, in this case, the respondent never declared any excess baggage nor its value at checking in and no additional sum was ever paid to her. Mr. Katende submitted that the compensation the respondent was entitled to was limited to what was stated under the Warsaw Convention.

Concerning notice of this limitation to the respondent, learned counsel pointed out that the respondent being a frequent flier ought to have been aware of the information on the ticket. Ignorance of the law is no defence. He was not entitled to the Illiterates Protection Act (cap 78) as claimed by his counsel in the lower court and agreed by the court. He cited *Thompson v London Midland & Scottish Railway Co (1930) 1KB 41,* where the railway company was held not liable for the injury to an illiterate passenger because limitation of liability was clearly stated in the ticket. Inability to read the ticket was irrelevant. Mr. Katende submitted that the appellant was not an illiterate within the meaning of the Illiterate Protection Act (cap 78) and nor was the Airlines ticket such a document as envisaged by the Act. It was never prepared for the respondent for use, in this trial, as evidence. Mr. Katende further contended that there was no wilful loss of the respondent's luggage as stipulated under article 25 so as to deprive the appellant of the protection. The duty lay on the respondent to show that the appellant wilfully and intentionally lost his luggage. This the respondent failed to do. The appellant was therefore entitled to rely on article 22(2) of the Warsaw Convention which limits liability.

Regarding the special damages claimed and awarded, Mr. Katende pointed out that these were not strictly proved. The receipts for the goods tendered in were of no probative value as they were never made in the names of the respondent.

Concerning the general damages awarded, learned counsel reiterated that the appellant's liability was limited by the Warsaw Convention. The appellant was ready and willing to compensate the respondent up to U$ 1120. There had been no need to file this suit. The money had been deposited in court before the suit. Mr. Katende prayed court to allow the appeal with costs.

Mr. Brian Othieno, learned counsel for the respondent, opposed the appeal, submitting that the learned Judge did not err to find that the appellant's liability was not limited under the provisions of the Warsaw Convention. Citing Articles 4(1) and (4) of the Warsaw Convention, the learned counsel argued that no luggage ticket was issued to the respondent as required under 4(1) in which case article 22 would not be available to the appellant. He pointed out that *"The baggage check"* relied on was only relevant in the Warsaw Convention as amended at the Hague. Under the amendment, the baggage check which article 4 talks of can be combined with the passenger ticket. This is not the same as under the Warsaw Convention.

He asserted that Uganda is not a High Contracting Party to the Warsaw Convention as amended at the Hague. She never ratified the Warsaw Convention and cannot therefore apply

(Continued)

(Continued)

their terms like "Baggage Check". In his view, since the luggage ticket was not issued, and luggage ticket is not a baggage check, article 22 was not available to the appellant.

Learned counsel contended that if a luggage ticket is issued under article 4(4), it contains particulars stipulated under article 4(d) (f) and (h) e.g. weight and liability limitation. He asserted that article 4(f) was thus not complied with by the appellant. The particulars required were not given. He sought to distinguish this case from the Ethiopian case (supra) relied on by Mr. Katende on the ground that in this case, the luggage ticket was not filled in as was done in the Ethiopian case. This means that the particulars in this case required to be given under article 4(d) (h) and (f) were not given. The respondent was given only a baggage tag which is not the luggage ticket envisaged under the Warsaw Convention. The learned Judge was thus correct in his conclusion that the Warsaw Convention limitations were not available to the appellant.

Concerning ground No.2, Mr. Othieno argued that no notice of the alleged limitations was ever brought to the attention of the respondent. The respondent's being a frequent flyer was not sufficient proof of the notice of limitations to the respondent. He further argued that the respondent was protected under the Illiterates Protection Act as ruled by the learned Judge. The airline ticket was a document as defined by the Act and the respondent was such an illiterate as he could not read and understand the terms on the air ticket and the Warsaw Convention. In his view, *Thompson v London Midland & Scottish Railway Co. (supra)* relied on by Mr. Katende was not applicable. Mr. Othieno asserted that there was wilful conduct on the part of the appellant in handling the respondent's luggage as evidenced by their letter endorsed "without prejudice" dated 10-03-03, (Ex P3), which was put in evidence with the consent of the appellant. In this letter the appellant admitted mishandling the respondent's luggage. He cited article 25 of the Warsaw Convention which provides that if the loss or damage is caused by such wilful misconduct or default by the appellant, then the limitations would not be available to the appellant.

Regarding special damages, Mr. Othieno contended that they were proved by the cash receipts tendered in as Ex P9-i-ii. These were never objected to. The fact that they were not in the respondent's names was never raised at the trial. It was therefore safe to infer that their contents and value were admitted. He stated that even the U$ 150 awarded for hotel expenses was not challenged. He prayed Court to find that the special damages had been satisfactorily pleaded and proved and to dismiss the appeal.

In reply Mr. Katende submitted that indeed no luggage ticket was issued to the respondent but that its absence did not affect the validity of the contract. He pointed out that a luggage ticket and a baggage check were all one document in this case. It was combined with the passenger ticket. It was a question of terminology. Furthermore, the air ticket lists all the particulars required. Learned counsel asserted that though the witness had poor eye sight, the appellant was still protected by the Warsaw Convention since they issued a proper document. The baggage check and luggage ticket being used interchangeably supports the appellant's contention that a luggage ticket and baggage check are the same thing (Ex P8). They are one document. Mr. Katende further stated that it is the respondent who tendered in the ticket at

(Continued)

(Continued)

the trial thus he cannot turn round and deny that he never had notice of the liability limitation. He had a document in which the limitation was embodied. He had accepted the ticket without any objection. He cannot, therefore, plead ignorance of its terms and conditions.

Regarding the letter endorsed *"without prejudice"* (Ex P3), Mr. Katende stated that it could not be relied on in court without the consent of the appellant. That is the law. However, it could be used by the appellant if it made an offer prior to filing the suit which was rejected. It (Ex P3) did not prove wilful misconduct as claimed by the respondent who had to prove wilful misconduct and not merely misconduct. The burden of proof is high and is akin to culpable negligence. Concerning the receipts, learned counsel pointed out that they were challenged in court (page 28 line 6).

Mr. Katende reiterated that both the 1925 Warsaw Convention and the amendment at the Hague were complied with. The appellant fulfilled all the requirements of the luggage ticket. This fits in with the Warsaw Convention, the luggage ticket and baggage check being on one document. He prayed Court to allow the appeal and set aside the judgement and orders of the High Court.

The learned Judge held:

> . . . it is the view of this court firstly that it is the Warsaw Convention and not the Hague amendment that is to be applied in this case. This Convention rationalises the generality that once a notice is said to be given that is final and requires that the Convention itself has to be notified (sic). This is logical given the fact that the Illiterates Protection Act Cap 78 does not exempt airline tickets. In the present case the literacy status of the plaintiff was demonstrated. Further still article 25 of the Warsaw Convention does not allow exemption where, as in this case, an element of wilful misconduct taking the form of mishandling baggage, has also been demonstrated. I have not been advised that the carriage By Air (Colonies Protectorates and Trust Territories) Order No. 144 of 1953 has been revoked or amended. The first schedule to that order is the Warsaw Convention which makes provisions in sections 2(article 4) and in chapter 3(article 25) that operate to liberate the plaintiff in this case from the clinical exclusion of the Airlines liability in any event.
>
> The plaintiff in my view has proved his case on the basis of breach of contract of carriage and/or in the mishandling of his baggage resulting in loss that he has proved by Exhibit P9(i) to (xi) as admitted by the defendant. He is entitled to judgement against the defendant for U\$ 17,963 or its equivalent in Uganda shillings with costs as prayed.
>
> Secondly, the plaintiff is entitled to general damages given the inconvenience he has gone through and the loss of his investment in trade goods. I will allow him to collect U\$ 4150 being special damages and Shs 3 million (Three million only) as general damages. He will recover the costs of this suit from the defendant. It is so ordered.

The first issue to resolve is whether it is the Warsaw Convention 1929 or the Warsaw Convention as amended at The Hague, 1955 which is applicable to this case. This has to be looked for from the four corners of the air ticket itself. The conditions of contract are set out

(Continued)

(Continued)

on a coupon of the ticket Ex P8 which appears on page 54 of the record of proceedings. Clause 1 thereof states, inter alia:

"...Warsaw Convention" means the Convention for the Unification of Certain Rules Relating to International Carriage by Air signed at Warsaw Convention as amended at the Hague, 28th September 1955, whichever may be applicable.

Clause 2 goes on:

2. Carriage hereunder is subject to the rules and limitations relating to liability established by the Warsaw Convention unless such carriage is not "International Carriage" as defined by that Convention.

I think it is quite plain, it is the Warsaw Convention applicable to this matter as the learned Judge correctly found. If it were the amendment at the Hague, it would have been so stated. It is trite that no extraneous evidence is admissible to vary and/or contradict the terms and conditions of the written contract (Ss 91 and 92 of the Evidence Act—chapter 6). I turn to the issue of liability for loss, delay etc, by the appellant. It is clear that the appellant issued one ticket comprising the passenger ticket and the baggage check all in one. Clause 1 of the conditions of contract clarifies:

1. As used in this contract 'ticket' means this passenger ticket and baggage check.

The liability for loss is set out on a coupon (page 55 of the record) and reads:

Notice of Baggage Limitations

Liability for loss, delay or damage to baggage is limited unless a higher value is declared in advance and additional charges are paid. For most international travel...the liability is approximately US$ 9.07 per pound (US $ 20.00per kilo) for checked baggage. Excess valuation may be declared on certain types of articles. ..... Further information may be obtained from the carrier.

This is a replication of Article 22(2) of the Warsaw Convention. Relying on the above provision, in the *Ethiopian Airlines case (supra)*, this Court declined to order compensation for undeclared excess baggage. The baggage tag the respondent seeks to base his claim on has nothing to do with the value or contents of the luggage. It simply reads:

"Limited Release" even if your baggage has been tagged to final destination, you may have to clear through customs at Point of Transfer. This is not the Baggage Check (Luggage Ticket) described in Article 4 of the Warsaw Convention or the Warsaw Convention as amended by the Hague Protocol, 1955.

It is an identification tag as stated by Ismail Nsubuga (DW) and by the writing on it.

I therefore find it impossible to read into this tag anything else other than what it says. It says nothing about the contents of the luggage. A clause in the liability limitations page 55 of the record of proceedings reads:

Excess valuation may be declared on certain types of articles. Some carriers assume no liability for fragile, valuable or perishable articles. Further information may be obtained form the carrier.

(Continued)

(Continued)

It is therefore only one document that was issued to the respondent under the conditions of the contract. This contains all the relevant information as required under article 4 of the Convention. I cannot therefore take the view that since no luggage ticket was issued, the protection under article 22(2) is not available to the appellant. I think, with respect, the learned Judge was in error over this point.

Another issue taken was that the respondent could not read the ticket and was therefore protected under the Illiterates Protection Act (cap 78). The learned Judge agreed with the respondent which I would take to be a misdirection. The air ticket was not the respondent's document. It was never prepared for him for use as evidence of any fact or thing as stipulated under the Act. Most importantly, the respondent could read though with difficulty as do most people. He could therefore not categorize himself as an illiterate even if the law stated otherwise.

Furthermore, it is well settled that the fact that the respondent could not read would not exonerate him from his obligation under the contract. Once he is handed the ticket and has accepted it, he is bound by it. *Thompson v London Midland and Scottish Railway Company, (1930)* 1 KB 41. Kenya Airways (KQ) made the offer by tendering the ticket to the respondent which he duly accepted fully, thus undertaking to be bound by its terms. Also see *McCutheon v David Mac Brayne Ltd (1964) 1 ALL ER 437.* (1964) 1 WLR 134. Where it is stated:

> ... when a party assents to a document forming the whole or part of his contract, he is bound by the terms of the document, read or unread, signed or unsigned, simply because they are in the contract...

The contractual terms on tickets have always been held to be sufficient notice to the holders handling them without objection. In *Mendelssohn v Normand Ltd (1970) 1 QB 177;* the attendant gave the plaintiff a ticket with printed conditions on it. The plaintiff had been to this garage many times and he had always been given a ticket with the self same wording. Every time he had put it into his pocket and produced it when he came back for the car. It was held that he may not have read it but that did not matter. It was plainly a contractual document and as he accepted it without objection, he must be taken to have agreed to it.

Similarly, the respondent explained:

> Yes I was a frequent traveller on K.Q. ..... I did not have to explain that was in my bag. I did not know I had to do this. I am a frequent traveller having travelled KQ so many times.

Apparently the respondent has only himself to blame. He used to take everything for granted. The law would not exonerate him.

This brings me to the question as to whether the appellant's conduct was equivalent to wilful misconduct under article 25 of the Convention thus disentitling him to the protection under article 22(2). Mr. Katende clarified that it was incumbent upon the respondent to prove that the luggage had been lost due to the appellant's wilful misconduct. Learned counsel submitted that this was a case of negligence and not wilful misconduct. The appellant took a lot of trouble trying to search for the lost baggage, even to the extent of arranging a trip to Nairobi for the respondent to try and locate it. In counsel's view, this was not conduct

(Continued)

(Continued)

amounting to wilful misconduct. Mr. Katende pointed out that the burden of proof is high and akin to culpable negligence. It was never discharged, he submitted. Mr. Othieno, in my view, did not attempt to counter this.

It has been clearly stated that in a case like this regarding carriage by air, "in order to establish wilful misconduct, a plaintiff must satisfy Court that the person who did the act knew at the time that he was doing something wrong and yet did it notwithstanding or alternatively, that he did it quite recklessly, not caring whether he did the right thing or the wrong thing quite regardless of the effects of what he was doing on the safety of the aircraft and of the passengers—to which should be added their property, for which he was responsible;" *Horaben v British Overseas Airways Corporation (1952) 2 ALL ER 1016.*

I hold the view that the appellants exhibited a high degree of diligence and concern over the respondent's luggage. By arranging a trip for the respondent to try and locate the luggage, the appellant's conduct passed the test of diligence. The letter Ex P3 cannot be regarded as an admission of wilful misconduct. It should not have been put in evidence without the consent of both parties. It can only be used when it contains an offer that has been accepted and also in criminal matters. That being the case the respondent failed to establish wilful misconduct whose burden is high.

I find the wording on the air ticket and the law on the matter so clear that the result is to allow this appeal with costs. The respondent is only entitled to the compensation as stipulated under the Warsaw Convention, of U$ 1120 i.e. U$ 20 per kg of 56 kg lost.

Notes

1. The gender parity index is "the ratio of female to male enrolment ratios." See UNESCO (2006).
2. The classic paper on these concepts was by Akerlof (1970).
3. Non est Factum is the Latin phrase meaning "it is not my deed." The principle permits a signing party to escape performance of the agreement by claiming that the signature on the contract was signed by mistake, without knowledge of its meaning, but was not done so negligently. Such a contract would be void ab initio (USLegal.com, n.d.).
4. *Tatiyia v. Waithaka & K-Rep Bank Limited*, In the High Court of Kenya at Nairobi, Commercial & Admiralty Division, Milimani Law Courts, Civil Case No 315 of 2013. "While the court appreciates the 2nd Defendant's position that the charge was created, perfected and registered strictly in accordance with the law and that the statutory power of sale crystallised, the court cannot ignore the principle of *non est factum* in arriving at a just resolution of this matter. The Plaintiff may have executed the Charge but the question that arises is whether or not his intention was to execute a Charge or a transfer to the 1st Defendant."
5. *Boakyem and Others v. Ansah*. Supreme Court of Ghana, 2nd July, 1963, "As I have already indicated the illiterate persons concerned in this appeal were attesting witnesses only and there is no presumption that an attesting witness has any knowledge of the contents of a document the execution of which he attests; indeed the presumption is the other way round, *and a much heavier onus* therefore rests upon the plaintiff in this appeal to prove that the first defendant and his head of family attested the document by appending their marks thereto with an intelligent knowledge of the fact that the land granted thereby was their stool land and that with that knowledge they consented to its execution in the manner alleged."

6. Similar sentiments were expressed in the case of *Kotokoli and Another v. Sarbah* (High Court, Accra), "However, where the document did not bear a jurat on the face of it but the party who executed it did not object either to it or the transaction which it sought to evidence, that general rule should not be allowed to defeat the document on the mere technical ground of lack of a jurat. In the instant case, the receipt which counsel sought to avoid was issued by one illiterate to another and it bore no jurat but it could be inferred from the evidence that the appellant understood and fully appreciated its meaning and effects and he was therefore bound by its contents. *Waya v. Byrouthy* (1958)" cited.

7. Several countries have codified the Common Law principle to protect illiterates in their dealings with literate parties. See, for example, the efforts in Nigeria that has the following laws in place, The Illiterates Protection Act. Cap 83. Laws of the Federation of Nigeria (1958). The Illiterates Protection Law Cap 64 Eastern Nigeria (1920); The Illiterates Protection Law Cap 51 Northern Nigeria; The Illiterates Protection Law Cap 47 Western Nigeria, and The Illiterates Protection Law Cap 70 Bendel State (Edo & Delta States). See Ayodele (2010).

8. Illiterates Protection Act 1918 (Ch 78) UGANDA.

9. [67.] J. 354 90.—7/1914. E.&S.A.

10. J. 354 B.

11. J. 354 C.

12. J. 354 D.

Questions

1. Would you say the illiterate−literate contractual issues impede or promote economic development?

2. Do you find any differences in the way courts in Ghana, Zambia, Nigeria, and other jurisdictions have interpreted the illiterates' protection laws?

3. Given the low adult literacy rates, how do you ensure that the market participants are making informed rational decisions?

4. What are suggestions to reduce the asymmetric information between literate and illiterate people?

5. Define adverse selection in your own words. Provide an example.

6. Define moral hazard in your own words. Provide an example.

References

Akerlof, G.A., 1970. The market for "Lemons": quality uncertainty and the market mechanism. Q. J. Econ. LXXXIV, 3.

Ayodele, G., 2010. An Overview of the plea of Non est Factum and Section 3 of the Illiterates Protection Law (1994) of Lagos State in Contracts made by Illiterates in Nigeria. The Nigerian Current Law Review 2007−2010. <http://nials-nigeria.org/journals/NCLR1.pdf>.

Huebler, F., 2008. International Education Statistics: Adult Literacy in Sub-Sahara Africa. <http://huebler. blogspot.com/2008/05/literacy.html> (accessed 13.09.10).

Jogwu, C.N.O., 2010. "Adult Illiteracy: The Root of African Underdevelopment." *Education*, Spring 2010. <http://findarticles.com/p/articles/mi_qa3673/is_3_130/ai_n54399185/> (accessed 13.09.10).

UNESCO Institute for Statistics, 2006. Education for All (EFA) in Least Developed Countries. <http://unesdoc. unesco.org/images/0014/001472/147259M.pdf> (accessed 13.09.10).

USLegal.com, n.d. Non Est Factum Law and Legal Definition. <http://definitions.uslegal.com/n/non-est-factum/>.

CHAPTER 6

Commercial Law

Keywords: Commercial law; sale of goods; market-led growth; structural adjustment programs (SAPs) Sale of Goods Act; Trademarks and Patents Act; warranties

6.1 Introduction

In response to poor economic performance in the 1970s and early 1980s, almost all countries in sub-Saharan Africa (SSA) embarked on structural adjustment programs (SAPs) in the mid-1980s. One principal component of the SAP was a commitment to market-led growth. The private sector was declared to be the "engine of growth," and government interference in markets was curtailed along with the privatization of state-owned enterprises. The success of the market-led growth policy is critically dependent on the availability of private investment which, in turn, is dependent on an enabling investment climate.[1]

Countries in SSA have worked hard to create an enabling environment for investors. According to the United Nations Conference on Trade and Development (UNCTAD), countries made regulatory changes in response to the change in economic conditions in 2007 to promote foreign direct investments (FDI), and "the number of changes more favourable to FDI clearly exceeded those that were less favourable" (UNCTAD, 2009). The positive policies "accounted for 75 per cent of the 16 measures adopted in Africa, and the 47 countries of sub-Saharan Africa attracted 73% in 2008, up from 64% in 2007" (*Id.* p. 42.). The response to the regulatory changes has been positive as FDI inflows to the SSA region "registered a net increase in inflows, from $22 billion in 2007 to $30 billion" (*Id.* at p. 45.). Despite the impressive performance, potential investors and academics have expressed concerns about the negative impact of poor contract enforcement on expanded market interaction.[2]

6.2 Commercial Courts in SSA Countries

As part of the transition to market-led growth policy, several SSA countries established commercial courts to deal with business-related litigation. Details of the legislative history of the commercial court in Ghana is described since the legislative histories in establishing

F.O. Boadu: Agricultural Law and Economics in Sub-Saharan Africa.
DOI: http://dx.doi.org/10.1016/B978-0-12-801771-5.00006-X

the commercial courts in the various SSA countries point to a common theme to facilitate efficient and speedy resolution of business disputes.[3]

Ghana established commercial courts in 2005 to specifically deal with general commercial litigation, for example, issues related to banking and finance, the restructuring of commercial debt, and intellectual property (Sandra Cofie, 2007). This was to reduce the time spent by businesses in seeking enforcement of contracts in the courts.[4] The rules establishing the commercial courts laid out clear guidelines and procedures to be followed in dealing with commercial cases.[5] As one legal expert succinctly puts it, "time is the greatest factor that can cause the success or the failure of any business, it is therefore necessary that commercial disputes are resolved quickly" (Beecham, 2010). The *Sales of Goods Act* enacted in various countries in SSA is an attempt to define and enforce property rights to facilitate market interaction.

6.3 Sale of Goods

The primary law governing commercial transactions in Ghana is the *Sales of Goods Act, 1962* (Act 137). The Act is similar to the English Sale of Goods Act, 1893, except that Ghana's law covers both sale of goods and hire-purchase contracts. Also, international conventions such as the United Nations Convention on Contracts for the International Sale of Goods (the Vienna Convention) are a part of the legal and regulatory regime governing the sale of goods in Ghana. Prior to enacting Act 137, the sale of goods in Ghana was based on the common law and customary law.[6] It must be noted that the enactment of Act 137 did not oust the application of the common law to sales transactions.[7]

The *Sale of Goods Act* defines a contract for the sale of goods as "a contract whereby the seller agrees to transfer the property in the goods to a buyer for consideration called the price, consisting wholly or partly of money.[8] A "Good" under the Act refers to anything that can be moved for sale. This means the sale of land will not come under the Act, but the sale of corn grown and harvested from the land will be governed by the Act.

The Sale of Goods Act provides considerable flexibility to parties in a contract. For example, the Act states that "the sale of a good may be in writing, or by word of mouth, or partly in writing and partly by word of mouth, or may be implied from the conduct of the parties."[9] A safe rule is for parties engaged in large commercial dealings to reduce their understanding to writing to avoid ambiguities.

Even though the Sales of Goods Act is intended to facilitate contractual interaction by reducing transaction costs, the question of who is bound by the Act can sometimes raise some difficult questions for courts. For example, certain provisions apply to merchants only and the issue arises as to who is a merchant. Specifically, are farmers merchants under the *Sale of Goods Act*? The Act defines a merchant as "an agent having in the ordinary course of his business as an agent authority to sell goods, or to consign goods for sale, or to buy goods, or to raise money on the security of goods."[10] Courts in Ghana have not addressed this issue but the Supreme Court in the State of Texas, USA, concluded that farmers are merchants within the meaning of the Uniform Commercial Code of Texas.[11]

The two cases, *VEHRAD Transport & Haulage Co. Ltd. v MISR. Co. for Trailers & Transport Means and Barclays Bank Ltd.* (Ghana) and *BEKA (Pty) Ltd. v Universal Builders Botswana (Pty) Ltd.* (Botswana) discuss the issue of contract performance and the obligation to deliver the exact goods contracted for under the Sale of Goods Act. The complex issue of warranties is discussed in the cases of *Krane Construction Ltd. v RANA Motors & Metal Works Eng. Co. Ltd* (Ghana) and *A. E. Machinjiri T/A Mapanga Passenger Services v Leyland DAF (Malawi) Limited* (Malawi). Another Malawi case, *David Castledine t/a Royal Oak Cleaners v. David Gatrell t/a Office Depot* addresses the measure of damages under the Sales of Goods Act. The Uganda case, *Abdul Basit Sengooba and Ors. v Stanbic Bank Ltd.* deals with the problem of contracts involving minors.

VEHRAD Transport & Haulage Co. Ltd v MISR. Co. for Trailers & Transport Means and Barclays Bank Ltd

High Court (Commercial Division)
Suit No. RPC/17/08, October 26th 2009
Cecilia H. Sowah, J.

Facts: The plaintiffs case is that in January 2007, it ordered six [6] trailers and four [4] tankers to specification from 1st Defendant, a company based in Egypt. The tankers were supplied first. After they had been cleared plaintiff says it discovered several variances with the agreed specifications. Plaintiff says it also discovered when the trailers arrived that they also did not meet all specifications. However the trailers were also cleared and put in a customs bonded warehouse because they were attracting demurrage. The 1st Defendant's attention had been drawn to the variances and it had agreed to correct them. Although, the 1st Defendant sent workers to Ghana, they did not complete the rectifications. It is also alleged that 1st Defendant failed to deliver a container of spare parts.

In its defence, the 1st defendant asserts that the vehicles conformed to the agreed specification. The defendant denies accepting that there were repairs to be done on the tankers and trailers and sending workers to rectify any defects. It is contended that the plaintiff had a statutory duty to ensure that pre-destination inspection and destination inspection were conducted on all the items before actual shipment and clearing of the goods at the destination port of Tema. It is also contended that the plaintiff could clear the goods because these inspections had been done and plaintiff had been satisfied that the items conformed to specification. 1st defendant therefore challenges the inspection alleged to have been carried outside the statutory requirements by an independent company.

(Continued)

(Continued)

The 2nd Defendant is plaintiff's bankers with whom letters of credit were opened for the two consignments. Payment for the tankers was effected before they were delivered, but plaintiff is seeking to stop the bank from paying out the US$159,400.00 for the trailers. The 2nd defendant filed a Statement of Defence stating that by the agreement between plaintiff and 1st defendant, it (2nd Defendant) can only remit the sum for the trailers after plaintiff has provided the necessary supporting documents. That as this condition precedent for transferring the funds has not been satisfied by the plaintiff, it has not been possible to transfer the funds.

Plaintiff raised several issues among which was whether or not 1st Defendant failed to deliver the tankers and trailers in accordance with the technical specifications given by plaintiff and so is in breach of the sale agreement.

Opinion: From all the evidence before court, the fundamental issue to be determined is whether technical specifications were agreed and whether 1st defendant is in breach of contract by failing to supply the vehicles to such specification. Ghassan Hussein testified that Plaintiff had a contract with Shell Ghana Ltd and that the 1st defendant was informed to produce the vehicles to conform with Shells' [SOPAF] specifications. He said the parties communicated mostly by E-mails. He tendered E-mails exchanged between 17th October 2006 and 16th June 2007 as exhibits A—A7. In exhibit A5, the plaintiff had stressed that the defendant should *"PLEASE FOLLOW SOPAF SPEC"*. Also in evidence are pro-forma invoices exhibits C1, C2 and D1 dated 13th October 2006 which defendant sent to the plaintiff in respect of the tankers and trailers. Mr. Hussein's testimony was that the plaintiff told the defendant what she needed and based on this the defendant prepared the pro-forma invoices which contain the specifications agreed. These important facts were admitted by Mr Abaza in his examination in chief. He said:

> We spoke a lot of times and they came to Egypt, they took specifications and returned them and asked for new specifications, it took a long time then they said they needed pro-forma invoice.

Defence counsel argues that as the plaintiff failed to lead evidence on the details of the SOPAF specifications, therefore no such specifications exist. I think that such an important issue ought properly to have been raised during the trial and not for the first time in counsels' address. I find it strange that the defendant never questioned the existence of these specifications in their E-mails or during the trial. The only conclusion I draw from defendants' failure to challenge the existence of the so called SOPAF specifications is that it is apparently well known in the industry. I am satisfied on the evidence and I find that specifications were agreed and that the pro-forma invoices which the defendant issued and which contain detailed specifications were based on previous discussions, and indicative of an agreement on the technical specifications for the vehicles.

The next question I will consider is whether the agreed specifications were met?

Exhibits F and G are the reports of inspections conducted by Road Safety Ltd. In his examination in chief, Mr. Hussein described this company as a company *contracted by Shell to make sure that all tankers and trucks conform with SOPAF specifications and standard.*

(Continued)

(Continued)

Plaintiff contracted this company to inspect the tankers and trailers and identify the variances based on the specifications contained in the pro-forma invoices.

I found PW1 Michael Kosi Dedei, the Managing Director of Road Safety Ltd to be a very credible witness. He gave detailed testimony of the discrepancies that he found and explained the significance of all the deviations. For example in respect of the 10 ton axle tankers which the defendant supplied instead of 14 ton axles, he testified as follows:

A. The 10 tons axle basically means that, that axle should be able to carry a maximum load of 10 tons that is different from when you say an axle should be able to carry a 14 tons axle load. This means that the strength of the axles is different.

In respect of the tankers, the specifications called for two fenders at the front coupling with 15 pins. They were not there. He explained their significance as follows:

A. Basically what it means is that some electrical attachment cannot be made. When you have the trailer and the head you need certain electrical signal to be sent to some part of the trailer, now depending on how many signals you want to send to that trailer you need a certain number of pins to send that signal to the trailer in terms of electrical signals, and if you don't have that [sic] pins you cannot send that signals to the trailer.

I find that the reports of the independent inspector were done systematically and in the same format as the specifications on the pro-forma invoices so that the variations are easy to see. In its statement of defence, the defendant had asserted that the vehicles met the agreed specifications. However, Mr Abaza in his evidence and under cross-examination admitted that hoses were not supplied for the tanker contrary to the agreement, that a 60 liter water tank was installed instead of a 150 liter tank, and that 8 twist locks were provided instead of 12. These show, and I accordingly find that the 1st defendant failed to deliver the tankers and trailers according to the agreed specifications. There were other issues with the vehicles like peeling paint, side and rear lamps, bumpers not installed, hoses not supplied etc. Instead of a 150 metric tank for water, the defendant supplied plaintiff with 60 metrics. Plaintiff's representative testified that they also transport sodium cyanide which is a hazardous chemical, and a bigger water tank is required in case of spillage to be able to wash the product away.

Whilst some of the variations do not appear to me to be significant in that they can be fixed, and plaintiff has in fact admitted to making repairs, it is apparent that some of the variations are significant. For example only 8 of the requested 12 twist locks on the trailer were supplied. The evidence is that the 12 are necessary for weight distribution and safety if the trailer has to carry one 20 foot container. Thus plaintiff has been denied the option of carrying a single 20 foot container on its trailers. Also, supplying a 13 ton and 10 ton axles instead of the requested 14 ton axles obviously means the loads the vehicles can carry are restricted.

In respect of the 10 ton axles that were supplied, Mr Abaza explained as follows:

We supplied to them 14 tons axle but it is written on it 10 tons axle because it is according to laws in Egypt, and here too it must be written 11.5 tons

(Continued)

(Continued)

Defense witness put forward a similar explanation although he, unlike Plaintiff witness had not examined the trailers. I must say that I find these assertions to be most unconvincing. If this claim was fact, it would be a material fact to be pleaded but it was not pleaded. Both defence witnesses also admitted that 10 tons was clearly embossed on the trailers. It would thus take more than the mere say so of the witnesses to displace the prima facie evidence that the trailers were 10 ton axles.

Both witnesses confirmed the seriousness of the variance between 10 and 14 tons. When defense witness was cross-examined on the issue, he stated that an axle can break if a greater load is carried, and that to change from a 10 to a 14 ton axle, you will have to order a 14 ton axle and a suspension. By all standards therefore, these are serious deviations from the agreed specifications and I hold that they amount to a fundamental breach of agreement.

The *Sale of Goods Act 1962 Act 137* provides at sections 11 that:

> In a contract for the sale of goods by description whether or not the sale is by sample as well as by description, there is an implied condition that the goods shall correspond exactly with the description.

Also, section 55 of the Act provides as follows:

> s. 55—Damages for Breach of Condition or Warranty.
> Where the seller is guilty of a breach of his fundamental obligation or of a condition or warranty of the contract the buyer may maintain an action against the seller for damages for the breach complained of or may set up a claim to such damages in diminution or extinction of the price.

These mean that a buyer may still maintain an action for damages even where the goods have been delivered. He may even under section 49 reject the goods for a breach which is not of a trivial nature. The plaintiffs' action for damages for breach of contract is therefore maintainable. I share plaintiff counsels view that the simpler course to take will be compensate the plaintiff in damages. The evidence also shows that such discrepancies as changing the 10 ton axles to 14 ton axles will be difficult to correct.

Section 56 of the Sale of Goods Act provides that the measure of damages in an action under section 55 is the loss which could reasonably have been foreseen by the seller at the time when the contract was made as likely to result from his breach of contract. In the instant case, as a result of defendant's breach, the trailers had to be warehoused whilst the defendant arranged for its men to come down to correct the defects. The defendant admitted at the trial that plaintiff complained about variations and its men were sent down to attempt to rectify some of the variations but did not complete work. The defendant should have foreseen the damage to the plaintiff.

Judgment: In conclusion judgment is hereby entered for the plaintiff. The plaintiff is hereby adjudged to recover from the 1st defendant US$68,840 which is 20% of the purchase price of the tankers and trailers. It is hereby further ordered that the 2nd defendant do pay the said sum of US$68,840 to the plaintiff from the amount being held by it and the balance remitted to the 1st defendant.

Plaintiff is awarded costs of GH₵8,000.00

BEKA (Pty) Ltd v Universal Builders Botswana (Pty) Ltd

High Court of Botswana, Lobatse
CC-286-04, June 2008.

LESETEDI, J:

1. The plaintiff's claim is for the sum of ZAR 73 602 or the Pula equivalent, being in respect of goods sold and allegedly delivered to the defendant. The issues raised herein are the rights and obligations of each of the parties to a purchase and sale agreement. Although the plaintiff's particulars of claim indicate the goods sold and delivered to be bathroom accessories it is clear from the evidence that the said goods were specified type of luminaires.

2. The background of this case is quite brief and I will henceforth proceed to outline it. At all material times the plaintiff was a manufacturer and supplier of luminaires. The amount claimed is in respect of goods delivered purportedly as part of an order or orders made by the defendant to the plaintiff for delivery of luminaires.

3. The defendant denies that the goods delivered were the ones it ordered. It argues that as the delivered goods are not what was ordered, plaintiff is not entitled to payment.

4. The plaintiff called one witness a certain Mr. Carlese who was its sales representative at the time of giving evidence. He had been in the employ of the plaintiff for about a year and some months at the time he gave evidence. He was not in the employee of the plaintiff when the transactions leading to the dispute took place. The defendant on the other hand called one of its directors a certain Mr. Jamali who represented the defendant at all material times and another officer of the defendant who also played the role at the time.

5. The following emerges from the plaintiff and the defendant's evidence and it is common cause. On 15th July 2002, the plaintiff dispatched a quotation to the defendant offering its products by description and the prices listed thereto. Among the products listed in the quotation were:

BEKA R/LBR 436 4X36W RECESSED FLUORESCENT C/W LAMPS WHITE LOUVRE AND
BEKA R/LBR 418 4X18W RECESSED FLUORESCENT C/W LAMPS WHITE LOUVRE.

Based on the quotation the defendant made an order of the goods including the ones specifically described above.

6. In November 2002, plaintiff delivered luminaires similar to the quoted ones but described as RDP/440/612 W 3C/WHITE LOUVRE.

7. The defendant's case is that what was delivered is not what was ordered but products of low quality which are locally available at a much cheaper price than what was charged by the plaintiff. The plaintiff contends otherwise. Through its witness Mr. Carlese, plaintiff stated that both products are of good quality and meet the SABS specification standards. The issue for determination therefore is whether the goods quoted for were the ones delivered.

8. But before dealing with that issue, there is an issue of misrepresentation raised by the defendant. In its plea and in the evidence of Mr. Jamali, the defendant maintains that prior to the quotation being issued by the plaintiff, the plaintiff's then salesman a certain

(Continued)

(Continued)

Mr. Matthew De Jongh approached the defendant's officers including Mr. Jamali himself and marketed BEKA produced luminaries. According to Mr. Jamali, Mr. De Jongh represented that the plaintiff manufactured and supplied very good quality light fittings. These fittings did not come cheap though as they cost more than ordinary fittings of the same range. Mr. De Jongh further represented to the defendant that the light fittings which the defendant obtained from a local dealer though much cheaper, were low quality fittings compared to those produced by the plaintiff. Mr. Jamali himself was aware of the good reputation of the lights produced by the plaintiff and was prepared to pay the quoted price for them. In his evidence, he in fact referred to such lights as the Rolls Royce of light fittings. Mr. Carlese did confirm the good reputation of the plaintiff's products. He could however not say whether at the material time, the plaintiff produced the light fittings quoted for.

9. It was on the basis of the representations by Mr. De Jongh that the defendant made an order of the quoted products. It is Mr. Jamali's evidence that the word "BEKA" that precedes the descriptions of the luminaries, is a reference to the manufacturer. It is accepted by both parties that what was delivered was not BEKA produced luminaires but were products produced by a different company by the name of R & S.

10. Close to a year after delivery of the products the defendant having paid for some products other than the ones in dispute, the plaintiff wrote a letter of demand on the 21st October 2003 authored by one Mr. Koster its Financial Director. The relevant part of that letter reads:

I wish to remind you that the goods referred to on the above invoice, were supplied and delivered, on Universal Builders (Botswana) (Pty) Ltd's specific, and written request/order form.

Quite clearly this contention by Mr. Koster is not correct in the light of the admitted differences in the quotation and invoice.

11. In answer to the plaintiff's demand, the defendant on the 4th of November 2003 wrote back:

"I kindly request you to discuss the entire transaction from the beginning till date with your Mr. Matthew De Jongh, Sales Executive. It was clearly understood by us that the price we agreed and the material we would receive from yourselves will be of good quality and not imported from China, Taiwan etc. Your sales representative agreed and delivered the material quoted does not correspond to the quality material [sic]. We also requested you to inspect the same and take them back.

Further the price you have charged in Rand 634.5/Unit which otherwise can be obtained at P122.00 from the reputed local retailer [sic]. We also came to know that you have purchased from the local reputed retailer and sold it to us, which we feel is a breach of trust and the support we had given you since 2001.

Under the circumstances it is not possible to pay Invoice No. 125574 at the price charged by yourselves.

Thank you,

Yours faithfully

Jamali Director"

(Continued)

(Continued)

12. In the reply to the above letter, the plaintiff reiterates that the products supplied were in accordance with the quotation. It denies that the goods supplied were from China or Taiwan but argues that they are of a South African manufacture and of excellent quality bearing the relevant SABS mark. The response also denies that the goods were purchased from a Botswana supplier.

13. During the trial, the defendant conceded that the goods were not Chinese make but produced by a South African company. It nonetheless continued to contend that those goods were of cheaper quality than the BEKA lights. It also continued to argue that they were not the goods ordered or quoted for. Further, the defendant maintained its position that what was delivered was easily available locally at very cheap prices.

14. Mr. De Jongh has not given any evidence to gainsay the defendant's evidence regarding the alleged representations and the defendant's early rejection of the goods. Mr. Carlese wasn't able to deny or shed any light on any communication between the defendant's officers and Mr. De Jongh. He clearly could not do so as these were not within his personal knowledge and there were no records thereof. But then the defendant had always contended, as is clear from the letter of 12th November 2003, that there had been discussions with Mr. De Jongh regarding the query on the delivery. That notwithstanding, no denial ever came forth from Mr. De Jongh even after the plaintiff received the defendant's letter of 4th November 2003.

15. The first question to address is whether, as pleaded by the defendant, there was a misrepresentation by De Jongh when he represented that the plaintiff dealt in genuine electrical goods of better quality than what defendant was then buying from a local dealer which the plaintiff was willing to supply to the defendant at a reasonable price. The defendant's evidence that it bought on the basis of that representation has not been seriously dealt with by the plaintiff. It is also not seriously disputed that the plaintiff manufactured good quality fittings which were of better quality than what the defendant had been obtaining locally. The question is whether De Jongh's representations that the plaintiff would supply the luminaries ordered amounted to a mispresentation.

16. It is pertinent to note at the outset that no replication was filed by the plaintiff to deny the plea of misrepresentation or to explain away the representations ascribed to De Jongh.

17. A party who has been persuaded by a misrepresentation to enter into a contract or to agree to terms to which he would otherwise not have agreed, is entitled to a relief whether the misrepresentation was fraudulent, negligent or innocent.
   See, JOUBERT'S LAWSA, First Re Issue, Vol 5(1) p201. Defendant pleads that the misrepresentation was fraudulent. But as it was stated in *Sampson v Union Rhodesia Wholesale Ltd (in Liquidation) 1929 AD 468 @ 480,*

   It makes no difference whether the person who induced the contract knew at the time he made the representation that it was false. The defendant is entitled to succeed if he can establish that the representation of the plaintiff was a material one and that he entered into the contract on the faith of such representation.

18. A contract induced by misrepresentation is voidable. See, *Moshawa Holdings (Pty) Ltd v John Burrows & Partners* [1994] BLR 70 (CA) @ 74. On this ground the defendant would succeed.

(Continued)

(Continued)

19. The other issue however is whether even in the absence of a misrepresentation, the delivery that was made was in terms of the order which was premised on the quotation.

20. A buyer's main object in entering into a contract of purchase and sale is to acquire the thing sold. It is of the essence of the contract that the seller is obliged to make the thing sold available to the buyer. See, Joubert's LAWSA, Vol 24 para 59.

21. A tender of goods other than those which were sold entitles the buyer to cancel the contract. LAWSA Vol 24 above citing *AYOB & Co. v Clouts [1925] WLD 199.*

22. It is also clear that if a specific thing is sold, the seller is obliged to make available that precise thing and not another thing even though the thing tendered is similar to the one sold. THE LAW OF SALE AND LEASE Third Edition AJ Kerr page 163. Where the goods delivered are not the ones ordered the purchaser cannot be compelled to agree to any terms other than those initially specifically agreed. *Robertson Municipality v Jansen [1944] CPD 526 @ 542.*

23. The defendant has in its submission also referred to a number of authorities to the same effect. See, MACKEURTAN, SALE OF GOODS IN SOUTH AFRICA, 5TH EDITION PAGE 48, 142−143.

24. In my view the plaintiff has failed on a balance of probabilities to show that it delivered to the plaintiff the goods ordered. The mere fact that the goods sold by R & S may be similar to those quoted for, does not in the absence of acceptance by the defendant, constitute delivery. It is clear from the defendant's letter of the 4th of November 2003, that upon realising that the delivery was of the wrong products, the defendant demanded proper delivery. These contentions were never denied by the person who was involved in the communication by the defendant.

25. In the absence of proper delivery of what was ordered, plaintiff's claim must fail and it is dismissed with costs.

Krane Construction Ltd v RANA Motors & Metal Works Eng. Co. Ltd

High Court (Commercial Division, Accra, Ghana)
Suit No. OCC/77/08
July 17TH 2009
Cecilia H. Sowah, J.

Fact: Plaintiff is a building construction company. Its case is that on 8th February 2007, it purchased a brand new Mazda Swaraj single cabin (2 × 4) 6 ton pick-up vehicle from the defendant at a cost of US$23,000.00. The vehicle was covered by a 12 calendar month warranty. It is alleged that after using the vehicle for 3 months and covering less than 12,000 km, it developed a mechanical fault which the defendant attributed to a damaged piston within the engine. Plaintiff says it was agreed between the parties that defendant would install a brand new engine to replace the faulty one. However, the defendant unilaterally decided to overhaul the faulty engine. The plaintiff has refused to accept the vehicle and sued for *inter alia* general Damages for breach of warranty.

(Continued)

(Continued)

The defendant in its statement of defence admits giving plaintiff a warranty of 12 months and admits that a mechanical fault due to a damaged piston occurred but says that the warranty was limited only to repairs. Defendant also denies that it agreed with plaintiff on 15th August 2008 that a brand new engine would be fitted for plaintiff, or that it was under any obligation to do so. Defendant pleads that the vehicle was repaired and plaintiff duly notified so denies that plaintiff was denied the use of its vehicle and is entitled to its claims for loss of use.

Opinion: In this instant case the basic facts relied on by plaintiff are admitted by defendant and have already been found as fact. The issue in contention is the terms of the warranty. The plaintiff denies defendant's assertion that the warranty was limited to repairs or that they had been so informed by the defendant. If the testimony of defendant's witness is to be believed, no warranty document from the manufacturer came with the vehicle. The question then, as rightly posed by plaintiff's counsel in his written address is — if there was no warranty document, what warranty did witness purportedly explain to plaintiff? What terms of warranty did the defendant purport to rely on to explain the terms?

In my view, the onus was on the defendant to prove the terms of the warranty. It is my view that a reasonable doubt as to the existence of a limited warranty or being informed of a limited warranty had been raised and the burden of producing evidence sufficient to avoid a ruling against it on this issue shifted to the defendant. The defendant failed to introduce any evidence in this regard, except for stating that a new engine was not covered by the warranty of this made in India vehicle. I think it is an undeniable fact of life that to attract customers, its natural to put forward only the favourable terms of the transaction in order to convince the buyer to make a purchase. As DW2 said, "So, as the seller, to convince the customer to buy I have explain to you what the warranty covers and the benefit".

I think there is no denying the fact that the performance of an overhauled engine cannot match a new engine especially considering the type of work i.e. construction, that plaintiff was engaged in. I cannot therefore accept defendant's contention that the overhauled engine is as good as new. I have considered defendant's unproven assertion that replacing the engine is not covered by the warranty on this vehicle, and it seems to me defendant is seeking to evade its contractual responsibility.

Section 13(1)(a) of the Sale of Goods Act 1962, Act 137 provides that there is an implied condition that goods are free from defects which are not declared or known to the buyer before or at the time when the contract is made. The condition is not an implied condition only where the buyer has examined the goods, or in respect of defects which should have been revealed by the examination, or in the case of sale by sample, or where the goods are not sold by the seller in the ordinary course of the seller's business, in respect of defects which the seller was not, and could not reasonably have been aware. These three provisos [that is, subsection (a)(i)(ii)(iii) of section 13 of Act 137] are inapplicable on the facts of this instant case.

By Section 49(1)(b) of Act 137, a buyer has the right to reject goods where the seller is guilty of breach, not being of a trivial nature, of a condition of the contract. As I have already

(Continued)

(Continued)

found, the defect in this case is not a trivial defect but a major engine problem. I accordingly hold that plaintiff is entitled to reject the goods that is, the truck in this case, for breach of implied condition. The defendant alleges that plaintiff's driver authorised the repair of the truck. It is however clear from exhibit 1 that plaintiff's driver just narrated what was wrong with the vehicle to defendant's mechanic. The engine oil, vibration when the truck was started, and pulling and smoke were to be checked. There is nowhere in that exhibit where it stated that after checking or diagnosing the faults, repairs were to be effected. Neither plaintiff nor defendant's mechanic knew the exact trouble with the vehicle at the time the vehicle was sent to the workshop. So it is most unlikely that plaintiff authorised opening of the engine to repair the broken piston.

The evidence led for plaintiff shows that they did not even reject the whole of the truck but merely asked for the engine to be replaced. I think it was a very reasonable request. Generally, warranties on brand new cars are usually described as limited warranties and cover repair and replacement of any original component that is found to be defective in material or workshop under normal use, except where items are specially stated as "Not Covered" by the General warranty. It is described as a limited warranty because normal maintenance service, normal deterioration or wear, and damage resulting from the owners' negligence etc are not covered.

Judgment: In conclusion, I hereby enter judgment for the plaintiff to recover from the defendant as follows:

1. A replacement of the vehicle with a brand new one within 3 months.
2. Failing 1 above, or in the alternative, a refund of the purchase price of U$23,000 plus interest thereon at the prevailing rate from 23rd July 2007 to date of payment.
3. General damages of GH¢8,000.00.
4. Costs of GH¢1,000.00.

A. E. Machinjiri T/A Mapanga Passenger Services v Leyland DAF (Malawi) Limited

High Court, Malawi — Principal Registry, Blantyre
Civil Cause No. of 2000
14th day of February 2006 at Blantyre.

Chimsula Phiri, J

Judgment

Chimasula Phiri J,

The plaintiff's claim is for damages for breach of contract in respect of implied warranty as to fitness and merchantability of goods; loss of income from the said breach; interest charges in respect of financing facilities and further consequential relief for causing or **inducing** the plaintiff to breach his contract with the Leasing and Finance Company of Malawi Limited.

(Continued)

(Continued)

The defendant denies the claim made by the plaintiff and prays for the dismissal of the action.

The Issues for Determination

1. Whether at the time of the contract the defendant knew the particular purpose for which the plaintiff required the bus?
2. Whether it was express or implied condition of the said contract that the bus shall be reasonably fit for the purpose it was acquired?
3. Whether or not the defendant has breached any express or implied term of the contract?
4. Whether or not the plaintiff has suffered any loss or damage and the nature and extent of any such damage or loss?
5. Whether the sale of the bus was by description.
6. Whether there was an implied condition and/or a warranty that the bus should correspond to the said description and be merchantable under the said contract?

Standard of Proof

The standard required in civil cases is generally expressed as proof on a balance of probabilities. "If the evidence is such that the tribunal can say: We think it more probable than not, the burden is discharged, but if the probabilities are equal it is not." Denning J in Miller vs Minister of Pensions *[1947] ALL E.R. 372; 373, 374.*

The Evidence

The plaintiff called one witness while the defendant summoned two witnesses. These witnesses adopted their witness statements and tendered in evidence documentary evidence. The evidence of the plaintiff was that on 23rd August 1999 the defendant offered to sell an Aeolous Coach Mini Bus to the plaintiff at the price of K2,500,000. The plaintiff accepted the offer. The plaintiff contacted Leasing and Finance of Malawi Company Limited (LFC) for a loan facility to be used in purchasing the said minibus. On 5th November 1999 LFC granted the plaintiff a loan of K2,500,000. The loan attracted interest of 50% per annum. The loan sum was paid to the defendant. The sole purpose of purchasing the bus was for the plaintiff to use it as passenger carrying business which fact the plaintiff claims to have made known to the defendant. Part of the money realised from the business was to be used for repayment of the loan.

The plaintiff stated that he noticed that there was demand for transport in terms of luxury travel between Lilongwe and Blantyre since the only coach service was provided by Stagecoach Malawi Ltd which had over-aged vehicles and constantly experiencing breakdowns. The plaintiff thought of buying a new bus which would serve those who desired to travel in executive class between Blantyre and Lilongwe.

He took the bus from the defendant in December 1999 and the plaintiff alleges that shortly afterwards some faults were discovered. In February 2000 the bus was returned to the defendant for repairs. Initial faults were air-locking in the fuel system, reverse gear hardness, improper adjustment to brake system and malfunctioning of the electrical system. The bus

(Continued)

(Continued)

remained in the defendant's garage until 3rd July 2000 when the plaintiff collected it for use. On 12th July 2000 the bus was again returned to the defendant's garage after developing faults relating to brakes, electrical system and excessive consumption of engine oil. The plaintiff collected the bus from the defendant's garage on 14th July 2000 after being assured by the defendant that the fault on the bus had been rectified. However, on 15th July 2000 the bus was taken back to the defendant's garage when the plaintiff discovered that the bus could not operate. When the plaintiff checked on progress on the bus on 17th July 2000 he was told that the gear box had been removed to rectify an inner problem. Further he was told that the high oil consumption could not be rectified.

On 8th August 2000 the plaintiff wrote to the defendant telling them that he was no longer interested in the bus as it had proved to be not commercially viable. On the other hand on 28th September 2000 Leasing and Finance Company terminated the lease agreement with the plaintiff on account of his failure to service his loan account for a period of 10 months which by then had accumulated to over K3,373,544.35. The plaintiff commenced this action because the defendant was not willing to compensate the plaintiff. The plaintiff stated that before taking delivery of the bus in December 1999, the defendant presented it to the Road Traffic Department for Certificate of Fitness and Registration formalities. The plaintiff applied for Road Service Permit and also took out a Comprehensive Insurance Cover.

In cross-examination the court was asked to take judicial notice of Civil cause 3659 of 2002 — *Leyland DAF (MW) Ltd v Mapanga Transport*; Civil Cause 2738 of 2002 — *Leyland DAF (MW) Ltd v Mapanga Transport* and Civil Cause 86 of 2003 — *Leyland DAF(MW) Ltd v Christobell Machinjiri*. The plaintiff agreed that Mapanga Passenger Service is not a limited liability company. The plaintiff indicated that the correct date of delivery of the bus is mid-December 1999. The plaintiff expressed his dissatisfaction in the way COF test is conducted. However, the plaintiff conceded that the Road Traffic Directorate would not issue a COF to a vehicle which is not fit to be on the road. The plaintiff further admitted that the defendant sent its Foreman with the bus to the Road Traffic Directorate for COF test. He also admitted that Exhibit D1 was a record for Mapanga Coachline registration number BL 5155. The plaintiff stated that he had employed a driver who was driving this bus and it was the same driver who was taking it to the defendant for repairs.

The plaintiff stated that he had 5 passenger service vehicles and all these were generating an income. If one of the vehicles broke down, the plaintiff would still generate income with the other buses. The plaintiff explained that an air-lock happens as a result of several factors including blockage of fuel passage, clogged fuel filters and dirty fuel tank. Whenever there is an air-lock, the engine does not receive the required amount of fuel for it to perform. He denied that in January 2000 the air-lock was caused because the vehicle was run on empty fuel tank. However, the plaintiff was quick to admit that he was not in the vehicle at the material time. Similarly, when the defendant's mechanics came to rectify the air-lock problem, the plaintiff was not present. The plaintiff indicated that he holds Grade III Motor Vehicle Mechanic Certificate as well as qualifications in general mechanical engineering. Before he took delivery of the bus it was shown to him when it was in the bonded warehouse. He was

(Continued)

(Continued)

shown the interior and exterior of the bus. He stated that the defendant pressed for payment so that the bus could be redeemed from the bonded warehouse.

As a result, the plaintiff asked Leasing and Finance Company to release the funds to the defendant before the plaintiff test-drove the bus. The plaintiff had the chance to test-drive it only at the time the bus was delivered to him. The plaintiff admitted that he did not specify to the defendant the type of coach that he wanted. The plaintiff stated that there was service warranty for 6 months given by the defendant. However, the bus was never delivered for such routine service because it was frequently breaking down and calling for repairs. The plaintiff denied that the bus is operating on the Mulanje-Muloza Road and he does not remember when the vehicle went off the road. The plaintiff stated that the air-lock problem was in January 2000 and the defendant gave back the vehicle to the plaintiff in February 2000 but no later than end of same month he took it back to the defendant for repair service.

The plaintiff indicated that he had his own mechanics who were maintaining his fleet. The plaintiff conceded that according to the Exhibits in court it is correct that the defendant never worked on the engine of the bus because it never developed an engine fault or problem. In re-examination the plaintiff insisted that the bus had continuous problems and was always in the possession of the defendant for repairs. The plaintiff indicated that he abandoned the LL—BT route and opted for the BT—Mulanje route when the bus proved that it could not stand a long journey without inconveniencing passengers.

The first witness for the defendant was Henry Jentala Nthukwa. He works for the defendant as an Auto-Electrician and Workshop Foreman. He joined in March 1976. He stated that the plaintiff bought an Aeolous bus registration BL 5155. Preparation Delivery Inspection (PDI) was done by the defendant in October 1999. The bus was then later delivered to the plaintiff. The bus came back to the defendant's workshop in January 2000 after a breakdown on the road. One of the mechanics was assigned to go to the breakdown recovery near Kamuzu Stadium. The mechanic came back and reported that the bus had run out of fuel. The mechanic came back to the workshop, collected fuel and went back to fill the tank and did bleeding of the air filled fuel system and the vehicle was back on the road.

The vehicle came again in May 2000 for replacement of bumper stop rubbers. The bus came again in July 2000 with problem of oils showing on the engine. The oil sump guard bolts were tightened by a mechanic. Since July 2000 the vehicle came back in June 2002 with brake failure problem. This was rectified and the plaintiff collected it. Later the plaintiff came with the bus again with a slave cylinder problem. It was removed and replaced. Since June 2002 the bus has never been taken back to the defendant's workshop but it is seen plying its trade. He stated that the faults which the plaintiff pointed out were serviceable or rectifiable and were actually rectified. Every time the faults were rectified the plaintiff took delivery of the bus. He stated that he has relatives in Mulanje and when he went to visit them in 2002 and mid-2004 he saw the bus carrying passengers. Further, the plaintiff still goes to the defendant to buy spare parts.

(Continued)

(Continued)

In cross-examination he stated that he holds a Form 4 MSCE certificate, Grade I Auto-Electrical Certificate, Advanced Certificate in Electrical Technology and Grade III Motor Vehicle Mechanic Certificate. Between 1999 and 2000 he was not the Workshop Foreman but was Workshop Chargehand. He was looking after mechanics and auto-electricians and before any matter was referred to the Workshop Foreman, it was routed through the Workshop Chargehand. He could not remember meeting the plaintiff at all. He does not know why the plaintiff bought the bus. He explained that Exhibit D1 which is a record for this bus was filled by a receptionist whenever the bus was delivered to the defendant's workshop. In re-examination he insisted that he has seen the bus plying its trade twice since 2002 and that the owner is the plaintiff.

The second witness for the defendant was Tobias Kapasule. He is employed by the defendant as a Grade I Mechanic. He joined as Assistant Mechanic in 1971. He stated that in October 1999 he did PDI of BL 5155 for the plaintiff. He corroborated the evidence of Mr Nthukwa.

In cross-examination he confessed that he was not aware of the contractual terms of sale of the bus between the plaintiff and the defendant. He does not know why the plaintiff bought the bus. He stated by doing PDI the defendant ensures that when a vehicle is bought and before it is delivered to the buyer, everything must be inspected and be in good working condition. He says that he was satisfied with the PDI which was done to the bus. About the January 2000 incident of air-lock he was not the one who rectified it but he was present when the Foreman was being briefed of the problem. He stated that after the air-lock problem had been rectified the bus was driven to the workshop for rectification of other faults.

He referred to the job card and stated that the bus was out on 15th February 2000 i.e. after 22 days. It came again in May 2000 and this time he was involved. It then came again in July 2000 for rectification of oil leaks. In June 2002 the vehicle was attended to in respect of brake failure. He admitted that he would not know much as the Foreman did. In re-examination the witness stated that his statement contains all the relevant material information.

Legal Analysis and Findings of the Court

According to Section 16 of the Sale of Goods Act — Cap 48:01 there shall be no implied warranty as to fitness except in certain cases. It provides as follows:-

16. *Subject to this Act and any written law in that behalf, there shall be no implied warranty or condition as to the quality or fitness for any particular purpose of goods supplied under a contract of sale, except as follows:*
    (a) *where the buyer, expressly or by implication, makes known to the seller the particular purpose for which the goods are required, so as to show that the buyer relies on the seller's skill or judgment, and the goods are of a description which it is in the course of the seller's business to supply (whether he be the manufacturer or not), there shall be an implied condition that the goods shall be reasonably fit for such purpose;*

(Continued)

(Continued)

(b) *where the goods are bought by description from a seller who deals in goods of that description (whether he be the manufacturer or not), there shall be an implied condition that the goods shall be of merchantable quality;*
Provided that if the buyer has examined the goods, there shall be no implied condition as regards defects which such examination ought to have revealed;

(c) *an implied warranty or condition as to quality or fitness for a particular purpose may be annexed by the usage of trade;*

(d) *an express warranty or condition shall not negative a warranty or condition implied by this Act unless inconsistent therewith.*

The remedies for breach of warranty are set out in Section 53 of the Act as follows:-

53. (1) Where there is a breach of warranty by the seller, or where the buyer elects, or is compelled, to treat any breach of a condition on the part of the seller as a breach of warranty, the buyer shall not by reason only of such breach of warranty be entitled to reject the goods; but he may —
(a) *set up against the seller the breach of warranty in diminution or extinction of the price; or*
(b) *maintain an action against the seller for damages for the breach of warranty.*
2. *The measure of damages for breach of warranty shall be the estimated loss directly and naturally resulting, in the ordinary course of events from the breach of warranty.*
3. *In the case of breach of warranty of quality, such loss shall **prima facie** be the difference between the value of the goods at the time of delivery to the buyer and the value they would have had if they had answered to the warranty.*
4. *The fact that the buyer has set up the breach of warranty in diminution or extinction of the price shall not prevent him from maintaining an action for the same breach of warranty if he has suffered further damage.*

According to Section 16 of the Sale of Goods Act, no warranty as to the quality or fitness for any particular purpose of goods supplied under a contract of sale can be implied except in the instances provided under sub-sections (a) and (b). Notwithstanding existence of exceptions aforesaid, it is apparent from the proviso to sub-section (a) that the condition as to fitness for any particular purpose cannot be implied in the case of a sale of a specified article under its patent or trade name.

The defendant in its Amended Defence has denied that the contract for the sale of the bus was subject to any condition or warranty. The sale of a bus was under its trade name AEOLOUS and it follows that there was no implied condition as to its fitness for the alleged purpose or any purpose. The plaintiff stated in his evidence that it was his intention to use the bus as a luxury coach between Lilongwe and Blantyre but there is nothing more than that by way of documental evidence. I do not believe that the plaintiff told the defendant that he wanted to use his bus in direct competition with Stagecoach Coachline. It is possible and I would not doubt it that the plaintiff indicated to the defendant that he wanted to use the bus for passenger service without specifying the route. The court will at a later stage determine whether or not the bus was fit for passenger service.

(Continued)

(Continued)

The plaintiff has alleged that the defendant was in breach of an implied term in relation to fitness for purpose or merchantability of the goods. It seems to be the plaintiff's contention the defendant was in breach of the alleged implied terms because barely within the period of a month after delivery the bus broke down four times with passengers on board and due to the fault and defects particularised under paragraph 8 of the Amended Statement of Claim. The burden of proof is on the plaintiff. The plaintiff merely made a statement. He did not even specify the dates of those breakdowns. The plaintiff who claims to have own mechanics for maintenance and service of his fleet did not even call any one such mechanic. Even as a wildest dream, no passenger was called to confirm the unfitness of the bus for passenger service. The plaintiff has alleged that the bus had faults or defects. In a way, he has challenged the roadworthiness of the bus as certified by the Road Traffic Directorate.

On the other hand, the witnesses for the defendant pointed out that some of the faults were rectifiable and were indeed rectified. For example, air-locking, electrical system faults and oil leaks just to mention a few. In fact, Exhibit D1 clearly records the faults for which the bus was taken to the defendant for repairs and the dates of such occurrence. The plaintiff did not challenge this exhibit. I believe the evidence of the defendant that air-lock to the bus was caused by running on empty fuel tank. The defendant cannot be blamed for the plaintiff's own shortcomings. In fact, from Exhibit D1 this was the entry point of problems for this bus. I find as a fact that the bus was on the road for a month without breakdowns confirms that the bus was fit for its passenger service. The service card for the bus shows long intervals between one fault that developed on the bus to another fault development. This is contrary to the plaintiff's claim.

The plaintiff has contended that this was sale of goods by description and that the plaintiff relied on the skills and judgment of the defendant as to merchantability of the goods. The plaintiff argues that the quotation which the defendant made to the plaintiff dated 23rd August 1999 described the AEOLUS MINIBUS and the plaintiff relied on it.

The question which calls for consideration in the present case is whether or not the bus sold to the plaintiff by the defendant was sold by description. Chanell J in *Varley vs Whipp* [1990] 1QB 513 at page 516 said:

> *The term 'sale of goods by description' must apply to all cases where the purchaser has not seen the goods but is relying on the description alone. The most usual application of that section, no doubt, is to unascertained goods, but I think it must also be applied to cases such as this where there is no identification otherwise than by description.*

In the head note to the case of *Varley v Whipp* cited above it is stated thus:

> *The expression 'contract for the sale of goods by description,' in the Sale of Goods Act, 1893, Section 13, applies to all cases where the buyer has not seen the goods, but relies solely on the description given by the supplier.*

> *This section is the same as Section 16 of the Sale of Goods Act which is now under consideration.*

(Continued)

(Continued)

Further Robert Lowe on *Commercial Law*, 5th Edition at page 175 in the footnote emphasises that for there to be a sale by description there must be reliance on the descriptive words i.e. the buyer must buy the goods because their identity is as described.

The foregoing being the legal position, the question which the court should consider is whether from the available facts it can be fairly concluded that there was a sale of the bus by description.

The plaintiff in cross-examination stated as follows:

> *The coach was first shown to me when it was in the bonded warehouse. It had not been cleared. I was only shown the inside looks and the external beauty of it. The authorities could not allow us to test drive it. After looking at the bus, Leyland DAF pressed me to push for the payment with Leasing and Finance Company of Malawi Limited so that they could have funds to redeem it from the bonded warehouse. I went ahead and asked Leasing and Finance Company of Malawi Limited to release funds to the Leyland DAF before the vehicle was tested.*

The foregoing evidence clearly shows that the sale of the bus in this action was not a sale by description. The plaintiff had first seen or ascertained the bus and had even gone inside it. It is in fact after this ascertainment that the bus was sold to the plaintiff.

Further the plaintiff in examination-in-chief which was in addition to the written statement said as follows:

> *I do not adopt Exhibit P1 as part of my evidence because it does not mention 'coach'. . . . . .it reads 'a minibus' when it should be reading Coach.*

This evidence fortifies the defendant's contention that the plaintiff did not rely on the description of the bus in Exhibit P1, but had physically seen or ascertained the bus.

Therefore, the plaintiff has failed to prove that the sale of the bus to him was a sale by description. The implied condition that the bus ought to have been of merchantable quality under Section 16(b) of the Sale of Goods Act could not be applicable to the sale in this action.

Conclusion

I am not satisfied that the plaintiff has proved his claim against the defendant and I dismiss it with costs.

Predieri Metalli SRL v Intrex Aluminum System Ltd

High Court (Commercial Division, Accra, Ghana)
Suit No. RPC/26/06
Cecilia H. Sowah, J.

Facts: Plaintiff is an Italian company engaged in the manufacture, distribution and sale of aluminium profiles whilst Defendant is a Ghanaian company engaged in the fabrication of

(Continued)

(Continued)

aluminium windows and doors. Plaintiff claims that the Defendant purchased aluminium profiles and accessories from her and as at the end of 2004, Defendant owed it EURO 212,994.73 in unsettled invoices despite several demands. Plaintiff is claiming the said sum together with interest, expenses and costs.

Defendant claims that Plaintiff granted it a 120-day credit facility and under that scheme Plaintiff supplied it material, which were found to be discrepant, and which Defendant has been unable to use. Further, that Plaintiff agreed to vary the credit supply scheme and defer her right to payment until such time that Defendant was paid for a project it had undertaken for the Law Faculty. Defendant contends therefore that Plaintiff's claim is premature. Defendant further avers that it had paid $45,000 out of the sum claimed.

The three (3) issues thus settled for trial are as follows:

1. Whether or not the Plaintiff is owed an amount of EURO 212,994.73 by the defendant.
2. Whether or not the amount owed to the Plaintiff is due.
3. Whether or not Plaintiff has made demands for the amount owed by the defendant.

Opinion: After answering all three questions in favor of the Plaintiff, the Court continued.... The other ground relied on by Defendant for its contention that Plaintiff's claim is premature is that aluminium profiles imported were found to be discrepant and could not be used. As Mr. Adote explained and demonstrated in his evidence-in-chief, by "discrepant" defendant meant that there were missing components, which needed to be supplied before the materials could be used. Vittio denied that any discrepant supplies had been made or that a complaint of such had been received, thus throwing upon defendant the proof of those assertions.

At paragraph 9 of its Statement of Defence, the defendants concern was that it had been unable to use the discrepant stock to date because plaintiff had refused to extend further credit to enable defendant import the missing parts. Paragraph 9 states as follows:

> *1st Defendant further says that it has since been holding the discrepant stock in its warehouse which it has been unable to use to date. Plaintiff has also refused to extend to the 1st Defendant further credit to bring in the missing components which will enable the Defendant sell same in the open market to other users.*

Whether or not profiles supplied were discrepant and has not been used was not even an issue set down for trial, and in his submissions on the issue, defendants counsel does not state any enforceable obligation or duty which the plaintiff had failed to perform, or indeed any relief it is seeking from the Court relating to the discrepant parts. The simple complaint of the defendant is that Adote approached the plaintiff and made proposals of how the missing parts could be brought in which were spurned. Was Plaintiff to blame for the discrepant supplies? Was plaintiff obliged to extend further credit to Defendant to bring in the missing parts? When were they supplied, How long after the supply did defendant discover the discrepancies? And when was plaintiff notified? All these are issues in respect of which sufficient evidence should have been adduced to support a finding for defendant.

(Continued)

(Continued)

The Statement of Defence is silent on claims made during the testimony of Mr. Adote that Plaintiff was somehow to be blamed for the discrepant stock, as plaintiff was technical advisor for the Defendant. Paragraph 6 of the defence merely states that 1st defendant imported a large quantity of stock that was found to contain the wrong components. I believe that this testimony was an afterthought, since were it true that plaintiff advised on the materials to buy, it would have been an important fact to be pleaded as forming the basis of defendant's contention that plaintiff must supply it with the missing parts for it to be sold before payment.

Under cross-examination Adote was asked:

Q: As you sit in the box have you written to Predierri complaining about the state of affairs
A: No I have not but I communicated to them through Ronado Nape
Q: I am suggesting to you that there has never been any communication between you and the plaintiff on this matter
A: Some of the key arrangements were oral agreement as in the course of such relationship if you send a message of a type I believe it is acceptable based on the relationship.

It is strange that if it was really on Plaintiff's advise that the material was supplied; Defendant has made no formal complaint, and has merely asked for further credit to bring in the missing parts. It appears to me, considering the dates of the unpaid invoices, and Adotey's testimony that the discrepancy was discovered late in 2004, that the Defendant held the goods for a long time despite its incompleteness. Indeed according to Mr. Adotey, the issue of discrepancy was not a problem until defendants credit facility was reduced as otherwise defendant could have brought in the missing components under the scheme. In the light of the above I do not find defendants contention with respect to the discrepant stock believable or supported by the evidence and I hold that plaintiff is under no liability to defer receipt of payment until after the defendant has been able to order the missing components, use the stock and receive payment.

Counsel for defendant also submits that by supplying discrepant materials, Plaintiff is in breach of section 13 of the Sale of the Goods Act 1962 Act 137 and is not entitled to the reliefs claimed.

I do not think that section 13 of Act 137 is applicable in this case. The defendant did not offer the necessary proof that the blame for the discrepant stock laid on plaintiff. No evidence was forthcoming as to how the order was placed, and whether there were express specifications from the Defendant or it was on the advice of Plaintiff. In any case Adote had explained that by discrepant it was not meant that the stock was defective, only that certain parts are missing.

In respect of the 3rd issue, I am satisfied on the evidence exhibits 'C' to 'C13' which are a series of fax and E-mails, which passed between plaintiff and defendant between 29th April 2003 and 21st July 2005 and were unchallenged, that several demands were made on the

(Continued)

(Continued)

defendant to pay the overdue invoices. Whether or not plaintiff would be entitled to interest if it were successful in proving its claim was not made an issue for trial so I assume the claim for interest is not disputed. I accordingly hold that in accordance with normal commercial practice, plaintiff is entitled to interest on the amount owed which the defendant had withheld since it became due.

Judgment: In conclusion, I find plaintiffs claim proved and hereby enter judgment for the plaintiff in the sum of Euro 212,994.73. Interest is hereby awarded on the said sum at the prevailing rate for Euros exigible in England and calculated from the due dates as per the statement of account exhibit B, up to and inclusive date of payment. Cost is assessed at One hundred million cedis (¢100,000,000.00.) considering among others the cost to Plaintiff of traveling down to testify in this suit.

David Castledine T/A Royal Oak Cleaners v David Gatrell T/A Office Depot

High Court of Malawi
Lilongwe District Registry
Civil Cause No. 116 of 2007
Coram: T.R. Ligowe: Assistant Registrar

Order on Assessment of Damages

The plaintiff got a judgment in default for the defendant to pay him K800 000, interest, damages for breach of contract and costs of the action. This is the assessment of the interest and damages.

Notice of appointment for the assessment was dully served on the defendant but he did not turn up for the hearing. No reason for the non attendance having been given, the court proceeded in the defendant's absence.

Mrs. Joyce Castledine, the plaintiff's wife gave evidence. The facts are simple and are that the plaintiff and his wife bought a house at Area 10. Around September 2006 they contracted the defendant to install a specified kitchen set in the house. They paid a deposit of K800 000 on 13th September 2006. Their agreement was that the kitchen set would be fitted within four weeks from that date. The Castledines were only waiting for the kitchen to be fitted and then occupy the house in October 2006. Four weeks passed without the kitchen being fitted. It would appear the works had started but they were not of the quality and colour specified. The parties corresponded several times between December 2006 and January 2007 over the issue. Eventually the plaintiff rescinded the contract. He gave the defendant notice to refund the deposit paid and remove the defective materials that were being installed. He commenced the present action when he saw that the defendant was neglecting to repay the deposit.

(Continued)

(Continued)
Assessment of the Interest

Interest is awarded where a party to whom money is owed is driven to legal proceedings to recover it. In the absence of any rate specified in the contract between the parties the interest is awarded at the minimum lending rate plus 1%. It is calculated from the date on which the cause of action arose to the date of judgment at compound interest. (See *Zgambo v Kasungu Flue Cured Tobacco Authority* 12 MLR 311.) It is compound interest because the wrongdoer is presumed to have made the most beneficial use of the money and it would in any case be adequate compensation to the party wronged.

In her evidence the witness gave the average lending rate of 25.5% instead of the minimum. Thus I have not been accorded with proper evidence on which to base my award. I can only award a nominal sum of K50 000.

Assessment of Damages

This is clearly a case of sale of goods. The seller delayed to deliver the goods and was in breach of the condition as to quality of the goods and the buyer rejected them. In **McGregor on Damages** 16th Edition paragraph 872, it is stated:

> If the buyer has lawfully rejected the goods the case becomes in effect one of non-delivery and the measure of damages is therefore the same as that applicable to non delivery, with the addition that where the seller wrongfully refuses to take back the goods the buyer may recover expenses incurred in keeping them either until the seller does receive them or until they can be resold on the market by the buyer.

There are cited two cases on that principle. *Chesterman v Lamb* [1834] 2 A. & E. 127 and *Ellis v Chinnock* [1835] 7 C. & P. 169.

The measure of damages for non-delivery of goods is prescribed by section 51 of the Sale of Goods Act Cap 48.01 of the Laws of Malawi. It provides;

(1) Where the seller lawfully neglects or refuses to deliver the goods to the buyer, the buyer may maintain an action against the seller for damages for non-delivery.

The measure of damages shall be the estimated loss directly and naturally resulting, in the ordinary course of events, from the seller's breach of contract.

Where there is an available market for the goods in question the measure of damages shall prima facie be ascertained by the difference between the contract price and the market or the current price of the goods at the time or times when they ought to have been delivered, or, if no time was fixed then at the time of the refusal to deliver.

McGregor on Damages 16th Edition paragraph 822 comments that the measure of damages as provided in subsection 3 "represents the amount that the buyer must obtain to put himself in the position he would have been in had the contract been carried out. For, to put himself in such a position, he must go into the market and buy equivalent goods; and even if he does not choose to rebuy in the market his loss will remain the same. If therefore there is no

(Continued)

(Continued)

difference between the contract and the market prices the buyer will have lost nothing and the damages will be nominal."

The plaintiff had to pay another contractor to fit his kitchen but the price at which that was done was not disclosed in evidence. That is another challenge to me as I have no basis for measuring the damage. I am going to award a nominal sum of K10 000.

The plaintiff is also entitled to damages for the defendant's delay in installing the kitchen set as agreed. This would be as a consequential loss of use of the plaintiff's house from the period he would have started using it had the defendant installed it in the four weeks agreed to the period the plaintiff employed another contractor. I would think that loss is logically reflected by the cost of continuing to stay in the rented house during that period. The witness gave it as from November 2006 to April 2007 at K31 700 to Malawi Housing Corporation which amounts to K190 200. I award the plaintiff that much for consequential losses.

In summary the plaintiff is awarded K50 000 interest and K10 000 plus K190 200 in damages. The total is K250 200. He is also awarded costs of the action.

Made in chambers this 11th day of July 2008.

Abdul Basit Sengooba and Ors v Stanbic Bank Ltd

High Court of Uganda, Kampala
(Commercial Division)
HCT - 00 - CC - CS - 0184 − 2001, Date: 06/07/06
HON. Justice Geoffrey Kiryabwire

Judgment

The first, second and third plaintiffs are adults while the fourth and fifth plaintiffs are minor children suing through their father Haji Suleiman Lule. All five plaintiffs are none the less children of Haji Suleiman Lule. The plaintiffs claim jointly and severally against the defendant bank for the refund of Shs.28,000,000/ = allegedly paid in 1996 for the purchase of a property comprised in Kyadondo Block 244 Plot 2485, at Kisugu Kampala (hereafter called the property). The property it is pleaded was advertised by the defendant bank for sale through a firm M/S Speedway Auctioneers as part of a bank debt recovery.

The plaintiffs allegedly paid for the property through a friend of their father Haji Kaddu Kiberu. It was the plaintiff's father's intention that the property would be bought for the benefit of the children who at the time were all minors. After payment the plaintiffs allegedly signed an agreement, took occupation of the property and asked for the title deed and papers showing that the mortgage there on had been discharged. However it is alleged that the defendant bank and their agents the auctioneer did not comply with this request.

(Continued)

(Continued)

However 3 years after the said purchase the defendant bank formally refused to have the property transferred to the plaintiffs. Instead the plaintiffs allege that the defendant bank re advertised the property and "resold" it for which reason the plaintiff's now seek a refund of their money and damages in lieu of specific performance.

For the defence it is pleaded that no sale of the said property took place on the said date by their agents M/S Speedway Auctioneers.

The defendant bank denies that the plaintiffs signed any valid agreement of sale and took occupation of the said property. The defendant bank further pleads that if a sale took place then it was done contrary to the bank's express instructions and that their agent auctioneers must have been on a frolic of their own.

This case has a long history before the Courts having come before two different Judges since it was filed in 2001. The file finally came up for trial before me in May 2005. At the scheduling conference before the first Judge Justice J. Ogoola (as he then was) the parties agreed to the following facts;

1. That Speedway Auctioneers were agents of the defendant for purposes of sale of the suit property.
2. That the suit property was advertised for sale.
3. That the suit property has since been sold (to another person as I understand it).

The parties agreed to 3 issues for trial namely;

1. Whether the suit contract between the parties is valid.
2. Whether Kiranda and Kabuuka t/a Speedway Auctioneers sold the suit property to the plaintiffs and if so whether the defendant is vicariously liable.
3. Whether the plaintiffs are entitled to the reliefs sought in the plaint.

Issues No. 1: <u>Whether the suit contract between the parties was valid.</u>

The contract in question (Exh. P.4) made between M/S Speedway Auctioneers (referred to in the said contract as "…as per instruction given to us by Uganda Commercial Bank pursuant to their mortgage rights") of the one part and Abdul Basit Sengooba, Haruna Nyanzi, Mariam Namawejje, Akram Lule and Umaama Namukwaya jointly of the other part. It is signed by one Mubiru — Kalenge (the second name is not clear) for Speedway Auctioneers in the presence of Kiranda Andrew and the signature of Haji Sulaiman Lule (PW1) appears on behalf of the buyers.

Paragraph 2 of the agreement provides the consideration as Shs.28,000,000/ = the buyers having been the highest bidder in the auction

   …*conducted on the 4th of December, 1995.*

Counsel for the plaintiff submitted that Haji Sulaiman Lule PW1 instructed his friend Haji Kaddu Kiberu PW2 by letter Exh. P5 to look around and purchase a property for his minor children at the time. This Haji Kiberu did by identifying and successfully bidding for the suit

(Continued)

(Continued)

property. Haji Sulaiman Lule then signed the agreement on behalf of his children as they were minors. Counsel for the plaintiffs submitted that this could be done as Haji Sulaiman Lule is the father of the plaintiffs and therefore did not need special authority to sign on their behalf. Mr. Kiberu then paid the purchase price. Counsel for the plaintiff then submitted

> ...*The payment was made and Speedway Auctioneers received the money. It was immaterial whether Kiranda or Kabuuka signed or not as sellers. What is important is that Speedway Auctioneers signed as the sellers to the plaintiffs. The contract of sale of the land was valid.*

Counsel for the plaintiffs challenges the assertion by the defendant that the plaintiffs were minors and therefore could not contract as they allegedly did when in reality the defendant's agents accepted and received their money. He submitted that this would constitute unjust enrichment and should not be condemned by Court.

Counsel for the plaintiff referred me to the case of *Davies v Beynan Harris* [1931] 47 TLR 424 for the proposition that contracts which give a minor a benefit of a permanent nature like a contract for property is voidable at the instance of the minor until he/she is of majority age. In this regard the plaintiffs are clearly still interested in the property.

Counsel for the plaintiff also argued that it was immaterial whether the plaintiff's father or their father's friend made the actual payment. Indeed Counsel for the plaintiff submits that PW2 Haji Kiberu has never requested a refund of the money. All this he argues showed that this was an investment made by a father for the benefit of his children.

Counsel for the defendant faults the agreement on several counts.

First of all Counsel for the defendant argues that none of the plaintiffs signed the agreement. He argued that it was the plaintiff's father Haji Sulaiman Lule PW1 who signed the agreement and yet he did not show Court any authorization to do so on their behalf. Counsel for the defendant argued that for a person to sign a contract on behalf of minors that person must be their legal guardian but not necessarily their parent. He therefore argued that this legal capacity had to be shown, I suppose through same legal documentation. Counsel for the defendant also wondered why Haji Sulaiman Lule having appointed Haji Kiberu as his agent vide Exh. P5 then went ahead to sign the agreement thereafter.

Counsel for the defendant submitted that it is PW1 Haji Lule who made the purchase and that is why he lodged a caveat in his personal names on the title of the suit property as the purchaser. Counsel for the defendant argues on that ground alone no cause of action has been established.

Secondly, Counsel for the defendant submitted that the agreement is invalid for lack of capacity to contract because the plaintiffs are minors. He submitted that under Section 2(2) of the Contract Act (Cap 73) a minor is a person who has not reached the age of eighteen. He further submitted that for minors Section 3 of the Sale of Goods Cap 82 only allows minors to contract for "necessaries" and in this case no evidence was led to show that the suit property would meet that definition. Counsel for the defendants argued that 3 of the plaintiffs are now adults and there was no reason for them not to come and testify in

(Continued)

(Continued)

the case. Indeed he observed that none of the plaintiffs testified and so to him the plaintiffs are not aggrieved parties and it is just their father.

I have perused the submissions of both Counsels and reviewed the evidence adduced in Court.

The legal arguments revolve around the validity of the contract. The contract or agreement in question is Exh. P4. The arguments presented to Court to my mind revolve first around capacity and then secondly agency which is really what the second issue is about. In this case the issue revolving around capacity relates to whether the plaintiffs as minors could and actually did enter into the agreement Exh. P.4. The evidence shows that the plaintiffs' father PW 1 Haji Lule signed the contract on their behalf by affixing his personal signature. It is therefore clear that Haji Lule is the one who entered into the contract on behalf of his children. Evidence was not lead as to the actual ages of the children and as to whether by reason of their infancy they could not actually sign the said agreement.

Indeed because a person is a minor does not ipso facto mean that he/she cannot sign an agreement and therefore must have his/her parent or guardian sign on his/her behalf.

A review of the legal authorities on the subject of the law of minors' contracts would suggest that the primary objective of the law is the protection of minors from the consequences of their own inexperience (see the Law Reform Commission of Western Australia Report on Minors Contracts May 1988 accessed through www.austlii.edu.au/an/other/walrc/25/P25-II-R.pdf on 24/06/04). This is the basis of the cited case *Davies V Beynon-Harris (1931) 47 TLR 424* which involved a minor paying rent.

However this present case is different in that the said minors did not actually sign the agreement and so the principles as to minors' contracts would not apply to them. The contractual obligations did not fall on the minors but rather their father PW1 Haji Lule and that is why he caused his friend PW2 Haji Kiberu to pay the contract sum and why PW1 Haji Lule then signed the agreement. During cross examination PW1 Haji Lule testified that

> . . .I appointed Kiberu as my agent. Kaddu Kiberu paid the money on my behalf with instructions to register the title in my children's names. . . .

Clearly if the agreement did not meet with problems it was the intention of PW1 Haji Lule that the beneficial interest as a result of the purchase would pass to his children at the time of transfer of title ownership as he was the actual buyer of the said property. I therefore find that the plaintiffs did not enter into the contract and therefore the issue of capacity or validity in their regard did not arise. In this regard I agree with the submissions of Counsel for the defendant that it is PW1 Haji Lule who has the proprietary interest and that the plaintiffs as named have no cause of action. This is sufficient to dispose of this case. However before I leave this issue entirely there is also a lot of confusion with regard to the contract as to when the auction actually took place. The agreement states that the auction took place on the 4th December 1995. However Exb. D. 1 a letter from M/S Speedway Auctioneers signed by

(Continued)

(Continued)

Kabuuka. J. and dated 10th January 1996 to M/S Mayanja Nkangi & Elue Co. Advocates would seem to suggest otherwise. It reads in part

> ... *we refer to your instructions to us dated 2nd December, 1995 ... we took the initial procedure of 30 days and on 4th December 1995 the advertisement were placed in the New Vision.*
>
> *On 4th January 1996, the notice elapsed and the sale would have been effected <u>had there been a ready buyer.</u>*
>
> *However in the circumstances above, we undergo a series of advertisements to attract buyer and at the same time search for them for private treaty sale...*

To my mind therefore there was no auction on the 4th December 1995 as there was no ready buyer. Clearly the agreement Exh. P4 and this letter Exh. D. 1 by the same auctioneers are contradictory. It is unfortunate that the auctioneers were not called by either party to shed light on this aspect of the contract. Be that as it may I find that the plaintiffs have no cause of action and therefore there was no valid contract between them and the defendants.

I also find that this issue disposes of the case so I make no further findings on issues 2 and 3.

I according dismiss the case.

As the suit was filed in the names of minors and young persons I will exercise my discretion under Section 27(2) of the Civil Procedure Rules not to award costs against them. Each party will bear its own costs.

Notes

1. The effects of the SAPs on countries are mixed. For example, "While African countries urgently need to increase spending on health care, education, and sanitation, IMF structural adjustment programs have forced these countries to reduce such spending. In African countries with ESAF programs, the average amount of per capita government spending on education actually declined between 1986 and 1996." See Robert Naiman and Neil Watkins (1999). Some studies have found some positive impacts of SAPS on a few individual countries, see, for example, Harold Alderman (1994).
2. For an excellent treatment of markets and contract enforcement in African countries, see Marcel Fafchamps (2004) (see especially Chapter 2).
3. The rationale for establishing a commercial court in Malawi is typical, "Malawi Government established the Commercial Courts Division in 2007 as part of efforts to improve the business climate and attract potential investors. The court was intended to expedite hearings and determinations of commercial cases following concerns that political issues were taking precedence over commercial and business matters and sometimes commercial cases were taking as long as two to three years before getting resolved." See remarks by Justice Frank Kapanda (2010).
4. For an excellent account of the history and performance of the commercial courts in Ghana, see Dateh-Bah (2007).
5. These rules are found under Order 58 which is part of the new High Court (Civil Procedure) Rules, 2004 (CI 47). *Id.*
6. See Date-Bah (1973). Some jurisdictions in sub-Saharan Africa still use the common law in resolving sale of goods conflicts. See, for example, "the contract of sale of goods in our present case, is governed by common law − not statute." *Kimberley Engineering Works (Pty) Ltd. v M.R.C. Building Construction* (High Court of Lesotho), CIV/T/460/03 (*per* Guni, K.J.J.).

7. Section 80 of the *Sale of Goods Act* states that the relevant rules of the common law will continue to apply in so far as such rules are not inconsistent with the provisions of the Sale of Goods Act.
8. Sale of Goods Act, 1962, § 1.
9. Sale of Goods Act, 1962, § 3.
10. Sale of Goods Act, 1962, § 81.
11. *Carroll Nelson v Union Equity Co-Operative Exchange*, 548 S.W. 2d 352 (Texas Supreme Court), 1977.

Questions

1. In your opinion should courts apply the current commercial laws in your country to farmers? If so, should they apply to all farmers (large and small)?
2. How well have commercial courts functioned in your country?
3. Explain what a market-led growth policy is, and how it has affected countries in SSA.
4. Why is time important as it pertains to business disputes in courts?
5. What is the definition of a "Good" under the *Sale of Goods Act*?

References

Alderman, H., 1994. Ghana: adjustment's star pupil? In: Sahn, D.E. (Ed.), Adjustment to Policy Failure in African Economies. Cornell University Press, Ithaca, New York.

Beecham, K., 2010. President of the Ghana Bar Association on the 5th Anniversary of the establishment of the commercial courts in Ghana. (viewed at <http://gbcghana.com/news/32581detail.html> (accessed 22.03.10).

Cofie, S., 2007. "Ghana-establishment of the commercial court," SmartLessons. Advisory Services. International Finance Corporation, <http://www.doingbusiness.org/features/GhanaCommercialCourt.aspx> (viewed 05.01.10).

Date-Bah, S.K., 1973. Aspects of the role of contract in the economic development of Ghana. J. Afr. Law. 17 (3), 254–270, 268.

Dateh-Bah, K., 2007. Developing a new commercial court in Ghana. Tex. Int. Law. J.viewed 21.03.10. at <http://findarticles.com/p/articles/mi_7753/is_200707/ai_n32256053/>.

Fafchamps, M., 2004. Market Institutions in Sub-Saharan African countries: Theory and Evidence. MIT Press, Massachusetts.

Justice F. Kapanda, 2010. Ambassador Bodde Hails Malawi's Commercial Court. U.S. Embassy, Lilongwe, Malawi at <http://lilongwe.usembassy.gov/events3.html> (accessed 12.09.10) (at opening of Malawi commercial court).

Naiman, R., Watkins, N., 1999. A Survey of the Impacts of IMF Structural Adjustment in Africa: Growth, Social Spending, and Debt Relief. <http://www.cepr.net/a-survey-of-the-impacts-of-imf-structural-adjustment-in-africa/#ES> (accessed 14.09.10).

United Nations Conference on Trade and Development (UNCTAD), 2009. World Investment Report, 2009. New York and Geneva, p. 30.

CHAPTER 7

Trademarks and Patents

Keywords: Intellectual property; patents; trademarks; biotechnology; plant breeding; African Regional Intellectual Property Organization (ARIPO); Consultative Group on International Agricultural Research (CGIAR); International Treaty on Genetic Resources for Food and Agriculture ("The Plant Treaty"); World Intellectual Property Organization (WIPO); nonrival good

7.1 Introduction

A vibrant agriculture sector is important to poverty alleviation in sub-Saharan Africa (SSA). The agriculture sector is a source of food, income, employment, and foreign exchange earnings that support the importation of manufactured goods and services from other countries. The 2014 populations of Western and Eastern Africa were 339 and 378 million, respectively. With growth rates of 2.7% in West Africa and also 2.7% in East Africa, populations are projected to reach 784 and 851 million by 2050 (Population Reference Bureau [PRB], 2014). To feed the expanding population and keep food prices within the budgets of households, countries have to expand the use of science and technology in agriculture.

The development of science and technology is being carried out at national research centers, private research institutions, and the Consultative Group on International Agricultural Research (CGIAR). The efforts at these various institutions are critically dependent on an enabling regulatory environment that promotes the protection of intellectual property rights (IPR).

7.2 Law and Economics of Trade Marks and Patents

According to the World Intellectual Property Organization (WIPO), "Intellectual property (IP) refers to creations of the mind: inventions, literary and artistic works, and symbols, names, images, and designs used in commerce" (World Intellectual Property Organization (WIPO), 2010). Trademarks and patents are types of IP classified as industrial property and are also two of the common ways of protecting IP legally in SSA.[1]

F.O. Boadu: Agricultural Law and Economics in Sub-Saharan Africa.
DOI: http://dx.doi.org/10.1016/B978-0-12-801771-5.00007-1

In economic theory, intellectual property rights law and regulatory regime exist to solve the problem of nonrivalry in the consumption of an individual creation. A nonrival good is a good for which the consumption of the good by one person does not diminish the quantity available to others. For example, beautiful scenery is a nonrival good because one's enjoyment of the scenery does not diminish the amount of the scenery that another person may enjoy.

In the absence of an IP law and regulations, the producer of an intellectual property is unable to exclude others from freely consuming the good, or to reproduce the good at minimum marginal cost. Society utilizes IP law and regulations to grant monopoly rights to the producer of intellectual property to protect against free-riding and to encourage more inventions.

There is a longstanding debate on whether society ought to protect inventions, and if so for how long to grant such exclusive rights (see, eg, Dutfield, 2003). In the context of developing countries, some researchers have argued that "IPRs are necessary to stimulate economic growth which, in turn, contributes to poverty reduction. By stimulating invention and new technologies, they will increase agricultural or industrial production, promote domestic and foreign investment, facilitate technology transfer and improve the availability of medicines necessary to combat disease" (Commission on Intellectual Property Rights, 2002). The counter-arguments are equally compelling, "IP rights do little to stimulate invention in developing countries, because the necessary human and technical capacity may be absent. They are ineffective at stimulating research to benefit poor people because they will not be able to afford the products, even if developed. They limit the option of technological learning through imitation. They allow foreign firms to drive out domestic competition by obtaining patent protection and to service the market through imports, rather than domestic manufacture. Moreover, they increase the costs of essential medicines and agricultural inputs, affecting poor people and farmers particularly badly" (Commission on Intellectual Property Rights, 2002).

Four main justifications have been suggested in support of granting patents to inventors.[2] First, is the "natural-law" thesis that argues that an inventor has an exclusive property right in their own ideas. These exclusive property rights must be protected with a patent as a moral obligation. Second is the "reward-by-monopoly" justification that suggests that society must reward the services rendered by inventors by granting them temporary monopoly so they may reap benefits from their invention. Third is the "monopoly-profit-incentive" justification that argues that only high profit expectations made possible through the granting of monopolies would encourage inventors to take risk and contribute to progress of society at large. The fourth justification is the "exchange-for-secrets" thesis that seeks to encourage inventors to release their secrets to society in exchange for granting the inventor exclusive use of the secret for the benefit of society.

All SSA countries operate under international, regional, and domestic intellectual property legal regimes. For example, in the international arena, there is the *International Treaty on Genetic Resources for Food and Agriculture* ("The Plant Treaty") approved in 2001. One important principle under the Plant Treaty is *Farmers' Rights* under which farmers are recognized as the guardians and holders of traditional knowledge and stewards of agricultural biodiversity. This recognized right demands that farmers share benefits arising from the utilization of plant genetic resources for food and agriculture (Food and Agriculture Organization (FAO)). At the regional level, the *African Regional Intellectual Property Organization* (ARIPO) handles patents and trademarks from member countries, and at the domestic level, Ghana is discussed as an example below.

Ghana's law is typical of what one finds in other SSA countries. Ghana's legislation covers patents, trademarks, and utility certificates. Patents are governed by the *Patents Act, 2003 (Act 657)* which defines a patent as "(1) the title granted to protect an invention, and (2) an invention as an idea of an inventor which permits in practice the solution to a specific problem in the field of technology."[3] Patents are issued for a period of 20 years.[4] Some important exclusion from patent protection that are relevant to agriculture include (1) plants and animals other than micro-organisms; (2) biological processes for the protection of plants or animals other than nonbiological and microbiological processes; and (3) plant varieties. The exclusion of plant varieties, plants, and animals generally is in recognition of the central role of agriculture in the economy. It may also be the case that since most plant and animal research is publicly funded, there is no rationale to make the use or further development of plants and animals exclusive.

Trademarks in Ghana are governed by the *Trademarks Act, 2004 (Act 664)*. The Act defines a trademark as "any sign or combination of signs capable of distinguishing the goods or services of one undertaking from the goods or services of other undertakings including words such as personal names, letters, numerals and figurative elements."[5] Trademarks are issued for a period of 10 years and may be renewed upon payment of appropriate fees.[6] A trademark may be removed from the Register of Trademarks if it is demonstrated that it has not been used for a period of over 5 years.[7]

Trademark infringement cases are common in common law jurisdictions in SSA. Most of the cases deal with the situation where an importer attempts to register a product in the domestic market as their own trademark. In the *Pulsart Impex Limited v. Dart Hills Limited* case (Ghana), the court was called upon to decide whether the mere fact of importing a good without any property right in the manufacture of the product, or a license, would entitle one to register the product as its own trademark. The case also discussed the type of information needed to prove damages in an infringement action. In the case of *Paterson Zochonis and Company Limited v. A.B. Chami and Company Limited*, the Nigeria Supreme Court discussed in detail the elements that go into the determination of what constitutes an infringement of a trademark. The case reveals how trademark law takes into consideration the factor of illiteracy, that is, a product that is likely to deceive an illiterate may not be registered as a trademark. The Kenya case, *Premier Food Industries Limited v. Al-Mahra Limited* discussed the test to use in determining whether a trademark infringement has occurred. In the case of *Tanzania Cigarette Company Limited v. Mastermind Tobacco Limited* (Tanzania) the court was called upon to decide the ownership of a the trade mark in the form of a sign and not similarities in the names of the products. The Zambia case, *Trade Kings Limited v. Unilever PLC, Cheesebrough Ponds (Zambia) Limited, Lever Brothers (Private) Limited*, deals with a situation where two parties have legitimately registered a trademark that could be confusing. The case turned on whether a trial court had the power to cancel a registration without going into the merits of the case.

Two patent cases are discussed. These cases raise several issues relevant to other countries in SSA. The Ghana case, *Rhone-Poulence s.a. and Another v. Ghana National Trading Corporation* addresses several important questions, namely, may a state institution be sued for patent infringement? Also, may a party that merely imports and sells in Ghana a patented drug infringe the patent of a patentee? And whether failure to file an action within a specified period amounts to laches? And, finally, how much proof is required to support damage claims? The Namibia case, *GEMFARM Investments (PTY)Ltd v TRANS HEX Group Ltd and Another* raises the complex issue of the applicability of the union laws of South Africa to an independent Namibia.

Pulsart Impex Limited v Dart Hills Limited

High Court (Commercial Division, Accra, Ghana)
June 10th, 2008
Cecilia Sowah, J.
SUIT No. IPR/4/07

FACTS

Plaintiffs' case is that she is the registered owner of the ONION and CROCODILE brands of door locks since 27th March 1994. That for the last three years she has been losing market to some importers who are duplicating the brands and bringing cheap quality products into the country from China and Hong Kong. Plaintiff avers that some of these infringing products were purchased from Defendant Company, and has sued the defendant for (1) an injunction to restrain defendant whether acting by themselves, the proprietors, officers, servants, agents or otherwise from infringing trade marks ART No. 910 for the CROCODILE BRAND and ART No. 693-2495 for the ONION BRAND both under class 6, (2) any inquiry as to damages, (3) costs.

(Continued)

(Continued)

The defendant denies that plaintiff is entitled to any of the reliefs claimed. It is asserted that the plaintiff dishonestly registered the ONION and CROCODILE trademarks and had no right to do so as it was aware that other companies were involved in the importation of these brands prior to the registration. It is defendant's case that it took over Dallashie Enterprise which was owned by the sole shareholder of Defendant Company, and that Dallashie Enterprise had been trading in the two brands in issue before their registration by the plaintiff. It is also contended that plaintiff is in breach of the Protection Against Unfair Competition Act, 2000 Act 589. Defendant counterclaims for the following: a) Declaration that the alleged registration of the Onion and Crocodile trademarks by the Plaintiff is dishonest and therefore invalid, and b) Such further or other reliefs this Honourable Court might deem fit.

OPINION

The following issues were set down to be tried:

1. Whether or not the Plaintiff's registration of the Trademark was dishonestly effected.
2. Whether or not the Plaintiff's action is in breach of the Protection Against Unfair Competition Act, 2000 (ACT 589).
3. Whether or not the Defendant has the vested right of the original manufacturers to trade in the 'Onion' and 'Crocodile' branded locks.
4. Whether or not the Defendant has been honestly concurrently dealing in the branded locks.
5. Whether or not the Plaintiff is entitled to its claim.
6. Whether or not the Defendant is entitled to its counterclaim.

The burden of persuasion or the legal burden usually lies on the party who has to prove an essential averment in order to get the remedy he seeks. In the instant suit, as it is the plaintiff's case that the defendant has infringed on his trademark, and that it has suffered loss thereby, the onus to establish the infringement and the loss lies on the plaintiff. As can be seen from the agreed issues, the fact that the brands have been registered by the plaintiff is not in issue. What is put in issue by defendant's counter-claim is whether the registration ought to be invalidated? Defendant thus carries the legal burden to show that the registrations are invalid and ought to be expunged from the register.

I think I should state my opinion that in trademark actions where a relief is sought for the invalidation of a registered mark, it is ideal, if not mandatory under sections 12, 20(1) and 38(1), that the Registrar of Trademarks be made a party to the action so that he may be heard on the matter and properly bound by the decision of the Court. Be that as it may, I shall proceed to determine the issues before the court.

I shall begin with a discussion of the issues which pertain to the onus borne by the plaintiff, namely issue 5 whether the plaintiff is entitled to its claim.

The owner of a registered trademark has an exclusive right to use the mark. The right is infringed if any person, without the owner's consent, uses the mark itself or a mark closely

(Continued)

(Continued)

resembling it in the course of trade. In its pleadings, the plaintiff alleged that its branded products were being duplicated. Paragraph 9 of the statement of claim states:

> Plaintiffs say that for the last three years or so, they have been losing the market in respect of their branded products to some importers who are duplicating the said brands and bringing cheap quality imported from China and Hong Kong to sell at reduced rates.

At the trial however, evidence in support of these alleged facts were not presented. Although plaintiff had averred that he had purchased some of the infringing products, none was put in evidence, and although plaintiff pleaded the particulars of infringement at paragraph 14 of the statement of claim, no evidence was led to prove the facts alleged. [See *Manu v. Kuma [1963] 2 GLR 462 where* Van Lare JSC held that "mere filing of particulars of expenditure does not constitute proof; particulars are allegations of fact which ought to be proved by evidence"]. For example, the issue of "similarity" was not addressed. None of the pieces allegedly bought from Defendant was put in evidence for purposes of comparison of the marks and the goods to determine if they were duplicates or infringed. Nor was plaintiff's packaging and labeling as against Defendant's proved. I accordingly hold that the plaintiff failed to establish one important aspect of infringement, namely that the goods were duplicates or cheap imports.

On the other hand, it is contended for the defendant that it imports from the manufacturer of the products in China and that plaintiff did not have the consent of the said manufacturer to register the marks. Defendant tendered import documents dated 1993 to support this assertion. In the event, as plaintiff failed to establish that the goods were infringing, I must accept the evidence adduced for the defendant and hereby find that the goods imported by the defendant bear the valid marks of the manufacturer and are genuine.

But, even if defendant's marks are genuine, can they still be considered as infringing the plaintiff's trademarks?

Mr. Arjun Khushiram Mahtani, Managing Director of Plaintiff Company testified for the plaintiff. He stated that the plaintiff imports hardware, namely door locks, hinges etc. for distribution in Ghana. That after studies which showed that the ONION and CROCODILE brands were acceptable on the market, he took steps to register the logos, which were duly gazetted. He tendered in evidence the Commercial and Industrial Bulletins and the Certificates of Registration for the ONION and CROCODILE brands as exhibits A and A1 and B and B1 respectively. He denied that the registration was dishonest as he went through the normal procedure for registration. Asked by his lawyer what the publication and the issuing of the certificates meant, he said:

It means the Registrar General has in effect given me the ownership of the trademark and logos and has allowed me to sell in the market under my name.

So in effect, does it exclude other people who intend to import that particular brand?

By virtue of the Trademark law, my company becomes the sole proprietor of this trademark and totally excludes other companies from importing or distributing in these two brands.

(Continued)

(Continued)

In cross-examination, Mr Mahtani said the plaintiff imports from Aimda International Trading Company. He was pressed further on the issue as follows:

Q. Have they been your manufacturers since 1992?
A. They have been the exporters.
Q. Are they the manufacturers of the brand?
A. They are the exporters.
Q. Do you know the manufacturer of the products?
A. I don't know.
Q. Are you aware that the manufacturer of the products is in China?
A. I am not aware.
Q. Have you heard of Shangani Mineral of Export and Import of China?
A. No my Lord.
Q. I suggest to you that the manufacturers of the products are Shangani Mineral of Export and Import.
A. You are making the statement. I am not aware.

I have set out this testimony because it sums up the basis and the reasoning behind plaintiff's claim. It will help in determining whether plaintiff was entitled to register the two brands and claim proprietorship to the exclusion of all other importers in Ghana.

The rationale behind trade marks is to protect the business reputation and goodwill of the proprietor. The law attempts to prevent traders from running their business in such a way as to steal a competitor's trade. A business may have spent years building a reputation and goodwill with customers and potential customers, and it would be unfair if a newly formed business attempted to capitalise on this by making out that its own products or services were those of the established business. That is the offence of passing off. An injured party is in a stronger position if he can rely on the law relating to trademarks as it is easier to prove that an infringement of a registered trademark has taken place. Thus the law of trademarks was developed from the common law of passing-off. That property right conferred by the act of registration under the Trademarks Act 2004 [Act 664] is therefore the right of the proprietor to take legal action to protect his business reputation and goodwill. In *Burberry's v. Cording [1909] 26 RPC 693*, Parker J said at 379:

> *If an injunction be granted restraining the use of a word or name, it is no doubt granted to protect property, but the property, to protect which it is granted, is not the property in the word or the name, but the property in the trade or goodwill which will be injured by its use.*

As far as the evidence adduced by the plaintiff goes, the corroborative evidence necessary to prove a connection in the course of trade in the branded goods was absent. I can only suppose that this was because as far as plaintiff was concerned, the mere fact of registration was sufficient to entitle her to her reliefs.

So I ask the question whether it is open to all and any person to apply to register the mark of a product which has not been registered in this country, and thus become the proprietor of that mark with all its privileges? I pose this question because it appears

(Continued)

(Continued)

from the evidence that this is exactly what the plaintiff did. Mr Addo—Atuah made a number of submissions relating to this issue in his written address. He contends that plaintiff had gone through all the processes of registration validly and did not have to consult anybody including the exporters or manufacturers in registering those trademarks. He concedes that the plaintiff does not know the manufacturer but argues that that does not affect plaintiff's right as the registered proprietor. He further contends that though Mr Mahtani had admitted that he knew defendant previously as Agyei Trading and that Agyei Trading was dealing in door locks, nothing stopped plaintiff from registering those trademarks validly in accordance with law. Counsel further contends that once there is a registered trademark, it excludes the dealing in it by all other persons within the jurisdiction with respect to that trademark or product. With all due respect to counsel, these contentions are all erroneous.

A fact established by the testimony of Mr Mahtani is that plaintiff is not the manufacturer of the products but merely imports and distributes the products. He admitted that he did not know the manufacturer.

These were his answers during cross-examination [See page 7 of the proceedings of 19th March 2008]:

Q. When you were going to register these Onion and Crocodile, did you speak to your exporters?
A. It was not necessary to speak to anybody.
Q. Did you find out who the manufacturers of the products were?
A. I did not need to find out. I registered my trademark.
Q. Did you find out whether there was any intellectual property right of your exporters or the manufacturers of the product?
A. I went to the Register General with the requisite papers. I did not find any further details. I applied through the normal procedure.

It is also important to note that plaintiff does not assert that it originated the marks in contention or that she is an exclusive licensee or that she has a sole distributorship agreement with his exporter. Its argument is that plaintiff does not need any permission from the originators of the mark or the manufacturers to register the marks.

Intellectual property law concerns legal rights associated with creative effort or commercial reputation and goodwill. It is a fallacy to think as Mr Mahtani does, that the Registrar gives ownership of a trademark. One does not obtain a property right by registering a mark you do not own or do not have title to. One must have title or ownership of the property to be entitled to register it as a trademark which then confers an exclusive right to its use.

Flipping through exhibit B, I find that the plaintiff is the registered proprietor of several other products. I also saw that KARAFI BITTERS is a registered mark in class 5. A simple analogy should help illustrate the point I seek to make. Suppose Mr Obi a Nigerian exporter discovered that Karafi Bitters is a best seller in Nigeria, would he be entitled to register that mark in Nigeria without reference to the manufacturer here in Ghana? And would Obi then

(Continued)

(Continued)

be entitled to stop all other persons who have bought the product from the registered proprietor in Ghana from importing Karafi Bitters into Nigeria?

In my view, it is eminently unreasonable to suppose that a person who does not own the property can register a proprietary right over that property. Property has been defined as the general property in goods and not merely a special property, as for example that which arises under a bailment or licence. Property connotes title or ownership. Blackstone's commentaries define "right of property" as "That sole or despotic dominion which one man claims and exercises over the external things of the world, in total exclusion of the right of any other individual in the universe." From the evidence, the plaintiff cannot claim to be the owner of the product or the original marks. Even had plaintiff succeeded in proving that she had traded in these brands over a number of years, the legal position will still be that one does not ordinarily acquire proprietorship of a trademark simply by using it with the consent of the owner over a period of time. *Travelpro Trade Marks [1997] RPC 864* cited by counsel for the defendant, which held that a sole distributor is a mere agent and can claim no ownership of the mark, supports my view.

It would be chaos if our Trademark law was reduced to a first come right. It could not have been the common law that anybody could claim the proprietary right in someone's goods just because the owner had failed to register it. In my view, the common sense approach is that a person must have a just or lawful claim to the property in order to register its logo and obtain an exclusive proprietary right which will be recognised and protected by law.

I do not see that plaintiff has any right to the marks and I hold that plaintiff has no lawful claim to the products or their marks, and was not entitled to register the ONION and CROCODILE brand of door locks. *Rhone-Poulence SA & anor v. GNTC [1972] 2 GLR 109* cited by counsel for plaintiffs as being on all fours with this case, is in fact a case about patents, and the holdings in that case are mostly inapplicable to this case. In any case, whilst that case is about an infringement of a valid patent, the main issue in contention in this suit touches the right to register the mark by a person who is neither the manufacturer or an exclusive licensee, and the validity of that registration.

From the facts as so far found, it seems to me that both the plaintiff and the defendant are involved in the parallel imports of goods bearing the same valid trademarks. The real complaint of the plaintiff is that goods bearing valid trademarks are being imported to compete with his locally registered mark. Counsel for the plaintiff contends that all persons within this jurisdiction are excluded from dealing in the product. That contention is not correct. Ghanaian trademark law does not prohibit the sale of parallel imports, and I believe that that is so even where the complainant has an exclusive right of the manufacturer to import into the Ghanaian market. This is because such a contract creates an exclusive contractual right only as between the proprietor of the mark and the licensee. The owner or proprietor of an intellectual property right who consents to the marketing of his goods cannot use that right to prevent the export of the goods or their subsequent sale. His right is said to be exhausted by the first consensual marketing. This is the doctrine of exhaustion of rights which was formulated by the European Court [See *Consten and Grundig v. Commission [1966] ECR 299*] and is in my view applicable in

(Continued)

(Continued)

Ghana since it captures the main principle behind those jurisdictions like Ghana where parallel imports are not prohibited. Therefore, if even a manufacturer of goods which are not infringing cannot stop their export after sale, I do not see how the plaintiff in this suit, not being the originator of the mark, or an exclusive licensee can persuade the court to grant it the injunction it seeks to restrain others from importing the products.

Plaintiff admitted in cross-examination that he did not find out whether there was any intellectual property right of his exporters or manufacturers of the products. I find on the evidence that plaintiff registered the two marks without reference to the originator of the marks and I hold that that Registration of the marks were dishonest. In my view, there is implicit in the fact of registration a claim by the plaintiff that it produced the goods. See *Travel pro Trade Mark [1997] RPC 864.*

In respect of its claim for damages, plaintiff failed to establish that it was entitled to damages when she failed to prove the infringement. In any case, she failed to lead any evidence on the basis of which an inquiry as to damages could be conducted. These were matters capable of proof. Plaintiff's market share in the trade, evidence to establish Plaintiff's prices or the cheap prices of others, loss of profits, plaintiff's audited accounts, monies were spent promoting the products, receipts, evidence of advertisement or other forms of marketing etc. could have shown the expenses of plaintiff which entitled it to damages. In *Faroe Atlantic v A G [2006] 1 GMLR 1* at 43, Dr Twum JSC cited with approval Ollennu J's statement in *Majolagbe v. Larbi [1959] GLR 190 at 192* on the requirements of proof in law and held that an award for loss of profit would be disallowed as the respondent had failed to quantify their alleged loss of profit.

I shall now turn to the defendant's counter-claim which encapsulates issues 1, 2, 3 and 4. The defendant bears the burden to prove the alleged facts therein.

Our Trademarks Act provides for challenge of the validity of a mark even after registration. Section 35 of the Trademark Act provides that the certificate of registration provides prima facie evidence of ownership. This means that that prima facie proof becomes conclusive evidence only when the party challenging the validity of the registration fails to discharge the onus. It was rightly contended for the defendant that if she was able to prove any of the three requirements set out in section 12 of the Act, then she had succeeded in proving that the registration was invalid.

Section 12 of the Act provides as follows:

(1) The High Court shall invalidate the registration of a trademark if the person requesting the invalidation proves that section 1 or a requirement of section 4 has not been complied with.
The Court may invalidate the registration of a trademark if because of an act or inactivity of the owner, it has become the common name in the trade for goods or services for which it is registered.
(3) The invalidation of the trademark is effective from the date of registration.
(4) The Registrar shall record the invalidation and publish the invalidation as soon as possible.

(Continued)

(Continued)

The first ground for invalidation argued for the defendant was that plaintiff's trademark failed to distinguish his goods from the goods of other undertakings, and therefore failed to pass the test of the definition of a trademark in section 1 of the Act. The basis of this contention was defendant's assertion that he and others were trading in the mark before the plaintiff registered it. The evidence adduced by the defendant in support of this claim were exhibits 1, 2, 3, 4 and 4A to show that Dallashie Enterprise was registered in June 1992 to trade in import and export of general goods, whilst defendant company was incorporated in October 2005 with one of its objectives being to acquire and take over as a going concern, the business then being carried on under the name and style of Dallashie. Defendant also tendered exhibits 5, 6 and 7 showing importations of Crocodile and Onion locks by Dallashie Enterprise between May and December 1993. Mr. Kwabena Agyei, the sole shareholder of Defendant Company testified that he was the sole proprietor of Dallashie Enterprise, which like his father's business Agyei Enterprise, dealt in hardware including the brands in issue.

I am satisfied by the evidence adduced for the defendant and make a finding of fact in respect of issue 4 that prior to the registration of the brands by the plaintiff, the predecessor of the defendant company was also concurrently dealing in the branded locks. During cross-examination of Mr. Mahtani, it was clear that he was aware that his company was not the only company dealing in the door locks. It is therefore not true that he got to know about Defendant's dealing only three (3) years previously.

I hold that the defendant had thereby acquired a vested right which would have disqualified plaintiff from registering the mark had it been brought to the attention of the Registrar. Plaintiff failed to distinguish his mark from the brands already on the market as required by sections 1, 5(b) of Trade Mark Act. As discussed earlier, it does not appear that plaintiff's mark is any different from the mark put on the product by the manufacturer and sold to anyone who would buy. I therefore hold that plaintiff's mark failed the distinctive test and on this ground also, the registration ought to be invalidated.

I shall next deal with issue 2 which is whether or not Plaintiff's action is in breach of the Protection Against Unfair Competition Act 2000, Act 589.

I have already made the following findings of fact: That plaintiff's allegation of infringement was not proved. That prior to Plaintiff's registration of the Trade Mark, Defendant had been lawfully importing these products from China for 15 years or so. I have also held that the Plaintiff cannot claim exclusive use thus depriving Defendant from carrying on his business. On the basis of these findings of fact and law, the Defendant is entitled to be protected under section 8 (2) of the Protection Against Unfair Competition Act 2000, Act 589

Finally, is the Defendant entitled to its Counterclaim which seeks a declaration that the registrations of the Onion and Crocodile brands were dishonest and therefore invalid?

It is contended for the plaintiff that it is too late for the Defendant to raise the issue of dishonesty since the registration should have been opposed under s.5 of Trade Mark Act. As already stated, this view is not tenable as the Act provides for invalidation of registered marks. [See sections 12, 20(1) and 38]

(Continued)

(Continued)

In Black's Law Dictionary, a dishonest act is akin to a fraudulent act, and strictly speaking ought to have been pleaded with particularity which defendant failed to do. However, "dishonesty" has often been used as meaning an unconscientious dealing, and in that sense I think that the defendant showed that the registration of the marks by the plaintiff when it did not have the consent of the manufacturers and was aware that other companies dealt in the products was unconscionable. Be that as it may, in my view, proof that the registration was dishonestly obtained is not a sine qua non for invalidation of a trademark, and I will make no findings of fact in that regard.

JUDGMENT

In conclusion, I find that the plaintiff failed to prove its claims and I hereby dismiss them. The defendant on the other hand has established that the plaintiff's mark ought to be invalidated by reason of its failure to distinguish it from other marks already on the Ghanaian market. Defendant is accordingly entitled to its counter-claim and I hereby accordingly declare the registration of the ONION trademark in Part A of the register under No 25,951 in Class 6, and the CROCODILE trademark also in Part A under No 25,984 in class 6 invalid and hereby Order rectification of the register by expunging these registrations and due publication of the invalidation.

Costs of One Thousand five Hundred Ghana Cedis (GH¢1,500.00.) to defendant.

Paterson Zochonis and Company Limited v A.B. Chami and Company Limited

Supreme Court of Nigeria
Lewis and Udoma, JJ. S.C., Sowemimo, Ag. J.S.C.
April 2nd, 1971

LEWIS, J.S.C., delivering the judgment of the court:

The appellants, Paterson Zochonis & Co. Ltd., were proprietors of a trade mark registered in Class 48 in respect of perfumery (including toilet articles, preparations for the teeth and hair, and perfumed soap) which was registered in Nigeria for a period of 14 years from February 2nd, 1960 as No. 10989. The trade mark has no name but is of a device in a horizontal rectangle of an elephant using its trunk to pull fruit from a palm tree with a hill in the background. No colour was registered.

The respondents for their part applied to register, in Class 48 in respect of perfumery (including toilet articles, preparations for the teeth and hair, and perfumed soap), a device in a vertical rectangle bearing the name "Asirire" (meaning "evening" in Hausa) in letters down the right hand side in an outer border, depicting, within a further vertical rectangle inside, an elephant in the background, bedecked and with a person riding in a howdah upon its back, with two palm trees on either side of the rectangle and water in the foreground.

(*Continued*)

(Continued)

The appellants objected to that registration, but on May 23rd, 1968 Adefarasin, J. in the Lagos High Court in Suit No. M/135/67 rejected the objection, allowed the application, and ordered the registration of the applicants' trade mark with 10 gns. costs. Against that decision the objectors have appealed to this court.

The first point taken by Mr. Souza for the appellants is that the learned trial judge in his judgment referred to the colour actually used in the device of the objectors, put in evidence as Exhibit 3, when he described the registered trade mark of the objectors and that he also referred to the colour in the applicants' device, yet colour was not mentioned in the registered trade mark or in the application to register. In the circumstances we agree that, as no question of the colour being used so as to be likely to deceive arose, the learned trial judge should have ignored the colours used, because they were not part of the existing registered trade mark and were not sought to be used as an integral part of the device which the applicants sought to register as a trade mark. It must always be kept in mind that a registered owner whose mark is registered without limitation of colour may use the trade mark in any colour.

The second point taken by Mr. Souza was that the learned trial judge in his judgment said (1968 (2) ALR at 74):

> *I have considered whether the mark of the applicants could deceive or confuse illiterate Nigerians living in the North into taking it for the product of the respondents. The respondents did not attempt to show by evidence how such a confusion or deceit could arise; they did not call any of their customers or show that there has been any exclusive association of their products with the elephant or palm tree. In the cases to which I have made reference above, evidence of the behavior of the dealers in the products in question in relation to the mark was led, and the court was satisfied in each case that the public could be deceived. It is not sufficient for an objector to allege deceit or confusion. Where resemblance is not so obvious on an examination of the two rival marks, evidence ought to be led to show that illiterates are or could be deceived. There is no evidence before me in the instant case that the applicants have adopted the essential feature of the respondents' trade mark or that the respondents' mark is known in illiterate Nigerian trading circles by that feature.*

This was putting an onus on the objectors of calling evidence that they did not have to hear. Once again, we agree with his submission, as in *Albah Pharmacy v. Sterling Prod. Intl.* (1), (be it noted decided after the judgment of the learned trial judge in the present case) we said (1968 (3) ALR Comm. At 314):

> *It is important to make it clear at the outset that we are of the opinion that the learned judge was in error when he tried to shift the onus of proof on to the appellants; he stated that they called no witness to prove that he was deceived by the product sought to be registered. We are unable to accept this proposition, and we do not think the onus shifts in these cases to the defendants. We refer to Kerly on Trade Marks, 8th ed., at 399 (1960), where the learned author, dealing with this point, stated:*
>
> *'In such cases, the onus is on the applicant to satisfy the Registrar that the trade mark applied for is not likely to deceive or cause confusion, so that refusal to register does not involve the conclusion that the resemblance is such that either an infringement action or a passing off action would succeed.'*

(Continued)

(Continued)

Mr. Souza then objected to registration being granted when there was no evidence of concurrent use, but Mr. Ogunlami for the applicants rightly pointed out that the case was never brought or fought by the applicants on the basis of concurrent use, and concurrent use only comes into issue if the court in fact finds that there was honest concurrent use, and it did not do so here. Compare 38 *Halsbury's Laws of England*, 3rd ed., para. 896 at 539, where it is stated:

> *The court or registrar may, in the case of honest concurrent use or of other special circumstances, permit the registration of identical or similar marks for the same goods or description of goods by more than one proprietor subject to such conditions and limitations, if any, as may be thought right. Each case must be considered on its own merits and where there would be real hardship in refusing the application, this may offset the possibility of confusion.*

Concurrent use arises under s.13 (2) of the Trade Marks Act, 1965, which came into force on June 1st, 1967 and so applied to the present application, but in this case the dispute was in respect of s.13 (1); and these sub-sections read:

> *13 (1) Subject to the provisions of subsection (2) below, no trade mark shall be registered in respect of any goods or description of goods that is identical with a trade mark belonging to a different proprietor and already on the register in respect of the same goods or description of goods, or that so nearly resembles such a trade mark as to be likely to deceive or cause confusion.*

> *(2) In case of honest concurrent use, or other special circumstances which in the opinion of the court or the Registrar make it proper so to do, the court or the Registrar may permit the registration of trade marks that are identical or nearly resemble each other in respect of the same goods or description of goods by more than one proprietor subject to such conditions and limitations, if any, as the court or the Registrar, as the case may be, may think it right to impose.*

Mr. Souza finally argued that the learned trial judge was wrong to permit registration, as the use of an elephant and palm tree in any form would deceive or confuse an illiterate, so that although the two devices were not identical the ordinary man in the street would be deceived or confused if the applicants' device was allowed to be registered. Mr. Souza asks us, if he be right, to order that the order of the learned trial judge, that the applicants' trade mark be registered, should be set aside and the application to register be refused.

The learned trial judge however immediately before the passage in his judgment which we have already quoted stated, quite correctly in our view, the principle to be applied when he said (1968 (2) ALR at 74) — "the principle is well-established that trade marks which were not likely to deceive literates or educated persons but could deceive illiterate Nigerians should be excluded from registration."

We must apply that principle to the facts of this case. We hear in mind the words of Brett, L.J. (as he then was) in the case In *re Worthington & Co.'s Trade Mark* (4), where he said (14 Ch. D. at 15–16; 49 L.J. Ch. At 649–650):

> *Therefore, it seems to me that the proper construction is that where a trade-mark is registered, it is not merely the outline or design as printed in the advertisement in black, or black and white, which*

(Continued)

(Continued)

is to be protected, but that which is to be protected is the trade-mark as it may be used or will be used in the ordinary course of trade, that is, in any colour. That being so, it seems to me that the proper test is this: assume both trade-marks to be registered, and let it be supposed that each person registering is ignorant of the other's trade-mark, would any fair use of the second be calculated to deceive? I quite agree that we ought not to take into consideration obliteration or a fraudulent alteration of the second design. The question is whether any fair use of the second would be calculated to deceive. Now, if the first may be used in any colour, so also the second if registered may be used in any colour, and, supposing the parties to be ignorant of each other's marks, they might both with a perfectly fair intention use them of the same colour. The question would then be whether, supposing them both to be fairly used with the same colour, would the second be calculated to deceive any person who only used ordinary observation? That brings us to a matter of fact to be considered in each particular case. The decision with regard to any two trade-marks cannot give any assistance as to what ought to be the decision with regard to any other two trade-marks. In each particular case you must do the best you can to come to a right decision as to what would be calculated to deceive, it being assumed that the two marks are not identical. Then one has to exercise one's own eyes.

What has to be considered, as was stated in *Kerly on Trade Marks*, 8th ed., at 156 (1969) when referring to *Bailey's* case (2), is whether "there is a real tangible danger of confusion of the mark which it is sought to register should be put on the Register."

It is clear here that in so far as the products in question are asked for by name there can be no confusion, as the applicants' alone bear a name — "Asirire." In the test by ear, therefore, the applicants' trade mark is clearly registrable.

So far as the test by eye is concerned, it is to be noted that not only is the name incorporated into the device of the applicants so that even an illiterate would appreciate that there was writing though he would not know what it meant, but more important the whole pictorial scene in the two devices is quite different, and indeed the shape of the two devices is dissimilar, the objectors' registered trade mark being a horizontal rectangle while the applicants' proposed trade mark is a vertical rectangle. Whilst size, unless incorporated specifically in the details of a registration, is not a factor to be considered, as a registered trade mark owner may use his device in any size, shape is one factor to be taken into consideration in determining whether registration of the applicants' device is likely to deceive or cause confusion with the objectors' registered device.

We cannot accept the submission of Mr. Souza that the registered device of an elephant and palm tree means that no other device incorporating in a wider overall design an elephant and palm tree could ever be used. Here the objectors' device appears as an elephant, apparently wild, without covering, whilst the applicants' elephant, apparently tamed, is portrayed with a man riding in a howdah on its back. Accepting, as Mr. Souza himself said, that the devices are not identical, the right test is not to place the two devices side by side but to consider, as we said in *Alban Pharmacy v. Sterling Prod. Intl.* (1) (1968 (3) ALR Comm. At 316), whether — "the person with imperfect recollection, the incautious and the illiterate as well as those who may place an order by telephone," would be likely to be confused

(Continued)

(Continued)

or deceived, and we think the devices are so dissimilar overall that, notwithstanding both incorporate an elephant and a palm tree, even an illiterate person with an imperfect recollection would not be confused or deceived. We think the applicants' trade mark is quite *distinctive* from the objectors' registered trade mark and, as Jessel, M.R. said in the case of *In re Jelley, Son & Jones's Application* (3) (51 L.J. Ch. At 640n.; 46 L.T. at 382n.):

> I have always had regard in these cases of registration of new marks to the question of distinctiveness; that is a very different question to the question of distinction as regards old marks.

Therefore, although the learned trial judge applied in part some tests in coming to the conclusion that he did, we are satisfied that, notwithstanding this, he in fact came to the right conclusion in the end, and that he rightly allowed registration of the applicants' trade mark, as it is not likely to deceive or cause confusion with the objectors' registered trade mark. The appeal is accordingly dismissed with 34gns. costs to the applicants, the respondents in this appeal.

Appeal dismissed.

Premier Food Industries Limited v Al-Mahra Limited

Republic of Kenya
High Court at Nairobi (Milimani Commercial Courts)
Civil Case No. 661 of 2005

RULING

This is an application dated 28th November, 2005. It is brought under Order XXXIX Rules 2 and 9 of the Civil Procedure Rules, Section 3A of the Civil Procedure Act, Section 36 of the Trade Marks Act Cap. 506 and all other enabling provisions of the Law. The application is seeking three primary orders. They are as follows:-

1) That the defendant's trade mark "**PEP-TOP**" registered as No.55633 with the registrar of Trade Marks in Class 30 (Schedule III) in respect of tomato sauce be expunged from the records of the trademarks registry.
2) An injunction be issued against the defendant restraining it, its directors, employees, agents and/or servants from using the trade mark name "**PEP-TOP**" or any other name or names similar to those of the plaintiff and the logo currently used by the defendant or any other logo similar to that of the plaintiff.
3) The defendant be restrained whether acting by its directors, officers, servants or agents employees or any of them or otherwise howsoever from packing, selling or offering or displaying for sale any products and/or goods which bear the name "**PEP-TOP**" or bear or use the device and/or shape of labels as applied on products and/or goods manufactured and sold by the plaintiff or any similar or colourably similar to the plaintiff's.

(Continued)

(Continued)

The grounds for the application are:-

1) The defendant's trade mark name "**PEP-TOP**" (the offending mark) is identical with or strikingly similar to those of the plaintiff's trade mark names "**PEP**", "**PEPTO**", and "**PEPTANG**" (the plaintiff's marks) and is therefore breaching the plaintiff's trade mark rights.

2) The offending mark creates confusion amongst the public as it can and is being passed off as that of the plaintiff's.

3) The offending mark further creates confusion and misleads the public into believing that the plaintiff is also selling products and/or goods in the trade mark name "**PEP-TOP**".

4) The defendant is using the device and shape on the labels of their products and/or goods which closely resemble the device on the plaintiff's products/goods which enhances the confusion amongst the public and results in a passing off the defendant's products and/or goods as associated with those of the plaintiff's.

5) The defendant is infringing upon the goodwill and good reputation that has been established by the plaintiff hence exploiting this goodwill and denying the plaintiff any rights and interests arising therefrom.

6) The defendant's instructions on their label contain similar words, description and colour as that on the plaintiff's label, furthering the passing off.

7) The defendant by the aforesaid actions seeks to pass off its products and/or goods as that of the plaintiff which infringes both upon the goodwill and good reputation established by the plaintiff in the market and further causes confusion among customers and the public in general which is consequently detrimental to the plaintiff's position.

8) It is just and equitable and necessary that the court grants the applicant an injunction in order to prevent any further infringement of the plaintiff's trademarks and abuse of goodwill or reputation by the defendant as the harm caused cannot be measured or compensated in damages.

The application is supported by an affidavit sworn by one Sundararaman Sharmajaran, the plaintiff's Operations Manager. To the said affidavit are annexed 4 exhibits. In the affidavit the grounds for the application are substantiated. The main points raised are that the plaintiff is the registered proprietor of the following trademarks hereinafter referred to as the "plaintiff's marks".

Trademark No.	Trademark	Class & Schedule	Expiry Date
2706	PEP	42 Schedule II	2011
2707	PEPTANG LABEL	42 Schedule II	2011
4717	PEP	44 Schedule II	2006
23632	PEPTO LABEL	32 Schedule III	2012

The plaintiff is a leading manufacturer and distributor of various consumer products which are well known in the Kenyan and East African Market to wit tomato sauces and ketchups. In or about August 2005, the plaintiff learnt that the defendant is the registered proprietor of

(Continued)

(Continued)

a Trademark registration number **55633** "**PEP-TOP**" in class 30 schedule III in respect of tomato sauce to subsist in the register for a period of 10 years with effect from 11.2.2004.

This Trademark is identical with or strikingly similar to those of the plaintiff's said marks and have the same pronunciation. Further that the defendant's said trade mark name, the device and shape of the label closely resemble the device and shape on the labels on the plaintiff's products to the extent that the public is most likely to believe that the defendant's products and/or goods are manufactured by or are otherwise associated with the plaintiff's products. The plaintiff further states that the defendant's labels contain similar words description and colour as those of the plaintiff's labels. The ingredients on the "**PEP TOP**" labels are identical to the plaintiff's labels in identical orders as those for the plaintiff's. In the premises the defendant will be able to pass off its goods and/or products as those produced by the plaintiff and the similar name and label will create confusion amongst the public and/or customers by leading them to believe that the plaintiff is trading as "**PEP TOP**" which is in fact not true and is detrimental to the business of the plaintiff which has established goodwill over a period of time in respect of its trade names, trademarks, logos and the get up, device and shape of its labels. The plaintiff contends in the said affidavit that the defendant is intentionally using a name, logo and device which are strikingly similar to that of the plaintiff and is unlawfully and unduly infringing on the said goodwill established by the plaintiff by misleading the customers and the public in general into believing that the plaintiff is trading as "**PEP TOP**" which is not true. There is also a contention that the products and/or goods sold by the defendant are of a different quality to that of the plaintiff and that the plaintiff's products are of much higher quality and the sale of any more products and/or goods by the defendant will cause great loss of reputation to the plaintiff and thereby cause irreparable loss and damages.

The defendant opposed the application and relied upon a Replying Affidavit of one Abdulrasul Swaleh Muhsin the defendant's Managing Director sworn on 7.12.2005. It is deponed in this affidavit that the mark "**PEP TOP**" is not identical with nor strikingly similar to the plaintiff's marks and does not bear the same pronunciation. To the contrary it is deponed that the said trademark is distinct and the distinction was appreciated by the Registrar before accepting the mark for registration. The defendant further contends in the said affidavit that the name "**PEP-TOP**" cannot mislead the public to believe that it is the plaintiff's or is associated with the plaintiff. According to the defendant a general look at the products shows that there exists no resemblance in shape and device between the products to warrant the plaintiff's concern. The fonts used on the trademarks names, the colour regime, the graphics and the labeling are so distinct that no reasonable person would consider the products similar. No confusion can therefore be caused. In the premises the defendant contends that it is not cashing in on the plaintiff's goodwill in respect of its trade names and marks, logos, gate up device and shape of the labels.

I have perused and considered the application, the affidavits in support and the annextures. I have also considered the replying affidavit. I have also carefully considered the able submissions of the Learned Counsels and all the cases to which I was referred as well as

(Continued)

(Continued)

the Law. Having done so I take the following view of this matter. The prerequisites to be established by the plaintiff were laid in the case of *Reckit & Colman Properties Ltd — vs — Borden In. (1990) 1WLR 491*. They are as follows:-

First (the plaintiff) must establish a goodwill or reputation attached to the goods or services which he supplies in the mind of the purchasing public by association with identifying 'get-up'. Secondly he must demonstrate a misrepresentation by the defendant to the public (whether or not intentional) leading or likely to lead the public to believe that goods or services offered by him are the goods or services of the plaintiff. Thirdly, he must demonstrate that he suffers or in a quia timet action, that he is likely to suffer damage by reason of the erroneous belief engendered by the defendant's misrepresentation that the source of the defendant's goods or services is the same as the source of those offered by the plaintiff.

*In the case at hand, there appears to be no dispute that the plaintiff is the registered proprietor of the trademarks "PEP", "PEPTANG LABEL", "PEPTO LABEL" which were registered way back in the year 1992. There is also no dispute that the plaintiff is a leading manufacturer and distributor of various consumer products which are well known in the Kenyan and East African market to wit tomato sauces and ketchups. At paragraph 10 of the supporting affidavit sworn by Sundararaman Dharmarajan it is deponed that the plaintiff has established a goodwill over a period of time in respect of its trade names and trademarks, its logos and the get up device and shape of its labels. The defendant's response to that argument is a denial contained in paragraph 6 of the replying affidavit of Abdulrasul Swaleh Muhsin sworn on 7th December, 2005. A second response is found in paragraph 13 of the same affidavit where it is deponed that "the fact that the defendant is still producing/manufacturing **"PEP TOP"** has nothing to do with the applicant's loss of reputation and/or business except in so far as **"PEP TOP"** is simply superior in quality and therefore more marketable."*

In my view this latter averment suggests that the defendant acknowledges the reputation of the plaintiff but says it is not responsible for the loss of the same. In the premises I find that the plaintiff has shown on a prima facie basis that it has created a goodwill or reputation attached to the goods or services which it supplies in the minds of the purchasing public.

I have observed the defendant's Trade Mark "**PEP TOP**" and the plaintiff's mark "**PEPTANG**". The similarities at a casual glance are as follows:

The 1st two syllables are identical; they are in white against a reddish background; they slant in the same manner. The only difference is in the last two letters. The similarities in the labels are as follows: There are pictures of tomatoes below the trademark names and the words "**Tomato Sauce**". The pictures of tomatoes are reddish on a yellow background. Ingredients are printed in capital letters on the left side of the labels. To an ordinary customer in my view the obvious similarities are striking and he would not easily notice the difference.

In *Parke Davis & Co. Ltd — vs- Opa Pharmacy Ltd [1961] EA 556* which was an action in passing off, the Court of Appeal held that since the first two syllables in the trade, names "*Capsolin*" and "*Capsopa*" were identical and there were resemblances in the containers there was a real probability of confusion and the appellant company was entitled to an injunction. That case

(Continued)

(Continued)

was followed by Mbaluto J in *Beierdorf AG —vs- Emirchem Products Limited: HCCC No.559 of 2002 (UR)*. In the latter case the trade mark "**NIVELIN**" was found to be strikingly similar to the trademark "**NIVEA**" and would probably cause confusion to consumers.

In *Brooke Bond Kenya Ltd —vs— Chai Ltd [1971] EA 10*, the Court of Appeal held inter alia that the general impression of the average customer is the test of passing off. In that case the appellant sued the respondent for infringing its trademarks and for passing off its goods as the appellant's. The infringement consisted in using the words "Green Label". The packets used by the respondent had been changed to make them nearly resemble those of the appellant.

In the premises, I am satisfied that the plaintiff has demonstrated a misrepresentation by the defendant to the public (whether or not intentional) leading or likely to lead the public to believe that goods or products or services offered by it are the goods or products or services of the plaintiff.

As regards the last test as to whether the plaintiff has suffered or is likely to suffer damage by reason of the erroneous belief engendered by the defendant's misrepresentation that the source of the defendant's goods or services is the same as the source of those offered by the plaintiff, I have found as follows:-

Sundaranaman Dharmarajan the Operations Manager of the plaintiff has in the supporting affidavit at paragraph 9 deponed that by its Trade Mark "**PEP-TOP**", the defendant will be able to pass off its products and/or goods as those produced by the plaintiff resulting in confusion amongst the public and/or customers by leading them to believe that the plaintiff is trading as "**PEP-TOP**" which is in fact not true and is detrimental to the plaintiff's business. Indeed, the affidavit further continues, some of the plaintiff's customers have enquired from the plaintiff as to whether "**PEP TOP**" is one of its products which shows confusion amongst the public and/or customers. The said Dharmarajan has further deponed at paragraph 12 of the same affidavit that the plaintiff's products are of a much higher quality and the sale of any more products and/or goods by the defendant will cause a great loss of reputation to the plaintiff and thereby cause irreparable loss and damages. I have already found that the similarities between the defendant's Trade Mark "**PEP TOP**" and the plaintiff's marks raise a real probability of confusion to customers. Such confusion is likely to cause damage to the plaintiff. The plaintiff's apprehension that it will suffer irreparable loss and damages is therefore not without basis. Actual loss in my view need not be proved. *In Banme & Co. Ltd —vs— A.H. Moore Ltd (2) [1958] 2 All E.R. 113* it was held:

> no man was entitled even by the honest use of his own name, so to descry by or mark his goods as in fact to represent that they were the goods of another person.

I respectfully adopt these wise words and hold in the case at hand that the plaintiff has shown on a prima facie basis that it is likely to suffer damage by reason of the erroneous belief engendered by the defendant's misrepresentation that the source of its goods is the same as the source of those of the plaintiff.

Having found as above, I have no hesitation in holding that the plaintiff has established the first and 2nd tests set out in the precedent setting case of *Giella —vs— Cassman Brown & Co. Ltd. [1973]*

(Continued)

(Continued)

E.A 358 to wit a prima facie case with a probability of success at the trial and that the injury complained of would not adequately be compensated in damages. Being of that persuasion, in my view the plaintiff was also entitled to the protection provided by Section 7 of the Trade Marks Act which gives the proprietor of a Trade Mark certain rights. The section reads:-

> *exclusive right to the use of the trade mark in relation to the goods or in connection with the provision of any services and without prejudice to the generality of the foregoing that right is infringed by any person who not being the proprietor of the trademark uses a mark identical with or so nearly resembling it as to be likely to deceive or cause confusion in the course of trade or in connection with the provision of any services in respect of which it is registered.*

In finding that the plaintiff has satisfied the conditions for the grant of interlocutory injunctive relief, I am alive to the fact that the plaintiff has inter alia sought the same prayers in its plaint. In my view it is not correct as argued by counsel for the defendant that this finding is a determination of the main suit at interlocutory stage. The plaintiff has in addition to the prayer for injunction sought several other prayers including declarations, permanent mandatory injunctions and general damages. In my view even if no other prayer was sought the court still has jurisdiction in appropriate cases to issue orders prayed for in the suit at interlocutory stage.

In the end the plaintiff's application dated 28.11.2005 is allowed in terms of prayers 3, 4 and 5 thereof. The injunction will be conditional on the plaintiff filing an undertaking under seal to pay damages if any to the defendant in the event that it is found at the trial that the injunction ought not to have been issued. The said undertaking to be fortified by a similar undertaking by a director of the plaintiff. The said undertakings to be filed within 7 days of today.

Costs shall be in the cause.

Orders accordingly.

Tanzania Cigarette Company Limited v Mastermind Tobacco Limited

High Court of Tanzania (Commercial Division), Dar es Salaam
Commercial Court Case No. 11 OF 2005, November 28th 2005
Massati, J

The Plaintiffs, MS Tanzania Cigarette Company, Ltd, filed a suit in this Court against the Defendants MS Mastermind Tobacco (T) Limited for the following reliefs:

In a simple language, the parties' claims against each other are for infringement of trade marks and passing off and unfair competition. For the purposes of this judgment, I will retain the description of Plaintiff and Defendant when dealing with the suit, and the parties in the counterclaim shall be baptized as *"MASTERMIND"* and *"TCC"* for the Counterclaimant and the counter defendant respectively.

(Continued)

(Continued)

At the beginning of the trial the following issues were framed for the suit, and the counterclaim respectively.

<u>For the Suit:</u>

1. Whether the Defendant has infringed the Plaintiff's trade mark?
2. Whether the Plaintiff registered trademark SAFARI graphic fraudulently?
3. Whether the Defendant has prior rights over MASTER trademark by virtue of making the application first?
4. Whether the Defendant has extensively marketed the MASTER brand cigarette so as to make it well known?
5. Whether the trade mark SAFARI was changed by the Plaintiff so as to resemble the trademark MASTER?
6. To what reliefs are the parties entitled?

<u>On the Counterclaim:</u>

1. Whether TCC has passed off MASTERMIND'S "MASTER" cigarettes by manufacturing SAFARI cigarettes?
2. Whether MASTERMIND has exclusive rights in "MASTER" trade mark?
3. Whether MASTERMIND has goodwill in the trade mark 'MASTER' to protect?
4. Whether TCC has engaged in unfair competition against MASTERMIND?
5. To what reliefs are the parties entitled?

The bone of contention here is that the Defendant has infringed the Plaintiff's trade mark registered in the name of SAFARI. S. 2 defines the term *"trade or service mark"* to mean: -

any visible sign used or proposed to be used upon in connection with or in relation to goods or services for the purposes of distinguishing in the course of trade or business the goods or services of a person from those of another.

The term *"visible sign"* is defined to mean -

Any sign which is capable of graphic reproduction, including a word, name, brand, device, heading, label, ticket, signature, letter, number, relief stamp seal, vignette emblem or any combination of them.

In the present case the name of the Plaintiff's registered trade mark is *"SAFARI"*, whereas that of the Defendant is *"MASTER"*. So the disputed visible sign is not in the form of a name, as the names are different. What the parties claim is the similarity in pictorial representation in the packet of the two products.

I gather this from the evidence of the parties on record. Thus PW1 testifies on p. 15 of the typed proceedings:

In SAFARI and MASTER LIGHTS there are circles in the middle. The words SAFARI and MASTER are similarly positioned in the same manner. The colouring of the labels (blue) is also similar. The characteristics and simulation of the above and lower lines are similar. The dress up of the packets are similar.

(Continued)

(Continued)

And PW2 at p. 20 of the proceedings says:

> *From a distance the colours the shapes and the positioning of different elements in the packets (are the same)*

Earlier on, PW2 had observed:

> *The invention of the SAFARI trade mark to indicate the introduction of either sunrise or sunset. The idea behind Master Mark is also the rising and setting of the sun on a dark blue background. So these and SAFARI virtually represent the same thing.*

And DW1, testified on p. 43 of the proceedings that:

> *There are certain similarities (between Exh.P9 and P11). The blue colour, the sun/moon, the lines at the top and bottom are almost similar.*

So, even as between the witnesses from each side, there is little doubt that the two brands of cigarettes *"SAFARI"* and *"MASTER"* (Exh.P9 and P11) are similar in appearance. That they are confusingly similar is amply demonstrated by PW1, PW2, PW4, PW5, PW6 and PW7. Having myself closely scrutinized them I too conclude that the two brands have similar visible signs or get up except for the names. Therefore each is a trademark by definition. The question is who is the owner of the trade mark in dispute leaving the names aside.

Section 14 (1) of the Trade and Service Marks Act stipulates:

> *14. (1) The exclusive right to the use of a trade service mark as defined in section 32 shall be acquired by registration in accordance with provisions of this Act.*
> *(2) Registration of trade or service mark shall not be considered validly granted until the application has fulfilled the conditions for registration.*

S. 20 (1) of the Act prohibits the registration of a trade or service mark which is identical with a trade or service belonging to different proprietor and already on the register in respect of the same goods, services or closely related goods or services or that so nearly resembles that trade or service mark as to be likely to deceive or cause confusion.

This takes me to the next question. Resemblance of the graphics apart which of the two trade marks is valid under ss. 14(1) and 20 (1) of the Act?

It is evident from the wording of that section, this will have to be decided by reference to the date of registration of each of the trade marks. From the evidence on record, the Defendant filed her application for registration of the trade mark on 24/6/2004 (Exh.D2) and the mark was finally registered on 20th May 2005 as per Exh.D7. According to Exh.D7, the registration became effective from 24/6/2004. It was registered in Class No. 34 under No. 30748. On the other hand the Plaintiff had filed her application for registration on 6/9/2004 (Exh.Pl) and was eventually registered on 20/1/2005 but with effect from the 6/9/2004 (Exh.P6).

According to s. 28 (1) (b) of the Act the date of application is deemed to be the date of registration if the application shall not have been opposed, or if opposed, the opposition has

(Continued)

(Continued)

been decided in favour of the application. True, in this case the Plaintiff filed an opposition to the application of the Master Mark on 4/5/2005. (Exh.P14). In that notice, the Plaintiff described herself as the registered proprietor of SAFARI registered on the 6th day of September 2004. It is also true that the opposition has not been determined in favour of the Defendant.

In my view in the light of the provisions of ss. 20 (1) and 28 (1) of the Act and the evidence of DW2 the Assistant Registrar of Trade and Service Marks, the Plaintiff's mark would appear to be not validily registered by reason of a prior application for registration of the Defendant's mark. So apparently in the words of s. 28 of the Act, the application of the Plaintiff's SAFARI trade mark and Exh.P6, was accepted/issued in error, and therefore apparently invalid. The reason is to be traced in the chronology of the events, which shows that in priority of time, the Defendant's MASTER trade became effective on 24/6/2004, whereas the Plaintiff's became effective on 6/9/2004. On the face of it therefore it appears that the Defendant is the lawful proprietor of the <u>MASTER Lights</u> trade mark (Ex.P 11).

But there is something else. The registration of SAFARI has been challenged for having been registered fraudulently. That allegation is found in paragraph 4:2 of the Defendant's written statement of Defence and opposed by the plaintiff in paragraph 4:2 of the reply. It forms the second issue in the main suit, which I will have to consider before returning to the first issue.

T.A. BANCO AND ROBIN JACOB'S took <u>KELLY LAW OF TRADE MARKS</u> (12th ed. and page 178) to define "fraud."

> It might be fraud for a person to procure the registration of a trade mark as . . . which he knows he is not entitled to claim the exclusive use of . . . if for instance he knows that it is used by another trader.

With that she concluded that by conceding their knowledge as to the existence or MASTER trade mark pending with the registrar and by proceeding to register the SAFARI with that knowledge, the Plaintiff must be deemed to have registered it fraudulently.

It is true that the term "fraud" is not defined in the Trade and Service Marks Act, although it is used in several provisions of the Act, such as ss. 37 and 50(2). In <u>BROOM'S LEGAL MAXIMS</u> 10th ed. at page 542 the mode of proving fraud is discussed.

> fraud is proved when it is shown that a . . . representation has been made (1) knowingly or (2) without belief in the truth or (3) recklessly without caring whether it be true or false.

In the present case, and on the facts and evidence on record there is no doubt that the Defendant's application for registration was lying pending in the office of the Registrar. It is evident from the testimony of PW1 that the Plaintiff knew of the pending application. The Plaintiff filed an application to register "MASTER" which was rejected on account of it being similar to a pending one. By proceeding to register the SAFARI the Plaintiff either knowingly or recklessly did so without caring whether or not the two marks resembled. After procuring registration the Plaintiff then filed an apposition to the registration of MASTER which the Plaintiff knew had been pending for over three months prior to the filing of their application. So I have every reason to conclude that by so doing the Plaintiff intended to violate the

(Continued)

(Continued)

Defendant's right and cause injury to her. Direct evidence of actual design or contrivance to perpetrate a positive fraud, may be wanting, but I am positive that constructive fraud has been established by the available strong circumstantial evidence.

For the above reason, I will answer the second issue in the affirmative. I find and hold that the registration of the SAFARI mark under dispute was procured fraudulently.

The combined effect of my finding in the second issue and my discussion on the first issue generally is that although the SAFARI mark has been registered, its registration was obtained by fraud, and in terms of section 50 (2) of the Act its registration was invalid. And since infringement only protects a registered trade mark and since in law registration is valid only if it complies with all the conditions of registration, and since DW2 has also shown that the SAFARI mark was registered by mistake I will proceed to hold that the Plaintiff cannot maintain an action on infringement.

On the other hand it is true that the Defendant's trade mark was eventually registered on 20/5/2005, and since it was pending since 24/6/2004, it is deemed to have been effective as from the latter date. However it is also true that when it was registered a notice of opposition against its registration was pending.

And it is clear that no registration in law could properly proceed without first deciding the opposition in favour of the applicant. By so proceeding to register, the Registrar violated section 28 (1) (b) of the Act. For the same reasons, therefore the Defendant is not the lawful proprietor of the Master trade mark under dispute either. Therefore it cannot be protected under section 32 (1) of the Act. The argument of the learned counsel for the defence therefore also fails.

So all said, the first issue is answered in the negative, not because the Defendant is protected under section 32 (1) of the Act but because the Plaintiffs trade mark now in dispute was registered fraudulently and by mistake and would not confer in law, exclusive right of use of that trade mark to the Plaintiff. And under section, 31 and 32 of the Act only valid registration can be protected by an action in infringement.

The third issue is whether the Defendant has prior rights over MASTER trade mark by virtue of making the application first? It was submitted by Ms. Kasonda, that the validity of a trade mark dates back to the date of the application for registration. She sheltered herself with the provisions of ss. 20 (1) and 28 (1) of the Act. She therefore asked the Court to hold that the Defendant has prior rights over the Master trade mark.

Mr. Mnyele, learned Counsel for the Plaintiff, while conceding the right of use of a prior applicant of a trade mark, submitted that that right would only be effective upon the application being registered. And since under S. 28 (1) of the Act the MASTER trade mark should not have been registered pending the determination of an opposition against its registration the Defendant had no prior rights over the mark. He reinforced his argument by citing an Indian case of the *Registrar of Trade marks and Another vs Kumar Ranjee Sen Air* [1966] Calcutta.

(Continued)

(Continued)

I have no doubt that the case cited by the learned Counsel, represents good law. **And** I have already held above that both <u>SAFARI</u> and <u>MASTER</u> were wrongly registered in law. And I have no doubt in my mind that a proprietor of a trade mark acquires exclusive use of the trade mark, upon registration. But the question here is, whether the person has a prior right of use of a trade mark which he has only applied for registration?

It was held by the Supreme Court of India in *N.R. Dongre vs. Whirlpool Corporation* [1996] 5 SCC. 714, quoted in <u>SARKAR ON TRADE MARKS</u> — Law and Practice 4th (ed.) at p. 172, that

> *A trader needs protection of his right to prior use of a trade mark as the benefit of the name and reputation earned by him cannot be taken advantage of by another trader by copying the mark and getting it registered before he could get the same registered in his favour.*

Therefore a trader's right of use to a trade mark is protectable before registration.

In the present case, the Defendant had filed her application for registration of her MASTER trade mark three months prior to the Plaintiff's application. Although the Plaintiff procured the registration of SAFARI graphic label earlier/before that of the Defendants, the Defendant nevertheless had prior rights over MASTER trade mark by virtue of making the application first. Therefore the third issue is answered in the affirmative.

The fourth issue is whether the Defendant has extensively marketed the MASTER brand cigarettes so as to make it well known?

Let me begin with Ms. Kasonda's submission in which she quotes a passage from MASTER's book. The passage was however, conveniently, not quoted in full. Whatever was available, the full passage reads:

> *A mark may become famous and well known almost overnight through modern advertising and advanced technology.*

That is the part quoted by Ms Kasonda. But the passage does not end there. It continues:

> *More frequently a mark will become well known with the passage of time by dint of the continued expenses of resources, time...*

My understanding of this passage read as a whole is that as a rule marks take time to be known although in exceptional cases, through modern technology **and** advertisement this could take a short time. So the fame of a trade mark is normally a function of time.

On the premises, I find that while there might be some evidence on record, that evidence is not sufficient to establish that that stint of promotion was enough to make the cigarettes well known. In fact, both PW2 and DW1 admit that a goodwill is acquired over a period of time. DW1 said in cross examination that no goodwill can be acquired within one week or one month. For all the above reasons I will answer the fourth issue in the negative.

(Continued)

(Continued)

The fifth issue is whether the trademark SAFARI was changed by the Plaintiff so as to resemble the trade mark MASTER?

Mr. Mnyele learned Counsel submitted that on the evidence on record, it cannot be said that the Plaintiff imitated the MASTER trade mark to make the SAFARI trademark. He relied on the evidence of PW1. He said the Defendant had a duty to prove the imitation and failed to do so. So he prayed that the issue be answered in the negative.

Ms. Kasonda, learned Counsel for the Defendant submitted that since the Plaintiff has quite a number of SAFARI labels (Exh.P7) some of which she does not use and which are distinct from MASTER, the Plaintiff's application of the SAFARI trade mark in dispute which resembles the MASTER was ill intentioned, as the Plaintiff was aware of the existence of MASTER's application for registration. She said this was admitted by PW2. So by rushing for the registration of a similar trade mark, the Plaintiff's intention was to prevent the Defendant's entry into the market. So in her opinion this was sufficient evidence to prove that the Plaintiff changed the SAFARI trademark to imitate the MASTER trademark, and so, argued that the fourth issue be answered in the affirmative.

I agree with Mr. Mnyele, that imitation is a question of fact and has to be decided on the basis of the evidence on record. It is true that according to Exh.P6 and P7, the Plaintiff had registered different types of SAFARI. The SAFARI KALI FILTER and SAFARI KING SIZE were graphically and colourably different from the SAFARI KING SIZE FILTER shown in Exh.P6. According to Exh.Pl, this type of SAFARI brand was submitted for registration along with MASTER on 6/9/2004. The MASTER LIGHTS trademark was by then pending registration. Looking at Exh.P8 (SAFARI KING FILTER) and Exh.P7 and P10 (MASTER LIGHTS) it is difficult to see the difference immediately. In fact, all the parties agree that the two brands are confusingly similar.

There is no direct evidence that the Plaintiff imitated the MASTER trademark from SAFARI label and resemblance per se does not prove imitation. But as I posed to answer the second issue, the 3 months prior existence of the application for registration of MASTER trade mark, together with the Plaintiff's admitted knowledge of MASTER and their intention to launch their products in the market, and the close resemblance of the two brands is not a mere coincidence. I think these factors build a strong circumstantial evidence that call for some satisfactory explanation from the Plaintiff. As I found in the second issue I find no satisfactory explanation for that coincidence from the Plaintiff as the existence of that coincidence is, I think, peculiarly within the Plaintiff's knowledge, and s. 115 of the Evidence Act requires that:

> *115. In civil proceedings when any fact is especially within the knowledge of any person the burden of proving that fact is upon him.*

The evidence of PW2, that she was involved in the SAFARI Trade Mark graphics does not assist the Court because she did not indicate the date of that *"invention"*. I suppose the intention of the evidence of PW3, and PW4, in mentioning an ex worker of the Plaintiff in the name of CHOMBA was to introduce that CHOMBA may have transferred that *"invention"* to

(Continued)

(Continued)

the Defendant Company. However, we don't know when did CHOMBA cease employment, with the Plaintiff; and since even PW2 did not indicate when that invention was made, the evidence of PW2, PW3 and PW4 is not sufficient to prove that the Plaintiff *"invented"* the graphic in dispute and thus offer some explanation for that coincidence. On the other hand, DW1 produced Exh.Dl to show that at least in point of time the Defendant was the first to apply for registration of that brand. I think an earlier application raises a rebuttable presumption that any subsequent application of a similar mark, may be a result of imitation. The burden of rebutting that presumption is, in this case on the Plaintiff, and I am not satisfied that the Plaintiff had discharged that burden. Therefore, I will answer the fifth issue in the affirmative.

The last issues for both the main suit and the counterclaim are, to what reliefs are the parties entitled?

The Plaintiff's claim is based on <u>infringement</u> on its SAFARI trade mark by the Defendant, for which it prays for perpetual injunction, delivery of all manufactured or imported cigarettes that infringe the trademark, general damages and costs. I have held above that although the Plaintiff had procured the registration of SAFARI label earlier than the Defendant's MASTER and since the two get ups are confusingly similar to each other, and since the application for registration of the MASTER was made prior to that of SAFARI and was still pending when the SAFARI was registered, I declare that the SAFARI trade mark was fraudulently and/or otherwise by mistake wrongly registered vis a vis the MASTER trade mark. And since infringement is protected by registration, and by that, I mean lawful registration, and since fraud vitiates everything the Plaintiff had no trade mark in law in the name of the disputed SAFARI which could be infringed. Therefore the Plaintiff has failed to prove its case on a balance of probabilities, and the suit is accordingly dismissed.

On the other hand, MASTERMIND's action is based on the common law tort of passing off and unfair competition. I had held above that under common law, a trader may maintain an action for passing off even if the trade mark is not registered. In the present case, although the MASTER trade mark was eventually registered, its registration was not in accordance with the law, and therefore unlawful, but by reason of it having filed an application for registration of the trade mark earlier than TCC's SAFARI MASTERMIND had a prior right of use to the trade mark which happened to be confusingly similar to SAFARI. Therefore MASTERMIND had a prima facie right to protect its trade mark from passing off. However to prove the tort of passing off, one has to further prove that he had goodwill in the products that are alleged to be passed off. In my judgment, MASTERMIND had not yet acquired any goodwill in the MASTER Cigarettes when it launched the counterclaim. Without a goodwill no action for passing off can succeed.

As to unfair competition since SAFARI Cigarettes had not yet been put on the market and its prices known, no predatory trade practice has been established under the Fair Competition Act 1994 and therefore there was no evidence of unfair competition. That leg of the counterclaim too fails. Consequently the whole of the counterclaim fails and it too, is dismissed.

(Continued)

(Continued)

Before I pen off let me make a few remarks. From the look of things it appears to me that the parties have instituted their claims prematurely without first exhausting the machinery established within the offices of the Registrar of Trade and Service Marks, instanced by the pending notice of opposition filed by the Plaintiff. Their claims are to some extent, like premature babies whose proper place is the incubator who for this purpose is the Registrar, so that their matters can be regularized. And the Registrar could do well to assume and exercise his statutory duties in whatever area that has not been finally determined in this judgment.

After so saying, I now proceed to pronounce that both the suit and the counterclaim are dismissed and each party shall bear their own costs.

Order accordingly.

Trade Kings Limited v Unilever PLC, Cheesebrough Ponds (Zambia) Limited, Lever Brothers (Private) Limited

Supreme Court, (S.C.Z. Judgment No. 2 OF 2000), Appeal No. 71 of 1999, 9th November, 1999 and 9th February 2000
Ngulube, C.J.

NGULUBE, C.J.: delivered the judgment of the court.

This case involves two popular and very well known bath soaps, namely GEISHA and GEZA BEAUTY SOAP.

On 15th May 1997, the respondents commenced an action in the High Court pursuant to Section 59 of the Trade Marks Act, Cap. 401 seeking an injunction to restrain the appellants from allegedly infringing their trade mark number 83/93 in respect of GEISHA and from passing off the soap GEZA as the respondent's soap. The respondents also sought ancillary relief by way of delivery up and destruction of the materials complained of; damages; and an account of profits. The facts were further compounded on account that this was not simply one registered proprietor of a trade mark suing a defendant who is a mere imitator: It was common ground and obvious on the face of the documents that the defendant in the action had followed the procedures under the Trade Marks Act, Cap. 401, and thereby also became a registered proprietor of their own trade mark number 547/94 GEZA BEAUTY SOAP AND FLOWER DEVICE. At the end of the day, the learned trial judge did not deal with the case as presented by the complainants but sought to re-open the registration process at a point where an objection has been received and ordered that the registration of GEZA be expunged and that the statutory processes consequent upon the receipt of a valid objection be proceeded with.

The appeal is against the decision to expunge and to allow the objection to be processed as if in the usual way under the statute, including the Regulations. We heard learned arguments and submissions on both sides. One point which immediately stands out and which emerged

(Continued)

(Continued)

and which appeared to be common cause was that the learned trial judge did not infact adjudicate upon the action and the issues actually presented by the respondents. As Mr. Lisulo argued, their case has not been adjudicated upon to date. The record shows that the respondents did not ask for their opponent's trade mark to be expunged. As we see it, any aggrieved person desirous of attacking a registration which is in force whether by rectification or by expunction has to follow the procedure ordained by the Act, especially Sections 37 (for expunction or rectification) and 38 (for expunging due to breach of conditions). It follows that Mrs. Mwenda was on firm ground when she submitted that it was a misdirection on the part of the learned trial judge to have granted remedies which were not even pleaded or applied for and when there were statutory procedures to be followed. As she pointed out, the court was bound to take heed of the provisions of Section 57 of the Act which is to the effect that registration constitutes prima facie evidence of the validity of the original registration.

We can immediately allow this part of the appeal; we reverse the learned trial judge and restore the appellants' registration of the trade mark GEZA.

Mr. Lisulo submitted quite correctly in some respects that issues of infringement and passing off are independent regardless whether there is registration of the trade mark or not. The submission has merit in so far as an action for passing off of goods may be concerned and to which we will return in a moment. However, we entertain serious reservations whether an action for infringement as such of a trade mark by one registered proprietor can be maintained against the registered proprietor of another trade mark which may be the same or confusingly similar. We are aware that, under Section 9 of the Act, the registration of a mark creates a statutory monopoly protecting the use of the mark in the course of trade for the goods or service for which the mark is registered. The section inures for the benefit of both registered proprietors and any resulting conflict appears to have been anticipated by the legislature in Subsection 4 of Section 9 which reads---

> *(4) The use of a registered trade mark, being one of two or more registered trade marks that are identical or nearly resemble each other, in exercise of the right to the use of that trade mark given by registration as aforesaid shall not be deemed to be an infringement of the right so given to the use of any other of those trade marks.*

As currently advised — since we did not have the benefit of hearing full submissions and arguments on the point — it is not feasible for one registered proprietor of a trade mark to maintain an action for infringement as such of that mark against another registered proprietor of another mark though the marks be identical or very similar.

The action for passing off is another matter altogether and Mr. Lisulo's submission that it is independent has support in the authorities. It is unaffected by the Trade Marks Act. As Christopher Wadlow puts it in his book "The Law of Passing-off", 2nd edition at page 2, ---

> *Passing-off and the law of registered trade marks deal with some overlapping factual situations, but deal with them in different ways and from different standpoints. Passing-off emphatically does not confer monopoly rights in any names, marks, get up or other indicia, nor does it recognise them as property in their own right.*

(Continued)

(Continued)

In the leading modern authority on passing-off, that is, in the case of *ERVEN WARNINK B. V and Others v J. TOWNEND & SONS (HULL) LTD and Others;* (1979) 2 All E.R. 927, their Lordships identified the main characteristics of a passing-off action. In the leading judgement, Lord Diplock said, at p. 932-3---

> My Lords, A. G. Spalding & Bros. v A. W. Gamage Ltd. *((1915) 32 R.P.C. 273) and the later cases make it possible to identify five characteristics which must be present in order to create a valid cause of action for passing off: (1) a misrepresentation (2) made by a trader in the course of trade, (3) to prospective customers of his or ultimate consumers of goods or services supplied by him, (4) which is calculated to injure the business or goodwill of another trader (in the sense that this is a reasonably foreseeable consequence) and (5) which causes actual damage to a business or goodwill of the trader by whom the action is brought or (in a quia timet action) will probably do so.*

These propositions should be read subject to Lord Diplock's wise caution at p. 933 where he said---

> *In seeking to formulate general proposition of English law, however, one must be particularly careful to beware of the logical fallacy of the undistributed middle. It does not follow that because all passing-off actions can be shown to present these characteristics. All factual situations which present these characteristics give rise to a cause of action for passing off. True it is that their presence indicates what a moral code would centure as dishonesty trading, based as it is on deception of customers and consumers of a trader's wares, but in an economic system which has relied on competition to keep down prices and to improve products there may be practical reasons why it should have been the policy of the common law not to run the risk of hampering competition by providing civil remedies to everyone competing in the market who has suffered damage to his business or goodwill in consequence of inaccurate statements of whatever kind that may be made by rival traders about their own wares. The market in which the action for passing off originated was no place for the mealy mouthed: advertisements are not on affidavit: exaggerated claims by a trader about the quality of his wares, assertions that they are better than those of his rivals, even though he knows this to be untrue, have been permitted by the common law as venial 'puffing' which gives no cause of action to a competitor even though he can show that he has suffered actual damage in his business as a result.*

We are taking some time on this because both Mr. Lisulo and Mr. Sikota, if we understood them correctly, suggested that this court should attempt to finally resolve the whole of the case or that the case be sent back to the High Court for rehearing. Arising from this, it is necessary to consider whether it is infact possible for this court to resolve the factual issues that have to be addressed merely on the record since an appeal operates as a rehearing on the record. In this case, each side organised people to swear that GEISHA and GEZA sounded the same and that the get-up would confuse and those to say they were not the same and would not confuse. What is certain is that the resolution of such a case would turn largely on issues of fact. It would of course be unpardonable for any court to assume that the average Zambian consumer is some kind of retard as suggested by some of the affidavits. Indeed in considering issues of get-up for example, a good summary is given in Wadlow's "The Law of Passing-Off" at paragraph 6.54 at page 433-4 which read---

(Continued)

(Continued)

A comprehensive summary of the issues involved in cases turning on get-up was given by Byrne, J. in Clarke v. Sharp: (1898) 15 R.P.C. 141)--

[F]irst, it must always be kept in mind that the actual issue is, not whether or not the judge or members of the jury determining it would, or would not, have personally been deceived, but whether or not, after hearing the evidence, comparing the articles, and having had all the similarities and dissimilarities pointed out, the true conclusion is that the ordinary average customer of the retail dealers is likely to be deceived.

This being the issue, it is obvious that the judgement of the eyesight is a most important, if not the most important, element in its determination; so much so, that there are many cases in which it practically determines the case, and that, notwithstanding the views of many witnesses and the most careful and elaborate discussion of difference of opinion. On the other hand, there are cases in which the evidence satisfies one that the eyesight, alone and unguarded, misleads. It is necessary to consider the nature of the article sold, the class of customers who buy; to remember that it is a question of likelihood of deceiving the average customer of the class which buys, neither those too clever, nor fools; neither those over careful, nor those over careless. One must bear in mind the points of resemblance and the points of dissimilarity, attaching fair weight and importance to all, but remembering that the ultimate solution is to be arrived at, not by adding up and comparing the results of such matters, but by judging the general effect of the respective wholes. A man may be entitled to use every single dissected item of the whole, and any of such items, and yet be disentitled to use the whole; being the items arranged in a particular form or manner. Another matter of vital importance to be considered is whether there is, or is not, some essential point of difference or resemblance which overcomes or establishes the effect of other points of resemblance; how much of the matter complained of is common to the world, how much to the trade in other similar articles, and how much to the trade in the specific commodity; colour; shape, form, originality of arrangement — all these have to be considered; but the ultimate decision must become to, having regard to all considerations, as a matter of judgement on a question of fact.

We respectfully agree with the foregoing. It follows that since this is largely still an un-adjudicated case in the High Court, the factual questions should be delved into there. We are mindful that we have not specifically alluded to all the arguments and submissions which we heard. For example, there were arguments whether a notice of opposition to the registration of the appellant's trade mark was validly lodged in time or at all. The starting point, as far as we are concerned was that the trade mark was duly registered and no one had asked for its expunction. The statute provides a procedure to be followed by aggrieved persons before registration as well as after registration.

The procedure before registration can not be resorted to here after the event and the registration process can not be re-opened in the fashion attempted below. We have already observed that the case below was diverted from being an inquiry into alleged infringement and passing-off to one dealing with registration of the appellants' trade mark. We are also mindful of a ground of appeal which complained about the condemnation of the appellant in costs when they had done nothing wrong and when the case of those considered to have been the successful party had infact been nicely skirted and bypassed. The resulting order for

(Continued)

(Continued)

a retrial is strictly speaking neither party's fault and it would be unfair to inflict an order for costs against either side in respect of the first trial.

In the sum the appeal is allowed; the order of expunction is quashed; the decision below is set aside and there will be a rehearing of the case before the same or another High Court Judge. The costs of the first trial and of this appeal will abide the outcome of the retrial.

Rhone-Poulence s.a. and Another v Ghana National Trading Corporation

HIGH COURT, ACCRA
26 May 1972
ABBAN J.

Abban J. In this application, the plaintiffs are asking for an order of interim injunction restraining the defendant from infringing the plaintiffs' patent rights in respect of the Ghana Patent No. 522, and from offering for sale a drug, called metronidazole, the product involved in the said infringement.

The two plaintiffs are limited liability companies. The first plaintiff is the owner of the United Kingdom Patent No. 836854. This patent was sealed in the United Kingdom Patent Office, on 28 September 1960, and it covered an invention entitled the "New imidazole derivations and processes for their preparation." The said patent was later registered in Ghana, under the Patents Registration Ordinance, Cap. 179 (1951 Rev.), as Patent No. 522, and dated 18 October 1962. Patents covering the said invention have also been sealed by the first plaintiff in other countries, namely, West Germany, United States of America, Soviet Union, Japan, Holland, Canada, Denmark and Sweden.

The second plaintiff is a manufacturer and it is registered in this country as an external company. It deals mostly in pharmaceutical and medical preparations. According to the plaintiffs, the second plaintiff is "a wholly owned subsidiary of the first plaintiff." The plaintiffs further aver that since the grant of the United Kingdom Letters Patent on 28 September 1960, the second plaintiff has been the sole and exclusive licensee of the first plaintiff in respect of that patent and of all the other patents sealed in other countries including the Ghana Patent No. 522. So that the rights of the patentee (the first plaintiff) deriving from the said invention are exclusively vested in the second plaintiff. From the photo-copy of the patent specification, attached to the affidavits of the plaintiffs, it is clear that one of the imidazole derivatives covered by the patent has the generic name of "metronidazole." This "metronidazole" is manufactured and sold by the second plaintiff in this country and in other parts of the world under the trade name Flagyl. This drug, according to the plaintiffs,

> has been an outstanding success since its introduction on the market in 1960; and until the introduction in 1969 of a chemically related substance, called nitrimidazine, metronidazole was the only product effective for the oral treatment of vaginal trichomoniasis.

(*Continued*)

(Continued)

Even after 1969, the drug has been, and still is, extremely useful in treating many infections.

The defendant's case is that it received the product in question from its manufacturer-supplier, called International Generics Ltd. of London, for sale in this country; and in the circumstances it cannot be held responsible for the production of the said drug. The defendant further averred, in paragraph 19 of its affidavit in opposition, that at the hearing [Page 114] of this application it would seek leave of the court to join the said International Generics Ltd. who

> have agreed by telex to indemnify the defendant and who would be sending their managing director from London to be present during the hearing of the application, in order to show what document this company [International Generics Ltd.] holds to justify the sale of the drug.

I should observe that the said managing director of the International Generics Ltd. was not present during the hearing of the motion. Also no document was tendered or shown to the court by the defendant to justify the manufacture and sale of metronidazole in this country by the International Generics Ltd. My view is that the International Generics Ltd. are not the patentees of the said metronidazole, neither are they licensees of the patentees.

It is perhaps worth pointing out that several preliminary objections were raised by learned counsel for the defendant. But the court decided to hear arguments on the merits as well, and to consider the application as a whole. The motion was therefore argued at great length.

Three bottles containing metronidazole tablets and purchased from the defendant's shops in Accra, Kumasi and Takoradi, respectively, were tendered by learned counsel for the plaintiffs without objection. The defendant's receipts issued in respect of those purchases were attached to one of the affidavits filed by the plaintiffs and were marked SAA3, SAA4 and SAA5, respectively. Learned counsel for the plaintiffs submitted that these exhibits show that the defendant has infringed the said patent. Counsel contended that all that is necessary at this stage is to make out a prima facie case, namely, that the plaintiffs are the owners or the exclusive licensees of the Ghana Patent No. 522, and that there is some infringement of that patent. Counsel submitted that the evidence so far produced by the plaintiffs before the court, justifies the making of an order of interlocutory injunction against the defendant, and the court ought to grant the application.

As I indicated earlier on, certain objections were raised and ably argued by learned counsel for the defendant. He contended that no prima facie case of infringement has been established, and even if it is held otherwise, there are many impediments which militate against the granting of the interlocutory injunction. The first objection put forward by learned counsel for the defendant is based on the State Proceedings Decree, 1972 (N.R.C.D. 59). Learned counsel argued that since the defendant is a statutory corporation, having been established under the Statutory Corporations Act, 1964 (Act 232), it comes within the ambit of section 1 of N.R.C.D. 59. Counsel said the International Generics Ltd. supplied the metronidazole tablets to the defendant for sale in Ghana under an agreement entered into between the defendant and the said International Generics Ltd., and that the International Generics Ltd., being a foreign company, the present case falls within section 1 (b) [Page 115] of N.R.C.D. 59.

(Continued)

(Continued)

Thus the Attorney-General's fiat was required before the defendant could be sued. But since the plaintiffs did not obtain that fiat before issuing the present writ, the action itself is a nullity, and in consequence, the application for the interlocutory injunction cannot be entertained. Learned counsel for the plaintiffs disagreed with this contention, and briefly submitted that the action herein has nothing to do with the alleged contract between the defendant and the said International Generics Ltd. and, as such, the fiat of the Attorney-General was not necessary in this case.

I think N.R.C.D. 59 is not applicable to the present action. This Decree came into operation on 19 April 1972 and section 1 thereof provides that: *[His lordship here read the provisions as set out in the headnote and continued:]* Careful reading of these provisions will show that the contracts being referred to in this Decree are those to which the intended plaintiff is or has been a party; and the legal proceedings in question must have arisen out of those contracts. An intended plaintiff who has not entered into any contract with any of the bodies or agencies mentioned in the Decree, and whose intended action will not be grounded on any such contract, does not require the Attorney-General's fiat under this Decree before he can issue his writ of summons. In my opinion, the Decree is very restricted in its application, and it is not open to this court to give it a greater field of operation. The plaintiffs are not parties to the alleged contract entered into by the defendant and the said International Generics Ltd.; and the proceedings herein are based on a tort alleged to have been committed by the defendant, independent of any such contract. The plaintiffs did not therefore require the fiat of the Attorney-General, and the present action commenced without the said fiat is quite in order.

The second objection raised by learned counsel for the defendant is that if there was an infringement, that infringement was authorised by the government. He contended that the Ghana National Trading Corporation Instrument, 1965 (L.I. 395), which laid down the objects of the defendant corporation, permitted the importation and selling of goods including all types of drugs. Thus, submitted counsel, if in the course of carrying out the said objects, there has been an infringement by the defendant of the plaintiffs' patent rights, that infringement ought to be taken to have been authorised by the government under the said L.I. 395.

The objects of the defendant are specified in paragraph I (a) to (d) of the said L.I. 395. I need not set them out *in extenso*. I will only say that there is nothing in these objects which bears out learned counsel's submission. Nothing in those objects gives the defendant the power or the right to operate its business without regard to the laws and regulations governing trade. The objects, indeed, do not say anything about infringement of patent rights. If the argument of learned counsel is accepted, it will have far reaching consequences, because the logical conclusion will be that so far as the G.N.T.C. is concerned, it has a standing [Page 116] authority of the government to breach any trade laws and regulations which may stand in its way.

I think L.I. 395 has not, either expressly or impliedly, authorised any such conduct. The defendant in carrying out its objects, as defined in the said instrument, will have to respect

(Continued)

(Continued)

the patent rights of others, and to conform to the laws of the land, as well as to the generally accepted trade practices as required of any trading firm or organization. Likewise, the provisions of section 4 of the State Proceedings Act, 1961 (Act 51), cannot avail the defendant. Because the defendant has not been able to produce any evidence, documentary or otherwise, showing that the Republic authorised the infringement in question. I therefore hold that the government did not at any time authorise the infringement of the Ghana Patent No. 522.

The *locus standi* of both plaintiffs was also challenged. Learned counsel for the defendant contended that the Ghana Patent No. 522 was registered in the name of a company, called Societe des Usines Chimiques Rhone-Poulence which is quite different from the first plaintiff whose name is Rhone-Poulence s.a. Learned counsel therefore submitted that the first plaintiff is not the patentee, and as such, cannot institute the present action. I think this objection is adequately answered by paragraph (3) of Mr. Anaman's affidavit which says:

> prior to 29 December 1961, the first plaintiff was named Societe des Usines Chimiques Rhone-Poulence but it was changed to its present name with effect from 29 December 1961. This change of name was communicated to the Patent Office of United Kingdom which office acknowledged the change and made record thereof in its register.

This assertion of Mr. Anaman is borne out by the certificate issued by that office and attached to Mr. Anaman's said affidavit and marked SAA1. The certificate states:

"Patent Office,

25 Southampton Buildings,

London.

I, the undersigned, being an officer duly authorised in accordance with section 62 (3) of the Patents and Designs Act, 1907 to sign and issue certificates on behalf of the Comptroller-General, *hereby certify that a Patent numbered 836, 854 and dated the 6 May 1958, was sealed to Societe des Usines Chimiques Rhone- Poulence, a French Body Corporate, of 21 Rue Jean-Goujon, Paris, France, on the 28 September 1960, for an invention entitled 'New imidazole derivatives and processes for their preparation.' I also certify that under date, the 25 July 1962, notification of the change of name of the said Societe des Usines Chimiques Rhone Poulence to Rhone-Poulence S.A. was recorded in the Register of Patents;* that under date, the 6 August 1971, notification of the change of address of the said Rhone-Poulence S.A. to 22 Avenue Montaigne, Paris, France was recorded in the Register of Patents; *that no other document affecting the proprietorship of the said Patent* [Page 118] *has been entered in the Register of Patents; that, subject to the payment of the prescribed renewal fees, the term for which the said Patent was granted will end at the expiration of sixteen years from the 6 May 1968; and that the said Patent is still in force.*"

(The emphasis is mine). There is therefore more than sufficient evidence to show that the first plaintiff is the owner of the United Kingdom Patent No. 836854 which has also been registered in Ghana as Patent No. 522. Learned counsel for the plaintiffs stated from the Bar that the registrar of patents in Ghana was also informed of the change of name. I have no reason to doubt the veracity of this statement of learned counsel. In any case, since the person who owns

(Continued)

(Continued)

United Kingdom Patent No. 836854 is the person who also owns Ghana Patent No. 522, and since it is proved that the first plaintiff owns the said United Kingdom Patent, it follows that no person other than the first plaintiff owns the Ghana Patent No. 522. Consequently, even if it is assumed, for the purpose of argument, that the registrar of patents in Ghana has not been notified of the change of name, or that the change of name has not been effected in the Ghana Patent, there is still some evidence before this court to hold that the first plaintiff is the same as the person whose name appears on the Ghana Patent No. 522.

As regards the second plaintiff, learned counsel for the defendant submitted that it has no cause of action. He contended that the second plaintiff is a bare licensee and, as a bare licensee, it ought to have asked the patentee of the invention, under the Patents Act, 1949 (12, 13 & 14 Geo. 6, c. 87), s. 35 (3), to bring this action; and if the said patentee failed to do so within two months, it is only then that the second plaintiff will have a cause of action, which will then entitle it to bring the present suit. It should be noted that the Patents Act, 1949, which is the foundation of counsel's argument, is a United Kingdom Act. It is a consolidating Act which came into effect on 1 January 1950, and it consolidated the Patents and Design Acts 1907 to 1946. It will therefore be seen that that Act is not a statute of general application. Neither have its provisions been adopted by the law-makers of this country. In the circumstances, the said Act is not applicable in Ghana. In any case, the plaintiffs deny that the second plaintiff is a bare licensee. They contend that the second plaintiff is the exclusive licensee of the first plaintiff. Mr. Rowley, in paragraphs (1) and (10) of his affidavit in support of the application, stated as follows:

> *(1) I am pharmaceutical chemist and am West Africa Area Manager of May and Baker Ltd. the second named plaintiff herein.... (10) Since the grant of United Kingdom Letters Patent No. 836854 on 28 September 1960, my company has been the sole and exclusive licensee of the patentee under this patent and numerous corresponding patents including Ghana Letters Patent No. 522 and in consequence, exclusive rights in the invention deriving therefrom, have been vested, not in the patentee, but in my company. [Page 119]*

Apart from being the exclusive licensee of the patentee, the second plaintiff further contends that it is "a wholly owned subsidiary of the first plaintiff." I am of the opinion that there is evidence that the second plaintiff is not a bare licensee. It is an exclusive licensee of the first plaintiff, and as such, the second plaintiff has every right to take proceedings in respect of infringements committed after the grant of its licence and the patentee can also join the suit as a plaintiff. See *Halsbury's Laws of England* (3rd ed.), Vol. 29, p. 93, para. 197, where the learned editor said:

> *The right to sue for infringement of a patent belongs to the registered proprietor of the patent, to his exclusive licensees, that is, persons on whom the patentee has conferred, to the exclusion of all other persons (including the patentee) any right in respect of the patented invention, and, in certain circumstances, to holders of compulsory licences and licences under patents endorsed 'licences of right.' When licensees sue alone, the patentee must be made a defendant, but is not liable for costs unless he enters an appearance and takes part in the proceedings. Where the patentee sues, it is usual to join exclusive licensees as plaintiff.*

(Continued)

(Continued)

(The emphasis is mine). In *Renard v. Levinstein (No. 2)* (1865) 11 L.T. 766, Wood V.C. at p. 767, held, inter alia, that the court could give redress in respect of an infringement of patent at the suit of those who were the exclusive licensees. I therefore hold that the second plaintiff properly joined the first plaintiff in bringing this action.

It was further submitted that since the second plaintiff did not register his licence or whatever interest was assigned to it by the patentee, in accordance with the Patents Registration Ordinance, Cap. 179 (1951 Rev.), s. 10, the second plaintiff cannot have any cause of action in this country. This submission, again, is misconceived. The section does not make the registration of such assignments or interests compulsory. The said section 10 provides that:

> *Where a person becomes entitled by assignment, transmission, or other operation of law to the privileges and rights conferred by a certificate of registration or to any interest therein, he may make application in the prescribed manner to the Registrar for the entry on the Register of such assignment, transmission, or other instrument, affecting the title, or giving an interest therein.*

(The emphasis is mine). I am of the view that the language used by the Ordinance in this section is permissive. The assignee of the patentee is invested with discretion and he can therefore decide either to register or not to register his assignment. The word "may" used in this particular context, to my mind, was not intended to be construed as "must" or "shall." Thus there is no obligation on the assignee to apply for the registration of his said assignment or interest. Since the section has not got compulsory force, I hold that the registration of the assignment of the rights of a patentee, as provided under section 10 of Cap. 179, is not mandatory. I further hold that failure of an assignee to register his said assignment or interest, as in the case of the second plaintiff herein, will not preclude that assignee from instituting an action when there is an infringement of his rights under the assignment, so long as the assignee concerned is the exclusive licensee of the patentee.

Learned counsel for the defendant also contended that the defendant had nothing to do with the processing or manufacturing of the metronidazole. Counsel stated that the defendant is a mere seller thereof, and that the action should have been brought in London against the International Generics Ltd. which actually manufactured the said drugs abroad and supplied them to the defendant in Ghana. I do sympathise with this submission. But what we are concerned with in this case is the sale of the metronidazole in Ghana, and not its manufacture in the United Kingdom by the International Generics Ltd. According to the plaintiffs, it is the sale of the drug in Ghana by the defendant which constitutes the infringement. In my opinion, where a patent has been granted in Ghana for processing a particular product, the importation from abroad and the sale in Ghana of that product, made according to the patented process by a person who is neither the patentee nor the licensee of the patentee, is an infringement. The case of *Elmslie v. Boursier* (1869) L.R. 9 Eq. 217 is in point. In that case, it was held that the importation and sale in England of articles manufactured abroad according to the specification of an English patent is an infringement [Page 121].

(Continued)

(Continued)

The case of *Elmslie* was cited with approval by the Court of Appeal in *Von Heydon v. Neustadt* (1880) 14 Ch.D. 230, C.A. In the subsequent case of *Badische Anilin und Soda Fabrik v. Hickson* [1906] A.C. 419, H.L., Lord Davey in the course of his judgment in the House of Lords said at p. 422 that:

> It has also been decided in a number of cases that to sell and deliver in this country the product of the invention was an infringement of the monopoly granted, whether such product was made in this country or abroad.

See also *Saccharin Corporation Ltd. v. Anglo-Continental Chemical Works* [1901] 1 Ch. 414 and *Wright v. Hitchcoch* (1870) L.R. 5 Exch. 37 at p. 47. It can therefore be seen that the fact that the defendant was not the manufacturer or had nothing to do with the processing of the metronidazole is irrelevant.

The defendant contended that the interim injunction should not be granted, because the plaintiffs delayed for two years before the issue of the writ and that that delay amounted to laches. It will be recalled that the second plaintiff first wrote to the defendant on 9 February 1970, drawing the defendant's attention to the patent rights of the second plaintiff in certain drugs, and requested the defendant not to infringe those rights. A copy of that letter attached to Mr. Anaman's affidavit, shows that at that time, that is, on 9 February 1970, the second plaintiff appeared not to have become aware of the defendant's infringement of the Ghana Patent No. 522, now in dispute. The infringement which the second plaintiff was aware of, and complained about in that letter, was in respect of the United Kingdom Patent No. 716207 which has been registered in Ghana as Patent No. 288. The said Patent No. 288 related to another product called chlorpromazine, which is also manufactured and sold by the second plaintiff under the registered trade mark "Largactil."

Apart from this particular drug covered by the said Patent No. 288, the second plaintiff did not complain of any infringement of the Ghana Patent No. 522 in dispute herein, or of any other patents. The second plaintiff in that letter, however, gave the defendant a list of the second plaintiff's other patented drugs, their trade marks and their patent numbers. The letter also requested the defendant, in case it had sold any of those drugs, to furnish the second plaintiff with a statement of those sales, and the stocks being held by the defendant in respect of any of the products listed in that letter. The list incidentally, included "metronidazole" with its Ghana Patent No. 522.

Contrary to expectation, the defendant did not reply to the second plaintiff's said letter. It seems to me that it was after that letter had been written, and the defendant had become aware of the second plaintiff's interest in the said Patent No. 522, that the defendant started selling the metronidazole in its shops. This conduct of the defendant leaves a lot to be desired, because the defendant set out to do an act which it knew was likely to be an infringement of the patent rights of the second plaintiff. Having regard therefore to the circumstances of this case, and to the fact that the actual infringements, which brought about the present suit, were the sales made by the defendant on 8, 9 and 20 September 1971, respectively, I do not think that the seven months that elapsed [Page 123] between

(Continued)

(Continued)

8 September 1971 and 18 April 1972, the date on which the writ of summons was issued, ought to be regarded as amounting to excessive delay. The plaintiffs are not therefore estopped by laches.

The last submission of the defendant's counsel was that assuming there has been an infringement of the patent, the plaintiffs have not been able to prove to the court the extent of harm or damage done to the plaintiffs' business or any financial loss incurred by them. The short answer to this submission is that the court will invariably grant an injunction even though no damage, pecuniary or otherwise, is proved, if the acts complained of will result in infringing the legal rights of the plaintiff. This was made quite clear by Parker J. in *Weatherby & Sons v. International Horse Agency and Exchange Ltd.* [1910] 2 Ch. 297 at p. 305, where the learned judge said:

> But, in my opinion, an unfair use may be made of one book in the preparation of another, even if there is no likelihood of competition between the former and the latter. After all copyright is property, and an action to restrain the infringement of a right of property will lie even if no damage be shewn.

In the case just cited, the dispute was about copyright, and I think the infringement of copyright and of patent, as in the present case, can be treated on the same footing, the question being one and the same, namely, whether the right of exclusive licensee has been infringed. See also *King v. Brown, Durant & Co.* [1913] 2 Ch. 416. I therefore hold that it is not necessary for the plaintiffs, at this stage of the proceedings, to prove actual damage. They are only to establish a prima facie case of infringement. This, in my opinion, they have been able to do. So that before they have the chance to establish their rights at law, it is the duty of this court to intervene to protect them by an interlocutory injunction.

Nevertheless, I have given thought to the question whether instead of granting the interlocutory injunction, I should rather order the defendant to keep an account of all the metronidazole tablets it will sell in this country, and the profits it will make on them, between now and the day of the final hearing and determination of the suit. But I am entertaining great doubts as to whether the defendant would keep proper accounts, especially because of its refusal even to acknowledge the receipt of the plaintiffs' letter of 9 February 1970; and in view of its refusal to comply with the plaintiffs' requests and to pay attention to the reasonable remonstrances contained in the said letter. I think in the circumstances of this case, to put the defendant upon terms of keeping an account, and to allow it to continue what may eventually prove to be an improper business, would be a very ineffective mode of recompensing the plaintiffs, if they should, in the long run, turn out to be in the right.

Again, I have cautiously considered the degree of convenience and inconvenience to the parties by granting or not granting the interim injunction. The business of the second plaintiff is mainly that of the manufacturer and dealer in pharmaceutical and medical preparations. But the defendant, on the other hand, trades in all sorts of goods and commodities, including every conceivable provision. So that the sale of this particular drug — metronidazole — forms

(Continued)

(Continued)

a negligible part of the defendant's vast business. This is amply borne out by paragraph (27) of the defendant's own affidavit which states that:

> *the defendant's business is wider than the distribution of International Generics Ltd. products which is very minimal in relation to the defendant's total operation which covers technical goods, motor vehicles as well as bottling and sale of soft drinks.*

I am therefore satisfied that it would be less inconvenient and less likely to produce irreparable damage, to stop the defendant from selling the said drug, than it would be if the defendant is permitted to sell it and merely keep account. Moreover, I firmly believe that if the defendant is prevented from selling the drug for the time being, the public will not in any way suffer or be affected, because whatever happens, the drug will continue to be available in the open market, or in the drug stores in Ghana through the agencies of the second plaintiff; only the price may differ from that of the defendant.

However, on the consideration of the whole matter, I have come to the conclusion that the course which will best meet the ends of justice is to grant the interlocutory injunction and then put the plaintiffs upon terms. Accordingly, the defendant, its agents, officers, servants, or workmen are restrained from infringing the Ghana Patent No. 522, by importing, purchasing, supplying or offering for sale the product called metronidazole, pending further order of this court. The plaintiffs are ordered to give an undertaking to abide by such order, if any, as to damages as the court may think fit to make, if they should ultimately turn out to be in the wrong.

The said undertaking should be in writing and must be deposited with the senior registrar of this court, and a copy thereof served on the defendant. The order of the interim injunction herein made should not be drawn up by the senior registrar until the said undertaking is given in the manner as indicated (*supra*), and the order should take effect as from the day on which it is formally served on the defendant or its solicitors.

The plaintiffs are awarded costs assessed at ¢85.00.

Application granted.

GEMFARM Investments (PTY) Ltd v TRANS HEX Group Ltd and Another

High Court (Namibia)
Case No. P I 445/2005, April 7th 2009
Coram: Damaseb, J.P. et Maritz, J.

MARITZ, J.: All the exceptions raised in this action concern the application or interpretation of probably the most neglected area of statutory regulation in Namibia: patent legislation. In a world increasingly driven by globalised economies and markets; in an age where more technological advances have been made in a single century than in all the centuries which

(Continued)

(Continued)

have preceded it combined; at a time when commerce and industries are increasingly based on and benefiting from the power of knowledge converted into ideas, inventions and technologies for the benefit of humankind and its environment, it should be a serious legislative concern that our statutory laws designed to record, preserve and protect those ideas, inventions and technologies are marooned in outdated, vague and patently inadequate enactments passed by colonial authorities in this country about a century ago. Yet, it is by those laws that this Court is called upon to adjudicate the defendant's exceptions to the plaintiff's Particulars of Claim.

The plaintiff, a Namibian company, claims that it is the patentee and registered proprietor of an invention for the "method of, and apparatus for, underwater mining" of mineral deposits known as a "pebble jetting system" (the "invention"). The invention is more fully described in the Complete Specification thereof which was accepted by the Registrar of Patents on 8 August 2001. It is not necessary for purposes of these exceptions to detail the specifications of the invention other than to state that, amongst others, the specifications describe a method of mining underwater mineral deposits which comprises an apparatus inducing an upwards stream of water, air and gravel in a pipe extending upwardly from the deposit to a mining vessel above it from where it is again pumped down to the deposit so that the water with the gravel entrained in it impacts on the deposit and breaks it up, thereby enhancing lifting thereof to the vessel with the upwardly flowing water and air. Letters Patent No. 2001/0050 for the invention were issued on 22 April 2002. On the face thereof, the Registrar of Patents in Namibia recorded under his hand that the Letters have been made patents and were dated and sealed as of 13 February 2002.

The Plaintiff avers that the defendants have infringed its patent for the invention by making, or causing to be made, an installation and an airlift comprising integers of the invention, more fully described in its Particulars of Claim, and fitting them (or causing them to be fitted) on the MV "Namakwa" and the MV "Ivan Prinsep", two motor vessels chartered by the first defendant (or caused to be chartered by it) from the second defendant. As a result of the infringement, the plaintiff avers, it suffered damages in the amount of US$8 416 950.00 (approximately N$ 80 million) for the loss of contracts and royalties pertaining to the exploration and exploitation of underwater mineral deposits in certain defined areas. The correction of an erroneous description of a particular component of the invention aside, the plaintiff, therefore, is seeking a declarator to the effect that the defendants have infringed its patent; an interdict restraining defendants from continuing to do so; an order for the payment of damages in the amount of US$8 416 950.00 plus interest thereon *a tempore morae* by the defendants jointly and severally and a *mandamus* directing the defendants and all those possessing any such equipment under them, to deliver up to plaintiff any and all made or used by them in contravention of Plaintiff's invention within ten days of the order.

The defendants excepted to the plaintiff's Particulars of Claim (as amplified by its further particulars) on the basis that it either does not disclose a cause of action or lacks the necessary averments to sustain the relief claimed and submits that the plaintiff's claims fall to be dismissed with costs.

(Continued)

(Continued)

The main thrust of the first exception is that the Patents and Designs Proclamation, No. 17 of 1923 (the "Proclamation") upon which the plaintiff relies for the registration of its patent had been repealed by the Patents Act, No. 37 of 1952 (the "1952-Act") and was therefore no longer in force in Namibia when the patent was sealed or granted. Hence, the recipients plead that the grant was a nullity and, consequently, that the letters patent purportedly issued thereunder were of no force and effect. Therefore, they aver, the plaintiff's reliance thereon cannot sustain its action and the relief claimed.

This exception invites the Court to examine the statutory basis for the granting of patents in Namibia and, in particular, to determine whether the Proclamation was still of application in 2002 when the patent was sealed and the letters issued.

The Proclamation is perhaps one of the earliest examples where the Union had one of its statutes applied to the Territory subject to local modifications — not by an express or implied provision contained in the statute itself, but by reference in legislation of local application promulgated by the Administrator, a delegated lawgiver installed in the Territory. In its original form, it was structured as follows: Sections 1—4 deal with the granting and registration of patents; sections 6—8 with the registration of designs; sections 10—12 with the registration of trademarks; sections 14—16 with copyright in registered works; sections 18—24 with general provisions and sections 5, 9, 13 and 17 apply the provisions of the "Union Act" in so far as they are applicable to the balance of matters mentioned in those sections, *mutatis mutandis* to patents granted and designs, trademarks and the copyright in works registered under the Proclamation.

It is of some significance in the determination of the issues which follow that the "Union Act" was not applied to the Territory by some or other provision in the Act itself but by the legislative act of a delegated lawgiver in the Territory and that the "Union Act" was not applied by the Proclamation to the Territory in its entirety but only in part and subject to the substantive provisions of the Proclamation dealing with the grant or registration of the various components of intellectual property. So, for example, is the right to apply for a patent; the contents of such an application; the granting of a patent by the Registrar and the keeping of a register of patents regulated in sections 1—4 of the Proclamation in a manner which is substantially different to the treatment of the same topics in the "Union Act". The "Union Act" is also applied in a truncated form: the limitation is apparent from the wording in s.5.

> 5. *The provisions of the Union Act with regard to the effect and duration of a patent, the renewal, extension, surrender and revocation of patents, the grant of compulsory licences, the amendment of Specifications, actions for infringement and the rectification of the register shall, in so far as such provisions are applicable, apply, mutatis mutandis, to patents granted under this Proclamation.*

The "Union Act" is defined in s.18 as "the Union Patents, Designs, Trade Marks and Copyright Act, 1916 (Act No. 9 of 1916) and any amendment thereof". The difficulty which presents itself in the first exception arises from the later repeal of sections 6-75 of the 1916-Act and so much of the rest of that Act (and of a 1947-amendment thereof) as relates to

(Continued)

(Continued)

patents in the Union of South Africa by s.103(1) of the 1952-Act. The 1952-Act, which comprehensively consolidated and amended the law relating to patents in South Africa, also expunged the reference to "patents" from the 1916-Act's title and long title. The net effect thereof in South Africa was that the remainder of the 1916-Act continued to be in force for the time being, but was limited in its application to designs, trademarks and copyrights. The excipients aver that the territorial and legislative sweep of the 1952-repeal extended beyond South Africa's borders and was not limited to the provisions of the 1916-Act: regard being had to the provisions of s.5 of the Proclamation and the definition of "Union Act" in s. 18 thereof, they plead that the 1952-Act also applied to the Territory and that it repealed and replaced both the 1916-Act (as it applied in the Territory) and the Proclamation.

It follows, that the most fundamental question to be answered for purposes of the first exception is whether the 1952-Act repealed the provisions of the Proclamation under which patents are being granted. Only if it did, can it be said that the patent relied on by the plaintiff for its cause of action was registered "in terms of legislation that was not applicable in the Republic of Namibia anymore" — as averred in the first exception.

Adv. Oosthuizen SC (assisted by Adv. Van Eeden) submits on behalf of the plaintiff that, even if it were to be accepted in favour of the recipients that the 1952-Act repealed the patent-provisions of the 1916-Act as it had been applied in the Territory, the repeal did not affect the validity of the Proclamation. He argues that there is no legal principle under which it could be contended that, where a specific Act incorporates, by reference, the provisions of another Act, the former is invalidated or repealed by the fact that the latter Act has been repealed. In the context of the constitutional and legislative dispensation applicable to this case, the submission is persuasive.

Although the South African Parliament had plenary powers to legislate for the Territory "as an integral portion of the Union" under Article 2 of the Mandate at the time, it had to do so "subject to local modifications as circumstances may require". For this reason, not every law made by the Union Parliament was applied without more to the Territory. There is nothing in the language of the 1952-Act which suggests that it was intended to have extraterritorial effect or to impose its provisions on the legislative dispensation in the Territory — neither expressly (as was done, for example, in the Copyright Act, No. 63 of 1965 and the Trade Marks in South West Africa Act, No. 48 of 1973) nor by necessary implication.

There is, in addition, also a second reason why it must be dismissed. It relates to the definition of "Union Act" in s.18 of the Proclamation and, more in particular, is to be found in the answer to the question whether the 1952-Act, which repealed the patent provisions of the 1916-Act in South Africa, also applied to the Territory and became the "Union Act" for purposes of patents. Originally, the "Union Act" was defined to "mean the Union Patents, Designs, Trade Marks and Copyright Act, 1916 (Act No. 9 of 1916) and any amendment thereof". Whilst it is clear that the words "and any amendment thereof" would include any amendment to the Act which might have been enacted prior to the promulgation of the Proclamation, there is a significant divergence of opinion on the application of subsequent enactments in the Union either amending or repealing its provisions. They range from one

(Continued)

(Continued)

school of thought which contends that none of the Acts passed by the Union Parliament to amend the 1916-Act in South Africa applied to the Territory and others which suggest that all of them, including the 1952-Act, are.

The need to publish Union statutes in the Territory before they obtained the force of law was a matter already raised and thoroughly argued in *Offen*'s case. Both in the court *a quo* and on appeal (reported as *R v Offen*, 1935 AD 4) it was held, in keeping with judicial thinking at the time, that publication of the law in question (the *Customs and Excise Amendment Act*, No. 36 of 1925) in the Union *Gazette* sufficed because, although the port and settlement of Walvis Bay was being administered "as if it were part of the mandated territory and as if the inhabitants of the said port and settlement were inhabitants of the mandated territory" (under s.1(1) of Act 24 of 1922), it nevertheless remained part of the territory of the Union of South Africa. Wessels, CJ quoted s.38(1) of Act 36 of 1925 and continued:

> *Sec. 38 of that Act reads as follows: 'The mandated territory of South-West Africa shall, for the purpose of the collection of customs and excise duties, be regarded as a part of the Union.' If that is so, then Union legislation which is valid Union legislation* ipso facto *applies to the mandated territory and is in force in Walvis Bay and sub-sec. (3) provides specifically that the provisions of the Act shall, apply to Walvis Bay, 'which for the purposes of this section shall be deemed to be a part of the mandated territory.' It is perfectly clear from that sub-section that it makes the Act applicable to Walvis Bay on promulgation in the Union Gazette, not as part of the Union territory only but as part of the Union territory which is deemed to be part of the mandated territory. There is therefore no need for it to be promulgated in the mandated territory if it is a Union Act of force in the Union and therefore of force in mandated territory and Walvis Bay.*

This approach was followed (again in respect of legislation applicable in Walvis Bay) in *R v Ackermann*, 1954(1) SA 95 (SWA) at 96F-H.

The matter again received scrutiny by Brebner J in an instructive judgement about the judicial thinking at the time in *Faul v S.A. Railways & Harbours*, 1949 (1) SA 630 (SWA). After considering the Governor-General's power to apply a Union law to the Territory; the principle in Roman-Dutch Law (as applied to the Territory by s.1(1) of Proclamation 21 of 1919) that promulgation of a law is required before such law can have a binding effect upon the subjects it pertains to; the meaning of the words "commencement" and "taking effect" in s.12(1) of the *Interpretation of Laws Proclamation*, 1920 and *Offen's*-case, he concluded (at 636 and 367):

> *It seems to me that legislation of the Union Parliament can only become operative in the Mandated Territory, if either on the one hand the Territory is, for the purposes of the particular Act, deemed to be part of the Union . . .or the expression 'the Union' is defined as including the Mandated Territory . . ., or on the other hand, the legislation is made applicable by proclamation by the Governor-General or the Administrator under delegated authority under and by virtue of the powers conferred by sec. 2 of Act 49 of 1919, and when such proclamation is stated to be issued under the authority of sec. 2 of Act 49 of 1919, it can only have the force of law within the Territory if it is published in the Gazette of the Territory in terms of sec. 44 (1) of Act 26 of 1925. So if the particular Act of the Union deals specifically with the Mandated Territory, it must be promulgated in*

(Continued)

(Continued)

the Official Gazette of the Territory before it can bind the inhabitants therein. Legislation is ordinarily territorial in its operation, and does not bind persons resident beyond the territorial boundaries of the law-giver, since such legislation cannot be made effective while the persons affected are resident abroad. ...

The Union Parliament has authority to legislate extra-territorially, but such legislation cannot be binding upon residents of a foreign territory except by convention or in the case of the Mandated Territory by promulgation of the legislation in the *Gazette* of the Territory. The Mandated Territory occupies a peculiar position: on the one hand it is a foreign country territorially *vis-à-vis* the Union, on the other hand, the Union Parliament has power of legislation in respect thereof, but the operative effect of such legislation within the Territory is not dependent upon conventions or treaty or international law, but upon promulgation of the legislation within the Mandated Territory, or upon the Union Act incorporating the Mandated Territory as part of the Union Territory.

Measured by any of the criteria in the cases of *Offen, Faul, Ackermann, Grundlingh* and *Ntoni* or by s. 22(5) of the *South West Africa Affairs Amendment Act*, No 23 of 1949, there is nothing in the language of the 1952-Act which either expressly or by necessary implication indicates that the Union Parliament intended to apply its provisions to the Territory: the Territory is not included in the definition of the "Union"; the Act does not contain a provision to the effect that the Territory is deemed to be part of the Union for purposes of the Act and it has not been applied to the Territory by proclamation of either the Administrator or the Governor-General. An allegation in the exception to the effect that the 1952-Act "was promulgated in a Gazette of the territory" remained unsubstantiated. No reference was made in argument to the *Official Gazette* referred to and I have not been able to find any.

If the Legislature intended Act No. 37 of 1952 to apply to South West Africa it would have said so. I am fortified in this view by the fact that this Court and its predecessor, the South West Africa Division of the Supreme Court of South Africa, have on several occasions since 1952 issued orders on the basis that Act 9 of 1916 remained in force in South West Africa.

It is very unsatisfactory that patent matters in South West Africa are still regulated by a South African Act which was repealed in its country of origin more than thirty years ago.

I agree. For these and the other reasons mentioned earlier, I find that the 1952-Act did not apply to the Territory and that the first exception must also fail on this ground.

The conclusion forced upon the Court by the language of the Proclamation, however out of tune it may be with patent laws in other countries, is inescapable: Only inventions in Namibia may be registered as patents and then only by persons who are not importers. Adv. Jansen argued that the reason for the limitation is to be found in the Administrator's desire not to hamper the development in the Territory by allowing foreign inventions to be patented here. Given the status of the Territory as a C-mandate at the time — a classification reserved in the submission Genl. Smuts (who, according to Verloren Van Themaat and Wiechers, *Staatsreg, supra*, at 407, designed the Mandate system adopted by the League of Nations) for German colonies inhabited by underdeveloped populations — it might well have been so. It may also

(Continued)

(Continued)

explain why the Proclamation, unlike the 1916-Act, does not allow patents to be granted to the actual inventors of imported inventions.

In the result, I am not satisfied that the averments made on the pleadings exclude, on all possible evidence that may be led thereon, that the patent for the invention has not been granted lawfully under the Proclamation to the plaintiff. For this reason, this exception must also fail. The following order is therefore made:

All the exceptions against the plaintiff's claim are dismissed with costs, such costs to include the costs consequent upon the employment of one instructing and two instructed counsel.

Notes

1. According to WIPO (2010), "IP is divided into two categories: Industrial property, which includes inventions (patents), trademarks, industrial designs, and geographic indications of source; and Copyright, which includes literary and artistic works such as novels, poems and plays, films, musical works, artistic works such as drawings, paintings, photographs and sculptures, and architectural designs. Rights related to copyright include those of performing artists in their performances, producers of phonograms in their recordings, and those of broadcasters in their radio and television programs."
2. This discussion is based on an abbreviated version of Fritz Machlup's famous paper on patents.
3. *Patent Act*, 2003 Section (1) and (2).
4. *Patent Act*, 2003, Section 12 (1). The life of a patent under Nigeria law is also 20 years, *Patents and Designs Act* Chapter 344, Laws of the Federation of Nigeria Section 7 (1). Also as in the case of Ghana, patents cannot be obtained for "plant or animal varieties, or essentially biological processes for the production of plants or animals (other than microbiological processes and their products)" in Nigeria, *Patents Act, Section* 1 (4)(a).
5. *Trademarks Act*, 2004 (Act 664), Section 1.
6. *Trademarks Act*, 2004 (Act 664), Sections 10 & 11.
7. *Trademarks Act*, 2004 (Act 664), Section 14.

Questions

1. According to the World Bank, "International policies toward protection of intellectual property rights (IPRs) have seen profound changes of the past two decades. Emerging trends and technologies — such as bio-informatics (mapping of the human genome), biotechnology (creation of designer plants), and the widespread availability of digital content and media via the Internet—have raised new questions about intellectual property law. How will developing countries fare in this globalized and challenging intellectual property environment?"

   How would you respond to the above observation based on the law on intellectual property in your country?
2. List the pros and cons on whether society ought to protect inventions.
3. Explain the difference between trademarks and patents.

4. How may a trademark be removed? Explain.

5. Several countries in SSA do not protect patents for plant varieties. What are the pros and cons for the failure to protect plant varieties?

6. Visit WIPO's *Facts and Figures* for the latest year. What factors may explain the very low IPR applications for SSA countries compared to other countries? See http://www.wipo.int/edocs/pubdocs/en/wipo_pub_943_2014.pdf.

References

Commission on Intellectual Property Rights, 2002. Intellectual Property Rights and Development Policy, Report of the Commission on Intellectual Property Rights, London, p. 1. <http://www.iprcommission.org/papers/pdfs/final_report/ciprfullfinal.pdf> (viewed 17.09.10).

Dutfield, G., 2003. Literature Survey on Intellectual Property Rights and Sustainable Human Development, UNCTAD, Geneva. <http://www.iprsonline.org/unctadictsd/docs/GDutfield_LiteratureSurveyOnIP_April2003.pdf> (viewed 17.09.10).

Food and Agriculture Organization (FAO), International Treaty on Plant Genetic Resources for Food and Agriculture, Article 9.2 (b). <ftp://ftp.fao.org/docrep/fao/011/i0510e/i0510e.pdf> (viewed 05.04.15).

Machlup, F., An Economic Review of the Patent System. <http://harmful.cat-v.org/economics/intellectual_property/An_Economic_Review_of_the_Patent_System> (viewed 26.05.10).

Population Reference Bureau (PRB), 2014. 2014 World Population Data Sheet. <http://www.prb.org/pdf14/2014-world-population-data-sheet_eng.pdf> (viewed 07.04.15).

World Intellectual Property Organization (WIPO), What Is Intellectual Property? <http://www.wipo.int/about-ip/en/> (viewed 17.09.10).

CHAPTER 8

Cooperatives in Sub-Saharan Africa

Keywords: cooperative; financial cooperative; agricultural cooperative; Coasian theory; free rider problem; International Cooperative Alliance; International Labor Organization

8.1 Introduction

The International Cooperative Alliance (ICA) defines a cooperative as "an autonomous association of persons united voluntarily to meet their common economic, social, and cultural needs and aspirations through jointly-owned and democratically-controlled enterprise" (ICA, 2006). Cooperatives are important institutions in the development of agriculture in sub-Saharan Africa (SSA) because they serve as a source of capital formation, employment, and acquisition of market power.[1] As the examples from Ghana show, agricultural cooperatives are found in both the input (Box 8.1) and output (Box 8.2) sectors. While financial cooperatives dominate the market in SSA countries, there are several major agricultural cooperatives including, production and marketing cooperatives, poultry and livestock cooperatives, fishing and fish marketing cooperatives, and food processing and marketing cooperatives. Agriculture is also important in the sustainability of other cooperatives such as gin-distilling cooperatives, handicraft cooperatives, transport cooperatives, consumer cooperatives, and credit unions.[2]

Cooperative institutions were introduced into African countries as part of overall colonial economic policy.[3] This government interference in cooperative activities continued after independence in several SSA countries until the structural adjustment programs of the 1980s.[4] The World Bank has identified government interference as a major source of failure for cooperatives around the world (World Bank, 2008).

8.2 The Law and Economics of the Cooperative Organization

The economics of cooperatives is based squarely on Coasian theory that explains how the assignment and costs of transferring property rights affect incentives and economic outcomes.[5] The basic idea is that organizational form matters when products and assets have different attributes and also belong to different people. The cooperative form of

---

BOX 8.1 Seed producers worry about poor use of improved seeds

General News Thursday, 21 August 2008.

Seed producers in the Eastern and Greater Accra regions have complained about the poor use of improved seeds by farmers, relying rather on flawed non-certified seeds, due to the poor regulation of the industry by the state. They said aside their businesses being bruised by the non-enforcement of regulations by government leading to low returns on investments; the poor reception by farmers on the use of certified seed was also having a negative effect on their businesses. They said although certified seed produced in Ghana is currently 10 per cent below the national seed requirements, almost half of the seed is left unsold thus serving as a major disincentive to producers to invest in improved crop varieties to increase yields. Mr McKeown Frimpong, President of the Eastern and Greater Accra regions Seed Growers Association (EGARSGA), told the GNA in Koforidua that a well-functioning seed policy must be the basis of dynamic agricultural business in the country as it could help promote continual improvement in productivity. "It is only in an atmosphere of well-laid down policies that would guide the production and distribution of certified seeds to enable members realize the sweat of their investments in the seed business," he said.

BOX 8.2 Sheanuts producers appeal for regulation of industry

Business News Saturday, 20 December 2008.

Members of Sunbawiera Sheanuts Producers Association at Kperisi, a farming community in Wa Municipality have called on management of Ghana Cocoa Board (COCOBOD) to speed up regulation of the industry to bring sanity into it. "Sheanuts production can alleviate the people of Northern, Upper East and West Regions from extreme poverty provided management of Ghana Cocoa Board see the industry as a great potential for the economic growth of the three Regions and offered the needed attention like cocoa," Alhaji Imoru Ayitey, Chairman of the association said. He was speaking to newsmen at Wa after addressing a meeting of the association at Kperisi. Alhaji Ayitey noted that the disorganized nature of the industry made it difficult for producers to benefit from their toil and destroy the industry if measures were not instituted to arrest the situation. Mr Yaw Agyei Acheampong, a Service Provider in the industry said Ministry of Trade, Industry and President's Special Initiatives planned to organize training programmes for the producers to acquire skills to enable them improve quality of their produce for the international market but could not materialise. He said the Co-ordinator of Sheanuts at COCOBOD was preparing a manual to regulate the industry next year and urged producers to organize themselves into groups or associations to benefit from the regulated industry.

organization arises to address problems that are not easily handled by the investor-owned firm. The economics of cooperatives is built on the "theory of agency, property rights, incomplete contracting, and Williamson's transaction cost economics."[6] The cooperative governance structure solves the information asymmetry and monitoring problems encountered in agency relationships. Cooperative contractual structures help address the free rider problems that arise when property rights are poorly defined. On the other hand, incomplete contracting problems are handled through the cooperative organization by carefully defining residual rights. The cooperative form of organization is also effective in reducing the transaction costs associated with contracting. Transaction costs economics help to explain how the cooperative form of organization reduces the incentives for opportunism. The unique characteristics of agricultural activity, especially the importance of coordination between growers, processors, wholesalers, and retailers suggest that a cooperative governance structure is most likely to maximize returns to society.

One institutional change driven by the transition from central government control to market-led development is the emphasis on the "rule of law." As one author succinctly puts it, "this era of 'cooperative freedom' has also witnessed a renewal in the integration of the sector as the previously state-imposed and non-viable federations as well as apex bodies have been rendered redundant and alternative voluntary, autonomous, strategic and more viable consensual cooperative networks based on members' needs in the unfolding new socio-economic environment are being formed."[7] The new legal and regulatory regime governing the revival of the cooperative movement emphasizes the autonomy of cooperatives is best summarized in the International Labour Organization's *Recommendation on the Promotion of Cooperatives, 2002*, (No. 193) (referred to as "Recommendation No. 193."[8]

While details of the cooperative laws and regulations in different SSA countries differ, these laws reflect their colonial experiences.[9] The cases from Ghana and Tanzania show how cooperatives have been able to use the courts to break down government control and solidify the independence of the cooperative movement. The two cases from Ghana, *National Co-operative Kente and Adinkra Weavers Association v. Registrar of Co-operatives* and *Manzah and Others v. Registrar of Co-operative Societies* addressed two main questions: (1) the extent of the powers of Registrar of Cooperatives, and (2) whether an injunction could be used to stop the Registrar from taking certain actions concerning cooperatives. The rulings in these cases point to Courts' desire to enhance the autonomy of cooperatives after the passage of N.L.C.D. 252.

The Tanzania case, *21st Century Food and Packaging Ltd*, also shows how cooperatives in SSA are functioning after market and political liberalization. The case shows that competition in the market place is not being promoted by government fiat, but by a producer group, the Tanzania Sugar Producers Association, challenging the fiscal power of the government to influence the market through the granting of subsidy to a firm. The ruling in the case is focused on the issue of *joinder*. Initially, the Producer Association brought an action against the Tanzania Ministry of Finance and the Attorney-General seeking the nullification of a subsidy to a firm to import sugar into Tanzania. The Association argued that the subsidy would hurt competition in the marketplace. In filing the action, the Association did not include 21st Century Food and Packaging Ltd., the beneficiary of the government tax subsidy, as a party to the suit. 21st Century Food and Packaging Ltd. brought this action for the court to join as a party to the suit. Our focus is not on the *joinder* issue but rather the bigger issue of the power of a cooperative to sue government for a fiscal policy affecting the market. It is particularly pertinent since historically, companies and governments have used the *infant* industry argument to justify subsidy payments to domestic firms.

National Co-operative Kente and Adinkra

Weavers Association v Registrar of Co-operatives
High Court, Accra, Ghana
28 July 1980

Facts: The plaintiffs in this suit are a co-operative association with limited liability registered under sections 4 and 5 of the Co-operative Societies Decree, 1968 (N.L.C.D. 252). The plaintiffs registered their bye-laws as required under section 8 of the Decree (N.L.C.D. 252). The Plaintiffs initially registered two unions from two regions of Ghana and made up of seven societies, but that after registration and in keeping with their bye-laws they admitted new societies which covered the Eastern, Volta and Ashanti Regions. According to the Plaintiffs, once they registered their association, they are entitled to conduct the affairs of the association in accordance with their registered bye-laws. According to their bye-laws, they have sole authority to admit new members, and the government or any other entity has the authority to admit new members. According to the Plaintiffs, the Registrar has been interfering with the conduct of their business and their affairs contrary to the bye-laws and the provisions of the Decree and that he has been usurping their powers of admitting new members by himself. The Plaintiffs brought this suit for "Perpetual injunction restraining the defendant, his servants or agents from interfering with the day-to-day affairs of the plaintiffs and also from registering non-members of the association."

The defendant, the Registrar, represented by the Government attorney objected to the Plaintiff's request for an injunction arguing that an injunction was not a permissible remedy for actions by a servant of the Republic. The objection was based on the proposition that the registrar was a civil servant whose remuneration was charged to the

(Continued)

(Continued)

Consolidated Fund and was thus holding a "public office" in terms of the definition of "public office" in the Constitution, 1979, art. 213 (1). Consequently, the registrar was by virtue of the State Proceedings Act, 1961 (Act 51), s. 24 a servant of the Republic and therefore by virtue of section 13 (2) of Act 51 an order of injunction could not be properly granted against.

Opinion: Under the provisions of article 211 of the Constitution, 1979, the citizen had a general right to enforce civil claims against the government as if the government were a private person of full age and capacity. There was no constitutional provision that a claim for an injunction was an exception to that general right. The provisions of the State Proceedings Act, 1961 (Act 51), denying the citizen a right to obtain an order of injunction against the Republic would seem to be inconsistent with the Constitution. And therefore by virtue of article 2 (1) of the Constitution, the said provisions of Act 51 were void and of no effect. Dictum of Apaloo J.A., as he then was, in *Benneh v. The Republic* [1974] 2 G.L.R. 47 at p. 79, C.A. (full bench) cited.

In my respectful opinion, before the promulgation of the Constitution, 1969, there was no power in the court to grant an injunction against the Republic having regard to the provisions of the State Proceedings Act, 1961 (Act 51). This is also the practice in England where section 21 of the Crown Proceedings Act, 1947, denied the citizen the right of an injunction against the Crown. As against public officers or public authority exercising statutory functions, the citizen affected by the exercises has always had a right under English law to restrain ultra vires acts alleged to be in purported exercise of statutory powers: see *Attorney-General v. Aspinall* (1837) 2 My. and Cr. 406 and the *Pride of Derby and Derbyshire Angling Association Ltd. v. British Celanese Ltd.* [1953] Ch. 149.

In the said *Pride of Derby* case the award of injunction against a local authority was called in question but the Court of Appeal re-affirmed in clear terms the propriety of such a remedy. It seems therefore that although the English Crown Proceedings Act dis-allowed injunctions against the Crown, this was never understood to extend to servants of the Crown as such. In any case, under the provisions of article 211 of the Constitution, 1979, provisions in substance adopted from article 170 of the Constitution, 1969, with no alteration in form or substance, the citizen has a general right to enforce civil claims against the government as if the government were a private person of full age and capacity. There is no constitutional provision that a claim for an injunction is an exception to this general right. The provisions of the State Proceedings Act, 1961, denying the citizen a right to obtain an order of injunction against the Republic would seem to be inconsistent with the Constitution and therefore by virtue of article 1 (2) of the Constitution, the said provisions of Act 51 are void and of no effect. Article 1 (2), also culled from the Constitution, 1969, provides:

1. "(2) This Constitution shall be the supreme law of Ghana and any other law found to be inconsistent with any provision of this Constitution shall, to the extent of the inconsistency, be void and of no effect."

(Continued)

(Continued)

I am persuaded in taking this view of the law by an examination of the majority decision of the full bench of the Court of Appeal in *Benneh v. The Republic* [1974] 2 G.L.R. 47. In that case in dismissing the further appeal of the appellant, the full bench then exercising the appellate function of the then abolished Supreme Court, was studiously silent about the ratio decidendi that found favor with the ordinary bench per Koi Larbi and Anin JJ.S.C. On the contrary at p. 79 Apaloo J.A., as he then was, in dealing with the jurisdiction of the High Court to grant the relief by way of injunction as arose in the case, did not even consider it necessary to canvass the reasons why the view of the ordinary bench of the Court of Appeal denying jurisdiction of the High Court must be considered erroneous. He very firmly and rightly stated, "We feel no doubt that the High Court was clothed with jurisdiction to determine and grant a relief in a claim such as the present." Indeed, in the *Benneh* case it seems, as appears at p. 97 of the full bench decision, that an interim order of injunction was given against the Republic and the court saw nothing wrong with it.

I must observe though that in this case the relief by way of injunction is against the registrar and not the Republic. The registrar has statutory functions to perform; if he misconceives these functions and proceeds to exercise functions contrary to the enabling statute, I conceive, he can be compelled by injunction to refrain from his purported exercise of non-existent statutory functions and can furthermore be compelled by mandamus as Jiagge J., as she then was, did in *Mould v. de Vine* [1962] 1 G.L.R. 533, to carry out his statutory functions.

I think, strictly speaking, the registrar in discharging his statutory functions is not acting as a servant of the Republic. He can be said to be a servant of the Republic in the broad context in which all public officers are servants of the Republic. But a servant, strictly speaking, must, in contemplation of law, be interpreted in the domain of master and servant relationship, where the servant is in fact an agent doing at a given moment of time, that which the master can also do but which he delegates to him to do. That is not so with the Republic and the registrar in regard to his functions under the Decree. In the absence of an enactment in that behalf, the Republic per any other person cannot perform the registrar's functions and therefore, vis-a-vis the registrar's functions, the relationship of master and servant does not exist. The registrar acts in his statutory capacity as registrar.

In the result, I hold that if he acts in a manner ultra vires the enabling provisions of N.L.C.D. 252 he can be restrained by re-course to the remedy of injunction. The preliminary point of law taken by counsel that the action be dismissed in limine is therefore misconceived.

The plaintiff-applicant is therefore entitled to apply for an interim order of injunction, but as the motion has not been fixed for hearing, I shall adjourn the matter for the vacation judge to deal with. The motion is therefore adjourned sine die for the registrar to fix it before the vacation judge. Order accordingly.

Judgment: *Preliminary objection overruled.*

Manzah and Others v Registrar of Co-operative Societies

In the High Court, Sekondi, Ghana
30 November 1971

The plaintiffs submitted an application to the Senior Co-operative Officer, Takoradi, for the registration of their society as a co-operative society. The Plaintiffs claim that in a reply, the Registrar of Co-operatives had imposed certain conditions on them which had not been provided for by the Co-operative Societies Decree, 1968 (N.L.C.D. 252). The plaintiffs brought this suit for the Court to answer the following questions:

(a) Whether under paragraph 4 of the Co-operative Societies Decree, 1968 (N.L.C.D. 252), the Registrar of Co-operative Societies, Accra, and the Senior Co-operative Officer, Western Region, Takoradi, have power to impose on the plaintiffs the prerequisites and pre-conditions laid down in their letters Nos. PR. 1711/6 of 26 April 1971, and WR/ UCSRS/6 of 24 March 1971, respectively.
(b) Whether the imposition of the said prerequisites and pre-conditions are not *ultra vires.*
(c) Whether the plaintiffs have not complied with paragraph 4 of N.L.C.D. 252, and
(d) Whether the plaintiffs are not entitled to have their proposed society registered.

Opinion: The plaintiffs submitted their application on 25 February 1971. The senior co-operative officer wrote back on 24 March 1971 setting out certain conditions or prerequisites which, in his view, were essential for the registration of the plaintiffs' society. His letter (exhibit B) reads as follows:

"Department of Co-operatives
P.O. Box 119,
Takoradi
24 March 1971.

Ref. No. WR/UCSRS/6

Dear Sir,

PROPOSED UNITY CO-OPERATIVE SPIRIT RETAILERS SOCIETY

I acknowledge receipt of your letter dated 25 February 1971 together with two copies of bye-laws and application for registration of the above-named society.

The application is being processed but meanwhile it has to be stressed that certain prerequisites are essential for registration of the society.

(a) There must be a group of at least ten persons who follow as a normal means of livelihood the occupation of distillation of akpeteshie.
(b) The persons must reside within or occupy lands within the area of operations as defined in the application.
(c) The society should be existent and will be inspected by officers from this department.
(d) Members should subscribe shares in the society.
(e) The society must keep proper accounts for inspection by this department

(Continued)

(Continued)

If the conditions above are satisfied, an economic survey will be conducted to establish the potential viability of the society. If the society is found to be an economic unit, a recommendation will be made to the Registrar of Co-operative Societies for registration of the society.

It would be appreciated if the points raised would be brought to the notice of your clients.

I will inform you of further developments in this exercise.

Yours faithfully,

(Sgd.) D. O. A. Akuffo
Senior Co-op. Officer
(Western Region)

Mr. James Mercer,
Bankole Chambers,
Post Office Box 26,
Sekondi.

cc: The Registrar of Co-op. Societies,

Department of Co-operatives,

Accra."

A copy of this letter was sent to the Registrar of Co-operative Societies, Accra, who in an undated letter wrote to the plaintiffs' solicitor and paragraphs 2 and 3 of his letter (exhibit C) are relevant to this application. Paragraph 2 of exhibit C reads as follows:

"The penultimate line of paragraph 4 (2) of the Co-operative Societies' Decree, 1968, (N.L.C.D. 252), namely: 'The application. . .shall furnish any information in regard to the society as the Registrar may require' empowers the registrar to demand certain conditions, the fulfillment of which facilitates eventual registration"; and paragraph 3 is also in these words, "The preparation and production of an economic survey report prior to registration is one such vital condition."

The Plaintiffs maintain that the conditions imposed by the senior co-operative officer and confirmed by the registrar are *ultra vires* because such conditions are non-existent in so far as the Co-operative Societies Decree, 1968 (N.L.C.D. 252) is concerned. It does seem to me that the conditions which are to be satisfied by a proposed society before registration are contained in paragraphs 3 (1) and 34 (1) (a) of N.L.C.D. 252. Paragraph 3 (1) is as follows:

"No society, other than a society consisting of co-operative societies which are registered in accordance with the provisions of this Decree (in this Decree referred to as 'registered societies'), shall be registered unless it consists of at least ten persons qualified for membership under paragraph 34 of this Decree."

(Continued)

(Continued)

Paragraph 34 (1) also reads as follows:

"In order to be qualified for membership of a registered society a person shall be -

(a) capable of entering into a legally enforceable contract;
(b) resident within or in occupation of land within the area of operations of the society as defined in its bye-laws."

This clearly shows that the society must consist of at least ten members who are capable of entering into a legally enforceable contract and are resident within or in occupation of land within the area of operation of the society as defined in its bye-laws.

Again paragraph 4 (1) of N.L.C.D. 252 requires an application for registration to be made to the registrar and such application ought to be signed by at least ten members qualified for membership as stated in paragraph 34 (1) of N.L.C.D. 252.

In their application to the registrar sixteen members have signed and it is interesting to note that the application form itself was provided by the defendant and it is a printed form in which it is stated that the members are "Ghanaians over 21 years old of sound mind who follow as a normal means of livelihood the occupation of distillation and retailing of akpeteshi." They also stipulated their area of operation to be in Takoradi. The sixteen members signed in one column, their names were written in another column and their place of abode in a third column. This means that there are only three columns shown on one side of the printed application. The three columns on the printed application do clearly comply with the requirements for registration, and there is nothing in the Decree requiring shares to be subscribed before registration can be considered, nor is it a condition precedent to registration that account books must be kept. There can be no doubt that proper accounts will have to be kept when operations of the society commence. It is equally true that shares will subsequently have to be subscribed by the members when they start distilling and retailing akpeteshi.

I can well imagine why the possession of account books and subscription for shares are not made pre-conditions for registration of a proposed co-operative society. The chief underlying principle of the co-operative movement in this country is to encourage and assist villagers to come together to form co-operative societies to sell their produce with a view to having for themselves the profits that will otherwise go to middlemen. In short the main object of a co-operative society is the promotion of the economic interests of its members in accordance with co-operative principles. To make it a condition for such poor villagers to subscribe shares initially before registration may be difficult for them, and they may not have money on hand to purchase account books immediately. But it is possible that the members may possess the raw materials to enable them to come together and organize themselves into a co-operative society. It is only when operations are in progress and proceeds from the sale of their produce start coming into the coffers of the society that they will have the financial capability to subscribe shares and purchase account books.

(Continued)

(Continued)

Counsel for the respondent referred the court to paragraph 4 (2) of N.L.C.D. 252 and submitted that that paragraph empowered the registrar to ask for any information. I have no quarrel with the learned state attorney in this regard: that the registrar has the power to ask for any information that may assist him in considering an application for registration of a co-operative society, but there is a distinction between asking for certain information from the plaintiffs and imposing conditions to be fulfilled by them before registration. Exhibit B did not ask for information but it imposed certain conditions to be complied with by the plaintiffs.

I think the registrar also fell into error when he stated in exhibit C that in view of paragraph 4 (2) of N.L.C.D. 252, he had power "to demand certain conditions, the fulfilment of which facilitates eventual registration." The preparation and production of an economic survey is not a condition imposed by the Decree either. The registrar in preparing his economic survey, as a purely administrative or departmental exercise, may ask for certain information which will assist him in determining the economic viability of the proposed co-operative society, but the preparation of an economic survey is not a pre-condition required by law. Co-operative officers inspect societies that have been registered by the registrar and condition 2 (c) in exhibit B relates to acts *in futuro* and I cannot see how it must be a prerequisite to registration: see paragraph 47 of N.L.C.D. 252. It does seem to me, however, that conditions 2 (a) and 2 (b) set out in exhibit B have been satisfied by the plaintiffs but the so-called conditions 2 (c), 2 (d) and 2 (e) contained therein and paragraphs 2 and 3 of exhibit C are *ultra vires* the registrar.

The plaintiffs therefore have complied with paragraph 4 (1) of the Decree but the registrar may do certain things under paragraph 4 (2). If the registrar thought these conditions as necessary prerequisites to registration, I think he should have recommended their inclusion in the Decree to the minister responsible for the department of co-operatives. Perhaps the registrar with his enormous experience in the field of co-operative movement in this country may consider it necessary to recommend to the appropriate authority to have the Decree amended to include such matters as would promote the advancement of the co-operative movement in the country.

The plaintiffs have asked me to decide "whether they are not entitled to have their proposed society registered." The question of registration is a matter that lies entirely within the discretion of the registrar, for paragraph 5 of the N.L.C.D. 252 says that "if the Registrar is satisfied that a society has complied with the provisions of this Decree and that its bye-laws are not contrary to the objects thereof he *may* register the society and its bye-laws." (The emphasis is mine). I can well envisage the registrar now asking for certain information in accordance with paragraph 4 (2) of the Decree before considering the plaintiffs' application for registration, and the court, in my view, will not be performing its function judicially and judiciously by attempting to fetter the registrar's hands at this stage if the court directs that the society is entitled to be registered now. In any event a refusal by the registrar to register the society gives the plaintiffs a right of appeal to the Minister responsible for Labour and Social Welfare: see paragraph 5 (2) of N.L.C.D. 252.

(Continued)

(Continued)

Application granted in part.

The decisions from the courts support the new policy direction to empower cooperatives in Ghana to contribute to the development of large-scale commercial farming. One such policy and program initiative is the assistance being given by the U.S. government to cooperative institutions in Ghana (Box 8.3).

John R. Dunn, "USDA co-op development efforts support commercial farming in Ghana" Rural cooperative Magazine, May/June 2004, (http://www.rurdev.usda.gov/rbs/pub/may04/ghana.htm)

BOX 8.3 USDA co-op development efforts support commercial farming in Ghana

By John R. Dunn, *Director*
Co-op Resources Management Division
USDA Rural Development

Since 2000, the Cooperatives Program of USDA Rural Development has been working in Ghana to build western style cooperatives that help Ghanaian farmers successfully market their farm products. The vital work in this poor, West African nation is carried out under the banner of the Consultative Committee on Agriculture and Rural Development (CCARD). CCARD is a formal, government-to-government relationship between USDA and the Ghana Ministry of Food and Agriculture (MOFA).

The purpose of the Ghana Cooperative project is to extend western cooperative models into a Ghanaian setting to help farmers there transition to a more commercial level of food production. The project operates with a two-pronged strategy of direct advisory assistance and training which targets existing cooperatives and intervenes with Ghanaian institutions that can help sustain the adoption of western cooperative models over the long haul.

CCARD conducts a series of joint activities that serve the agricultural and trade interests of both nations. USDA agencies with active involvement in CCARD include: Rural Development; Cooperative Research, Education and Extension Service, Foreign Agricultural Service; Natural Resources Conservation Service; and the Agricultural Marketing Service. Activities conducted by CCARD are funded primarily by the U.S. Agency for International Development (USAID).

The Ghana Cooperative Assistance project, managed by the Cooperatives Program of USDA Rural Development, was initially funded under USAID's African Trade and Investment Program (ATRIP), but has since been adopted by USAID's mission in Ghana. The ATRIP-funded project covered work both in Senegal (in partnership with the Federation of Southern Cooperatives) and in Ghana (in partnership with OIC International). Current efforts focus exclusively in Ghana and parallel Rural Development's Nigeria cooperative development project (see Rural Cooperatives, Jan./Feb. 2004 issue).

(Continued)

BOX 8.3 USDA co-op development efforts support commercial farming in Ghana (Continued)

The Ghana Cooperative College is a small institution in Kumasi, the Ashanti region capital. It is charged with training managers and directors of Ghana's cooperative system in basic cooperative principles and business skills. This college is extremely lacking in resources and was sliding into decline, a result of diminishing public funding and, more significantly, of reliance on the teaching of outdated and ineffective top-down models of cooperative enterprise. Reform and rejuvenation of the Cooperative College became one of the centerpiece projects under CCARD. As a first step, former USDA Cooperatives Program staff member Rosemary Mahoney was contracted to conduct a curriculum review and assessment for the college. This resulted in a series of recommendations and strategies for improving the overall conditions of the college.

In February, one of the centerpiece recommendations was implemented with the opening of a new computer training facility at the college. The new computer lab will provide students with basic training in business software and IT methods essential to contemporary business operations. The opening of the center represents a true public-private partnership. Partially funded by USAID, with computer donations from the National Cooperative Bank, National Rural Telecommunications Association and the Cooperative Development Foundation, the center is managed by volunteers of the U.S Peace Corps. Future activity will include staff development, planning, and cooperative course designs, to be done in partnership with the Cooperative Center at the University of Wisconsin.

Source: http://www.rurdev.usda.gov/rbs/pub/may04/ghana.htm (Rural Cooperative Magazine, May/June 2004).

21st Century Food and Packaging Ltd v Tanzania Sugar Producers Association (1st Respondent); The Ministry of Finance (The Tanzania Government) (2nd Respondent); The Hon. Attorney General (3rd Respondent)

The Court of Appeal, Tanga
Civil Appeal No. 91 of 2003, April 14th 2004
Coram: Lubuva, J.A., Munuo, J.A., and Nsekela, J.A.

JUDGMENT

Lubuva, J. This appeal arises from the decision of the High Court, Commercial Division (Kalegeya, J.) dismissing the appellant's application for leave to be joined as a co-defendant in Civil Case No. 85 of 2003. In the High Court, Commercial Division, the first respondent in this appeal, Tanzania Sugar Producers Association, had instituted a suit against the second and third respondents, the Ministry of Finance and the Attorney General respectively, challenging the government's tax remission granted to the appellant for the importation of 7,000 tons of refined industrial sugar. The tax remission was published in the Government Notice No. 68 of 28.3.2003.

(Continued)

(Continued)

The gravamen of the complaint by the first respondent was that the tax remission granted to the appellant would result in unfair competition with other local sugar producers in the country. The first respondent also claimed that while enjoying such tax remission, the appellant had also applied to the Sugar Board of Tanzania for the importation of another 36,000 tons of refined industrial sugar which it was further alleged, would frustrate the government policy of promoting and protecting local sugar industry.

Consequently, as already observed, the first respondent instituted the suit seeking the following reliefs: First, a permanent injunction to restrain the second respondent from issuing tax remission to any person for the importation of refined industrial sugar. Second, a declaration that any tax remission issued by the second respondent for the importation of refined industrial sugar null and void.

As the appellant was not made a party to the proceedings in the suit but was touched in one way or the other in the reliefs sought, leave to be joined as a co-defendant in the suit was sought. Invoking the provisions of Order 1 Rule 10 (2) of the Civil Procedure Code, the learned trial judge was settled in his view that the applicant, the appellant in this appeal, was neither a necessary nor a proper party in the proceedings in Civil Case No. 85 of 2003. The application was dismissed. Being dissatisfied, the appellant has instituted this appeal.

At the hearing of the appeal, Dr. Lamwai, learned counsel, appeared for the appellant, Mrs. Kashonda and M/S Mnguto, learned advocates, represented the first respondent and for the second and third respondents, Mr. Kamba, learned Principal State Attorney, appeared. Initially, Dr. Lamwai had filed four grounds of appeal, however, at the commencement of hearing of the appeal, he opted to abandon ground four. He therefore argued the following grounds:

1. The Learned Judge erred in law and in fact in holding that the orders in Miscellaneous Civil Case No. 114 of 2002 would not be affected by any order which would be given in Commercial Case No. 85 of 2003;
2. That the Learned Judge erred in law and in fact in holding that the Appellant would not be affected by any order passed in Commercial Case No. 85 of 2003 while it was clear from the record that the Appellant was one of the importers of white sugar as industrial sugar;
3. That the Learned Judge erred in law and in fact in holding that the Appellant had no interest in Commercial Case No. 85 of 2003 worth making it a party in the suit, while there was a subsisting order of temporary injunction which specifically ordered the 2nd Respondent not to issue a tax exemption order in favour of the Appellant.

Arguing these grounds together, Dr. Lamwai vigorously criticized the learned trial judge in dismissing the application. First, he said it was erroneous on the part of the trial judge to hold this view because from the record and the circumstances of the case, it was abundantly shown that the appellant was a necessary and proper party to be joined in the proceedings. For instance, he said in paragraphs 8, 9, 10, 11 and 12 of the plaint, the appellant featured extensively in the pleadings. According to Dr. Lamwai, in these paragraphs, the plaintiff,

(Continued)

(Continued)

the first respondent in this appeal, is central in the complaint raised by the first respondent. The complaint is that the remission of tax for the importation of the consignment of 7,000 and 36,000 tons of refined industrial sugar by the appellant not only would adversely affect fair trade competition but also would not promote and protect local sugar production in the country. Nonetheless, Dr. Lamwai stressed, the appellant was not made a party to the proceedings in which he could be heard. In that situation, the appellant was a necessary and proper party in the proceedings, Dr. Lamwai urged.

Secondly, Dr. Lamwai submitted that the appellant's rights accruing from Government Notice No. 68 of 28/3/2003 regarding 7,000 tons of Industrial Sugar had not been concluded in Miscellaneous Civil Cause No. 114 of 2002 as urged by the second and third respondents. On the contrary, Dr. Lamwai countered, the appellant's rights under Government Notice No. 68 of 28.3.2003, which were confirmed in Miscellaneous Civil Cause No. 114 of 2003, would be affected by the decision sought in Civil Case No. 85 of 2003. For this reason, the appellant was therefore an interested and proper party in Civil Case No. 85 of 2003, he insisted.

Thirdly, Dr. Lamwai said that the trial judge correctly set out the position of the law under the provisions of Order I Rule 10 (2) of the Civil Procedure Code 1966, the equivalent of which was commented by the distinguished Indian author, Mulla in The Code of Civil Procedure, 16th Edition, Vol. II pages 1567–8. However, Dr. Lamwai further submitted that the judge misapplied the law as extracted in the passage from the learned author. Had the learned trial judge properly construed and applied the law to the circumstances of the case, he would have found that the appellant was a proper party to be joined as a co-defendant.

In turn, Mrs. Kashonda and M/s Mnguto, learned advocates for the first respondent, responded to these submissions. Mrs. Kashonda said that the trial judge's correct finding that the appellant was not a necessary party in Civil Case No. 85 of 2003 cannot be assailed for the following reasons: First, the appellant's interests realized in Civil Cause No. 114 of 2002, are separate and distinct from those involved in Civil Case No. 85 of 2003. Therefore, there was no basis for the claim that the appellant was a necessary party. Furthermore, she said the consignment of 7,000 tons of industrial sugar, subject of the Government Notice No. 68 of 28.3.2003 concerned a previous transaction which was different from the 36,000 tons consignment for the year 2003. On this ground, Mrs. Kashonda maintained that there was no ground for joining the appellant as a party in Civil Case No. 85 of 2003. Like the learned trial judge, she was of the firm view that even if the appellant was not joined as a party, its interests would be taken care of by the Attorney General, the Principal Legal Adviser to the government who would leave no stone unturned. On her part, M/S Mnguto, learned counsel, also addressed the Court. Essentially, she reiterated the submissions by Mrs. Kashonda.

For the second respondent, Ministry of Finance and the third respondent, the Attorney General, Mr. Kamba, learned Principal State Attorney, made two pertinent observations: First, that there were two transactions undertaken by the appellant which involved tax remission for the importation of sugar. The first transaction whose tax remission was gazetted in Government Notice No. 68 of 28/3/2003 had nothing to do with Civil Case No. 85 of 2003. The second transaction related to a future prospective importation of 36,000 tons of

(Continued)

(Continued)

industrial sugar by the appellant which was touched upon in Civil Case No. 85 of 2003. With regard to this transaction, Mr. Kamba conceded that as the orders sought in Civil Case No. 85 of 2003, were directly linked with the appellant which was not made a party in the suit, it was fair and just that the appellant should have been made a party. Secondly, he said the granting of tax remission is not as of right on the part of the appellant, it is a matter of discretion on the part of the second respondent's officials concerned.

The determination of this appeal turns on a narrow scope, namely whether the appellant was a necessary party to be joined in the suit, in Civil Case No. 85 of 2003. It is common ground that the question of joining a party or otherwise to the proceedings is a matter of applying the applicable law. In the case of Tanzania, the procedural law is set out under the provisions of Order 1 Rule 10 (2) of the Civil Procedure Code, 1966. To this, the learned judge directed his mind. It provides:

> *"10. - (2) The court may at any stage of the proceedings, either upon or without the application of either party, and on such terms as may appear to the court to be just, order that the name of any party improperly joined, whether as plaintiff or defendant, or whose presence before the court may be necessary in order to enable the court effectually and completely to adjudicate upon and settle all the questions involved in the suit be added."*

In an effort to construe the law, and as stated by Dr. Lamwai, learned counsel for the appellant, the learned judge correctly set out the legal position as elaborated by the distinguished author, Mulla in The Code of Civil Procedure, 16th Edition, Vol. II, pages 1567−8. Quite extensively, the judge extracted and relied on the learned author's commentary on the provision of the Indian Code of Civil Procedure, the equivalent of Order I Rule 10 (2) of the Civil Procedure Code, 1966. Applying Mulla's (supra) commentary, to the instant case, the learned judge as indicated earlier, was of the firm view that the appellant was not neither a necessary nor a proper party. Having regard to the circumstances of the case as a whole, we pause to consider whether that was a proper application of the law. Dr. Lamwai was quick to respond that the judge misapplied the law while on the other M/S Kashonda and Mnguto, held the contrary view.

This issue has engaged our minds considerably. In resolving it, we shall briefly examine some aspects of the facts which we think, are generally not seriously disputed. From the plaint, the core base of the suit, by the first respondent against the second and third respondents, it is apparent that the appellant is abundantly referred to. Centrally, what is averred in the plaint relates to the tax remission granted for the importation of industrial sugar in which the appellant was one of the beneficiaries. This is evident from paragraph 8, 9, 10, 11 and 12 of the plaint. Therefore, in these circumstances, the question falling for consideration is whether the learned judge in his decision considered the averment in the plaint touching on the appellant.

From a cursory glance through the record and the ruling in particular, it is at once apparent that the learned judge did not take into account what was averred in the plaint. It is to be observed that in the plaint, the prayers sought by the plaintiff, the first respondent in this

(Continued)

(Continued)

appeal, seeks a permanent injunction to restrain the second respondent, Ministry of Finance from issuing tax remission for the importation of industrial sugar. Furthermore, a declaration is also sought that the issuance of tax remission by the second respondent for the importation of industrial sugar is null and void. This is an aspect in which the court is called upon to resolve one way or the other in Civil Case No. 85 of 2003.

There is no gainsaying that it is an aspect which directly affect the interests of the appellant. In that situation, we think it would be in the interest of justice that the appellant is given an opportunity of being heard in order to enable the court to settle the issues raised in the suit. To do so, we also think that not only would this accord with the spirit of the provisions of Rule 10 (2) of Order 1 of the Civil Procedure Code but would also be in conformity with the principles of natural justice i.e. according an opportunity to a party to be heard in a matter which directly affects the party.

In this case, while the learned judge concedes that the appellant would adversely be affected in its interest if the government is restrained as sought in the suit from issuing **tax** exemption, with respect, he takes too narrow a view of the application of the extracted paragraphs from Mulla (supra). Had the learned judge taken a broad view of the principles set out in Mulla (supra) on the relevant section of the Indian Code of Civil Procedure which as stated earlier is in *pari materia* with Order 1 Rule 10.(2) of the Civil Procedure Code, 1966 of Tanzania, we think he would have come to a different conclusion.

On a proper construction of Order I Rule 10 (2) of the Civil Procedure Code and application of the guiding principles as discerned from Mulla's commentaries to the facts of the case, we are increasingly of the view that the appellant's presence before the court was necessary in Civil Case No. 85 of 2003. In our view, the appellant's presence in court in this case would enable the court to effectually and completely adjudicate upon the issues raised in the suit regarding tax exemption of imported industrial sugar. All the more so, where, as in this case, the appellant centrally featured in the plaint and had applied to be joined in the suit.

Then there was the learned judge's line of argument that the appellant's interest in the case pertains to other interests and not existing legal interest in which case, Rule 10 (2) of Order 1 does not come to play. While it is common ground that the first consignment of 7,000 tons of imported industrial sugar subject of Government Notice No. 68 of 28/3/2003 for which tax remission had been granted, the second consignment of 36,000 tons was yet to be imported in future. Dismissing the applicant's application the learned judge held that the applicant was not a necessary party because the interest involved pertained to the future.

We need not be delayed in this point. As already indicated, one of the reliefs sought in Civil Case No. 85 of 2003 was a declaration that any issuance of tax remission for the importation of industrial sugar is null and void. From this order, it appears to us that no fine distinction could be made between existing and future legal interests. If the order is granted and the remission is declared null and void, both the existing interests as well as the others based on the exemption may well be affected. In that situation, either way, the applicant would be affected and hence an interested and necessary party in the suit. It is our view therefore that

(Continued)

(Continued)

this was no ground for the learned judge to hold that the appellant was not a necessary and proper party to be joined in the suit.

Next we wish to comment briefly on the learned judge's casual observation that even if the appellant was not joined as a party, it would be ably represented in the suit by the Attorney General. This point was also reiterated by Mrs. Kashonda supported by M/S Mnguto, learned counsel. It is common knowledge that the Attorney General as Principal Legal Adviser to the government, ordinarily represents government ministries, departments or other government agencies. In this case, he represented the second and third respondents. Apart from these, we can see no basis for the appellant, a private agency being represented by the Attorney General.

In any case, in this case, as correctly stated by Mr. Kamba, learned Principal State Attorney, from the pleadings, the issues raised in relation to the tax remission are better suited to be answered or clarified by the appellant. With respect, we are in agreement with the learned Principal State Attorney on this submission. This is for the obvious reason that the Attorney General would, in our view, competently represent the views of the government on behalf of the second and third respondents with regard to the government policy on the sugar industry and the procedure followed in granting tax remission. Otherwise, we are unable to see how the Attorney General can hazard any views on behalf of the appellant regarding the adverse effect on the appellant if tax remission was not granted. For this reason, we find no merit in the claim that the Attorney General would leave no stone unturned in representing the appellant.

For the foregoing reasons, we allow the appeal and set aside the High Court decision dismissing the appellant's application to be joined as a party to the suit in Civil Case No. 85 of 2003. The matter is remitted to the High Court with direction to proceed with the hearing of the case from the stage reached on 6.11.2003 after joining the appellant as a party to the proceedings.

Costs granted to the appellant.

Notes

1. According to the International Labor Organization (ILO, 2009), Cooperatives in Kenya mobilized 31% of national savings in 2007, and 63% of Kenyans derived their livelihood from cooperative activities, while 250,000 people were directly employed by cooperative-based institutions. There were 11,000 cooperatives registered in Kenya in 2007. Membership in cooperatives grew from 750,000 in 2005 to 1,600,000 in 2007. Zambia has 15,929 registered cooperatives countrywide as of March 2008, and in Rwanda 211 of the 228 registered micro-finance institutions were cooperatives in 2006. See International Labor Organization. Also, "approximately seven per cent of the African population reportedly belongs to a cooperative, though some countries like Egypt, Senegal, Ghana, Kenya and Rwanda report a higher penetration rate of over ten per cent" (Theron, 2010). There are a total of 1080 agricultural cooperatives out of a total of 2200 cooperatives in Ghana (Cooperatives in Ghana are governed by the *Cooperative Societies Decree, 1968*), National Liberation Council, *Gazette* No. 11, 28th February, 1966).
2. There are an estimated 147 cooperatives having 100,000 members in Botswana. The focus of cooperatives includes: cattle marketing, savings and credit, detailing, handicraft, and multipurpose. See ILO, *id.*

3. Theron, *op. cit.* "During that period, cooperatives in Africa were used by the colonial powers as a strategic tool to group rural producers into clusters, so that essential export commodities such as coffee, cocoa and cotton, could be collected more cost-effectively."

4. "After independence, the governments of the now sovereign States accorded an essential role to cooperatives, in particular for the development of rural areas. Cooperatives enjoyed preferential treatment and were granted supply and marketing monopolies which protected them from competition. They paid for these privileges with the total loss of autonomy, democratic control and business efficiency. Cooperatives degenerated into tools of government, or mass organizations of the ruling party." *Id.*

5. This discussion is based primarily on a paper by Sykuta (2001).

6. id at 1274.

7. Theron, *id.*

8. "The new emphasis on cooperative values and principles (as outlined in Recommendation No. 193) reflects a reaction to an approach that saw cooperatives in developing and post-command economies regarded as accountable to the state rather than their membership. In the African context, this approach also meant that cooperatives were often utilized as instruments of government policy, and cooperative autonomy was often severely compromised. Cooperative autonomy must thus be regarded as representing the litmus test for evaluating the policy and legislative framework." See Develtere (2008).

9. "In fact there is already a degree of convergence between cooperative legislation in different countries of the region. This is due to the fact that most of the countries of the region have similar legal traditions, as a result of a common colonial heritage. It is therefore relatively easy to commence such a dialogue, while not neglecting to engage with the experiences of countries from different legal traditions." Develtere, *op. cit.* Also, these four colonial powers (British, French, Portuguese, and Belgium) did, in different ways, introduce modern cooperation in their former colonies. As a matter of fact, it is not difficult to discover similarities in the cooperative systems in Kenya and Ghana, both former British colonies. *Id.*

Questions

1. Explain how cooperatives are tools for acquisition of market power.
2. Define a "cooperative" in your own words.
3. Perform an Internet search of the International Cooperative Alliance. List the values and principles on the ICA website. In your opinion, is the ICA achieving its stated objectives?
4. What types of cooperatives are in your country, and what laws govern these cooperatives? What economic activities are allowed to operate as cooperatives, and why are some economic activities barred to be performed under a cooperative system?

Challenge Questions

What is COOP AFRICA? How would you assess their contribution to cooperative development in SSA?

One study concluded, "The 'collapsing' of the cooperative movement in Zambia can be attributed to lack for planning for policy transition on behalf of the government as well as a manifestation of fragile cooperative institutions, whose internal organization was not robust enough to withstand the liberalization reforms."

In what ways did liberalization affect cooperative institutions? How would you assess this statement in the context of the 21st Century Foods case from Tanzania?

See Peter K. Lolojih (2009) "Bearing the brunt of a liberalized economy: A performance review of the cooperative movement in Zambia," *CoopAFRICA* Working Paper No. 16.

References

Develtere, P., 2008. Chapter one - Cooperative development in Africa up to the 1990s. In: Develtere, P., Pollet, I., Wanyama, F. (Eds.), Cooperating Out of Poverty: The Renaissance of the African Cooperative Movement. International Labour Office, Geneva.

ICA, 2006. "What is a Cooperative?" <http://www.ica.coop/coop/index.html>.

International Labor Organization, COOP Africa: Cooperative Facility for Africa (dated 13.08.2009) at <http://www.ilo.org/public/english/employment/ent/coop/africa/about/index.htm>.

Sykuta, M.E., Cook, M.L., 2001. A new institutional economics approach to contracts and cooperatives. Amer. J. Agr. Econ. 83, 1273–1279.

Theron, J. 2010. "Cooperative Policy and Law in East and Southern Africa: A Review," Coop Africa Working Paper No. 18.

World Bank, 2008. World Development Report, p. 154.

CHAPTER 9

Contracts Governed by International Conventions or Treaties

Keywords: International conventions; international treaties; commercial contracting; Contracts for the International Sales of Goods (CISG); Warsaw Convention

9.1 Introduction

Countries in sub-Saharan Africa (SSA) are party to several international treaties and conventions governing commercial contracts. Membership in these international institutions presents an opportunity to countries to participate in the global market system. There has been an impressive growth in world trade since the World War II. In 1950, exports accounted for 8% of worldwide production but today accounts for 26% (Business Roundtable, 2006). One explanation for this impressive growth is the availability of treaties and conventions that have reduced the cost of doing business. Today, there are a large number of international commercial treaties and agreements that support modern commercial interaction between parties from different countries (Alford, 2005).[1] This chapter discusses two international treaties that have been instrumental in promoting commercial contracting between residents of different nations.

9.2 United Nations Convention on Contracts for the International Sale of Goods (CISG)

The United Nations Convention on Contracts for the International Sale of Goods (CISG), accepted by the representatives at the Vienna Convention for the International Sale of Goods (CISG) on April 11, 1980, is probably the most significant of all the international commercial treaties (Eiselen, 1996). According to one expert, the CISG has "surpassed all expectations," and the treaty "represents the most successful attempt to unify an important part of the many and various rules of the law of international commerce" (Flechtner, 2008). The CISG has been discussed as a success story despite some shortcomings.[2] The role of the CISG in international commercial interaction has been to significantly reduce the transaction cost of doing business. The benefits include "a simplification of the legal

F.O. Boadu: Agricultural Law and Economics in Sub-Saharan Africa.
DOI: http://dx.doi.org/10.1016/B978-0-12-801771-5.00009-5

environment within which international sales operate by having available one set of domestic rules which is internationally accepted; A global uniform approach to international sales, independent of the intricacies of private international law; a reduction in the number of foreign legal systems that may potentially apply to the international contracts of sale of South African traders; The opportunity to unify the law of sale applicable in the southern African region; and saving of legal expenses; the removal of unnecessary trade barriers, supporting the growth of international trade; and the acceptance of a legal regime which is already applicable in many instances" (Eiselen, 1996).

The application of the CISG to countries in SSA is quite limited. Even more significant is the unavailability of any cases where the CISG has been applied to inter-regional trade between SSA countries. This may reflect the low level of commercial interaction between countries in SSA.[3] One of the few cases that required the application of the CISG involved a used shoes importer from Uganda.[4] The case required an interpretation of Article 39 dealing with nonconforming goods.[5] The Ugandan importer lost the case, a decision that has been severely criticized by one commentator.[6] Another case also dealt with the problem of nonconformity with contract terms. Even though the parties are not from SSA, the subject matter, the importation of cocoa, could well have been an issue involving an exporter of cocoa from SSA.

District Court (*Landgericht*) Frankfurt (Main)

11 April 2005 [2-26 O 264/04]
Translation by Linus Meyer
Edited by Institut für ausländisches und Internationales
Privat- und Wirtshaftsrecht der Universität Heidelberg
Daniel Nagel, editor

SUMMARY OF THE DECISION

The court has, on the basis of the written proceeding decided: The claim by the Plaintiff [Buyer] is rejected. The Buyer has to bear the costs of the proceeding. This judgment is provisionally enforceable. The enforcing party has to provide security in the amount of 110% of the costs which are still to be set.

CASE

The Plaintiff [Buyer] is a society that has its place of business in Kampala, Uganda. Because of an announcement on the Internet placed by the Defendant [Seller], it bought from the Seller 360 bags of used shoes, quality class one and 360 bags of used shoes, quality class two (9,000 kg each) at a price of 27,000 EUR plus C&F FOB Mombasa, Kenya (3,750 EUR), thus at a total price of 30,750 EUR. Quality class one consists of used shoes in a very good condition, i.e., without rips or holes and if at all with only slight, minor signs of use.

(Continued)

(Continued)

Quality class two means shoes of good quality, i.e., with slight signs of use, but also without rips or holes. The goods sent by the Seller arrived in Mombasa on 26 April 2004. After the Buyer had paid the last installment of the purchase price on 18 May 2004, it received the original Bill of Lading document from the Seller on 24 May 2005. [*Translator's note: The date "24 May 2005" appears to be in error, with the date "24 May 2004" intended.*] The Buyer had the goods transported to Kampala then, Uganda, where it examined them on 16 June 2004. On 17 June 2004, the Buyer reprimanded the Seller for the bad condition of the goods. The Buyer complained about the condition of the goods again by a letter of 23 June 2004 and set an extension until 22 July 2004. The Uganda National Bureau of Standards declined the import of the shoes by letter of 24 June 2004. For the wording of that statement, reference is made to page 14 of the record. The Bureau stated that the shoes were not acceptable for the Ugandan market because of their bad and unhygienic condition. It declared the shoes to be unfit for usage and recommended their destruction at the parties' cost.

The Buyer declared avoidance of the contract by letter of 2 July 2004.

The Buyer contends that the shoes that were delivered had not been in conformity with the contract. Instead of the quality agreed upon, the bags had only contained defective and unusable shoes, among them high-heel woman's shoes, inline-skates and shoe trees. With respect to the timeliness of the notice of non-conformity, it states that the Seller had known that the shoes would be forwarded from Mombasa to Uganda. Buyer also states that the goods could not be examined in Mombasa because of international regulations on freight and customs, as the containers had been sealed in Germany. An examination in Mombasa would have required damage to the customs seal and would thus have caused a payment of customs duty for the goods in Kenya. The Buyer argues that paying additional customs in Kenya would have been an unreasonable burden.

The Buyer demands reimbursement of the purchase price as well as of the costs incurred such as customs, handling fees and freight costs.

The Buyer has requested the court to order the Seller to pay EUR 62,301.63 plus interest 8% above the base interest level on:

— EUR 10,000 since 11 March 2004;
— EUR 5,000 since 6 April 2004;
— EUR 10,000 since 28 April 2004;
— EUR 5,000 since 30 April 2004;
— EUR 475 since 18 May 2004;
— EUR 4,4475.17 since 10 July 2004; and
— EUR 27,351.46 since the claim has been served upon the Seller.

The Seller has requested that the claim be dismissed. The Seller argues that the notice of non-conformity of the goods was not sent in time. It also contests the amount of the damage. In addition to the parties' arguments stated here, reference is made to the memoranda that have been added to the file.

(Continued)

(Continued)
REASONS FOR THE DECISION

The Buyer's claim is admissible but not justified.

1. The Convention on Contracts for the International Sale of Goods (CISG) is applicable to the present dispute, as the contract is for the sale of goods and the parties have their place of business in different States which are parties to the Convention (Art. 1(1)(a) CISG). The Federal Republic of Germany has been party to the Convention since 1 January 1991, Uganda since 1 March 1993.

2. The Buyer is not entitled to any payment under Arts. 45(1)(b), 74, 8[4](1) CISG nor under any other provision.

   a) The Seller has fundamentally breached the contract concluded between the parties by delivering shoes not in conformity with the contract. This can be inferred from the letter by the Uganda National Bureau of Standards of 24 June 2004 (page 14 of the record) according to which the shoes were in a bad and unhygienic condition and not acceptable for the Ugandan market. The fact that this document refers to the goods delivered can be inferred from the wording of the letter and the enclosure, which states the number of the bags as well as the sender and recipient of the goods. According to this letter, the shoes delivered were not in conformity with the quality classes one and two agreed upon in the contract. As the Seller itself has stated that shoes are not perishable items and therefore cannot "rot" in a container in a warehouse (page 55 of the record), it is assumed that the goods had been in the same bad condition before they arrived in Mombasa.

   b) The Buyer is, however, precluded from relying on a lack of conformity (Art. 39(1), 38 CISG). This is because the Buyer did not examine the goods soon enough and also did not give notice of the non-conformity of the goods within a reasonable period of time.

   The Buyer detected the non-conformity of the shoes delivered on 16 June 2004 in Kampala, Uganda and gave notice to the Seller on 17 June 2004. The Seller was thus given notice of the lack of conformity only one day after it had been detected. The examination of the goods, and consequently the notice was, however, too late.

   According to Art. 38(1) CISG, the Buyer was obliged to examine the goods within the shortest period practicable under the circumstances. Mombasa, Kenya was the goods' contractual destination. Therefore, the examination of the goods was to be conducted there, Art. 38(2). The goods arrived in Mombasa on 26 April 2004. The court will, however, assume in favor of the Buyer that the period for examination did not begin before 24 May 2004 as this is the date when the Buyer received the original Bill of Lading document after having paid the last installment of the purchase price. But even under the assumption that this was the date when the time to examine the goods began, the notice was made too late, as it was only made on 17 June 2004, which is three weeks after the time for examination started. Art. 38(1) CISG does not give a special period of time but only states that the goods have to be examined "within as short a period as is practicable in the circumstances." The strict measure of § 377 HGB

   (Continued)

(Continued)

[translator's note: "immediately"] cannot be applied here (Schlechtriem/Schwenzer, Handbuch zum Einheitlichen UN-Kaufrecht, 4. ed. Art. 38 para. 16; MüKo / Benicke, Handelsgesetzbuch §§ 373-406, CISG Vol. 6, before Art. 38, 39 para. 1).

However, an examination that did not take place until more than three weeks had passed has to be regarded as too late and unreasonable in international commerce. The Buyer had known for several weeks that the goods had arrived in Mombasa and would have been able to organize an examination (*cf.* Achilles, Kommentar zum UN-Kaufrechtsübereinkommen (CISG), Art. 38 para. 9). The goods were neither complicated technical equipment nor was it necessary to assemble or process them in order to examine them (Schlechtriem/Schwenzer, Art. 38 para. 17).

The non-conformity of the goods could have been detected by only looking at a sample. As the examination did not require much effort, the Seller could expect that it would be conducted within a short period of time (MüKo/Benicke, Art. 38 para. 7). The Buyer has not presented any facts that would justify a longer period. Consequently, the Buyer had no right to postpone the examination until the goods had arrived in Uganda.

The Buyer cannot rely on Art. 38(3) CISG according to which the examination can be postponed until the goods have arrived at their final destination. Article 38(3) would only be applicable if the Buyer did not have a sufficient possibility to examine the goods and if the Seller knew or ought to have known the possibility that the goods would be forwarded. Art. 38(3) is generally applicable in this case, because the Buyer redirected the shoes to Kampala, Uganda, after they had arrived in Mombasa and the goods were examined immediately after their arrival in Uganda. It is, however, questionable, whether the Seller knew or ought to have known of the possibility that the goods would be forwarded to Uganda at the time the contract was concluded. The Seller has contested this. The fact that the Buyer has its place of business in Uganda is insofar insufficient. The e-mail of 13 April 2004 (page 91 of the record) is irrelevant in this context as it was sent after the conclusion of the contract.

This question, which is in dispute between the parties, does, however, not need to be decided. The Buyer has not convinced the court that it did not have a reasonable opportunity to examine the goods before they were forwarded (Art. 38(3) CISG). As shown above, the Buyer had sufficient time to organize and conduct the examination of the goods in Mombasa. It was under no pressure of time as the goods were not forwarded immediately after their arrival in Mombasa. Eventually, the goods were forwarded three weeks after the Buyer had received the Bill of Lading and seven weeks after their arrival in Mombasa. In addition, the packaging did not have any distinct features that would have made an examination on the spot unreasonable. The shoes were packed in simple plastic bags which could be opened without difficulties and without destroying the packaging (Schlechtriem/Schwenzer, Art. 38 para. 25; Honsell, Kommentar zum UN-Kaufrecht, Art. 38 para. 31).

Repacking which could have caused costs was not necessary as well (Achilles, para. 15). In addition, the court cannot see why opening the containers would have been

(Continued)

(Continued)

inadequate or unreasonable in the present case. The argument presented by the Buyer that it would have been unreasonable to fly from Uganda to Kenya to examine the goods is not convincing. The Buyer, or respectively its manager, did not need to fly to Kenya itself to examine the goods. It could have ordered somebody else to examine the goods (Art. 38(1) CISG—"cause them to be examined"). In addition, the inconvenience of a flight from Uganda to Kenya cannot be an argument against the Seller, as the Buyer itself has chosen Mombasa as the goods' destination. It was free to agree upon a different destination with the Seller.

The Buyer's argument that the goods could not be examined in Mombasa because of international regulations for freight and customs as the customs seal would have been damaged which would have caused an obligation to pay customs duties in Kenya is not convincing. The argument that paying the customs duties would have been unreasonable, cannot be followed because the obligation to pay customs duties does not represent a lack of a reasonable opportunity in the sense of Art. 38(3) CISG which could be used to construct a disadvantage for the Seller. The number and the amount of customs duties that would have to be paid were factors that the Buyer had to take into account in its commercial consideration. The Buyer had to consider whether the deal would be profitable with respect to the purchase price and the resale price. In addition, it would have been possible for the Buyer to agree upon Kampala, Uganda and not Mombasa, Kenya as the destination of the goods.

Apart from that, it is doubtful whether the buyer would have needed to pay additional customs duties if the customs seal had been damaged in Kenya for an examination of the goods. This has not sufficiently been demonstrated by the buyer. Even if double customs duties would have had to be paid, this does not automatically make the examination unreasonable. Reasons for unreasonableness have not been presented by the Buyer.

The Buyer has not even specified how high the customs duties in Kenya would have been. Consequently, Art. 38(3) CISG does not lead to an extended period for examination and notice.

3. The Buyer also cannot reduce the price. The lack of a timely notice of non-conformity has not been supported by an acceptable excuse by the Buyer (Art. 44 CISG). Accordingly, the claim had to be declined.

The decision on costs is based on § 91 ZPO, the decision on provisional enforceability on 709 ZPO.

b. *Convention for the Unification of Certain Rules Relating to International Carriage by Air* (Warsaw Convention.[7])

Another application of international commercial conventions and rules to resolve domestic commercial conflicts is the *Royal Dutch Airlines (KLM) and Another v FARMEX, Ltd.* case, where a court in Ghana applied the *Warsaw* convention to resolve a contract dispute between a local company and a foreign-based company with offices in Ghana. The *Kenya Airways Limited v. Ronald Katumba* involves two domestic parties. The case shows how an international convention is being used to resolve a domestic conflict. This case raises the important issue of the extent to which international governance institutions are increasingly being used to address domestic issues.

Royal Dutch Airlines (KLM) & Another v Farmex Ltd

Court of Appeals, Accra, Ghana
27 June 1989

FACTS

FARMEX, the plaintiffs are exporters of fruits and the defendants are two air carriers, Royal Dutch Airlines (henceforth KLM), and British Caledonian Airlines (henceforth BCal). The plaintiff arranged to ship a consignment of mangoes to a consignee in London in November 1985. They did their booking with BCal which confirmed the booking. However, "at the last minute," as the plaintiff put it, BCal could not take the cargo because there was a fuel shortage in Lagos. The sales manager of BCal, one Mr. Macasuley, gave the plaintiffs an alternative means to ship the mangoes on KLM to Kano for transit connection with the BCal flight the next day. This arrangement was agreed to by KLM, the first defendants herein. The evidence indicates that the cargo left Kotoka International Airport, Accra on 29 November 1985. However Bcal did not receive the goods on the expected day so a telex message was sent to the plaintiffs indicating that the goods had not reached them. The plaintiffs contacted KLM from whom they learnt that the purser of KLM had mistakenly taken the relevant documents to Amsterdam instead of handing them over to their office in Kano. The mangoes did get to London eventually but were declared unwholesome and unfit for human consumption. The plaintiff held KLM and BCal liable jointly and severally in the amount of £23,800.

OPINION

Both defendants deny liability. The first defendants pleaded in paragraph 2 of their statement of defence that they "agreed to transport the plaintiffs' said goods to Kano on the understanding that the plaintiffs had arranged for collection of the said goods on arrival in Kano by British Caledonian for transportation from Kano to London." They argued that "the plaintiffs' negligence in not advising the second defendants to take immediate delivery of the plaintiffs' said goods as agreed and in not properly marking the packages containing the said goods caused a delay of three days before the second defendants could take delivery of the said goods." The second defendants also concede that there was delay in the delivery of the goods but blamed the first defendants for the delay. Their contention was that the delay in transshipping the consignment from Kano to London was due solely to the default of the first defendants in that: "(a) the first defendants failed to mark or cause to be marked the consignment with proper identification; and (b) the first defendants purser overcarried all papers on the consignment to Amsterdam and therefore making it impossible for the second defendants to take immediate delivery of the consignment for shipment to London."

They did not end there. They also contended that the plaintiffs ignored their advice against shipping their mangoes by the route chosen and by this the plaintiffs agreed to take the risk and to waive any claim in respect of any damage or loses occasioned by delays in the shipment or delivery of their consignment. The second defendants therefore pleaded that they would rely on the principle of *volenti non fit injuria*.

(Continued)

(Continued)

The issues set down for trial by the plaintiffs were:

(1) Whether or not in law the defendants are liable as carriers for damages in not delivering the cargo of mangoes to London as instructed in the air way-bill.

(2) Whether the defendants are jointly and severally liable to the plaintiffs for the sum of £23,800 being the value of cargo in question.

To my mind, the issues pose one main question: who should be blamed for the delay which resulted in the mangoes getting rotten?

Just before evidence was taken on 17 October 1986 the first defendants sought and obtained leave from the court to amend their pleadings by adding the following new paragraph:

In further answer to the averments contained in paragraphs 6 and 7 of the plaintiffs' statement of claim, the first defendants will deny that they were responsible for any delay in the transportation of the plaintiffs' goods or at all and will say that in any case they took all necessary means to avoid damage or loss to the plaintiffs' goods and that any damage which might have occurred in relation thereto was caused by or contributed to by the plaintiffs' negligence and that accordingly the first defendants are not liable or are exonerated from liability in relation thereto having regard to articles 20 and 21 of the Warsaw Convention, 1929, the terms of which are binding on the parties.

The trial judge did not agree to have the case disposed of by legal argument, instead she took evidence and I must say that in my opinion she was right. After a detailed analysis of the evidence adduced before her, the learned judge held both defendants liable and awarded damages in the sum of £23,800 sterling against them jointly and severally. Both defendants have appealed to this court on several grounds of appeal. In my opinion the appeal raised three main issues for determination. These may be stated as follows:

(a) Did the plaintiffs lead sufficient evidence to establish the liability of either or both of the defendants?

(b) Did the plaintiffs prove their damage?

(c) Was the judge right in awarding damages in foreign currency instead of in the Ghanaian currency, the cedi?

I shall deal with the issue of liability first. As I have said the parties involved in this litigation agree that their relationship is governed by the Warsaw Convention which by virtue of the Carriage By Air (Colonies, Protectorates and Trust Territories) Order, 1953 (LN 155) of 1954 is part of the laws of this country. Article 1 of the Convention provides in part: "(1) this Convention applies to all international carriage of persons, luggage or goods performed by aircraft for reward ..." The facts show that the plaintiffs had contracted with the defendants to convey their consignment of mangoes by air for reward to a consignee in London. Thus rightly the parties herein are bound by the terms of this Convention. Article 19 of the Warsaw Convention provides that, "The carrier is liable for damage occasioned by delay in the carriage by air of passengers, luggage or goods." The trial court judge did not only find the

(Continued)

first defendants liable but also found the second defendants liable as well. Concerning the first defendants, she said (see *Farmex Ltd v KLM* [1987-88] 2 G.L.R. 650 at 655):

I am of the view that from the evidence, the first defendants were under an obligation or duty not merely to air freight the goods to Kano and rest at that, but to deliver same to British Caledonian Airways (BCal) for onward carriage to London; and to deliver along with the cargo, the relevant documents covering it, especially the air waybill, exhibit A, and so also they were under an obligation to deliver the goods before 1 December 1985 to enable BCal ship the goods via flight No BR 366 of 1 December 1985.

There is overwhelming evidence on record to support these findings by the trial court and I hold that these findings accurately spell out the contractual relationship between the first defendants and the plaintiffs.

I pause to ask the question: in the face of this evidence what further proof does one need to establish that the first defendants, KLM, delayed the delivery of the goods to BCal on time to enable the latter ship the consignment of mangoes to London on 1 December 1985? Since the goods were delivered after the flight had left Kano, can the first defendants escape blame for having delayed the delivery of the goods? My answer is that they cannot. I therefore affirm that the first defendants delayed the plaintiffs' cargo of mangoes and in my view they will be liable unless they can justify the delay. They had made capital out of their contention that the plaintiffs failed to telex BCal, Kano to take delivery of the goods. Even if there was that lapse on the part of the plaintiffs, that was not the reason why the first defendants did not deliver the goods to BCal on time. In their own evidence they said they did not attempt to deliver until they got the air way-bill, a document which their purser had failed to leave at Kano. I hold therefore that the first defendants delayed the goods and thereby failed to comply with the shipping instructions. On their own showing it was the absence of the air way-bill which made them delay the delivery of the goods and not the absence of information to BCal at Kano.

I now turn to consider the case of the second defendants, BCal. They had agreed in Accra with the plaintiffs to ship the mangoes from Kano to London on 1 December 1985. They had agreed to inform their Kano office by telex about this. The evidence is that the first attempt by KLM to deliver the goods to BCal, Kano was 2 December 1985. They declined to accept the goods because they had received no information about it. Suffice it to say that the telex message sent from Accra by BCal to their Kano office reached them on 4 December 1985. There had been a delay of five days. The evidence shows that the only reason why BCal, Kano refused to accept the goods was that they had no information about it.

In his evidence-in-chief the airport manager for British Caledonian Airways had testified that:

All that I know was my representative in Kano did not accept the cargo because they had no notification of the arrival and also there was no proper mark to accompany the cargo. What I mean is, the air way-bills and notices of the final destination of the cargo did not arrive in Kano. I learnt all the papers were on the KLM flight but the purser did not hand the paper back to Kano. At the time I sent the telex I did not think the air way-bill would be overcarried by KLM. From my information there was no identification to show the final destination of the cargo. Had the telex message arrived in Kano early enough the people in BCal would have accepted the cargo even without the air way-bill. The other way is true too . . .

(Continued)

(Continued)

(The emphasis is mine.) There is no doubt that the telex message did not arrive early enough. However, the air way-bill was available on 2 December and yet they refused to accept the goods until after 4 December when they received the telex. There is evidence that attempts were made to deliver the goods to BCal, Kano on 2 and 3 December. They refused to accept them. In the face of their evidence in court that the goods could be accepted even without the telex message once the air way-bill was available, I find their refusal to accept the goods together with the air way-bill quite strange and even unreasonable.

I now proceed to examine the evidence and the relevant law in an effort to see whether the defendants should not be held liable for the loss which the plaintiffs have suffered by the destruction of the mangoes. I begin with the first defendants. Their contention is that their contract with the plaintiffs is independent of what the plaintiffs had with the second defendants and that they carried out the terms of the contract. I have already dealt substantially with this issue. In so far as they failed to deliver the goods on time to enable same shipped by BCal on 1 December 1985 as clearly stated on the air way-bill, they cannot claim to have carried out their side of the contract. It was submitted by counsel on behalf of the first defendants that exhibit A does not indicate that they should deliver the goods to anybody and that it was not pleaded that they (the first defendants) have committed any breach.

The first defendants knew or ought to have known that in terms of exhibit A they were to deliver the goods to BCal, Kano to enable the latter ship it on "BR 366 of 1 December 1985." Indeed their representative who gave evidence on their behalf before the court below was in no doubt that they were to deliver to BCal by 1 December 1985. Their failure to deliver in terms of what was stated on exhibit A constitutes breach of the agreement they had with the plaintiffs. Exhibit 2, the air way-bill, leaves the first defendants in no doubt that the goods they carried were "goods in transit", "that the consignee was Coulsavalis Ltd" of Cheshire and that "BCal, Kano was to connect with BR 366 of 1 December 1985" as I have already pointed out. In my view these submissions ignore the evidence on record and I reject them.

The first defendants also rely on articles 20 and 21 of the Warsaw Convention to say that they are not liable. The two articles provide that:

Article 20:

> (1) The carrier is not liable if he proves that he and his agents have taken all necessary measures to avoid the damage or that it was impossible for him or them to take such measures.
> (2) In the carriage of goods and luggage the carrier is not liable if he proves that the damage was occasioned by negligent pilotage or negligence in the handling of the aircraft or in navigation and that, in all other respects, he and his agents have taken all necessary measures to avoid the damage.

Article 21:

If the carrier proves that the damage was caused by or contributed to by the negligence of the injured person the Court may, in accordance with the provisions of its own law, exonerate the carrier wholly or partly from his liability.

(Continued)

(Continued)

It is their case that "they took all necessary measures to avoid the damage." The burden is on them to prove this. The evidence on record is that they made the first attempt to deliver the goods after the date they were expected to deliver same. They were already in breach of the terms of the contract. In my opinion they delayed delivery and since we are dealing with perishables, they cannot escape blame. Article 20 therefore does not avail them.

They invoke article 21 of the Convention because they say the plaintiffs failed to arrange for the collection of the goods at Kano and also failed to mark the goods with the consignee's particulars which also made it impossible for them to deliver. Here again these two contentions cannot be sustained. The first part of the contention would only be true if they themselves had complied with the terms of the contract within the time they were expected to deliver. Secondly, the second defendants gave evidence that the shipper does not have the responsibility of marking or identifying the goods. This is part of the representative's cross-examination by the first defendants.

In my view it was not the negligence of the plaintiffs which made the first defendants delay delivery. I therefore hold that article 21 of the Convention does not help them either. In the end I conclude that the first defendants are not exonerated from liability.

The second defendants seek to avoid liability on two main grounds. It was contended on their behalf that in terms of article 30 (1) of the Convention the plaintiffs had not been able to show that the damage was caused during the second defendants' period of carriage. It was also contended that the plaintiffs failed to prove that the mangoes got damaged during the carriage of the goods because there is no evidence as to the condition of the mangoes at the time the consignment left Accra. It was also urged on us during argument, as was also pleaded by the second defendants, that the plaintiffs took a risk and that by the maxim *volenti non fit injuria* they cannot be heard to complain about the loss suffered.

The next issue is whether or not the plaintiffs took such risk as to entitle the second defendants to rely on the maxim *volenti non fit injuria* to escape liability. The second defendants' case is that they warned the plaintiffs about possible delay in the receipt of the telex message that BCal would send to their Kano office. The facts of this case do not justify a conclusion that the plaintiffs took a risk and therefore absolved the second defendants and for that matter the first defendants as well from liability arising out of delay in the delivery of the goods to the consignee. The main suggestion is that the plaintiffs could have sent the goods by a more expensive but safer route. Having regard to the cause of delay which resulted in the loss of the mangoes I am not persuaded that the maxim *volenti non fit injuria* applies to the case. On the application of the maxim one reads from *Salmond on Torts* (18th ed), at 468:

> ... it is in each case a question of fact whether a real consent to the assumption of the risk without compensation can be deduced from all the circumstances of the case. For the issue is not whether the plaintiff voluntarily and rashly exposed himself to the risk of injury, but whether he agreed that if injury befell him, the loss should be on him and not on the defendant.

I therefore hold that the plaintiffs did not take any risk that would exonerate the second defendants from liability in respect of the loss which the plaintiffs have suffered in this case.

(Continued)

(Continued)

My view then is that neither the first nor the second defendants are exonerated from liability. They are jointly and severally liable to make good the loss suffered by the plaintiffs. To this extent I affirm the decision of the trial judge.

I now turn to the question of damages. There are clear principles both in the decided cases and in the textbooks which govern the award of damages in these circumstances. In *Shawcross and Beaumont On Air Law* (2nd ed), at 363 the learned authors discussed the measure of damages when dealing with the carrier's liability for delay. They noted:

> At common law the measure of damages for delay is prima facie *the difference between the value of the goods at the time when they ought to have been delivered and the time when they were delivered.*

In the instant case, we are dealing with a situation of total loss. In Cheshire and Fifoot, *Law of Contract* (4th ed), at 504 the learned authors stated the view that:

> *In all cases the law first determines the normal loss caused to the plaintiff and then puts him in the position that he would have occupied had that loss not occurred. It indemnifies him in full for that loss and to that extent but only to that extent, it insists upon* restitutio in integrum.

The plaintiffs therefore are entitled to be indemnified in full for the loss they have suffered. It is however the duty of the plaintiffs to establish by evidence the total loss suffered. In their evidence before the trial court the plaintiffs through their managing director informed the court that they had taken the action to claim the value of the mangoes from the defendants. The legal position is that the plaintiffs are entitled to be indemnified to the full extent of their loss. That being the case, I am of the view that the trial judge was justified in awarding the plaintiffs the sum of £23,800 which from the evidence represents what they have lost by the loss of the mangoes.

It was strenuously argued on behalf of the defendants that the trial judge erred in awarding damages in foreign currency. I have considered the points raised in argument and I am of the view that there is no legal impediment to the award of damages in foreign currency in appropriate cases. In the instant case, the court is to indemnify the plaintiffs in full for the loss they have suffered. What they have lost is the sum of £23,800 as established by the evidence. They are entitled to it.

The trial judge was also criticised for awarding interest on the damages awarded. I think that criticism is sound. The damages awarded in my view represent the full market value of the consignment of mangoes. The plaintiffs have been indemnified in full and there is no justification for awarding the interest on that sum of money. I therefore uphold the appeal on that ground and set aside the order awarding interest. Subject to this I am of the view that the appeal must fail.

LAMPTEY JA. I have had the advantage of reading the judgments of my brothers Osei-Hwere and Essiem JJA. I cast my lot with the judgment read by Essiem JA.

(Continued)

(Continued)

In the instant appeal, the plaintiff company is a Ghanaian company. Both defendant companies are internationally reputable and respectable airline companies with branches spread over the face of the whole earth. I have no doubt that the plaintiff company is aware of the interests the defendant airline companies have outside the shores of Ghana. Having regard to the current currency laws of this country I wish to state in the language of Lawton LJ in *Schorsch Meier GMBH v Hennin* (supra) at 431, CA that "the plaintiff company must be left to extricate itself from the intricacies of the law relating to execution and exchange control." I am satisfied that in all the circumstances the trial judge was right in awarding damages in foreign currency. I would dismiss the appeal.

Osei-Hwere JA.

JUDGEMENT

I am satisfied from the foregoing that by the failure of the plaintiffs to fulfil the condition precedent (either express or implied) of making an advance reservation, BCal, Kano were disabled from accepting the cargo immediately when tendered and that that was, in the circumstance, the real cause of the delay. In my opinion it will be immoral to allow the plaintiffs seize the handle of the default of the overcarriage by KLM and attack them thereby. I would, accordingly, wholly exonerate BCal from liability. If my judgment had prevailed I would have allowed the appeal and set aside the judgment and costs of the court below and in place thereof I would have dismissed the plaintiffs' action and entered judgment for the defendants.

Kenya Airways Limited v Ronald Katumba

Court of Appeal of Uganda, Kampala
Civil Appeal No. 43 of 2005
(Appeal from the judgement and decree of the High Court of Uganda at Kampala before Honourable Mr. Justice R. O Okumu Wengi, dated the 28th day of February 2005 in civil Case No. 75 of 2005)

Judgement of Hon Justice A.E.N Mpagi-Bahigeine, JA

This appeal arises from the judgement and orders of Okumu Wengi, J, dated 28-02-05. The respondent sued the appellant seeking special and general damages arising out of breach of contract and negligence. The appellant denied the allegations, relying on the terms of the said contract. The learned Judge preferred the respondent's story. Hence this appeal.

The facts, briefly, are that the respondent was a frequent passenger on the appellant's airline from Dubai to Entebbe and vice versa. On 30-01-2003, armed with a return air ticket to Dubai, the respondent checked in his luggage weighing 56 kilograms, on flight No. KQ413H and KQ310H. He, however, did not declare any special value for the baggage, nor did he pay any sums over and above that indicated on the ticket for the said special value of the baggage.

(Continued)

(Continued)

On arrival back at Entebbe, the respondent's baggage was found to be missing. At the request of the appellant, the respondent filled in a property irregularity form, informing the appellant that he had not retrieved his luggage; it was missing. The appellant took steps to try and locate the missing luggage. Arrangements were made to fly him to Nairobi in an effort to trace the missing luggage. It was, however, irretrievably lost. The appellant thus offered to compensate the respondent in the sum of US. $ 1120, in accordance with the terms and conditions stated on the Air ticket, under the Warsaw Convention, which is US $ 20 per kilogram lost, for the 56 kgs.

The respondent declined the offer and opted to file a suit seeking U$ 17963 as the value of the goods lost together with U$ 150 additional cost for the flight to Nairobi, with general damages and costs.

The appellant denied liability beyond the limit of US $ 1120.

The learned Judge held that the appellant's liability was not limited as claimed and ordered it to pay US $ 17,963 to the respondent as prayed.

The memorandum of appeal is dated 30-06-05 and comprises the following grounds:

1. The learned trial Judge erred in law in finding that the appellant's liability was not limited under the Warsaw Convention.
2. The learned trial Judge erred in law and in fact in finding that notice of the limitation of the appellant's liability was not brought to the attention of the respondent.
3. The learned trial Judge erred in law in holding that the Illiterates Protection Act cap 78 applies to airline tickets.
4. The learned trial Judge erred in fact in holding that the respondent was illiterate.
5. The learned trial Judge erred in law and in fact in holding that there was an element of wilful misconduct on the part of the appellant.
6. The learned trial Judge misdirected himself on the law governing the award of special damages and erred in awarding the sum of US$ 150 to the plaintiff as special damages.
7. The learned trial Judge misdirected himself in evaluating the evidence on record and arrived at a wrong decision.

At the conferencing, three issues emerged for determination by the court:-

1. Whether the appellant's liability is limited. (This issue covers grounds 1, 2, 3, 4, 5 and 7 of the Memorandum of Appeal).
2. Whether the trial Judge properly directed himself on the remedies available to the respondent. (This issue covers grounds 6 and 7 of the Memorandum of Appeal).
3. What remedies are available to the parties.

Regarding issue No.1, Mr. Sim Katende, learned counsel for the appellant, citing Article 22 (2) of the Warsaw Convention, pointed out that its wording limiting the appellant's liability was replicated on the airline ticket issued to the respondent and that the respondent was aware of it. In support of this submission learned counsel relied on *Ethiopian Airlines v Olowu Motunrola*, Court of Appeal Civil Appeal No. 30 of 2005, where this court held that in the absence of any special declaration of excess baggage, the airline's liability for lost baggage

(Continued)

(Continued)

was limited to US$ 20 per kg under the Warsaw Convention. Similarly, in this case, the respondent never declared any excess baggage nor its value at checking in and no additional sum was ever paid to her. Mr. Katende submitted that the compensation the respondent was entitled to was limited to what was stated under the Warsaw Convention.

Concerning notice of this limitation to the respondent, learned counsel pointed out that the respondent being a frequent flier ought to have been aware of the information on the ticket. Ignorance of the law is no defence. He was not entitled to the Illiterates Protection Act (cap 78) as claimed by his counsel in the lower court and agreed by the court. He cited *Thompson v London Midland & Scottish Railway Co* (1930) 1 KB 41, where the railway company was held not liable for the injury to an illiterate passenger because limitation of liability was clearly stated in the ticket. Inability to read the ticket was irrelevant. Mr. Katende submitted that the appellant was not an illiterate within the meaning of the Illiterate Protection Act (cap 78) and nor was the Airlines ticket such a document as envisaged by the Act. It was never prepared for the respondent for use, in this trial, as evidence. Mr. Katende further contended that there was no wilful loss of the respondent's luggage as stipulated under article 25 so as to deprive the appellant of the protection. The duty lay on the respondent to show that the appellant wilfully and intentionally lost his luggage. This the respondent failed to do. The appellant was therefore entitled to rely on article 22(2) of the Warsaw Convention which limits liability.

Regarding the special damages claimed and awarded, Mr. Katende pointed out that these were not strictly proved. The receipts for the goods tendered in were of no probative value as they were never made in the names of the respondent.

Concerning the general damages awarded, learned counsel reiterated that the appellant's liability was limited by the Warsaw Convention. The appellant was ready and willing to compensate the respondent up to U$ 1120. There had been no need to file this suit. The money had been deposited in court before the suit. Mr. Katende prayed court to allow the appeal with costs.

Mr. Brian Othieno, learned counsel for the respondent, opposed the appeal, submitting that the learned Judge did not err to find that the appellant's liability was not limited under the provisions of the Warsaw Convention. Citing Articles 4(1) and (4) of the Warsaw Convention, the learned counsel argued that no luggage ticket was issued to the respondent as required under 4(1) in which case article 22 would not be available to the appellant. He pointed out that *"The baggage check"* relied on was only relevant in the Warsaw Convention as amended at the Hague. Under the amendment, the baggage check which article 4 talks of can be combined with the passenger ticket. This is not the same as under the Warsaw Convention.

He asserted that Uganda is not a High Contracting Party to the Warsaw Convention as amended at the Hague. She never ratified the Warsaw Convention and cannot therefore apply their terms like "Baggage Check." In his view, since the luggage ticket was not issued, which luggage ticket is not a baggage check, article 22 was not available to the appellant.

Learned counsel contended that if a luggage ticket is issued under article 4(4), it contains particulars stipulated under article 4(d) (f) and (h) e.g. weight and liability limitation.

(Continued)

(Continued)

He asserted that article 4(f) was thus not complied with by the appellant. The particulars required were not given. He sought to distinguish this case from the Ethiopian case (supra) relied on by Mr. Katende on the ground that in this case, the luggage ticket was not filled in as was done in the Ethiopian case. This means that the particulars in this case required to be given under article 4(d) (h) and (f) were not given. The respondent was given only a baggage tag which is not the luggage ticket envisaged under the Warsaw Convention. The learned Judge was thus correct in his conclusion that the Warsaw Convention limitations were not available to the appellant.

Concerning ground No. 2, Mr. Othieno argued that no notice of the alleged limitations was ever brought to the attention of the respondent. The respondent's being a frequent flyer was not sufficient proof of the notice of limitations to the respondent. He further argued that the respondent was protected under the Illiterates Protection Act as ruled by the learned Judge. The airline ticket was a document as defined by the Act and the respondent was such an illiterate as he could not read and understand the terms on the air ticket and the Warsaw Convention. In his view, *Thompson v London Midland & Scottish Railway Co.* (supra) relied on by Mr. Katende was not applicable. Mr. Othieno asserted that there was wilful conduct on the part of the appellant in handling the respondent's luggage as evidenced by their letter endorsed "without prejudice" dated 10-03-03, (Ex P3), which was put in evidence with the consent of the appellant. In this letter the appellant admitted mishandling the respondent's luggage. He cited article 25 of the Warsaw Convention which provides that if the loss or damage is caused by such wilful misconduct or default by the appellant, then the limitations would not be available to the appellant.

Regarding special damages, Mr. Othieno contended that they were proved by the cash receipts tendered in as Ex P9-i-ii. These were never objected to. The fact that they were not in the respondent's names was never raised at the trial. It was therefore safe to infer that their contents and value were admitted. He stated that even the U$ 150 awarded for hotel expenses was not challenged. He prayed Court to find that the special damages had been satisfactorily pleaded and proved and to dismiss the appeal.

In reply Mr. Katende submitted that indeed no luggage ticket was issued to the respondent but that its absence did not affect the validity of the contract. He pointed out that a luggage ticket and a baggage check were all one document in this case. It was combined with the passenger ticket. It was a question of terminology. Furthermore, the air ticket lists all the particulars required. Learned counsel asserted that though the witness had poor eye sight, the appellant was still protected by the Warsaw Convention since they issued a proper document. The baggage check and luggage ticket being used interchangeably supports the appellant's contention that a luggage ticket and baggage check are the same thing (Ex P8). They are one document. Mr. Katende further stated that it is the respondent who tendered in the ticket at the trial thus he cannot turn round and deny that he never had notice of the liability limitation. He had a document in which the limitation was embodied. He had accepted the ticket without any objection. He cannot, therefore, plead ignorance of its terms and conditions.

(Continued)

(Continued)

Regarding the letter endorsed "without prejudice" (Ex P3), Mr. Katende stated that it could not be relied on in court without the consent of the appellant. That is the law. However, it could be used by the appellant if it made an offer prior to filing the suit which was rejected. It (Ex P3) did not prove wilful misconduct as claimed by the respondent who had to prove wilful misconduct and not merely misconduct. The burden of proof is high and is akin to culpable negligence. Concerning the receipts, learned counsel pointed out that they were challenged in court (page 28 line 6).

Mr. Katende reiterated that both the 1925 Warsaw Convention and the amendment at the Hague were complied with. The appellant fulfilled all the requirements of the luggage ticket. This fits in with the Warsaw Convention, the luggage ticket and baggage check being on one document. He prayed Court to allow the appeal and set aside the judgement and orders of the High Court.

The learned Judge held:

> . . . it is the view of this court firstly that it is the Warsaw Convention and not the Hague amendment that is to be applied in this case. This Convention rationalises the generality that once a notice is said to be given that is final and requires that the Convention itself has to be notified (sic). This is logical given the fact that the Illiterates Protection Act Cap 78 does not exempt airline tickets. In the present case the literacy status of the plaintiff was demonstrated.
>
> Further still article 25 of the Warsaw Convention does not allow exemption where, as in this case, an element of wilful misconduct taking the form of mishandling baggage, has also been demonstrated. I have not been advised that the carriage By Air (Colonies Protectorates and Trust Territories) Order No. 144 of 1953 has been revoked or amended. The first schedule to that order is the Warsaw Convention which makes provisions in section 2(article 4) and in chapter 3(article 25) that operate to liberate the plaintiff in this case from the clinical exclusion of the Airlines liability in any event.
>
> The plaintiff in my view has proved his case on the basis of breach of contract of carriage and or in the mishandling of his baggage resulting in loss that he has proved by Exhibit P9(i) to (xi) as admitted by the defendant. He is entitled to judgement against the defendant for U$ 17,963 or its equivalent in Uganda shillings with costs as prayed.
>
> Secondly, the plaintiff is entitled to general damages given the inconvenience he has gone through and the loss of his investment in trade goods. I will allow him to collect U$ 4150 being special damages and Shs 3 million (Three million only) as general damages. He will recover the costs of this suit from the defendant. It is so ordered.

The first issue to resolve is whether it is the Warsaw Convention 1929 or the Warsaw Convention as amended at The Hague, 1955 which is applicable to this case. This has to be looked for from the four corners of the air ticket itself. The conditions of contract are set out on a coupon of the ticket Ex P8 which appears on page 54 of the record of proceedings. Clause 1 thereof states, inter alia:

> ". . .Warsaw Convention" means the Convention for the Unification of Certain Rules Relating to International Carriage by Air signed at Warsaw Convention as amended at the Hague, 28th September 1955, whichever may be applicable.

(Continued)

(Continued)

Clause 2 goes on:

> "2. Carriage hereunder is subject to the rules and limitations relating to liability established by the Warsaw Convention unless such carriage is not "International Carriage" as defined by that Convention.

I think it is quite plain; it is the Warsaw Convention applicable to this matter as the learned Judge correctly found. If it were the amendment at the Hague, it would have been so stated. It is trite that no extraneous evidence is admissible to vary and or contradict the terms and conditions of the written contract (Ss 91 and 92 of the Evidence Act—chapter 6).

I turn to the issue of liability for loss, delay etc, by the appellant. It is clear that the appellant issued one ticket comprising the passenger ticket and the baggage check all in one. Clause 1 of the conditions of contract clarifies:

> 1. As used in this contract 'ticket' means this passenger ticket and baggage check.

The liability for loss is set out on a coupon (page 55 of the record) and reads:

> NOTICE OF BAGGAGE LIMITATIONS.
>
> Liability for loss, delay or damage to baggage is limited unless a higher value is declared in advance and additional charges are paid. For most international travel. . .the liability is approximately US$ 9.07 per pound (US $ 20.00per kilo) for checked baggage. Excess valuation may be declared on certain types of articles. . . .. Further information may be obtained from the carrier.

This is a replication of Article 22(2) of the Warsaw Convention. Relying on the above provision, in the *Ethiopian Airlines case (supra)*, this Court declined to order compensation for undeclared excess baggage. The baggage tag the respondent seeks to base his claim on has nothing to do with the value or contents of the luggage. It simply reads:

"Limited Release" even if your baggage has been tagged to final destination, you may have to clear through customs at Point of Transfer. This is not the Baggage Check (Luggage Ticket) described in Article 4 of the Warsaw Convention or the Warsaw Convention as amended by the Hague Protocol, 1955.

It is an identification tag as stated by Ismail Nsubuga (DW) and by the writing on it.

I therefore find it impossible to read into this tag anything else other than what it says. It says nothing about the contents of the luggage. A clause in the liability limitations page 55 of the record of proceedings reads:

> Excess valuation may be declared on certain types of articles. Some carriers assume no liability for fragile, valuable or perishable articles. Further information may be obtained from the carrier.

It is therefore only one document that was issued to the respondent under the conditions of the contract. This contains all the relevant information as required under article 4 of the Convention. I cannot therefore take the view that since no luggage ticket was issued, the protection under article 22(2) is not available to the appellant. I think, with respect, the learned Judge was in error over this point.

(Continued)

(Continued)

Another issue taken was that the respondent could not read the ticket and was therefore protected under the Illiterates Protection Act (cap 78). The learned Judge agreed with the respondent which I would take to be a misdirection. The air ticket was not the respondent's document. It was never prepared for him for use as evidence of any fact or thing as stipulated under the Act. Most importantly, the respondent could read through with difficulty as do most people. He could therefore not categorize himself as an illiterate even if the law stated otherwise.

Furthermore, it is well settled that the fact that the respondent could not read would not exonerate him from his obligation under the contract. Once he is handed the ticket and has accepted it, he is bound by it. *Thompson v London Midland and Scottish Railway Company*, (1930) 1 KB 41. Kenya Airways (KQ) made the offer by tendering the ticket to the respondent which he duly accepted fully, thus undertaking to be bound by its terms. Also **see** *McCutheon v David Mac Brayne Ltd (1964)* 1 ALL ER 437. (1964) 1 WLR 134. Where it is stated:

> . . . when a party assents to a document forming the whole or part of his contract, he is bound by the terms of the document, read or unread, signed or unsigned, simply because they are in the contract. . .

The contractual terms on tickets have always been held to be sufficient notice to the holders handling them without objection. In *Mendelssohn v Normand Ltd* (1970) 1 QB 177; the attendant gave the plaintiff a ticket with printed conditions on it. The plaintiff had been to this garage many times and he had always been given a ticket with the self same wording. Every time he had put it into his pocket and produced it when he came back for the car. It was held that he may not have read it but that did not matter. It was plainly a contractual document and as he accepted it without objection, he must be taken to have agreed to it.

Similarly, the respondent explained:

> Yes I was a frequent traveller on K.Q. . . . I did not have to explain that was in my bag. I did not know I had to do this. I am a frequent traveller having travelled KQ so many times.

Apparently the respondent has only himself to blame. He used to take everything for granted. The law would not exonerate him.

This brings me to the question as to whether the appellant's conduct was equivalent to wilful misconduct under article 25 of the Convention thus disentitling him to the protection under article 22(2). Mr. Katende clarified that it was incumbent upon the respondent to prove that the luggage had been lost due to the appellant's wilful misconduct. Learned counsel submitted that this was a case of negligence and not wilful misconduct. The appellant took a lot of trouble trying to search for the lost baggage, even to the extent of arranging a trip to Nairobi for the respondent to try and locate it. In counsel's view, this was not conduct amounting to wilful misconduct. Mr. Katende pointed out that the burden of proof is high and akin to culpable negligence. It was never discharged, he submitted. Mr. Othieno, in my view, did not attempt to counter this.

(Continued)

(Continued)

It has been clearly stated that in a case like this regarding carriage by air, "in order to establish wilful misconduct, a plaintiff must satisfy Court that the person who did the act knew at the time that he was doing something wrong and yet did it notwithstanding or alternatively, that he did it quite recklessly, not caring whether he did the right thing or the wrong thing quite regardless of the effects of what he was doing on the safety of the aircraft and of the passengers—to which should be added their property, for which he was responsible;" *Horaben v British Overseas Airways Corporation* (1952) 2 ALL ER 1016.

I hold the view that the appellant's exhibited a high degree of diligence and concern over the respondent's luggage. By arranging a trip for the respondent to try and locate the luggage, the appellant's conduct passed the test of diligence. The letter Ex P3 cannot be regarded as an admission of wilful misconduct. It should not have been put in evidence without the consent of both parties. It can only be used when it contains an offer that has been accepted and also in criminal matters. That being the case the respondent failed to establish wilful misconduct whose burden is high.

I find the wording on the air ticket and the law on the matter so clear that the result is to allow this appeal with costs. The respondent is only entitled to the compensation as stipulated under the Warsaw Convention, of U$ 1120 i.e. U$ 20 per kg of 56 kg lost.

Notes

1. Hoffman (2002) has also published an excellent guide to conducting research on international commercial laws. Prior to the CISG, international commercial transactions were governed by the Convention relating to a Uniform Law on the Formation of Contracts for the International Sale of Goods (ULF) and the Convention relating to a Uniform Law on the International Sale of Goods (ULIS) done at The Hague on 1 July 1964. See Univ. Prof. Dr Peter Schlechtriem, "Uniform Sales Law—The UN-Convention on Contracts for the International Sale of Goods."

2. "Today the CISG has 72 member states; nine out of ten leading trade nations being member states. It can be estimated that about 17−18% of all international sales transactions are potentially governed by the CISG." See Schwenzer and Pascal Hachem (2009).

3. For an authoritative assessment of inter-regional trade in sub-Saharan Africa, see United Nations Economic Commission for Africa (2010). Excellent commentaries on the CISG and its relevance to developing countries are available from Date-Bah, Samuel K. (*Delegate to Vienna Diplomatic Conference*) in the following articles: Date-Bah (1979, 1980, 2004).

4. [Party names omitted], District Court (*Landgericht*) Frankfurt (Main), 11 April 2005 [2-26 O 264/04], [Translation by Linus Meyer] *Edited by Institut für ausländisches und Internationales, Privat- und Wirtshaftsrecht der Universität Heidelberg, Daniel Nagel, editor.*

5. When goods are delivered, Article 38(1) imposes an obligation on the buyer to "examine the goods, or cause them to be examined, within as short a period as is practicable in the circumstances." Article 39(1) requires a buyer to give the seller notice specifying a claimed lack of conformity in delivered goods "within a reasonable time after [the seller] has discovered it or ought to have discovered it." This is one of the most litigated sections of the CISG. Flechtner (2008).

6. "A substantially more egregious example—perhaps more properly described as an 'outlier'—illustrating the stiffly formalistic and pro-seller approach that some German courts have taken to the buyer's obligation to notify the seller of breach can be found in a 2005 trial court decision involving the sale of used shoes to an

Ugandan buyer. *Also*, This decision represents an almost willful misreading of the notice requirements of the Convention, and a gross miscarriage of justice. Its approach violates the normal canons of interpretation because it renders Article 38(3) a dead letter: *Furthermore*, The result of the court's long series of misinterpretations and mistakes was a truly stunning injustice. *Also*, The result in the *used shoes case* is an extreme example of what strikes me as a strange fixation by some courts on forcing buyers to follow a rigidly-defined process for discovering and notifying the seller of a lack of conformity. This fixation manifests itself by visiting upon buyers the direst consequences—a complete loss of any rights relating to the breach—for the least failure to follow that process."

7. Convention for the Unification of Certain Rules relating to International Carriage by Air (with Additional Protocol), known as "The Warsaw Convention" is an international convention which regulates liability for international carriage of persons, luggage or goods performed by aircraft for reward. It was originally signed in 1929, amended in 1955 at The Hague, and in 1975 in Montreal. See United Nations Treaty Collection, Registration No. LoN-3145

Questions

1. What is the importance of the United Nations Convention on Contracts for the International Sale of Goods (CISG)?
2. What are some of the transaction costs associated with international trade and in what ways does the CISG reduce transaction costs associated with international trade?
3. Give examples of situations and disputes in which the CISG has been effectively applied in resolving the dispute in your country.

References

Alford, D., 2005. A guide on the harmonization of international commercial law. <http://www.nyulawglobal. org/globalex/Unification_Harmonization.htm> (accessed 22.09.10).

Business Roundtable, 2006. World Trade Organization (WTO), builds on historical success. <http://trade. businessroundtable.org/trade_2006/wto/success.html>.

Date-Bah, S.K., 1979. The United Nations convention on contracts for the international sale of goods, 1980: overview and selective commentary. Ghana Law Rev. 11, 50−67.

Date-Bah, S.K., 1980. Problems of the unification of international sales law from the standpoint of developing countries. Problems of Unification. Oceana, New York, = 7 Dig. Com. L. (1980) 39−52.

Date-Bah, S.K., 2004. The UNIDROIT principles of international commercial contracts in West and Central Africa—reflections on the OHADA project from the perspective of a common lawyer from West Africa. Unif. Law Rev. 9 (2), 269−272.

Eiselen, S., 1996. Adoption of the Vienna Convention for the international sale of goods (the CISG) in South Africa. S. Afr. Law J. 116 (Part II), 323−370.

Flechtner, H.M., Spring 2008. Funky mussels, a stolen car, and decrepit used shoes: non-conforming goods and notice thereof under the United Nations Sales Convention ("CISG"). Boston Univ. Int. Law J. 1−28.

Hoffman, M., 2002. Features—revised guide to international trade law sources on the internet. <http://www. llrx.com/features/trade3.htm> (accessed 23.09.10).

Schwenzer, I., Hachem, P., Spring 2009. The CISG—successes and pitfalls. Am. J. Comp. Law. 57, 457−478.

United Nations Economic Commission for Africa, 2010. Assessing Regional Integration in Africa IV: Enhancing Intra-African Trade. Addis Ababa.

CHAPTER 10

Tort Law

Keywords: Entitlement; transaction cost; negligence; duty of care; breach of duty; causation; res ispa loquitur; damages; liability; trespass; balance of probabilities; statute of limitations

10.1 The Economics of Tort Law

Calabresi and Melamed's seminal paper on entitlements is central to an understanding of the law and economics of torts (Calabresi and Melamed, 1972). According to the authors, law in all societies must address two fundamental questions when a dispute arises between two members of that society. First, as between the two parties, who must prevail, that is entitled? Second, once the entitlement has been determined, how should it be protected?[1]

According to the authors, an entitlement may be protected by *property*, *liability*, or *inalienability* rules. When an entitlement is protected by a property rule, then one must negotiate with the holder of the entitlement if they seek to destroy the entitlement. For example, if one wishes to use land belonging to another, one must seek the landowner's permission and pay appropriate compensation to use the land. If an entitlement is protected by a liability rule, one does not need to obtain permission to destroy the entitlement but they must compensate the holder of the entitlement once they have destroyed the entitlement. For example, one is free to drive their car on the road but if they hit another car they must pay compensation for any damages and injury caused. Under the liability rule parties do not negotiate *ex ante* to have an accident. An entitlement cannot be destroyed in any way if it is protected by an inalienability rule. For example, the right to have a child is inalienable.

But what explains the choice of rule protecting an entitlement? According to the authors, the choice of rule is explained by the transaction costs associated with enforcing the rule.[2] In the case of a property rule for example, the owner of the land is known, land prices can be determined, and there are active land markets. In this sense, transaction costs are low enough to encourage private parties to engage in negotiations for acquiring the land. On the other hand, if the right to operate a car was protected by a property rule instead of a liability rule, then one who seeks to operate a car would have to search for all potential parties who may be injured by him and negotiate with them before getting on the road. The transaction cost of

F.O. Boadu: Agricultural Law and Economics in Sub-Saharan Africa.
DOI: http://dx.doi.org/10.1016/B978-0-12-801771-5.00010-1

seeking out all potential victims is very high. In this case, a liability rule is best. In the case of the right to have a child, the cost of policing parties to prevent them having a child is prohibitively high. In this case society simply makes the right inalienable.

10.2 Negligence

It has been suggested that "the positive economic theory of tort law maintains that the common law of torts is best explained as if judges are trying to promote efficient resource allocation" Parisi and Dari-Mattiacci (2006).[3] One common tort is *negligence*.[4] A party who has been injured by the conduct of another party may bring a negligence action to recover damages. For the injured party (plaintiff) to be successful, they must prove that (1) the defendant owed a duty of care; (2) defendant breached the duty of care; (3) the breach was the proximate cause of the plaintiff's injury; and (4) damages. Failure to prove any of these elements may lead to a finding of no negligence on the part of the defendant. The Botswana case, *Nash Sebina v Gobatlwang Kgwakgwe* lays out the general principles of a negligence action.

a. *Duty*

"Duty" has been described as a "person's responsibility not to destroy another person's initial entitlement" (Hirsch, 1979). Duty may be based in common law or imposed by statute.[5] Unless one owes a duty of care to another party, they cannot be found negligent in their actions towards those parties. For a landowner, the duty owed depends on the status of the individual. If the person is on your land without your consent, that is, a *trespasser*, the landowner's duty is limited to not intentionally injure the trespasser. If the person is on the land with permission, that is, a *licensee*, the landowner must warn of known dangers on the land, and if the person is on the land for the benefit of the landowner, that is an *invitee*, the landowner must make the premises absolutely safe for the use of the invitee.[6] In the case of *Attraah v Aboaah*, the court discussed the duty of care owed by a farmer to his neighbor when a fire set by the farmer destroyed the neighbor's farm.

b. *Breach of duty*

Breach of duty is establishing fault or negligence. A plaintiff may prove breach of duty owed to them in several ways. One way is to establish that the defendant's conduct falls below what a reasonably prudent person would do under same or similar circumstances. In the case of *Sebina v Kgwakgwe* the High Court of Botswana in deciding the negligence of a driver of a vehicle stated: "I hold that the plaintiff has proved all his heads of negligence on a balance of probabilities, save only that of failing to avoid a collision when by the exercise of reasonable care he could have done so. There was in fact no collision. He could however, have avoided the accident by such exercise of reasonable care. He should have slowed down upon encountering the donkey cart, and have passed it at a speed where there was no danger of skidding and losing control on the gravelly surface."[7] The same principle was used to dismiss a negligence suit against a hospital where the court concluded, "The true test for establishing negligence in diagnosis or treatment on the part of a doctor was whether he had been proved to be guilty of such failure *as no doctor of ordinary skill would be guilty of if acting with ordinary care.*"[8]

A plaintiff may also use defendant's violation of a relevant statute as evidence of breach of duty. Violation of a statute is *prima facie* proof of breach of duty of care. In the case of *Dzamboe v Mark*, the court stated "The rule regulating overtaking or turning vehicles then in force was to be found in regulation 46 of the Road Traffic Regulations, 1957 (L.N. 135). Failure to observe those rules was prima facie evidence of negligence, and the question whether a driver had driven prudently and reasonably in accordance with the regulations was one of fact."[9] Violation of statute as evidence of negligence was also cited in the case of *Yamusah v Mahama* "the use of one head lamp only as well as driving with defective headlights are offences under the existing Road Traffic Regulations. And thus if by using defective or no lights an accident occurs it will be prima facie evidence of negligence, as I hold in this case."[10]

Plaintiffs may also rely on the doctrine of *res ipsa loquitor* ('thing speaks for itself') to prove negligence on the part of the defendant. As explained in the case of *Vanderpuye v Pioneer Shoe Factory Ltd*, *res ipsa loquitor* "is not a doctrine of substantive law but merely a rule of evidence, i.e. a forensic technique in proving negligence."[11] A plaintiff may rely on this doctrine under clearly defined circumstances. Generally, the source of the damage must be in the sole control of the defendant. Also, the type of accident in issue does not happen unless someone was negligent, and the plaintiff was not contributory negligent. If these conditions are met, the burden shifts to the defendant to prove that they were not negligent, "All the facts leading to the destruction of the plaintiff's goods entrusted to the care of the defendants were within the peculiar knowledge of the defendants who had custody of the goods. They had control of the warehouse in which the goods were kept. Like other cases founded on negligence such as running-down actions, where the facts leading to the accident are unknown or when the facts are within the peculiar knowledge of the defendant, the onus of proof rests on the defendant to establish by evidence that the accident occurred without any want of care on his part. The doctrine of *res ipsa loquitur* applies in such circumstances."[12]

Causation

In a negligence action, the plaintiff must show that the defendant is negligent, and the negligence is the cause of injury. Legal causation requires a "*causal connection between the defendant's* carelessness and the damage."[13] In the case of *Sarpong v Fibre-Bag Manufacturing Co.* the court stated that "the plaintiff must prove not only negligence or breach of duty, but that the fault of the defendant *caused or substantially contributed* to his injury."[14]

Damages

In economic theory, damages are "to compensate for the destruction of initial entitlements through the imposition of negative externalities." Courts in Ghana recognize *Special damages*, that is, damages that "cover out of pocket expenses and loss of earnings from the date of the accident to the date of the trial."[15] Special damages include hospital costs, transportation, and lost wages.[16] The courts also recognize *general damages*, which includes pain and suffering and punitive damages.[17] Damages for fatal injuries are provided by statute.[18] The *Yamusah v Mahama* case discusses these general damages and also the availability of compensation when an injured party uses native treatment for injuries from an accident. The Zambian case, *Continental Restaurant and Casino Limited v Arida Mercy Chulu* emphasizes the need to present credible evidence in support of injury claims in tort. The Nigerian case of *Messrs Dumez* (Nig.) *Ltd v Patrick Nwaka Ogboli* addresses issues in trespass and crop damage. The Zimbabwe case, *Panhowe Farm (PVT) Ltd. v J Mann & Company* (Zimbabwe) also discussed determination of crop damage due to cattle trespass.

Defenses

The following defenses are often invoked by defendants in negligence suits.

i. Assumption of risk: Some individuals may assess danger and decide that they could increase their welfare by taking the risk. In this case, the law refuses to hold a defendant liable for any injuries that the plaintiff suffers (Hirsch, p. 137).

ii. Contributory negligence: *The Civil Liability Act*, 1963 (Act 176) contains the rules on contributory negligence. Contributory negligence arises in the situation where the injured plaintiff also failed to exercise due care and his conduct contributed to the injury. Under common law, contributory negligence was a complete bar to recovery. The common law rule was changed by Act 176 to what is known in most jurisdictions as *comparative negligence*. In this case, the court will apportion the fault and compensate the plaintiff accordingly based on relative fault.[19] For example, suppose a plaintiff sues for Cedi 100.00 as damages caused by a defendant. If a court determines that the plaintiff was 20% responsible for the accident, plaintiff shall receive Cedi 80.00. Part III of the *Civil Liability Act*, 1963, (Act 176) contains the damages rules for fatal injuries. Any member of the deceased's family may bring an action to recover both compensatory and punitive damages. The Act abolishes the *last opportunity rule*.[20] There is a 2-year *Statute of Limitations* for wrongful death actions.[21]

iii. Statute of Limitations: The beginning point for a lawyer handling a particular lawsuit is to check the relevant statute of limitations. Statute of limitation has been defined as "legislative act restricting the time within which legal proceedings may be brought, usually to a fixed period after the occurrence of the events that gave rise to the cause of action. Such statutes are enacted to protect persons against claims made after disputes have become stale, evidence has been lost, memories have faded, or witnesses have disappeared" (Encyclopedia Britannica, 2010). The statute of limitations promotes efficiency in litigation by reducing the transaction costs associated with finding the information needed to resolve conflicts.[22] The statute protects the quality of evidence, see Listokin (2002). There have always been issues regarding when the limitations period "begins to run." Should the limitations period begin when the "cause of action" arose, or when the plaintiff "discovered the injury"?[23] The High Court of Uganda in *J. A. Osma v TRANSOCEAN (U) Ltd.* discussed the application of the statute of limitations. The case of *Republic v High Court, Koforidua; Ex Parte Nsowaa* (Ghana) interpreted the limitations provisions under the Ghana Civil Liabilities Act, 1963 and discussed the circumstances under which a party may be granted an extension of the limitations period.

Nash Sebina v Gobatlwang Kgwakgwe

High Court of The Republic of Botswana, Lobatse
CC-1580-05, November 14th 2008
Kirby J:

FACTS

Kirby J: In this action the plaintiff claims damages of P899,000 plus interest thereon and costs, arising from injuries sustained by him in a motor accident which occurred on 2nd June 2002 along the fenced tarred road which links Molepolole, Lephepe, Shoshong and Serowe. It is the plaintiff's case that the accident (and his resultant injuries) was caused by the negligence of the defendant, who was the driver of the accident vehicle, in which the plaintiff was a passenger, in one or more of the following respects:

(a) He failed to keep a proper lookout.
(b) He drove at an excessive speed having regard to the prevailing circumstances.
(c) He failed to apply his brakes timeously or at all.
(d) He failed to have adequate regard to other road users.
(e) He failed to avoid a collision when by exercise of reasonable care he should have done so.
(f) He failed to keep his vehicle under proper control.

The defendant denies liability. He pleads that he was not negligent at all. He is excused from liability since he acted reasonably when faced with a sudden emergency, namely an encounter with an unlit donkey cart on the road, which he had to avoid, thus leading to his loss of control of the vehicle, and the accident.

OPINION

I do not place much importance on the apparent controversy as to whether the defendant lost control after moving to the right to avoid the cart, or whether he first overtook the cart before losing control. On the evidence, the donkeys drawing the cart were walking, and it

(Continued)

(Continued)

would take only a moment for a vehicle even traveling at 80 km per hour to pass. All agree that it was the stone chippings which rendered the road surface slippery, and caused the car to skid, and it is common cause that by the time the truck skidded across the road, it was past the donkey cart.

In my judgment the probabilities are that the defendant saw the donkey cart too late to slow down or stop. Instead he moved quickly to his right, without slowing down, and so got into a skid on encountering the loose chippings on the right of the road. In attempting to correct the skid, he lost control of the vehicle and overturned, after passing the donkey cart.

It is on those facts that the court must determine whether or not the defendant was negligent. Both counsel are agreed that even the slightest degree of negligence is enough to establish liability in this case, even if the conduct of the donkey cart driver, and the cart's condition contributed materially, as they obviously did, to the accident. The fact that the plaintiff was not wearing a seatbelt may be relevant on the question of damages, but it is irrelevant in relation to the accident itself.

In cross-examination the defendant readily conceded that he had a duty at night to drive at such a speed as to be able to stop within the range of his lights if confronted with an obstruction on the road. This was something he knew. He knew from his previous trip on the road, and from travelling on it that night, of the presence of the three lines of loose stone chips, which could render the road slippery if driven over. He was also keeping a lookout for animals on the road after his previous accident just two nights previously. His explanation for not being able to stop in time was that the donkey cart was masked from view at a distance by the curve of the road.

There are a number of legal principles which apply to a case of this nature, and it seems to me that the application of each one of them points to negligence on the part of the defendant. First, negligence has been defined as the failure to exercise that care and skill which would be observed by a reasonable man in order to prevent harm to others as a result of his acts or omissions. See *R v Meiring* [1927] AD 41 at 46. Whether negligence is or is not present will depend upon the facts and circumstances of each case. See *South African Railways v Symington* [1935] AD 37 at 45.

Second, the fact that a driver skids is not per se evidence of negligence. If he could reasonably anticipate that a skid may occur and he fails to take the necessary precautions to avoid this, he is negligent. See *R v [White]* [1940] (1) P.H.O (8), where a driver skidded on a corrugated gravel road and struck a vehicle parked beside the road. The court held that:

> . . . *it was his duty to reduce his speed below skidding speed before he reached those cars. He did not do so and it was impossible to avoid the conclusion that he failed to exercise reasonable care in not reducing his speed and thereby averting a skid under road conditions which he knew would tend to cause a skid.*

So too in this case the defendant was well aware of the slippery state, due to loose stones, of parts of the road surface, yet he overtook, or swerved, at a speed which led not only to a skid, but one which endured for almost 100 metres, and led to his car rolling more than once.

(*Continued*)

(Continued)

Third, while it has been held that there is no absolute rule of law which states that a driver who drives at night must proceed only at such a speed that he is able to stop within the range of his lights, generally this is so and his failure to do so may in the circumstances provide evidence of negligence, either in that he failed to keep a proper look out or that he traveled at an excessive speed in the prevailing conditions. See *Morris v Luton Corporation* [1946] I AER I (C.A); *Hoffman v SAR & H* [1955] (4) SA 476 AD. So, where a driver is blinded by the lights of an on-coming vehicle, this may, depending on the circumstances, mitigate or excuse his blame if he collides with an unlit obstruction or animal. But normally, it will not do so. See *Manderson v Century Insurance* [1995] (1) SA 522 AD.

In *Price & Quality Bakery (PTY) LTD v Bophelo (George's Bakery & Another)* [1997] BLR 1282, a driver collided at night with an unlit stationary vehicle. Gyeke Dako J. remarked at p. 1289:

> *When a man drives a motor vehicle along a road, he is bound to anticipate that there may be people or animals or things, including a motor vehicle in the way, at any moment; and he is bound to go no faster than will permit of his stopping, or deflecting his course at any time from anything he sees after he has seen it.*

I respectfully agree with this statement, although I would add that he must travel at such a speed that he can safely deflect his course from an obstruction after he has seen it. In this case there was no on coming vehicle to reduce visibility in any way. In this case too the defendant was well aware of the danger of encountering animals on the road as only two nights previously he had been in collision with a cow in similar circumstances. By definition a stray animal, especially when approached from the rear, is unlit, just as the donkey cart was. Despite his protestation to the contrary, in my judgment he was not keeping a proper lookout, and that is why he only saw the cart when it was too late even to safely apply brakes. He was driving without due care and attention, and his admission of guilt was properly made.

He was also, in my view, driving at a speed which was not safe in the circumstances. The length of his skid marks and the fact that he rolled his vehicle twice indicate that he was travelling faster than the 80–90 km per hour of his own estimate. He admitted that his vision was limited by pitch darkness and the fact that his vehicle was entering a bend made his lights less effective, yet he failed to apply brakes or to slow down to ensure that the road ahead was clear. Even 80 km per hour can be an excessive speed where visibility is not good. See *Baoki v The State* [2001] 2 BLR 164.

Finally, it is only permissible to overtake another vehicle when it is safe to do so, and in a manner and speed which is also safe. See *Tonyela v SAR & H* [1960] (2) SA 68 (a case involving the overtaking of a horse and cart). Here the cart was given no warning of the defendant's intention to overtake so as to enable it to move further to the left, and the defendant began to overtake when he was too close, or alternatively going too fast to enter the area of slippery gravel at an angle, and so got into the skid which caused the accident.

JUDGMENT

I hold that the plaintiff has proved all his heads of negligence on a balance of probabilities, save only that of failing to avoid a collision when by the exercise of reasonable care he could

(Continued)

(Continued)

have done so. There was in fact no collision. He could however, have avoided the accident by such exercise of reasonable care. He should have slowed down upon encountering the donkey cart, and have passed it at a speed where there was no danger of skidding and losing control on the gravelly surface.

The defence of sudden emergency also does not avail the defendant, because there was no sudden emergency — only a foreseeable occurrence; namely encountering animals or an animal drawn conveyance on a road at night where the defendant knew these were likely to be encountered, and which road was known to have a slippery surface at its verges. See, for a similar case where the defence failed, *Baoki v The State* (supra).

Liability is accordingly established and I find for the plaintiff, with costs.

Dzamboe v Mark

High Court, Accra
4 March 1980
[1981] G.L.R. 350, 350 (1980)

FACTS

This is a claim for general damages for personal injuries sustained by the plaintiff in a collision between his Honda motor-cycle and the defendant's car. The collision occurred on 26 April 1974 at 6 p.m. The plaintiff's case is that he was riding from Legon along the road linking Legon with Achimota School towards Achimota. At the main junction to Christian Village, he rode past it, but attempted to turn right at the second junction which is about 150 metres from the other junction. In the act of turning, the defendant came from behind and collided into him. The defendant was attempting to overtake the motor-cycle. The plaintiff suffered a compound fracture of the right tibia and fibula which took ten months to heal.

The defendant's case is that on the same day and time he was driving from Legon along the same road and in the same direction. He saw the plaintiff as soon as he came out of a bend to a straight stretch of the road which stretches for a distance of about 300 metres to the Christian Village junction. The defendant followed the motor-cycle along this straight stretch of the road to the Christian Village junction. The plaintiff rode past the junction without evincing any intention to turn right. The defendant then decided to overtake. He sped up and caught up with the plaintiff, while gradually shifting to the right lane. At the time, Ghana drove left. When he was about a metre to the plaintiff the latter swerved right, suddenly and by reflex action, he also swerved right to avoid him but he could not do so completely. As the defendant was already in the right lane the motor-cycle came along and collided into the front left mudguard of the car. The handle of the Honda was trapped between the mudguard of the car and the tyre, so by the time the car came to a complete stop the Honda had been dragged for a short distance. The plaintiff was thrown off the Honda by the impact, but the Honda dropped on the

(Continued)

(Continued)

road. Later it was carried off the road and placed at the roadside. The plaintiff himself was lying prostrate on the road. The defendant sought and obtained assistance from two people who came to the scene and they put the plaintiff in his car, and took him to the Korle-Bu Teaching Hospital where he was admitted for treatment. Then he reported the accident at the Tesano Police Station and an officer was detailed to go to the scene of the accident with him. The police officer made a plan which was tendered in this case as exhibit B.

OPINION

The plaintiff's witnesses maintained that by usage and custom of the people, the first junction is regarded as an exit from the village, and the second junction as the entrance to it. There are no traffic sign posts to give such directions and the road from both turnings are untarred. Both parties conceded that the second turning was a bushy path of about six feet wide at the time of the accident. The road, as the court saw it, had been widened and resurfaced. But the first junction has always been regarded as the main entrance to the village. Even with the facelift given to the road from the second junction, the first junction still stands out as the main entrance to the village. The second junction is not quite visible from the Legon end of the road, one gets to it before one is aware there is a turning. The impression I formed was that it would be easier and more reasonable for intending travellers to Christian Village from the Legon end to turn at the first junction. The inference I make of the plaintiff's conduct is that he missed the first turning and tried to make it at the second. I do not believe that he deliberately went past the first turning because it was by custom plied on as a one-way traffic road for vehicles making their exit from the village.

The parties in this case have shifted blame for the accident on each other. The plaintiff maintains he indicated by his trafficator sign that he was turning right, and that the defendant ignored the sign and drove into him. The defendant contends that the plaintiff had not shown by any sign whatsoever his intention to turn right. On the contrary he said the plaintiff was riding close to his nearside, and it was after he had moved to the right ready to overtake when the plaintiff swerved suddenly to the right. The only issue in this matter therefore is who is to blame for this accident.

There is no hard and fast rule as to how and where a vehicle should overtake another, but the Highway Code prohibits overtaking at road junctions. However; such a prohibition if it were stretched to cover every side-road, would make driving in towns and cities, which have so many side-roads, intolerable. The mere fact of an accident occurring at a junction while a leading vehicle is being overtaken should not, ipso facto, make the person in charge of the overtaking vehicle liable. Each case must be taken on its own peculiar facts. Where the condition of the road permits, a following vehicle should feel free to overtake if the leading motorist behaves in a way which indicates that he is going straight. The driver of a leading vehicle owes an equal duty of care to the driver of the vehicle coming from behind as the latter owes to the former. If the driver of a leading vehicle intends to change his course, he must indicate this intention to other users of the road. This includes vehicles approaching from behind and on-coming vehicles. From decisions on cases involving overtaking vehicles, that duty is not discharged by merely giving the indication; the driver of the turning vehicle must see

(Continued)

(Continued)

that his signal has been observed and appreciated by the driver of the vehicle behind him. The rules which ought to be observed at the date of this accident are to be found in the Road Traffic Regulations, 1957 (L.N. 135). Regulation 46 deals with overtaking or turning vehicles. These the regulations which were in force when Ghana drove left. Every motor vehicle was required to be driven on the left or nearside of the road and a vehicle overtaking traffic moving in the same direction was to pass on the right, but if the leading vehicle was turning right and had signalled accordingly, the overtaking vehicle would pass on the left. As was held in *Chaplin v Howes* [1928] 3 C. & P. 554 and applied in *West African Bakery v Miezah* (supra) failure to observe these rules is prima facie evidence of negligence, and the question whether a driver has driven prudently and reasonably in accordance with the regulations is one of fact.

The plaintiff has made a big issue of the fact that the defendant overtook at a road junction, and his counsel submitted this was an act of negligence. The plaintiff has also made capital out of the fact that the defendant came from behind him and that hitting him in those circumstances amounts to prima facie evidence of negligence. At paragraph 3 of the statement of claim the following particulars of negligence were charged against him:

"(1) excessive speed;
(2) failure to exercise proper control over the vehicle;
(3) failure to have regard for a vehicle in front;
(4) ignoring signal of a vehicle in front; and
(5) failure to make a proper use of brakes."

The case for the defendant has been that the plaintiff misled him into thinking he was going on a straight course and as the road was clear of other traffic, he found it safe to overtake. The defendant said he was familiar with the road. He knew there was the junction to Christian Village so he lagged behind the plaintiff to watch his intentions. The plaintiff was not riding fast so the defendant who followed for some time could not have driven faster than the plaintiff. The charge of excessive speed made against the defendant could have no basis. The damage caused to the respective vehicles is not very serious. According to exhibit C, the vehicles examiner's report, the defendant's vehicle had dents at the fore-end of the nearside mudguard, a dent at the radiator, and a graze at the front bumper. The plaintiff did not even find it worthwhile to make any claim for damages for his motor-cycle. He did not mention any damage on it. It could not have been substantially damaged. If the defendant had driven at excessive speed the impact would have been more traumatic than it was recorded in both injury to plaintiff and damage to the vehicles.

With regards to the failure to exercise proper control, the evidence does not support such an allegation and nothing needs be said about that. On failure to have regard for a vehicle in front, I accept the defendant's case that the plaintiff misled him into thinking that he was going straight and not turning right. The plaintiff himself said he did not see the defendant at all before he turned, he just noticed that he had been hit by something. Yet he said he looked both ways — back and front — before he turned. That evidence could not be true. The accident happened towards the Achimota side of a straight portion of the road which stretches for a distance of about 440 metres. If the plaintiff did not see the defendant in the

(Continued)

(Continued)

bend, he was bound to notice him while they were on the straight stretch. As he did not, the only inference I can make of this omission was that he, the plaintiff, was not keeping a proper look-out on the road.

The way to determine whether one's signals have been observed is to watch the other's reactions. The way he reacts will be indication that he appreciates the course of action one wants to take. It is important that before one turns across the road, one looks into the driving mirror to see that one has been observed by vehicles from behind. That should be the behaviour of a reasonable and prudent man. That is the yardstick to measure the conduct of a careful driver.

The conduct of the plaintiff in this case fell short of this. He completely disregarded the presence on the road of approaching vehicles. But whether this conduct wholly caused or merely contributed to the accident would depend on whether the plaintiff gave any signal at all of his intention to turn. If he did not, and misled the defendant to think that it was safe to overtake, then the conduct of the defendant in overtaking in those circumstances could not be faulted.

JUDGMENT

Held, dismissing the plaintiff's claim for negligence: the driver of a leading vehicle owed an equal duty of care to the driver of the vehicle coming from behind as the latter owed the former. If the driver of a leading vehicle intended to change his course, he had to indicate this intention to other users of the road. That would include vehicles approaching from behind and oncoming vehicles. That duty was not discharged by merely giving the indication; the driver of the turning vehicle had to see that his signal had been observed and appreciated by the driver of the vehicle behind him. The rule regulating overtaking or turning vehicles then in force was to be found in regulation 46 of the Road Traffic Regulations, 1957 (L.N. 135). Failure to observe those rules was prima facie evidence of negligence, and the question whether a driver had driven prudently and reasonably in accordance with the regulations was one of fact. It was important that before one turned across the road one looked into the driving mirror to see that one had been observed by vehicles from behind. That should be the behaviour of a reasonable and prudent man.

Republic v High Court, Koforidua; Ex Parte Nsowaa

Supreme Court, Accra
25 April 1990
[1989–90] 2 G.L.R. 677, (1990)
Sowah CJ, Adade, Francois, Wuaku and Amua-Sekyi JJSC

FACTS

One Kwame Peprah (KP) died on 11 October 1980 from injuries he sustained when he was knocked down by a motor vehicle earlier that same day. Thereafter the applicant,

(Continued)

(Continued)

representing the dependants of KP, engaged the services of an insurance claims agent to pursue their claim for compensation for the death of KP but she was eventually informed by the State Insurance Corporation on 5 November 1985 that the insurance cover note was a forgery and that the insurance company would therefore not accept liability on behalf of the assured. Subsequently, the applicant, recognising that they were caught by the statutory time limit of 3 years from the death laid down under section 3 (2) of the Limitation Decree, 1972 (N.R.C.D. 54) for bringing an action for damages for the benefit of the dependants of a deceased person pursuant to section 16 of the Civil Liability Act, 1963 (Act 176), brought an ex parte application before the High Court, Accra under sections 23 (1) and (2) and 25 (2) of N.R.C.D. 54 for leave to sue after the statutory period laid down under section 3 (2) of N.R.C.D. 54 had expired. The application was in April 1986 granted by Ampiah JA sitting as an additional judge of the High Court. The applicant therefore issued a writ on 26 May 1986 as administratrix of KP, claiming damages against the driver and owner of the vehicle which had knocked down KP. Upon being served with the statement of claim, the respondents in their defence, contended that the action was statute-barred and that at the time the writ was issued the applicant was not the administratrix of the estate of KP. Thereafter the respondents brought an application under Order 25 of the High Court (Civil Procedure) Rules, 1954 (L.N. 140A) before the High Court, Koforidua (to which court the suit had then been transferred for hearing) to strike out the suit brought by the applicant. In his ruling, the trial judge, Abakah J, held that as the order extending the time within which to sue was made by Ampiah JA, sitting as a judge of co-ordinate jurisdiction, he could not interfere with it. He however upheld the objection that at the time the writ was issued the applicant was not an administratrix and therefore dismissed the action. The applicant therefore brought the instant application for an order of certiorari to quash the decision of Abakah J for an error of law on the face of the record.

OPINION

Amua-Sekyi JSC: The cause of action of the dependants is derived from section 16 of the Civil Liability Act, 1963 (Act 176) which states:

> "16 (1) Where the death of a person is caused by the fault of another such as would have entitled the party injured, but for his death, to maintain an action and recover damages in respect thereof, the person who would have been so liable shall be liable to an action for damages for the benefit of the dependants of the deceased."
>
> Sections 3 (2) of the Limitation Decree, 1972 (N.R.C.D. 54) sets a time limit of 3 years from the death for the bringing of an action under section 16 of Act 176. Thus, if the applicant desired to sue she had up to 10 October 1983 to do so. In the absence of any enabling provision in the law she would have no right to sue after that date.
>
> Sections 23 (1) and (2) and 25 (2) of N.R.C.D. 54 give to a person in the position of the applicant, a right to apply for leave to sue after the period of limitation laid down in section 3 (2) has expired. By section 24 (1) if the application for leave is made before the issue of the writ it shall be made ex parte. The applicant put in one which came before Ampiah JA sitting as an additional judge of the High Court, Accra. He granted

(Continued)

(Continued)

    it and the applicant issued a writ against the driver and the owner of the vehicle on 26 May 1986. The applicant sued as administratrix of the estate of Kwame Peprah.

The law then requires that the facts must be material, relate to the cause of action, be of a decisive character and be outside the knowledge of the plaintiff until 2 years or more after the commencement of the 3-year limitation period. Assuming that the plaintiff got to know that the insurance cover note was a forgery only in 1985 the last requirement would have been met; but it cannot be seriously argued that in an action against the driver and owner of a motor vehicle the fact of insurance or no insurance is material, or relates to the cause of action, or is of a decisive character. It is only when judgment has been obtained against the tortfeasors and it is sought to bring an action (for the satisfaction of the judgment debt) under section 10 of the Motor Vehicles (Third Party Insurance) Act, 1958 (No 42 of 1958) that the question of insurance becomes material or relevant. There were thus no facts on which the applicant could properly go before the High Court to ask for leave to sue.

The refusal of Abakah J to interfere with the order made by Ampiah JA is understandable having regard to the decision of the Court of Appeal in *Dankwa v Fuller*. However, the order having been obtained on an *ex parte* application under Order 52, r 3 of L.N. 140A any party affected by it could move the court to set it aside. The application is by motion and, ideally, ought to be taken by the judge who made the order; but, as can be seen from Order 39, r 4 of L.N. 140A, the application can, in case of necessity, be taken by another judge. In April 1986 when the order was made Ampiah JA had just been elevated to the Court of Appeal and was in the course of winding up his work in the High Court. What was more, the suit was transferred from Accra to Koforidua. It is our belief that the circumstances were such that if a proper application had been made Abakah J would have been competent to deal with it and set aside the order. Be that as it may, this court is not inhibited by any rule of law or practice from declaring that the facts did not justify the exercise of the power to grant leave to sue out of time.

The evidence put forward by the applicant to answer the defence that she was not an administratrix at the time she issued her writ was a search filed in the High Court, Accra. This showed that the application for letters of administration was granted on 21 May 1986 subject to the filing of notices for three days. No caveat having been lodged, the grant took effect from 21 May 1986. In my view, Abakah J's strictures on the search were not justified. If he had any doubts about the matter, he ought to have adjourned the proceedings for the applicant to obtain amended letters from the court which made the grant. The dismissal of the action of the applicant on this ground was therefore wrong.

After the dismissal of the suit the applicant went back to the High Court, Accra and obtained an amended letter of administration which stated correctly that the date of the grant was 21 May 1986. Next, she obtained another extension for time before Lutterodt J and filed a fresh writ for the same reliefs. Six months later, she lodged this application for an order of certiorari to quash the decision of Abakah J. Thus, if we were to grant her the order she seeks and restore the original action there will be two suits before the courts for the same reliefs.

(Continued)

(Continued)

Clearly, such a situation cannot be countenanced as it will amount to an abuse of legal procedure. In any event, being satisfied that the order granting leave to issue the original writ ought not to have been made, this court would not revive that still-born action even though Abakah J was in error when he dismissed it on the ground that the applicant had obtained her letters of administration on 28 May 1986.

JUDGMENT

Held, dismissing the application: (1) sections 23 (1) and (2) and 25 (2) of the Limitation Decree, 1972 (N.R.C.D. 54) gave to the person in the position of the applicant, a right to apply for leave to sue after the expiration of the 3-year period laid down in section 3 (2). However, the facts on which an applicant could properly come before the court to seek leave to sue out of time must be material, relate to the cause of action, be of a decisive character and be outside the knowledge of the applicant as the plaintiff until 2 years or more after the commencement of the 3-year limitation period. If the applicant (in the instant case) got to know that the insurance cover note was a forgery only in 1985 the last requirement would have been met. However, it could not be contended that in an action against the driver and owner of a motor vehicle the fact of insurance or no insurance was material, or related to the cause of action, or was of a decisive character. It was only when judgment had been obtained against the tortfeasors and it was sought to bring an action (for the satisfaction of the judgment debt) under section 10 of the Motor Vehicles (Third Party Insurance) Act, 1958 (No 42 of 1958) that the question of insurance became material or relevant. There were consequently no facts on which the applicant could properly go before the High Court to ask for leave to sue out of time.

(2) Since the order extending time within which to sue was made by a judge of co-ordinate jurisdiction on an ex parte application under Order 52, r 3 of the High Court (Civil Procedure) Rules, 1954 (L.N. 140A), any party affected by it could move the court to set it aside. The application, by motion, ought to be taken ideally by the judge who made the order; but under Order 39, r 4, the application, could, in case of necessity, be taken by another judge.

Yamusah v Mahama and Another

High Court, Tamale
[1991] 1 G.L.R. 549, 549 (1988)
30 June 1988
Benin J

FACTS

The plaintiff was a farmer and an anaesthetist assistant at the Tamale Hospital whilst the first and second defendants were driver and transport owner respectively. In 1985 whilst the

(Continued)

(Continued)

plaintiff was a pillion rider on a motor bike, a vehicle driven by the first defendant collided with the motor bike. The first defendant was arraigned before the district court on criminal charges of careless driving and negligently causing harm to the plaintiff. He pleaded guilty to both counts and was convicted on his own plea and sentenced. The plaintiff, in the instant action, sued the defendants jointly and severally for general and special damages for bodily injuries, pain and suffering caused by the negligence of the first defendant. The plaintiff contended that the first defendant's plea of guilty at the district court being an admission against interest was a conclusive presumption of his liability for the plaintiff's injuries under the Evidence Decree, 1975 (N.R.C.D. 323), s 26 and was thus estopped from denying liability for negligence. The court found that the vehicle was being driven by the first defendant at night with only one head lamp which was also defective because it was not bright.

OPINION

Benin J.: The plaintiff's claim against the defendants jointly and severally is for general and special damages for bodily injuries, pain and suffering arising from a motor accident caused wholly by the negligence of the first defendant by the manner he drove, managed or controlled Mercedes cargo truck No UR 2453 owned by the second defendant and driven by him in the course of his employment as servant or agent or both of the second defendant on 8 May 1985. The facts of the plaintiff's case may be gathered from the pleading as amended containing the following relevant averments:

Particulars of Negligence

(a) Driving too close to his off side.
(b) Paying no proper attention at all to other users of the road.
(c) Driving too fast or at a speed that is unreasonable having regard to the nature of the road.
(d) Failing to so drive, manage or control his said vehicle in such a way as to avoid colliding with the plaintiff's motor cycle.
(e) Driving at night with defective headlight.

And as far as the same may be consistent with the facts the plaintiff will in addition rely on the maxim res ipsa loquitur.

Particulars of Injuries

(a) Head injury (contusion).
(b) Body contusion (chest, neck and waist pains).
(c) Crushed injury to left leg (with compound comminuted fracture of tibia and fibula with loss of some bones).
(d) Loss of skin anterior aspect of tibia.

As a general result of the accident the plaintiff now suffers recurrent waist, chest and neck pains, shortening of his left leg, swelling of the left leg and can no longer weed or do other farm operations and cannot also indulge in his favourite hobby of playing volley.

(Continued)

(Continued)

Particulars of Special Damage

(a) Cost of drugs (gentamicin injection)	¢12,000
(b) Travelling to Accra for routine checks (once every six weeks)	¢50,000
(c) Cost of farm labour for two farming seasons (1985 and 1986)	¢30,000
(d) Native treatment	¢8,000
(e) Loss of shoe and damage to wearing apparel	¢8,000
Total	¢108,000

After finding the defendant guilty of negligence, the court continued. . .

Next, to the damages claimed. I shall first deal with the special damages. Special damages normally cover out of pocket expenses and loss of earnings from the date of the accident to the date of the trial. They are usually based on facts within the peculiar knowledge of the plaintiff so he must first plead them and then go on to prove them strictly in court, and finally it must not be too remote. I shall place the special damages under three headings, viz: medical, transport and farm labour expenses.

Medical. I must mention here that the plaintiff's injuries were not disputed. The plaintiff is entitled to recover any medical or similar expenses incurred as a result of the injury. And if as a result of the injury the plaintiff has to receive special attendance at home or elsewhere the additional expenses thereby incurred may be recovered. The plaintiff candidly told the court that as a hospital staff himself he was treated free of charge and got all the drugs free with the exception of only one injection, gentamycin, which he had to buy from outside at a total cost of ¢12,000. Counsel for the defendants submitted that the plaintiff should have produced a receipt to support it. I think apart from the defence counsel's failure to challenge the cost of the drug in cross-examination and the defendants' failure to lead any rebuttal evidence, and having regard to the circumstances surrounding this particular claim, I have no doubt the claim must be accepted. He could well have said he bought all or most of the drugs and he could have got away with it on ground of shortage at the material time. Production of a receipt is not a strict requirement of the law. Obtaining a receipt for goods purchased is desirable but not compulsory, what matters is effective possession of the goods purchased. I find that the plaintiff spent ¢12,000 to purchase gentamicin injections.

Under this head of claim, the plaintiff said he also underwent native treatment. Counsel for the defendants submitted that since (i) this treatment was not on the recommendation of the medical officer; and (ii) no receipt was produced, the court should not accept this claim. On the second ground, I think my earlier position will still stand valid. At any rate how many of our local medicine men know of receipts in their activities at all, let alone to possess and issue them? Was it necessary to require that the plaintiff could only go in for native medical treatment upon a recommendation from the medical officer? I must confess I am not aware of any rule to that effect and counsel did not refer me to any, nor did he profess to base his submission on any rule. I am thinking that since the plaintiff himself submitted himself

(Continued)

(Continued)

voluntarily to the medical officer(s) for treatment, common sense will surely dictate that he be at liberty to go elsewhere for additional or further treatment. In line with my thinking I believe the plaintiff did not need anybody's recommendation or advice or otherwise to go for native treatment. This claim not having been at all or seriously disputed, I accept it and find as a fact that the plaintiff underwent native treatment at a cost of ¢8,000.

Transportation. The plaintiff said he had to travel to Accra and back by air transport to receive treatment. Whilst it is the duty of the plaintiff to mitigate his loss by travelling by the cheapest available transport, I think it will be stretching the rule too far to demand that a person who had suffered broken bones to his leg should go by road from Tamale to Accra and back just to mitigate his loss. I think it will rather have the effect of increasing loss because it would cause him greater pain and suffering and thereby extend the period of treatment. I think the pain and suffering if it persists is a better reason for increasing costs than to endure it to save costs to the tortfeasor. In the absence of any evidence to the contrary as to the quantum of damage claimed, I accept and find that the plaintiff spent ¢50,000 on transportation which I find was reasonable in the circumstances with regard to the fare, frequency of travel and mode of travel.

There was also a claim for loss of shoe and damage to wearing apparel through the accident. We were not told what type of shoe and apparel they were to enable us assess their value. In view of this I do not think, the plaintiff is entitled to the entire amount claimed, for he could well have over-stated the price. I will allow him ¢5,000 under this head.

Farm labour hired. The plaintiff pleaded and led evidence that he was a farmer doing the farming himself. But as a result of the accident he could not farm and so hired labour at a total cost of ¢30,000 for the 1985 and 1986 farming seasons. This comes under loss of earnings. That he was also a farmer and engaged labourers during the period of his incapacitation was not disputed. But being a full time civil servant, if the plaintiff says he was farming himself then it meant he could effectively farm only during the week-ends. For that matter any labour he hired could only be during the week-ends and for one labourer at a time in place of himself. He did not tell us that prior to the accident he had additional labour to assist his efforts. I think therefore that the farm labour expenses, in the absence of detailed information as to what type of labour was engaged, how much was paid per each labourer, or how many labourers were engaged and for what duration, should be reduced by a third. I therefore enter judgment for the plaintiff to recover ¢20,000 by way of farm labour expenses.

General damages. The medical report, exhibit A, records the following relevant facts as to injuries sustained:

(1) Head injury (contusion).
(2) Body contusion (chest, neck and waist pains).
(3) Crushed injury to left leg (with compound comminuted fracture to tibia and fibula with loss of some bones).
(4) Loss of skin anterior aspect of tibia.

(Continued)

(Continued)

The patient was rushed to theatre and the compound fractured wound was thoroughly cleaned and the leg put in long leg Plaster of Paris for daily wound dressing. He was discharged back to Tamale to continue with treatment and to be followed up at the out-patients department clinic. The medical report states:

> On examination today, he complains of pains on the left knee with stiffness, still wound discharging pieces of bones. Waist, chest and neck pains. Two inches shortening of left leg. On and off headaches; the left leg swells a lot. X-ray examination: left tibia and fibula revealed malunion comminuted fracture one third of tibia and fibula. In view of present functional disturbances as elaborated above which will persist for a long while, I assess incapacity at 45 per cent.

The injuries sustained by the plaintiff have not been disputed at all and I accept them as proved in evidence. The result being that he suffered pain, deformed body, physical incapacitation and loss of enjoyment of amenities, namely volleyball. He is entitled to recover damages for these, keeping in mind the principle that the amount awarded must represent a reasonable and fair compensation. On loss of amenities, the law is that if the plaintiff's injuries deprive him of the capacity to engage in some sport or pastime which he hitherto enjoyed, he is entitled to damages for loss of enjoyment. The plaintiff's claim was that he played volley as a hobby. In other words, he only played it for his entertainment or for exercises; he made no money therefrom as professionals do. The plaintiff has not told us his age to enable us determine how long he could continue engaging in volley playing. I think a sum of ¢20,000 should be adequate to cover this head of claim.

On pain and suffering and injuries, I take note of the nature of the injuries he suffered, the persistence of the pain, the length of time he had to be at the hospital to undergo treatment and other related factors, and having made comparative award study, I have come to the conclusion that the plaintiff be allowed ¢120,000 on these heads of claim. Judgment is entered for the plaintiff accordingly to recover the following from the defendants jointly and severally:

(i) Total special damages	¢95,000
(ii) Pain and suffering	¢120,000
(iii) Loss of amenities of life	¢20,000
Total	¢235,000

I award the plaintiff costs of ¢8,000 in this action.

JUDGMENT

(1) the use of one head lamp only and driving with defective headlights were offences under the existing Road Traffic Regulations. Thus if by using defective or no lights an accident occurred (as in the instant case), it would be prima facie evidence of negligence. (2) The plaintiff was entitled to recover any medical or similar expenses such as expenses for native treatment (as in the instant case assessed at ¢8,000) incurred as a result of injuries arising from negligent driving. *Judgment for the plaintiff.*

Continental Restaurant and Casino Limited v Arida Mercy Chulu

Supreme Court, Zambia. Judgment No. 28 of 2000, 20th July and 24th August, 2000
Appeal No. 77/99
Sakala, A.D.C.J.

JUDGMENT

Sakala, Acting D.C.J.: delivered the judgment of the court.

This is an appeal against a judgment of the High Court awarding the Respondent, a sum of K85 million as damages for injury suffered after eating food which contained a foreign matter. For convenience, the Appellant will be referred to as the Defendant and the Respondent as the Plaintiff, the designations which they were at trial.

The Plaintiff, who is a Magistrate, was on 22nd July, 1998, together with other Magistrates, invited for lunch by the Chief Administrator at Polo Grill, a restaurant run and owned by the Defendant Company. While at the restaurant, the Plaintiff was served with some mushroom soup. This soup contained a cockroach.

The evidence of the Plaintiff was that while she was taking her soup, she felt something hard and rough in her mouth which she mistook for a piece of mushroom, but after she pulled it out from her mouth she noticed that what she thought was a piece of mushroom, was in fact a cockroach with its legs and wings intact. The Plaintiff hereafter failed to continue with her lunch. She alerted one of the Defendant's waiters. The Plaintiff remained at the restaurant when her friends had left. One of the management staff apologized to her and offered her fresh food to cook at home, but she refused. The Plaintiff also testified that she has since continued to suffer from nausea. The Plaintiff subsequently sued the Defendant Company for damages.

The learned trial Judge identified issues for determination as to whether the Defendant company owed any duty of care to the Plaintiff and if so, whether the duty was breached and whether the breach occasioned the Plaintiff any damage. After citing the provisions of Section 3(b) of the Food and Drugs Act, Cap. 303, the Court found that the Defendant company owed the Plaintiff duty of care. The court further found that this duty was breached. The Court had no difficulty to hold that Plaintiff suffered damage or injury as a result of having been served with the soup containing a cockroach.

In determining the amount of damages to be awarded, the court noted that a cockroach is an insect known to be one of the dirtiest insects. The Court pointed out that the damages to be awarded had to take this element into account. The court also observed that the injury suffered by the Plaintiff was such that it could not be completely forgotten hence entitling the Plaintiff to aggravated damages. Although the Plaintiff did not claim for exemplary damages in her statement of claim nor endorsed it in the writ, the learned Judge was still satisfied that this was one of the cases where damages to be awarded had to take into account the element of exemplary damages. The Court awarded a sum of K85 million as damages plus costs.

Mr. Lungu, on behalf of the Plaintiff, did not file heads of argument and indicated that he conceded to all the arguments on behalf of the Defendant Company except on quantum of damages awarded.

(Continued)

(Continued)

On behalf of the Defendant, Mr. Mutemwa filed written heads of argument. In his brief oral submissions, Mr. Mutemwa pointed out that the actual damage suffered by the Plaintiff was that she felt nauseatic and had stomach pains that led her not to enjoy food for a week. He submitted that there was no evidence of medical attention and that the damage, if any, was merely nausea. Counsel also submitted that the condition suffered by the Plaintiff did not warrant an award of colossal damages and that she should be entitled only to nominal damages of K500,000.00.

Counsel concluded his submissions by pointing out that in cases of this nature, medical evidence is necessary to justify the award. Alluding to the case of *Donohue v Stevenson (1)*, he submitted that in that case the Plaintiff was actually hospitalised. In his brief submissions on behalf of the Plaintiff, Mr. Lungu submitted that the evidence of the injury suffered by the Plaintiff was not challenged. He pointed out however, that if the Court had to reduce the amount of K85 million, which he conceded was on the higher side, a sum of K50 million should be awarded.

The only issue for determination in this appeal is the amount of damages. But we wish to point out that in including exemplary damages in the award, which damages were not pleaded, the learned Judge overlooked the many decisions of this court where we have said that exemplary damages should be specifically pleaded. This had always and is still the law on exemplary damages. These damages were not pleaded here. The important point to stress, however, is that in cases of this nature, the basis of awarding damages is to vindicate the injury suffered by the Plaintiff. The money was to be awarded in the instant case not because there was a cockroach in the soup, but on account of the harm or injury done to the health, mental or physical of the Plaintiff. Thus in the *Donoghue* case the Plaintiff was hospitalised. Mild condition is generally not enough a basis for awarding damages.

The Plaintiff has, therefore, a duty to bring credible evidence of illness. The award in the instant case comes to us with a sense of shock as being wrong in principle and on the higher side. We want to take advantage of this case to point out that in future, nothing will be awarded if no proper evidence of a medical nature is adduced. In this instant case, the learned trial Judge flew overboard in the award of damages. Accordingly, we set the award of K85 million aside. In its place, we award a sum of K2 million. We make no order as to costs in this court.

Mensah v National Savings and Credit Bank

Supreme Court, Ghana
[1989–90] 1 G.L.R. 620, 620 (1990)
4 December 1990

Wuaku, Amua-Sekyi, Aikins, Edward Wiredu JJSC and Amua JA

FACTS

Under a contract of bailment, the plaintiff in April 1978 delivered some imported goods to the defendants for safekeeping in their warehouse for a fee. By clause 19 of the insurance

(Continued)

(Continued)

contract any action to recover moneys under the policy had to be commenced within twelve months of the loss or damage. On 5 June 1979 fire broke out in the warehouse and burnt down the plaintiff's goods the declared value of which was ¢1,988,320. There was evidence that the warehouse was constructed of sandcrete blocks, roofed with asbestos, locked and guarded night and day by paid security officers and was equipped with fire extinguishers. But it was an old building with old, corroded and exposed electrical wires near the beach where there had been frequent outbreak of fire as a result of electrical short-circuiting. It was not however positively proved that the fire was caused by electrical short-circuiting. The defendants had delayed the claim against the insurers until the twelve-month limitation period had elapsed. Although they informed the plaintiff about the loss of his goods, they did not notify him about the rejection of the claim by the insurers before the expiration of the limitation period. Instead they assured him they were pursuing the claim. After several abortive attempts to get the defendants to pay him for the value of his goods, he instituted an action against them claiming damages for the loss of the goods. The defendants joined the insurers as third parties. The trial judge dismissed the claim against the insurers on the ground that it was time-barred. He however found the defendants liable in negligence on the ground that they should have foreseen that electrical wires in such old premises near the sea would corrode and might cause an electrical short-circuit resulting in fire. On appeal by the defendants, the Court of Appeal reversed the decision of the trial judge on the grounds, inter alia, that the evidence on which negligence was founded was most unsatisfactory as none of the witnesses could say positively that the fire was caused by an electrical short-circuit and that the defendants bore no responsibility to make the warehouse absolutely safe. This case is a further appeal to the Supreme Court by the plaintiff.

OPINION

Amua-Sekyi JSC: On liability, the trial judge held that the defendants had been negligent. It seems that the basis of the finding was that the defendants should have foreseen that electrical wires in the old premises near the sea would corrode and that such corrosion might cause an electrical short-circuit resulting in fire. But, as the Court of Appeal pointed out. The evidence was most unsatisfactory as none of the witnesses who spoke to this could say positively that the fire was caused by an electrical short-circuit. The evidence was, to say the least, speculative and ought not to have found favour with the trial judge. Moreover it seems to me that even if it had been proved satisfactorily that the fire was caused by an electrical short-circuit arising from corroded wires, this would not have been sufficient unless there were evidence that the defendants knew of the poor state of their electrical wires and took no steps to remedy the defects.

I cannot find a better statement of the law than that contained in the following passage of *Halsbury's Laws of England* (3rd ed), Vol 2, para 225 at p. 116.

> *The bailee is not, apart from special contract, an insurer, and, therefore, in the absence of negligence on his part he is not liable for the loss or damage to the chattel due to some accident, fire, the acts of third parties, or the unauthorised acts of his servants acting outside the scope of their employment.*

(Continued)

(Continued)

The liability of the defendants was not absolute. It was to take care of the goods in the manner a prudent man of business would of his own property. In this case, they kept them in a warehouse constructed of sandcrete blocks, roofed with asbestos, locked and guarded night and day by paid security officers. To guard against the possibility of fire, the warehouse was equipped with fire-extinguishers. I am in complete agreement with the Court of Appeal that the defendants did all that could reasonably have been expected of them to see that the plaintiff's goods were safe.

In spite of the conclusion I have come to, I am satisfied that the defendants are liable to the plaintiff because they failed to notify him of the repudiation of liability by the insurers. In *Ranson v Platt* [1911] 2 KB 291, CA. the plaintiff, a married woman living apart from her husband, deposited certain goods belonging to her with the defendant, a warehouseman. Subsequently, the plaintiff's husband went to the premises and claimed to be the owner of the goods. The defendant refused to deliver them to him except under a magistrate's order. A summons was issued against him, he attended and an order was made. In compliance with the order he delivered the goods to the plaintiff's husband. The Court of Appeal held the defendant liable in damages on the ground that he ought to have given notice to the plaintiff of her husband's claim to the goods and of the summons.

The value of the plaintiff's goods as declared to the insurers was ₵1,988,320. That sum represents the maximum sum that can be recovered under the policy, even if the loss exceeded it. The evidence being clear that the plaintiff's goods were worth ₵1,988,320 that is the only sum he can lawfully claim or be awarded. I would therefore allow the appeal and enter judgment for the plaintiff against the defendants for the sum insured less ₵20,000 with costs in this court. The order for costs made in favour of the defendants in the Court of Appeal should stand.

Wuaku JSC: I have had the privilege of reading the opinions of my brothers Amua-Sekyi and Edward Wiredu JJSC, both of whom had ably stated the facts of this case. I need not repeat them. I agree with the view expressed by my learned brother Amua-Sekyi JSC that the plaintiff would only be entitled to recover ₵1,988,320.

Edward Wiredu JSC [dissenting]: Since writing this judgment in this case, I have had the privilege of reading the opinions of my brothers Amua Sekyi and Aikins JJSC but I have not been able to persuade myself to agreeing with their views expressed on the issue of liability. I will therefore proceed to read my judgment in which I have expressed a dissenting view.

To me the core of this appeal rests on the answer to the question: on which of the parties rests the onus of proof? And whether this duty was discharged. This is a clear case of bailment for valuable consideration, and the law is that "a custodian for reward is bound to use due care and diligence in keeping and preserving the article entrusted to him on behalf of the bailor." All the facts leading to the destruction of the plaintiff's goods entrusted to the care of the defendants were within the peculiar knowledge of the

(Continued)

(Continued)

defendants who had custody of the goods. They had control of the warehouse in which the goods were kept. Like other cases founded on negligence such as running-down actions, where the facts leading to the accident are unknown or when the facts are within the peculiar knowledge of the defendant, the onus of proof rests on the defendant to establish by evidence that the accident occurred without any want of care on his part. The doctrine of *res ipsa loquitur* applies in such circumstances: see the case of *Ansah v Busanga* [1976] 2 G. L.R. 488, CA. It has also been held that it is unnecessary to plead the words *res ipsa loquitur*: see *Asantekramo alias Kumah v Attorney-General* [1975] 1 G.L.R. 319 and *Halsbury's Laws of England* (3rd ed), Vol 28 at 79.

In the present action like cases of *res ipsa loquitur* the burden of proof is on the defendant-bank (the custodian) to show that the loss or the destruction of the plaintiff's goods did not happen in consequence of his neglect to use such care and diligence as a prudent or careful man would exercise in relation to his own property: see *Phipps v Cleridges Hotel Ltd* [1905] 22 LTR 49 and *Brooks Wharf and Bulls Wharf Ltd v Goodman Brothers* [1937] 1 KB 534 at 538-539, CA. If the custodian of the goods succeeds in showing that he is not negligent then he is not bound to show how the loss or damage occurred: see *Bullen v Swan Electric Engineering Co* [1907] 23 TLR 258, CA and the *Wharfs* case (supra).

So the question to be answered here is whether in the instant case the defendants on whom the onus rested to show that they had on the particular facts of this case exercised such care and diligence as a prudent person or a careful man would have exercised in relation to his own property as they pleaded to paragraph 6 of the defence (supra) discharged that onus.

The facts revealed in this case by the first defendant's witness show that the ignition which resulted in the fire outbreak was the result of an electrical fault. This is what he said:

> *The cause of the fire was stated as fire by electrical short-circuit. Short-circuit is a break in the path provided for carrying an electrical current. We found that the building was an old one and that the electrical wiring has stayed for a long time. And since it is nearer to the sea, the sea breeze formed moisture to deteriorate the insulators and rendered the wires naked. Fires can be caused by many factors. Some of which are crash and collision, matches, children with fire or other lighters, spontaneous ignitions and doubtful causes.*

The Fire Service report, exhibit B, states:

SOURCES OF IGNITION: (1) There was no item in the warehouse that could have ignited by itself than electricity. *As the warehouse was very old and the position of it is exposed to the sea breeze, coupled with the raining season, there was the likelihood of moisture and water disturbing electricity and resulting to arcing and short-circuit which finally gave out smoke and set the warehouse on fire on application of air by the soldiers opening the doors.*

(2) In support of the above I have to state that many stores and wholesales including Makola Number One Market, Two Guys, Rose Pillars, Indian Bazaar just to mention a few were looted but

(Continued)

(Continued)

there was no fire. There were indications at some of the doors that they were forced open by intensive shots from guns, but as there was no fire before the looters or the soldiers approached them, they did not burn, therefore it was concluded that the supposed cause of fire was electrical fault. (The emphasis is mine.)

Apart from the above evidence the defendants produced no evidence as to the measures taken to ensure the safety of the electrical wiring of the warehouse. The evidence shows that the wiring of the warehouse was external. The warehouse itself was old with corroded electrical wires exposed. This defect cannot be said to be latent which a vigilant custodian would have allowed to remain unchanged and not rewired. Having regard therefore to the above can it be said that the defendants succeeded in showing that they exercised the duty of care they assumed by not replacing defective old and exposed electrical wires? Is this not a neglect on their part? I hold in my judgment that in the particular circumstances of this case, taking into consideration the locality where the warehouse is situate and the frequent fire outbreaks caused by electricity in that area, the defendants failed to discharge the onus on them as pleaded. I further hold in my judgment that the learned trial judge of the High Court was right in his conclusion in favour of the plaintiff. For the above reasons, I would allow the appeal.

JUDGMENT

A bailee was not, apart from special contract, an insurer and therefore in the absence of negligence on his part, he was not liable for the loss or damage to the chattel due to some accident, fire, the acts of third parties, or the unauthorised acts of his servants acting outside the scope of their employment. Therefore the liability of the defendants as bailees was not absolute but only upon proof of negligence. It was to take care of the goods in the manner a prudent man of business would of his own property. On the facts, the Court of Appeal had rightly held that the defendants did all that could reasonably have been expected of them to see that the plaintiff's goods were safe.

Contra per Edward Wiredu JSC dissenting. All the facts leading to the destruction of the plaintiff's goods entrusted to the care of the defendants are within the peculiar knowledge of the defendants who had custody of the goods. They had control of the warehouse in which the goods were kept. Like other cases founded on negligence such as running-down actions where the facts leading to the accident are unknown or when the facts are within the peculiar knowledge of the defendant, the onus of proof rests on the defendant to establish by evidence that the accident occurred without any want of care on his part. The doctrine of *res ipsa loquitur* applies in such circumstances. In the present action, like cases of *res ipsa loquitur*, the burden of proof is on the defendant-bank (the custodian) to show that the loss or the destruction of the plaintiff's goods did not happen in consequence of his neglect to use such care and diligence as a prudent or careful man would exercise in relation to his own property ... [on the facts] the defendants failed to discharge the onus on them.

Appeal allowed in part.

J.A. Osma v TRANSOCEAN (U) Ltd

High Court of Uganda, Kampala
Civil Suit No. 1385/86, October 30th 1990
Hon. Mr. Justice G. M Okello

FACTS

When this suit was called for hearing before me, Mr. Malinga for the Defendant raised a preliminary objection in point of law contending that the suit is time barred misconceived, bad in law and does not disclose a proper cause of action against the defendant and prayed that it should be rejected under O 7 r 11(d) of the CPR. The Defendant had raised this point under paragraph 4 of their W.S.D.

For the Plaintiff, Mr. Donge opposed the preliminary objection hence this ruling.

The principle applied in determining whether or not a plaint discloses a cause of action is that the court must look only at the Plaint. See *Onesforo Bamuwayira and 2 others. v A.G* [1973] HCB p. 87; *Nagoko. v Sir Charles Turyahamba and Anor* [1976] HCB 99.

In the instant case the relevant parts of the pleadings are as follows:

Plaint

1.   Plaintiff's action against the defendant is in detinue for the wrongful detention of his vehicle Dutsun Station wagon.

2.   In late 1978 the Plaintiff imported a reconditioned Dutsun Station Wagon, Engine number CLS.625367 Chassis number p. 610 — 831976 from Yokohama Japan which vehicle arrived at the Port of Mombasa on or about 14th March 1979 as indicated in the defendant's Cargo Dispatch Certificate referred to above an annexure 'A.'

3.   The said vehicle was cleared from the port of Mombasa by the defendant company and the vehicle arrived in Kampala on 10th September 1979 as per the defendant's cargo Dispatch Certificate referred to above as annexure 'A'.

4.   To date the said vehicle has not been handed over to the plaintiff and no explanation offered to him despite the numerous efforts the plaintiff made to get his vehicle released.

5.   Notice of Intention of begin the suit was served on the defendant on 29th July 1986".

Paragraph 4 of the defendant's W.S.D reads thus;-

"5.   Without prejudice to the foregoing, the defendant shall aver that the suit is time barred, misconceived and bad in law, does not disclose a proper cause of action against the defendant".

OPINION

Mr. Malinga argued that under section 4 of the Limitation Act Cap 70 Laws of Uganda, actions in torts should be instituted before the expiration of 6 years from the date when the cause of action accrued. He submitted that in the instant case, the suit being in tort of detinue, the action must be instituted before the expiration of 6 years from the date when the cause of action accrued. Counsel pointed out that in the instant case, the plaint does not

(Continued)

(Continued)

aver the date of effective demand by the plaintiff for the delivery of the vehicle to him after its arrival in Kampala on 10th September 1979. He submitted that in that case, the date of demand is taken to be 10.9.79 because in his view detinue is not a continuing tort for the purpose of limitation. That his date therefore constitutes the date when the cause of action accrued, That the action hiving been instituted on 14/11/86 as shown the "Received" stamps of the court on the Plaint, the suit is instituted well after the 6 years period from the date when the cause of action accrued, That the suit having been barred by Limitation Act must be rejected under O 7 r 11 (d) CPR.

For the Plaintiff, Mr. Donge contented that the suit is not statute barred because the tort of detinue is based on wrongful detention of the Plaintiff's chattel by the defendant. That so long as the wrongful detention of the Chattel continues, the cause of action also continues. He submitted that detinue is a continuing tort.

As regards the of effective date of demand by the Plaintiff for the delivery of the vehicle, Mr. Donge submitted that the demand was made on 27.9.86, when the defendant, was given notice of intention to sue as indicated in paragraph 7 of the Plaint, He submitted further that even if the cause of action is taken to have arisen on 10.9.79, there was still a cause of action because detinue as a tort is continuing since the defendant still continues to wrongfully hold the chattel.

Mr. Malinga replied that the effect of Limitation Act was not to abolish the cause of action but to deny the Plaintiff remedy through court action because of his delay in instituting the suit.

From the above argument, I am of the view that the issue of the dispute between the parties is whether detinue is a continuing tort. What is detinue? Detinue may be stated to be a wrongful retention by the defendant after demand of possession of a chattel which the Plaintiff is entitled to immediate possession of. It is significant to note that there must be a demand by the Plaintiff of the release of the chattel and a refusal by the defendant to release the same in order to constitute a cause of action in the tort of Detinue.

As to whether this type of tort is a continuing one for the purpose of Limitation Act, it is important to consider the nature of the tort because those torts like nuisance, false imprisonment and occasionally trespass to land which though may he done once but which consequences and damages arising from them are continuous are regarded as continuing torts (Winfield and Jolowicz on Tort 12th Ed., Pages 648–9). In those types of torts, a fresh cause of action arises de die dem (from day to day) so long as the wrongful state of affairs continues. In such event the Plaintiff can recover for such portion of the tort as lie within the time allotted by the statute of limitation although the first commission of the tort occurred outside the period prescribed by the statute of limitation (see Winfield and Jolowicz on Tort 12th Ed., Page 649).

The gist of the wrong in a tort of detinue therefore lies in the wrongful detention of Property by the defendant after demand by the Plaintiff for its release. So long as the wrongful detention of the chattel continues, the cause of action arises de die dem (from day to day)

(Continued)

(Continued)

and in that event the plaintiff can recover for such portion of the tort as lie within the limitation period prescribed by the statute of Limitation even though the first commission of the tort occurred out side the time prescribed by law.

For the reasons stated above, I find myself in agreement with Mr. Donge that detinue is a continuing tort for the purpose of limitation.

In the instant case, the Plaint does not contain the date when the Plaintiff demanded from the defendant the release of the vehicle after its arrival in Kampala on 10.9.79, Mr. Malinga submitted that in the event of such a failure to make the averment, the date of demand should be to be taken to be the 10.9.79 when the vehicle arrived in Kampala and that this should constitute the date of the cause of action. I agree with that argument because for there to be a cause of action for tort of detinue, there must be a demand by the Plaintiff for the release of the chattel and a refusal by the defendant to release the same. In a continuing tort like in this one, this date constitutes the date of first commission of the tort but so long as the wrongful detention continues the cause of action arises from day to day,

JUDGMENT

In this case it is averred in paragraph 6 of the Plaint that the defendant still continues to wrongfully retain the vehicle to date. It means that the cause of action also continues. It follows that the action is not time barred for the portion of the tort which lies within the limitation period of 6 years. For the reasons given above, the preliminary objection is over-ruled.

Attraah v Aboaah

High Court, Kumasi, Ghana
30th September, 1963
Apaloo J.

FACTS

The plaintiff and the defendant own farms contiguous to each other at a place called Witreso at Odumasi, Ashanti-Akim. The preponderance of the evidence is that both were cocoa farms. Some time in September 1961, the defendant set fire to his own farm. This fire was spread by the force of a strong wind and caused damage to the farm. It is agreed by the witnesses that it was exceptionally dry weather and dry winds were blowing from Agogo towards Konongo Odumase. In an action against the defendant before a circuit court, the plaintiff claimed that the defendant was negligent in setting fire to his own farm in these circumstances and in failing to prevent its spread to her (the plaintiff's) farm. The learned circuit court judge found as a fact that before setting the fire the defendant had cleared the edges of his farm and held that to be the known and accepted farming practice. He ruled

(Continued)

(Continued)

that the burning of the plaintiff's farm was an "Act of God" and therefore the defendant was not liable to the plaintiff. The plaintiff appealed to the High Court. This is an appeal from the judgment of a circuit court which on the 11th April, 1963, dismissed a claim by the plaintiff against the defendant for damage suffered by the former as a result of the destruction by fire of the plaintiff's cocoa farm.

OPINION

The plaintiff claimed that the defendant was negligent in setting fire to his own farm and in failing to prevent its spread to her farm. The defendant pleaded that he took all reasonable precautions to avoid the spread of the fire and accordingly claimed that the fire spread accidentally and also by "Act of God." The precaution which the defendant said he took was that he cleared the confines of his own farm before lighting the fire.

His counsel has urged in this court that that is the ordinary farming practice and beyond that the defendant need not go. The learned circuit court judge found as a fact that before setting the fire, the defendant cleared the edges of his farm. He held that to be the known and accepted farming practice. He therefore concluded "the burning of the plaintiff's farm was therefore an 'Act of God' and the defendant is not liable to the plaintiff for any damages, if any, suffered by her."

Not unnaturally, the plaintiff appeals to this court on two grounds. Firstly, it was submitted on her behalf that the judgment was unreasonable having regard to the evidence. The way in which the judgment failed to conform to reason, counsel pointed out, was that although the court wholly cleared the defendant from making reparation, he was himself offering by his letter, exhibit 1, to pay compensation for the damage.

The second ground of appeal, which counsel argued with rather more conviction, complains that the "learned circuit court judge erred in holding that the burning of the plaintiff's farm was an 'Act of God'." Counsel referred to and relied on the definition of an "Act of God" in *Winfield on Tort* (6th ed.), p. 54 which defines it as "an operation of natural forces so unexpected that no human foresight or skill could reasonably be expected to anticipate it." It was said that such a defence could not fit in with the facts of this case. To show the extent to which the operation of natural forces must be unexpected to make a successful defence of an "Act of God" counsel refers to the well-known case of *Nichols v Marsland*.

I do not understand counsel for the respondent to attempt to support the conclusion of the learned circuit court judge that the burning of the plaintiff's farm on the known facts of this case was an "Act of God" in the accepted legal connotation of that term. To conclude that where the weather was known to be exceptionally dry and windy and a man took the risk of lighting fire which then spreads in the ordinary course of nature and causes damage, that damage was caused by an "Act of God" is to throw reason to the winds. It is a fallacy which I should have thought was self-evident. In my judgment, there is nothing remotely resembling an "Act of God" in this case and in so far as the learned circuit court judge concluded this case in the defendant's favour on that basis, I cannot feel any doubt that he was in error.

(Continued)

(Continued)

The facts of this case suggest plainly to my mind that the defendant was negligent in lighting the fire in the state of the weather which was known and which was narrated by the witnesses. His counsel, however, argued with force that there was no negligence and pointed to the finding of the learned circuit court judge that the defendant before lighting the fire took the precaution of clearing the edges of his farm. The only object of clearing the confines of the farm was to prevent the spread of the fire. But if the weather was known to be exceptionally dry and windy, I should have thought commonsense would suggest that such a course would be a wholly ineffectual preventative. A man who takes the risk of lighting fire in those circumstances must at his peril contain the fire within the confines of his land or take the consequences of its spread. I think the defendant ought reasonably to have envisaged that the precaution which he took was wholly unequal to the risk which he ran and that in the state of the weather, the fire would spread to neighbouring farms precisely as it did. There can be no doubt that he owed a duty to his adjoining farmers not to cause damage to their property. I am satisfied he committed a breach of his duty to the plaintiff and is liable to her for the damage she sustained.

Counsel for the respondent has urged on me not to see with what he called English eyes what ought properly to be looked at with native eyes and not to impose liability where conduct conforms with what local farmers themselves regard as blameless. In view of the impact which the common law has made on our indigenous law and also our own administration of justice, I think this is a just and right-minded observation. But it is to be remembered that the parties themselves considered this particular conduct to be blameworthy and the defendant himself offered to pay monetary compensation for the damage. It would be a little surprising if a rational system of law denied any remedy to a person in the plaintiff's position who, through no fault of her own was damnified by the culpable conduct of her neighbour. Indeed the defendant himself said, "The farming practice in these matters is that I should go and inspect the farm and pay for the damage." Accordingly as I said, the plaintiff is entitled to damages which I must proceed to assess.

The plaintiff pleaded that the number of cocoa trees destroyed in her farm amount to 300 and claimed an aggregate sum of £G150 for them. When the farm got burnt, the parties appointed a date to inspect the farm and to check the number of damaged trees as is customary. The agreed dates did not eventually prove suitable to the defendant. The plaintiff, however, sent Kwasi Adae and one Yaw Barimah to count the trees. The former gave evidence and said the damaged cocoa trees numbered 300. I did not read the cross-examination of this witness by counsel as disputing that number. The defendant himself was not in the position to dispute that number. He failed to avail himself of two opportunities to check these trees. The only person who said anything about the number of cocoa trees burnt in the plaintiff's farm on the defendant's behalf was the defendant's third witness by name Kwasi Beyden. He estimated the number as 40. He did not claim to have checked them and was obviously engaged in a form of guesswork. In so far as it is necessary to credit one person as against the other, I certainly prefer the evidence of the man who swore that he was sent for the express purpose of checking the trees and found them to be 300 to the man who merely guessed the number. It follows that I am prepared to find and do find that the number of

(Continued)

(Continued)

matured cocoa trees burnt in the plaintiff's farm was 300. The total sum of £G150 claimed by the plaintiff as the value of the damaged cocoa trees works out at ten shillings per tree. I think that is reasonable and indeed in the case of *Serwah v Darkwa* in which I gave judgment, I accepted ten shillings as a fair value of a matured cocoa tree. It follows therefore that I hold the plaintiff entitled to the sum of £G150 as damages for the destruction of the cocoa trees.

The plaintiff also testified that foodstuff was damaged in her farm and estimated its value as £G50, which sum she also claimed. The defendant is an adjoining land owner with the plaintiff and if no foodstuff was damaged or destroyed by him, he would have said so. He himself said in cross-examination that the plaintiff planted cocoyam, plantain and few cocoa trees. Far from disputing liability to the plaintiff in respect of the foodstuff, he wrote a letter to the plaintiff (exhibit 1) agreeing to pay for the foodstuff as well as the cocoa. It is not at all easy to assess damage for an unspecified quantity of foodstuff destroyed along with 300 cocoa trees. But a wrongdoer does not get away because the assessment of damages is difficult. In all the circumstances of this case, I think the fairest way of determining this matter is to split the plaintiff's claim on this head of damage into two equal halves and award her one half of the £G50 claimed, that is, £G25. The plaintiff will therefore recover from the defendant the total sum of £G175 as damages.

JUDGMENT

Held, allowing the appeal: (1) where the weather was known to be exceptionally dry and windy and a man took the risk of lighting a fire which then spreads in the ordinary course of nature and causes damage, such damage cannot be said to have been caused by an "Act of God." (2) The defendant was negligent in lighting the fire in view of the known state of the weather at the time. (3) A farmer owes a duty of care to his adjoining farmers not to cause damage to their property. Therefore a farmer who, before setting fire to his farm takes a precaution which he knows or ought to have known would be ineffective in preventing the spread of the fire, must at his peril contain the fire within the confines of his land or take the consequence of its spread. In this case the defendant ought reasonably to have envisaged that the precaution which he took was wholly unequal to the risk which he ran and that, in the state of the weather, the fire would spread to neighbouring farms precisely as it did. He committed a breach of his duty to the plaintiff and was therefore liable to her for the damage which she sustained. (4) An award of ten shillings would be a fair value for each mature cocoa tree destroyed. It is, however, not easy to assess damages for an unspecified quantity of foodstuff destroyed. But a wrongdoer does not get away because the assessment of damages is difficult. In all the circumstances of this case the fairest way of assessing the damages was to split the plaintiff's claim on this head of damage into two equal halves and award the plaintiff one half of the damages claimed. *Serwah v Darkwa*, High Court, 29th June, 1962, unreported, followed.

Accordingly, the judgment of the circuit court dismissing the plaintiff's claim is set aside. For it, I substitute judgment for the plaintiff against the defendant for the sum of £G175. The plaintiff will have her costs in the circuit court assessed at 25 guineas and in this court assessed at 30 guineas. Any costs paid pursuant to the judgment of the circuit court to be refunded to the plaintiff-appellant.

10.3 Strict Liability

Another tort theory that a Plaintiff may rely on to recover for injuries caused by a defendant is the theory of *strict liability*.[24] It has been suggested that the "difference between negligence and strict liability is a difference in *the content of the underlying duty of care*.[25] For example, in the case of blasting, an activity generally considered ultra-hazardous and therefore subject to strict liability, "the blaster has a duty-not-to-harm-by-blasting."[26] Compare the duty on the blaster to the duty for a motorist covered under negligence rule. The motorist has "a duty-not-to-harm-by-faultily-motoring."[27] So regardless of the care taken by a blaster they are held responsible if they injure someone. A motorist is held responsible only if they behaved negligently. Both negligence and strict liability can induce efficient behavior so in economic terms, the difference lies in their distributional consequences. In the case of strict liability, the injurer bears all the cost, that is the activity cost plus the injury cost. In the case of negligence, an injury bears the activity cost but may not bear the injury cost unless the activity was performed negligently.

Strict liability has been applied to a limited number of injuries. Injuries by wild animals are subject to strict liability. For example, injuries cause by a lion owned by a party may subject the party to a strict liability action. Another area of application is what are considered "abnormally dangerous" activities such as blasting, explosives, and in some cases spraying of crops, see Prosser et al. (2005). In the 1970s strict liability became popular in suits against manufacturers of products in what is currently referred to as "products liability" law.

Strict liability has been applied in Ghana to hazardous activities. There is no products liability law as found in the United States, for example, under the *Restatement of Torts*.[28] Ghana law applies strict liability to ultra-hazardous activities under the *Rylands v Fletcher* rule, as discussed in the case of *Vanderpuye v Pioneer Shoe Factory Ltd*.[29] In the case of *Acropolis Bakery Ltd v ZCCM Ltd* the Zambia Supreme Court refused to apply the strict liability rule announced in *Rylands v Fletcher* to the conduct of striking miners that caused injury to another party.

Vanderpuye v Pioneer Shoe Factory Ltd

Court of Appeal, Accra, Ghana
28 July 1980
[1981] G.L.R. 181, 181 (1980)
Archer, Anin and Charles Crabbe, J.J.A.

FACTS

The appellant, a landlord, let a warehouse in a complex of buildings, known as Derby Works, in Accra, to the respondents, manufacturers of shoes and other footwears under

(Continued)

(Continued)

an oral agreement, at a monthly rent of ¢200. The premises were used by the respondents mainly for the storage of manufactured footwear and raw materials like leather, rubber soles and rubber sheets. In November 1972, there was a fire outbreak which damaged the warehouse and an annex used as offices (but not let to the respondents). The respondents lost all goods in the warehouse and the sparks from the fire damaged property in an adjoining house. The respondents continued to pay rents for ten months but refused to pay any more rents thereafter because they had lost the use of the warehouse.

The appellant therefore sued in the High Court claiming, inter alia, (a) damages for negligence — relying on *res ipsa loquitur* and the doctrine in *Rylands v Fletcher* and (b) recovery of the unpaid rents since the fire outbreak. The appellant called witnesses including the fire officers and the warehouse-keeper, an employee of the respondents. Whilst the fire officers, as experts, could not state what caused the fire, the warehouse-keeper testified that none of the employees in the warehouse smoked cigarettes and that he had locked up the warehouse intact after close of work at 5 p.m. and that the fire was discovered after 6 p.m. The effect of the whole evidence of the warehouse-keeper was to exonerate the respondents from any liability in negligence. No evidence was given by the respondents neither did they call any witnesses.

The trial judge, on these facts, held, inter alia, dismissing the action that: (1) the appellant had failed to prove negligence and that *res ipsa loquitur* could not apply to the case; (2) the doctrine in *Rylands v Fletcher* was also inapplicable because there was no "non-natural use" of the warehouse by the respondents; and (3) since the tenancy was not a demise for a term certain, the respondents were under no obligation to pay rent after the destruction of the warehouse. On appeal, counsel for the appellant argued, inter alia, that the trial judge had misapplied the rule in *Rylands v Fletcher* to the facts of the case. He also drew the attention of the appellate court to the provisions of Act 328 and the regulations made thereunder and submitted (even though not pleaded at the trial) that the respondents had not complied with the provisions of the Act.

The appellant's case therefore rested on the common law ranging from the law of negligence, the doctrine of *Rylands v Fletcher* [1868] L.R. 3 H.L. 330, nuisance and to the law relating to recovery of rent.

Was there negligence? The fire officers could not, as experts, state what caused the fire. The insurers and their adjusters maintained that the cause of the fire was fortuitous, meaning accidental or caused by chance. The warehouse-keeper who was the last person to leave the warehouse testified that none of the employees in the warehouse smoked. He locked up the warehouse with padlocks and keys which were handed over to the workshop manager. There was no evidence that the watchman or an intruder thereafter opened the warehouse. There was no overt act on the part of the respondents or their servants and agents to suggest that the fire was caused by the negligence of the respondents. In such a case it seems to me that the learned trial judge was right when he held that the appellant had failed to establish negligence.

(Continued)

(Continued)

Was negligence established by the rule of evidence popularly known as *res ipsa loquitur?* The real complaint of the appellant was that after he had concluded his evidence and closed his case, the respondents should have given evidence by explaining how the accident happened or could have happened. In other words, the respondents did not rebut the presumption of negligence. Learned counsel for the appellant cited the cases of *Kesiwah v Jaja* and *Ansah v Busanga* and submitted that the respondents' failure to give evidence should have tilted the scales in favour of the appellant. In the recent and latest decision of this court in *Boateng v Oppong* it was held that whenever the rule of res ipsa loquitur was relied on by the plaintiff, then a defendant had to discharge the evidential burden of displacing the inference of negligence against him. In the present appeal, failure by the respondents to enter the witness-box is not the sole and paramount consideration. What matters in my view is whether there was evidence during the trial to suggest that the respondents had been negligent, or whether the facts as stated by the appellant were such that an inference of negligence could be drawn from those facts. Erle C.J. in *Scott v London and St. Katherine's Docks Co.* [1865] 3 H. & C. 596 at p. 600 in propounding this rule of evidence chose his words very carefully thus:

> There must be reasonable evidence of negligence. But where the thing is shown to be under the management of the defendant or his servants, and the accident is such as in the ordinary cause of things does not happen if those who have the management use proper care, it affords reasonable evidence, in the absence of explanation by the defendants, that the accident arose from want of care.

It follows that absence of an explanation is a sine qua non for the operation or the applicability of *res ipsa loquitur.* This was emphasised by Lord Porter in *Barkway v South Wales Transport Co., Ltd.* [1950] 1 All E.R. 392 at p. 394, H.L.:

> The doctrine is dependent on the absence of explanation, and, although it is the duty of the defendants, if they desire to protect themselves, to give an adequate explanation of the cause of the accident, yet, if the facts are sufficiently known, the question ceases to be one where the facts speak for themselves, and the solution is to be found by determining whether, on the facts as established, negligence is to be inferred or not,

Fortunately for the respondents, the vital witness, that is their warehouse-keeper, Bamfo Sampong, who could have been called by the respondents to give evidence (because he had control and management of the warehouse and was the last person to leave the warehouse) was called by the appellant. The effect of the whole evidence of this witness in examination-in-chief and in cross-examination was to exonerate the respondents from any liability in negligence. He was emphatic that nobody smoked in the warehouse — a possible theory for the cause of the fire which was suggested by the fire officers in their reports and also by the insurers and their adjusters. It seems to me therefore that where the evidence of explanation expected from the respondents has already been furnished by the appellant's own witness *res ipsa loquitur* cannot automatically apply by the mere physical absence from the witness-box of the respondents or their witnesses.

As a follow-up, learned counsel for the appellant further argued that the learned trial judge erred in law by misinterpreting the decision in *Sochacki v Sas* [1947] 1 All E.R. 344, D.C. to

(Continued)

(Continued)

mean that *res ipsa loquitur* has no application to tortious liability arising from outbreaks of fire. In his judgment, the learned trial judge quoted the last paragraph of Lord Goddard C.J.'s judgment in the *Sochacki* case (supra) at p. 345:

> *Counsel for the defendants argued that I am bound to apply the doctrine of* res ipsa loquitur, *but I do not think this is a case of* res ipsa loquitur. *Everybody knows fires occur through accidents which happen without negligence on anybody's part. There is nothing here to show that the plaintiff left any improper fire in his room, any larger fire than usual, a fire which was too large for the grate, or anything like that. There was a fire burning in his room. He left his room for two or three hours. I do not consider that the doctrine of* res ipsa loquitur *could possibly apply to a case such as this. I come to the conclusion here that there is no evidence of negligence against the plaintiff in this case, and without evidence of negligence there is no liability on the plaintiff for the fire. Consequently, there will be judgment for the plaintiff against both defendants, with costs.*

Nowhere in this passage, did Lord Goddard C.J. state expressly or impliedly that *res ipsa loquitur* has never applied to cases of fire since the enunciation of the rule in 1805. The two sentences in the passage, "but I do not think that this is a case of *res ipsa loquitur*" and "I do not consider that the doctrine of *res ipsa loquitur* could possibly apply to such a case as this," clearly demonstrate that Lord Goddard was considering the particular facts of the case before him and no more. In that case the lodger had left in his room a fire in his grate and neighbouring rooms had been damaged by fire spreading from the lodger's room. Lord Goddard C.J. thought the fire in the grate was not improper, the fire was not larger than usual or too large for the grate. From such facts, he thought a presumption of negligence could not be inferred.

However, the learned trial judge after considering the *Sochacki* case (supra) expressed himself as follows: "In my view the contention that in a case of fire, negligence must be proved, and that the doctrine of *res ipsa loquitur* has no application is unanswerable." A cursory reading of this passage is capable of giving the impression that in fire cases *res ipsa loquitur* is inapplicable. However, if the passage is split to reflect the contention referred to, it becomes obvious that the learned trial judge was dealing with the submission of learned counsel for the respondents in his address when he said that mere exclusive possession and control of the warehouse could not be circumstance from which negligence could be presumed if a fire broke out and that in all cases of fire, negligence must be proved. The learned trial judge's view then was that in a case of fire, negligence must be proved and that *res ipsa loquitur* did not apply to the circumstances before him. I think that was what the learned trial judge meant. He was referring to the contention of learned counsel for the respondents and no more. I do not think the learned trial judge was attempting to lay down a new rule. He did not misinterpret Lord Goddard's decision. He referred to "contention" and that contention could only be the one advocated by learned counsel for the respondents, namely, that *res ipsa loquitur* had no application to the facts presented by the appellant.

Even if my interpretation of the learned trial judge's passage is untenable, sitting in an appellate court I am entitled to find out for myself, whether from the evidence adduced by the appellant and his witnesses an inference of negligence can be drawn. My view is that there

(Continued)

(Continued)

is nothing from the evidence which "makes the thing speak for itself." If one bears in mind that *res ipsa loquitur* is not a doctrine of substantive law but merely a rule of evidence, that is, a forensic technique in proving negligence, then the court below was right in refusing to presume negligence at the close of the appellant's case. *Res ipsa loquitur* as a rule of evidence can apply to highway accidents where a vehicle has landed in a ditch or has gone off the road. But is the rule inapplicable where a vehicle, while on the highway, becomes ablaze and is burnt down completely in the middle of the road? Surely, if all the relevant facts for establishing negligence on the part of the defendant cannot be proved, the plaintiff is at liberty to invoke *res ipsa loquitur* and rely on the facts of the accident raising the inference of negligence. But it must be remembered that previous cases where *res ipsa loquitur* has been relied on, are not precedents invariably or inflexibly binding in subsequent cases. Lord Goddard L.J. in *Easson v London and North Eastern Railway Co.* [1944] K.B. 421 at p. 423, C.A. made the position clear when he said:

> None of the reported cases, however, really laid down any principle of law. They only show that in the circumstances of the case there was evidence on which the jury could find a verdict for the plaintiff.

I do not therefore think that the court below misinterpreted the decision in *Sochacki v Sas* (supra) where the court refused to apply *res ipsa loquitur*.

I shall now deal with the fourth ground of appeal, that is:

> The learned trial judge erred in law by making the finding that the defendants' user of the warehouse was not a nonnatural user thereof and that the storage thereon of footwear and the materials for the manufacture and packing thereof was for the natural benefit of the plaintiff and the defendants. The rule in Rylands v. Fletcher *was thereby misapplied to the facts of this case.*

What is the rule in *Rylands v Fletcher?* Blackburn J. delivering the judgment of the Court of Exchequer Chamber said as reported in (1866) L.R. 1 Exch. 265 at p. 279:

> We think that the true rule of law is, that the person who for his own purposes brings on his lands and collects and keeps there anything likely to do mischief if it escapes, must keep it in at his peril, and, if he does not do so, is prima facie answerable for all the damage which is the natural consequence of its escape.

The facts have already been stated and the evidence indicates clearly that the wholesale room contained only materials for the manufacture of shoes, that is, manufactured shoes in cases, rubber soles, and rubber sheets. If Blackburn J.'s exposition of the law is applied, one can only say that leather shoes cannot be mischievous. So also are the rubber soles and rubber sheets — these cannot be described as mischievous or dangerous things. In affirming Blackburn J.'s judgment, Lord Cairns in the House of Lords (see (1868) L.R. 3 H.L. 330) thought there must be "non-natural use" of the land. This expression was clarified in *Rickards v Lothian* [1913] A.C. 263 at p. 280, P.C. to mean:

> It must be some special use bringing with it increased danger to others, and must not merely be the ordinary use of the land or such a use as is proper for the general benefit of the community.

(Continued)

(Continued)

The House of Lords in *Read v Lyons* [1947] A.C. 156, H.L. has emphasised that in deciding the question whether the user is natural or not, all the circumstances of the time and place and practice of mankind must be taken into consideration so that what might be regarded as dangerous or non-natural may vary according to those circumstances: see the judgment of Lord Porter at p. 176.

In the present appeal, the evidence shows that the appellant let the premises to the respondents to be used as a warehouse and the respondents did use the premises as a warehouse for storing manufactured shoes and raw materials for the same purpose. The articles stored were not mischievous or dangerous things. Indeed these were manufactured in a factory adjoining the warehouse in the same building complex. What are the circumstances in the evidence capable of suggesting that the user of the warehouse was non-natural? I think the court below was right in holding that the use of the warehouse was natural.

The real complaint of the appellant was that when the fire started, steps were not taken by the respondents to stop the fire or to contain it so as to prevent it from spreading to the annex and the residential parts of the complex. The appellant complained of defective fire-fighting equipment. The evidence of the warehouse-keeper was that after he had locked the doors of the warehouse, the keys were kept in the manager's office. Nobody during that night had access to the warehouse. The watchman could not have opened the doors because he did not have the keys. The fire was first detected by the appellant's relatives who wasted no time in calling in the Fire Brigade who were on the spot within a few minutes and fought the fire throughout the night.

Although the cause of the fire was not established, did the respondents allow the fire to continue through their negligence? In *Musgrove v Pandelis* [1919] 2 K.B. 43, C.A., petrol in the carburettor of the defendant's car caught fire and the driver could have prevented the fire from spreading by turning off the tap from the petrol tank. He failed to do this and the fire spread to the plaintiff's rooms. The defendant was held liable. Scrutton L.J. explained the rationale behind this principle in *Job Edwards, Ltd. v Birmingham Navigations* [1924] 1 K.B. 341 at p. 357, C.A. as follows:

> There is a great deal to be said for the view that if a man finds a dangerous and artificial thing on his land, which he and those for whom he is responsible did not put there; if he knows that if left alone it will damage other persons; if by reasonable care he can render it harmless, as if by stamping on a fire just beginning from a trespasser's match he can extinguish it; that then if he does nothing, he has 'permitted it to continue,' and become responsible for it. This would base the liability on negligence, and not on the duty of insuring damage from a dangerous thing under Rylands v. Fletcher.

This dictum was approved by the Privy Council in *Goldman v Hargrave* [1967] 1 A.C. 645, P.C. in which it was held that an occupier of land was under a general duty of care, in relation to hazards whether natural or man-made occurring on his land, to remove or reduce such hazards to his neighbour and that the existence of such duty must be based on knowledge of the hazard, ability to foresee the consequences of not checking or removing it, and the ability to abate it; and that the standard of care required of the occupier is founded on what it was reasonable to expect from him in his circumstances.

(Continued)

(Continued)

In the *Goldman* case lightening had struck a one hundred feet tree in the centre of the defendant's land. The fire had started in the fork of the tree about 84 feet from the ground. It was impossible to deal with the blaze at that height and so pending the arrival of fire control officers, the defendant caused the tree to be felled. Unfortunately, he did not bother to extinguish the fire with water. The fire kept on burning until a few days later there was a strong wind that fanned the fire and caused it to spread from the defendant's land to the plaintiff's land. The defendant was held liable for damage caused by the fire to the plaintiff's properties.

In the present appeal, what has to be considered is whether in all the circumstances the respondents could have prevented the fire from destroying the annex and parts of the residential portion. It seems to me that by applying the test laid down in *Goldman v Hargrave*, the respondents cannot be held liable on the ground that they were negligent in permitting the fire to spread from the warehouse.

As the appellant failed to prove negligence on the part of the respondents either before the outbreak of the fire or after the outbreak of fire, then, if he wants to succeed on the principles of *Rylands v Fletcher*, he must satisfy all the conditions laid down in that doctrine. First of all, the respondents did not start the fire and it cannot be said that they kept fire on their land which escaped.

At common law, liability for fire is governed by the doctrine of *Rylands v Fletcher* and it is not obligatory that the plaintiff should prove negligence; in other words it is not necessary to prove lack of care on the part of anyone. At common law, the liability was originally absolute without qualification until the rule was enunciated in its present form by Blackburn J. And in *Collingwood v Home and Colonial Stores Ltd.* [1936] 3 All E.R. 200, Lord Wright explained the rule at p. 203, C.A. as follows:

> ... if a fire spread from a man's premises and did damage to adjoining premises, he was liable in damage on the broad ground that it was his duty at his own peril to keep any fire that originated on his premises from spreading to and damaging his neighbour's premises.

As already pointed out, there is no evidence that the respondents kept any fire in the warehouse or that by their conduct they permitted the fire to spread to the annex.

The real fascinating and attractive decided case which the appellant regards as his trump-card is *Mason v Levy Auto Parts of England Ltd.* [1967] 2 Q.B. 530. The headnote at pp. 530–531 reads:

> The defendants, in connection with their business as dealers, stored large quantities of combustible materials in their yard up to its common boundary of some 210 feet with the plaintiff's garden in which stood his house, and they provided fire-fighting equipment and access lanes substantially as recommended by the local fire brigade, although some access lanes were narrower than recommended. A railway station was close by the yard. A severe fire of unknown cause started in the yard; it was detected at an early stage by the defendants, but the fire-fighting equipment was ineffective to control it, and it spread to the plaintiff's land. He brought an action for damages against the defendants ...

MacKenna J. applied the decision in *Musgrove v Pandelis* (supra) and held that on the principle of *sic utere tuo ut alienum non laedas* the defendants had brought into their yard combustible

(Continued)

(Continued)

materials which were kept in such conditions that if they ignited, the fire would be likely to spread to the plaintiff's land and as the defendant's use of the land, was non-natural, they were liable to the plaintiff in damages. At pp. 542–543, MacKenna J. disclosed what factors influenced him by saying:

> *I have regard (i) to the quantities of combustible material which the defendants brought on their land; (ii) to the way in which they stored them; and (iii) to the character of the neighbourhood.*
>
> *It may be that those considerations would also justify a finding of negligence. If that is so, the end would be the same as I have reached by a more laborious, and perhaps more questionable, route.*

It is significant to note that MacKenna J. confessed to taking a more laborious and perhaps questionable route. What was the route? At pp. 541–542 he reasoned as follows:

> *A defendant is not held liable under* Rylands v. Fletcher *unless two conditions are satisfied: (i) that he has brought something onto his land likely to do mischief if it escapes, which has in fact escaped, and (ii) that those things happened in the course of some non-natural user of the land. But in Musgrove's case the car had not escaped from the land, neither had the petrol in its tank. The principle must be, Romer L.J. said, the wider one on which* Rylands v. Fletcher *itself was based, 'sic utere tuo' . . .*

Then the learned judge continued at p. 542:

> *If, for the rule in* Musgrove's *case to apply, there need be no escape of anything brought onto the defendant's land, what must be proved against him? There is, it seems to me, a choice of alternatives. The first would require the plaintiff to prove (1) that the defendant had brought something onto his land likely to do mischief if it escaped; (2) that he had done so in the course of a non-natural user of the land; and (3) that the thing had ignited and that the fire had spread. The second would be to hold the defendant liable if (1) he brought onto his land things likely to catch fire, and kept them there in such conditions that if they did ignite the fire would be likely to spread to the plaintiff's land; (2) he did so in the course of some non-natural use; and (3) the things ignited and the fire spread. The second test is, I think, the more reasonable one. To make the likelihood of damage if the thing escapes a criterion of liability, when the thing has not in fact escaped but has caught fire, would not be very sensible.*
>
> *So I propose to apply the second test . . .*

It must be remembered that in *Musgrove's* case the court found that the fire was due to negligence. But as already mentioned, common law liability for fire is based on the principle of absolute liability and no proof of negligence is necessary. What actually compelled MacKenna J. to follow his laborious route in the *Mason* case was the plaintiff's allegation that the defendants "so used their land by cluttering it with combustible material closely packed that the plaintiff's land was endangered." What were these combustible materials? At pp. 533–534 of the report the following is stated in MacKenna J.'s judgment:

> *At the time of the fire almost the whole of the defendants' yard, up to its boundaries, including that which runs with the plaintiff's garden, was stacked high with cases of machinery. Inside the cases the machinery was either coated with oil or grease or wrapped in waxed or greased papers as a*

(Continued)

(Continued)

protection against rust. The cases were of wood, and some had broken open. Tarpaulins had been put over the stacks and some of these were torn. Flammable materials were stored for use in the defendants' business, including petroleum, acetylene and paints. All those materials, including the wooden boxes and the grease, the oil and the waxed and greased papers, were, in the opinion of an assistant station officer at Lyndhurst Fire Station, highly combustible. His evidence satisfied me that the yard, used as it was by the defendants, was a serious fire-risk to the adjoining occupiers.

What were the combustible materials in the warehouse in this appeal? According to Bamfo Sampong, the warehouse-keeper, there was:

a quantity of men's and women's footwear, rubber soles of shoes, rubber sheets. The shoes were kept in cardboard boxes, 24 pairs in each cardbox. The cardboxes were more than 200. All the shoes were in boxes. The rubber soles were loose ones. There were about 5,000 pairs of rubber soles. There were about 250 rubber sheets. The rubber sheets were about three feet square. These were all the things kept in the warehouse by the defendants.

If one compares the present case with the *Mason* case, it is clear that the facts are distinguishable. In the present case, there was no petroleum, no acetylene, paints, grease, oil or waxed and greased papers in the warehouse which could be regarded as a danger or risk to adjoining premises. In the *Mason* case, MacKenna J. asked himself two questions: (1) did the defendants in this case bring to their land things likely to catch fire, and keep them there in such conditions that if they did ignite, the fire would be likely to spread to the plaintiff's land? If so (2) did the defendants do these things in the course of some non-natural user of the land?

In the present appeal, the answer to each question should be No! The fourth ground of appeal is therefore untenable. I must confess that I have had some anxious moments over this appeal with a feeling of sadness for the appellant's plight. However, in view of the reasons I have given, I have no option but to dismiss the appeal and affirm the decision of the court below.

Anin J.A. I agree.

Charles Crabbe J.A. I also agree.

Acropolis Bakery Ltd v ZCCM Ltd

Supreme Court, (S.C.Z. Judgment No. 30 of 1985), (1985) Z.R. 232 (S.C.), 10th September and 10th October, 1985
Ngulube, D.C.J., Gardner and Muwo JJ.S.

Ngulube, D.C.J.: delivered the judgment of the court.

FACTS

The facts accepted by the learned trial commissioner were that there was in July 1981, an illegal strike staged by some miners working for the respondents at Kitwe. It appears that the

(Continued)

(Continued)

miners had some dispute with their employers, the respondent, over working conditions and, without going through the procedures required by the Industrial Relations Act, Cap.517, they went on what is popularly referred to as a wild-cat strike. On 23rd July, 1981, there was assembled in the Mindolo Mine Compound, a large crowd of people found by the learned trial commissioner to have been striking miners and this crowd was in riotous mood. At that point in time, the appellant's driver and helper arrived with a bread van to make deliveries of bread to customers in the compound. The crowd attacked the bread van with sticks and stones and finally set it on fire, resulting in the total destruction of the vehicle, valued at K36,000, and the bread, valued at K1,200.

OPINION

It was argued at the trial on behalf of the appellants that the respondents ought to be made answerable to the appellants for the loss which they suffered, broadly speaking, on any one of three alternative footings. The first was that the respondents must be vicariously liable for the acts of their striking employees, since when they vented their anger on the appellant's property, they did so in connection with a grievance against their employers and as such complaint was related to their work, it was in the course and within the scope of their employment and their actions attached vicarious liability to their employers. The learned trial Commissioner had no difficulty in rejecting this argument. After carefully reviewing the authorities he found that what the strikers did was neither within the scope nor in the course of their employment. In fairness, it should be stated that Mr. Mkandawire does not, before this court, seek to rely on vicarious liability which depends on the employee, inter alia, acting in the course of his employment.

All the authorities are agreed that acts of personal or collective vengeance and violence unrelated to the proper or improper but bonafide purported performance of a job will not be regarded as falling within the course of employment. In particular, an act amounting to a criminal offence committed by an employee which has no conceivable connection with his employment will not attract vicarious liability and will not be in the course of employment. Thus in *Poulton v Kiesall* (1), a case under the repealed Workmen's Compensation Act, 1906, of the United Kingdom an assault was held not to have been suffered in the course of employment when striking workers assaulted a fellow worker who was on his way home from work and who had been specifically requested by his employers to continue to work despite the strike. If the worker who was the victim of the assault was not in the course of employment then the more reason to say that the striking workers who assaulted him were even more outside the course of employment. And in *Warren v Henlys* (2), the employers were not liable for the act of personal vengeance when a garage employee assaulted a customer out of personal dislike.

One of the considerations for attaching vicarious liability these days is that the employer is better able to make good the plaintiff's loss and to bear the cost of the damages inflicted by the employees' wrongful conduct. But even on this rationale there must be a proper foundation and an arguable connection between the conduct complained of and the employment. When the strikers attacked and burnt the bread van they were clearly not engaged on their employers' business. They were wholly on an orgy of their own

(Continued)

(Continued)

and any connection between their violence and the grievances they had against their employers is so tenuous as to be wholly insufficient in law to bring about vicarious liability. We agree entirely with Mr. Mkandawire's approach that the question of vicarious liability does not arise for our consideration.

The second proposition advanced at the trial and repeated here was that the respondents themselves had a primary liability to the appellants on the basis of strict liability under *Rylands v Fletcher* (3). The argument can be summarised as saying that, because the employers failed to attend to the workers' grievances, this brought about the violent mood in their employees and when the latter vented their feelings on the appellant's property, their employers must be answerable for the consequences. The third proposition was that the respondents were under a primary liability for their own negligence in that they owed the appellants a duty of care not to do anything in relation to their workers which would incense them and cause them to injure third parties. Neither the second nor the third proposition found favour with the learned trial commissioner. He determined, as Mr. Masengu submits before us, that liability could only arise on the principles of vicarious liability. We agree that the principles of strict liability under *Rylands v Fletcher* cannot possibly be extended to the keeping and collecting of miners in mine compound. We agree also that the proposed duty of care is not one which can be recognised.

Mr. Mkandawire's major submission has been to say that this court should take a bold step and either recognise a new principle of law or extend the application of the existing principles so that employers must be liable for the wrongful actions of their employers which actually cause damage to a third party where the injury is suffered as a direct reaction to provocation by the employer or his failure to handle an industrial dispute in such manner that the employees do not lose their tempers and resort to indiscriminate violence against the person or property of innocent passers-by. It is common cause that the existing principles for attaching liability to one person for the wrongful deeds of another do not apply in the appellant's favour in this case, where it is sought to attach liability for riot damage to the respondents simply because it was their employees who rioted and destroyed the appellants' property. It is also not in dispute that we do not have in this country any legislation establishing any fund from which compensation can be paid to victims of riots or other crimes such as the fund under the Riot (Damages) Act, 1886, of the United Kingdom. Of course, we used to have such a law in the past, namely the Riot Damages Ordinance, Cap. 261 in the 1962 Edition of the Laws.

That ordinance established a Riot Damage Fund Administered by a Riot Damage Commissioner who could settle claims such as that in this case from funds raised by imposing a levy on rioters and any other people aged 16 years and above who resided in the compound (riot damage area) where the destruction by rioters took place. This ordinance was repealed in 1965 and the mischief which did occur in this case is no longer remedied by any of our statutes. So far as we are aware the only safeguard available to innocent victims of riots in this country would appear to be protection of a suitable insurance policy extending cover to riot damage which can be taken out. Further we do not understand Mr. Mkandawire to have been seriously suggesting that the

(Continued)

(Continued)

principle in *Donoghue v Stevenson* (4), which he cited can be applied so as to enable us to say that there was in a case such as this a duty of care which can be recognised by the law which employers shall owe generally to third parties not to incense the workers.

The argument in this regard assumes that the court is expected to inquire into the merits or demerits of workers' grievances and to declare whether the employer was or was not in the wrong so as to determine whether the employer should or should not be blamed for acts of violence by workers on strike. We are quite certain that the court cannot properly be expected to undertake such an exercise. The court can also not be expected to hold, in effect, that violent and riotous conduct is a natural and foreseeable consequence of conduct on the part of the employers allegedly amounting to provocation of the workers.

We agree that the law should be responsive to changing circumstances. In a proper case, we do not see why an established principle cannot be extended to cover a novel situation: we would not hesitate to do justice on the merits of the case where a new situation arises for which there is no precedent but where it plainly appears that the legitimate rights of one person have been unfairly or wrongfully injured by another, since the recognition of those rights would presuppose the availability of remedies for their enforcement and protection. But where a victim of a riot seeks to recover from another whose only known connection with the actual wrong-doer, or the wrongful act, is that he is the wrong-doers' employer, and where the implications of acceding to such a novel proposition would be to make employers generally liable, on wholesale scale, even for all the criminal or purely private frolics of their workers, then we must decline to take the bold step suggested by Mr. Mkandawire. Such a drastic innovation is best left to the legislature since, as presently advised, the exclusion of an employer's vicarious liability and indeed the application of such vicarious liability are all founded on good sound principles of common sense and considerations of fair play. In any case, it would be far easier to attach new heads of liability to actual wrongdoers than to extend vicarious liability, which in effect the proposition seeks to bring about though couched in terms suggesting some sort of novel primary liability.

JUDGMENT

In the result, this appeal must fail. Costs follow the event.

Appeal dismissed

10.4 Intentional Tort—Trespass

Trespass has been defined as an "invasion of right to exclusive possession of land."[30] Trespass is one of the most common forms of tort, especially in rural areas in sub-Saharan Africa. The two cases, *Emmanuel Basaliza v Mujwisa Chris* (Uganda) and *Herbst Feeds (PTY) Limited v Tebogo Radithotse* (Botswana) point to the difficulty in determining when a trespass has occurred and if so the amount of damages to award.

Emmanuel Basaliza v Mujwisa Chris

High Court of Uganda at Fort Portal
Hct-01-cv-cs-0016 of 2003
Hon. Justice Lameck N. Mukasa

FACTS

The Appellant, Emmanuel Basaliza was the plaintiff in Fort Portal Chief Magistrates Court Civil Suit No. MFP 1 of 2000. The Appellant brought the said original suit against the Respondent, Chris Mujwisa, to recover general damages, compensation of shs3,3000,000 interest and costs.

The appellant's cause of action was founded in trespass. The parties had neighbouring farms separated by a barbed wire fence. The appellant's claim was that in the month of July 1998 the Respondent's cows strayed into the Appellant's banana plantation trespassing thereon and destroyed banana plants valued by a field extension officer at shs1,200,000. Also in the month of November 1999, the respondent's cows trespassed upon the appellant's farm and pasture, destroying thereon pasture and banana plants and broke a wooden bridge causing damage all valued at shs1,200,000 On a third occasion, also around November 1999 the Respondent's animals trespassed and destroyed the Appellant's banana plants valued at shs600,000. Also on 10th December 1999 the Respondent's animals trespassed into the Appellant's property and on this occasion the Respondent's bull illegally mounted the Appellant's pregnant heifer which aborted as a result. The value of the would be calf was put at Shs300,000.

In his defence the Respondent denied that his cows had ever strayed onto the Appellant's banana plantation, denied that his bull had illegally mounted the Appellant's pregnant heifer and contended that no heifer of the Appellant had aborted and further that the Appellant had sent his workers to the Respondent's farm who drove out his cows and took them to the Appellant's farm and detained them until the area L.C. I chairman intervened and they were released.

OPINION

In his judgment the learned Chief Magistrate found that there was no proved trespass on all occasions and dismissed the Appellant's claim with costs. The Appellant was dissatisfied with the judgment thus this appeal on the ground that:-

The learned trial Chief Magistrate erred in law and fact when he failed to properly evaluate the evidence before him and came to the wrong conclusion.

In his submissions Counsel for the Appellant stated that the trial Magistrate did not properly address the issue of trespass, the subject of the main suit raised by the Appellant. He pointed out that PW1 John Kasaija had directly witnessed the trespass of the respondent's cattle on the appellant's banana plantation as per the July 1998 incident. That as to the November 1999 incident PW3 Johnson Kaganda had recognized the invading cows as those of the respondent. That the cows first destroyed the appellant's banana plantations, drunk water in

(Continued)

(Continued)

the water trough and ate salt. That a bull had mounted the Appellant's cow which was pregnant. Counsel contended that had the learned Chief Magistrate properly considered and evaluated the above evidence he would had found that the appellant had proved his case on the balance of probabilities.

In his judgment the learned trial Chief Magistrate first considered the alleged acts of trespass committed in July 1998. He then considered the trespass of 1999 wherein he identified the following acts of trespass:

(a) The coming of cows of the defendant to the plaintiff's farm.
(b) The damaging of the bridge.
(c) The trespass on the plaintiff banana plantation and eating of the grass/pasture.
(d) The defendant's bull mounting the plaintiff's cow and the cow's abortion.

While considering the trespass allegedly committed in 1998 the learned trial Chief Magistrate considered contradictions in the evidence of the plaintiff and that of his witness and as result he did not believe their evidence. It was an agreed fact from the evidence adduced by both parties that the two owned farms which at one point shared a common boundary. Further that there was a barbed wire fence between the two farms at that point. They both kept cattle on their respective farms.

Regarding the incident which was alleged to have taken place in July 1998, PW1 John Kasaija stated that while at work in the appellant's farm at around 11:00 a.m. about 20 to 25 cows of the respondent entered into the appellant's farm and destroyed the appellant's banana plantation by eating the banana stems. Both the appellant and this witness stated that the incident was reported to the L.C. I officials who came in to assess the damage. Both named Bernard Rwaheru as being among the L.C. officials who came over. However, there were contractions as to whether he was the chairman of the area or not at the material time. While being cross-examined Leonard Rwaheru denied going to the appellant's farm in July 1998. John Kasaija also named Kaganda among the people who had come in to see the damage but in his testimony the said Johnson Kaganda did not talk about the July 1998 incident. The Assistant Veterinary Officer, Michael Businge testified that on 27th July 1998 he was called by the appellant to carry out an assessment of the appellant's crops destroyed by animals. This witness came in after the event he therefore did not witness the trespass being committed. That leaves only John Kasaija who testified that he had actually seen the Respondent's cows trespass on the Appellant's plantation and destroying the banana plantation. However while being cross-examined this witness contradicted himself when he stated:

We do not stay in the farm after leading our cows, we go away. I was not present when the cows trespassed upon the banana plantation.

Also when being re-examined he stated:

I was not present when the defendant's cows trespassed on the plaintiff's farm in July 1998.

(Continued)

(Continued)

The above were contradictions in the evidence of a key witness which should not be disregarded as they went to the root cause of action. I accordingly find that the learned Chief Magistrate properly evaluated the evidence before him and came to the right conclusion that the appellant had failed on a balance of probabilities to prove the alleged act of trespass committed by the respondent's cows in July 1998.

With regard to the trespass stated to have been committed in November 1999 the record shows that the evidence adduced by both sides indicated that about 25 to 30 cows of the Respondent including a bull entered the appellant's farm. The issue is how the Respondent's cattle gained entry into the Appellant's farm.

John Kaganda stated that one day in the month of November 1999 at around 9.00 a.m. he met visiting cows mixed with the Appellant's cows drinking water. The appellant's cows were of the exotic Fresian type while the visiting cows were a mixture of the local breed and cross breed. The visiting cows numbered about 28 to 30. According to him the visiting cows had gained entrance by breaking into the barbed wire fence. He recognized the visiting cows as those of the Respondent because on several occasions the same cows would trespass onto the appellant's farm and the witness would drive them back. The witness reported to the herdsman Kasaija and to the appellant. This witness did not see the cows enter the farm. He found the cows while they had already trespassed the banana plantation and crossed the bridge.

John Kasaija testified that on the material day after milking the cows he went home. Shortly after he was called by Tadeo who informed the witness that strange cows had entered the appellant's farm. The witness saw the cows which had mixed with the appellant's cows. He separated the two herds. Took the appellants herd home and left the invading herd in the farm. This witness also did not see how the invading herd had entered the farm. However, he stated that the cows had broken through the Respondent's fence and entered the appellant's farm.

The defence version is that it was the appellant's workmen who had cut his fence and drove his cattle from his farm into the appellant's farm. The witness Irene Kabanyaha stated that she would occasionally visit the Respondent at his farm and stay for about two or three months. That at the material time on 26th November 1999 while cutting trees for a broom in the defendant's farm at around 9.00 a.m. or 10.00 a.m. she was attracted by noise coming from the side of the Respondent's farm where cattle was grazing. She moved towards the noise and saw strange people driving the Respondent's cattle and crossing into the Appellant's farm. That he over heard the appellant thanking those people for having brought in the cattle. This witness informed Yakobo Kasaija, the Respondent's herdsman, who went after the cattle. Yakobo Kasaija testified that he was called by his mother and when he came he found that cattle had been taken away. That he followed the cattle which he found in the appellants farm. The witness stated that he had found that the Respondent's barbed wire had been broken. The witness contradicted himself when said he had not seen the appellant's workers taking the cattle to the appellant's farm, but later stated that he had seen he

(Continued)

(Continued)

appellant, Lakwena, Kalinda and Kaganda and other people driving the Respondent's cows from the Respondent's farm and he followed them.

Yakobo Kasaija stated that when he followed the cows onto the appellant's home, the appellant arrested, tied and assaulted him. Irene Kabanyaka stated that after waiting for Yakobo Kasaija return in vain, she also went to the Appellant's farm. The witness found Yakobo Kasaija beaten and tied on a tree in the compound, she untied him.

Irene Kabanyaka testified that at around 7.00 p.m. she together with Rwaheru went to the appellant's home to seek the release of the cattle. The appellant released to them the cows but retained the bull which he released after three days.

In his plaint, the appellant claimed for 3,300,000 as compensation for the property damaged. This claim is comprised of:

(i) Banana plants destroyed in the course of July 1998 trespass — Shs1,200,000.
(ii) Banana plants damaged during another trespass in November 1999 — Shs1,2200,000.
(iii) Banana plants damaged during another trespass in November 1999 — Shs600,000.
(iv) Value of would be calf — Shs330,000.

In essence this is a claim for special damages and as such must not only be specifically pleaded but must also be strictly proved. See *Kyambadde v Mpigi District Administration* [1983] HCB 44, *Asuman Mutekanga v Equator Growers (U) Ltd* S.C.C. A No: 7 of 1995.

As for the trespass allegedly communicated in July 1998 I have already upheld the learned Chief Magistrate's finding that the appellant failed on the balance of probabilities to prove the alleged acts of trespass. Consequently, the appellant could not recover any damages, special or general, alleged to have resulted therefrom.

In his testimony the appellant stated that during the November 1999 trespass the Respondent's cows destroyed his banana plantation, broke a bridge on his farm, consumed his improved pasture which had special legumes for exotic cattle. Both John Kasaija and Johnson Kasanda testified that the Respondent's cows broke the fence passed through the appellant's banana plantation and entered the farm. Johnson Kaganda stated in his evidence that the cows destroyed the banana plantation, drunk water in the water troughs and ate salt. John Kasaija only talked about the bridge during cross-examination when the stated:

> *Normally the plaintiff's cows pass the bridge, which was broken . . .. When the worker came he found the cows had broken the bridge.*

Similarly John Kaganda only talked about the bridge during cross-examination when he stated:

> *The cows used to use a bridge for a long time. The cows of Mujwisa damaged Basaliza's bridge. The cows broke the bridge because they came mating while passing the bridge. I found when the cows had passed the bridge, they had just passed you could tell by the hoof marks*

(Continued)

(Continued)

Michael Busingye testified that he was an Assistant Veterinary Officer holding a Diploma in Animal Husbandry from Bukalasa Agricultural College, 1995, an attendant certificate from Tororo DFI covering crop Husbandry 1995 and a Certificate in Artificial Insemination from Entebbe Veterinary Institute 1998. He was in charge of overseeing animal husbandry and fish farming in Hakibale sub-county. That on 27th November 1999 in the presence of the LCI Chairman he visited the appellant's farm with instructions to assess the damage caused on the farm by straying animals. The witness tendered in evidence two reports both dated 27th November 1999. In his report three acres of banana plantation had been damaged and he put the damage at Shs600,000. There was a broken bridge but no value was put on it. In the other report the witness indicated that 4.0 acres of paddock with improved pasture had been over grazed. The area was explained as the area where the appellant had held the straying cattle for between 8 to 12 hours. The damage caused by the overgrazing was put at shs.1,200,000. In both reports the witness stated that he had estimated the value on the basis of the Area Compensation Committee Meeting of 27th February 1996. The resolution or minutes of this meeting were not produced in evidence so as to guide court on how the estimates were arrived at by the witness. Though this witness stated that the L.C. I chairman, Leonard Rwaheru was present when he was carrying out the valuation. All that Leonard stated in his testimony about the grass and banana plantation was:

--- The farm is covered with grass, I saw grass.----

The following morning I was called after the Veterinary Officer had come -- I met them in the banana plantation when they were coming back. -----

On the 1st day when I was called, we briefly went around, the cows had excreted in the farm. ---

This witness does not talk about any damaged bridge, banana plantation or pasture. In *Yosefu Kashongoize v China Sickman Corporation* [1995] IKALR 64 the plaintiff claimed compensation for soil excavated from his land as murram Justice AN Karohora held:

As regards soil which was removed, I must state that this item was not proved on the balance of probabilities. It was not enough to write down particulars and so to speak, to throw them at the head of court, saying this is what I have lost. I ask you to give these damages. They have to be proved. See Boham Carter vs Hyde Park Hotel (1994) 64 TLR 178. The onus of proof was on the plaintiff to prove by calling quantity surveyors to tell how much soil in cubic meters had been removed and costs of each cubic meters but there was no such evidence. In the circumstances this head of claim for damages would fail.

In the instant case the formula used to assess the loss was not availed to court. The evidence of the Assistant Veterinary Officer contradicted that of the other plaintiff's witness, particularly that of the L.C. I. Chairman who never testified about the damage to a bridge, banana plantation or pasture. I find that the learned Chief Magistrate came to the right conclusion when he found that the appellant had on the balance probabilities failed to prove his claim on the above three items.

Before I take leave of the claim relating to the banana plantation and the pasture I must point out that though the learned Chief Magistrate came to the right conclusion considering

(Continued)

(Continued)

the evidence on record, his Worship largely based his conclusion on his findings at the locus. The court record shows that Court visited the locus on 1st August 2002 and the proceedings were recorded as follows:

A Locus

1.8. 2002

Both parties present

Both Advocates present

Mr. Kihumuro — interpreter

Court: We were shown the plaintiff's farm land. — The pasture can not be said to be improved when it is covered with 'Teete' grass which is very old. The plaintiff is clearing it now. We did not see salt troughs. There is a water trough and not damaged. The wooden bridge is intact. Plaintiff says he repaired it after the damage.

The learned Chief Magistrate drew two sketch plans.

The purpose of visiting the locus in quo is for each party to indicate what he is claiming. Each party must testify on oath and be cross examined by the opposite party. The purpose is for the witness who has already testified in court to clarify what they were stating in court and to indicate features and boundary marks, if any, to the court. Any observation made or noted by the court at the locus in quo must be noted and recorded and must form part of the record. See *J. W. Ononge v Okallang* [1986] HCB 63, *Erukana Jawangara v Anderea Obbo — Ogolla* [1976] HCB 31. Save for observations of court the record does not show any testimony by any of the witnesses at the locus in quo. In *Badiru Kabalega v Sepiriano Mugangu* [1992] 11 KALR 110 it was held that if the trial Court fails to follow the accepted procedure at the locus in quo and bases its judgment on the trial at the locus in quo, that omission is fatal to the whole trial.

In *Yaseri Waibi v Edisa Lusi Byandala* [1982] HCB 28 Justice Manyindo held that the usual practice of visiting the locus in quo is to check on the evidence given by witnesses and not to fill gaps for then the trial magistrate may run the risk of making himself a witness in the case. Such situation must be avoided.

That being the position of the law as regards evidence at the locus in quo, in the instant case the alleged acts of trespass were committed in July 1998 and November 1999. The locus was visited on 1st August 2002. With lapse of time a lot must have changed at the locus. There was no dispute over boundaries. The visit to the locus was in the circumstances a useless exercise. This case could have been decided without visiting the locus. Without basing himself on his findings at the locus, the learned Chief Magistrate would have properly come to the same decisions on a proper evaluation and security of the evidence which was already available to him on record.

The appellant also claimed for Shs330,000/ = being the value of a would be calf. In his report of 27th November, 1999 the Assistant Veterinary Officer stated that when he visited the appellant's farm that day he saw one cross breed bull of breeding age tethered by a rope to a tree, that he also looked over several cows belonging to the appellant and observed that

(Continued)

(Continued)

one had dried mucal discharge as from natural breeding. In his report of 10th December 1999 the officer stated that on that day he had checked the appellant's cow for a retained placenta. That he found the cow had aborted on 6th December 1999, the foetus was between 4 to 5 months old and the cause could have been due to forced mounting of a bull. In cross examination the witness explained that by "natural breeding" in his report he meant a bull mounting a cow. The witness said that he did not see all of the appellant's cows that day and that he did not see the appellant's bull. The witness stated that he did not know when the bull mounted the appellant's cow.

The issue is whether on the material day of the trespass this cow had been mounted by the Respondent's bull. Did any witness see the mounting and identify the bull? John Kasaija stated that the Respondent's bull also mounted the appellant's cows which had a miscarriage. He said that he saw the Respondent's bull mounting the appellant's cow. However, this witness while being cross examined contradicted himself when he said that he did not bother to keep looking at the cows and when he said that he saw the bull after it had mounted the cow. This puts doubt to his testimony on whether he actually saw the appellant's cow being mounted by the respondent's bull.

John Kaganda stated that there was a bull which mounted the appellant's cows which were pregnant. In cross examination he stated that the cows broke the bridge because they came mating while passing the bridge. Yet he goes on to say that he had found when the cows had passed the bridge. Therefore this witness could not have seen the cows mating as they passed the bridge.

There was no evidence to show that the appellant did not have a bull on his farm so as to exclude any other bull from being responsible for the mating which could have resulted into the abortion. The appellant failed on a balance of probabilities to prove that the abortion was a result of his cow having been mounted by the respondent's bull. That put aside, the appellant did not adduce any evidence to show how he had arrived at the value of the would have been calf. It is trite that special damages must be strictly proved. Therefore the learned Chief Magistrate came to the right conclusion when he dismissed the appellant's claim under this item.

In his final judgment the learned Chief Magistrate found that there was no proved trespass on both occasions and dismissed the appellant's claim. I have already upheld the learned Chief Magistrate finding with regard to the alleged trespass of July 1998. I have however found that the Respondent's cattle in November 1999 trespassed onto the appellant's farm. In his pleadings the appellant had prayed for general damages and interest thereon at 60% from the date of cause of action until payment in full.

As a general principle damages in tort are compensatory in nature. A party who suffers damages due to the wrongful act of the other must be put in the position he would have been had he not suffered the wrong. The appellant was entitled to the exclusive use of his farm and pasture thereat by his cattle. His right was interfered with when the Respondent's cattle was left unattended which enabled it to break the barbed wire fence between the appellant's farm and that of the respondent, and while on the appellant's farm intermingle with his cows and inevitably feed on pasture intended for only the appellant's herd. The appellant was in the

(Continued)

(Continued)

circumstance entitled to reasonable compensation for the damage and inconvenience suffered. At the court below the appellant had prayed for general damages of Shs6,000,000. However this was in respect of trespass on the two incidents. This Court's finding is that the appellant adduced evidence to prove only one incident that is of November 1999. In the circumstances I find that general damages of Shs2,500,000 is reasonable and the appellant is awarded the same. The appellant's entitlement to that money has only arisen upon the pronouncement of this judgment. The appellant is therefore awarded interest at the rate 25% per annum from the date of this judgment until payment is full.

The appellant is awarded costs for the proceedings before this court and the court below. I so order.

Herbst Feeds (PTY) Limited v Tebogo Radithotse

High Court of Botswana, Lobatse
CC 2258-05
February 25, 2008.
Dingake J:

1. By combined Summons registered with this Court on the 19th of October, 2005, the plaintiff sued the defendant for failing to keep his cattle under control with the result that the plaintiff suffered damages in the sum of P91977.50 (Ninety One Thousand Nine Hundred and Seventy Seven Pula and Fifty Thebe) which represents plaintiff's loss of income due to the destruction of its crops.
2. The plaintiff alleges that during or about the period January 2005 until 17th October, 2005, the defendant in defiance of plaintiff's rights, allowed his cattle, bearing brand PT over R to wrongfully and unlawfully enter upon the plaintiff's property, **Farm Tsinani**, Lobatse, invading plaintiff's property without the knowledge and/or consent of the plaintiff and that although repeatedly warned to desist, the defendant defiantly and in willful disregard of plaintiff's rights, refused to keep his cattle under control.
3. The plaintiff avers in its Particulars of Claim that the defendant has acknowledged his liability in writing to plaintiff in a document annexed to the Summons marked "HF1". This document was produced in evidence by the plaintiff and was admitted as evidence and marked "P1". Exhibit "P1" is central to plaintiff's claim to the extent that the plaintiff says it amounts to acknowledgment of liability to the plaintiff. For completeness, I reproduce hereunder in its entirety the said Exhibit "P1".

"Tebogo Radithotse
P.O. Box 400
Lobatse

L.A. Herbst (Herbst Feeds (Pty) Ltd)
P.O. Box 744
Lobatse

(Continued)

(Continued)

To Whom It May Concern

I Tebogo Radithotse we are taking our cattle from you Louis Herbst today 9/10/05 from your lands where you have impounded them. I hereby give the surety that if you release them today I will take them away and after this day they wont come back again and damage your crops again. I will take them away today to a safe place where I can look after them so that they don't come and damage your crops again.

Signed
T Radithotse

Signed for owner of Lands
L.A. HERBST
(signed)

Witness:
(1) Clemence Mafuka
(2) Isaac Murhawo
(3) Oscar M. Malama"

4. The plaintiff called three witnesses to prove its claim.
5. PW1 was Louis Herbst. He is the director of the plaintiff. His evidence was that the plaintiff plants Lucerne crops which upon harvesting are sold to customers as cattle feeds. PW1 testified that plaintiff's cattle are in the habit of entering plaintiff's farm and destroying the crops.
6. It was PW1's evidence that the defendant's cattle would enter the farm through some holes in the fence of the farm. Mr. Herbst testified that he knew that the cattle belonged to the defendant because he once took the brands of the cattle while they were in the farm and he went to Gaborone to find out who the owner of the brand is, and he found out that it was the defendant's.
7. Mr. Herbst told the court that on several occasions he would send his workers to inform the defendant that his cattle were in the habit of entering plaintiff's farm and destroying the crops, but to no avail. It was PW1's evidence that some time in October on a Sunday, he saw the defendant removing his cattle out of the plaintiff's farm.
8. According to Mr. Herbst the defendant admitted liability that his cattle were damaging plaintiff's crops, and he made him sign an acknowledgement of liability, in the form of exhibit "P1". It was PW1's evidence that notwithstanding the defendant's undertaking to keep his cattle under control, following the signing of Exhibit "P1" above, the defendant failed to keep the cattle under control because a week later, on or about the 14th of October 2005, his cattle invaded plaintiff's farm again.
9. With respect to how the claim of P91977.50 (Ninety One Thousand Nine Hundred and Seventy Seven Pula and Fifty Thebe) being damages, was constituted, it was PW1's evidence that he worked out the amount on the basis of the stock feeds that he lost and also because his returns for the period the defendant's cattle invaded the farm was less than what he usually makes for the same period. It was his evidence that this much is clear if one has regard to the VAT Forms which he produced as evidence and were admitted as such and marked "P2" to "P17" respectively.

(Continued)

(Continued)

10. Under cross-examination, the plaintiff told the Court that the defendant's cattle started invading plaintiff's farm from January to October 2005, but other than the date appearing on exhibit "P1" and the 14th of October, 2005 no other specific dates were mentioned for the period it is alleged the defendant's cattle destroyed the plaintiff's farm.

11. Still under cross-examination, the following questions were posed to PW1:
    "MR. MONCHO: Was it only his cattle -- the defendant's cattle that had the skill to break and enter into your fields?
    PW1: No.
    MR. MONCHO: How many other people do you know whose cattle entered into your fields?
    PW1: About four to six who I ended up summoning at the kgotla (customary court).
    MR. MONCHO: How may cattle belonging to the defendant entered your field?
    PW1: At one stage, it was between 100 and 130 -- you can't really count them they run around.
    MR. MONCHO: Are you referring to the defendant's cattle only or were they mixed with other people's cattle?
    PW1: I would say they were mixed. The other people's cattle other than his were 4, 5, 6 or perhaps 10, but they were not many.
    MR. MONCHO: The defendant says at that stage, he had 30 cattle including calves. What do you say to this?
    PW1: I don't know.
    MR. MONCHO: Besides defendant's cattle, were there instances where other people's cattle entered your field without defendant's cattle?
    PW1: Yes.
    MR. MONCHO: Just to clarify, we are talking about the period under which you are claiming?
    PW1: Yes.

12. PW1 was also asked why he attributed the damages to the defendant alone when he has earlier on said the defendant's cattle were mixed with other people's cattle. PW1's answer was that the other people he summoned at the kgotla and they paid. He said they were about six of them.

13. Still under cross-examination, PW1 was asked the following question:
    "MR. MONCHO: I am told that there are wild animals like Kudus that feast on your crops?
    PW1: That is true.

14. PW2 was Clemence Mafuka. He is employed by plaintiff. He commenced employment with plaintiff in 2002 and he has been in the employ of plaintiff for 6 years. He drives tractors, cultivates, and ploughs. He told the Court that defendant's cattle used to invade plaintiff's farm. He said defendant's cattle were more than 100. He said these cattle damaged plaintiff's farm. He also confirmed that he signed the document marked "P1" as a witness.

15. Under cross-examination, he was asked when defendant's cattle entered the plaintiff's farm. His answer was that it was in 2005, but he does not remember the months. He said it was only the defendant's cattle that they used to take out of the farm.

16. PW3 was Oscar Malama. He is employed by plaintiff. He told the Court that from January to October 2005 he was working for the plaintiff. He knew the defendant and said that the defendant's cattle used to invade plaintiff's farm. He said he was not sure of the number of the cattle, but they were in excess of 60. He said the defendant's cattle

(Continued)

were almost chased away from the plaintiff's field almost every morning. He said these cattle used to graze on plaintiff's Lucerne crops. He also confirmed that he signed the document marked "P1" referred to earlier as a witness.

17. At the end of PW3's testimony, the plaintiff closed its case, and Mr. Moncho, learned counsel for the defendant, made an application for absolution from the instance. The test to be applied by the court in deciding an application made by Mr. Moncho, has been traversed by this court on countless occasions. The question which the court has to ask itself is whether the plaintiff has adduced evidence upon which a reasonable court could or might find for the plaintiff. If the answer is in the negative, then, the application for absolution from the instance is entitled to succeed. (See *Gascoyne v Paul and Hunter* [1917] T.P.D 170.)

18. In the case of *Mazibuko v Santam Insurance Co Ltd and Another* [1982] (3) S.A 125B, the court, per, Corbett J.A, stated the position as follows at pages 132 H−133 A:

> *In an application for absolution made by the defendant at the close of the plaintiff's case the question to which the court must address itself is whether the plaintiff has adduced evidence upon which a court, applying its mind reasonably, could or might find for the plaintiff; in other words whether plaintiff has made out a prima-facie case. This is trite law.*

19. As the pleadings would indicate, the plaintiff is claiming damages occasioned by the destruction to its crops by the defendant's cattle for the period January to the 17th October 2005. It was therefore incumbent upon the plaintiff to lead cogent evidence that would establish *prima-facie*, that, for the period appearing in its particulars of claim, the defendant's cattle destroyed his crops resulting in the plaintiff suffering damages in the amount claimed.

20. The situation that obtains at the end of plaintiff's evidence is that there is no evidence led, that establishes *prima-facie*, that the Defendant's cattle entered the plaintiff"s farm and caused the damage amounting to P 91 977.50 (Ninety One Thousand Nine Hundred and Seventy Seven Pula Fifty Thebe). No evidence has been led, whatsoever, with respect to the quantities of the crops that the defendant's cattle destroyed and the estimated value per unit or whatever measurement may be used.

21. There was also no evidence led how the damage was apportioned to various other people whose cattle were part of the defendant's cattle when they entered the plaintiff's farm for the period under consideration being January to 17th October 2005. Nor was there any evidence led of the damage that was occasioned by wild animals which PW1 conceded used to "feast" on plaintiff's crops.

22. It was the evidence of PW1 that the damages that the plaintiff seeks are the difference between what plaintiff ought to have made by selling the cattle feed and what it actually made after the defendant's cattle invaded the farm. But no evidence was led as to what ordinarily the plaintiff would make for the same quantities of the crops that were damaged or destroyed by the cattle belonging to the defendant and other people.

23. Exhibits "P2" to "P17" shed no light on the above, nor do they shed any light on the quantities that were destroyed and prices per unit.

24. It was the plaintiff's evidence that "P1" amounted to an acknowledgement of liability. I think this conclusion is not correct. Reading exhibit "P1" I do not get a sense that, it is an unequivocal statement by the defendant that his cattle damaged the plaintiff's crops

(Continued)

on the 9th of October, 2005, or for the period claimed in the Particulars of Claim, and that he is liable for the damages thereof. On plain reading the thrust of "P1" is that the defendant simply says that he undertakes that if the plaintiff releases his cattle which it had impounded, he will ensure they don't come back again to damage his crops. I am aware that the precise phrase used in the letter signed by the defendant is that: "**I hereby give the surety that if you release them today I will take them away and after this day they wont come back again and damage your crops again.**" That in my opinion cannot constitute admission of liability for the amount claimed, nor can it be construed as admitting liability that the plaintiff's cattle damaged the plaintiff's crops on the 9th of October, 2005, admittedly the letter acknowledges some damage in the past, but it is not clear when. The time period is important having regard to the evidence of PW2 that the defendant's cattle used to come "every day" to the plaintiff's farm. Further, although counsel for the plaintiff says I must construe exhibit "P1" to be an admission of liability, his own witness, PW3, says "P1" was simply a warning to the defendant not to allow his cattle into the field again. This much, I must say, appears to accord more with the thrust of the letter. It is for the above reasons that, I cannot accept, *prima-facie*, that "P1" constitutes an admission of liability.

25. The question that I have to determine is whether on the basis of the evidence led could or might a reasonable Court hold for the plaintiff? I do not think so. The plaintiff was obligated to prove his loss or damage or at least lead *prima facie* evidence of the damage and loss. In my view the plaintiff dismally failed to lead material evidence, as I earlier said, on the quantity of the crops that were destroyed particularly by defendant's cattle and the ordinary market value for that particular quantity of crops that were destroyed. There was no attempt, whatsoever, in this direction. There was not even any attempt also to isolate or to apportion in a reasonable manner the destruction occasioned by the other people's cattle and wild life.

26. In view of the failure of the plaintiff to establish a *prima facie* case on the loss or the damage that it sustained as indicated earlier, I am left with no choice but to uphold the application of absolution from the instance which I hereby do. The application succeeds with costs.

Messrs Dumez (Nig.) Ltd v *Messrs* Patrick Nwaka Ogboli

In The Supreme Court of Nigeria
On Thursday, the 30th day of March 1972
S.C. 60/1970

Judgment of the Court

Delivered by

Lewis. J.S.C.

In Suit No. A/3/66 in the High Court at Agbor the plaintiff claimed damages in the sum of £565 for trespass which he alleged in his writ the defendant committed about March 1965 at Issele-Azagba in Utulu village and adjoining the new Otulu-Illah road and there "used their

(Continued)

(Continued)

road implements and destroyed a large quantity of the plaintiff's farm crops and economic trees." Paragraphs 4, 5 and 6 of the statement of claim read:

4. The defendant company undertakes road construction and road repairs as one of its major duties.

5. The plaintiff has been farming on the aforesaid piece or parcel of land since November 1929 and right from that time planted and owned palm trees, kola nut trees, banana trees, rubber trees and also owned Iroko trees on the land.

6. On or about March 1965, the defendant company in the course of their duty entered into the aforesaid land of the plaintiff and used their road implements and destroyed a large quantity of the plaintiff's farm crops and economic trees namely:

Particulars of Damages

(1)	Special Damage	£	s	d
21	Palm trees uprooted value £5 each	105	0	0
5	Kola nut trees destroyed value £5	25	0	0
10	Banana trees destroyed value £1 each	10	0	0
15	Plantain trees destroyed value £1 each	15	0	0
4	Iroko trees destroyed value £25 each	100	0	0
60	Rubber trees destroyed value £4 each	250	0	0
	Total special damage	£495	0	0
(2)	General Damages	70	0	0
	Grand Total Damages	**£565**	0	0

The defendants admitted in their statement of defence paragraph 4 of the statement of claim, denied paragraphs 5 and 6 and then in paragraphs 7 and 8 of their statement of defence pleaded:

7. The defendants aver that in pursuance of a representation made to the Controller of Works Services, Ministry of Works and Transport, Benin City, by the plaintiff, the said Controller of Works Services caused the District Engineer, Ministry of Works and Transport, Asaba, to investigate the plaintiffs claim. That the said District Engineer, in a letter ref: No. AS/RE. 17/32/DE of the 5th July, 1966, and copied to the plaintiff and defendants, stated 'that the crops involved were within the 50 feet limit measured from the centre of the old existing road'. The defendants will rely on the said letter during the trial of this action.

8. The defendants shall at or before the trial contend as a matter of law that:

(i) they acted within the ambit of section 9 of the Building Lines Regulation Law Cap. 14 of the Western Region of Nigeria;

(ii) in the premises, the defendant cannot be liable to the plaintiff's claim:
  (a) for special damages and
  (b) for general damages as claimed by paragraph 6(1) and (2) of the statement of claim;

(iii) whereof the plaintiff's claim discloses no cause of action and therefore it is frivolous and should be dismissed with substantial costs."

(Continued)

(Continued)

On the 18th November 1968 Uche Omo Ag. J. *(as he then was)* gave judgment for the plaintiff in the sum of £295-5s-0d and in his judgment said *inter alia:*

> *I am satisfied further on the evidence that the defendant company did destroy some of the plaintiff's crops on his plantation. I accept his evidence that he has a large plantation on the site alleged which he has been working on since 1929. That this damage was done in the process of carrying out a Mid-Western Nigeria Government contract is admitted by all. I also find that the plaintiff's plantation begins about 32 feet from the centre of the road and extends far beyond 50 feet from it. In some respects the evidence led by the plaintiff and the defendant company falls rather short of what each side was in a position to adduce; this is not unimportant having regard to the submissions made by counsel at the end of the case.* The plaintiff did not lead any *evidence to show* (a) *when crops were planted on the part of his plantation immediately abutting (nearest) the road;* (b) *what economic trees were planted thereon;* (c) *no independent evidence of enumeration and/or valuation has been called.* The defendant company has failed to lead *positive evidence* (a) *to show whether or not there was authority given by anyone to it to remove the crops on the land; and if so* (b) *why it was necessary to damage these crops;* (c) *to state, if that is so, that in order to carry out the contract it was necessary to clear as much as 30—100 feet from the centre of the road on each side of it*

Having so found he then considered the provisions of the *Building Lines Regulations Law* (Cap. 14 of the Laws of the Western Region of Nigeria, 1959) applicable in the Mid-West and came to the conclusion that the defendant could not rely on the provisions of either section 4, 6, 7(1) or 9 of that Law and that there was no need for him to consider whether the exemption set out in section 10 of that Law applied and he accordingly held that that Law did not justify the defendants' action and thus he found them liable for the destruction of the plaintiff's permanent crops. He then went on to consider the damages resulting therefrom and concluded his judgment with the words:

> *I accept the plaintiff's enumeration of the other trees destroyed as correct. Even though the plaintiff impressed me as an experienced plantation owner his case would have benefited from the evidence of an independent valuation which was not called. Having regard to the statement of claim, Exhibit 1 and other evidence before me I am unable to accept plaintiff's valuation in its entirety. I amend the valuation to read as follows:*

		£	s	d
21	Palm trees at £4 each	84	0	0
5	Kolanut trees at £2-10s each	12	10	0
10	Banana trees at 15s each	7	10	0
15	Plantain trees at 15s each	11	5	0
60	Rubber trees at £3 each	180	0	0
	Total	295	5	0

(Continued)

(Continued)

Accordingly there will be judgment for the plaintiff in the sum of £295-5s-0d.

The defendants have appealed to this Court against that decision and two main issues were raised in the appeal, namely whether the defendants were exonerated from liability for the destruction of the plaintiff's permanent crops because of the provisions of the *Building Lines Regulations Law*, and whether even if not so exonerated the learned trial judge rightly awarded £295-5s-0d as special damages as he did. Mr. Ogunsanya for the appellants argued a ground of appeal that read:

That the learned trial judge having found in essence:

(a) that the plaintiff/respondent's crops were damaged in the process of carrying out a Mid-Western Nigeria contract along the Otulu-Atuma road;

(b) that the Ministry of Works and Transport, Mid-Western State of Nigeria was the defendant company's employer for the purposes of this contract by reference to exhibits 1, 2, and 4 in his finding;

(c) that the Otulu-Atuma road enjoys an obstruction-free zone of 50 feet from the centre of the road on either side thereof under the Building Lines Regulation Law Cap. 14 Laws of Western Region of Nigeria (Schedule to the Law);

(d) that the plaintiff/respondent's plantation starts 32 feet from the centre of the road;

(e) that 'any other obstruction' includes permanent crops;

(f) that the plaintiff/respondent's crops in question are permanent crops;

> *misdirected himself in fact and in law when he said that there was no evidence before him that anyone authorised the defendant company to pull down or remove the said crops from the land thereby failing to apply section 7(1) of the said Law in favour of the defendant/ appellant."*

This ground of appeal clearly relied on section 7(1) of the *Building Lines Regulation Law* which reads:

> *The Provincial Engineer may cause any building or part thereof which has been or is being created or any other obstruction which has been created or is being created in contravention of section 4 or of an order under section 5 or any natural obstruction within one hundred feet of the centre of any road to which this Law applies to be pulled down or removed.*

but, when we pointed out to Mr. Ogunsanya that though having regard to the definition of 'create an obstruction' in section 2(1) of the Law it would cover 'permanent crops,' the difficulty, as we saw it, was that there was no evidence that the Provincial Engineer had caused their removal, Mr. Ogunsanya then conceded that this was so and first of all asked that he be allowed to substitute a reference to section 9 for the reference to section 7(1) in the ground of appeal. However, on examining section 9 which reads:

> *the authorities responsible for the up-keep of any road to which this Law applies may take from within one hundred feet of the centre line of such road or such lesser distance as may be substituted by order under section 5 such materials as may be necessary for the maintenance of the road and*

(Continued)

(Continued)

may construct and maintain within the area aforesaid all drainage works necessary for the maintenance of the said road,

it was clear to us that that section applies only to taking materials necessary for the maintenance of the road or constructing and maintaining drainage works necessary for such maintenance and there was no evidence on the record that the defendants were either taking materials for the maintenance of the road or constructing and maintaining drainage work for such maintenance as the only evidence was that they were constructing the road so in our view section 9 was of no assistance. Mr. Ogunsanya did not then pursue his request to substitute a reference to section 9 for the reference to section 7(1) in the wording of the ground of appeal but asked us to interpret the reference to the Provincial Engineer in section 7(1) as embracing the defendants in the same way that it was held in *Itambong and Others v Akonye* [1964] N.M.L.R. 128 that the Ministry of Works could delegate its power under section 9(1) of the Law to the respondent there. To our mind, however, that submission misunderstands the position and the effect of that case, as in that case there was evidence that for the purposes of section 9 "the authorities responsible for the up-keep" of the road in question were the Ministry of Works and there was further evidence that they had delegated their powers to the respondents, but in the present case there was no evidence whatsoever that the Provincial Engineer had delegated his powers (always assuming that the Provincial Engineer could so delegate) and when the section refers specifically solely to the 'Provincial Engineer' and not to "the authorities responsible for the up-keep of any road' as in section 9(1), we cannot interpret the words 'Provincial Engineer' to mean the Ministry of Works as if the Ministry was intended to have the power it would either have been named specifically in the subsection or a phrase would have been used such as is used in section 9(1) that would allow evidence to be led as though the Ministry was the authority responsible for the up-keep of the road but this was not done in section 7(1).

Mr. Ogunsanya then sought to argue that under section 4 of the *Building Lines Regulation Law* which reads:

No person shall, otherwise than as may be allowed by an order under section 5, create an obstruction within one hundred feet of the centre line of any road to which this Law applies to plant any crop which requires to be sown and reaped within a period of twelve months upon any ground occupied by any such road or the drains adjacent thereto,

it was forbidden to create an obstruction and as under section 5(1) of the Law an order had been made in respect of the road in question namely Route 499 making the obstruction-free area 50 feet on either side from the centre line of the road (see page 218 of volume 1 of the Laws of Western Region of Nigeria, 1959) and as the learned trial judge had found that the plaintiff's permanent crops began 32 feet from the centre line of the road therefore the plaintiff was committing an illegal act and could not rely on it to claim damages. He further submitted that the onus lay on the plaintiff to prove, if he could, that he was exonerated from the provisions of section 4 by virtue of the provisions of section 10 which reads:

The provisions of sections 4, 6 and 7 shall not apply to any structure of a permanent nature erected or to any permanent crops planted on any land before the provisions of this Law have been applied to that land,

(Continued)

(Continued)

and in his submission, the plaintiff had not done so. In our view, however, when a person is found to be in possession of land, as here the plaintiff was, then the onus is on the person going on that land and causing damage to establish affirmatively his entitlement to do so and if as here he is relying for his entitlement on a Law then he must show, reading the provisions of the Law together, that he has such entitlement and this the defendants certainly failed to do here as there was evidence to the contrary which the learned trial judge accepted in his judgment when he found "that he has a large plantation on the site alleged which he has been working on since 1929," and the first Order in Council listed under the subsidiary legislation following the Building Lines Regulation Law at page 213 of Volume 1 of the Laws of the Western Region of Nigeria, 1959 was made in 1940 so that there were permanent crops on the land at the time the Law applied to the road in question and section 10 therefore exempted the plaintiff from being liable for creating an obstruction in respect of those permanent crops under section 4 of the Law. Once again therefore we see no merit in this submission.

Finally Mr. Ogunsanya argued a ground of appeal that read:

> That the learned trial judge, having found that:
>
> 'The plaintiff did not lead any evidence to show

(a) when crops were planted on the part of his plantation immediately abutting (nearest) the road;
(b) what economic trees were planted thereon;
(c) no independent evidence of enumeration and/or valuation has been called',

> had no basis upon which to award the plaintiff/respondent special damages as he did and so erred in law.

It was his submission that in the final passage of the judgment of the learned trial judge which we have quoted and in particular to the words "having regard to the statement of claim, exhibit 1 and other evidence before me I am unable to accept plaintiff's valuation in its entirety," it was clear that the learned trial judge rejected the plaintiffs own valuation of his permanent crops yet in Mr. Ogunsanya's submission the learned trial judge gave judgment for a figure for each of the items of special damages claimed without having any evidence before him of the figures that he awarded. Mr. Emordi for the respondent in reply conceded that not only was there a conflict between the value put on the permanent crops in the pleadings with the evidence adduced but also conceded that there was no evidence on the record of the value of the crops in the sums awarded by the learned trial judge. He nonetheless asked this Court not to hold against the plaintiff the failure to call satisfactory evidence of the special damages and sought to say that the learned trial judge should anyway not have rejected, as he did, the plaintiff's claim for general damages. We pointed out to him, however that there was no appeal by the plaintiff against the refusal of his claim for general damages so counsel could not now be heard to argue that the learned trial judge was in error in refusing them.

(Continued)

(Continued)

To our mind it is clear that the learned trial judge, having rejected the evidence of the plaintiff as to the value of the permanent crops, could not set himself up as a valuer to make an assessment of their value without evidence on the record upon which he could act enabling him to do so. The plaintiff not having seen fit to appeal against the refusal of the award for general damages must stand or fall on the award of special damages and on Mr. Emordi's own concession, quite rightly in our view, the learned trial judge was in error in coming to the conclusion that he did as he made an assessment without evidence before him of the amount at which he valued the respective permanent crops when he had already rejected the plaintiff's valuation thereof.

It is axiomatic that special damages must be strictly proved and unlike general damages where, if the plaintiff establishes in principle his legal entitlement to them, a trial judge must make his own assessment of the *quantum* of such general damages and on appeal to this Court such general damages will only be altered if they were shown to be either manifestly too high or manifestly too low or awarded on a wrong principal, so far as special damages are concerned, a trial judge cannot make his own individual assessment but must act strictly on the evidence before him which he accepts as establishing the amount to be awarded, just as a trial judge when for instance he is assessing compensation to be paid for land compulsorily acquired must do, as we indicated in *The Governor of Mid-Western Province and Ors. v Eluaka and Ors.* S.C. 181/67 (unreported) of the 23rd October, 1970 when we said:

> Now we have indicated before and we must re-iterate that in determining compensation a judge must make his assessment on the evidence before him and not make guesses based on matters upon which he has not received specific evidence.

That special damages must be strictly proved has been repeatedly emphasised by this Court as for instance in *Oshinjinrin and 5 Ors. v Elias and Ors.* S.C. 63/68 *(unreported) of the 3rd April, 1970* when we said:

> Undoubtedly the rule that special damages must be strictly proved applies to cases of tort. In effect the rule requires anyone asking for special damages to prove strictly that he did suffer such special damages as he claimed. This however does not mean that the law requires a minimum measure of evidence or that the law lays down a special category of evidence required to establish entitlement to special damages. What is required is that the person claiming should establish his entitlement to that type of damages by credible evidence of such a character as would suggest that he indeed is entitled to an award under that head, otherwise the general law of evidence as to proof by preponderance or weight usual in civil cases operated. In the case in hand, learned counsel for the defendants concedes that there was evidence concerning the special damages claimed and that the learned trial judge accepted the evidence thus given in that respect. He however complained that the evidence should not have been accepted and acted upon by the learned trial judge and submitted that for the evidence to be acceptable it should have been cumulative and not based on the ipse dixit of the claimant alone. We are of course unable to accept this submission and no authority whatsoever has been cited to us in support of it. A court trying such a case should give adequate consideration to the evidence offered in support of a claim for special damages and if the accepted evidence possesses such a probative

(Continued)

(Continued)

> *value as preponderates the case in favour of the person claiming, then award would certainly be justified (see* Agbaje v. National Motors 20/68 of 13th March, 1970).

In our view therefore the plaintiff having failed to prove his claim for special damages his claim must fail and this is not a case where we see any reason why the justice of the case is such that it calls for us to enter a non-suit or order a rehearing, and we accordingly allow the appeal, set aside the judgment awarding the sum of £295-5s-0d together with the order of costs to the plaintiff of £51-1s-0d and we do order that the plaintiff's claim be dismissed with 30 guineas costs to the defendants in the High Court. The defendants/appellants are entitled to the costs of this appeal which we assess at 70 guineas.

Notes

1. Note that if entitlements are not assigned and protected, then the law of the jungle will prevail with the strongest imposing their will on the weak—"might makes right."
2. The authors also mention other justice reasons for choosing a particular rule.
3. Hirsch (1979) also tells us that "the tort system has a price-system rationale. Individual tortfeasors may meet their tort duties for a price, for an appropriate compensation."
4. One theory in torts that is not discussed in this chapter is the theory of "intentional torts" such as battery, defamation, assault, etc. Battery is an offensive touching of a person or their property. Intentional torts are not common in agriculture. The only intentional torts relevant to agriculture are trespass, trespass to chattel, and conversion. As in the case of other theories of tort law, Landes and Posner have pointed out that, "the common law treatment of intentional torts can be explained on the hypothesis that the common law attempts to promote efficiency." See Landes and Posner (1981).
5. As an example of the duty based in common law, the Court held in the case of *Attraah v Aboaah* [1963] 2 *G.L.R. 340, 340 (1963)* that, "A farmer owes a duty of care to his adjoining farmers not to cause damage to their property. Therefore a farmer who, before setting fire to his farm takes a precaution which he knows or ought to have known would be ineffective in preventing the spread of the fire, must at his peril contain the fire within the confines of his land or take the consequence of its spread. In this case the defendant ought reasonably to have envisaged that the precaution which he took was wholly unequal to the risk which he ran and that, in the state of the weather, the fire would spread to neighbouring farms precisely as it did. He committed a breach of his duty to the plaintiff and was therefore liable to her for the damage which she sustained." An example of duty based in statute, regulation 46 of the Road Traffic Regulations, 1957 (L.N. 135) defined the duty owed by drivers of turning vehicles at an intersection. See *Dzamboe v Mark* [1981] G. *L.R. 350, 350 (1980)*.
6. A landowner owes no duty to an undiscovered trespasser. However, the law does not permit the setting of traps that may injure a trespasser. A dinner guest is considered a licensee, while a bailiff that comes to your property to serve you with a summons to court is considered an invitee under the law.
7. *Nash Sebina v Gobatlwang Kgwakgwe*, High Court of The Republic of Botswana, Lobatse CC-1580-05, November 14th 2008. The most famous definition of the "reasonable person" was offered by Learned Judge Hand (*the Hand Rule*). According to Judge Hand, three variables enter into the determination of reasonableness: (1) the probability that the incident would occur; (2) the gravity of the resulting injury; and (3) the burden of adequate precaution. In algebraic terms, if the probability be called P; the injury L; and the burden B: liability depends upon whether B is less than L multiplied by P; that is, whether B is less than PL. *United States v Carroll Towing Co.*, United States Circuit Court of Appeals, Second Circuit, 1947. 159 F.2d 169.

8. *Gyan v Ashanti Goldfields Corporation* [1991] 1 G.L.R. 466, 466 (1990).

9. *Dzamboe v Mark, op. cit.*

10. *See Yamusah v Mahama* [1991] 1 G.L.R. 549, 549 (1988) (Benin, J.).

11. *Vanderpuye v Pioneer Shoe Factory Ltd.* [1981] G.L.R. 181, 181 (1980).

12. *Mensah v. National Savings & Credit Bank*, [1989–90] 1 G.L.R. 620, 620 (1990). Also *Ansah v Busanga* [1976] 2 G.L.R. 488, CA and *Asantekramo alias Kumah v Attorney-General* [1975] 1 G.L.R. 319.

13. *Asantekramo alias Kumah v Attorney-General* [1975] 1 G.L.R. 319, 319 (1975).

14. Cited in *Asantekramo alias Kumah v Attorney-General, supra.*

15. See *Yamusah v Mahama and Another* [1991] 1 G.L.R. 549, 549 (1988).

16. *Id.*

17. *Id.*

18. *The Civil Liability Act*, 1963 (Act 176).

19. Where any person suffers damage as the result partly of the fault of any other person and partly of his own fault or the fault of someone for whom he is responsible (in this part referred to as contributory negligence), a claim in respect of that damage shall not be defeated by reason of the fault of the person suffering damage, but the damages recoverable in respect thereof shall be reduced to such extent as the court thinks just and equitable having regard to the plaintiff's share in the responsibility for the damage. *The Civil Liability Act*, 1963 (Act 176), Part I, §1.

20. The fact that a person (1) had an opportunity of avoiding the consequences of the act of another but negligently or carelessly failed to do so; or (2) might have avoided those consequences by the exercise of care; or (3) might have avoided those consequences but for previous negligence or want of care on his part, shall not free that other from responsibility for such consequences. *The Civil Liability Act*, 1963 (Act 176), Part V, §29.

21. *The Civil Liability Act*, 1963 (Act 176), Part IV, §26.

22. "We realize that statutes of limitations are statutes of repose designed to promote stability in the affairs of men and to avoid the *uncertainties and burdens inherent in defending stale claims*" (emphasis ours). *Teeters v Currey* (518 S.W. 2d 512, 513 (Supreme Court of Tennessee, 1974)).

23. For example, suppose one undergoes a medical procedure and discovers 5 years later that the procedure was not properly performed and has led to some injury. Should the limitations period begin from when the party performed the procedure or when the party discovered that they had been injured?

24. The discussion of the economics of strict liability is summarized from *The Stanford Encyclopedia of Philosophy*, available at http://plato.stanford.edu/entries/tort-theories/ (accessed 20.04.10).

25. *Id.*

26. *Id.*

27. *Id.*

28. Section 402 A of the *Restatement of Torts* (Third). The Restatements are treatises on various American law topics and are published by the American Law Institute.

29. [1981] G.L.R. 181, 181 (1980).

30. *Restatement of Torts* (Second) 165.

Questions

1. Provide your definition of inalienable rights.

2. List and explain each of the steps for a plaintiff to be successful in a negligence case.

3. Why is proving causation important?

4. What types of damage awards are available in tort law? What explains the different types of damage awards in tort?

5. Explain how the statute of limitations reduces transaction costs.

References

Calabresi, G., Melamed, A.D., 1972. Property rules, liability rules and inalienability: one view of the cathedral. Harv. Law Rev. 85, 1089–1128.

Encyclopedia Britannica, eb.com "Statute of Limitations" 2010.

Hirsch, W.Z., 1979. Law and Economics: An Introductory Analysis. Academic Press, New York.

Landes, W.M., Posner, R.A., 1981. An economic theory of intentional torts. Int Rev Law Econ. 1, 127–154.

Listokin, Y., 2002. Efficient time bars: a new rationale for the existence of statutes of limitations in criminal law. J Legal Stud. XXI, 100.

Parisi F., Dari-Mattiacci, G., 2006. The Economics of Tort Law: A Précis. George Mason University Law and Economics Research Paper Series, No. 03-49. <http://papers.ssrn.com/sol3/papers.cfm?abstract_id=458701> (accessed 04.05.10).

Prosser, W.L., Wade, J.W., Schwartz, V.E., 2005. *Torts*; Cases and Materials. 11th ed. University Casebook Series, Foundation Press, New York.

CHAPTER 11

Eminent Domain

Keywords: Eminent domain; private land; post-independence; public use requirement; just compensation requirement

11.1 Introduction

The power of government to take private land for various purposes including economic development is well recognized around the world. The power to take private land is known as the power of eminent domain, and for countries in sub-Saharan Africa (SSA), the exercise of this power has been fraught with difficulties. The difficulties arise because post-independence SSA countries have needed private lands for building infrastructure, and other development projects, and yet the process of acquiring the land, especially consultation with landowners during the eminent domain process and compensation for land taken by the government have been problematic.[1] Land ownership is an important property right (see de Soto, 2003). Given the significance of land in a society, government acquisition must proceed cautiously to avoid social upheaval.

Most countries have defined the power of eminent domain in their constitutions. There is consistency in the overall thrust of eminent domain power in SSA countries, but there are some differences in language, stringency, and reach. For example, Article 20(1) of Ghana's 1992 Constitution empowers government to take land for *public interest* or *public purpose* (Government of Ghana and Ghana Constitution, 1992). As explained by one expert, where the government takes land for a school building, hospital, food distribution center, warehouse, etc. the acquisition is for a *public purpose*. On the other hand, the government may acquire the land in a *public interest* for a public body, private companies, and individuals.[2] For example, the Ministry of Agriculture maintains a register of government-acquired lands that investors may lease for long-term projects. In Kenya, eminent domain power may be exercised "in the interest of defense, public safety, public order, public morality, public health, town and country planning or the development or utilization of property so as to promote the public benefit."[3]

There is always concern about the fairness in taking land from one private owner and passing it on to another private entity that may profit from the use of the government-acquired land

F.O. Boadu: Agricultural Law and Economics in Sub-Saharan Africa.
DOI: http://dx.doi.org/10.1016/B978-0-12-801771-5.00011-3

under the cloak of *public* interest. The expansive grant of power to SSA governments has important implications not only for lands acquired for agriculture and industrial development purposes, but also for addressing problems of preventing urban sprawl and congestion.[4] However, if courts in SSA follow the path taken by the Supreme Court of the United States decision in 2005, governments may take land from one private entity and give to another private entity for development purposes. In the United States, the decision in the case that made such government action legal generated considerable controversy and discontent among scholars and the public.[5]

A second issue concerns compensation for the land taken. Ghana's experience with compensation for land taken is typical of what happens in other SSA countries. Compensation for land taken has been the practice in Ghana since colonial times, and is today captured under Article 20(2) of the 1992 Constitution. However, as Larbi explains, there has been a shift in implementing the compensation requirement. Historically, the payment of compensation was part of the process in acquiring the land. This practice shifted to where the government could acquire the land and later discuss the issues associated with compensation.[6] The effect is that "compensation for lands acquired ceased after 1966 and the NRC/SMC policy of repudiation of national debts worsened the situation. Compensation has not been paid for 90% of all lands acquired since 1966, and the government's indebtedness to land owners stood at approximately US$94.1 million in 2004."[7]

Another source of tension between landowners and the government is the change in the purpose and use of the acquired land. Again, Ghana's experience is typical of what one finds in other SSA countries. While the 1992 Constitution (Section 20(5)) requires that acquired lands be used for the purposes stated in the acquisition, and gives the previous owner of the land the first right to re-acquire the land should the government not use the land for the stated purpose (Article 20(6)), the government still follows a policy announced in 1953, "to reserve to Government the right to use any land compulsorily acquired for any purpose which in the opinion of the Government would be for the benefit of the country as a whole.[8] Following this policy would frustrate the implementation of the provisions under the 1992 Constitution.

11.2 The Economics of Eminent Domain

There is an extensive literature on the economics of eminent domain.[9] The economics literature examines two key elements underpinning the concept of eminent domain, (1) the public use requirement and (2) the just compensation requirement.

The Public Use Requirement

Economists have suggested two rationales in support of the public use requirement under eminent domain. First, it has been suggested that due to the *free rider* problem, it is efficient for government to use the power of eminent domain to acquire property for public use. Consider the building of a major highway. Since a private individual will not be able to exclude others from using the road (free rider problem), or face difficulties in getting payments for use of the road, the road may not be built at all. The government must step in and build the road using general tax revenues. As Miceli and Segerson point out, the free rider problem justifies "government provision of public goods but does not in itself justify the acquisition of land by eminent domain (Miceli and Segerson, 2007, p. 12)."

The second problem is the *holdout problem and land assembly*. Consider the Volta River Development Project that was implemented under the Volta River Development Act, 1961 (Act 46) in Ghana. The project covered an area of 8515 hectares across land from five regions—Ashanti, Brong-Ahafo, Eastern, Northern, and Volta regions (Larbi et al., 2004). In the absence of government power to acquire the land, individual landowners may *holdout* and demand values for their land that are far in excess of the true value of the property. Excessive demands could make the implementation of the project very costly. Furthermore, the wide array of property rights across regions (private lands, stool lands, community lands, family lands, etc.) would pose significant transaction costs (Coasian sense) to bargaining and render the project infeasible. To deal with the holdout problem, Miceli and Segerson suggested that "the power of eminent domain should be granted to any developer, public or private, engaged in assembly, a conclusion that seems contrary to the plain meaning of *public use*" (Miceli and Segerson, *op. cit.*, p. 15). The expansive nature of the power of eminent domain under the 1992 Ghana Constitution seems consistent with the suggestion by the two authors.[10]

The Just Compensation Requirement

The Constitution of Ghana requires that government pays just compensation to the person whose land has been taken. The Land Valuation Board (LVB) in Ghana is responsible for determining the value of land. It is not exactly clear whether the LVB represents what may be considered "fair market value" or not. Economists have concluded that the fair market value is "systematically less than the amount owners would ask for their land in a consensual transaction" (Miceli and Segerson, 2007, p. 19.). In effect the use of fair market value measures of compensation hurts landowners and since the value is low, transfers excessive private land to public use (Miceli and Segerson, 2007, p. 23). Economists have also suggested that "payment of full, market-value compensation leads to a moral hazard problem that causes landowners to overinvest in their property" (Miceli and Segerson, 2007, p.48). Economists have an important role to play in providing information that would improve government's eminent domain practice in Ghana. The large number of court cases, the massive encroachment on acquired land, and the failure to utilize acquired land for their stated purposes are the result of the compensation problem in Ghana (see Larbi, Antwi, and Olomolaiye, *op. cit.* at pp. 124–125).

In the case of *Goldmark Nigeria Limited & Ors v Ibafon Company Limited* the Supreme Court of Nigeria addressed the question of whether land acquired by the federal government and subsequently leased parts of the land to private entities, disqualified these leased lands as being used for "public purpose." Two cases from Ghana involving compulsory acquisition of land by the government are presented below. The case of *Chief Lands Officer v Opoku* (Ghana) addresses the circumstances under which the failure to develop acquired land within the stipulated conditions of acquisition could lead to a termination of the contract. In the case, it is a governmental entity that is suing to cancel a lease for non-performance. In the case of *Owusu and Others v Agyei and Others*, the Supreme Court of Ghana addressed two important questions: (1) did the government have the right to compulsorily acquire the property in question and (2) did the ordinary citizens of the area where the land was located have standing to sue their Chief for accounting for the compensation received from the government? In *Namibia Grape Growers and Exporters Association and Others v The Ministry of Mines and Energy & Mineral Ancillary Rights Commission & Northbank Diamonds Limited*, the Namibian Supreme Court discussed the application of sections of the Namibian constitution in resolving a conflict between a private mineral company and a farming community holding surface rights to land. The Court had to determine the regulatory authority of the Ministry of Mines and Minerals.

Goldmark Nigeria Limited & Ors v Ibafon Company Limited

In the Supreme Court of Nigeria
On Thursday, the 4th Day of October 2012

SC421/2001

Judgment of the Court

Delivered by Olufunlola Oyelola Adekeye. JSC

This is a further appeal to the Supreme Court by the 1st—4th appellants against the judgment of the Court of Appeal Lagos Division delivered on the 30th day of March 2000. This judgment affirmed the judgment of the Lagos High Court entered in favor of the 1st—2nd plaintiffs now 1st—2nd respondents on the 31st of March 1994.

The appeals lodged by the four appellants were consolidated pursuant to Order of the Supreme Court on 2/2/2009, whereupon the names of the parties as stated on the Motion on Notice dated 25th of May 2006 were adopted.

The parties were re-designated as follows —

1. Goldmark Nigeria Ltd — 1st Appellant
2. Electron Holdings Ltd — 2nd Appellant
3. Nigerian Ports Plc — 3rd Appellant
4. Landgold Holdings Ltd — 4th Appellant

(Continued)

(Continued)
And

1. Ibafon Company Ltd — 1st Respondent
2. Kolawole Abayomi Balogun — 2nd Respondent
3. Attorney-General of the Federation — 3rd Respondent
4. The Minister of Transport — 4th Respondent
5. The Minister of Works & Housing — 5th Respondent

The Federal Government of Nigeria now represented by the Attorney-General of the Federation, the 3rd respondent in this appeal acquired a large tract of land at Ibafon off Apapa-Oshodi Expressway, Lagos through its agencies the Ministry of Transport, Ministry of Works and Housing, the 4th and 5th respondents, in July 1976 by the Public Notice 901 of 22nd of June 1976. The 1st and 2nd respondents, Ibafon Company Limited and Kolawole Abayomi Balogun took a Writ of Summons on the 14th day of August 1990 challenging the acquisition of their land by Public Notice No 901 of the 22nd of June 1976. The beneficiary of the acquisition was the Nigeria Ports Authority now the 3rd appellant in this appeal. The Statement of claim was amended on the 22nd of June 1992.

By the amended statement of claim, the 1st and 2nd respondents claimed before the Lagos State High Court as follows-

1. A declaration that alienation by the 1st defendant to the 5th, 6th, 7th, 8th and 9th defendants and other private business concerns for private business/commercial use of lands acquired by the Federal Government from the plaintiffs on the ground of "public purpose" and the use of these lands by the said defendants and/or other private concerns for their own profit-making business/commercial ventures, is not a "public purpose" under the Public Lands Acquisition Act Cap 167 and consequently such alienations are illegal, unlawful, null and void and of no legal effect whatsoever.
2. A declaration that the two parcels of land measuring 2,835 and 1,333 hectare & originally belonging to the 1st and 2nd defendants respectively before the purported compulsory acquisition of the same since June 1976 by the Federal Military Government of Nigeria have ceased to be under any valid legal acquisition and should automatically revert to the 1st and 2nd plaintiffs, the same having not been used for any public purpose.
3. An order of inquiry/account into the total sum of rents collected so far from the alienation of the said parcels of land by the 1st defendant since June 1976 to the date of judgment and a direction that the said total sum be paid over to the 1st and 2nd plaintiffs in proportion to the respective lands.
4. An order of perpetual injunction restraining all the defendants either by themselves, their servants, agents and/or privies from further trespassing upon, alienating, transacting business or doing anything whatsoever in respect of or on the said parcels of land forming the subject matter of this suit. In the alternative only
   i. A declaration that the plaintiffs are entitled to compensation for the said acquisition should this honorable court find same to be legal, and

(Continued)

(Continued)

    ii. An inquiry as to the amount of compensation payable to the plaintiffs by the 2nd to 4th defendants. The 1st and 2nd respondents filed a 2nd amended Statement of Claim paragraphs 2—7 read as follows-

2. "By two separate Deeds of lease dated 6th of January 1978 and 20th of January 1976 and registered as No 99 at page 99 in Volume 1794, No 16 in Volume 1806 the land registry in Lagos, the 1st and 2nd plaintiffs respectively became leaseholders for 99 years each of the parcels of land being, lying and situate Ibafon off Apapa-Oshodi Expressway Araromi, Apapa measuring 2,835 hectares and 1,383 hectares and more particularly described in survey plans No KE/L/914 dated 20th May 1976 by Alhaji Y.O. Keshinro Licensed Surveyor and No DB/26/P of 17th January 1976 by Ogunmekan Licensed Surveyor respectively. The plaintiffs shall rely on the said Deed of Lease, survey plan and the two purchase receipts each dated 6th January 1976 at the trial of this suit.

3. At all material times, the plaintiffs were in possession of the said parcels of land and have been exercising ownership rights until when by government Notice No 601 of 22nd of June 1976, the Federal Military Government purported to acquire the said parcels of land for public purpose and in particular for the Nigerian Ports Authority took possession of the said lands.

4. No Notice of the acquisitions was ever served on the plaintiffs nor were they given the opportunity of being heard.

5. To the plaintiffs' total shock the plaintiffs discovered that rather than use the said lands for its own purposes, the Nigerian Ports Authority has since then leased out the said lands to private individuals and companies particularly the 5th, 6th, 7th, 8th and 9th defendants who now use the parcels of land for their own personal businesses such as the selling of sand and other businesses which are totally private and which have nothing to do with the purpose for which the lands were acquired.

6. Upon realizing that the said lands were no longer used for public purposes, the plaintiffs by several correspondents appealed to the 1st, 2nd, 3rd and 4th defendants to release the lands back to the plaintiffs who needed the lands for their own business purposes rather than leasing them out to other third party businessmen, all to no avail. The plaintiffs shall rely upon all relevant correspondences between the plaintiffs, the plaintiffs' solicitors and the defendants at the trial.

7. The plaintiffs by their solicitors letter dated 26th February 1990 gave notice to the 1st defendant pursuant to Section 97 (2) of the Ports Act Cap 155 Laws of the Federal Republic of Nigeria before commencing this suit."

The 1st—4th appellants as defendants filed their statement of defence and the 3rd—5th respondents. The case of the 1st and 2nd respondents was that the 2nd respondent purchased two parcels of land from the Oluwa family, the receipts of payment issued were tendered as Exhibits A and B. The parcel of land 2,835 hectares was purchased for the use of his company the 1st respondent which he intended to register at a future date and another 1,333 hectares for himself. He took possession of the land and fenced the entire area. He surveyed the properties in 1978 and beacons were erected on the land. Deeds of leases were executed to cover the parcels of land which were registered at the Lands Registry. They were marked

(Continued)

(Continued)

Exhibits A and B and Exhibits C and D. At the time Exhibit A was prepared, the 1st respondent was not incorporated as a company. When Exhibit D was executed, the 1st respondent had been incorporated and it was expressly contracted to ratify and adopt the benefit of the contract incorporated in Exhibit A. The 2nd respondent was in possession of the parcels of land when agents of the 4th and 5th respondents entered the land to demolish the walls erected thereon and ejected the 1st and 2nd respondents. The agents claimed that the land had been acquired by the Federal Government. The 1st and 2nd respondents claimed that no notices of acquisition were served on them. The plaintiffs testified that the 3rd—5th respondents through the Nigerian Ports Authority had been employing the land for purposes other than public use; as activities like selling sand, leasing and fishing were carried on there.

The 1st and 2nd respondents tendered survey plans in support of their claim to the land in dispute. The defence of the appellants and the 3rd—5th respondents in a nutshell are:

1. That by Public Notice 901 Exhibit F, the 3rd—5th respondents compulsorily acquired the land for the use of the Nigerian Ports Authority in perpetuity. Acquisition was published in the Federal government official gazette No35 Volume 63 of 8th July 1976.
2. The lands are being used for ports related activities on the areas not presently required by Nigerian Ports Authority like sand dredging and piling which could only be carried out within the area under the control of Nigerian Ports Authority.
3. The claim of the 1st and 2nd respondents are spurious as all the parcels of land in the foreshore of all areas where there are lagoons and seas belong exclusively to the Nigerian Ports Authority.
4. The area in question is land reserved for port development acquired by NPA Plc and as it is the practice in other parts of the world over this land had been laid out into a new industrial layout, the lease the next 13—15 years. The NPA Plc acquired 2,500 hectares as owner for present and future development of the ports.
5. The lands of the 1st and 2nd respondents were part of the land for future expansion of the Nigerian Ports Authority Plc.
6. That the 2nd respondent/4th appellant is also a lease holder over the lands before the acquisition and disputes the plaintiff's claim. It took a lease of the piece of land in 1987.
7. The 1st respondent cannot benefit from Exhibits A and D not being in existence or properly incorporated when they were executed.
8. The trial court should not have proceeded against it having dismissed the respondents' case against the 3rd appellant who is the predecessor-in-title.

The 3rd appellant as 1st defendant, the Nigerian Ports Authority brought a motion on Notice under Order 22 rules 2 and 3 of the Civil Procedure Rules 1972 to dismiss the suit. The grounds for the application were that the 1st and 2nd respondents did not commence the action in compliance with the provisions of Sections 97 and 98 of the Ports Act 1990. The action against the Nigerian Ports Authority was statute-barred not having been instituted within twelve months of the act of acquisition. The statutory pre-action notices prescribed in Section 97 of the Ports Act were not served on the Nigerian Ports Authority prior to the

(Continued)

(Continued)

institution of the action. The court took argument and a considered ruling was delivered on the 22nd of March 1991 in which the court struck out the case against the 3rd appellant.

The matter went on to trial without the 3rd appellant the Nigerian Ports Authority. Trial ended on 26th of May 1993. On the 31st of March 1994, the court entered judgment in favour of the 1st and 2nd respondents. The learned trial judge declared that the compulsory acquisition effected by the Federal Government on behalf of the Nigerian Ports Authority was null and void. The 1st and 2nd respondents were the parties vested with title to the property on or before June 1976 when the Notice of acquisition was purportedly issued. There was no evidence that acquisition notice was served on the 1st and 2nd respondents by the Federal Government agencies; the 4th and 5th respondents. The entry upon the land of the 1st and 2nd respondents constituted actionable trespass for which damages should be awarded. The learned trial judge went further to pronounce that the use of the land as proved before the court does not constitute use for public purpose under the Public Acquisition Act Cap 167.

In view of the fact that the act of the appellants constitutes actionable trespass for which damages are payable, trial courts then ordered an account of how much had been collected on the land which should be paid over to the 1st and 2nd respondents in proportion of their holdings. Vide pages 289—290 of the Record. Though the learned trial judge found that the 1st and 2nd respondents had proved their case and were entitled to an order of perpetual injunction restraining further trespass onto the property but declined to make an order against the appellants and 3rd and 4th respondents so as not to compel the government to legislate on its behalf more so as the lands have been leased out to other people by the appellants.

The 1st and 2nd respondents being dissatisfied with that part of the judgment, by which the court declined to make an order of perpetual injunction against the appellants, filed an appeal to the Court of Appeal. The 7th defendant now 1st appellant filed a cross-appeal on the ground that the High court was in error in entering judgment for the plaintiff/1st—2nd respondents when the claim against the 1st appellant and its predecessor-in-title had been dismissed on the ground that the action was incompetent.

The 1st appellant; Goldmark Nigeria Limited argued that the Lagos High Court lacked the jurisdiction to entertain the suit after the 26th August 1993. The 2nd appellant; Electra Holdings Limited also filed a cross-appeal on similar ground and further that the acquisition was within the competence of the 4th and 5th respondents and finally that the 1st and 2nd respondents failed to prove that the 2nd appellant was in occupation of the property within their holdings.

The Court of Appeal delivered its judgment on the 30th of March 2000 whereby the appeal of the 1st and 2nd respondents was allowed and the cross-appeals of the 1st and 2nd appellants dismissed. The Court of Appeal held that a dismissal of the action against the 3rd appellant was not a bar to the continuation of the case against the other appellants who derived then title from the 3rd appellant. The Court of Appeal emphasized that from the Amended Statement of Claim, there was no doubt that it is the acquisitior of land by the

(*Continued*)

(Continued)

3rd—5th respondents that constitute the substratum of the entire case before the trial High Court. In view of the foregoing findings of the Court of Appeal, the 2nd appellant who did not participate in the proceedings at the Court of Appeal sought leave to appeal as an interested party and was so permitted by the order of court dated the 19th of January, 2004. The 1st, 2nd and 4th appellants filed their appeals to this court against the judgment of the Court of Appeal.

The 1st appellant in the brief filed on 9/11/2010 formulated four issues for determination as follows:

1. Whether the learned justices of the Court of Appeal were right in holding that the Lagos State High Court had jurisdiction to adjudicate over the matter after August 26th 1993.
2. Whether the action against the 1st appellant was maintainable in view of the dismissal of the claim against the 1st respondent/3rd appellant (ie, NPA) for reasons of the claim being statute-barred.
3. Whether the learned justices of the Court of Appeal were right in upholding the declaration granted in favor of the plaintiffs/1st—2nd respondents in the face of the incontrovertible evidence that the 1st respondent's company was not in existence, that is, had not been incorporated at the time the land was purportedly conveyed to it by Oluwa chieftaincy family.
4. Whether the learned justices of the Court of Appeal were right in granting an order of perpetual injunction against the appellants in substitution for the direction by the learned trial judge that evidence should be adduced on the said issue of compensation.

The 2nd appellant settled two issues for determination as follows:

1. Whether the learned justices of the Court of Appeal were right in holding that the High Court had jurisdiction to continue with the action after the 26th of August 1993.
2. Whether the Court of Appeal was right in holding that the action in the High Court was maintainable against the 3rd appellant (former 1st defendant) and other appellants who all derived their titles from the 3rd appellant (former 1st defendant) notwithstanding the dismissal of the action against the 3rd appellant on the ground that the action against it was incompetent.

The 3rd appellant (interested party) formulated two issues for determination in the following terms:

1. Whether the learned justices of the Court of Appeal were incorrect in holding that the High Court of Lagos State possessed the jurisdiction to continue determination of the action after the 26th of August 1993.
2. Whether the learned justices of the Court of Appeal were incorrect in holding that the action was maintainable against the defendants who were successors-in-title to the 1st defendant (now 3rd appellant), notwithstanding the dismissal of the action against the 1st defendant now 3rd appellant on the ground that the action against it was incompetent.

(Continued)

(Continued)

The 4th appellant distilled three issues for determination as follows:

1. Whether the lower court was correct to have allowed the plaintiffs/1st and 2nd respondents appeal on the grounds of non-service of notice of acquisition contrary to the case put forward by them at the trial court which was based on the allegation of use of the land for a purpose other than public purpose and whether same did not amount to formulating a case for the party different from that put forward by it.
2. Whether the lower court did not err in law when it upheld the decision of the trial court in favor of the 1st plaintiff/respondent despite the fact that the 1st plaintiff/respondent had not yet been incorporated at the time it purportedly acquired interest in the subject matter of this appeal and whether in view of its lack of capacity it was entitled to the service of notice of acquisition.
3. Whether the claims against the 8th defendant/4th appellant were maintainable in view of the dismissal by trial court of the plaintiff/1st and 2nd respondents' claims against the 1st defendant/4th appellant who is the predecessor-in-title to the 8th defendant/4th appellant.

All the respondents distilled four issues for determination as follows:

1. Whether the learned justices of the Court of Appeal were right in holding that the Lagos State High Court had jurisdiction to adjudicate over the matter after 26th August 1993.
2. Whether the action against the 1st appellant was maintainable in view of the dismissal of the claim against the 1st defendant/3rd appellant Nigerian Ports Authority for reasons of the claim being statute-barred.
3. Whether the learned justices of the Court of Appeal were right in upholding the declaration granted in favor of the plaintiffs in the face of the incontrovertible evidence that the 1st defendant company was not in existence (ie, had not been incorporated) at the time the land was purportedly conveyed to it by the Oluwa Chieftaincy Family.
4. Whether the learned justices of the Court of Appeal were right in granting an order of perpetual injunction against the defendants in substitution for the direction by the learned trial judge that evidence should be adduced on the said issue of compensation.

I intend to be guided by the four issues raised by the 1st appellant for the resolution of this appeal.

Issue One[11]

Issue Two

Issue Three

Issue Four

Whether the learned justices of the Court of Appeal were right in granting an order of perpetual injunction against the defendants in substitution for the direction by the learned trial judge that evidence should be adduced on the said issue of compensation. The 1st appellant submitted that the learned trial judge granted the declaration sought by the 1st and

(Continued)

(Continued)

2nd respondents but declined to grant the order of injunction sought and directed the respondent to adduce evidence on the issue of compensation. The trial court declined to grant injunction in the circumstance of the case, in view of the hardship which would be occasioned by the grant of an injunction vis-a-vis the fact that the plaintiffs were asking for compensation in the alternative. The decision of the trial judge in refusing to grant an injunction cannot be faulted having regards to the peculiar facts of this case. The land in dispute was acquired in 1976. It was leased to six other companies for a term of 21 years for monetary values. The companies had moved into possession and invested on the land. The 1st and 2nd respondents did not file an action until 14 years after the acquisition. Publication of the notice of acquisition was in the Gazette. Delay defeats equity. The 1st appellant cited cases to buttress the submission.

The court is urged to grant the alternative claim of compensation sought by the 1st and 2nd respondents. The 1st and 2nd respondents replied that the lower court entered judgment in their favor declaring the appellants and anybody deriving possession through them as trespassers on the properties in dispute and declared the acquisition of the properties as void. It is trite that a victim of an act of trespass is entitled to an order of injunction to restrain continuance of a further trespass. This court had in similar cases of declaring acquisition to be illegal and void, had upheld the grant of ancillary relief of injunction. The ground given by the trial judge for declining to make the order does not justify a refusal of the order. The appellants have been declared trespassers. They have been ordered to render accounts to the 1st and 2nd respondents for the use of their properties. They are now entitled to their properties as if the acquisition did not take place. If this court does not make an order of injunction, there will arise from this decision of the trial court multiple suits against various parties to enforce the order declaring the respondents the owners of the properties. Since a perpetual injunction is granted in a final judgment determining the concluding right of the parties, there was no basis for the trial court to refuse to make the order and to order the 1st and 2nd respondents to lead evidence on their alternative claim for compensation as though the acquisition was legal. The justices of the Court of Appeal were right in granting the order of perpetual injunction against the defendants.

The 3rd—5th respondents contended that the justices of the Court of Appeal were right in upholding the 1st and 2nd respondents appeal on the issue of the grant of perpetual injunction. The learned trial judge of the trial court found that the 1st and 2nd respondents had successfully proved their case on the preponderance of evidence and are also entitled to perpetual injunction in the action being sought. The learned trial judge then declined to grant perpetual injunction on the grounds:

1. So as not to legislate for the Federal government.
2. Because all the lands had been leased to other parties.

The perpetual injunction should have been granted in the circumstance of this case especially since the acquisition was declared null and void against the 1st appellants. The 3rd to 5th respondents urged this court to dismiss the appeal.

(Continued)

(Continued)

The grant of the relief of perpetual injunction is a consequential order which should naturally flow from the declaratory order sought and granted by court. The essence of granting a perpetual injunction on a final determination of the rights of the parties is to prevent permanently the infringement of those rights and to obviate the necessity of bringing multiplicity of suits in respect of every repeated infringement. Compensation was a relief sought as an alternative claim by the 1st and 2nd respondents. A court will proceed to make an order in respect of an alternative claim where the main or previous claim did not succeed but where a court grants the claim of a successful party to a suit there will be no need to consider an alternative claim.

The trial court found in favour of the 1st and 2nd respondents and declared the acquisition of their properties by Public Notice 901 of 1978 illegal, null and void for reasons of fundamental breach of the provisions of Public Acquisition Act Cap 167 of the law of the Federation of Nigeria and Lagos 1958. These are for failure to serve the requisite notice on the occupiers of the property and to acquire for public purpose. The appellants were declared trespassers on the properties and liable to render accounts to the 1st and 2nd respondents of the profits made on the use of the properties. The learned trial judge ought to have granted perpetual injunction restraining the appellants their servants and privies from further trespassing upon, alienating or doing anything whatsoever on the parcel of land, the subject matter of the suit. It was wrong of the trial court not to make the order in the circumstance and to order the claimants to lead evidence on their claim for compensation after declaring the acquisition illegal, null and void. The order contradicted his findings in the suit.

The trial court declined granting the perpetual injunction in the following words:

> Therefore, to restrain the defendants perpetually on the use of the parcels of land is to legislate for the present executive as to what use to make for a particular Scheme. The defendants are not averrs to the plaintiffs using the land but there is no parcel of land available to be leased out. The alternative is to compensate the plaintiffs.

The Court of Appeal was therefore right in granting the order of perpetual injunction to rectify that anomaly. I resolve this issue in favor of the 1st and 2nd respondents.

The 4th appellant raised the issue as to "whether the lower court was correct to have allowed the 1st and 2nd respondents appeal on the grounds of non service of notice of acquisition contrary to the case put forward by them at the trial court which was based on the allegation of use of land for a purpose other than public purpose and whether same did not amount to formulating a case for a party different from that put forward by it."

The 4th appellant grouped the claims of the 1st and 2nd respondents into primary and secondary claims. The primary claim was for declaration that the alienation of their lands by the 3rd appellant to the 1st, 2nd and 4th appellants was null and void on the basis that it was not being used for public purpose for which it was compulsorily acquired. The secondary claims are as follows:

1. A declaration that the land be reverted to the 1st and 2nd respondents.
2. An order for inquiry/account of the rent collected by the 3rd appellant.
3. An order for perpetual injunction against the 1st, 2nd and 4th appellants.

(Continued)

(Continued)

The 4th appellant submitted that the 1st and 2nd respondents at the trial court did not specifically claim for a declaration that the acquisition was null and void for the reason of non-service of notice of acquisition, though it pleaded non-service of the notice of acquisition. In order to succeed under this claim, it must be so pleaded. This court is urged to resolve this issue in favor of the 4th appellant.

The 1st and 2nd respondents replied that this issue is germane to all the appeals. It is apparent from the claims and pleadings of the 1st and 2nd respondents that the acquisition of their properties at Ibafon along Apapa Oshodi Expressway Lagos executed by the 3rd—5th respondents by Public Notice No 901 of 22nd June 1976 was challenged on two grounds:

1. No notice of acquisition was ever served on the plaintiffs
2. The use of the land in particular by the 1st, 2nd, and 4th appellants does not constitute a public purpose under the public lands acquisition Act Cap 167, laws of the Federation of Nigeria 1967.

The 1st and 2nd respondents sought a declaration that the acquisition was void and sought for enquiry into damages and perpetual injunction. Parties testified in support of their cases. It is not disputed that the 3rd to 5th respondents to the appeal carried out the compulsory acquisition exercise of the land and transferred the land to the 3rd appellant the Nigerian Ports Authority. The evidence before the trial court by the 2nd respondent that he was occupying the land and he was not served with any Notice of Acquisition was uncontroverted. The 3rd and 5th respondents that carried out the acquisition did not establish any proof in the course of trial that the 1st and 2nd respondents were served the required Notice of Acquisition. In essence the 3rd—5th respondents failed to comply with the provisions of Sections 5 and 9 of the Public Land Acquisition Act, Cap 167, Laws of Nigeria and Lagos 1958.

I regard this issue raised by the 4th appellant in this appeal as being over meticulous in the face of overwhelming evidence before the court about the process of acquisition. It is an attempt by a desperate appellant to save its appeal.

The claim of the 1st and 2nd respondents challenged the breach of the Public Land Acquisition law in the acquisition of their properties by the Federal Government Agencies. The twin pillars of a valid acquisition according to the provisions of the Public Lands Acquisition Act Cap 167 Laws of Nigeria and Lagos 1958 particularly Sections 5 and 9 were infringed by the 3rd, 4th, and 5th respondents at Ibafon Lagos. It was the case of the 1st and 2nd respondents that no Notice of Acquisition of their land was served on them and that the acquisition was not for public purposes as required by law but for the private benefit of the 1st, 2nd and 4th appellants. The 3rd—5th respondents did not put forward before the trial court any concrete evidence of notice being served on the claimants — 1st and 2nd respondents.

There was ample evidence of transfer to the 3rd appellant the Nigerian Ports Authority and the purported lease for a term of 21 years at the payment of rents to the 1st, 2nd, and 3rd appellants.

Further there was evidence that the 1st, 2nd, and 4th appellants engaged the land for their private gains and not for Ports related matters. It is imperative to re-state the provisions of

(Continued)

(Continued)

Section 5 and 9 of the Publics Lands Acquisition Act 1967 Laws of Nigeria and Lagos which reads:

Section 5:

Whenever the government-general resolves that any lands are required for a public purpose of the Federation the Minister shall give notice to the persons interest or claiming to be interested in such lands or to the persons entitled by this ordinance to sell or convey the same or to such of them as shall after reasonable inquiry be known to him (which notice may be as in Form A in the schedule or to the like effect).

Section 9(1):

Every notice under Sections 5 and 8 shall either be served or left at their last usual place of abode or business if any such place can after reasonable inquiry be found and in case any such parties shall be absent from Nigeria or if such parties or their last usual place of abode or business after reasonable inquiry cannot be found, such lands or if there be no such occupier shall be affixed upon some conspicuous part of such lands.

Section 9(2):

Prescribes method of notice to Corporation, Company or Firm to be served on the principal office or if not known on principal officer or agent of such Corporation, Company or Firm.

Section 9(3):

All notices served under the provisions of this ordinance shall be published once at least in the gazette.

If the forgoing is not complied with, such acquisition shall be illegal, unlawful, null and void. The law equally empowers such acquisition when it is required for public purpose.

What is public purpose is not defined in the Act but has been identified by the courts in numerous cases. The acquisition must be for bona fide public purpose. It is suggested that for a particular purpose to qualify as public purpose or public interest it must not be vague and the way it benefits the public at large must be capable of proof. The test is whether or not the purpose is meant to benefit the public and not just to aid the commercial transaction of a company or a group of people for their own selfish or financial purposes.

On the issue of notice this court pronounced several decisions that the publication in the gazette does not constitute sufficient notice there must be personal service of same on the person. This court had always emphasized that government has the right to compulsorily acquire property on payment of compensation.

There is no argument about such constitutional power. There are statutes which provide for the procedure of acquiring property by the government. Government is expected to comply with those statutes which it has enacted. Where government disobeys its own statutes by not complying with this the laid down procedure for acquisition of property it is the duty of the

(Continued)

(Continued)

courts to intervene between the government and the private citizen. The trial court found in favour of the 1st and 2nd respondents. The Court of Appeal held that based on the testimony of the parties there was nothing to controvert the findings of the trial judge that notice of acquisition was not served. Both courts declared the public acquisition of the properties of the 1st and 2nd respondents invalid, null and void. This court has no reason or exceptional circumstance to interfere with the concurrent findings of fact of the lower courts.

In sum the appeals lack merit and I accordingly dismiss them. The costs of the appeal is assessed at N50,000.00 in favour of the 1st—2nd respondent.

Judgment delivered by

Walter Samuel Nkanu Onnoghen. JSC

Chief Lands Officer v Opoku

High Court, Accra, Ghana
17th July, 1962
Djabanor, J.

Facts: On taking a lease of a piece of land at Kumasi from the Government Lands Department, the defendant signed an undertaking on the 4th July, 1956, agreeing to develop the land "for the purpose approved . . . by the Kumasi Planning Committee." It was further agreed that the defendant "shall within one year from the date hereof commence to erect and within two years complete buildings on the said plot. . .". The defendant made a few cement blocks early in 1957. The Kumasi Planning Committee did not grant a development permit to the defendant until the 14th October, 1958. Thereafter he actively began to build. On the 24th July, 1959, the Lands Department by its agents re-entered the plot and purported to terminate the lease for breach of the undertaking, contending that the defendant failed to commence the building within one year of the 4th July, 1956, and in any case he did not have on the plot a completed building by the 4th July, 1958. The Lands Department refused to accept any rent tendered to them relating to the period subsequent to the 24th July, 1959.

Opinion: Djabanor, J: By his statement of claim filed on the 30th September, 1961, (writ issued on the 9th August 1961) the plaintiff claimed as follows:

> "(1) The plaintiff is entitled to the possession of the plot of land and premises known as No. 22 Block VIII, North Zongo, Kumasi, now in occupation of the defendant Joseph Opoku or his sub-tenants.
> (2) The defendant entered into an undertaking on the 4th July, 1956, to develop the said plot by building a main residential house on it within two years from that date and to pay on the 1st day of April in each year a rent of £G18 5s. *per annum.*

(Continued)

(Continued)

(3) The defendant having failed to comply with the terms of the above-mentioned undertaking the said Plot No. 22 Block VIII North Zongo was lawfully and duly re-entered upon on behalf of the plaintiff with the intent of determining the said undertaking on the 24th day of July, 1959.

(4) After the said re-entry the said Joseph Opoku the defendant wrongfully went into occupation and is still in occupation thereof.

And the plaintiff now claims:

(1) Possession of the said premises.

(2) A declaration that the defendant has no interest in the said plot."

In his defence the defendant admitted that he entered into an undertaking on the 4th July, 1956, as stated in paragraph (2) of the plaintiff's statement of claim but denied that the plaintiff is entitled to the possession of the plot. The plot has now been built upon. The plaintiff claims to be entitled to the possession of the plot on two main grounds; first that the defendant failed to pay the annual rent of £G18 5s. reserved, and secondly that the defendant in breach of the covenant in the undertaking failed to complete the building on the plot within two years from the 4th July, 1956. The written undertaking, the breach of which is the subject of this action had been lost, but by consent a similar undertaking, made between the plaintiff's predecessors in title and another party was tendered.

As I understand it the plaintiff's case is that in breach of paragraph (2) of the undertaking the defendant failed to complete a building on the plot within two years from the 4th July, 1956, and that therefore the plaintiff in accordance with paragraph (7) of the said undertaking re-entered the land and thus determined the tenancy. The defendant's contention is that the plaintiff has not re-entered, and that even if he has, he has done so wrongfully, or else the plaintiff should not be allowed to re-enter.

Paragraphs (1) and (2) of the undertaking read as follows:

"(1) That I shall use the said plot for the purpose approved by the Development Permit No. 603 dated 23rd day of June, 1948, issued by the Kumasi Planning Committee.

(2) That I shall within one year from the date hereof commence to erect and within two years complete buildings on the said plot such buildings to be erected in accordance with plans and specifications to be approved by the Kumasi Town Council on behalf of the Asantehene."

It is to be observed that the plot was to be used for the purpose approved by the permit granted by the Kumasi Planning Committee on a certain date.

In the absence of the defendant's own undertaking I can only supply this date (ie, the date of the permit to develop) from exhibit 4. From this exhibit the permit was dated the 14th October, 1958. That means that the plot must be developed in compliance with the permit issued on the 14th October, 1958. Now according to paragraph 2 the building is to commence within one year and be completed within two years of the "date hereof." The plaintiff maintains that the relevant date of commencement is the 4th July, 1956, the date of the signing of the undertaking, and the defendant contends that it cannot be other than the

(Continued)

date when the permit to develop was granted. It is not known precisely when the plan was approved as having complied with the building regulations, but in my view it does not matter.

This undertaking was entered into by the defendant. The document is not an agreement. The defendant is saying to the plaintiff: "In consideration of your permitting me to enter forthwith into occupation of this plot I undertake that I shall use the said plot for the purpose approved by the Kumasi Planning Committee." It seems to me that this is the main undertaking, and that until the purpose for which the plot is to be used is approved by the appropriate committee the defendant cannot really say how long it will take him to undertake the development. I think that it is for that reason that the date of the approval of the purpose for which the land is to be used is inserted in the undertaking. In the instant case the plot was approved for the purpose of building a dwelling-house thereon on the 14th October, 1958. I hold, therefore, that the date of commencement and completion of the dwelling-house must be computed as from the said 14th October, 1958, and not the 4th July, 1956.

The evidence is that the defendant started to make cement blocks on the plot within one year of the signing of the undertaking. In my view that constituted a commencement of building operations. By exhibit C5 the defendant reported to the senior valuer, Lands Department, that he had completed the building on the plot. That letter was dated the 6th February, 1960. If that is correct then the defendant had completed the building within two years from 14th October, 1958, and the purported re-entry on that ground is unlawful and of no effect. If the defendant did not complete before October 1960 (which I think is the truth), the re-entry taking place as it did before October 1960, is irregular and of no effect.

The plaintiff also purported to have re-entered on the ground of breach of covenant to pay rent. The law on this is settled. At page 493, para. 378 of Hill and Redman's *Law of Landlord and Tenant* (12th ed.) appears the following:

> *The proviso for re-entry on non-payment of rent is regarded in equity as merely a security for the rent, and accordingly, provided that the lessor and other persons interested can be put in the same position as before, the lessee is entitled to be relieved against the forfeiture on payment of the rent and any expenses to which the lessor has been put. . . .. If the lessor has brought an action to recover possession, the lessee or his assigns may, at any time before trial, pay or tender to the lessor or pay into Court, all the rent in arrear, together with costs, thereupon all further proceedings are stayed and the lessee or his assigns hold the demised lands under the lease, without any new lease.*

By section 212 of the Common Law Procedure Act, 1852, if the tenant pays all the rent in arrear before trial, the relief against forfeiture will be granted, but this provision applies only when the rent was six months in arrear. Wilberforce, J., so held in the recent case of *Standard Pattern Company Limited v Ivey*. In this instant case the rent was in arrear for only four months, and in any case the evidence is that the rent for that whole year was tendered to the plaintiff but he took an amount of £G5 11s. 7d. for rent from 1st April, 1959 to 20th July, 1959, and rejected the rest. In the circumstances I will not allow the plaintiff to take possession of the plot on the ground of the breach of this covenant either.

(Continued)

(Continued)
Judgment

(1) As the defendant was to develop the plot "for the purpose approved by the Kumasi Planning Committee," a body over which he had no control, the two-year period in the undertaking must be calculated from the time when the said planning committee approved the proposed development and granted a permit for that purpose. This date is the 14th October, 1958. The re-entry by the department on the 24th July, 1959, before the expiry of the two-year period in October 1960, is wrongful and of no effect.

(2) The making of cement blocks constitutes a commencement of building operations. The defendant sufficiently honoured his undertaking to commence the building within one year when he made some blocks early in 1957.

(3) Where a lessee pays or tenders all rent in arrears, including costs if there is a case pending, the lessee is entitled to relief against forfeiture, for the proviso for re-entry on non-payment of rent is regarded in equity as nothing more than a security for rents.

The plaintiff's action is accordingly dismissed and there will be judgment for the defendant as he is still entitled to the possession of the plot. The defendant will have the costs of this action assessed at 40 guineas.

Owusu and Others v Agyei and Others

Supreme Court, Ghana, Accra
11 December 1991

Francois JSC

Sometime in 1971, the Government of Ghana was minded to acquire two parcels of land at Digya and Kogyae in the Kumawu Traditional Area, for the purpose of establishing a national park and a game reserve. Acquisition processes were set in train and the park and the reserve respectively were acquired on 20 September 1971, and subsequently established. But the modalities for the said acquisition have not gone unquestioned, and the circumstances surrounding the lodgment of claims and the payments thereon have neither passed without protest nor criticism. The protest which took the form of a legal suit mounted by some citizens of Kumawu, as the plaintiffs representing the Oman of Kumawu, attempted to halt an illegality perpetrated by the chiefs and traditional title holders of Kumawu in enriching themselves at the expense of the state. The plaintiffs' concern seems to have revolved round the illegality that made the said chiefs beneficiaries in their personal right, of claims arising out of the acquisition of the said lands, to the detriment of the Oman itself. They consequently urged the disgorgement of all payments made to the said chiefs; and a refund of the said moneys to the stool's coffers.

The initial success of the plaintiffs in the High Court: see *Owusu v Agyei* [1980] G.L.R. 1 per Roger Korsah J suffered a reverse at the Court of Appeal. The plaintiffs foundered mainly on the attack on their representative capacity and the fundamental viability of the acquisition

(Continued)

(Continued)

itself. It seems to me that the issues provoking serious debate are within a very small compass. They relate firstly, to the validity of the acquisition, and secondly, to the credentials of the plaintiffs, that is, whether they possessed the requisite representative capacity to sue. Lesser issues like fraud and illegality would be discussed in the course of this judgment. The record of this appeal is contained in four massive tomes distinguished only by extensively indifferent typescript and the prolixity of matter not essential to the resolution of the dispute.

The first inquiry is to ascertain whether there was a viable acquisition of Digya and Kogyae lands. There is no doubt that the enabling legislation for a valid acquisition was either under the Administration of Lands Act, 1962 (Act 123) or the State Lands Act, 1962 (Act 125). Since both could not be employed at the same time, it is necessary to restate the essential provisions of these enactments to ascertain the appropriateness of choice. Section 7 of Act 123 is as follows:

> *7.(1) Where it appears to the President that it is in the public interest so to do he may, by executive instrument, declare any Stool land to be vested in him in trust and accordingly it shall be lawful for the President, on the publication of the instrument, to execute any deed or do any act as trustee in respect of the land specified in the instrument.*

> *(2) Any moneys accruing as a result of any deed executed or act done by the President under subsection (1) shall be paid into the appropriate account for the purposes of this Act.*

Section 1 (1) of Act 125 provides as follows:

> *1.(1) Whenever it appears to the President in the public interest so to do, he may, by executive instrument, declare any land specified in the instrument, other than land subject to the Administration of Lands Act, 1962 (Act 123), to be land required in the public interest; and accordingly on the making of the instrument it shall be lawful for any person, acting in that behalf and subject to a month's notice in writing to enter the land so declared for any purpose incidental to the declaration so made.*

(The emphasis is mine.)

A cursory reading of the two Acts would suggest that the acquisition of undisputed land could be readily accomplished by invoking Act 123, while Act 125 was more apposite where contentious claims requiring the determination of ownership, among other things, arose. It would be noticed that Act 125 excepts from its purview "land subject to the Administration of Lands Act, 1962 (Act 123)." This singular phraseology has generated diverse statutory interpretations. It is said that by excluding Act 123 in the body of Act 125, the latter Act could not deal with stool lands. The alternative contention is that the section only relieves the President from publishing an executive instrument where the land is stool land within the meaning and intendment of Act 123.

The trial judge, Roger Korsah J, in a painstaking analysis of the two Acts and the evidence before him, came to the conclusion that a proper acquisition had taken place. Had the defendant-respondents not made initial claims to the lands at Digya and Kogyae as their personal properties, the Lands Department might have proceeded under Act 123 to acquire

(Continued)

(Continued)

them as uncontroverted Kumawu stool lands. The said chiefs having perpetrated the illegality could not be permitted to take advantage of their fraud.

The Court of Appeal while not condoning fraud, thought differently. It felt that no viable acquisition of the two parcels of land had taken place. The court held that the modalities for a proper acquisition under Act 123 had not been performed. Act 125, according to the court, was completely ruled out since the subject of acquisition was stool land. Again, the instrument giving legal sanctity to the acquisition was the Wild Life Reserves Regulations, 1971 (LI 710) which was made under a power conferred not by Act 123 or Act 125 but by the Wild Animals Preservation Act, 1961 (Act 43). To the court, then, there should have been the strictest compliance with the requirements of Act 123 or Act 125. The court held that:

> No instrument for the acquisition of the land was, in fact made, as required by the provisions of section 7 of Act 123. Nor was one made under the provisions of section 1 of Act 125. The relevant provisions of the law had not been complied with. There is no acquisition, in law, for which compensation could have been paid."

Under Act 123, the management of stool lands was placed under the control of a minister (now Lands Commission) who by section 17(1) and (2) was empowered to collect all revenues from stool lands and initiate actions to accomplish this end. On the basis that where an Act prescribes the modalities for its operation, no other avenue is available for obtaining the same end, the Court of Appeal, per Charles Crabbe JA (as he then was) held:

> Under the statute law, as it now is, the minister is the proper person to maintain the action for the recovery of the moneys paid to the co-defendant-appellant and his vassals.

In effect, if the minister did not exercise the statutory duty imposed on him of gathering all revenue due to the stool from whatever source — including capital gains — no one else could do so. This interpretation dealt a death blow to the plaintiffs' capacity to represent the Oman, as the plaintiffs' stance suffered from the fatal defect of usurping ministerial functions. With respect, and with deference to the Court of Appeal, I do not share their enthusiasm to dismiss the plaintiffs' case on the grounds that the acquisition of Digya and Kogyae failed from procedural incompetence, or that the plaintiffs lacked capacity to sue. The paramount objective of the acquisition of the said parcels of land was to transform them into a strict nature reserve and a national park respectively.

On the ground this objective was largely achieved with a physical transformation of the two parcels of land despite any shortcomings that bedevilled the exercise of acquisition en route. Moreover, the government for its part has substantially honoured its obligations by paying compensation after claims had been lodged in due compliance with LI 710. That the claims were irregularly made or that the sums fell into wrong hands, are different issues altogether which should not becloud the validity of the acquisition.

It is said that there is no principle of justice, convenience or logic which should permit procedural law to encroach upon substantive rights: see Dicey and Morris, *Conflict of Laws* (8th ed), p 883. That statement is supported by equally potent expressions of legal presumptions.

(Continued)

(Continued)

For instance the maxim, "that which ought to have been done, is presumed to have been done": see its illustration in *Engineering Industry Training Board v Samuel Talbot* [1969] 1 All ER 480 at 482, CA per Denning LJ (as he then was): "…we no longer construe [Acts of Parliament] according to their literal meaning. We construe them according to their object and intent *[omnia praesumuntur rite esse acta]*." The principle is restated in our own Evidence Decree, 1975 (N.R.C.D. 323), s 37(1): "It is presumed that official duty has been regularly performed."

The question whether provisions in a statute are directory or mandatory is generally resolved by examining the known objectives of the statute. The court will not permit the mischief of splitting hairs on the true construction of a statute to undo accomplished objectives of the statute. Thus was it held in *Montreal Street Railway Co v Normandin* [1917] AC 170 at 175, PC:

> When the provisions of a statute relate to the performance of a public duty and the case is such that to hold null and void acts done in neglect of this duty would work serious general inconvenience, or injustice to persons who have no control over those entrusted with the duty, and at the same time would not promote the main object of the Legislature, it has been the practice to hold such provisions to be directory only, the neglect of them, though punishable, not affecting the validity of the acts done.

(The emphasis is mine.)

It seems to me also clear that the Court of Appeal somehow overlooked the amendment to section 1 of Act 125 by the State Lands Act, 1962 (Amendment) Decree, 1968 (N.L.C.D. 234). That amendment states:

> Provided that where the National Liberation Council is satisfied that special circumstances exist by reason of which it appears to the Council to be expedient that any particular land which is subject to the Administration of Lands Act, 1962 (Act 123) should be declared under this subsection to be land required in the public interest, the Council may by writing declare that it is so satisfied and thereupon it shall be lawful for the said land to be declared under this subsection to be land required in the public interest and the Administration of Lands Act, 1962 shall not apply to any such land in respect of which an executive instrument has been made in accordance with this subsection.

(The emphasis is mine.)

It will be noted that in N.L.C.D. 234 as also in Acts 123 and 125 the permissive "may" has been employed in relation to the President's discretionary powers of publication or declaration of a necessary public acquisition or utility. In the instant case, the President did declare and publish the government's intention, but by a legislative instrument, that is, LI 710, rather than an executive one. If my reading and understanding are not faulty, the legislative instrument became a permissive alternative to an executive expression which could by presidential discretion have remained silent and unpublished.

The criticism of LI 710 by the Court of Appeal, consequently does not appeal to me even if that legislation came under the aegis of Act 43. The observations on the presumptions of

(Continued)

(Continued)

regularity and the ambit of discretionary powers which negate any strict application of mandatoriness are more potent arguments for conferring viability. Indeed, the wide discretionary powers conferred on the President by Acts 123 and 125 to do any act for the furtherance and legitimisation of an acquisition seems, with respect, to have been missed. Accordingly, I find legal validation of the acquisition from statute law, that is, the amendment to Act 125 by N.L.C.D. 234, by statutory presumption, as also by case law. In my view, the factum of acquisition of the Kumawu lands, Digya and Kogyae, cannot be assailed with any degree of success.

The Court of Appeal overturned the decision of the High Court also on another ground, namely a disabling incapacity in the plaintiffs to launch their claim. The court felt they had no locus standi and could not urge the ground of necessity to clothe them with capacity, under the exceptions in *Kwan v Nyieni* [1959] G.L.R. 67, CA. It was the court's view that such an extension could only be by judicial fiat, that is, by legislation. Moreover, since under section 17 of Act 123 the management of stool lands was assigned to a minister, it was only the minister who had authority to bring an action concerning revenue from stool lands. It was the court's view that such revenue would be held in trust by the minister for the stool and since the minister performed his duties as a public rather than a private trustee, it was only the Attorney-General who could enforce the trust, or permit a relator action.

Turning first to the principle as set out in the headnote in *Kwan v Nyieni* (supra) at 68—69, the following are the criteria for its application:

> "(1) as a general rule the head of a family, as representative of the family, is the proper person to institute a suit for recovery of family land;
> (2) to this general rule there are exceptions in certain special circumstances, such as:
> (i) where family property is in danger of being lost to the family, and it is shown that the head, either out of personal interest or otherwise, will not make a move to save or preserve it; or
> (ii) where, owing to a division in the family, the head and some of the principal members will not take any steps; or
> (iii) where the head and the principal members are deliberately disposing of the family property in their personal interest, to the detriment of the family as a whole.

In any such special circumstances the Courts will entertain an action by any member of the family, either upon proof that he has been authorised by other members of the family to sue, or upon proof of necessity, provided that the Court is satisfied that the action is instituted in order to preserve the family character of the property."

The principle is not confined to land. It is applied where the assets of a family are being dissipated and the inactivity of the head of family has provoked an extreme exigency calling for unusual measures to redress the wrong. Nor is it confined to monetary assets. A dignity or status that is being sullied to the detriment of the family as a whole, because those entrusted with authority to curb the wrong lack the enthusiasm to do so, may be appropriately dealt with by those family members more conscious of the evil and possessing the necessary will to

(Continued)

(Continued)

abate it. Thus in *Sarkodee I v Boateng II* [1977] 2 G.L.R. 343, CA (full bench) the majority opinion while restating the principle that a single kingmaker could not file destoolment charges, still held, as stated in the headnote at 344, that where it was uncontroverted that the essential prior consultations had taken place:

> ...but that the majority of the kingmakers had unreasonably withheld their support or that they had been actuated by oblique motives, the single kingmaker must be deemed to have satisfied the requirements of the customary law as to acquire the right to commence proceedings under section 33 of the Chieftaincy Act, 1971 (Act 370).

The cases seem to illustrate the commonsense view of the customary law. Where those clothed with authority to protect family interests fail to do so, and as it were, form an unholy alliance or conspiracy to damage the interests of the family, an urgent situation must be deemed to have arisen allowing for a relaxation of rules and permitting more responsible members of the family to protect the endangered family interests. I find in this appeal that the three exceptions to the *Kwan v Nyieni* (supra) rule may fruitfully be pressed into service to clothe the plaintiffs with capacity. The respondents who should have protected Kumawu stool revenue, formed an unholy alliance to enrich themselves at the expense of the state. Their conduct, amounting to fraud, disabled them from performing their duty in preserving Kumawu stool revenue. It could hardly be expected that they would take steps of their own volition to refund moneys they had illegally appropriated or rather misappropriated. A more apposite example of the application of the exceptions to the *Kwan v Nyieni* (supra) principle would be hard to find. In my view, the categories of the application of the exceptions have yet to be exhausted. They may never close.

It seems to me also that the provisions of Act 123 transform moneys arising from the acquisition of stool lands into a trust fund. Section 7(2) of Act 123 requires moneys accruing from the President's act of vesting stool land in himself upon trust "to be paid into the appropriate account." It follows that whoever holds such trust funds can be proceeded against to disgorge the sums for payment into the "appropriate account."

Trust funds can be followed and retrieved wherever they are illegally diverted under the equitable doctrine of following or tracing trust property. I am yet to learn that barricades can be legally erected to sustain rank or status, while subverting and undermining this trust principle. The co-defendant-respondent makes no secret that he has retained and applied the trust fund for purposes of his own and in defiance of statutory directions. He has failed to deposit the sum in the appropriate account as ordained by law. He can receive no protection for his illegal conduct by relying on the traditional immunity from accountability. That principle cannot be urged as a cloak for fraud.

Since it is a statutory imperative that moneys from stool land acquisition should be lodged in a designated fund, it would be improper for this court to overlook a defalcation that illegally subverts this rule. The principle of non-accountability cannot be projected above statutory requirements to afford a viable protective umbrella. Above all, the co-defendant-respondent entered the fray not as a chief, but in a private personal capacity. The dichotomy is useful,

(*Continued*)

(Continued)

since it insulates the stool while at the same time permitting the money to be traced to him and recovered without any breach of constitutional proprieties.

In my view, the traditional rule of not proceeding against a reigning head on issues of accounting has not been violated. An issue of accounts imports some legitimacy in the use of part of a sum demanded, albeit in questionable proportions. The claim for accounts then seeks to straighten out the books and set the record of legitimate income against legitimate expenditure on an unimpeachable basis. That is not the issue in this case. Here, it is the recovery of an entire sum which the law requires to be lodged in an "appropriate account." But if the circumstances may be construed as affording an example of such a violation, then it is, in my view, sanctioned under the authority of Act 123 and the legally permissible quest to restore trust funds where they belong.

Another hurdle upon which the plaintiffs stumbled in the Court of Appeal related to their locus of representing the oman. *Banahene v Hima* [1963] 1 G.L.R. 323 defines oman in a legal constitutional context. It also explains Order 16, r 9 of the High Court (Civil Procedure) Rules, 1954 (LN 140A) which deals with representation. Three ingredients of common interest, common grievance and common benefit must be abundantly present to validate a representation of the oman. In the *Hima* case (supra), the representation was only of farmers who were pursuing a peculiar interest, namely a breach of contract relating to felled timber trees. In the present case, however, it is the citizens of the town who have a fundamental, traditional role to play in constitutional issues of the state, and who by virtue of their citizenship have a stake in all moneys payable on the acquisition of stool land and its proper utilisation, who have issued out a writ.

In the special situation where the natural rulers have disqualified themselves by permitting fraud to stain their hands, it is only the plaintiffs who are the remaining entity capable of championing the rights of the state. I find the tests of representation in this regard amply satisfied.

Finally, there is the issue of section 17 of Act 123. Is the minister or the Lands Commission the sole vehicle for pursuing revenue claims in respect of stool lands? The question has only to be formulated to provoke an answer in the negative. There are often contested claims between various stools. How does the minister or the Lands Commission achieve the split entities necessary to deal dispassionately with competing claims of various stools?

In my view, section 17 of Act 123 seeks to regulate and promote the orderly management of stool revenues. It does not encroach on inalienable rights of stools to their title to land. I differ from those who think title to stool properties has been effectively sequestrated by legislation. Section 17 only maps out revenue administration but does not edge out rights appertaining to ownership of stool lands. It should not be forgotten that N.L.C.D. 234 erodes the force of Act 123 by making that latter Act inapplicable in certain acquisitions, and consequently abating the force of section 17.

In the result, I see no warrant for disturbing the judgment of the High Court. I shall restore the decision of Roger Korsah J and allow the appeal.

(Continued)

(Continued)

Wuaku JSC: The facts and the law involved in this appeal are so well dealt with by my learned brother Francois JSC that I feel reluctant to say anything lest I unwittingly reduce the weight which I attach to the judgment. I am entirely in agreement with everything said. Nonetheless, I find it necessary to say something in support because to some people the judgment would appear to have abandoned the well-known trodden path of non-accountability of stool occupants to their subjects.

The appeal concerns the Digya and Kogyae forest lands belonging to the Kumawu stool. The undisputed facts which have come out from the trial and the appeals as I can see them are:

(1) No matter whatever process the government had adopted, properly or improperly, the government had compulsorily acquired, or shall I rather say, taken over the Digya and Kogyae forest lands.
(2) The government had paid the necessary compensation for the said acquisition.
(3) The compensation was paid to the co-defendant or through his accredited agents or both who took *dominion* of it and misappropriated it to their own use.
(4) The co-defendant and his agents are not entitled to receive the compensation and to make use of it as they had done.

Charles Crabbe JSC: read the leading judgment of the Court of Appeal and although the other two judges concurred, they each expressed an opinion which I consider not only very interesting but also very important. First Charles Crabbe JSC. He said:

> The general customary principles of non-accountability of stool occupants did not apply in the Kumawu Traditional Area. There was sufficient evidence to that effect that there was such a custom although it had fallen into desuetude. The custom was not dead. Statutes could not be used as instruments of fraud, and although there was no legal textbook to support the custom in Kumawu, the court should rely on evidence on the Kumawu Traditional Area.

Archer JSC (as he then was) had this to say:

> The settled law in this country is that an occupant of a stool, ie a chief, cannot be called upon by his subjects to account during his reign as a chief. The advent of the Anglo-Saxon system of jurisprudence into this country did not affect this principle of law. . .

> If there is to be any eminently desirable change in this aspect of customary law as regards chieftaincy then I think only chiefs themselves through their own enlightenment, dignity and reserve, with the welfare of their subjects at heart and in mind, can alter the law to be in consonance with this age and the spirit of accountability as enshrined in the present Constitution.

Mensa Boison JA, the third judge, lamented:

> The decision of this court is that the plaintiffs cannot question the co-defendant directly or indirectly by their action against the three defendants, the three defendants being self-confessed agents of the co-defendant. That is a decision that leaves the man in the street in bewilderment. He cannot understand.

(Continued)

(Continued)

Archer JSC (as he then was) and Mensa Boison JA referred to the case of *Owusu v Manche of Labadi* (1933) 1 WACA 278 which is the leading authority that only the occupant of the stool has the right to claim compensation in respect of stool land. May I say in parenthesis that the immunity of a head of family and which was later extended to cover chiefs was enunciated by Sarbah in his book *Fanti Customary Laws.* The authorities on this matter are many, both for and against the immunity proposition. The three learned judges held that the plaintiffs who were the respondents before them had no capacity to sue the defendants and therefore reversed the judgment of the High Court which was in favour of the plaintiffs now the appellants.

I would have thought that the judgment of the High Court having been reversed, the judgment would have ended there. On the contrary, the Court of Appeal deprived the successful defendants and co-defendant-appellants of the fruits of their judgment except as to costs. The successful appellants who are the respondents before us were ordered to refund the compensation, the subject matter of the plaintiffs' plaint, into court to await the publication of a valid instrument vesting the lands in the Republic for the public interest and that when the instrument is published the amount of compensation paid into court shall then, upon request of the Administrator of Stool Lands, be paid into the appropriate stool land account. In my opinion, that was a legal nicety all right.

The law does not exist in a vacuum, it is the very life we live. If the defendants have no right to keep the compensation wrongly paid to them, then they should have no remedy against persons who had made honest claim against them for the benefit of the oman, who, in any event, are the beneficiaries. In the circumstances, I hold the view that the Court of Appeal could have in the exercise of their power under section 32 of the Court of Appeal Rules, 1962 (LI 218) made the necessary order that the compensation paid into court should be paid into the appropriate stool account. It is stated that the co-defendant has not complied with the order made by Roger Korsah J in his judgment dated 19 October 1977 that the co-defendant should deposit the sum of ¢1,029,592 being the judgment debt with the registrar of the court within ten days from the date of his said judgment. I would suggest that the co-defendant pay the said sum of money within fourteen days from the date hereof into court at simple interest and at the current bank rate from the date of Roger Korsah J's judgment.

This case has a rather unfortunate history behind it. It could not be settled amicably before the Kumawu Traditional Council because the plaintiffs were treated with contempt. An attempt to make it a police case was frustrated. In the case of *Republic v Aduku V alias Ampah,* Court of Appeal, Accra, 21 May 1984, unreported, the Omanhene of the Mankessim Traditional Area was summarily tried for stealing the total sum of ¢1,573.34 contained in six counts. He was convicted and sentenced to prison. His appeals to the High Court, Cape Coast and the Court of Appeal were dismissed. He failed to prosecute his further appeal to the Supreme Court and it was struck out on 28 May 1990. Had the Omanhene agreed for the matter to be settled amicably he might not have lost his stool and would not have earned the stigma of an ex-convict.

(Continued)

(Continued)

My question is, which is better, to ask the occupant of a stool to account civilly and honourably or to be reported to the police by the very people whom the chief had refused to account to, and thereby face a criminal trial with its possible consequences. The fear of embarrassment to a chief should not be the ground for a chief not to account when a genuine demand for an account is made by his subjects.

It was Mensah Sarbah who enunciated the principle of immunity of head of family from accountability which was later extended to cover occupants of stools. Now that by the Head of Family (Accountability) Law, 1985 (P.N.D.C.L. 114) a head of family is made accountable to his family, I would recommend a similar law be made by the legislature to cover occupants of stools or chiefs. It is for those several reasons given above that I concur in allowing the appeal.

Osei-Hwere JSC: I have had the privilege of reading beforehand the judgment of my brother Francois JSC and I agree with him that the appeal ought to succeed. If there ever was any animated issue on which the two courts below vied for concurrence it was the finding of fraud against the second defendant and the co-defendant. The employment of this fraud which enabled them to collect and squander part of the compensation money for the acquisition was found to have been masterminded in its origin and fuelled in its propulsion by the co-defendant. Although a charge so serious as fraud should have been the subject of a cross-appeal by the co-defendant if he was minded to leave his honour and reputation unstained, he failed to do so. At the hearing of the appeal before us, his counsel rather sidled over it and invited us to restore his sullied name. This invitation must be declined precisely for the reason that he has remained contented with the judgment of the Court of Appeal.

The spectral presence of section 1(1) of the State Lands Act, 1962 (Act 125) so haunted the two courts below that it influenced their decisions in a manner diametrically opposed to each other. To the trial judge, Roger Korsah J, he seemed to have found the provision in the subsection which sought to exempt stool lands from compulsory acquisition so irksome that he had to embark on an ingenious reasoning from which he derived the conclusion that the lands for which the compensation was paid could not, having regard to the representations of the defendants who put in the claims, be regarded as stool lands. On the contrary, the Court of Appeal (per Charles Crabbe and Archer JJSC and Mensa Boison JA, a reluctant concurrent) held that as all were agreed that the lands concerned were stool lands, they could only have been acquired under the Administration of Lands Act, 1962 (Act 123) and, that being so, the court further held that section 17 of Act 123 denied the plaintiffs any locus standi.

As it will be realised hereafter, the reasoning of Roger Korsah J supportive of his conclusion that the lands acquired were not stool lands was, despite its ingenuity, rather vacuous. On the other hand, the Court of Appeal, in my view, was in error when it held that Act 123 was the operative statute for the compulsory acquisition of stool land. This was because both courts were eluded by the impact of the subsequent amendment to section 1 of Act 125 contained in the State Lands Act, 1962 (Amendment) Decree, 1968 (N.L.C.D. 234) which has been fully quoted in the able judgment of Francois JSC. The provision in the amending

(Continued)

(Continued)

Decree that "the Administration of Lands Act, 1962 shall not apply to any such land..."
seems clearly to mean that the regimen of the administration contemplated under Act 123
(such as sections 7, 17, 21, 22, and 23 which the Court of Appeal thought were relevant)
cannot be called into service in respect of such stool lands compulsorily acquired under
section 1(1) of Act 125. The acquisitions herein, accordingly, fell under the scheme provided
for under Act 125. The result is that Roger Korsah J came to the correct conclusion that Act
125 applied but gave the wrong reasons.

The view that section 17 of Act 123 is inapplicable by reason of the compulsory acquisition
of stool land under section 1(1) of Act 125 commends itself to practical reality because if the
substratum or foundation (ie, the stool land) is gone then there is nothing to be
administered. I disagree with the opinion maintained by the Court of Appeal that the locus
standi of the plaintiffs was struck down by the statutory provision in section 17 of Act 123. It
now remains to consider whether the customary law impediments which was also espoused
by the appellate court below was valid to deny the plaintiffs the right to sue.

The proposition of the customary law put forward was that the occupant of a stool could not
be called upon by his subjects to account whilst he is still in office and that the exceptions in
Kwan v Nyieni [1959] G.L.R. 67, CA could not be extended to clothe such subjects with
capacity to sue. It was hinted that the customary law securing the immunity of chiefs from
such actions was so immutable that not even the Supreme Court has the power to explode
that law. It must be emphasized that insofar as this court is concerned, it is only the hallmark
of justice that ensures the permanence of customary law declared by the courts. Any
customary law that sanctions fraud can have no place in our jurisprudence.

To clothe the plaintiffs with capacity, the analogy of the "derivative action" employed in
company law practice can usefully be applied. There a minority shareholder, dogged by the
rule in *Foss v Harbottle* [1843] 2 Hare 461, is powerless to prevent those in control of the
company from pursuing a course of which he disapproves even though such a course has
been an admittedly negligent one: see *Pavlides v Jensen* [1956] 2 All ER 518. Where those in
control go further, however, and behave fraudulently, the rule in *Foss v Harbottle* (supra) that a
wrong done to a company (for example those in control of the company expropriating the
company's property) can be redressed only by the company, will afford no defence to the
wrongdoers. Such a situation, that is, fraud on the company, is recognised as an exception to
the rule, thus enabling a minority share-holder to bring the action against the wrongdoers
which the company, by reason of the wrongdoers' control, is itself unable to bring.

The derivative action, providing as it does the escape from the rule in *Foss v Harbottle* (supra),
is therefore an action in the best interest of equitable principles. It was explained in
Wallersteiner v Moir (No 2) [1975] 1 All ER 849, CA that such a minority share-holder's action
brought to obtain redress, whether brought in the plaintiff's own name or on behalf of
himself and the other minority shareholders, and even though brought without the company's
authority, was in substance a representative action on behalf of the company to obtain
redress for the wrong done the company. In the instant case on appeal, the defendants (as
the stool elders or kingmakers) who should have initiated moves to bring the co-defendant to

(Continued)

(Continued)

account were themselves steeped in the fraud and as the compensation money expropriated was for the benefit of the oman, any member of the oman in the circumstance of the situation, had the capacity to seek redress by an action.

Alternatively, and on a more secure platform, the plaintiffs were entitled to justify their locus standi by virtue of the class representation or representative action or proceedings permitted under Order 16, r 9 of the High Court (Civil Procedure) Rules, 1954 (LN 140A). These proceedings trace their origin to the old Court of Chancery and were devised as an exception to the general rule that all parties interested in a cause or matter should be made parties to the record since the general rule itself became a barrier to expeditious litigation where the parties were numerous: see *Chancey v May* [1722] Prec Ch 591. In these circumstances, it was considered a matter of convenience that a number of plaintiffs could come to court as representing themselves and other persons with similar claims to their own. It was established that the persons represented are not required to give their consent to the proposed action: see *Bromley v Smith* [1826] 1 Sim 8; although they would be bound by the result of the case.

The policy of the early cases was not to restrict the employment of the representative action and this endures even today. In *John v Rees* [1969] 2 All ER 274 at 284, Megarry J stated that the proceedings should not be treated as a "rigid matter of principle but a flexible tool of convenience in the administration of justice." This allows for a liberal interpretation of the rules which serves to establish the confines of representation. The representative action under the rule is limited by one principle, that is, all persons on whose behalf the action is brought should have one common interest. This means that the class plaintiff can only include, in the class he seeks to represent, persons with whom he shares a "community of interest." This "community of interest" theory has been shown to have three inter-related consequences, each considered essential to the litigation and re-affirmed by Vinelott J in *Prudential Assurance v Newman Industries* [1979] 3 All ER 507. These are: (a) that the action should not confer upon class members a right which each could not have asserted in separate actions; (b) that all class members should have a "common interest" in the litigation; and (c) that the relief must benefit all whom the plaintiff purports to represent. It must be remarked that each of these consequences constituting the "community of interest" theory has been liberally interpreted with the result that a class plaintiff can be relatively ambitious in the definition of his class.

As to (a), it would seem at first sight that in order to share a "community of interest" with class members, the representative plaintiffs must enjoy the same cause of action against the defendants as the members of the class. But there has been quite forthright House of Lords authority that this is not a necessary mandate of the "community of interest" theory and it is arguable that a representative plaintiff does not have to share the cause of action he asserts on behalf of the class members. In the case of *Duke of Bedford v Ellis* [1901] AC 1, the propriety of representation by several plaintiffs of a wide and indeterminate class was considered by the House of Lords. It was contended that the plaintiffs were seeking to assert a public right and could proceed only after obtaining the *fiat* of the Attorney General. This contention was rejected and the representation upheld.

(Continued)

(Continued)

For the purpose of the liberal interpretation of the "community of interest" theory, the decision of the House of Lords raises two issues: first, the validity of representation despite the width of the class; and secondly, whether or not the representative plaintiffs could have proceeded even if they had had no interest in the suit. As to the first of these issues, mere numerosity is, by itself, no ground for holding that representation is improper, but when the class seems comprisive of at least the majority of all members of the public, it does imply that there is a real possibility that there will be differences between the interests of the class members which could be seen as undermining any "community of interest" that might otherwise exist between them. Moreover, as to the question whether or not the representative plaintiff can proceed without any interest of his own in the action, it has been suggested that he can. Lord Macnaghten stated at 7 of the *Duke of Bedford* (supra) decision that:

> If the persons named as plaintiffs are members of a class having a common interest, and if the alleged rights of the class are being denied or ignored, it does not matter in the least that the nominal *plaintiffs may have been wronged or* inconvenienced *in their individual capacity. They are none the better for that and none the worse. They would be competent representatives of the class if they had never been near the [defendant].*

(The emphasis is mine.)

The most literal interpretation of the above view that the *"nominal"* plaintiffs need not even have been themselves "inconvenienced," far less actually wronged, suggests that class plaintiffs can assert the claims vested in each individual class member without being required themselves to demonstrate an interest in the subject matter of the proceedings. The judgment of Lord Macnaghten was affirmed as "classic" authority on representative action by Megarry J in *John v Rees* (supra).

In *John v Rees* (supra), representation was achieved, although the class plaintiff had been so ambitious in defining his class that he included within it many of those who were opposed to his action. The plaintiff here was the chairman of the Pembrokeshire Division Labour Party who had been ousted by the defendants. He brought a representative suit on behalf of all members of the association except the defendants seeking, inter alia, a declaration that their election to positions of responsibility within the association were of no effect. Many of the class members supported the defendants against the plaintiff. Megarry J nonetheless held that the action was properly framed. He found a common interest in all class members insofar as they all belonged to the association. The decision of Megarry J illustrated the liberal interpretation of the inter-related consequence (b). Again, it may be argued that one has to look no further than *John v Rees* (supra) to see how little the requirement in (c) above serves to define the class represented. It is difficult to see how, in circumstances where many class members wished to join the other side, the relief sought by the plaintiff could be said to "benefit" them.

With the flexibility of the rules for class definition (and even without any such flexible approach in the definition), I find that the plaintiffs' right to sue by class representation was amply vindicated. It was for the above reasons, and my general agreement with my brother

(Continued)

(Continued)

Francois JSC on the points not raised by me, that I gave my concurrence that the appeal ought to be allowed.

Aikins JSC: I agree that the appeal be allowed for the reasons ably set out in the judgment of my brother Francois JSC. The appeal involves a number of legal points and the salient ones have been skilfully dealt with by him, but there is one point I would like to advert to, that is, whether the statutory provision of article 164(1) of the Constitution, 1969 embraces the customary law relative to "Chiefs' traditional holding of land in trust for their people", thereby exploding the air of sanctity surrounding the traditional rule prohibiting accountability of a reigning chief.

Article 164(1) provides that "All stool lands in Ghana shall vest in the appropriate Stool on behalf of, and in trust for, the subjects of the Stool", and to ensure that the funds are not carelessly dissipated, sub-article (2) provides for the establishment of a stool lands account into which all such moneys shall be paid. At customary law, chiefs in this country had always held land on behalf of their subjects, and a careful reading of paragraphs 705—709 of the *Proposals of the Constitutional Commission* which drafted the Constitution, 1969 shows that the intention behind the inclusion of article 164(1) was to stop the government from interfering with the chiefs' traditional holding of land in trust for their people.

What had happened was that even though the chiefs had from time immemorial been holding lands on behalf of their respective communities, the government in 1958 promulgated the Akim Abuakwa (Stool Revenue) Act, 1958 and the Ashanti Stool Lands Act, 1958 ostensibly to provide for the control of revenue and property of the stools of Akyem Abuakwa State and Ashanti and for the administration of those revenues. In actual fact the main purpose was to create:

> a stool revenue account for each stool into which stool land revenue was paid, and out of which account amounts determined by the Minister of Local Government were paid to the urban and local councils in these areas.

It was almost a well-known fact that after the moneys had been paid into the urban and local councils, the moneys secretly found their way into the pockets of party activists and functionaries of the government of the day, leaving insufficient money for the maintenance of the traditional authorities. The legislators made it clear that it was to stop this state of affairs from gaining root that article 164(1) was proposed, and they emphasised this in paragraph 709 of the *Proposals* thus:

> *709. We do not think that that state of affairs should be allowed to continue in the new Ghana in which we live.* We therefore propose that there should be a provision in the Constitution which should vest all stool lands in Ghana in the appropriate stool on behalf of, and in trust for, the subjects of the Stools. Here we include skin lands in stool lands.

There is nothing in the *Proposals* which indicates that article 164(1) was included merely to declare what the customary law had been for ages, that is, the unaccountability of chiefs in their traditional holding of land in trust for their people, as held by the Court of Appeal. In

(Continued)

(Continued)

my view, the holding of the Court of Appeal that the Constitution, 1969 had introduced nothing new is unfortunately a wrong assessment within the context of the true legal position. But even if it is said to be a declaration of the customary law, did the customary law still prevail and supersede the statutory provision in the Constitution, 1969? I think not. It seems to me, under the circumstances, that the customary law was embraced by the statutory provision of article 164(1). It definitely ceased to exist, giving way to the statute, and the beneficiaries had the right to seek the intervention of the court, and require the trust fund to be brought into court: see *Bastlett v Bastlett* [1845] 4 Hare 631.

From the foregoing, I hold the view that the appellants have the constitutional right to call on the co-defendant-respondent who stands in a fiduciary relation to them to account for any profit that he makes out of his trust: vide *Bray v Ford* [1896] AC 44, HL. It therefore follows that it is not only the Attorney-General who has the prerogative either *suo motu* or by a relator action to enforce the trust in this case under section 17 of the Administration of Lands Act, 1962 (Act 123). In sum, in my judgment, the appellants have a clear and unambiguous legal claim to the compensation paid in this case, and their appeal must be allowed.

Adjabeng JA: I have had the privilege of reading beforehand the judgments of my learned brothers, and I agree with them that the appeal be allowed.

Appeal allowed.

Namibia Grape Growers and Exporters Association and Others v The Ministry of Mines and Energy & Mineral Ancillary Rights Commission & Northbank Diamonds Limited[12]

Case No. SA 14/2002, 25/11/2004
Supreme Court of Namibia
Coram: Strydom, A.C.J., O'Linn, A.J.A., et Shivute, A.J.A.

Strydom, A.C.J.: This is an appeal from a judgment of a single Judge dismissing the application brought by the appellants. This matter concerns, more particularly, certain provisions of the Minerals (Prospecting and Mining) Act, Act No. 33 of 1992 (the Minerals Act). Among the challenges raised by the appellants are that the actions by the Ministry of Mines and Energy:

1. would have the effect of interfering with the Applicants' constitutional right and entitlement to fair administrative justice, as enshrined in clause 18 of the Constitution of the Republic of Namibia
2. the provisions of Part XV of the Minerals (Prospecting and Mining) Act, No 33 of 1992 to be *ultra vires* the provisions of clause 16(2) of the Constitution of the Republic of Namibia, and null and void an of no effect
3. that Northbank Diamonds Limited has, for the above reasons, no rights and/or *locus standi* in the proceedings before the Second Respondent purportedly in terms of Part XV of the Minerals Act.

(Continued)

(Continued)

Facts

It seems that an Exclusive Prospecting Licence with number 2101 (EPL 2101) was granted to a company with the name of Leotemp. Leotemp in turn transferred its rights to the third respondent. This happened on 25 June 1997. Thereafter the licence was again renewed until 25th April 2000. It is alleged that this renewal took place without any notice to the landowner and it is alleged that the *audi alteram partem*-rule was not complied with. The concession area, known as "block 9", is situated on the Aussenkehr farm.

The farm Aussenkehr is extremely suitable for the growing and marketing of grapes and all of the applicants are in some way or another involved in this industry or represents workers so involved. It is further alleged that up to March 1998 prospecting was done by the third respondent in terms of a "surface owners' agreement" as required by the Minerals Act. It is alleged that in terms of this agreement the owner expressed its intention to expand its farming operations and to that extent demarcated certain areas for such further expansion. The prospector undertook to use its best endeavours to prospect all such areas as soon as possible in order that these areas would become available for further grape cultivation.

This, however, did not happen. Instead it became clear that third respondent intended to excavate 4 pits of which pits 3 and 4 were situated within the area demarcated for further grape cultivation. Pits 1 and 2 would effectively fall within an area designated for the development of a township for the workers of Aussenkehr. In fact Pit 1 would be situated in an already existing portion of the informal settlement, housing some of the inhabitants of the village. Hence the application for the relief set out in paragraph 1.4 of the order.

The result of this was that when the "surface owners" agreement expired in 1998 the Sixth appellant was not without more prepared to enter into a new agreement covering the renewal of EPL 2101. Attempts were made to solve the impasse but when this was unsuccessful, third respondent invoked the provisions of section 52(3) of the Minerals Act by an application to the second respondent to have the dispute resolved in terms of the provisions of section 110 (Part XV) of the Minerals Act. Third respondent thereupon launched an application to second respondent in terms of section 109(1) of the Minerals Act. The outcome of this application was in favour of the third respondent but was later, by agreement between the parties, set aside by the High Court because the Commission was, at one stage during the proceedings, not properly constituted. A fresh application was thereafter launched by the third respondent. It is this application that forms the subject matter for the relief claimed and set out in paragraph 1.5 of the interim order.

It was further alleged by the applicant that the activities by the third respondent were a breach of the applicant's constitutional rights in terms of Articles 16 and 98(2)(b) of the Constitution and the applicant consequently asked the Court to declare Part XV of the Minerals Act, which sanctions such activities, to be *ultra vires* the provisions of the Constitution.

When the matter was argued Counsel on all sides were, notwithstanding the voluminous documentation and evidence placed before the Court, able to crystallize the main issues and

(Continued)

(Continued)

to confine their arguments to those issues. Apart from an appeal against certain costs orders and the question of who was responsible for the costs of the postponement of the appeal in April 2003, the appeal turned on three main issues, namely the constitutionality of Part XV of the Minerals Act, the review application in regard to the renewal of EPL 2101 in 1998 and the application based on the provisions of section 52 of the same Act.

A. Constitutionality of Part XV of the Mines and Minerals Act

The heading of Part XV of the Act reads 'Ancillary Rights'. In terms of sec. 108 a Minerals Ancillary Rights Commission (the Commission) is established consisting of a chairperson and two members. It furthermore applies the provisions of the Commissions Act, Act No. 8 of 1947, to the proceedings of the Commission. Sec. 109 is the *raison d'etre* of the Commission. It states that where it is reasonably necessary for the holder of a non-exclusive prospecting licence, a mineral licence or a mining claim to obtain a right:

> "(a) to enter upon land in order to carry on operations authorized by such licence or mining claim on such land;
> (b) to erect or construct accessory works on any land for purposes of such operations;
> (c) to obtain a supply of water or any other substance in connection with such operations;
> (d) to dispose of water or any other substance obtained during such operations;
> (e) to do anything else in order to exercise any right conferred upon him or her by such licence or mining claim;"

And such holder is prevented from carrying on such operations by, e.g. the owner of the land or any person competent to grant such right, then the holder of the licence can apply to the Commission to grant him such right. The section further provides for the procedure to be followed, the notices to be given to the owner or other interested party or parties and call upon them to make representations in opposition to such application. Sec. 110 provides for a hearing of the application and further states that the interested party or parties shall be heard either personally or through a legal representative and further provides for the cross-examination of any witnesses. If the Commission is on reasonable grounds satisfied that it is reasonably necessary for such holder to obtain such a right it may grant the right subject to such terms and conditions and for such period as the Commission may think fit. Under certain circumstances the chairperson may also, as an interim measure, and before a hearing takes place, grant to the holder such right which shall lapse on the date that the application, made in terms of sub-sec. (1), is considered and decided upon by the Commission. Sec. 112 empowers the Commission to determine an amount for compensation in regard to any right granted by it which shall be payable before the exercise thereof if security therefore has not been given. Sec. 113 gives to any person aggrieved by an order of the Commission a right of appeal to the High Court of Namibia.

The Court was asked to draw certain inferences from the provisions of sec. 107 of Part XV and it is therefore necessary to set out this provision in full, namely:

> 107. The provisions of this Part, in so far as they provide for a limitation on the fundamental rights contemplated in subarticle (1) of Article 16 of the Namibian Constitution in order to authorize,

(Continued)

(Continued)

subject to an obligation to pay just compensation, the holder of a non-exclusive prospecting licence, a mineral licence or a mining claim to enter upon any land of any person for purposes of carrying on operations authorized by such licence, are enacted upon the authority conferred by sub article (2) of that Article.

Article 16 of the Constitution, to which reference is made in sec. 107 of the Act, is part of the Bill of Rights contained in the Namibian Constitution and forms the basis of the attack launched by the appellants on the constitutionality of Part XV of the Minerals Act. This Article provides as follows:

Article 16 Property

(1) All persons shall have the right in any part of Namibia to acquire, own and dispose of all forms of immovable and movable property individually or in association with others and to bequeath their property to their heirs or legatees: provided that Parliament may by legislation prohibit or regulate as it deems expedient the right to acquire property by persons who are not Namibian citizens.

(2) The State or a competent body or organ authorized by law may expropriate property in the public interest subject to the payment of just compensation, in accordance with requirements and procedures to be determined by Act of Parliament.

Various other articles of the Constitution are also relevant to the question concerning constitutionality. These are articles 131, 22 and 25(1). These articles provide as follows:

Article 131 Entrenchment of Fundamental Rights and Freedoms:

No repeal or amendment of any of the provisions of Chapter 3 hereof, in so far as such repeal or amendment diminishes or detracts from the fundamental rights and freedoms contained and defined in that Chapter, shall be permissible under this Constitution, and no such purported repeal or amendment shall be valid or have any force or effect.

Article 22 Limitation upon Fundamental Rights and Freedoms

Whenever or wherever in terms of this Constitution the limitation of any fundamental rights or freedoms contemplated by this Chapter is authorized, any law providing for such limitation shall:

(a) be of general application, shall not negate the essential content thereof, and shall not be aimed at a particular individual;

(b) specify the ascertainable extent of such limitation and identify the Article or Articles hereof on which authority to enact such limitation is claimed to rest.

Article 25 Enforcement of Fundamental Rights and Freedoms

Save in so far as it may be authorized to do so by this Constitution, Parliament or any subordinate legislative authority shall not make any law, and the Executive and the agencies of Government shall not take any action which abolishes or abridges the fundamental rights and freedoms conferred by this Chapter, an any law or action in contravention thereof shall to the extent of the contravention be invalid provided that:...

The above provisions of the Constitution stipulates, firstly that the Rights and Freedoms, set out in Chapter 3, cannot be repealed and can only be amended in so far as such amendment

(Continued)

(Continued)

does not diminish or detract anything from the Rights and Freedoms so set out in that Chapter. Secondly the limitation of the Rights is only permissible where this is authorized by the Constitution and then only to the extent set out in Article 22. Thirdly any Act of Parliament which abolishes or abridges any of the Rights or Freedoms shall to that extent be invalid.

On behalf of the appellants it was submitted by Mr. Barnard that there could not be any question that the provisions of Part XV of the Act limits the property rights of a landowner and as the Minerals Act is an Act of Parliament it is subject to the above limitations. Referring to Article 22 Counsel submitted that the Legislator was aware of the effect of the provisions of Part XV and in order to find some authorization for the limitation of Article 16 it enacted the provisions of sec. 107 of the Minerals Act. Counsel however submitted that Part XV was not saved by sec. 107 as Article 16(2) deals with expropriation and sanctions the expropriation of land under certain circumstances. Part XV, so it was submitted, falls short of expropriation and only limits the use and enjoyment of his property by a landowner. Consequently Part XV, which limits the property rights of a Landowner without there being any authorization for such limitation, results in the provisions of Part XV being unconstitutional.

Counsel further submitted that the argument by the respondents that Article 16 only entrenched and safeguarded the framework within which property could be acquired, can be owned and disposed of and nothing more, was flawed. Counsel submitted that Article 16 safeguarded the component rights of ownership and not only certain of those rights as argued by the respondents. Counsel further submitted that even if Part XV of the Minerals Act was a reasonable legislative act then the provisions thereof were not saved because, unlike the South African Constitution, the Namibian Constitution did not contain a general limitation clause based on the reasonableness of the legislation. (See sec. 36(1) of the South African Constitution, Act 108 of 1996).

Mr. Chaskalson, on behalf of the 1st and 2nd respondents, submitted that Article 16 had to be interpreted in harmony with Article 100 of the Constitution. In this regard it was firstly argued by Counsel that, seen in this way, the encroachment on the interests of a surface owner by the owner of the mineral rights did not impact on property within the contemplation of Article 16. Alternatively, and if the Court should find that the encroachment did impact on the property of the surface owner, then Counsel submitted that Article 16(2) expressly permitted the appropriation of property by a competent body authorized to act in terms of the law and on payment of just compensation. Article 16 tacitly permits the reasonable regulation of property rights in the public interest. To that extent the Article authorizes interference with property rights which falls short of expropriation and therefore provides for a reasonable regulation of competing interests of surface owner and mineral rights holder. Counsel confirmed that ownership protected by Article 16(1) was not limited to the instances mentioned in the Article or to some "sticks in the bundle" of property rights. However the Article did not exclude reasonable regulation by the State in regard to property rights.

(Continued)

(Continued)

Mr. Chaskalson further pointed out that on the argument of Mr. Barnard an intransigent surface owner would be able to render the right of a holder of mineral rights nugatory. If Part XV was unconstitutional, as submitted by Mr. Barnard, then there was no means whereby a holder of mineral rights might, e.g. enter on the property to exercise his rights, if permission to enter on the property was not granted by the surface owner. That meant that the right, which was regarded as property, and was protected similarly by Article 16, was unprotected. Mr. Chaskalson submitted that the contentions by the appellants were absurd and would bring about a result not intended by the Constitution.

Mr. Gauntlett associated himself with the argument of Mr. Chaskalson for the first respondent. He pointed out that the appellants sought three declaratory orders and he referred the Court to the applicable law. Referring to the argument by Counsel for the appellants Mr. Gauntlett said that what Counsel was contending for was that Article 16 established an absolute right of surface ownership incapable of regulation. What was protected by the article was, on the interpretations given by this Court in regard to purposive interpretation of the Constitution, the full ownership in property. Mr. Gauntlett pointed out that the history of Namibia showed that mineral rights always vested in the State which was then free to licence mining operations. Reading Articles 16, 100, and 140 together, what the Constitution is providing for in its scheme was that the existing dispensation on mining laws, as one form of property rights, was carried through. The right to mine carries with it the ancillary rights set out in Part XV of the Minerals Act and is, if sensibly interpreted, intended to alleviate the position of the surface landowner.

The interpretation of Article 16 of the Constitution read with Articles 22 and 131 leads, according to Counsel for the appellants, to the inevitable conclusion that the ownership in property, be it movable or immovable, is not capable of regulation where such regulation abolishes or abridges any of the rights comprising ownership in property. The only limitation on ownership provided for in Article 16 is expropriation by the State, or a body set up in terms of the law, for public purposes and against payment of just compensation. This, so it was submitted by Counsel, was due to an oversight by the founding fathers when they drafted the Constitution. On the one hand Mr. Barnard submitted that the Constitution was immutable and that Part XV of the Mines and Minerals Act infringed the rights of a landowner and was therefore unconstitutional. On the other hand the enormity of such a submission forced Counsel to further submit that the Constitution was not cut in stone and such an obvious *lacuna* would be capable of correction by the Legislature, although it was conceded that any subsequent drafting to provide for regulation would itself diminish or abridge Article 16.

Certain issues crystallized during argument and became common cause. One such issue concerned the content of ownership in property. It was submitted by Mr. Barnard that the protection given by Article 16 extended over all rights included in property ownership and not only in some of the rights. During argument both Counsel on behalf of the respondents explained their stance and only qualified the protection so granted to ownership being subject to reasonable regulation. I agree that the protection granted by the Article

(Continued)

(Continued)

encompasses the totality of the rights in ownership of property. This Article, being part of Chapter III of the Constitution, must be interpreted in a purposive and liberal way so as to accord to subjects the full measure of the rights inherent in ownership of property. (See in this regard *Minister of Defence v Mwandinghi* [1993] NR 63 SC).

Another issue on which there was unanimity between the parties was the issue whether an exclusive prospecting licence was property. In my opinion the parties correctly agreed that such licence was property in the hands of the holder thereof. (See in this regard *Minister of Defence v Mwandinghi, supra,* p. 75.)

Thirdly the parties were *ad idem* that Article 100 of the Constitution vested mineral rights, for so far as they were not privately owned, in the State. In regard to Namibia mineral rights vested in the State since Colonial times. (See in this regard Imperial Mining Ordinance for German South West Africa, 8th August 1905 and Proc. 21 of 1919, Proc. 4 of 1940, Ord. 26 of 1954, Ord. 20 of 1968 and presently Act 33 of 1992).

I agree with Counsel, on behalf of the Respondents, that the question whether Part XV of the Minerals Act is constitutional must be determined on the provisions of the various Articles of the Constitution read with Article 100. The source for the enactment of the Minerals Act is to be found in Article 100 of the Constitution itself which vests those rights in the State. Constitutionally these rights never formed part of ownership in landed property and can therefore not be seen as *ex post facto* limiting the right of ownership of a landowner in regard of which the provisions of Article 22 of the Constitution must apply. The Minerals Act regulates the granting and the exercising of those rights and the relationship between the State and any holder on which such rights are conferred in terms of the Minerals Act. Because of a possible conflict between the exercise of such rights and the rights of the owner of landed property, the Act provides for machinery by means of which it attempts to resolve any dispute by balancing the competing rights and thereby relieving the tension so created. It is in this regard that Part XV of the Act, and to a certain extent also sections 51 and 52, play a role.

The contention by the appellants' Counsel that Part XV of the Minerals Act is unconstitutional carries in its wake the logical result that all and any regulation in regard to property, in so far as such regulation may abridge, in the least, one or any of the "bundle" of rights, of which ownership in property consists, such regulation will be invalid as it conflicts with the provisions of Article 16 of the Constitution. This was conceded by Counsel for the appellants. According to Counsel no provision was made for regulating of property in this regard. This caused Mr. Gauntlett to remark that whenever the State wanted to impose some or other regulation in regard to property, for example, to regulate the possession of arms and ammunition, they would not be able to do so except to expropriate all arms and ammunition.

Mr. Gauntlett, on the other hand, submitted that it was not the intention of the founding fathers to change the property regime in Namibia. The purpose of Article 16 was to protect the right of individuals and body corporates to acquire and possess property and did not intend this to change on the advent of Independence. Both Counsel for the respondents

(Continued)

(Continued)

further pointed out that an interpretation of Article 16 as an absolute and rigid provision, incapable of accommodating reasonable regulation of property, was untenable. Counsel also pointed out that, because of the provisions of Article 131, there was no way in which the situation could be corrected if the interpretation of Mr. Barnard was correct.

There is no doubt in my mind that if Mr. Barnard is correct we are facing a major crisis. His submission that the failure to provide for regulation, as far as property was concerned, as a mere oversight which could always be amended is all but reassuring, more particularly bearing in mind that such a correction itself would be, on his argument, an abridging of the provisions of Article 16 and would thus be in conflict with Article 131. No authority was cited by him in support of the proposition that amendment would be possible.

The owner of property has the right to possess, protect, use and to enjoy his property. This is inherent in the right to own property. It is however in the enjoyment and use of property that an owner may come into conflict with the rights and interests of others and it is in this sphere that regulation in regard to property is mostly needed and in many instances absolutely necessary. Such regulation may prohibit the use of the property in some specific way or limit one or other individual right without thereby confiscating the property and without thereby obliging the State to pay compensation. There are many such examples where, to a greater or lesser degree, the use or enjoyment of property, be it movable or immovable, is regulated by legislation and which would, on the argument of Mr. Barnard, constitute a limitation on the right of ownership which will then render such legislation unconstitutional and can be challenged by anyone against whom such legislation is enforced.

A search through the legislative publications of Namibia, as well as legislation taken over from the previous dispensation, support the above statement. Examples of these are, Ordinance 19 of 1957 controlling the eradication of weeds on land; Act 59 of 1968, controlling the sale of agricultural products; Act 3 of 1973, controlling agricultural pests; Act 12 of 1981, controlling the meat industry and Act 24 of 1995 making it compulsory to brand cattle; Act 13 of 1956, controlling animal diseases; Act 76 of 1969, dealing with soil erosion and Act 70 of 1970, prohibiting the subdivision of land under certain circumstances. All the above legislation is aimed at the use of land and agricultural products.

Examples of control over other property are Act 6 of 1998, the sale of alcohol; Act 7 of 1996, the control of arms and ammunition; Ord. 30 of 1967 and Act 22 of 1999, the control over the use of motor vehicles; Act 25 of 1964, control over the price of certain goods and Act 54 of 1956, control over the use of water under certain circumstances.

The above are only examples of the control by the State over the property of its subjects and inhabitants in Namibia. It is in my opinion inconceivable that the founding fathers of our Constitution were unaware of the vast body of legislation regulating the use and exercise of rights applicable to ownership or that it was their intention to do away with such regulation. Without the right to such control it seems to me that it would be impossible for the Legislature to fulfil its function to make laws for the peace, order and good government of the country in the best interest of the people of Namibia. (Art. 63(1) of the Constitution.)

(Continued)

(Continued)

It therefore seems to me that, like the right to equality before the law (Art. 10(1) of the Constitution), the right to ownership in property is not absolute but is subject to certain constraints which, in order to be constitutional, must comply with certain requirements.

In Constitutional Law of India by H.M. Seervai, 3rd Edition, Vol. II, pa. 14.24, the Author, discussing Arts. 19(1)(f), and 31, before these articles were amended, of the Indian Constitution, dealing with the right of citizens to acquire, hold and dispose of property both movable and immovable, pointed out that the sovereignty of the State involves three elements, namely the power to tax, "police power" and "eminent domain." The author further stated that 'police power' was defined as "the inherent power of a government to exercise reasonable control over person and property within its jurisdiction in the interest of general security, health, safety, morals and welfare except where legally prohibited (as by constitutional provision)." The accepted definition for 'eminent domain' is "the power of the sovereign to take property for public use without the owner's consent upon making just compensation." The distinction between an exercise of the State's police power and its power of eminent domain is familiar to South African expropriation law. (See in this regard: Davis, Cheadle and Haysom: Fundamental Rights in the Constitution: p. 243.)

It seems to me that in so far as a comparison can be drawn this distinction between the State's police power and its power of eminent domain is to a certain extent inspirational for Art. 16 of our Constitution and that Art. 16(1) can be compared to the State's police powers and Art. 16(2) its powers of eminent domain. If it is then accepted, as I do, that Article 16 protects ownership in property subject to its constraints as they existed prior to Independence and that Article 16 was not meant to introduce a new format free from any constraints then, on the strength of what is stated above, and bearing in mind the sentiments and values expressed in our Constitution, it seems to me that legislative constraints placed on the ownership of property which are reasonable, which are in the public interest and for a legitimate object, would be constitutional. To this may be added that, bearing in mind the provisions of the Constitution, it follows in my opinion that legislation which is arbitrary would not stand scrutiny by the Constitution.

To the extent set out above I agree with the submissions by Counsel for the respondents. This case, as far as I know, is the first concerning the interpretation of Article 16. I therefore do not want to imply that the requirements in the previous paragraph are a closed list and the final interpretation of the Article. It should in my opinion be allowed to develop as the need arises, if any.

This brings me to Part XV of the Minerals Act. In my opinion the constitutionality of this legislation can be approached on two grounds. Firstly, and as was pointed out previously, mineral rights vested in the State by virtue of Article 100 of the Constitution. As such the inroad into the property right of the landowner is created and sanctioned by the Constitution. In so far as the mineral rights may be transferred by the State into private ownership, it is, as property, also protected by Article 16 of the Constitution.

However, because of the origin of the right, being the Constitution itself, it cannot be said that it is the Minerals Act, or for that matter Part XV thereof, which abolishes or abridges

(Continued)

(Continued)

(see Article 25), the fundamental right of ownership protected under Article 16. The Minerals Act does no more than give effect and content to the right so vested by the Constitution and Part XV contains reasonable provisions for the balancing of this right *vis-à-vis* any other interests or rights, e.g. that of the landowner. Providing, as it does, for a proper hearing, the payment of compensation where necessary and control by the Courts of the land in regard to any order made by the Ancillary Rights Commission, there is no basis upon which the provisions of Part XV can be said to be unreasonable. I also do not understand Counsel for the Appellants submitting that the provisions are unreasonable.

Secondly, and bearing in mind the inherent power of the State over persons and property to exercise reasonable control, Part XV is enacted in the public interest and for a legitimate object and is a reasonable mechanism whereby similar contesting rights are balanced to ensure equal protection of those rights in terms of the Constitution. On this basis also it cannot be said that the provisions of Part XV of the Minerals Act are unconstitutional.

The interpretation of Counsel for the appellants will inevitably lead to the absurdity that it pre-supposes that any regulation in regard to ownership which controls to any extent one or other of the rights in ownership of property will be unconstitutional. In regard to the particular provisions of the Minerals Act the interpretation of Counsel is to the effect that a landowner could, *ad infinitum*, frustrate the rights of the holder of a mineral licence and that notwithstanding the fact that such right was property and was sanctioned by the Constitution itself. The owner, by refusing permission to a licence holder to enter upon his land, can effectively circumvent such right.

Reference was made to the provisions of sec. 107 of Part XV and it was submitted by Counsel for the appellants that the legislature itself was aware that the provisions of this Part of the Act would impact on the rights of ownership and that they therefore attempted to save the provisions by referring to Article 16(2) of the Constitution as authority for the abridgement of ownership rights protected by sec. 16(1). It was however submitted that Article 16(2) could not save the situation as it dealt with expropriation proper and did not cover the instance where only one or other of the rights inherent in ownership of land was diminished. However, on the reasoning set out above it seems to me, as was also submitted by Counsel for the respondents, that the Legislator was perhaps over-cautious in enacting sec. 107. As was further pointed out by Counsel for the respondents the possibility of an expropriation was always present and that it was thought prudent to include reference to Article 16(2) of the Constitution. In my opinion the inference Counsel for the appellants wanted us to draw from the inclusion of sec. 107 is not justified. In any event it is for the Court, and not the Legislator, to interpret the provisions of the Constitution and the Minerals Act.

I am, for the above reasons, of the opinion that the appeal cannot succeed on this ground.

Notes

1. According to Veit et al., the post-independence laws in Africa "emphasized state powers to promote development over the government's duty to protect private property rights." See Veit et al. (2008).
2. Larbi et al. (2004), at p. 117, citing Kotey (2002).
3. Government of Kenya, 1992, Constitution, 75(1)(a) cited in Veit et al. "In Uganda, eminent domain can be used when, 'the taking of possession or acquisition is necessary for public use or in the interest of defense, public safety, public order, public morality or public health' (Government of Uganda, 1995, Constitution, 26(2)(a))." *Id.*
4. In Tanzania, the Land Acquisition Act (LAA) allows for a broader use of eminent domain authority than in Kenya and Uganda, authorizing the president to "acquire any land for. . .any public purpose" (Government of Tanzania 1967, LAA, 2(a) 4(1)). Veit et al. *Id* at p. 11. On the other hand in Uganda and Kenya, the courts have interpreted "public interest" narrowly to mean that the targeted property must be used to promote the general interests of the community, not the particular interests of any private individuals or institutions." *Id* at p. 10.
5. The case that generated so much discussion is *Kelo v City of New London* [545 U.S. 469 (2005)]. See, for example, "It remains to consider why the Supreme Court in *Lingle*, *Kelo*, and *San Remo Hotel* placed such a crabbed interpretation on the Takings Clause and the rights of takings claimants. As discussed above, the Court has abandoned the vision of the Framers, who believed that robust protection of the rights of property owners affirmed liberty by diffusing power and shielding individuals from governmental control" (Ely, 2005).
6. Harrison C. Dunning has an excellent historical account of the issue of compensation in eminent domain actions in countries in SSA, see Dunning (1968).
7. Larbi et al., (2004) at p. 124. The quoted figure is only an approximation.
8. Larbi et al., *Id quoting* statement by the Minister for Local Government and Housing, 1953. Also, see Dunning, (1968).
9. See, for example, Miceli and Segerson (2007). The authors provide an extensive list of literature on the subject. The discussion in this section is based on the Miceli and Segerson paper.
10. See discussion under note 9 *supra*.
11. Issues one, two, and three addressed jurisdictional issues beyond the scope and focus of this chapter.
12. The 9 Appellants are the Namibia Grape Growers and Exporters Association as 1st appellant and the following 2nd through 9th appellants: Namibia Farm Workers Union; FTK Holland BV; Exotic International (PTY) Ltd.; Aussenkehr Town Developers (PTY) Ltd.; Grape Valley Packers (PTY) Ltd.; Namibia Nurseries (PTY) Ltd.; Nagrapex (PTY) Ltd. The Respondents are The Ministry of Mines and Energy as 1st Respondent, and the Mineral Ancillary Rights Commission, and the Northbank Diamonds Limited as 2nd and 3rd Respondents respectively. The Court consisted of Strydom A. as Chief Justice, and O'Linn A and Shivute A. as Associate Justices.

Questions

1. How should compensation be determined when a government takes the land of a farmer for public purposes?
2. How should compensation be determined if the government takes only a part of private property for public use?
3. May the government take private property and give to another party, and be able to justify the public purpose requirement?
4. Would you consider the taking of land under eminent domain to eliminate urban blight a justifiable taking for public purposes?

5. What recommendations do you have to compensate rural communities whose lands have been taken for economic development or public use purposes?

References

de Soto, H., 2003. The Mystery of Capital: Why Capitalism Triumphs in the West and Fails Everywhere Else. Basic Books.

Dunning, H.C., 1968. Law and economic development in Africa: the law of eminent domain. Colum. Law Rev. 68 (7), 1286−1315.

Ely J.W. 2005. "Poor Relation" Once More: The Supreme Court and the Vanishing Rights of Property Owners. <http://object.cato.org/sites/cato.org/files/serials/files/supreme-court-review/2005/9/poorrelation.pdf>.

Government of Ghana, Ghana Constitution, 1992. Article 20 (1).

Kotey, N.A., 2002. Compulsory acquisition of land in Ghana: does the 1992 constitution open new vistas? In: Toumlin, C., Delville, P.L., Traoré, S. (Eds.), The Dynamics of Resource Tenure in West Africa. James Currey, Oxford, pp. 203−214.

Larbi W.O., Antwi A., Olomolaiye P., 2004. Compulsory Land Acquisition in Ghana − Policy and Praxis, Land Use Policy, 21, 115−127, p. 117.

Miceli T., Segerson K., 2007. Private Property, Public Use, Just Compensation: The Economics of Eminent Domain, University of Connecticut, Department of Economics Working Paper Series, Working Paper 2007−12. Indexed at <http://repec.org/> (March 2010).

Veit P., et al. 2008. Chapter 4, Protected Areas and Property Rights: Democratizing Eminent Domain in East Africa, WRI Report, World Resources Institute, p. 11.

CHAPTER 12

Forest Resources

Keywords: Forest resources; sustainable development; wood industry; illegal logging; renewable resource; optimal use of forest resource; net present value; concept of legitimate expectations

12.1 Introduction

The total land area of Africa is approximately 3030 million hectares and the forests area is over 635 million hectares, representing 21.4% of total area and 16% of global forest area (International Union of Forest Research Organizations [IUFRO], 2010).[1] There are several definitions of "forest" and in this book we use the definition offered by the UN Framework Convention on Climate Change (FCCC), "Forest is a minimum area of land of 0.05–1.0 hectares with tree crown cover (or equivalent stocking level) of more than 10–30 per cent with trees with the potential to reach a minimum height of 2–5 metres at maturity in situ." (Noeff et al., 2006).[2] Forests are important in providing livelihoods to several populations, providing protection for important ecological resources including watersheds, soils, fauna, and species of flora (IUFRO, 2010, p. 15). An important role of forests is in maintaining social relationships, for example, community participation in managing unique forest resources, and specification of property rights.[3] Forests are also the sources of traditional medicines derived from plants for over 70–80% of Africans (IUFRO, 2010). Forests provide timber and timber products that are exported by countries to earn foreign exchange.[4] Studies have also examined the importance of forests to the overall well-being of forest inhabitants (IUFRO, 2010).

Concerns about sustainable development, especially after the 1992 Earth Summit (*Rio Summit*), expanding food demand due to population growth, climate change impacts, technological advancement, globalization, and energy availability have rekindled the debate about forest management policy options.[5] These concerns have led to new thinking about what an appropriate forestry policy ought to be. Ghana's forestry policy (1948 Forest Policy), for example, has shifted away from the historical emphasis on timber production for the wood industry and for export markets to a policy that, "recognizes the interdependency of forests and wildlife and the need to take appropriate measures to optimize resource

F.O. Boadu: Agricultural Law and Economics in Sub-Saharan Africa.
DOI: http://dx.doi.org/10.1016/B978-0-12-801771-5.00012-5

utilization, to ensure future supplies of wood and non-wood products and to manage national forest and wildlife resources so as to maintain the ecological balance and the diversity of the natural environment" (Ministry of Wildlife and Forestry, 1994).

Forest laws and policies in African countries are shaped by domestic, regional, and international forces. Ongoing political decentralization policies in some countries are elevating the role of local, community, and cultural practices in protecting forests. While the details of forest laws and policies differ in the various countries, there are some common themes addressing the need to protect forest biodiversity, prevent forest fires, insect pests and diseases, natural disasters and invasive species. Illegal logging, and more recently climate change concerns have become a part of the regulatory and policy regimes governing the forestry sector in African countries.

The physical location of countries, differences in precipitation, temperature, soil, cultural and different property rights relationships have combined to create very diverse forests in Africa. One forest region of major interest is the Congo Basin (Box 12.1).[6] The importance of the region in addressing climate change problems will become even more prominent in the future. Forests clean the air by sucking carbon dioxide from the atmosphere,

---

BOX 12.1 The Congo Basin

Congo Basin Forest Partnership

The Yaoundé Summit

The Congo Basin Forest Partnership (CBFP) originated at the September 2002 World Summit on Sustainable Development in Johannesburg, South Africa; the partnership had its roots in the 1999 Yaoundé Declaration. CBFP is the embodiment of one of the major principles that the declaration was founded upon — *that a regional approach and coordinated policies extending beyond national borders are necessary for the protection of the Congo Basin.*

The partnership is composed of 36 governmental organizations, intergovernmental groups, and NGOs — including the WWF — and is cofunded by a $128 million investment from the United States. The six basin countries in the partnership are — Chad, Cameroon, the Central African Republic, the Republic of Congo, Equatorial Guinea, and Gabon.

Yaoundé Declaration Goals

1. Creation of transboundary protected areas
2. Development of adequate taxation policies
3. Harmonization of national forest policies
4. Enhancement of the participation of rural populations in forest management
5. Enhancement of the participation of economic operators in forest management
6. Adoption of measures to harmonize forest policies with policies in other sectors
7. Tackling of high-level poaching

(Continued)

BOX 12.1 The Congo Basin (Continued)

8. Promotion of industrial wood processing
9. Promotion of national regional forums for the exchange of experiences
10. Adoption of sustainable strategies for financing the forestry sector through both internally and externally generated funds
11. Organization of further summits dedicated to the conservation and sustainable management of forests
12. Revival of the Organization for Wildlife Conservation in Central Africa (OCFSA)

A Brief Overview of Accomplishments Include

- 34 protected areas, 61 community-based natural resource management areas, and 34 extractive resource zones have been zoned for conservation management, covering 126 million acres (51 million hectares) or more than a third of the Congo Basin forests
- More than 11.5 million acres of forest have been certified as sustainably harvested by the Forest Stewardship Council (FSC)
- Over 5000 local men and women have been trained in conservation, land use planning, and related conservation capacities
- Although logging and forest degradation remain serious problems, the overall rate of deforestation in the Congo Basin is estimated to be a relatively low 0.17% — a third of that of Brazil and a 10th of that of Indonesia
- Indicators for the survival of some endangered species are also improving. Despite years of conflict and poaching, the population of mountain gorillas in Virunga, between the Democratic Republic of Congo, Rwanda, and Uganda, is up 17% over a previous census taken 20 years ago
- Studies of landscapes and wildlife have improved conservation planning, exemplified by the discovery of 125,000 previously unknown western lowland gorillas in northern Congo

Source: World Wildlife Federation, The Congo Basin: Large Scale Conservation in the Heart of Africa. *http://www. worldwildlife.org/who/media/press/2009/WWFPresitem13929.html (accessed 10.08.10).*

---

provide food, water, and shelter for people, and support biodiversity and ecological balance. The Congo Basin is a major potential source for improving the physical condition of the world and at the same time supporting the production of goods and services that yield incomes for individuals, especially those in rural areas in Africa.[7]

12.2 The Economics of Forest Resource Management

Economists consider forests as a form of capital.[8] Forests are a renewable resource and their contribution to sustaining life on earth is dependent on both natural regeneration and human management. It is in this context that forest management has emerged as a central theme in the public discussion of sustainable development. Forest land provides several economically useful products such as timber, plant medicinal resources, genetic materials, and more recently as a source for generating carbon credits.[9] Economists are interested in issues surrounding forest resource use and management both from the perspective of market opportunities and sustainability of the environment.

The basic issue in forest economics is the optimal use of forest resources. The key to answering this question is what has been defined as the *rotation interval*, that is, the period between one cut and the next. Certainly, the rotation interval is driven by both biological, and market factors. The optimal use of forest resources is obtained by maximizing the net present value of a stream of benefits. The most popular benefit is timber, but there are also non-timber benefits, such as game animals, eco-tourism, medicinal plants, genetic materials, forest reserves, and ambience. In the simple case of timber, the benefit comes from the plantings and harvestings. Since the measurement is the *net present value*, there is a need to identify costs that ought to be subtracted from the benefits to be maximized. These costs include planting, harvesting, management, transportation, and land.[10] The costs will also include the opportunity cost of money, that is, the interest on money before the timber is harvested.

The determination of optimal use of resources pre-supposes that markets are efficient and functioning properly. This is not the case. As Box 12.2 shows, there is considerable illegal logging of timber[11] in restricted forest areas in Ghana. In addition, poor definition of property rights to land has led to a large number of conflicts leading to a land case backlog in the courts.

BOX 12.2 Fulani Herdsmen Blamed for Chainsaw Operation in the North

Regional News of Monday, 20 July 2009

Tamale, July 20, GNA — Naa Bob Logga, President of the National Forest Forum, has attributed the wanton depletion of the forest through chainsaw operations in the northern sector to the activities of the Fulani herdsmen in the area.

"The Fulani herdsmen are the ones who know where all the big trees for lumber are and they lead the chainsaw operators to cut such trees without paying anything to landowners," he said. Naa Logga said this at a workshop on the International Forest Instrument that is aimed at promoting good environmental practices. The instrument is to strengthen political commitment and actions at all levels for sustainable forest management to enhance the contribution of forest to the development of the nation.

Some 60 participants from Upper East, Upper West and Northern regions attended the one-day forum. Naa Logga said the northern savannah woodland forests play an important role in stopping the desert from moving southwards and that the Volta Basin also needed much protection to ensure that the Volta River does not overflow its banks.

(Continued)

BOX 12.2 Fulani Herdsmen Blamed for Chainsaw Operation in the North (Continued)

Dr Atse Yapi, Food and Agriculture Organization representative, stressed the importance of protecting the forest and gave the assurance that FAO would continue to give assistance and support to protect the industry. Mr. David Guba Kpelle, Notional Project Coordinator, said charcoal burning, chainsaw operations and activities of Fulani herdsmen were some negative actions on the environment and stressed the need for affirmative measures to address the problem.

Source: GNA.

12.3 The Legal and Regulatory Framework of the Forest Sector in Sub-Saharan Africa

Several sub-Saharan African (SSA) countries have produced new forest management laws and policies since 1990, partly as a result of the awareness generated after the *Rio Summit*. In Africa, forest legislation was heightened after the Yaounde Summit of 1999. While there are some common themes, countries have placed different emphasis on integration of forestry into development and environment polices; participation and new role of stakeholders; diversification of management systems; valuing forest products and services; forest conservation; measures for an appropriate institutional framework for the forestry sector.[12]

Forestry laws and policies in SSA are based on international, regional, and domestic practices. There is no general framework for forestry at the international level so forestry issues are addressed in a series of treaties, declarations, and protocols. These international regimes influence domestic policies especially in cases where forest development funding is tied to compliance with the international protocol.[13] The Yaounde Summit is an example of a regional arrangement to protect forests.

For example, Nigeria's forest policy of decentralized government has led to laws and regulations affecting forestry being significantly influenced by local communities (Federal Ministry of Environment (Abuja), 2006). Box 12.3 shows how a lower level court in the Gambia enforced the law on illegal logging. At the domestic level, culture, norms, and social practices play an important role in the protection and management of forests. In most countries, the primary law affecting forestry is contained in the Constitution of the country and supported within the Constitution by a series of Acts and policies.[14]

Several cases have been brought before Courts to enforce laws protecting forests but disposition of cases has been low, for example, in Ghana, as shown in Fig. 12.1. The cases

BOX 12.3 Gambia: Niani District Tribunal Court Fined Men for Logging

The Daily Observer *(Banjul)* 26 February 2014

Lamin Sm Jawo

CRR — The Niani District Tribunal court, presided over by Chief Alh. Pierre Bah on Wednesday convicted and fined one Baboucarr Nyang of Gentehburr village in the sum of three thousand dalasi, in default to serve three months imprisonment, for cutting down live bombax-buonopozenfe and cordyla-africana trees from Niani Maru forest park. The district court further fined the convict to pay another five thousand dalasi for causing damages in the forest. Baboucarr Nyang will pay eight thousand dalasi (D8, 000), in default he will serve six months imprisonment.

The court also fined Abdoulie Njie, Amadou Njie and Haruna Sey, all of Nyakoi village, each two thousand dalasi for transporting the logs to Wassu, in default to serve three months imprisonment. According to the particulars of the offense read by the regional forestry officer for CRR north, Pa Demba Jeng, the accused person in the month of January illegally entered the Niani Maru forest park and cut down life bombax-buonopozenfe and cordyla-africana trees from the forest park which is against the Forest Act.

While passing the judgment, the district Chief Alh Pierre Bah strongly condemned this barbaric act, saying that people in his district should do their utmost to protect the forest cover. He pointed out that illegal activity in the forest has been rampant for the past few months thus leading to court cases. Chief Bah urged the residents of his district to desist from such barbaric acts, adding that the forest is important to our daily lives.

He spoke at length on the importance of the forest, stressing that frequent bushfires and cutting down trees had destroyed a significant portion of the forest cover and contribute equally to the problems in forest resource management. Illegal logging and bush fire, he pointed out, are not only damaging to agricultural products but trees as well; and more severely to the young trees. He thus enjoined people to put preventive and control mechanisms to protect the forest against bush fires and cutting down trees. Representing the forestry department, the regional forestry officer for CRR north, Pa Demba Jeng explained that forest Act section 109 states that whoever in a forest park expect authority of an officer not below the rank of regional forestry officer or an officer mandated by him to cut or take away any forest produce will be charged at least six thousand dalasi (D6,000) which are minimum fines for setting fire or cutting down keno trees without license in the forest. He noted that the said Baboucarr Nyang who entered the forest without permission and cut down life trees is against forest Act and whoever is caught will face the full force of the law. While calling on the people in the area to protect the forest against bushfires and cutting down trees, Nyang cited that more wood is consumed than the forest can replace. He thus challenged the people in CRR south to protect the forest against illegal activities.

Source: http://allafrica.com/stories/201402261523.html.

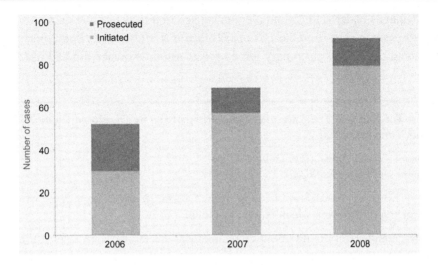

Figure 12.1

Illegal logging cases in Ghanaian courts 2006—2008. *Source: Chatham House: The Royal Institute for International Affairs, London. http://indicators.chathamhouse.org/illegal-logging-cases-ghanaian-courts-2006% E2%80%9308 (accessed 10.01.15).*

that have been brought before courts in SSA have focused on problems of interpreting existing laws and regulations regarding forest resources and land use within the context of the interaction between customary laws, statutes, stool lands, private lands, and government lands. The success of new forestry legislative and regulatory regimes in SSA will depend on how well the regimes address the cutting-edge issues of climate change and forests, energy and forests, community-based forest management, and resolution of forest land ownership conflicts as the value of forest resources (species, recreation, eco-tourism) increases.

The Nigeria Supreme Court's ruling in the case of *Bale Adedire & 6 Ors. v 1. The Caretaker Committee of the Ife Divisional Council; 2. Aderawos Timber Co. Ltd.* introduces the complex question of equitable balancing of the rights of indigenous land owners against those of concessionaires. The case addresses the issue of whether an entity who holds land in trust for a community may grant such land to a private entity.[15] The *Gliksten v Appiah* case involved two private entities. The case addressed the following issues—rights of a concessionaire and rights of a customary land owner; the measure of damages where a concessionaire's operation destroys landowner property (crops); and whether damages were properly awarded given the facts in the case. The *Kwadwo v Sono* case also examined the issue of damages and its measurement. The court recognized that there were customary rights and privileges of the local population to hunt and snare game, to gather firewood for domestic purposes, to collect snails and to till and cultivate farms and plantations on land being used for logging. The Court went further to explain the relationship between the measure of damages under statute, and a court's discretion to determine damages given the language in the statute. The third case, *Nana Hyeaman II v Osei and Others* puts to rest any doubts about the role of customary law in forest resource ownership and use.

Bale Adedire & 6 Ors v 1. The Caretaker Committee of the Ife Divisional Council; 2. Aderawos Timber Co. Ltd

Federal Supreme Court, Nigeria: 28th January, 1963
[Ademla, Taylor and Bairamian, F.J.J.]

Taylor FJ: − This is an appeal from the judgment of Kester J., of the High Court of Ibadan, dismissing the plaintiffs' claim which reads as follows:

The plaintiffs, members of the Ife Community, jointly and severally claim against the defendants jointly and severally:

(i) A declaration that the Deed of "Concession" dated 6th January, 1954, and registered as Instrument No. 16 at Page 16 in Volume 54, Register of Deeds, Lands Registry, Ibadan, purported to have been entered into by the Ife District Native Authority on the one part and 2nd Defendant on the other part is irregular and contrary to equity and liable to be set aside.

(ii) An order to set aside the aforesaid Deed.

(iii) Against the 2nd Defendant, an account of all profits derived pursuant and by virtue of the "Concession" conferred on them by the aforesaid Deed, and an Order that the sum found on such account be paid into Ife Divisional Council Treasury for public use and benefit.

(iv) Against the 2nd defendant, an injunction to restrain them from further exploiting of the "Concession," the subject matter of the aforesaid Deed.

The main ground on which the plaintiffs seek the declaration set out above is contained in paragraph 8 of the S/Claim which states that:

> 8. *Sir Adesoji Aderemi, the Oni of Ife concluded the said instrument on behalf of each side to the purported contract purporting to act in a dual capacity.*

This is followed by paragraph 9 in which it is averred that:

> 9. *The aforesaid Deed of concession is in the circumstances unfair, irregular and contrary to equity and liable to be set aside in that the Oni of Ife acted on both sides in a transaction in which he had a personal interest in possible conflict with his duty as trustee of communal lands.*

The case for the plaintiffs, as can be gathered from the pleadings, is that they are members of the Ife Community and that a lease of certain forest-area in Ife which was the communal property of the Ife Community, measuring some 53 square miles, was granted by the Ife District Native Authority to Aderawos Timber Trading Company Limited for a term of 25 years, subject to the conditions and stipulations contained in the Deed, and marked

(Continued)

(Continued)

exhibit "A" in these proceedings. The plaintiffs further say, and I would here quote paragraphs 3 to 5 of the S/Claim, that:

3. *The aforesaid property was held in trust for the said Community by the Ife District Native Authority, the successor of the rights and duties of which is now the 1st defendant.*

4. *At all dates material to the Deed of "Concession" registered as No. 16 at page 16 in Volume 54 Register of Deeds, Land Registry, Ibadan, Sir Adesoji Aderemi, the Oni of Ife was the trustee of Ife Communal Lands.*

5. *At all times material to the aforesaid Deed of "Concession", Sir Adesoji Aderemi, the Oni of Ife was a Principal member of the Aderawos Timber Company Limited.*

In their defence, both defendants made a general traverse of all the allegations contained in the S/Claim and the 1st Defendant goes on to set up the defence that the plaintiffs' claim to relief is barred or extinguished by s.62 of the Native Authority Ordinance Cap. 140 Laws of Nigeria and/or s.242 of the Local Government Law 1957 which contains identical provisions The 2nd Defendant Company aver in paragraphs 2 to 4 of the S/D that:

2. *The second defendants aver that the forest area comprised in the instrument described in paragraph 2 of the Statement of Claim was duly constituted a forest reserve under the Forestry Ordinance.*

3. *With further reference to paragraphs 2 and 3 of the Statement of Claim the defendants aver that the plaintiffs have no right in or over the area of land in dispute in this case.*

4. *The second defendants aver that the Deed described in paragraphs 2, 4, and 7 of the Statement of Claim was duly made in pursuance of powers vested in the Native Authority by law.*

From the pleadings the issues raised were these:

(1) Have the plaintiffs a locus standi? Have they any interest in the property in dispute which will entitle them to bring this action?

(2) If they have a right of action, did the Oni of Ife act in a dual capacity both as grantor and grantee or as once of the grantors and one of the grantees?

(3) Is the transaction one that a Court of Equity will set aside as being contrary to well established principles or rules governing dealings between parties to a contract or persons placed in a fiduciary or quasi-fiduciary position?

(4) Is the action barred by virtue of s.62 of the Native Authority Ordinance Cap. 140 Laws of Nigeria?

(5) Was the Deed of Concession made in pursuance of power vested in the 1st Defendant?

The appellants have filed seven grounds of appeal with their notice of appeal; and these grounds though couched in different forms, deal with the issues I have set out above. I shall deal with them in the order in which I have set them out.

On the first, the only witness who gave evidence at the hearing was the 1st appellant, and there was no evidence adduced by the respondents controverting the facts deposed to by this witness.

(Continued)

(Continued)

He said inter alia that:

I am Adedire Ogunleye. I am also the Bale (Head) of Adedire Agbedegbede Compound, Ile-Ife. I was formerly an elephant hunter. I was a member of the Hunters Guild at Ile-Ife. My ancestor's name is Ogunleye. I know the forest which is the subject matter of this case. I am a native of Ile-Ife. I am tax payer at Ile-Ife. I was born and bred in that forest. This was before it was made a Forest Reserve.

And under the cross-examination he said that:

I am the Head of the Ogunleye family. Some members of the Ogunleye family still farm in part of the reserve. Some members of the Ogunleye family are still hunting in this part of the reserve.

In addition to this evidence which as I have said is unrebutted, Mr. Kayode for the appellants drew our attention to the 1941 Laws of Nigeria, the Forestry Ordinance No. 38 of 1937 dealing with Ife Native Authority Forest Reserve. In the Second Schedule at page B270 under the Sub-head "Rights to Reside" appear the following provisions:

The holders of farming rights have the right to reside within their respective farm enclaves as described in this Schedule. The following have the right to reside temporarily for the purpose of the enjoyment of their hunting and fishing rights in the following camps respectively: — (There is no right to grow crops round those camps which are not covered by farming rights): Ogunleye and those of his successors who are members of the hunters guild of Ile-Ife and recognized by the heads of that guild as successors to the camps named.

Finally at page B272 certain farming rights in respect of certain areas are also reserved to the Ogunleye family.

Chief Williams has urged that the plaintiffs were unable to show the identity of the Community they represent; that there was no evidence that the Community owned the forest, and that the evidence of P.W.I. was confined mainly to the Ogunleye family, and that even then he is not shown as claiming on behalf of the family. Mr. Kayode in his reply said that the plaintiffs were not suing on behalf of the Community and as far as that point is concerned is content to put his case no further than that the 1st Plaintiff as a member of the Hunters' Guild and head of Ogunleye family has both hunting and "farming rights" in the Ife Native Forest Reserve.

It was further argued by Chief Williams that when the Native Authority takes over the management and control of a forest reserve, it in fact, becomes the owner of such reserve with the result that the plaintiffs have no rights over the area so declared a reserve. Our attention was drawn to various sections and definitions of words, both in the Forestry Ordinance No. 38/37, and Cap. 75 of Volume 3 of the 1948 Laws of Nigeria. I do not intend in this judgement to embark upon a discussion of the rights of the Community as a result of these Ordinances, for, as Mr. Kayode has said, he has not brought this action, the subject matter of this appeal, for and on behalf of the Ife Community. We are here concerned with the rights of the seven individual Plaintiffs/Appellants. As I have said, only the first appellant gave evidence and on his own showing, coupled with the reservation of certain rights to his family of farming, and of hunting rights to a guild of which he is a

(*Continued*)

(Continued)

member, it is beyond doubt that he has certain rights over portions of the conceded area, both as head and as member of the Ogunleye family. In this case on appeal, the 1st appellant as the head of the Ogunleye family is the person in whom by established Native Law and Custom, is vested the management and control of family property. Had exhibit "A" dealt only with rights of cutting timber, the argument might be put forward that the plaintiffs' rights of hunting, fishing and farming would in no way be affected by the felling of logs, but Clause 1*b* gives the 2nd defendants the following additional rights over the whole area:

> to make such roads, railways, and bridges, and to erect such buildings as are necessary within the Concession Area for the felling conversion and extraction of all such logs, timber, and firewood.

In my view, the 1st appellant has in his own right shown that he has an interest in portions of the conceded area, and that the 2nd defendants have been granted rights of felling timber, making roads, railways, bridges, and erecting buildings where required over the whole area conceded.

I now pass on to the second issue. At the hearing of the suit, Exhibit "B" the register of members of the 2nd defendant Company was put in by consent. Folios 4 and 5 show the only two members as being Sir Adesoji Aderemi, Oni of Ife, and one Lasisi S.A. Awoshiyan. The Articles of Association, Exhibit "C" together with the other exhibits tendered at the hearing, that is, G.5, D.4, and D.5 make it abundantly clear that Sir Adesoji Aderemi holds the largest share in this Company and that in 1957 he became a Director on the cessation of one Moronfolu Adedapo Aderemi of the Afin Ife from the directorship of the Company. In the Agreement Exhibit "A" the Testimonium reads thus:

> In Witness whereof the Oni of Ife and Council for and on behalf of the Ife District Native Authority. . . . .

Sir Adesoji Aderemi executed this Deed together with four others for the Oni of Ife and Council. There can therefore be no doubt, and in fact Chief Williams did not seek to argue to the contrary that the Oni of Ife did execute this Deed in a dual capacity being one of the grantors and at the same time the major shareholder of the grantee Company. Both the first and second issues must therefore be resolved in favour of the appellants.

I now come to the third point as to the effect of such a transaction in equity. Mr. Kayode has referred us to the case *of Regal (Hastings), Ltd. v Gulliver* [1942] 1.A.E.R. p. 378 in which Lord Sankey puts the duties and liabilities of persons occupying a fiduciary position as follows (at p. 381):

> As to the duties and liabilities of those occupying such a fiduciary position, a number of cases were cited to us which were not brought to the attention of the trial Judge. In my view, the respondents were in a fiduciary position and their liability to account does not depend upon proof of mala fides. The general rule of equity is that no one who has duties of a fiduciary nature to perform is allowed to enter into engagements in which he has or can have a personal interest conflicting with the interests of those whom he is bound to protect. If he holds any property so acquired as trustee, he is bound to account for it to his cestui que trust.

(Continued)

(Continued)

In the case of *Thomson, in re Thomson v Allen* [1930] 1 Ch. 203 at 214 Clauson J. says:

> *In order to find the principle I have to apply I turn to the judgment of Cranworth L.C. in the House of Lords in the case of* Aberdeen Ry. Co. v. Blaikie Brothers *(1). This case dealt with a fiduciary relation which arose from the fact that the person concerned in the case was the director of a corporate body. "A corporate body," says the Lord Chancellor, "can only act by agents, and it is of course the duty of those agents so to act as best to promote the interests of the corporation whose affairs they are conducting. Such agents have duties to discharge of a fiduciary nature toward their principle. And it is a rule of universal application, that no one, having such duties to discharge, shall be allowed to enter into engagements in which he has, or can have, a personal interest conflicting, or which possibly may conflict, with the interests of those whom he is bound to protect. So strictly is this principle adhered to, that no question is allowed to be raised as to the fairness or unfairness of a contract so entered into." And further: "The inability to contract depends not on the subject matter of the agreement, but on the fiduciary character of the contracting party, and I cannot entertain a doubt of its being applicable to the case of a party who is acting as manager of a mercantile or trading business for the benefit of others, no less than to that of an agent or trustee employed in selling or letting land."*

In this case on appeal before us the evidence, unchallenged, is abundant that the Oni of Ife was the major shareholder, and is the Chairman of the Board of Directors of the 2nd defendant Company who are the grantees. It has further been established by exhibit "A" that the Oni of Ife and four others for and on behalf of the Ife District Native Authority signed in the capacity of grantors. The grantors are, as a result of s.33 (1) of the Forestry Ordinance Cap. 75 Vol. 3 of the 1948 Laws of Nigeria empowered with full rights of control and management of the Native Authority Forest Reserve. While the rights of individuals in the Native Authority Forest Reserve are extinguished, certain rights are by s.27 preserved. The section reads thus:

> *Every right in or over land within an area constituted a Native Authority Forest Reserve under section 22, other than the rights set forth in the order constituting such reserve, shall be extinguished upon the coming into operation of the order, save as provided in section 23.*

I have pointed out in an earlier part of this Judgment the rights possessed by the 1st appellant and the Ogunleye family in certain parts of this reserve. It therefore stands to reason that in the management and control of the whole of the reserved area, the Oni of Ife and Council must exercise their rights or powers in a way that is not inconsistent with or detrimental to the rights and interests reserved in favour of those persons referred to in the 2nd Schedule to the Forestry Ordinance of 1937, and one of whom is the 1st appellant. In my view, the position of the Oni of Ife and Council vis-à-vis the 1st appellant is covered by the two cases to which I have made reference; and equity will not allow him so to put himself in a position in which his interests as the major shareholder of the 2nd respondent Company will be or may be in possible conflict with the duties imposed on him and his Council, as already indicated. He is placed in a quasi-fiduciary position as the Oni of Ife in the Ife District Native Authority which executed the Deed Exhibit "A" through the Oni of Ife and Council.

(Continued)

(Continued)

The fourth issue is whether the claims of the 1st appellant are barred by virtue of s.62(1) of the Native Authority Ordinance Cap. 140 Col. 4 of the 1948 Laws of Nigeria which provides that:

> *When any suit is commenced against any Native Authority for any act done in pursuance, or execution, or intended execution of any such Ordinance, duty or authority such suit shall not lie or be instituted unless it is commenced within six months next after the act, neglect or default complained of, or in a case of á continuance of damage or injury, within six months next after the ceasing thereof.*

There is a proviso to this section, but it is not relevant for the purposed of this appeal. Chief Williams Q.C., for the respondent argues that the granting of the concession was an act done in pursuance or execution of an Ordinance and that as such any Suit in respect thereof must be brought within six months after the 6th of January, 1954. Mr. Kayode Q.C., for the appellants contended that the section did not apply for the following three reasons:

 (i) That the duty imposed on the Native Authority was not one that it was obliged to carry out;
 (ii) Than an act in breach of a trust cannot be one done in the execution of a duty; and
 (iii) That even if these points were resolved against him, the period of six months would not begin to run until six months after the cessation of the damage or injury to the appellants, which he said was a continuous one.

I shall deal firstly with the second point argued by Counsel for the appellants, for, if this is answered in his favour, there will be no need to consider the other points raised by him and by the learned Counsel for the respondent. In dealing with this point, I shall also have covered the fifth issue set out earlier in this Judgment. As has been conceded, the *Native Authorities Ordinance Cap. 140* is identical with the Public Authorities Protection Act 1893. The Learned Author of Halsbury's Laws of England Vol. 23, the 1st Edition says at page 343 that:

> *The act, or omission, need not be directly justifiable, as this would reduce the protection to a nullity. It is sufficient if the defendant has a bona fide belief, even without reasonable foundation, in a state of facts, which, if true would give him a right to act as he does, or if he acts in pursuance of his office and has an honest intention of putting the law into force.*

> *He must, however, have acted colore officii and not for his own benefit; and the act complained of must be in execution of the duty and not merely contemporaneous with such execution.*

Again in paragraph 696 of the same work, the Learned Author says this:

> *In every case the defendant must have acted in good faith.*

In the case of *Sharpington v Fulham Guardians* [1904] 2 Ch. 449 Farwell J. says that:

> *Public authorities now perform many functions which compel them to enter into all sorts of contract; but this is the first time it has been suggested that on any construction the Act could apply to contracts of this nature. The defendants' counsel had not the courage to follow their argument to its logical conclusion, and say that every contract entered into by a public body is within the Act. But every contract entered into by a public body is necessarily in a sense entered into in discharge of a public duty or under statutory authority, for otherwise it would be ultra vires. And I think it would*

(Continued)

(Continued)

necessarily follow, if I decided in the defendants' favour, that every contract entered into by a public authority is an act done in pursuance of a public duty or authority, and therefore is one to which the Act applies. I do not see where to draw the line.

The point was, however, found against the defendant. In my view that must be so, for a contract is not protected merely because it is one entered into by a public authority. As Lord Buckmaster L.C., said in the case of *Bradford Corporation v Myers* [1916] 1. A.C. 242 at 247:

In other words, it is not because the act out of which an action arises is within their power that a public authority enjoy the benefit of the statute. It is because the act is one which is either an act in the direct execution of a statute, or in the discharge of a public duty, or the exercise of a public authority. I regard these latter words as meaning a duty owed to all the public alike or an authority exercised impartially with regard to all the public.

As I have said earlier, the Oni of Ife in particular and the respondents in general did not choose to give evidence at the Court of Trial. On the other hand, the appellants have shown that the Oni of Ife is benefited, as the substantial shareholder in the 2nd respondent Company, by the contract entered into between the respondents. Equity looks upon such a contract with disfavour and in the words of Clauson J., to which I have already referred, equity does not allow questions to be raised as to the fairness of the Agreement for the inability to contract depends not on the subject matter of the Contract, but the relationships of the parties. In my view, the Native Authority Ordinance does not protect an act such as this, done not in execution of an Ordinance, but in pretended execution of an Ordinance. The Ordinance was never meant to allow a member or members of a public Authority to put on the cloak provided by such Ordinance in order to enter into private contracts to the benefits of such member or members. I therefore hold that the defence does not avail the 1st respondent body, and it is not necessary for me to consider the other two points raised by Learned Counsel for the appellants.

In my view this appeal must succeed, the decision of the Court below is hereby set aside, and the following order is proposed:

(1) The deed of "Concession" dated the 6th of January, 1954, and registered as No. 16 at page 16 in Volume 54 of the Register of Deeds, Lands Registry, Ibadan, is hereby set aside.
(2) An account of all profits derived by the 2nd respondent pursuant to and by virtue of the said deed as from the said 6th January, 1954, to the date of this Judgment be rendered by the 2nd respondents within 90 days of this Judgment.
(3) All profits found to have been made by the said 2nd respondents are to be paid into the Ife Divisional Council Treasury.
(4) An injunction is granted restraining the 2nd respondents from further acting under the said Deed of Concession.

The Appellants are entitled to their costs in this Court which I make payable by the 2nd respondents only in the sum of 60 guineas and in the Court below at £290-10s-0d. I also order that the expenses of the taking of the account be borne wholly by the 2nd respondents.

Gliksten (West Africa) Ltd v Appiah

Court of Appeal, Accra, Ghana
27 June 1967

FACTS

This is an appeal by Messrs. Gliksten (West Africa) Ltd. (Plaintiff) after an adverse ruling at the trial court level. Gliksten operated a timber concession over an area which included Appiah's (Defendant) cocoa farms. The concession contained the usual clause for the protection of customary rights which includes farming. Appiah's complaint is that some time in 1959, Gliksten caused extensive devastation to his farms at Sankore No. 2 and Sankore No. 3 as a result of felling timber in the farms and also constructing roads and passes through the farms for the caterpillars which carted the felled timber. All these activities were undertaken by Gliksten without the permission of the Appiah who is now asking for both general and special damages for the unlawful acts by Gliksten. The Court addressed three important questions: (1) what is the legal relationship between a concessionaire and customary land owner; (2) whether general damages can be awarded against a concessionaire (Gliksten) and in favour of the holder of customary rights (Appiah) for acts done by the concessionaire in promotion of the objects of his concession; and (3) whether the special damages awarded in this particular case were properly assessed.

OPINION

(1) *What is the legal relationship between a concessionaire and customary land owner?*

Section 32 (1) and (2) of the Concessions Ordinance, Cap. 136 (1951 Rev.), are so sweeping in their conferment of rights on the concessionaire, that fraud apart, his title is good against the whole world. The provision reads as follows:

(1) A certificate of validity shall be good and valid from the date of such certificate as against any person claiming adversely thereto, and shall be effective in respect of the whole area of land contained by the boundaries stated in such certificate, whether or not any discrepancy exists between such area and the area indicated by the notice and plan of the concession referred to respectively in subsections (1) and (3) of section 8.
(2) A certificate of validity (whether issued under the provisions of this Ordinance or of any Ordinance repealed by this Ordinance) shall be conclusive evidence that all the requirements of the Ordinance under which it was granted or purported to be granted and all matters precedent and incidental thereto have been complied with, and shall not be liable to be impeached by any person by reason of any lack of notice of the boundaries or extent of the land in respect of which it is given, or for any other reason or on any other ground save that of fraud to which the holder of the concession is proved to be a party.

Thus even if the holder of customary rights is on the land before the grant of the certificate of the court validating the concession, the title of the concessionaire takes precedence over the holder of customary rights. And only such rights as are preserved by the law or in the concessions agreement will continue as against the concessionaire.

(Continued)

(Continued)

(2) *Whether general damages can be awarded against a concessionaire*

    a. General damages

Obviously the special damages are in respect of the economic trees, in this case cocoa, which were actually destroyed by the appellants. The general damages cannot but be for the alleged trespass committed by the appellants. The following is the manner in which the learned judge dealt with the question of general damages:

With respect to the plaintiff's claim for general damages in view of the defendants' validated concession over the area, the plaintiff cannot claim prospective damages in the sense of a loss which it may reasonably be anticipated he will suffer thereafter in consequence of the defendants' permanent devastation; it is plain that by virtue of the defendants' validated concession the plaintiff's rights over the area have been extinguished, and therefore, any loss which the plaintiff has suffered as a result of the defendants' devastation or destruction of his cocoa trees must be limited to the time damage was caused in 1959.

It follows that on the facts of this case damages must be measured by reference to the position of the plaintiff at the date when the damage or loss was sustained; any damage done at all, other than loss of cocoa trees, must have been suffered in 1959, and therefore any award must be limited to that period only. This must be so because the plaintiff's claim for general damages is based on the assumption that the defendants committed the trespass by their entry upon the land in 1959.

The plaintiff's claim for general damages is for the wanton and permanent devastation caused to his farm land by the construction of motorable roads and other caterpillar passes through his farm; this amount of damage, which by its nature is general, depends upon the extent and its permanent character. On this issue both the plaintiff and the defendants have disagreed on the evidence. However, in my opinion, it is irrelevant for the purpose of the plaintiff's claim to examine the different views in detail. I have to say this because, as I have already held, it seems to me that the defendants have a validated concession over the area of the plaintiff's farm; that fact is admitted by the plaintiff himself in paragraph (2) of his statement of claim and the only doubt left in my mind on the evidence is that the date on which the certificate of validity was granted to the defendants to operate in the area has neither been mentioned in the statement of defence nor in the evidence of the defendants' representative.

The evidence I have before me is that the defendants entered the plaintiff's farm and caused the devastation complained of sometime in 1959, the same year in which they prepared exhibit 7. I am therefore inclined to find on the evidence led before me that the defendants' concession over the area of the plaintiff's farm must have been validated some time in or about 1959 when they started operations. I find further support for this view I have taken from the fact that the plaintiff himself has not asked for the relief of an order of a perpetual injunction to restrain the defendants from further entering the area in question. In my view any permanent devastation which the defendants might have done to the area could not operate to the detriment

(Continued)

(Continued)

or loss of the plaintiff after 1959. For these reasons, I think the sum of £G200 would be quite sufficient to compensate the plaintiff for any damage suffered as a result of the defendants' trespass to his farm in 1959.

With all due respect to the learned judge, I have the greatest difficulty in understanding the principle upon which he based his award of general damages. To award general damages is to state that a wrong has been committed by a defendant and that these damages are what the law presumes to flow from the wrong complained of. But how can a wrong be committed on land by someone who is entitled to go on the land to carry out the activities which form the subject-matter of the alleged wrong?

The appellants had a timber concession over the area in dispute. The only way they could exploit it was to enter the land, cut and carry away the timber. This must entail some destruction to other vegetation because the felling of the timber in itself would cause some damage to adjacent trees and roads would have to be built for the purpose of transporting the timber. They proceeded to do exactly this. The law then holds them liable in damages for their action. If that is right, one may well ask, of what use is a concession? The law has been attacked at times for being inconsistent, but an inconsistency of this magnitude, if allowed to stand, would deprive the law of all pretence to principle. If the law allows a person to go on land to carry out certain activities, it cannot be a wrong for the person to act in accordance with that permission. I do not think the appellants committed any wrong for which general damages could be awarded.

b. Special damages

Different considerations apply to the award of the special damages for the actual destruction of the cocoa trees. Under section 13 (6) of the Concessions Ordinance, a concession may be certified as valid only if the court is satisfied that the customary rights of natives (and here I use the word as it appears in the Ordinance) are reasonably protected in respect of cultivation, collection of firewood, and hunting and snaring game. As I said earlier, this particular concession contained the usual provision for the protection of these customary rights. The cultivation by Appiah of cocoa and other crops on the land was therefore preserved. In the circumstances it is only reasonable that Appiah be compensated for the actual destruction of such economic trees as he had cultivated in pursuance of his protected rights. Indeed there is no dispute as to his entitlement under this head, for the appellants themselves made an offer on this basis to him. The only dispute here must be as to the quantum.

Appiah refused to accept the offer made, obviously because he thought the £G57 9s. 8d. assessed as the damage, contemptuous. In his evidence he stated that he and some helpers had done an actual count of the trees destroyed. The total they arrived at was 5,164 trees. He therefore claimed £G5,164 damages at the rate of £G1 per tree. The learned trial judge did not accept the number of trees as given by Appiah on the ground that "in such a case one cannot exclude the possibility of exaggeration and the counting cannot be fairly accurate." Appiah also called a surveyor who gave the area devastated on the farm by Gliksten as 7.89 acres. According to this surveyor such

(Continued)

(Continued)

an area should contain approximately 13,744 trees but allowing for thinning and damage done to young cocoa trees due to natural causes the area could contain at least 7,000 cocoa trees. Without rejecting the calculation of the devastated area the learned judge rejected the estimated number of trees: "the surveyor's figures were also not to be relied upon as he said he could not tell exactly the number of trees destroyed," said the learned judge. In the event the method of assessment of damages that the learned judge adopted did not require knowledge of the actual number of trees destroyed.

It has before been the practice of the courts to find out the number of such trees and then translate this figure into money by multiplying that number by the compensation per tree. This monetary conversion element may be anything between seven shillings to one pound per tree. As the learned judge said: "I myself have recently awarded ten shillings per a mature cocoa tree yielding fruits and seven shillings per young cocoa tree in similar cases which have come before me in this court." However, in the instant case he thought it better to abandon this method for a "safer and more satisfactory basis for awarding compensation for damage caused." This is the practice adopted by the Ministry of Agriculture in awarding compensation not for the number of trees, but for the acreage of trees destroyed.

The rationale for this method of calculation is that according to good agricultural practice an acre should contain a certain number of trees to give maximum production and this number would depend on the optimum spacing between any two trees of that species. If one plants the trees too closely and therefore exceeds the number of trees, this will not increase the yield per acre. All other factors remaining the same, the yield per acre would remain the same. In other words a farmer does not increase the yield per acre from his farm by ignoring sound agricultural principles and growing more trees therein than the acre can take. But the result of the old method of calculation of damage is that the farmer with more trees per acre, though not making more out of the acre than his model farming brother, was bound to reap more than his brother out of the devastation of the farm. This, I think, is sufficient justification for the abandonment of the old method. The learned trial judge was right in basing his computation upon the acreage devastated and not the number of trees destroyed.

There was some dispute about the extent of the devastation. Against the figure of 7.89 acres put forward by the surveyor called by Appiah, Gliksten put forward a devastated area of 2.206 acres, of which only 1.4866 acres was supposed to be grown with cocoa. Gliksten's figures were computed by their deputy general manager who is a civil engineer upon details prepared by his assistant after the respondent had pointed out the affected areas to the assistant. Unfortunately for Gliksten, the learned judge took a dim view of the expertise of the assistant who had no professional qualification, "but said he acquired his knowledge on these matters from mere experience." It is not my view that experience always provides a worse teacher than the classroom, but this was a question of fact on which two contrary views were put forward. The acceptance of

(Continued)

(Continued)

one necessarily involves the rejection of the other. Much as I doubt the soundness of the principle by which the one view was preferred to the other, I am not in the position to reverse the finding because there is nothing at this stage which leads me to the conclusion that the other figure is necessarily right. Reluctantly, therefore, I accept the area found by the learned judge as that which was devastated.

Having decided on the area devastated in favour of the respondent the learned judge took the figure of £G50 per acre given by the appellants' witness from the Ministry of Agriculture as the compensation per acre paid to farmers whose farms are destroyed by the Ministry and with it he computed the actual damage to the cocoa trees. His resulting figure was £G394 10s. The respondent in his cross-appeal complains that this figure is too low. I think there is some justification in this complaint. This witness from the Ministry clearly said that his department only dealt with diseased cocoa trees cut down by government. At times the department caused accidental damage to healthy cocoa trees. The £G50 per acre was paid irrespective of the size of trees destroyed and was applicable to both diseased and healthy trees. In any event the compensation paid by government was ex gratia.

To my mind it is quite wrong to use a compensation figure paid by government as an ex gratia award to encourage farmers to replant their destroyed farms which were disease-afflicted; a compensation figure which in any case is based primarily upon the thinking that the trees destroyed were diseased to calculate the damage to a farmer whose trees, of which not one has been suggested to be diseased, have been destroyed by a private person. There was at hand a fairer basis for the calculation. For the appellants had in an exhibit given the Ministry of Agriculture's view of the rate per acre which they thought timber concessionaires like the appellants should pay to farmers. In that exhibit the rate is given as £G100 per acre. I am inclined to the view that this is a fairer assessment for the devastation of a farm of healthy trees. I accordingly accept it in preference to the lower figure used by the trial judge. On that basis the damages for the destruction of the trees should be £G789 (N¢1,578.00).

JUDGEMENT

In the result I would allow the appeal to the extent of having the general damages of £G200 set aside. Otherwise, the appeal fails. The respondent's cross-appeal should succeed to the extent of having special damages of £G789 (N¢1,578.00) substituted for the £G39410s. (N¢789.00) awarded.

Azu Crabbe J.A.: I agree.

Concurring Opinion (Apaloo J.A.): I also agree that the appeal and cross-appeal be allowed to the limited extent proposed in the judgment of Amissah J.A., but as the appeal raised two somewhat novel points, I thought, I should express my concurrence in my own words.

There is, I think, nothing unique about a cocoa farmer bringing an action against a person who caused devastation to his farms seeking general and special damages. In my opinion,

(Continued)

(Continued)

in the cocoa growing areas of this country, such actions are commonplace. The right of an aggrieved farmer to recover both general and special damages against an ordinary tortfeasor for destruction of his farm and cocoa trees has not, in my experience, ever been questioned nor could have been questioned with anything approaching reason. But in this case, the appellants cannot be regarded as tortfeasors in any sense of that word. They are entitled to enter the land by reason of the fact that they are concessionaires and the right which the Concessions Ordinance confers on them is almost all-embracing. As I see it, the only basis on which they could properly be mulcted in general damages must be that their entry upon the land was per se a wrong redressible by the award of pecuniary compensation. If I am right in thinking that a concessionaire commits no wrong in entering land in respect of which he holds a validated concession, then there can be no rationale for awarding general damages.

I think the learned trial judge was himself alive to the problem which the award of general, as opposed to special damages, posed in this case and he attempts in a somewhat verbose passage which my brother Amissah has quoted, to explain the basis on which the award was made. I share the difficulty which my brother Amissah experienced in comprehending the principles on which the learned judge acted. Whatever those principles are, they must, I think, be wrong. I agree therefore that the general damages be set aside.

By common consent, the respondent was entitled to be compensated for the actual damage he sustained by reason of the activities of the concessionaires. Put in familiar terminology, the respondent was entitled to special but not general damages. This might seem curious but the reason for this has been explained in the very lucid judgment of my brother Amissah. I cannot improve upon that reason and I must say that he so effectively expressed my own views that I do not find it necessary to add anything.

With regard to the method of assessing damages for a devastated cocoa farm, two methods were suggested to the learned judge, first, to put a pecuniary value on each cocoa tree destroyed or secondly, to fix a composite sum per acre. The first method which was urged on behalf of the respondent, was the more familiar of the two and the one in which the learned judge could derive a great deal of assistance from decided cases. Indeed, the judge himself said he had assessed damages on that basis in the past. But the judge broke away from the past and expressed preference for the alternative and less familiar method of assessing compensation by the acreage. He did not give anything like a convincing reason for his departure from well-established precedent and I, who like him, have also assessed compensation on that basis in the past, was inclined at the initial stages of this appeal, to think that the newer method of assessing compensation by the acreage, was likely to result in diminished compensation to farmers and was, on that account, less than fair to them.

I think differently now. Having listened to the argument of Mr. Franklin, counsel for the appellants, I am persuaded that the better method of assessment is by the acreage since the yield per acre is the same irrespective of the number of trees. Modern scientific equipment makes it easy for the acreage to be determined with great precision and if all the trees are, as in this case, healthy and of comparable age, the damage could be ascertained with practically

(Continued)

(Continued)

no effort. I venture to hope, that like the learned trial judge in this case, judges faced in the future with the problem of assessing damages for devastated cocoa farms will discard the old method in favour of the new.

With regard to the quantum of the compensation, I agree with the figure proposed.

Kwadwo v Sono

Court of Appeal, Accra
27 February 1984

FACTS

A timber concession agreement between the defendant and the government required the defendant to compensate owners of any fruit-bearing or cocoa trees damaged as a result of the working of the concession; the amount of compensation payable was to be determined by the Administrator of Stool Lands. A cocoa farmer S, brought action for damages against the defendant in respect of, inter alia, cocoa trees destroyed in 1977 as a result of the defendant's operation. An inspection team from the Lands Department accompanied by the parties or their agents found that 11.68 acres and a total of 5,067 cocoa trees had been destroyed. The trial judge however rejected the compensation rate of ¢1.50 per cocoa tree fixed in 1974 by the Chief Lands Officer and which had been applied by the inspection team in calculating the compensation on the ground that it was ridiculously low.

Taking into consideration the fact that the price of a load of cocoa had risen from ¢30 in 1974 to ¢80 at the time of judgment, the annual yield and age of the trees destroyed coupled with the existing economic conditions he fixed the price of a cocoa tree at ¢12 each. The total award therefore came up to ¢60,804. The defendant appealed against the judgment on the grounds that (i) by the provisions of the Concessions Act, 1962 (Act 124), s 16 (4) and (5) the demise to the defendant under the concession agreement extinguished the rights and interests of the local farmers saved what had been reserved under the concession agreement.

Since the concession agreement which was binding on all persons on the land had stipulated that compensation was to be assessed by the Administrator of Stool Lands, the court erred in disregarding his assessment and in taking the age and yield of the trees destroyed in fixing the rate; and (ii) the court erred in not applying the acreage method in assessing the number of trees destroyed. In his reply counsel for the Plaintiff submitted, inter alia, that the assessment by the acreage was a rule of practice not a principle of law and therefore the court was not bound by it. The court found that the defendant did not seriously challenge the evidence in respect of the number of cocoa trees destroyed and that he had given the impression that he had accepted the figure of 5,067. Besides, he subsequently called the common witness who gave that evidence to give evidence for him.

(Continued)

(Continued)

It is provided by the Concession Act, 1962 (Act 124), s 16 (4) and (5) that:

(4) All rights with respect to timber or trees on any land other than land specified in the preceding subsections of this section are vested in the President in trust for the stools concerned.

(5) It shall be lawful for the President to execute any deed or do any action as a trustee in respect of lands or rights referred to in this section.

OPINION

This is an appeal by the defendant at the court below against an award of ¢61,252 special damages for his destruction of cocoa trees and other crops on the plaintiff's farm. The damage occurred in 1977 in the course of the defendant's timber and logging operations on Dormaa stool land, over which the defendant had concession rights. The trial took place at the High Court, Sunyani in March 1980 before Ampiah J who dismissed the additional claims for general damages for "capsid infestation, rehabilitation and other incidental damage as a result of the defendant's acts." The plaintiff's claim for an order of perpetual injunction restraining the defendant from further felling on the plaintiff's farm was similarly dismissed. This part of the decision is not questioned. For on authority where a person enters upon the land of another by lawful authority or license, acts done in pursuance of the authority or licence cannot be the subject for general damages in trespass: see *Gliksten (West Africa) Ltd v Appiah* [1967] G.L.R. 447, CA.

Different considerations, however, apply to the award of the compensation now appealed against. Exhibit 1, the defendant's concession agreement, was executed on 31 May 1965 and was obtained by virtue of the Concessions Act, 1962 (Act 124), hereafter referred to as the Act. Both at the trial and in this court, the rights conferred on the defendant by exhibit 1 and the exceptions in favour of the local inhabitants were not disputed. In particular that exhibit 1 preserves the customary rights and privileges of the local population to "hunt and snare game, to gather fire-wood for domestic purposes only, to collect snails ... and to till and cultivate farms and plantations on the demised land." It is also conceded that any farmer on the demised land whose crops suffer damage as a result of the timber operations of the concessionaire is entitled to compensation. Indeed, when the plaintiff complained of damage to his crops, the defendant was ready to offer compensation, but for lack of agreement on the figures. Consequently, upon the case coming before the court, a consent order requesting the Regional Lands Department to inspect and assess the extent of damage to the plaintiff's crops was made at the start of the proceedings.

The plaintiff by counsel filed inspection instructions, and the parties attended on the inspection team. In due course the Lands Department submitted its report, exhibit A, to the trial court, to be followed by evidence from the senior valuation officer, who led the inspection team. What is here relevant is that the parties accepted and the trial court found that an area of 11.68 acres of the plaintiff's cocoa farm was damaged or destroyed involving a total of 5,067 cocoa trees. His evidence, however, that he valued the 5,067 trees at ¢7,351.70, a figure which had been approved by the Chief Lands Officer, Accra became a

(Continued)

(Continued)

bone of contention. In his judgment the learned trial judge rejected the compensation rate of ¢1.50 per cocoa tree fixed in 1974 by the Chief Lands Officer and which the witness had applied. The learned judge was of the opinion that it was ridiculously low and that that rate did not reflect the economic realities of the times. There was evidence from the witness that it was the policy of the Chief Lands Officer to have compensation rates reviewed periodically and to bring them in line with economic trends in the country. That evidence was contained in exhibit X, the relevant paragraph of which reads:

(2) In the past, compensation rates as used in the department were restricted to land acquisition cases where the government acquired land and crops. From the basis of calculation in arriving at the present (1974) rates it is clear that prominence has been given to the estimated useful life of every crop in question and this will necessarily imply a major change in the valuation assessments in land acquisition cases where crops are also encountered and compensation paid separately therefor.

Exhibit X further adds in paragraphs (4) and (5):

(4) I shall be grateful if you give the matter your serious consideration and let me have your comments without prejudice to the operations of the new rates with effect from 1 March 1974 ...

(5) A review of the crop compensation rates in respect of the under mentioned crops is still being undertaken and the finally agreed rates will be communicated to you in due course ...

But even at the time of the trial in 1980 no such review had taken place, and the rate of ¢1.50 for a cocoa tree still prevailed. The witness was unable to tell on what basis the rates in exhibit X were arrived at, and the learned judge was obliged to rely on the economic trends in the country to work out a reasonable rate when he delivered himself thus:

"The price of cocoa has rocketed so high from ¢30 to almost ¢80 per load at the time of the incident. Looking at the age, and the annual yield of the destroyed cocoa, coupled with the economic conditions existing at the time, I think a price of ¢12 per cocoa tree would not be unreasonable. I would therefore award the plaintiff ¢60,804 damages for the cocoa trees damaged."

Awards for other crops destroyed brought up the total amount to the ¢61,252 mentioned earlier; but it is as to the ¢60,804 for the cocoa trees that the appeal is directed. Mr. Totoe, counsel for the defendant, has attacked this award on the ground that: "Because clause 2 (1) of the concession agreement, exhibit 1, stipulates that compensation payable to farmers for damaged crops should be assessed by the Administrator of Stool Lands the court erred in disregarding the assessment by the administrator." The burden of learned counsel's argument was that compensation under the concession was limited to payment of the actual value of the crops damaged, which is the rate as fixed and recommended by the administrator; that any consideration of age or yield of the trees affected was in the nature of prospective damages.

To this, Mr. Amofa's reply was that the proposition that the court was limited to the administrator's determination amounted to denying the citizen access to the courts in seeking

(Continued)

(Continued)

relief where he has suffered damage to his crops by the default of another, insofar as the court could not act according to its own lights and discretion. That, learned counsel for the plaintiff contended, was contrary to the Constitution, 1979 which gave the judicial power of the State to the courts.

Now clause 2 (1) of exhibit 1 relied on by Mr. Totoe enjoins the defendant:

> To compensate the owner of any fruit-bearing trees or cocoa trees growing thereon for any damage done by the lessee or his agents or contractors. Provided always that the amount of compensation payable shall be that determined by the Administrator of Stool Lands.

Mr. Totoe also refers to the provisions of the Concessions Act, 1962 (Act 124), s 16 (4) and (5) as the source of competency of the administrator. Those provisions recited that:

> (4) All rights with respect to timber or trees on any land other than land specified in the preceding subsections of this section are vested in the President in trust for [the] stools concerned.
>
> (5) It shall be lawful for the President to execute any deed or do any act as a trustee in respect of lands or rights referred to in this section.

What Mr. Totoe says is that by force of the above subsections of the Act, a demise to the defendant of the specified land overrides and extinguishes the rights and interests of the local farmers save as to what interests are preserved or of compensation payable therefor. This position, he submitted, was brought about because the concession agreement, exhibit 1, was binding on all persons on the demised land. Consequently he added that since 1962 the assessment of compensation had been given to or determined by the administrator. Mr. Totoe found support in a passage in the judgment in the case of *Gliksten (WA) Ltd v Appiah* (supra) when at 449, the court said:

> Thus even if the holder of customary rights is on the land before the grant of the certificate of the court validating the concession, the title of the concessionaire takes precedence over the holder of customary rights. And only such rights as are preserved by the law or in the concessions agreement will continue as against the concessionaire.

Besides having the land vested in him, I think the provisions of section 16 (4) and (5) of Act 124 do no more than empower the President to grant leases for timber rights only. Such a demise affects a person like the plaintiff only insofar as the concessionaire's rights extend as well to timber standing in the plaintiff's farm. This is so because the lease was for the entire specified land. And it is for this reason that the entry by the defendant into the plaintiff's farm was held not to be a trespass. But the defendant's right of precedence to timber on the land does not in any way abridge the plaintiff's legal rights and protection to his crops.

It may be observed with interest that the Act does not spell out the customary rights, privileges and interests of the local population over the demised land, as did the Concession Ordinance, Cap 136, s 13 (6)–(9). Nonetheless those rights, in my view, are legal. Not because they are declared so by an enactment but because they are

(Continued)

(Continued)

immemorial customary rights and privileges which members of the local population of the stool land have always enjoyed; whether their possession of the land was by right of occupation or by permission from the stool. Specifically those customary rights, in my opinion, are preserved not because they are excepted from the defendant's lease, exhibit 1, but rather that they are rights of the subjects which cannot be alienated by the stool for which the President acts.

Further if it were noted that exhibit 1 was contractual only between the President and the defendant, there could be no question that the plaintiff, was not bound by its terms. Consequently, I think the plaintiff's redress for the damage to his crops was not dependent on the terms and conditions of the lease, but based on his common law rights against an infringement of his proprietary interest. I therefore take the view that the onus is on the defendant, and not on the plaintiff, to show that the compensation clause, 2 (1) of exhibit 1, was binding on the plaintiff. I am satisfied that learned counsel has not been able to show that the provisions of section 16 (4) and (5) of Act 124 import a power for the administrator to determine the compensation rates. It follows that the trial court was not bound by the compensation clause in exhibit 1. In my opinion, the learned trial judge's approach to the assessment of the special damages was right in principle; save as to what we shall say on the quantum.

The appellant's second ground of appeal was that "because the acreage method of assessing the special damages could be applied in the instant case the court erred in not applying that method." Computation by the acreage of the number of cocoa trees destroyed in claims for damages appears to have been in recent times first ventured upon in these courts in the unreported case of *Appiah v Glikstein (WA) Ltd* before Lassey J (as he then was) at the High Court, Sunyani. The merits of this mode of calculation are lucidly explained in the judgment of this court delivered by Amissah JA in *Glikstein (WA) Ltd v Appiah* (supra) on the appellate hearing of that case. At 452−453 of the judgment this is what the court said:

> The rationale for this method of calculation is that according to good agricultural practice an acre should contain a certain number of trees to give maximum production and this number would depend on the optimum spacing between any two trees of that species. If one plants the trees too closely and therefore exceeds the number of trees, this will not increase the yield per acre. All other factors remaining the same, the yield per acre would remain the same. In other words a farmer does not increase the yield per acre from his farm by ignoring sound agricultural principles and growing more trees therein than the acre can take. But the result of the old method of calculation of damage is that the farmer with more trees per acre, though not making more out of the acre than his model farming brother, was bound to reap more than his brother out of the devastation of the farm. This, I think, is sufficient justification for the abandonment of the old method.

I however, agree as advanced by Mr. Amofa, that assessment by the acreage is a rule of practice and not a principle of law, and that this court is not bound to follow it as precedent. But I also think that where a rule of practice has the merit of scientific approach, and thus more likely to result in greater fairness to the parties, the lawyer's conservatism might do well to employ science as a handmaid of legal reasoning to advantage. I would

(Continued)

(Continued)

permit myself to add quickly that care must always be taken that a rule of practice should not become a rule of thumb with a danger to override any conflicting general principles of law relating to damages in such claims. In the instant case, two items of instructions filed by counsel for the plaintiff were to request for (a) acreage of the damage caused either by loading, felling or by way of caterpillar, etc, trucks; and (b) estimated number of cocoa trees damaged.

The acreage of 11.68 and the total of 5,067 damaged trees found by the court were based on the evidence of the leader of the inspection team. Questioned as to how he arrived at the number of cocoa trees, this witness deposed: "where cocoa measures 10′ × 10′ we have 400 cocoa trees or approximately 400 cocoa trees in 1 acre..." This evidence was not seriously challenged. Indeed, the defendant was present at the inspection by his agent, and all along the impression was given that the defendant accepted the figure of 5,067. Besides, the defendant later called this very witness, after his evidence as a common witness, to give evidence for him. That I think shows faith in the credibility of that witness.

Assessment by the acreage as I understand it is a means of ascertaining the number of trees affected in a case of devastation to crops. If that number is agreed upon by the parties, then I do not think there is room for preference between actual numeration and calculation by the acreage. In the *Appiah* case (supra) the respondents disputed the figures obtained by actual count, and so arose the question of choice between actual counting and computation by the acreage. In the instant case, the learned trial judge was not faced with any choice because there was after the inspection no dispute on the figure of 5,067 arrived at. I am of the opinion that there is no substance in this complaint.

To revert to the award of special damages of ¢60,804, it is complained, in essence, that the learned judge acted on wrong principles when he took into account the age and annual yield of the cocoa trees. It is said that a consideration of those matters made the award partake of prospective damages, which will then be general damages.

I think there is no argument that here it is the actual value of the cocoa trees that the plaintiff is entitled to as compensation. And on principle, a plaintiff is required to prove such loss. But the evidence in support will of course depend on the nature of the subject matter among other things. What is the price of a cocoa tree on the market? How many loads does a 5-year-old tree bear as compared with a 10-year old? These questions seem to defy practical answers; but certainly the value of a 5-year-old bearing tree may differ from that of a fully matured tree. These I think are factors which might help determine the economic usefulness of the crop and its pecuniary value. For that is what the plaintiff wants as compensation. The price per load of cocoa is a useful index of the value of trees lost, and that cannot be divorced from age and yield. In my opinion, the learned judge was right in principle in considering the factors as he did. His reasoning cannot be faulted.

(Continued)

(Continued)

By the nature of the subject matter, the evidence in support of value called for the exercise of the judge's discretion in arriving at a fair and reasonable rate. While we do not seek to substitute our discretion for his, it seems to us that the figure arrived at was excessive and therefore an erroneous assessment of damage. We think the rate of nine cedis per tree and not twelve cedis would be a fair and reasonable figure. In the result, the award of ¢60,804 is reduced by ¢15,201 and the sum of ¢45,603 is substituted for the judgment in favour of the respondent here. Save as to that variation the appeal would be dismissed.

JUDGMENT

Appeal dismissed. Damages reduced.

Nana Hyeaman II v OSEI and Others

High Court, Sekondi
6 April 1981

FACTS

The plaintiff, the divisional chief of Gwira Banso in the Gwira Traditional Area, instituted an action for the cancellation and setting aside of a timber lease of a parcel of land attached to his stool. Counsel for the defendant and co-defendants, however, raised a preliminary objection as to the capacity of the plaintiff to institute such an action on the ground that by virtue of the Concessions Act, 1962 (Act 124), particularly section 16 thereof, only the President could institute such proceedings on behalf of the stools concerned. Counsel argued in concert that the effect of the words "vested in the President in trust for the stools concerned" used in Act 124, s.16 was to take away the tradition-clothed powers of chiefs over stool lands.

OPINION

The preliminary question that erupted in this proceeding is whether the plaintiff, who is the divisional chief of Gwira Banso in the Gwira Traditional Area, has capacity to institute an action for the cancellation and setting aside of a timber lease of a piece or parcel of land attached to his stool. Counsel for the defendants and co-defendants submitted that there is no such capacity and referred to the Concessions Act, 1962 (Act 124) in substantiation of their submission, particularly section 16 thereof. The answer to the question therefore requires the interpretation of section 16 of Act 124 which provides:

> 16. (1) All lands referred to in subsection (2) or subsection (4) of section 4 of the Forests Ordinance (Cap. 157) and which have been constituted or proposed to be constituted as forest reserves under that Ordinance and all lands deemed to be constituted as forest reserves under subsection (7) of this section are hereby vested in the President in trust for the stools concerned:

(Continued)

(Continued)

Provided that all rights, customary or otherwise, in such lands validly existing immediately before the commencement of this Act shall continue on and after such commencement subject to this Act and any other enactment for the time being in force.

(2) All lands which in the future shall be proposed to be constituted as forest reserves under the Forests Ordinance (Cap. 157) shall become vested in the President in trust for the stools concerned with effect from the date of the publication of the notice relating to such land and prescribed under section 5 (1) of that Ordinance.

(3) Any land, other than land referred to in the preceding subsections, subject to the Administration of Lands Act, 1962 and in respect of which rights have been granted with respect to timber or trees under any concession and in force immediately before the commencement of this Act are vested in the President in trust for the stools concerned, subject to the terms of the concession, this Act and any other enactment for the time being in force.

(4) All rights with respect to timber or trees on any land other than land specified in the preceding subsections of this section are vested in the President in trust for stools concerned.

(5) It shall be lawful for the President to execute any deed or do any act as a trustee in respect of lands or rights referred to in this section.

(6) Any revenue from lands or rights vested in the President under this section or derived under subsection (11) shall be collected, paid in and disbursed as provided by the Administration of Lands Act, 1962.

As seems clear from their plausible submissions, counsel for the defendant and co-defendants were apparently influenced in their view by the magic words "vested in the President in trust for the stools concerned" used in the section and were thus induced to opine that the Act had in effect taken away the tradition-clothed powers of our chiefs over stool lands. They submitted in concert that only the President could institute proceedings, as trustee, on behalf of the stools concerned. That there has been in the pre- and immediate post-independence decades, a sustained legislative incursion into the traditional powers of our chiefs over their stool lands needs hardly be over-emphasised. The policy rationale assignable to this piecemeal legislative nibbling of the authority of our chiefs has been the compelling need to ensure efficient administration of stool lands for the public benefit because land has ever been and still is the fulcrum to our economic survival. It seems therefore necessary to throw a searchlight on the amplitude of the relevant statutes and case law in order properly to appraise their impact and effect on the traditional authority of our stools.

In *Ofori Attah II v Mensah* [1957] 3 W.A.L.R. 32 at pp. 34–35, Ollennu J. (as he then was) said:

In my opinion the powers of management of stool lands given to local government bodies by statute and the statutory provisions that transfer of any stool land in a state should be with the consent of the state council has not changed the native custom as to who is entitled to litigate in respect of stool lands. The position remains as it was; title in stool land is vested in the particular stool, and definitely it is only the occupant of that stool who is vested with authority to litigate the stool's title to the land.

(Continued)

(Continued)

The next important legislation was the Stool Lands Control Act, 1959 (No. 79 of 1959), s.7 of which transferred to the Governor-General the powers of urban and local councils over stool lands. In interpreting this section, Akainyah J. (as he then was) held in *B.P. (West Africa) Ltd. v Boateng* [1963] 1 G.L.R. 232 at p. 237 that the statute did not take away the ownership of stool land from the stools concerned. The Administration of Lands Act, 1962 (Act 123), followed in sequence and by its section 1, the management of all stool lands was vested in the minister to whom functions under the Act were assigned by the President. On the authority of *Ofori Attah II v Mensah* (supra), the management of stool lands by the minister did not imply that the rights of the occupants of a stool land had been taken away by the Act. Three sections of the Act are most germane to our inquiry. These are sections 2, 7, and 8 respectively of Act 123 which read as follows:

2. The President may direct the institution or defence of, or intervention in, any proceedings relating to any Stool land in the name of the Republic, on behalf, and to the exclusion, of any Stool concerned, and may compromise or settle any such proceedings...

7. (1) Where it appears to the President that it is in the public interest so to do he may, by executive instrument, declare any Stool land to be vested in him in trust and accordingly it shall be lawful for the President, on the publication of the instrument, to execute any deed or do any act as a trustee in respect of the land specified in the instrument ...

8. (1) Any disposal of any land which involves the payment of any valuable consideration or which would, by reason of its being to a person not entitled by customary law to the free use of land, involve the payment of any such consideration, and which is made,

(a) by a Stool;

(b) by any person who, by reason of his being so entitled under customary law, has acquired possession of such land either without payment of any consideration or in exchange for a nominal consideration, shall be subject to the concurrence of the Minister and shall be of no effect unless such concurrence is granted.

In my opinion, any interpretation of sections 2, 7, and 8 of Act 123 to the effect that the Act takes away completely the ownership rights of a stool to lands attached to it would be an unwarranted detour from well-articulated judicial opinion on the legislative intention in enacting such laws. A careful look at the words "in trust" or "as a trustee" used in sections 2 and 7 of Act 123 reveals that they are not intended to mean that the stools have no rights whatsoever over stool lands. For example, under section 8 of the Act, the stool can make grants of stool land vested in the President. The only fetter on this right is that the concurrence of the minister is required to validate the grant. If the legislature intended that all rights vested in a stool should be taken away, it would not have enacted section 8 of the Act. In *Frimpong v Nana Asare Obeng II* [1974] 1 G.L.R. 16 at p. 20, Edward Wiredu J. (as he then was) had this to say:

... I am of the view that section 2 of Act 123 does not take away the inherent right of occupants of stools to maintain actions in respect of their respective stool lands. The very wording of section 2 of Act 123 recognises this fact...

(Continued)

(Continued)

Now it becomes crystal clear, when section 2 of Act 123 is read in conjunction with sections 7 and 8 of the Act, that the words "in trust" used in section 7 do not exclude the inherent right of stools to maintain actions in respect of stool lands even though the Act says that stool lands are vested in the President in trust for the stool. The views of Edward Wiredu J. (as he then was) on the construction of Act 123 are unexceptionable and I fully indorse them.

Having perhaps hopefully succeeded in prying into the ambit of statutory provisions affecting stool lands, the problem facing us becomes a good deal narrower than it initially was because the statutes so far examined bear close affinity to Act 124. The juxtaposition of Acts 123 and 124 is in itself of tremendous significance, for they reflect a continuing legislative response to one identifiable problem, namely how best stool lands can be administered to optimum public advantage. Under section 16 (3) of Act 124 all lands subject to Act 123 and all lands referred to in the subsection are vested in the President in trust for the stools concerned. The sole purpose of the Act was to provide that the Concessions Ordinance, Cap. 136 (1951 Rev.), with certain exceptions spelled out in section 1 of the Act shall cease to apply to stool lands. The Concessions Act therefore did not in any way affect the operation of Act 123. Rather, the Act extended the Presidential trusteeship idea to cover lands subject to existing or future concessions.

There is one sure way of grasping the nettle in this case and it is by no means difficult. One just has to identify the areas of material similarities in the congeries of statutes affecting lands. I prefer to subsume them under what I call "praedial legislation," that is to say, legislation pertaining to land. It becomes obvious, if we adopt the purpose-oriented policy of statutory interpretation, that the legislature had never had the intention of depriving the stools of this country of their inherent right to ownership of stool land, notwithstanding statutory provisions entrusting stool lands to the President for the stools. This is made manifest by the fact that in one statute, Act 123, there is a provision in section 8 to the effect that stools can make grants of stool lands even though the same lands may have been entrusted to the President. The meaning of such words as "vested in the President in trust for the stools concerned" should be construed univocally in both Acts 123 and 124. The provisions are "in pari material" and ought to bear the same construction. As Lord Mansfield enunciated with typical lucidity in *R. v Loxdale* [1758] 1 Burr. 445 at p. 447:

> *Where there are different statutes in pari materia though made at different times, or even expired, and not referring to each other, they shall be taken and construed together, as one system, and as explanatory of each other.*

After an incisive study of the provisions of Acts 123 and 124, I am impelled irresistibly to the firm conclusion that there is nothing, open or esoteric, in the two statutes which would suggest, even faintly, that the legislature by enacting that stool lands including those subject to existing or future concessions shall be vested in the President in trust for the stools concerned intended that the stools should be denuded of their inherent rights to ownership of stool lands. The statutory powers of the President must be

(Continued)

(Continued)

construed as running side by side with the powers of the stools as the allodial owners of stool lands.

No doubt a stool land can lawfully be taken away to a concessionaire under the provisions of the Concessions Act, but before such a process is brought into fruition, the right of the stool to deal with the land in a manner not inconsistent with the provisions of Act 123 still persists. For example, the stool can sue in trespass to the land. It follows that the occupant of the stool can without any inhibition challenge the validity of a purported concession affecting his stool land. This is exactly what the plaintiff in this case seeks to do. He cannot be hamstrung by facile arguments that stool lands are vested in the President. For these reasons I hold that the objection to the capacity of the plaintiff is untenable and is accordingly overruled. The plaintiff is awarded ¢300 costs.

JUDGMENT

Preliminary objection overruled.

Notes

1. Inland water resources cover over 62 million hectares with the rest of the area classified as "other wooded land" or "other land." (International Union of Forest Research Organizations, 2010, page 9 (Table 4).
2. "A forest may consist either of closed forest formations where trees of various storeys and undergrowth cover a high proportion of the ground or open forest. Young natural stands and all plantations which have yet to reach a crown density of 10–30 per cent or tree height of 2–5 meters are included under forest, as are areas normally forming part of the forest area which are temporarily unstocked as a result of human intervention such as harvesting or natural causes but which are expected to revert to forest; [FCCC/CP/2001/13/Add.1] (Noeff et al., 2006, Page 3).
3. "The primary functions of forests globally include production (34.1% of area), protection of soil and water (9.3%), conservation of biodiversity (11.2%), multiple purposes (33.8%), and other unknown functions (7.8%)" (IUFRO, 2010, p. 16).
4. Revenues from the forest sector are key components of the balance of payments of several African economies. It is estimated that, on average, forests account for 6% of Africa's GDP (NEPAD, 2003). The contribution of the forest products sector to Africa's GDP was 1.5% in 2000; in monetary terms this amounts to about US$7.7 billion. Exports of timber products contribute more than 60% of GDP in Central and Western Africa. In Ghana, the forest sector contributes about 6% of GDP, while in Uganda this figure is as high as 23% (IUFRO, 2010, p. 16).
5. Sustainable development was defined by the Brundtland report as "development that meets the needs of the present without compromising the ability of the future generations to meet their own needs" (WCED, 1987).
6. The Congo Basin holds up to one-quarter of the world's tropical forests. Its mosaic of ecosystems—rivers, forests, Savanna, swamps and flooded forests—are teeming with life, the region harbors lush lowland forests, highland Montane forests, swamp forests, and Savanna and grasslands. Its dense forests extend almost 500 million acres, spanning the boundaries of Cameroon, the Central African Republic, the Democratic Republic of the Congo, Equatorial Guinea, Gabon and the Republic of the Congo. The Congo Basin is home to the most spectacular and endangered wildlife in Africa. There are 1000 bird species and 400 mammal species. Most of the world's forest elephants and great apes including chimpanzees, bonobos, and lowland and mountain gorillas, inhabit its forests. The Congo River is one of the last intact tropical rivers in the world, boasting 700 species of fish (World Wildlife Federation).

7. "The Congo Basin forests are estimated to contain between 25–30 billion tons of carbon. This is roughly equal to 4 years of current global anthropogenic carbon dioxide emissions. Protecting an additional 1% of forests in Central Africa would preserve 230 million tonnes of carbon, or about a third of the UK's annual greenhouse emissions, and which in today's market is worth more than USD 500 million" (CARPE, 2005).

8. The World Commission on Forestry and Sustainable Development has succinctly stated, "Forests are a capital asset that sustains the global habitat. To manage this capital for the public good, societies need indicators of the status of the world's forests, and estimates of their ecological and socio-economic value" (World Commission on Forest and Sustainable Development, 1999).

9. The UN Framework Convention on Climate Change (UNFCCC) stressed the linkage between forest resources and climate change under Article 4 of the Convention, "Article 4, paragraph 1(d): Promote sustainable management, and promote and cooperate in the conservation and enhancement, as appropriate, of sinks and reservoirs of all GHGs not controlled by the Montreal Protocol, including biomass, forests and oceans as well as other terrestrial, coastal and marine ecosystems." See United Nations (2006). For a scholarly discussion between forests as capital resources, rural economic development, and climate change, see Saunders et al. (2002).

10. These costs are analogous to what one would find in a partial budget for crops in farm management.

11. Illegal logging has been defined as, "when timber is harvested, transported, bought or sold in violation of national laws." See University of Copenhagen (2008). The brief concluded that "illegal logging constitutes a serious problem in Ghana. The annual harvest is conservatively estimated at approximately 3.3 mm^3 against the annual allowable cut 1.0 mm^3, that is, 70% of the annual harvest in Ghana is illegal."

12. The themes based on which forestry laws and policies are compared is based on a study by Kohler and SchmithÜsen (2004).

13. The International Tropical Timber Agreement that entered into force in 1997 controls sale of timber in international trade. Another example of an International Law that affects domestic legislation is the Convention of Biological Diversity (CBD) affecting forest management to protect against loss of plants and animals. For an excellent review of International Forestry Laws, see Lesniewska (2005).

14. Ghana's Acts include: the *Timber Resources Management Act* 1997 (Act 547); the *Forestry Commission Act of 1999* (Act 571); and the *Timber Resources Management Act 617 (Amendment) Act, 2002* (Act 617). Zimbabwe uses the *Revised Forest Act*, 1996 and the *Communal Lands and Forest Produce Act*; Malawi uses the *Forestry Act* 1997; and Zambia uses the *Forestry Act*, 1999. See Eastaugh (2010).

15. The problem in protecting the interests of indigenous communities when governments grant lands for large-scale developments in Africa will intensify. One source of tension is climate change where some have advocated the setting aside of large tracts of land for use in a *Clean Development Mechanism* to capture carbon credits as proposed under the Kyoto Protocol. Saunders et al. (2002) raised the critical issue of how to safeguard the interests of the indigenous people who own the forests in developing countries when these forests are transformed from carbon property into social capital, and the general problem of property and land rights. See Saunders et al. (2002).

Questions

1. What does the Constitution of your country say about customary law, chieftaincy, and land rights?

2. There is always the tension between rural people and central government over the distribution of benefits from forest resources. How in your opinion may countries achieve equitable distribution of resources?

3. Some have suggested that there is both policy failure and market failure in the management of forest resources. What is your understanding of these failures and how best to address them.

References

CARPE, 2005. Forests of the Congo River Basin: A Preliminary Assessment. Balmar, Washington, DC, <http://assets.panda.org/downloads/congo_forest_cc_final_13nov07.pdf> (accessed 10.08.10.).

Eastaugh, C., et al., 2010. Climate Change Impacts on African Forests and People. IUFRO Occasional Paper No. 24, Austria, Vienna.

Federal Ministry of Environment (Abuja), National Forest Policy. 2006, p. 18. (Extracted from <http://www.fao.org/forestry/15148-0c4acebeb8e7e45af360ec63fcc4c1678.pdf> (accessed 21.09.15).

International Union of Forest Research Organizations (IUFRO), 2010. Climate Change Impacts on African Forests and People. IUFRO Occasional Paper No. 24, Austria, Vienna.

Kohler, V., SchmithÜsen, F., 2004. Comparative Analysis of Forest Laws in Twelve Sub-Saharan African countries. FAO Legal Papers online #37. <http://www.fao.org/legal/Prs-OL/lpo37.pdf>.

Lesniewska, F., 2005. Laws of the Forest. International Institute for Environment and Development, Discussion Paper. <http://www.iied.org/pubs/pdfs/13505IIED.pdf>.

Ministry of Wildlife and Forestry, Forest and Wildlife Policy (FWP), 24th November 1994. Accra.

Noeff, T., Luepke, von, H., Schoene, D., 2006. Choosing a Forest Definition for the Clean Development Mechanism. FAO, Rome, Forests and Climate Change Working Paper Vol. 4.

Saunders, L.S., Hanbury-Tenison, R., Swingland, I.R., 2002. Social capital from carbon property: creating equity for indigenous people. Philos. Trans. A Math. Phys. Eng. Sci. 360 (1797), 1763−1775.

United Nations, 2006. Reporting of the LULUCF sector by Parties included in Annex I to the Convention. Available at: http://unfccc.int/methods_and_science/lulucf/items/4127.php (viewed 14.03.10).

University of Copenhagen, 2008. Ghana: Illegal Logging and Policy Brief by University of Copenhagen. Forest Policy Research, Development Brief, Vol. 5.

WCED, 1987. Report of the World Commission in Environment and Development: Our Common Future. Oxford University Press, Oxford.

World Commission on Forests and Sustainable Development, 1999. Our Forests, Our Future. Summary Report. p. 28. <https://www.iisd.org/pdf/wcfsdsummary.pdf>.

World Wildlife Federation, (n.d.). Congo Basin. <http://www.worldwildlife.org/places/congo-basin>.

CHAPTER 13

Wildlife Resources

Keywords: Wildlife management; market failure; social costs; open access; property rights; non-market values; safe minimum standard; precautionary principle; invasive species

13.1 Introduction

The evidence on wildlife populations in sub-Saharan Africa (SSA) is not impressive.[1] Wildlife protection and management has become a subject of major policy scrutiny with "more than 14% of species across the sub-Saharan African region threatened" (IUCN, 2015). Countries in the region are using several policy tools to respond to this threat. These tools include the setting aside of land for wildlife conservation, controlling the use of wildlife resources, such as the consumption of bushmeat, enacting laws to control hunting, and the imposition of taxes and fees on the consumption of wildlife resources such as hunting (Asibey and Child, 2010). The primary policy concern pertaining to wildlife is *extinction*, defined as "when the last individual organisms of the species die" (Kahn, 1995).

Several factors have contributed to the loss of wildlife populations in SSA. Some of the factors are overgrazing of the habitat supporting wildlife populations, the introduction of invasive/non-native species,[2] and excessive harvesting of species, such as bushmeat for consumption and trade.[3]

13.2 Economics of Wildlife Management and Conservation

The problems encountered in addressing wildlife extinction in SSA are summarized in the concept of *market failure*, the situation where "people make economic decisions that do not incorporate the full social costs of their actions" (Kahn, 1995). The habitats supporting wildlife populations are usually held as a common property or considered open access, where there are no defined property rights. The absence of defined property rights leads to overgrazing and destruction of the habitat for wildlife. This is an example of Hardin's *tragedy of the commons* where the absence of defined property rights leads to overuse of a resource. The introduction of invasive or non-native species is another example of an externality because the person introducing the species has not factored in or considered the

F.O. Boadu: Agricultural Law and Economics in Sub-Saharan Africa.
DOI: http://dx.doi.org/10.1016/B978-0-12-801771-5.00013-7

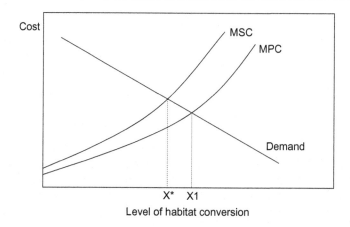

Figure 13.1
Market and Optimal Levels of Habitat Preservation.

cost others will bear should native species be threatened. Likewise, excessive hunting of wildlife may lead to extinction given the absence of property rights.

Fig. 13.1 explains the divergence between social and private costs and the implications of market failure. The marginal private cost (MPC) is lower than the marginal social cost (MSC). The level of habitat conversion is higher, X1, than the equilibrium level, X*.

13.3 Approaches to Estimating the Benefits of Wildlife Preservation

Several economic approaches have been suggested to explain and quantify the benefits and costs associated with the design and implementation of wildlife conservation policies and programs. Economists have sharpened the computation of benefits and costs. The approach is that for goods and services bought and sold in the market, the benefit is simply the market price multiplied by the quantity sold. However, there are other benefits that do not have market prices because they are not bought and sold in the market.

Some goods and services do not have a market because they are indivisible in consumption (eg, bird-watching), or are non-exclusive, such as an open grazing area. Economists have used different theoretical and quantitative approaches known as "non-market valuation" to compute non-market values.[4] The computation must also include *existence value*, that is, "the knowledge that the environmental resource continues to exist" (Randall, 1981, p. 413). For example, one may never get to visit the Victoria Falls but still derive utility from knowing that the Falls and the scenery it provides is not destroyed. The computed benefits are compared to costs to determine whether a particular conservation policy must be pursued. Both actual and opportunity costs are included in determining the total cost of wildlife preservation. Another economics-based approach to conservation is the use of a

Safe Minimum Standard, defined as "a level of conservation sufficiently high to reduce the probability of extinction (or irreversible loss) to a very low level" (Randall, 1981).

13.4 The Safe Minimum Standard (SMS) and the Precautionary Principle

Effective policies to protect environmental resources must address problems of risk and uncertainty. There are situations where the use of the popular benefit–cost assessment (BCA) is not adequate to address the problem at hand due to an inability to account for risk, uncertainty, and the long time period involved in using particular environmental resources. In such situations, economists have based evaluations on *Safe Minimum Standards* (SMS) and the *Precautionary Principle*. The "SMS is a level of conservation sufficiently high to reduce the probability of extinction (or irreversible loss) to a very low level" (Randall, 1981; see also Margolis and Naevdal, 2004).

The precautionary principle has been described as "when an activity raises threats of harm to human health or the environment, precautionary measures should be taken even if some cause and effect relationships are not fully established scientifically. There are four main components of the principle: taking preventive action in the face of uncertainty; shifting the burden of proof to the proponents of an activity; exploring a wide range of alternatives to possibly harmful actions; and increasing public participation in decision making" (Kriebel, 2001). The SMS and the precautionary principle point to a need to use a holistic approach in valuing environmental resources and to manage resources in a manner that ensures future generations have access to these resources.

13.5 Poaching, Illegal Wildlife Trade, and Invasive Species

Poaching, illegal wildlife trade, and invasive species are examples of market failure because in all cases the market system has failed to allocate resources in a socially efficient manner. Poaching occurs because property rights are poorly defined for the land on which animals are found. Illegal wildlife trade is closely tied to poaching, leading to negative externality such as the possible extinction of some species due to uncontrolled harvest of animals. The perpetrator gains benefits in the short run, but society suffers possible long-term damage such as irreversibility.

The *GREENWATCH v Uganda Wildlife Authority and Attorney General* case is an emerging trend whereby advocacy and volunteer groups file action against governmental entities to enforce natural resource laws. Local communities do not have the resources to challenge government for not enforcing laws and regulations protecting natural resources. GREENWATCH was seeking to block the export of chimpanzees because removing the animals from their natural habitat hurts the environment and also because the number of chimpanzees in Uganda was declining. In the Botswana case, *Roy Sesana* & (1st Applicant) & *Keiwa Setlhobogwa & Others*) (2nd Applicant) *v The Attorney General* the court examined the constitutionality of a government action to refuse game licences on property owned by the government.

The *Waterberg Big Game Hunting Lodge Otjahewita (PTY) Ltd. v The Minister of Environment & Tourism* addresses how Namibian authorities are trying to protect against potential negative externalities associated with invasive species. There are not many lawsuits by private entities against government agencies in SSA. This is due partly to the pervasive state control of all aspects of the economy. With countries moving towards market reforms, constitutionalism, and the rule of law, it is likely that challenges to state economic power will increase as private entities seek to expand their opportunities in the marketplace. The *Waterberg* case is an example of a challenge to administrative power and delegated authority.

Greenwatch v 1. Uganda Wildlife Authority; 2. The Attorney General

In the High Court of Uganda at Kampala
Miscellaneous Application No. 92 of 2004
(Arising from Misc. Cause No. 15 of 2004)

Before Honourable Justice Gideon Tinyinondi

RULING

In this application preferred under *037*, rr 2(1) and 9 of the Civil Procedure Rules the Applicant sought "an order of temporary injunction to issue against the Respondents, their agents attorneys and assigns anybody or person acting in that or such similar capacity from exporting, transporting, removing, relocating any Chimpanzee from Uganda to the Peoples Republic of China or any other place or country in the world until the hearing and determination of the main application herein or until further orders of this Court."

The grounds of the application were stated to be:

1. That there is a pending application seeking a permanent injunction against the 1st Respondent and for declaration that the decision of the 2nd Respondent in respect of the subject matter herein is null and void ab initio and the same is pending hearing in this Court.
2. That the pending application against the Respondents has great likelihood of success.
3. That activities the Applicants seek to restrain the Respondents from doing are illegal and ultra vires the powers.
4. That on a balance of convenience it is just and equitable that this application be granted.
5. The Respondents will not be prejudiced if the application is allowed but the Applicants will be prejudiced if the Order is not granted as it will render nugatory the main suit herein.

(Continued)

(Continued)

One Sarah Naigaga swore an affidavit in support of the application stating:

1. That I am the Executive Director of the Applicant and the person in charge of running its day to day affairs and swear affidavit in that capacity.
2. That the Applicant is a limited liability company limited by guarantee and incorporated under the laws of Uganda, and it is also registered in Uganda as a non-governmental institution under the Laws of Uganda.
3. That the Applicant members are all Ugandan citizens of age and sounding.
4. That the objectives of the Applicant include among others the protection of the environment, including but not limited to flora and fauna, increasing public participation in the management of the environment and natural resources, enhancing public participation in the enforcement of their right to a healthy and clean environment.
5. That I have learnt from the 1st Respondent that it intends to export Chimpanzees, from Uganda to China or elsewhere.
6. That we have had to take Court action in view of the urgency of this matter and the fact that the Executive Director of the 1st Respondent and its official Mr. Daniel Ankankwasa refused to talk to me about this.
7. That this followed press reports that the 1st Applicant and other official of Government have already finalised plans to export Chimpanzees from their Sanctuary to Zoos in The Peoples' Republic of China see annexture "A1 to A5."
8. That the decision would fundamentally affect the Chimpanzees and in turn impact negatively on the environment.
9. That by removing Chimpanzees from their natural habitat and exporting them to China the Respondents would violet the Applicants right to a clean and healthy environment as enshrined in the constitution.
10. That the Constitution demands that state and all its organs protect the natural resources of Uganda including flora and fauna and as the decision to export Chimpanzees from Uganda contravenes this directive principle of state policy.
11. That the decision to export Chimpanzees in null and void as it was made *ultra vires the powers* of *the Applicants.*
12. That the law empowers the Applicants to protect flora and fauna where they are and have no powers to alter the environment or move flora and fauna in a way that is not in the best interest of the environment.
13. That the decision to export Chimpanzees contravenes the Constitution directive principle of state policy that requires the state to ensure conservation on all natural resources.
14. That it is the duty of all the people of Uganda including the Applicants to uphold and defend the Constitution and that this application is made in that spirit.
15. That Applicants, and all other citizens of Uganda cannot enjoy a clean and healthy environment unless it had all its amenities, to wit air, water, land and mineral resources, energy including solar energy and all plant and animal life.
16. That the Applicant would therefore be aggrieved by the decision and the action of the Respondents in exporting Chimpanzees from Uganda, which action subtracts an essential ingredient of their environment.

(Continued)

(Continued)

17. That it is estimated that there are only 5000 Chimpanzees left in Uganda and therefore any further reduction in this number significantly affects the fauna component of the environment in Uganda.

18. That Chimpanzees are not goods, or chattels, they do not belong to the Government of Uganda but are Uganda's natural heritage, and a gift from God and the Respondents are only protecting them as trustees of the people of Uganda.

19. That it is just and equitable that this application be granted to maintain the *status quo* pending the final determination of the main application herein.

20. That if the *status quo* is not maintained and the Chimpanzees are exported it will be more difficult to revere and therefore on a balance of convenience this application ought to be granted.

21. That I swear this affidavit in support of the Applicants' application herein.

22. That all I have stated hereinabove is true and correct to the best of my knowledge.

At the hearing Dr. Joseph Byamugisha appeared for the Respondent while Mr. Kenneth Kakuru represented the Applicant. Dr. Byamugisha raised a preliminary objection. He submitted that this application which arose out of Miscellaneous Cause No. 15/2004 between the same parties should be struck out under 07, r11 (d) of the Civil Procedure Rules. His bases for this were

(a) *The 1st Respondent is a scheduled corporation under the civil Procedure and Limitation [Misc. Provisions] Act, Cap.72 of the Laws of Uganda 2000. Section 2 thereof provides that no suit shall lie or be instituted against a scheduled corporation until the expiry of forty-five days after written notice has been delivered or left at its office etc.*

(b) *Before Miscellaneous Cause No. 15/2004, out of which this application arises was filed, no such notice as required in the Act (ante) was served on the Respondent.*

Therefore Counsel's preliminary objection, he argued, was not directed against this application alone but also against Miscellaneous Cause No. 15/2004 which latter application was itself an incompetent suit on account of violating section 2 of the Act (ante).

In support of his submissions learned Counsel cited *Lyakiye v Attorney General* [19731] ULR 124 and *Kayondo v Attorney General* [1988/90] HCB 127. He prayed that this application and Miscellaneous Cause No. 15/2004 be struck out.

Mr. Kakuru replied as hereunder. He agreed that service of statutory notice on a corporation was mandatory. He also agreed with the Legal position in the cases cited by Dr. Byamugisha. He, however, pointed out that position obtains in ordinary suits brought under the Civil Procedure Act and the Civil Procedure Rules.

That this application and the cause out of which it arises were not one of such suits. That Miscellaneous Cause No. 15 of 2004 was brought under section 50 of the Constitution and Statutory Instrument No. 26 of 1992. That in *DR. J.W. Rwanyarare and 2 Others v Attorney General Misc. Application No. 85 of 1993* the High Court held that in matters concerning the enforcement of human rights under the Constitution no statutory notice was required because to do so would result in absurdity as the effect of it would be to condone the violation of the right and deny the Applicant the remedy.

(Continued)

(Continued)

Learned Counsel further argued that the Rules (under Statutory Instrument 26 of 1992) are specific for the enforcement of the rights and there is no statutory provision for a notice.

He cited:

> *Miscellaneous Application No. 140 of 2002: Greenwatch vs. Attorney General and MEMA and Miscellaneous Application No. 139 of 2001: Greenwatch vs. Attorney General and NEMA.*

Finally learned Counsel referred to the decision of the Constitutional Court in *Uganda Association of Women Lawyers and 5 Others v Attorney General* where the *"thirty days"* rule under the provision of rule 4(1) of the Fundamental Rights and Freedoms [Enforcement Procedure] Rules 1992 (legal Notice no. 4/1960 was discussed.

Dr. Byamugisha's reply was as follows. Article 50 of the Constitution was clear. It had two heads:

(a) whether a right has been infringed;
(b) where the right is being threatened with infringement.

That in the former the reasoning by the High Court that a statutory notice would delay the infringement of the right would not be right. That therefore if that reasoning cannot stand in (a) so also it cannot stand in (b). That section 2 of Cap. 72 was mandatory despite the Fundamental Rights and Freedoms (Enforcement Procedure) Rules.

Learned Counsel maintained that he would concede the point if the Constitutional Court had declared section 2 of Cap. 72 (ante) unconstitutional as taking out the suits under Article 50 of the Constitution. But that Court had not done so. And the High Court had no power to declare that this Act did not apply to Article 50 suits. Such a declaration by the High Court would have no effect of declaring the Act unconstitutional.

It is pertinent that I reproduce the provisions *of Article 50(1) of (4) the Constitution.*

> *(1) Any person who claims that a fundamental or other right or freedom guaranteed under this constitution has been infringed or threatened, is entitled to apply to a competent Court for redress may include which compensation.*
>
> *(2). . . . .*
>
> *(3). . . . .*
>
> *(4). Parliament shall make laws for the enforcement of rights and freedoms under this Chapter.*

I will also reproduce the provisions of *the Fundamental Rights and Freedoms (Enforcement Procedure Rules 5.1. 26 of 1992).*

This is one of the *laws* envisaged in Article 50(4) above. *Rule 7 reads*

> *7. Subject to the provisions of these Rules, the Civil Procedure Act and the rules made thereunder shall apply in relation to the application.*

(Continued)

(Continued)

In *The Environmental Network Ltd. v The Attorney General and NEMA:* HC Misc. Appl. No. 13/ 2001 J.H. Ntabgoba, PJ. considered a similar preliminary objection as the present one. He stated:

> --------*Although Rule 4 provides that no motion under Rule 3 shall be made without notice to the Attorney General and any other party affected by the application, Rule 7 clearly stipulates that----.*

Applying the so-called golden rule of interpretation, we assumed that besides Rule 7 of S.1. 26 of 1992, Parliament meant that any other rule of procedure should be applied. It is for this reason that I think that applications pursuant to Article 50 of the Constitution must be strictly restricted to the Civil Procedure Act and the rules thereunder and not under section 1 of Act No. 20 of 1996 (read Cap. 72, S.2)............

I agree with this requirement that the Respondent usually the Government or a scheduled corporation needs sufficient period of time to investigate a case intended to be brought against it so as to be able to avoid unnecessary expense on protracted litigation. This rationale cannot apply to a matter where the rights and freedoms of the people are being or are about to be infringed. The people cannot afford to wait forty-five days before pre-emptive action is applied by Court. They need immediate redress. They need a short period which is one provided under the ordinary rules of procedure provided by the Civil Procedure Act and its Rules. To demand from an aggrieved party a forty-five days' notice is to condemn them to infringement of their rights and freedoms for that period which this Court would not be prepared to do............

I have no better words to use than these in order to overrule the preliminary objection before me. It is accordingly overruled.

Roy Sesana & Keiwa Setlhobogwa & Others v The Attorney General

High Court, Lobatse
Misca. No. 52 of 2002, December 13th, 2006

M. Dibotelo, J

FACTS

On the 19 February 2002, the Applicants filed an urgent application on notice of motion seeking at paragraphs 2 and 3 thereof an order declaring, inter alia, that:

> *(a) The termination by the Government with effect from 31 January 2002 of the following basic and essential services to the Applicants in the Central Kalahari Game Reserve (CKGR) (namely):*
>
> *the provision of drinking water on a weekly basis; the maintenance of the supply of borehole water; the provision of rations to registered destitutes; the provision of rations for registered orphans; the*

(Continued)

(Continued)

provision of transport for the Applicants' children to and from school; the provision of healthcare to the Applicants through mobile clinics and ambulance services is unlawful and unconstitutional; the Government is obliged to:

(i) restore to the Applicants the basic and essential services that it terminated with effect from 31 January 2002; and

(ii) continue to provide to the Applicants the basic and essential services that it had been providing to them immediately prior to the termination of the provision of these services;

(c) those Applicants, whom the Government forcibly removed from the Central Kalahari Game Reserve (CKGR) after the termination of the provision to them of the basic and essential services referred to above, have been unlawfully despoiled of their possession of the land which they lawfully occupied in their settlements in the CKGR, and should immediately be restored to their possession of that land.

3. the Respondent pays the Applicants' costs.

The Application was supported by the founding affidavit of the First Applicant.

2. On the 4 March 2002, the First Applicant filed a supplementary affidavit seeking additional declaratory orders ". . ... that the refusal by the Government's Department of Wildlife and National Parks to:

(a) issue special game licences to the Applicants; and

(b) allow them to enter the CKGR unless they possess a permit, is unlawful and unconstitutional."

The application was opposed by the Respondent who filed several opposing affidavits.

OPINION

[After extensive discussion of the case background, the Court continued. . ...]

The concept or principle or doctrine of legitimate expectation has been accepted as part of our law. In *Mokokonyane v. Commander of Botswana Defence Force and Another* [2000] 2 BLR 102, the Appellant was, in terms of Regulation 4(5)(b) of the Defence Force (Regular Force) (Officers) (Amendment) Regulations 1996, given three months' notice in writing that he was being compulsorily retired on the ground that there were no future prospects for his promotion in the force. Regulation 4(4) of the said Regulations gives the Commander of BDF discretion to require any officer below the rank of Lieutenant-Colonel who has attained the age of 45 years to retire from the force. The compulsory retirement age in the BDF is 55 years. When the Appellant was given notice, he was 47 years and was not given prior notice of the decision to retire him nor was he given the opportunity to contest the decision.

The Appellant applied to the High Court for an order to set aside the decision of the Commander of the BDF to retire him but the application was dismissed. He appealed to the Court of Appeal where it was argued on his behalf that he had a legitimate expectation that he would not be compulsorily retired until he reached 55 years and that if his retirement at an early age was being considered he would be advised of this and be given the right to be heard before the decision to compulsorily retire him could be made. It was further contended

(Continued)

(Continued)

on his behalf that as he was not afforded such right, the decision to retire him was invalid and had to be set aside. It was held by Zietsman, J.A., dismissing the appeal, at page 107 F-G that:

> As was pointed out by Amissah, J.P. in his judgment in the MOTHUSI case, the claim of legitimate expectation and the claim of a right to be heard fall to be considered in relation to each other as the claim of legitimate expectation is the basis which gives standing to the claim of the right to be heard. His judgment deals fully with the legitimate expectation principle which has been accepted as being part of the law of this country,

and further on same page at letters G-H that:

> The essence of the principle (of legitimate expectation) is the duty to act fairly, and to give a person the right to be heard before a decision is made by a public official which decision may prejudicially affect the person in his liberty, his property, or his rights, unless the statute empowering the public official expressly or by implication indicates to the contrary.

The principle of legitimate expectation, I should stress, is founded on fairness in that public authorities or officials are expected to act fairly when they make decisions which are likely to affect or prejudice the interests of other people. In MOTHUSI v THE ATTORNEY GENERAL [1994] B.L.R 246 Amissah, J.P. (as he then was) at page 260 A—C described the principle of legitimate expectation thus —

> The concept of legitimate expectation has developed in administrative procedures to protect those who have been led either by contract or practice to expect a certain course of action in cases where the expected course of action has been altered without giving them the right to make representations. Starting from a procedural concept by which the requirement of natural justice could be brought into operation, it has been in some cases . . . ... not merely to cover the procedural concept, but to require the fulfillment of a promise made by authority.

. . . . . .

In my view, the issue of termination of services is the most important of them all because it triggered all the other issues or events that followed; its importance is borne out by the fact it is issue number one in both the Applicants' notice of motion and the order of the Court of Appeal. The thread running through all the Applicants' contentions that the termination of services was unlawful and unconstitutional is that they were not consulted before the decision to terminate the services provided to them in their settlements in the CKGR was made notwithstanding that they had a legitimate expectation that the government would consult them before making such a decision which was likely to adversely affect them or their interests or to prejudice them.

The Respondent maintains that the residents of the settlements in the CKGR were consulted before the services were terminated and has adduced or placed evidence before the Court in an endeavour to show that consultations took place over a number of years before the provision of services to the residents in the CKGR was finally terminated in early 2002.

(Continued)

(Continued)

The burden of proof is on the Applicants to prove that the government did not consult them before the services were terminated; that burden of proof in our civil proceedings is required to be discharged by the Applicants on a balance of probabilities. The basic principle in civil proceedings on the onus or in regard to the burden of proof is that he who alleges must prove. The Respondent, it must be stressed, bears no burden to prove that the government consulted the Applicants before terminating the services in the absence of any evidence by the Applicants showing that they were not consulted before the services were terminated. It is only when the Applicants have placed evidence before the Court showing that they were not consulted that it becomes necessary for the Respondent to adduce evidence in rebuttal to prove that the government consulted the Applicants before terminating the services. The standard of proof required of the Respondent in that rebuttal evidence is also on a balance of probabilities.

As I have already stated, a strong and consistent thread running through the Applicants' submissions in support of their contention that the termination of services was unlawful and unconstitutional is that they had a legitimate expectation that the government would consult them before the decision to terminate the provision of basic and essential services provided to them in their settlements in the CKGR was made, which consultation they maintain was not done. I pause here and observe that in their founding affidavit, the Applicants allege an ulterior motive on the part of the government as the reason for terminating the services, and that allegation is foreshadowed in paragraphs 79 to 85 of the First Applicant's founding affidavit wherein he alleges, inter alia, as follows:

> *Their legal claim is not to ownership, but to a right to use and occupy the land they have long occupied, unless and until that right is taken from them by constitutionally permissible means.*

This first question is in two parts in that it requires the Court to determine (a) whether the Applicants were in possession of the land, and (b) whether the Applicants occupied that land lawfully in their settlements in the CKGR at the time of the 2002 relocations.

On the first leg of this question, the Applicants maintain that they were in possession of the land in question. Initially, the Respondent adopted a somewhat ambiguous or equivocal position when in terms of the "Notice to Admit Facts" dated 5th June 2003 he was called upon by the Applicants to admit the allegation that the Applicants were in possession of the land they lawfully occupied in the CKGR prior to and subsequent to 31st January 2002. I say the Respondent's answer was ambiguous because while admitting this allegation, he went on to qualify his answer by adding that the Applicants "were preferably in occupation and not in possession" of that land. The Respondent has however now admitted without reservation that the Applicants were in possession of that land in his written submissions by stating that:

> *We concede that Applicants were in possession of their settlements in the CKGR as at 31st January 2002.*

I therefore find as a fact that the Applicants were in possession of the land they occupied in their settlements in the CKGR before the 2002 relocations.

(Continued)

(Continued)

The second leg of the first question is whether the Applicants lawfully occupied the land in their settlements in the CKGR before the 2002 relocations. The Respondent has argued that the occupation by the Applicants of the land in the settlements in the CKGR was unlawful because the CKGR is owned by the Government as it is state land. In the submission of the Respondent, this is so because the Applicants have not only claimed that they were unlawfully dispossessed of the land by the government but have also gone further to claim that their occupation of the land in question was lawful which the Respondent disputes. According to the argument of the Respondent, as the Applicants do not only claim that their dispossession was unlawful but also want the Court to declare their occupation lawful and want to be restored to that lawful occupation as a matter of right, this has led to a competition of rights of the owner and those of a possessor and in the submission of the Respondent "a claim of the restoration of possession cannot be stronger than that of ownership unless such possession was lawful", (vide paragraphs 86.4 to 87 of Respondent's written submissions). As I have already stated the Applicants have submitted that:

> Their legal claim is not to ownership, but to a right to use and occupy the land they have long occupied, unless and until that right is taken from them by constitutionally permissible means (vide para. 134 of their reply to Respondent's written submissions).

In the premises, the Government's refusal to issue special game licences to the Applicants was unlawful and is set aside.

Although the Applicants argue that the Government's refusal to allow them to enter the CKGR unless they have been issued with a permit is unlawful and unconstitutional, the difficulty in deciding this issue is again caused by the fact that none of the Applicants has come forward to give evidence in regard to how and when he or she was denied entry into the CKGR; what is before the Court are the allegations by the First Applicant on this issue who has elected not to give evidence so that his allegations may be tested in open Court; and who notwithstanding his allegation that he was denied entry into the Reserve did enter the Reserve in any event without a permit. It is one of the Respondent's witnesses who gave evidence which was not refuted by the Applicants and which I therefore believe that it was only when some of the former residents tried to enter the Reserve at an ungazetted point that they were prevented from doing so.

It will be recalled that the Applicants have conceded, and it is now common cause, that the CKGR is state land. This means that ownership of the CKGR is vested in the Government. It follows therefore that as owner of the CKGR, the Government can exercise all rights of ownership in respect of the CKGR, including the right to determine who may come into the CKGR and under what terms and conditions, and the right to decide who may or may not go into the CKGR. Based upon the Applicants' admission that the CKGR is owned by the Government, it follows that the Government has the right to impose conditions as to how any person, including the Applicants, may enter the CKGR. The position now is that the Government as owner of the CKGR wants the Applicants to obtain permits before they can enter the CKGR, and this is a proper exercise of one of the rights of ownership on the part of Government which the Government is entitled to do.

(Continued)

(Continued)

I have found that the termination of the provision of services to the Applicants by the Government in the CKGR was not unlawful. I have also found that the Government did not forcibly or wrongly deprive the Applicants of the possession of the land they occupied in the settlements in the CKGR. When the Applicants relinquished possession of the land they occupied in the settlements in the CKGR and relocated to the new settlements of Kaudwane and New Xade outside the CKGR, they were allocated plots in the new settlements. Furthermore, the Applicants were compensated for the structures they had erected on the land they occupied in the CKGR. They were then allowed to dismantle those structures and the material they had used to construct those structures was transported to the new settlements where the Applicants used it to build their dwellings on their new plots. The Applicants are not challenging the adequacy of the compensation they received for the structures they had built in their settlements in the CKGR.

It has been suggested in evidence by PW5 that she did not know what they were being compensated for on the ground that it was not explained to her what the compensation was for. However, I have no doubt that the Applicants knew and understood that the land they were allocated in the new settlements was in replacement of the land whose possession they had relinquished in the CKGR and further that the money they were paid was for the materials they had used to build their structures, including dwelling huts, in the CKGR. The evidence of the Respondent that since 1997 the relocation was a continuous process has not been disputed by the Applicants. After the first relocations in 1997 up to before the 2002 relocations, some residents relocated outside the CKGR from the settlements where the Applicants resided and those relocated were paid compensation.

I therefore find it improbable that the Applicants would not have known what those other residents who previously relocated were paid compensation for. The law accords equal treatment to all in that every person who desires to enter the Reserve must have a permit. In my view, therefore, there is nothing offensive in requiring the Applicants who relocated to obtain permits like everybody else in order to enter the CKGR. Further, "The New Shorter Oxford English Dictionary" defines the word "compensate" inter alia as to "make amends to, recompense" which last word it defines as to "make amends (to a person for loss, injury"). "The Concise Oxford Dictionary" defines the word "compensation" as "2 something, esp. money, given as recompense" while recompense is defined therein as "1 to make amends (to a person) or for (a loss etc.)." From these definitions, I have no doubt that the Applicants were paid the money they received and given plots they built their residences on at Kaudwane and New Xade for the loss of the sites or plots they occupied in the CKGR before the relocation. The receipt of compensation in the form of money as well as new plots in the settlements outside the CKGR was in replacement of the rights of the Applicants to occupy and possess land in the settlements inside the Reserve. I therefore do not agree that the Government's refusal to allow the Applicants to enter the CKGR unless they have been issued with a permit is unlawful and unconstitutional.

(Continued)

(Continued)

Lastly, on the issue of costs, the general rule is that costs follow the result. The Applicants have succeeded in two out of the six issues that I had to determine in that I have found they were in lawful possession of the land they occupied in the settlements before the 2002 relocations and that the Government's refusal to issue special game licences to the Applicants was unlawful. However, the First Applicant has elected not to give evidence in this matter notwithstanding that he initiated the action in which he made detailed allegations but has not come forward to support them.

The other Applicants may well have genuinely believed that as their leader he would take on the responsibility and testify on their behalf in these proceedings which he has not done. They may never have thought he would jump ship. It may therefore be contended that he personally should pay a portion of the costs of the Respondent in this action. In my view, however, justice will be better served if each party pays their own costs in this action. Before I conclude, I would like to make an observation that it is probable that the result of this litigation will not end the dispute between the parties. It is therefore to be hoped that, whatever the outcome of this case, the parties will after this litigation come together to resolve their differences.

The result is that, save for the two issues in which the Applicants have succeeded, their action in respect of the remaining four issues is dismissed.

Finally, in view of the decisions reached by each of us, the court makes the following Order:

1. The termination in 2002 by the Government of the provision of basic and essential services to the Applicants in the CKGR was neither unlawful nor unconstitutional. (Dow J dissenting).
2. The Government is not obliged to restore the provision of such services to the Applicants in the CKGR. (Dow J dissenting)
3. Prior to 31 Jan 2002, the Applicants were in possession of the land, which they lawfully occupied in their settlements in the CKGR. (unanimous decision)
4. The Applicants were deprived of such possession by the Government forcibly or wrongly and without their consent. (Dibotelo J dissenting)
5. The Government refusal to issue special game licenses to the Appellants is unlawful. (unanimous decision)
6. The Government refusal to issue special game licenses to the Applicants is unconstitutional. (Dibotelo dissenting)
7. The Government refusal to allow the Applicants to enter the CKGR unless they are issued with permits is unlawful and unconstitutional. (Dibotelo dissenting)
8. Each party shall pay their own costs. (Dow dissenting)

Delivered in open court at Lobatse this 13th day of December 2006.

M. Dibotelo
Judge

Waterberg Big Game Hunting Lodge Otjahewita (PTY) Ltd v The Minister of Environment & Tourism

Supreme Court of Namibia
Case No. SA 13/2004, November 23rd 2005
Coram: Shivute, C.J., O'Linn, A.J.A., Chomba, A.J.A

O'Linn, A.J.A.:

This judgment is divided for the purpose of easy reference into various sections namely:

  I: Introductory Remarks
 II: The confusion about the Parties involved, the failure to comply with Rule 53 of the Rules of the High Court and Article 18 of the Namibian Constitution relating administrative justice and the doctrine of reasonable expectation.
III: The lack of authority to decide
IV: Concluding remarks
    I: Introductory Remarks

This is a judgment on appeal from the High Court to the Supreme Court. The appellant is Waterberg Big Game Hunting Lodge Otjahewita (Pty) Ltd, a company conducting business as a hunting and safari lodge with its main place of business at Farm Otjahewita 291, District Otjiwarongo, Namibia. It does business under the name "WABI Lodge" or "Wabi (Pty) Ltd."

The appellant cited the Minister of Environment and Tourism in his official capacity as respondent, pursuant to his duties, powers and functions as set out in the Nature Conservation Ordinance No. 4 of 1975, particularly his duty to consider and decide on the importation of live game from South Africa in accordance with Section 49(1) of the said Ordinance as amended by Section 12 of Act 5 of 1996.

The said parties will hereinafter be referred to respectively as "Waterberg Lodge" and "the Minister." The Ministry of Environment and Tourism will be referred to as "the Ministry." The present appeal is against a decision of the High Court of Namibia, per Mainga J, delivered on 2 July 2004, in which the learned judge dismissed an application by Waterberg Lodge for the review and setting aside of a decision by the Cabinet, alternatively the Minister, refusing applications by WABI Lodge for the importation from South Africa into Namibia of Mountain Reedbuck as per application dated 19.9.2002 and 27.9.2002.

 II: The confusion about the Parties involved, the failure to comply with Rule 53 of the Rules of the High Court and Article 18 of the Namibian Constitution relating administrative justice and the doctrine of reasonable expectation.
    The applications for the importation of the Mountain Reedbuck were made on the form provided by the "Ministry of Environment and Tourism" and referred to as Annexures B2 and A1 to the founding affidavit of Mr Mark Egger, in his capacity as a shareholder and managing director of "Waterberg Lodge."
    It is unclear what precisely is meant by the term the "Ministry." I will assume for the purpose of this judgment that the meaning of the term is as defined in the Oxford Advanced Dictionary of current English, namely: "Department of State under a Minister."

(Continued)

(Continued)

It is further unclear on the available evidence, whether the Ministry or Mr. Beytell, Director of Parks and Wildlife Management in the Ministry of Environment and Tourism, or Mr. Beytell and the Ministry collectively, took the decision to decline the application. What is clear however is that neither the Cabinet nor the Minister took the decision. Furthermore there is no suggestion whatever that the Minister was consulted or was in any way a party to the decision-making process.

The Minister made no statement in the proceedings. However, Mr. Barend Johannes Beytell, hereinafter referred to as Beytell, stated in his answering affidavit that he is "duly authorized to oppose this application on behalf of the respondent and to depose to this affidavit on its behalf." (My emphasis added.)

In the aforesaid answering affidavit Beytell cites the respondent in the heading to the affidavit as "Ministry of Environment and Tourism." (My emphasis.) It follows that the allegation by Beytell is thus in effect that he is authorized by the "Ministry" to oppose the application and is authorized by the "Ministry" "to depose to the affidavit on its behalf." This adds to the confusion caused by correspondence from the "Ministry" as well as Beytell in reaction to the two applications by Waterberg Lodge under the name of Wabi Lodge and one application by Mr. Dries Malan.

The letter dated 4 September 2002 but only signed by Mr. S. Simenda, acting Permanent Secretary of the Ministry of Environment and Tourism on 30.9.2002, reads as follows:

Dear Mr Egger,

In response to your application to import Mountain reedbuck the following is our answer. After the bushbuck importation discussions, we in the Ministry reviewed the list of species that are imported and are busy with drafting a Cabinet submission making essentially the following recommendations:

(a) That certain species which have been imported in large numbers, such as waterbuck and Black wildebeest, may be imported in future as stopping their importation now, serves no real purpose.

(b) That certain species such as Cape bushbuck and Mountain reedbuck, although they have been imported in small numbers, should no longer be allowed to be imported as they never occurred naturally in Namibia and some pose real biodiversity conservation risks because of potential inbreeding with Namibian subspecies. Similar springbok colour variants will no longer be allowed to be imported.

It was therefore decided to decline your application to import Mountain reedbuck. We trust that you accept our decision as being in the best interest of conservation in Namibia and want to again encourage you and others like minded to explore ways of promoting our rare Namibian species and conserving them effectively in a co-operative manner.

Yours sincerely

S Simenda — Acting Permanent Secretary.

The letter dated 17th October 2002 by Mr. Beytell to Mr. Dries Malan reads as follows:

Your letter dated 3rd October 2002 refers.

(Continued)

(Continued)

You are granted permission to continue transporting game from the RSA until 31 December 2002 as requested.

Your application to import 50 common bushbuck and Nyale has also been approved.

Please report the bushbucks specifically to our staff at the border post or the nearest office of the Ministry during official working hours. The bushbuck and Mountain reedbuck may not leave the farm which receives them without prior approval from the Ministry.

Please report back farms who received these species and members delivered at each.

Please note that a Cabinet submission has been prepared for the Minister to motivate the refusal of further import of these two species into Namibia. No further permits will be issued for import of common bushbuck and mountain reedbuck until we have received a response from Cabinet. Furthermore no extension of permits not fully utilised will be considered.

Yours sincerely

B Beytell

Director

Parks and Wildlife Management

The last paragraph of the above stated letter relating to Bushbuck and Mountain Reedbuck corresponds to some extent to the earlier letter by the Acting Permanent Secretary in so far as the intended submission to the Cabinet is concerned.

The latter letter by Beytell however gives the impression that the applications for import of Bushbuck and Mountain Reedbuck will be declined "until we have received a response from Cabinet." (My emphasis added.)

It was clearly implied in this letter that the decision by the Ministry was a preliminary and temporary measure pending the awaited response of the Cabinet to the submission by the "Ministry."

This letter by Beytell indicates that at the time when Beytell wrote his letter dated the 17th October 2002 he was under the impression that the Cabinet was the decision maker. Beytell in paragraph 48 of his aforesaid answering affidavit says that the draft submission, Annexure B7 to his affidavit, was in fact never sent to Cabinet.

Why it was not sent after it was prepared and after Beytell had referred to it in his letter of the 17th October to Malan was never explained. There was no indication whatever in the papers before the Court *a quo* and in this Court, that there was any "response" from the Cabinet as envisaged in Beytell's letter to Malan dated 17th October 2002. That makes nonsense of Beytell's said letter.

As a matter of fact there is no indication whether the Minister or the Cabinet was ever consulted in regard to the Ministry's new policy to refuse the import of Bushbuck and Mountain Reedbuck. Further confusion of this policy was created, when Beytell, according to Annexure BB6, annexed to his answering affidavit, on 29.8.2002 approved a permit to Dries Malan for the import of 100 Mountain Reedbuck on 31st October 2002.

(Continued)

(Continued)

The main difference between the Simenda letter of refusal purporting to have been written on 4th September and signed only on 30th September and Beytell's allegations in his answering affidavit are the following:

The letter by Simenda	Beytell's allegations
1. The Ministry decided to decline the application.	1. Beytell decided.
2. That certain species such as Cape bushbuck and Mountain Reedbuck, although they have been imported in small numbers, should no longer be allowed to be imported as they never occurred naturally in Namibia and <u>some</u> pose real bio-diversity conservation risks, because of <u>potential inbreeding with Namibian subspecies.</u> (My emphasis added.)	2. It is submitted that the term "inbreeding was mistakenly used and should read <u>crossbreeding</u>. It was intended in that way and would have been understood in that way. This did not form any part of my reasoning. I also admit that there is no potential for <u>crossbreeding</u> between Mountain Reedbuck and any Namibian subspecies. This likewise did not form part of my reasoning. The potential crossbreeding referred to in Annexure "A" to the applicant's papers relates only to the Cape bushbuck mentioned therein. Any confusion in this regard is due to the unintended poor grammatical construction of paragraph (b) of the letter with regard to the decision sought to be reviewed.

It is astonishing that Beytell, who contends that he was the sole decision-maker and not the Cabinet, the Minister or the Ministry, did not write or draft or ensure the correctness of the letter signed by the Acting permanent Secretary Mr. Simenda and purportedly drafted by Mr. Erb, both of whom were obviously part and parcel of the Ministry of Environment and Tourism, as was Mr. Beytell, the alleged sole decision-maker.

As the decision to refuse the import of Bushbuck and Mountain Reedbuck was a decision based on a new policy, which could be expected to be controversial and not acceptable to entrepreneurs in the live game trade and the hunting and tourist industry, one could expect that the decision-maker, whoever that was, would have taken care to explain correctly and carefully, the new policy and the reasons for the decision to Waterberg Lodge, being the first applicant to be refused on the ground of the new policy. He or she would not have left it to someone else, to do and say what he or she deems fit on the purported behalf of the decision-maker.

It is improbable that Simenda, a senior official, would just usurp Beytell's power and function to write and formulate the letter of refusal and would suck the contents from his thumb. The letter was apparently formulated by Erb. Neither Simenda nor Erb submitted affidavits regarding circumstances in which the letter was written. The inference can thus be drawn that Simenda and/or Erb was not given the opportunity by respondent to submit an affidavit, because he could not support Beytell's version.

(Continued)

(Continued)

The principle applicable was set out in various decisions and recently again applied by this Court.[5] The formulation in the Elgin Fireclays case was as follows:

It is true that if a party fails to place the evidence of a witness who is available and able to elucidate the facts, before the trial Court, this failure leads naturally to the inference that he fears that such evidence will expose facts unfavourable to him. See Wigmore, (section 285 and 286). But the inference is only a proper one if the evidence is available and if it would elucidate the facts.

I may add that if the witness is not available, the party whose duty it is to place the evidence of such witness before Court, should place an explanation to that effect before Court. In the instant case, no such explanation is before Court. This is the second time in the recent past when a respondent who is a Minister of the Namibian Government and/or his or her legal representative has failed to place such evidence before Court and where an adverse inference had to be drawn against the case put forward by such respondent. The previous case was that of *Dresselhaus Transport v the Government of Namibia.*[6]

Not only do such tactics not avail the government in the litigation before the Court but they militate against the principle and policy of transparency to which the Government of Namibia has committed itself and by which the Government is bound.

Mr. Beytell in his answering affidavit sets out a number of reasons for his decision, not contained in Simenda's letter of refusal and according to Beytell, also conveyed by him to the representatives of Waterberg Lodge, including Mr Egger, the managing director of Waterberg Lodge, at a meeting subsequent to the taking of the decision to refuse an importation permit, but prior to the institution of proceedings. At this meeting Beytell did not offer a reconsideration of the applications.

When review proceedings was instituted in this case in accordance with Rule 53 of the Rules of the Namibian High Court, the notice was supported by the affidavits of Mark Egger, Mark Kutzner, Dr H.O. Reuter and Dr Herman Scherer in which the case of applicant was set out in detail.

It also cited the Ministry of Environment and Tourism as the respondent. This was probably induced by the fact that applicant at that stage was influenced by the Simenda letter of refusal, wherein it was indicated that the "Ministry" had taken the decision. However in applicant's founding affidavit, the respondent was clearly cited as the "Minister of Environment and Tourism."

In the notice, the respondent was also called upon in terms of Rule 53(1)(b),

to dispatch, within 15 days of receipt of the notice of motion, to the Registrar of this Honourable Court, the record of the proceedings and decisions sought to be corrected or set aside, together with such reasons as they are by law required or desired to give and that such respondents are to notify the applicants that they had done so.

It is common cause that the respondent did not submit any reasons at all in response to the aforesaid notice in terms of Rule 53(1)(b) supplementing or correcting the reasons contained in Simenda's aforesaid letter of refusal. Only in the answering affidavit Beytell

(Continued)

(Continued)

alleged that he and he alone took the decision to refuse the permit and that it was in no sense a "collective decision."

The applicant as a consequence was placed at a disadvantage because it had no opportunity to respond in terms of Rule 53(4) to these new reasons contained in respondent's answering affidavit, unless applicant applied to Court for leave to submit additional replying affidavits in terms of Rule 6(5)(e) of the <u>general</u> rules applying to applications.

It may also be argued persuasively, that the implication of Rule 53 was that if reasons were given by a decision-maker at the time of notifying the decision to the applicant, the reasons so given by such decision-maker as appears from the record of the decision, should bind respondent in an application for review. The only excuse by Beytell for not supplementing or correcting the reasons given by Simenda is that he, Beytell orally explained his reasons to representatives of Waterberg Lodge <u>subsequent</u> to the taking of the decision and the notification thereof to applicant in Simenda's letter signed on the 30th September 2002.

This is no justification for the failure. It may be that Beytell also relied on his contention in paragraph 47 of his answering affidavit to the effect that an applicant cannot claim a right to a permit and that part of Section 83(1) of Ordinance 4 of 1975 read with Section 12 of Act 5 of 1996 which provides *inter alia* that the decision-taker shall not be obliged to furnish any reasons for the refusal by it to grant or issue any permit. This section, if relied on, however does not afford any justification for such an attitude in view of Article 18 of the Namibian Constitution and the many decisions of this Court interpreting and applying that article.

It is further clear from the affidavits that even though the refusal was in terms of a new policy based on formerly undisclosed grounds, neither Beytell nor the Minister or any other official applied the *audi alterem partem* <u>rule</u>, by notifying the applicant, before taking the decision, of the intended new policy and the grounds thereof and giving the applicant an opportunity to make representations in regard thereto before the decision was taken, as required by the aforesaid Article 18 of the Namibian Constitution and the decisions of the Court in regard thereto.[7]

It was also pointed out by Mr Frank in argument that a considerable number of permits for the importation of Mountain Reedbuck had been issued prior to the disputed refusal to Waterberg Lodge, without any objection by the Ministry. That this is so, is quite clear from the affidavits and the documentary evidence placed before Court.

Furthermore, a number of factual allegations regarding the type of fencing of the property of Waterberg Lodge and the adjoining property, the water facilities available and the issues relating to biodiversity were only raised in Beytell's answering affidavit. These allegations, held against Waterberg Lodge, were never put to the representatives of Waterberg Lodge, before the decision was taken, notwithstanding the fact that these allegations and arguments were clearly controversial and not admitted by Waterberg Lodge. Its representatives should have been apprised of such alleged facts and arguments based thereon, before the decision was taken and an opportunity given to controvert such facts before the decision was taken.

(Continued)

(Continued)

Mr Frank also pointed out correctly that the entity that decided, be it Beytell and or the Ministry, applied a pre-determined policy, which militated against the exercise of a discretion in each case as envisaged by Section 49 (I) of the Ordinance and Article 18 of the Namibian Constitution. If the policy was merely used as a guideline, it would have been in order if applied by the decision-maker, provided that the applicant had knowledge of the policy and had been given the opportunity to respond to it before the application was decided. In the circumstances applicable to this application, no discretion was in fact exercised as envisaged by section 49 (I) and article 18 of the Constitution.

Mr Frank further contended that in the circumstances pertaining to the application in this case, the applicant had a legitimate or reasonable expectation to be heard before the taking of the decision and to be granted the importation permit.

The ratio of this "doctrine of legitimate expectation" is consistent with the thinking and principles contained in Article 18 of the Namibian Constitution. The said doctrine, as well as Article 18, are based on reason and justice in the exercise of administrative discretion. The doctrine was overtaken by the later incorporation of Article 18 in the Namibian Constitution. Nevertheless the doctrine can serve a useful purpose in supplying some specifics to the broad and general norms set out in Article 18 and be used as a tool for the implementation of Article 18. As such it should be applied by our Courts in conjunction with Article 18.

Although neither Article 18 nor the decisions of the High and Supreme Court of Namibia require the application of the *audi alterem partem* rule in every case of the numerous routine administrative decisions that must be taken by officials from day to day, the rule must be applied to ensure administrative justice where for example facts adverse to an applicant are relied on by the decision-maker not known to the applicant and where the doctrine of "reasonable expectation" applies.

In my view the circumstances of this case are such that the *audi alterem partem* rule should have been applied. In addition there are several other shortcomings in the decision-making process referred to above which justify a setting aside of the decision.

Any doubt regarding the justification of such setting aside on the aforesaid grounds, is removed by the fact that Beytell had no legal authority to take the decision. As a consequence I have declined to deal in more detail with the failure to comply with Article 18, the *audi alterem partem* rule and the doctrine of legitimate expectation and will deal in the following section with this decisive and fatal ground for setting aside the decision.[8]

III: The lack of authority to decide

During argument before us, certain incisive questions were posed by members of the Court relating to the delegation of powers.

As the issue appeared to be decisive and Mr Smuts for the respondent appeared to have become uncertain of the correctness of his original submissions as contained in written heads of argument, the Court allowed respondent's counsel to submit additional argument and gave leave to appellant's counsel to reply thereto.

There then followed the filing of supplementary heads of argument which were very helpful and narrowed the field of dispute on this decisive issue. There was no further

(Continued)

(Continued)

dispute about the legal requirements for a valid delegation as will appear from my further analysis of the legal issues.

Counsel for the respondent accepted that where "a delegation is raised, the onus rests upon the party asserting it, to prove it." Counsel referred to the decision in *Chairman, Board of Tariffs and Trade v Teltron (Pty) Ltd* [1997] (2) SA 25, (AD) where it was stated at p 31 F-G:

The Board is, after all, a creature of statute, and where the statute creating it gives it the right to delegate its duties, there is an onus on the Board to show that that delegation has been properly made. It may well be that the onus has not been discharged by the mere allegation that there had been a delegation. The terms of the delegation have not been disclosed. There is furthermore no proof that the formalities required for a resolution to that effect had been complied with, that the requisite quorum had been present and that the resolution had been properly recorded. None of this has been done.

Counsel also referred to other decisions and then concluded: "The approach of the Courts has thus been that a delegation is to be restrictively construed and that the person asserting it bears the onus of establishing the delegation as a question of fact."[9]

Mr Smuts further correctly conceded: "The overriding principle is that where the legislature has vested powers and functions in a subordinate authority it intends the power to be exercised by <u>that</u> authority..."[10]

After making the aforesaid concessions, counsel for respondent attempted to save its case by submitting, without any supporting authorities, that "the fact that the Legislature has taken the power from Cabinet and placed it in the hands of the Minister,.... would not in our submission mean that valid administrative action undertaken by the Cabinet and its predecessors would be undone and fall away by virtue of the amendment......"

I have no problem with this statement if restricted to <u>valid</u> administrative action, such as, for example, applications for permits granted or refused by an authority, properly authorized by law, to decide on such applications. Where the amending law however removes the power to decide from the previous entity to another entity, such as in the instant case, applications for permits <u>subsequent to such transfer of power</u>, will have to be decided by the new entity, unless that new entity validly, that is, in terms of a law allowing such entity to delegate, has in turn delegated such power to another entity.

I also disagree with counsel for respondent where they submit: "A delegation is after all administrative action which, we submit, would remain in place until withdrawn by the new repository of power." This contention applies to <u>subordinate legislation</u> such as regulations, because regulations are laws which, it may be argued, remain operative, until repealed. However, delegations of the power to decide on applications for the import of game must be distinguished from applications already decided by a previous delegatee, who acted at the time in terms of a valid delegation of power.

If prior delegations remain in place until the new entity appointed by law of Parliament revokes that delegation, it would make nonsense of Parliament's <u>express</u> appointment of the new entity to exercise the power in question. This is even more apparent where as in this case, neither the new 1996 Act nor any other legislation empowered the Minister to delegate his/her power under Section 49(1) of Ordinance 4 of 1975 as amended.

(Continued)

(Continued)

Even if respondent counsel's above submission was arguable, respondent's case is fatally flawed because as appears from the following analysis, there is no sufficient proof of a lawful delegation to Beytell.

It is important to keep in mind that the respondent — being the Minister of Environment and Tourism, has not filed any opposing affidavit and there is no defence or explanation by the Minister before the Court *a quo* and before this Court.

Beytell, does not in his answering affidavit allege that he was authorized by the Minister to oppose the application on behalf of the Minister or to file the answering affidavit on behalf of the Minister. (See par. 1 of the affidavit.)

Furthermore, Beytell nowhere sets out or purports to set out, the defence or opposition if any, of the Minister but only his own opposition to the application and his reasons for the disputed decision, allegedly taken by himself. In the circumstances the application for review must be regarded as unopposed by the respondent.

There can also be no doubt that, regardless of what the position was before the enactment and promulgation of Act 5 of 1996, the incumbent Minister of Environment and Tourism in terms of Section 12 of that Act, became the undisputed functionary to take decisions for the granting or refusal of any permit for the importation of game from South Africa in terms of Section 49(1) of Ordinance 4 of 75, unless of course, his authority was subsequently lawfully delegated to another official.

Although Beytell alleged that the said authority was lawfully delegated to him by the pre-independence Executive Committee and thereafter by the Cabinet of the pre-independence "Cabinet of the Interim Government" he could not and did not allege a delegation by the Minister in pursuance of Section 49(1) as amended by Section 12 of the aforesaid Act 5 of 1996, enacted by the Parliament of an independent Namibia.

Mr. Beytell did allege a delegation in 1992 or as at 1992 by reference to a document marked BB9 containing a list of office bearers, in terms of which the "Head of the Permit Office" is indicated as the office bearer who could exercise the powers given under Section 49(1). Beytell claimed that he filled that position at the time.

The list is not signed by any person and there is no indication on it or in Beytell's affidavit who had issued the list and in terms of which law it was issued. The vagueness of this and other allegations by Beytell in this application is indeed worrying. Whether or not he was not properly advised by his legal advisers, remains an open question.

Be that as it may. Beytell nowhere alleges or suggests that the Minister of Environment and Tourism delegated or purported to delegate his powers under Section 49(1) of Ordinance 4 of 1975 to him in any capacity. The only statutory provision for delegations of authority referred to by counsel for respondent, was a general authority to delegate powers of the Executive Committee of the pre-independence period as contained in Sections 2—6 of the Delegation of Powers Ordinance 24 of 1973 as amended by Section 1 of Ordinance 20 of 1975.

It must be noted that Section 6(2) of Ordinance 24 of 1973 as amended contains a typical savings clause by providing:

Any power, authority or function delegated to any person in terms of the Ordinance repealed by Section (1) shall be deemed to have been delegated to such person in terms of this Ordinance.

(Continued)

(Continued)

There is no similar savings clause in Section 12 of Act 5 of 1996 and it consequently appears that at least as from the enactment and promulgation of Act 5 of 1996, the Minister of Environment and Tourism is the only authority to exercise the power under Section 49(1) of Ordinance 4 of 1975 to grant or refuse permits for the importation of live game from South Africa into Namibia.

I have considered Articles 140 and 141 of the Namibian Constitution which may be regarded as serving the purpose of a savings clause dealing with the law in force at the date of Namibian Independence on 21/3/1990. The said Ordinance 24 of 1973 as amended was never expressly repealed or amended by Act of Parliament or declared unconstitutional by a competent Court and consequently remained in force in terms of Article 140(1) of the Namibian Constitution.

For the purpose of argument I will assume that any delegation of power validly ceded in terms thereof will remain valid even after Namibian Independence on 21 March 1990, unless expressly or impliedly revoked by Act of Parliament after Namibian Independence. Neither respondent nor counsel for respondent relied on the aforesaid provisions of the Namibian Constitution for supporting the argument that any pre-independence delegation relating to Section 49(1) of Ordinance 4 of 1975 was not only in force at the date of independence but continued in force even after the promulgation of Act 5 of 1996.

Although Mr Beytell in his answering affidavit alleged that there was in fact a delegation of the power to his post by the pre-independence Executive Committee, he produced no documentary proof of such delegation.

Nevertheless, even if I assume for the purpose of argument that a proper delegation did in fact take place, and continued in force for some time after Namibian Independence by virtue of Article 140 and 141(1) of the Namibian Constitution, I am convinced that such delegation could not survive the coming into force of Section 12 of Act 5 of 1996. This legislation unambiguously and expressly vested the power in the Minister of Environment and Tourism. There is no law in terms of which the Minister could delegate his power and no savings clause in terms of which an existing delegation could remain effective. There is also no allegation that the said Minister delegated or even purported to delegate his power.

It follows from the above that any purported exercise of the power by Mr Beytell or even the "Ministry" would be *ultra vires* their powers and null and void.[11]

IV: Concluding Remarks

I have shown in the previous section that the purported decision of Beytell and/or the Ministry had to be set aside as null and void.

The question then arises what should be the further course of events. There are two possibilities:

1. That the original application by Waterberg Lodge be referred to the Minister for consideration and decision. Or
2. That the Minister is directed to grant the two applications by the applicant.

(Continued)

(Continued)

I have come to the conclusion that in the particular circumstances of this case the second option should be followed.

Since writing my proposed judgment, I have had the benefit of reading the proposed additional judgments of my learned brothers Shivute, CJ AND Chomba, AJA followed by incisive discussions between us.

We all agree that the appeal must succeed and that the Minister must be ordered to pay the cost.

We differ however in regard to the issue whether or not the Minister must be directed to grant the permits in question or whether the application must be referred to the Minister to consider the applications *de novo*. On this issue I was of the opinion that the Minister should be ordered to issue the permits applied for. My learned brothers on the other hand are of the opinion that the applications must be referred "back to the Minister to consider and decide after complying with the principles of natural justice including the *audi alterem partem* rule."

I will attempt to summarize the main points relied on by my learned brothers:

1. The effect of my proposed order is that the Minister is penalised by not being given an opportunity to properly consider the applications and such penalisation is not justified.
2. The Minister did not take part in the previous decision making process and had no opportunity to do so as a result of the unilateral action of Mr. Beytell and/or the Ministry.
3. The Minister did not file an opposing affidavit, probably because he did not know of the court action against him.
4. The issues raised in the papers are complicated and in such a case the Court should not usurp or unduly interfere with the powers of the Minister to exercise his/her discretion. Such action will also be in conflict with the devision of powers between the Legislature, Executive and the Judiciary.
5. The delays in the case are not substantial and were in any case not caused by delays on the side of the Minister and/or Ministry.
   5.1. The further delays in obtaining a binding final decision will not be unduly prejudicial to the applicant.
6. To order the Minister to grant the application and issue the requested permit, without giving him the opportunity to exercise the discretion given to him under section 49(1) of the Nature Conservation Ordinance 4 of 1975 as amended by section 12(b) of Act 5 of 1996, will in effect deprive the Minister of his authority. Section 49(1) reads in effect:

No person shall import . . . any game or wild animal . . . except under a permit granted by the Minister. . .

I regret to have to state that I continue to disagree with my learned brothers on the issue of referral to the Minister to consider the applications *de novo* and adhere to my original point of view. I find it necessary however to supplement and then consolidate my original reasons in

(Continued)

(Continued)

the light of the points made by my learned brothers. The supplemented reasons are as follows:

1. This is a unique case which must be distinguished from the vast majority of administrative cases where the Minister or other office bearers who had to exercise an administrative discretion according to law, purported to exercise such function and such discretion, but had not done so properly, for example, where such functionary had failed to comply with the empowering law and/or had failed to comply with art 18, 25, 40, and 41 of the Namibian Constitution. In this case the incumbent of the post of Minister had failed to consider and decide applications since the enactment of section 12 of Act 5 of 1996, which unequivocally placed on the Minister, the duty to decide applications for permits.

   The question arises: Which of the above two failures, is the most serious failure of duty? In my respectful view, the last type amounts to a total abrogation by disuse of the said power and function to decide and is the most serious of the two abovementioned failures.

2. Neither the Minister nor the Courts should pass or attempt to pass the buck to the Ministry, or any official of the Ministry. This is so because the Namibian Constitution provided for and entrenched the Rule of Law. It abolished the system of <u>parliamentary</u> supremacy and replaced it with the principle of <u>constitutional</u> supremacy.

   Although the constitution also incorporated the principle of the division of powers between Legislature, Executive and the Judiciary, it strengthened the role of the Courts compared with that role in the pre-independence dispensation. When considering the relevance and applicability of decisions of the Courts prior to the implementation of the Namibia Constitution in 1989, the the Namibian Courts must always consider the impact, if any, of the Namibian Constitution on those decisions.

   The same principle applies to decisions of South African Courts. Although the Namibian Courts are not bound by such decisions, their persuasive effect plays a part in the decisions of Namibian Courts. Moreover, South African decisions based on the new South African Constitution which came into effect in 1996, must be considered in the light of the Namibian Constitution and differences if any between these constitutions.

   The Courts play a pivotal role in the enforcement of the Chapter on fundamental human rights and freedoms. The freedoms included in article 21(1)(j) "the right to practice any profession, or carry on any occupation, trade or business" subject to "the law of Namibia, in so far as such law imposes <u>reasonable restrictions</u> on the exercise of the rights and freedoms conferred by the said sub-article, which are necessary in a democratic society and are required in the interests of the sovereignty and integrity of Namibia, national security, public order, decency or morality, or in relation to contempt of Court, defamation or incitement to an office."

   It is not only the abolition of such rights which are prohibited in terms of article 25(1), but the <u>abridgment</u> of such rights. The Executive and the agencies of Government are included in this prohibition. Sub-article (2) of article 25 provides that the Courts can be approached by aggrieved persons to enforce or protect a right which has been "<u>infringed or threatened</u>." This right is not limited to rights which have been abolished or abridged.

(Continued)

(Continued)

Sub-article (3) of Article 25 provides specifically that the Court "shall have the power to make all such orders as shall be <u>necessary and appropriate</u> to secure the applicants the enjoyment of the rights and freedoms conferred on them under the provisions of this Constitution, should the Court come to the conclusion that such rights and freedoms have been unlawfully <u>denied</u> or <u>violated</u>. . . ."

Art. 18 provides for Administrative Justice and reads as follows:

Administrative bodies and administrative officials shall act fairly and reasonably and comply with the requirements imposed on such bodies and officials by common law and any relevant legislation and persons aggrieved by the exercise of such acts and decisions shall have the right to seek redress before a competent Court or Tribunal.

It must be clear from the above that the Honourable incumbent Minister had failed completely to decide on applications for permits for almost ten years. The incumbent Minister thus acted not only in breach of Ordinance 4 of 1975 as amended, but also in conflict with art. 18 of the Constitution, by not at all performing the functions and duties imposed by law for the benefit *inter alia* of persons in the position of WABI Lodge, carrying on the business of keeping a lodge on a farm stocked with game. The failure of the incumbent Minister becomes even more exposed when art. 40 and 41 of the Constitution is considered. These articles provide:

Art. 40 <u>Duties and Functions Members of the Cabinet</u>

The members of the Cabinet shall have the following functions:

to direct, co-ordinate and supervise the activities of Ministries and Government Departments including para-statal enterprises, and to review and advise the President and the National Assembly on the <u>desirability and wisdom</u> of any prevailing subordinate legislation, regulations or orders pertaining to such para-statal enterprises, regard being had to the public interest;

to initiate bills for submission to the National Assembly; . . .

to carry out such other functions as are assigned to them by law or are incidental to such assignment;

to issue <u>notices, instructions and directives</u> to facilitate the implementation and administration of laws administered by the Executive, subject to the terms of this Constitution or any other law; . . .

Art. 41: <u>Ministerial Accountability</u>

All Ministers shall be <u>accountable individually</u> for the administration of their own <u>Ministries</u> and <u>collectively</u> for the administration of the work of Cabinet, both to the President and to Parliament.

Section 12 of Act 5 of 1996, placing the function to consider and decide on applications for permits, squarely on the shoulders of the incumbent Minister, had to be initiated in Parliament by the incumbent Minister in terms of par (b) of Art. 40 of the Namibian Constitution. This specific provision, in conjunction with the general provision in par (a) "to direct, coordinate and supervise the activities of the Ministries," and par (k), the obligation to issue, notices, instruction and directives to facilitate the implementation and administration of laws administered by the Executive, makes it impossible for the Minister

(Continued)

(Continued)

to plead ignorance of the law and to shield behind members of his Ministry for the Minister's failure to exercise his/her functions in accordance with the constitution and the law. But it must be said immediately in favour of the incumbent Minister, that he/she did not attempt to shift the blame.

The incumbent Minister just did not file any answering affidavit. This omission is aggravated by the fact that officials such as Simenda, the Acting Permanent Secretary and Erb, who were involved in the decision making process and/or the explanation thereof, did not submit any affidavits.

3. It seems to me therefore with the greatest respect to my learned brothers, that the Court should not shift the blame on behalf of the Minister who failed to take the Court into his confidence. Similarly the Court should not make the excuse on behalf of the incumbent Minister, that he/she may not have known about the legal proceedings in which the applicant cited the Minister as the respondent. Although there were initial discrepancies in the formal citation which appear to be due to the negligence of applicant's attorneys, this point was not taken by counsel for the Minister in the appeal, obviously because it was without substance.

4. It is obvious from the above that although Beytell should have known better, he did not intentionally usurp the powers and functions of the Minister. Rather, it was the incumbent Minister, himself/herself who abrogated his/her function and power <u>by disuse</u>.

5. In the circumstance it cannot be said that if my proposed order is issued by the Court, the Court would be usurping the function of the Minister. It is rather the incumbent Minister himself/herself who had the duty to function over many years, but who deprived himself/herself of the opportunity to function. The <u>Court</u> would consequently also not be "penalizing" the Minister by making an order as proposed by me, but rather rectifying a grave neglect by the said incumbent in this regard in accordance with the provisions of the Namibian Constitution above referred to.

Should the matter be referred to the Minister for his consideration *de novo*, he would probably rely on officials of his Ministry to come to a decision. Beytell, in his answering affidavit, demonstrated a strongly held opinion and adherence to a fixed policy decided upon by the Ministry. He will probably convey that opinion to the Minister when the Minister considers the applications. There is no indication that the Honourable Minister is an expert on the issue. The possibility of bias of the officials and the effect of the predetermined policy on the Minister, is rather strong.

6. The applicant/appellant will be severely prejudiced if the applicant/appellant is now compelled by the order of Court to put its case *de novo* to a Minister who had failed for many years to exercise the power and function allocated to him/her.

It is not only the three years that have elapsed since the making of its application, but the time needed and the expenses entailed to get finality that have to be considered. This time and cost will not necessarily end with the decision of the Minister, because if the applications are again refused, review proceedings may again have to be instituted by the applicant, delaying finality for a further period of years.

After having had to endure the chaotic position of confusion and neglect caused by the actions and omissions of the Minister and his Ministry, the question must be squarely put

(Continued)

(Continued)

and answered: Is it fair and reasonable to require the applicant to submit its case *de novo* to the said Minister and Ministry in such circumstances?

On the other hand, the granting of the said applications by the Minister in execution of the order of the Court, in due course, will not prejudice the State's interest and duty to protect the bio-diversity of Namibian wildlife but will enable the Minister and the Ministry, in conjunction with and in consultation with the joint stakeholders, to decide on a policy and procedures which will sufficiently protect such bio-diversity as well as the public interest and the interest of the wild game farmers, traders and businessmen and women. They are entitled in terms of the fundamental freedom enshrined in art. 21 (j) of the Namibian Constitution, to practice their trade, business or profession subject to the law of Namibia, in so far as such law imposes reasonable restrictions, on the exercise of such right or freedom.

Section 49(1) of Ord. 4 of 1975 and art. 18 of the Constitution, are part of the aforesaid law of Namibia. Section 49 does impose reasonable restrictions, such as veterinary control for the importation of any game and in issuing the permit, <u>additional</u> conditions may be imposed other than a total ban to safeguard biodiversity and to prevent the spread of sickness by imported game.

7. This is not a case where the alleged complications of the issue of bio-diversity and the division of powers between the Legislature, the Executive and the Courts should be overemphasized.

   7.1 After all, several similar applications were apparently approved over many years for several applicants until the applications of applicants were suddenly refused, in execution of a new policy adopted by an unauthorized Ministry under the control of the Minister.

   During this period the issue of protecting the biodiversity was never raised and at no stage was it alleged that the imported game had infected the indigenous game with any disease or had any adverse effect on such game in practice.

   7.2 As to the alleged infringement of the principle and theory of division of powers and the alleged need not to unduly interfere with division of powers, the following points must be kept in mind:

i. <u>Art. 1(3)</u> of the Constitution, merely provides that "the main organs of the State shall be the Executive, the Legislature and the Judiciary." The functions and powers of these organs are dealt with separately in other provisions of the constitution, but although distinct they overlap.

ii. As to the power of one organ to interfere in the powers and functions of another, it is obvious that Parliament can and will interfere in the functions of the Executive.

As far as the Courts are concerned, the Courts are mandated specifically to interfere not only with the Legislature in regard to the constitutionality of laws, but with the Executive in regard to its actions and/or omissions which are in conflict with art. 18, 25, 40, and 41 and/or in conflict with the provisions of other laws.

It follows from the above that no principle of non-interference can be derived from the Namibian Constitution at least not in regard to "interference" by the Courts in the functions

(Continued)

(Continued)

and powers of the Executive, in the case of acts and omissions in conflict with the Constitution and/or other applicable laws.

8. There can be no doubt that the Minister and the Ministry, although not abolishing the freedom of the applicant/appellant to conduct a business of its choice, it has by its actions and omissions "abridged" such right in terms of art. 25(1) or "infringed" it in terms of art. 25(2) of the constitution. That abridgment or infringement will be exacerbated by the Court, if the Court prolongs the agony by referring the matter to the Minister for consideration *de novo*.

9. The Court has a wide discretion as to whether it should refer the matter back to the functionary who had failed to exercise his/her function properly, for a rehearing, or whether the Court should direct the functionary to issue an order as defined by the Court in order to achieve an expeditious, reasonable and just solution.[12]

   However, in the present case, where the incumbent Minister had failed to perform the function allocated to the Minister by law, without any excuse or justification, it will, in my respectful opinion not only amount to a failure to act in accordance with the letter and spirit of articles 12, 18, 21(j) and 25 of the Namibian Constitution, but also a failure of justice, should this Court refer the applications to the said Minister for a hearing and decision in which the applicant is expected to submit to such process at this late stage.

10. I have taken note of the decision in *Minister of Environmental Affairs and Tourism & Ors v Phamhill Fisheries Pty Ltd* [13] quoted by my learned brother Shivute CJ in which the Court held:

Judicial deference is particularly appropriate where the subject-matter of an administrative action is very technical or of a kind in which a Court has no particular proficiency...

This is obviously only one of the considerations. Furthermore, a lot of material and opinions have already been placed on record relating to the issues involved and in regard to the applicable facts relevant in this particular case.

It is accepted that the biodiversity of the Namibian wildlife must be protected but whether or not, accepting that principle, the sudden adoption of a policy behind the scenes and arbitrarily choosing the applicant as the first victim, is justified in the case before us, is a completely different issue. On this issue the Court is surely in as good a position as the Minister to decide, if not in a better position.

Furthermore, there is no evidence or indication at all, that the Minister is an expert or would have other unbiased expertise available to place him in a better position to decide than the Court, on the issues, factual and legal, which have emerged in this case.

After all, the main consideration as stated by my learned brother Shivute CJ, on the authority of the case law, is – "In essence ... a question of fairness to both sides."

(Continued)

(Continued)

My learned brother Shivute, CJ, has also adopted the *dictum* in the decision of *Minister of Environmental Affairs & Tourism v Phambili Fisheries (Pty) Ltd* wherein it was stated:

> *Judicial deference does not imply judicial timidity or an unreadiness to perform the judicial function. It simply manifests the recognition that the law itself places certain administrative action in the hands of the Executive, not the Judiciary.*

This broad principle is subject to the provisions of the Namibian Constitution discussed *supra*. Furthermore, the problem in this case is that the Minister had failed completely to perform the "administrative action" placed in the hands of the Executive by the Namibian Constitution and section 49(1) of the Nature Conservation Ordinance, as amended by Act of Parliament. In such circumstances the Judiciary must not fail to make the appropriate order because of "judicial timidity" or "an unreadiness to perform the judicial function."

I fear that a decision by this Court ordering the applications to be heard de novo by the incumbent Minister may well be seen by many as "judicial timidity" or "unreadiness to perform the judicial function."

For these reasons I adhere to the order proposed by me in my draft judgment being:

1. The appeal succeeds.
2. It is declared that the refusal by Mr Beytell and/or the Ministry of Environment and Tourism to grant the appellant's applications of 19th and 27th of September 2002 for the importation of Mountain Reedbuck, is *ultra vires* and null and void.
3. The respondent, the Minister of Environment and Tourism, is directed to issue the permits applied for.
4. The respondent is ordered to pay appellant's costs of the appeal as well as that in the Court *a quo*.

Notes

1. According to the African Conservancy (n.d.), only 1% of the 5–10 million elephants that existed in 1930 exist today; only 2070 of the over 100,000 black rhinos that existed on the plains of Africa remain; 10,000–15,000 free-roaming African lions remain today; and there are only 4000–5000 wild dogs in Africa today.
2. The introduction of alien species can have a profound and devastating impact upon an ecosystem. Lake Victoria remains one of the best examples of the effect that invasive species can have on an ecosystem from anywhere in the world. Before the 1970s Lake Victoria contained hundreds of species (350–500 +) of fish in the cichlid family, of which 90% were endemic, comprising 80% of the fish biomass and much of the fish catch. This represented one of the diverse and unique assemblages of fish in the world. Since the introduction of the Nile perch and Nile tilapia, half the species are either extinct or only occur in very small populations. Nile perch now comprise 60% of the fish biomass. Their introduction has probably led to the extinction of 200 species of fish (IUCN, 2015).

3. "Communities living near a forest in Nigeria obtain 84 percent of their animal protein from bushmeat. In Ghana, approximately 75 percent of the population consumes wild animals regularly; in Liberia, 70 percent; and in Botswana, 60 percent" (Asibey and Child, 2010).

4. "Nonmarket Valuation is used to infer values for items that are not subject to markets like environmental services or health. Generally people are not charged for swimming in a public river or cleaner air. . . Widely-used approaches include Willingness-to-pay (WTP); Travel Cost Method (TCM); Contingent Valuation Method (CVM)," see Loomis (2005).

5. *ELGIN Fireclays Ltd v Wehls* [1947] (4) SA 744 AD at 749–750. *Minister Estates (Pty) Ltd v Killarney Hills Pty Ltd* [1979] (1) SA 621 (AD) at 624 B-H.

6. *Dresselhaus Transport v Government of the Republic of Namibia* SA 20/2003, NmS delivered 11.5.2005 p 44.

7. *Chairperson of the Immigration Selection v Frank & Another* [2001] NR 1075 SC at 109E–110B; 116F–121G; 170F–176I.

    Government of the Republic of Namibia v Sikunda [2002] NR 2003 SC at 226G–229 F. See also High Court decision; 2001 NR 181 *Mostert v Minister of Justice* [2003] NR 11 SC at 22J–29 D. *Cronje v Municipal Council of Mariental* [2004] (4) NLLP 129 at 175–182. *Du Preez & Another v Truth and Reconciliation Committee* [1997] (3) SA 204 AD at 231–234I and 233F–234. *President of RSA v SA Rugby Football Union and Others* [2000] (1) SA 1(CC) at 93I–99D. *Bel Porto School Governing Body & Others v Premier Western Cape & Another* [2002] (3) SA 265CC at 291C–295H, 300C–16E.

8. See *Bel Porto School Governing Body and Others v Premier Western Cape and Another* [2002] (3) SA 265 (CC) at 332–333, paragraphs 209–212. For the relationship between the doctrine of legitimate expectation and Article 18, see also: *The Chairperson of the Immigration Selection Board v Frank*, Asibey and Child (2010).

9. *Kasiyamhuru v Minister of Home Affairs & Others* [1999] (1) SA 643 (W) at 651 D-E. *Attorney-General, OFS v Cyril Anderson Investments (Pty) Ltd* [1965] (4) SA 628(A) at 639. *Shidiack v Union Government* [1912] AD 642 at 648.

10. Baxter, *Administrative Law*, at 434/435 *Martin v Overberg Regional Services Counsel* [1991] (2) SA 651 at 656 G-H.

11. *Opperman v Uitvoerende Komitee van die Verteenwoordigende Owerheid van die Blankes en Andere* [1991] (1) SA 372 (SWA) at 380 D-E. *Shidiack v Union Government (Minister of Interior)* [1912] at 642. *Wasmith v Jacobs* [1987] (3) SA 629 (SWA). *Yannakom v Apollo Club* [1974] (1) SA 614 (AD) at 623 F-H. Baxter, *Administrative Law* at 433–439.

12. See the decisions quoted by my brother Shivute, CJ in regard to the discretion to be exercised by the Court. See in addition: Erf 167, *Orchards cc v Greater Johannesburg Metropolitan Council & An* [1999] (1) SA 92 (SCA) at 109 C-G and the decision therein referred to. *Airoad Express (Pty) Ltd. v Chairman Local Road Transportation Board, Durban and Others* [1986] (2) SA 663 AD at 680 E-F in regard to bias, gross incompetence and/or where the outcome appears to be foregone. *The Namibian Health Clinics cc v Minister of Health and Social Services*, unreported judgment of the High Court of Namibia dated 10 September 2002.

13. 2003(6) 407 (SCA) at 432 par 53.

Questions

1. Define extinction and explain why this is a major concern.
2. What are the risk and uncertainty problems relevant to wildlife conservation?
3. Go to http://worldwildlife.org/threats/illegal-wildlife-trade. Give two examples of how the WWF is working to prevent illegal wildlife trade.

4. What are property rights and why are they important to the problem of wildlife extinction?
5. In what ways, if any, may criminal and civil sanctions be combined with an economic incentive system to check illegal poaching?

References

African Conservancy, n.d. Wildlife and Conservation Statistics. Available at: <http://www.africanconservancy. org/about/documents/Facts.pdf>.

Asibey, E.O.A., Child, G.S., 2010. Wildlife Management for Rural Development in Sub-Saharan Africa. Unasyla No. 161. <http://www.fao.org/docrep/t8850e/t8850e03.htm> (viewed 10.09.10).

International Union for Conservation and Nature (IUCN), 2015. The IUCN Red List of Threatened Species; Major Threats: Invasive Species, 2015-4. [Online 23 February 2016] <https://www.google.com/search? q=iucn&ie=utf-8&oe=utf-8>.

Kahn, J.R., 1995. The Economic Approach to Environmental and Natural Resources. The Dryden Press, Fort Worth.

Kriebel, D., et al., 2001. The precautionary principle in environmental economics. Environ. Health Perspect. 109, 871–876 [Online 15 August 2001] <http://ehpnet1.niehs.nih.gov/docs/2001/109p871-876kriebel/ abstract.html>.

Loomis, J., 2005. Economic values without prices: the importance of nonmarket values and valuation for informing public policy debates. Choices, 20 (3).

Margolis, M., Naevdal, E., 2004. Safe Minimum Standards in Dynamic Resource Problems – Conditions for Living on the Edge of Risk. Resources for the Future, Discussion Paper 04-03.

Randall, A., 1981. Research economics: An economic approach to natural resource and environmental policy. Grid Publication Inc., Columbus, Ohio.

CHAPTER 14

Water Resources

Keywords: Water resources; water demand; water pricing; legal and regulatory regime; water rights; urban water; irrigation water

14.1 Introduction

The law and economics of water resources in sub-Saharan Africa (SSA) presents complex analytical challenges. The challenges arise because of the nature of water itself. Water is found in streams, rivers, lakes, underground, in solid form as ice, in the atmosphere, in plants, and in soils, etc. Water may also be put to different uses such as for drinking, agriculture, industry, manufacturing, power generation, recreation, and navigation. Water is subject to different quality standards, and may be supplied to the population through a public, private, public—private partnership, community supply such as a public standpipe, or it may be a stream or village pond, with appropriation subject only to custom social norms. These varied characteristics influence the economics, laws, and regulations governing water resources. For countries in SSA, a major challenge is balancing urban and agricultural needs for water in the future.

Water covers 70% of the earth's surface but only 2.8% is fresh water and 97.2% is saline water.[1] Actual Renewable Water Resources per Capita available in SSA is about 8 (1000 m^3/year; World Bank/WRI, undated). SSA countries have the lowest freshwater withdrawal rates among all the regions of the world.[2] The population of SSA is projected to increase from 840 million in 2010 to 1.3 billion in 2030, and further to 1.7 billion in 2050 (World Bank, undated). This increasing population will increase water demand to meet municipal, agriculture, mining, industrial, energy (hydropower), watershed management, coastal ecology and biodiversity, fisheries, and recreational uses. These varied demands for water are the sources of potential conflicts in water markets. To address poverty issues and raise incomes in rural areas, the medium-term water conflict will center on urban and irrigation uses.

F.O. Boadu: Agricultural Law and Economics in Sub-Saharan Africa.
DOI: http://dx.doi.org/10.1016/B978-0-12-801771-5.00014-9

14.2 Urban Water Use

The urban population in SSA is expanding rapidly and the expansion is putting pressure on social amenities such as water, sanitation, housing, and health facilities. Table 14.1 shows that piped water and stand posts are the major sources of water supply in urban areas.

Public utilities charge urban water users a fee to build and maintain the infrastructure supporting water supply.[3] The public utility is usually a governmental entity and its fee is set by government. For example, in Ghana, water tariffs are set by the Public Utilities Regulatory Commission (PURC) based on guidelines set by government.[4] Water use in rural communities is controlled by the community and fees are not set by a formal public utility entity.[5]

14.3 Irrigation

Irrigation use in SSA is low. According to one report, only 5% of the total cultivated area in SSA is irrigated, even though irrigation could raise yields by at least 50% (You, 2008). The irrigation potential and its implications for food security, the expanding urban population, and the impact of climate change bring the allocation of water to urban and agricultural uses to the forefront of public policy. Countries in SSA have to make difficult decisions about future pricing of urban and irrigation water.[6] The analysis presented below explains the narrow theoretical issue associated with pricing water for irrigation and urban uses.[7]

Fig. 14.1 presents a dual-pricing analysis for urban and irrigation water demand and supply. The vertical axis is the price of water and the horizontal axis is the quantity of water available for urban and irrigation uses. D^u represents urban demand for water and D^a represents agricultural demand. D^t represents the total (urban and agricultural) demand for water. S represents the supply of water and it is vertical because there is only a fixed quantity of water available at any point in time. p represents water price set by the government. At this price, the quantity of water demanded, W_d^t is less than the quantity supplied W_s.

Over time, due to expanding urban population demand, the urban demand curve shifts to $D^{u'}$ and total demand for water shifts to $D^{t'} (D^{u'} + D^a)$. The economy will experience a

Table 14.1: Urban water supply sources in Africa (Banerjee, 2008)

	Percentage of Urban Population Accessing Various Water Sources				
	Piped Water	Stand Posts	Wells/Boreholes	Surface Water	Vendors
1990−1995	50	29	20	6	3
1996−2000	43	25	21	5	2
2001−2005	39	24	24	7	4

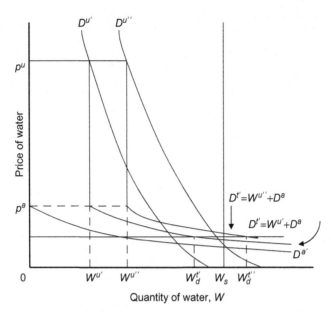

Figure 14.1
A Two-price System for Water.

water shortage since total water demand, $W_d^{t'}$ is greater than available supply W_s. The government may decide to establish a dual water price system for urban and agriculture uses. Suppose the urban price is set at p^u and the agriculture price remains at p^a. Urban users will satisfy their demand at $W^{u'}$ leaving the quantity of water remaining to agricultural uses. The dual-pricing system allocates water effectively to the urban and agriculture users since the total demand $W_d^{t'}$ is less than the total supply W_s. Note that we are measuring water demands based on the total water demand curve, $D^t (D^{u'} + D^a)$. However, the solution may be temporary because as the urban population expands further, with an urban water demand curve now represented as $D^{u''}$, the total water demand curve shifts up to $D^{t''} = W^{u''} + D^a$. Once again pressure from urban demand will lead to a shortage of water since $W_d^{t''}$ is greater than available supply, W_s.

The analysis of urban and rural water demand point to important policy challenges that governments must address. At the top of the challenges is the need for credible overall rural−urban policies that stem the flow of the population to urban centers. Governments also have to take on the problem of irrigation water pricing in anticipation of expanded irrigation water demand in support of several large-scale agriculture projects to meet the food security objectives of countries. The pricing of small-scale irrigation water demands special attention given the large number of small farmers and the critical role they play in the supply of foodstuffs, especially vegetables.

14.4 Legal and Regulatory Regime Governing Water Resources in SSA

The laws and regulations affecting the water economy in any society are influenced by the interaction between natural conditions such as precipitation, location, political, economic, and social conditions. Given the differences in these conditions, discussion of the water laws and regulations in SSA has to focus on themes that are common to all countries. One common theme is that countries have passed Acts or statutes that vest ownership of all public water in the head of state, and control of water resources in a Minister of State. Public water in all the countries includes both surface and groundwater and requires a permit for withdrawal. Countries have also set up utility boards or commissions that set user fees, issue permits for water use, and define priority in water allocation. Water for domestic purposes is the top priority in all the statutes. Water laws and regulations make a distinction between urban and rural communities' water use, leaving control and management of the former to the public utilities and the latter to communities.

All the SSA countries have exemptions that allow small farmers to use water for agricultural and livestock purposes. Some statutes require a small farmer to register water usage with the local district office, especially if the small farmer constructs a dam for irrigation purposes. The institutional mechanisms for water distribution in the urban areas vary across countries. Countries use corporatized state-owned enterprises, public–private partnerships, private entities, or sometimes contract out a private company to distribute water. Rural communities take water from rivers and ponds and are not subject to the formal laws and regulations operating in urban areas. All countries have included provisions in the water law to address water quality and pollution issues. In some countries, separate legislation is used to address water quality and pollution problems, for example, pollution prevention may be under the Environmental Protection Agency. In the rural communities, water quality protection is the collective responsibility of the community under the leadership of a chief or community leader.

14.5 Case Law on Water Resource Use and Quality Control

There are only few court cases on water regulation violations in SSA because the water market is not developed. A developed market is characterized by active transactions between private parties, and between enforcement agencies and private parties. While enforcement agencies issue citations for violations of regulations, these do not end up as formal court actions. There is no documentation of water conflict resolution before a chief or community leader, but in a situation where a formal court is available, for example, at the district level the community may use the formal legal apparatus as Box 14.1 shows.[8] Box 14.1 is not a case of water pollution from agriculture use of a pesticide. Due to the low level of pesticide and fertilizer use, agriculture has not been a major source of water quality

---

BOX 14.1 Farmer Gets 1 Year for Polluting River

A 32-year-old farmer has been sentenced to 24 months imprisonment for polluting the Mankran River with DDT insecticide. The river serves as the community's main source of water. Stephen Dogbe pleaded guilty and was convicted on his own plea.

The Prosecutor, Police Inspector Abraham Agyei-Mensah, told the court presided over by Mr Frank Owusu-Afriyie that Dogbe and the complainants lived in separate cottages near Egyanso where the river serves as their source of drinking water.

He said on March 30, this year, at about 2100 hours, some inhabitants went to fetch water and saw the accused polluting the river with the insecticide, thus killing large quantities of fish. The prosecution said the complainants arrested Dogbe with the dead fish and the rest of the insecticide in a bottle and handed him over to the police.

During interrogation, the accused admitted the offence, the prosecution added.

Source: GNA

Story from Myjoyonline.Com News

http://news.myjoyonline.com/news/200704/3165.asp

Published: May 4, 2007

---

deterioration in SSA. The participation of local communities in enforcing water quality regulations is efficient because it reduces the transaction costs facing the national enforcement agencies often located at urban centers and far from rural areas.

The *Allan Sugar case* discussed below reiterates the idea that courts frown on the introduction of extraneous information to change the terms of a written contract. As the court ruled, an easement or prescriptive right to an irrigation system is unavailable where a party purchases part of a large piece of land but fails to explicitly negotiate rights to an irrigation system that is located on the land. The case is a reminder of the need for contracting parties to reduce their intentions in writing. The *Namibia Water Corporation Limited v AUSSENKEHR Farms (PTY) Ltd* case is another example where poor contract specification could have adverse consequences for a party. In addition to the terms of the contract on its face, note the issue of who is entitled to a permit for irrigation water under the policies of the government. The *Charliewell, Kakweni Chunga v City Council of Lusaka* case raises issues that several countries in SSA will face with expanding urbanization and population expansion. The spatial expansion of cities may bring lands formerly designated as agricultural under the jurisdiction of municipalities. While the annexation of farmlands may by statute extend property tax powers to new communities, the financial constraints facing municipalities may not support the provision of social services, such as health facilities, schools, water, roads, and security to the annexed areas.

Allan Sugar (Products) Ltd v Ghana Export Co., Ltd
COURT OF APPEAL, ACCRA

30 March 1983

FACTS: The appellants (hereinafter referred to as the plaintiffs) as their name implies, are a company engaged in sugar-cane production. Their dispute with the respondents (hereinafter referred to as the defendants) is over irrigation rights on land they acquired from the National Investment Bank (N.I.B.) for the cultivation of their canes. The facts of the dispute can be shortly stated. N.I.B. in an apparent drive to sustain agriculture, provided funds to a vegetable marketing body called the Mankesim Co-operative Vegetable Growers Marketing Society Ltd. The project was an unmitigated disaster, and N.I.B. lost ¢300,000. To call a halt to further losses, N.I.B. foreclosed their mortgage with the society and re-allocated the 200 acres of land involved in the venture to the protagonists in this appeal. On the land were buildings and an irrigation system that were the society's assets which N.I.B. also disposed of.

The plaintiffs obtained 50 acres of land and all the buildings previously occupied by the co-operative society and they were indeed prepared to pay any price to keep those buildings in their exclusive possession. They do not quarrel with this disposition. The plaintiffs, for the sum of ¢25,000 acquired the rights for the unexpired term of the co-operative society's lease. For their 150 acres of land, the defendants on the other hand, had to pay ¢75,000. But they sought and obtained from N.I.B. the exclusive right to the use of the irrigation system. The terms of their agreement with N.I.B. were embodied in an exchange of letters culminating in exhibits 3, 4 and 6. For the better appreciation of the defendants' contract with N.I.B., I would set these out fully. Exhibit 3 states:

"Ghana Export Co., Ltd.
P.O. Box 7663,
Accra-Ghana.
6 April 1979.
National Investment Bank,
P.O. Box 3726,
Accra.

Dear Sir,

MANKESIM FARMS LIMITED

We are writing with reference to your letter of 21 March addressed to the Secretary to the S. M.C. and copied to us. As previously indicated, we consider the settlement figure of ¢75,000 unfair as it represents 75 per cent of the total acquisition price, when in fact we have been allocated only 50 per cent of the project land and facilities. In addition the project buildings are occupied exclusively by Allan Sugar Products Ltd.

We however wish to confirm our discussions (Anteson/ Bentil) of 5 April 1978 that we accept the assessment of ¢75,000 subject to the following:

(1) that we are given title to 150 acres of the project land;

(Continued)

(Continued)

(2) we have exclusive use of the entire irrigation facilities attached to the project;

(3) in view of the satisfactory agreement reached; the settlement proposals as contained in letter Ref. No. SMC/CR. 10741 V.4 of 24 May 1977 is withdrawn.

Meanwhile, we enclose our cheque for ¢40,000 in the hope that you will be able to accept our proposals to enable the balance of ¢35,000 to be paid.

Yours faithfully,
(Sgd.) Henry Bentil
Managing Director."

And exhibit 4 also states:

"National Investment Bank
P.O. Box 3726,
Accra.
25 April 1978.
The Managing director,
Ghana Export Co., Ltd.
P.O. Box 7663,
Accra.

Dear Sir,

MANKESIM FARM LAND

We acknowledge receipt of your letter dated 6 April 1978 and the cheque for ¢40,000 sent therewith. Upon receipt of the remaining ¢35,000 we shall transfer title to the remaining 150 acres of the farm land with exclusive use of the irrigation facilities. As we agreed at our discussions held in my office on 5 April 1978 you will obtain withdrawal of letter No. SMC/CR. 10741 V.4 date 4 May 1977.

Yours faithfully,
(Sgd.) P. F. O. Anteson
Chief Legal Adviser."

And finally exhibit 6 provides:

"National Investment Bank
P.O. Box 3726
Accra

10 January 1979

(Continued)

(Continued)

Dear Sir,

MANKESIM FARM LAND

We acknowledge receipt of your letter Ref. MI/MB/SAO dated 20 November 1978 together with your clients' cheque for ¢10,000 being payment on account.

The bank will assign to your clients the 150 acres together with the irrigation facilities after full payment has been made by your clients.

Yours faithfully,

(Sgd.) G. A. Mustapha

for Chief Legal Adviser

The Managing Director
Ghana Export Co., Ltd.
P.O. Box 7663,
Accra."

The defendants' insistence on the exclusive use of the irrigation system was to protect their young vegetables grown on a very large scale for the export market. For the healthy husbandry of vegetables it was necessary, they argued, that they retained absolute and exclusive control of the system. Joint control, especially in the atmosphere of bad blood that existed between the parties, would spell the doom of their venture. Apparently, their grantors, N.I.B. appreciated the position and granted them what they sought.

The plaintiffs were dissatisfied with the turn of events. They brought the regional administration and the central government into the matter to intervene to ensure that they were not denied the irrigation facilities. Before the plaintiffs exercised that extraneous lever, they were well aware of the understanding the defendants had reached with N.I.B. This is clearly brought out in all answer to the question:

> "Q. Before you started your negotiations with the Castle, did you know that the National Investment Bank had negotiated with the defendants for the sale of the 200-acre farm with the irrigation system and the buildings?
> A. Before I went to the Castle I knew about it."

The Castle, that is the central government, was not a contracting party; all it could do was to make recommendations. In exhibit B which was a suggested compromise, the government stated:

"After further study of the various decisions reached at the meeting, and following consultations with the Bank of Ghana on same, this office is convinced that the following should be adopted as a satisfactory settlement of the issue:

(1) (i) that the Ghana Export Co., Ltd. be allocated 100 acres of land for its vegetable project;

(Continued)

(Continued)

(ii) that Allan Farms (Products) Ltd. be allocated 60 acres of the lowland area;

(iii) that the remaining 40 acres be allocated to the local farmers; and

(iv) that the new Irrigation Development Authority should take over in due course and rehabilitate the installed irrigation facilities to be hired out to all users in the area.

(2) By a copy of this letter, the Ministry of Agriculture is being advised to take note of the decision in paragraph 1 (iv) above for implementation in due course."

This letter, dated 24 May 1977 was signed for the Secretary of the Supreme Military Council.

OPINION: In my view, the language is one of exhortation and not of compulsion. It was not an edict which could have any legal viability. The deed of assignment that followed and upon which the plaintiffs' rights were founded is dated 8 May 1978. It does not even reflect the recommended shares. It is completely silent about the irrigation facilities. The argument that the settlement terms suggested by the government in exhibit B were never effectuated and were indeed abrogated by the actual terms of agreement between the respective parties is clearly borne out by exhibit 3, which was the defendants' final offer that was accepted by the National Investment Bank in exhibit 4. The express demand that the government's suggestion in exhibit B be ignored was implicitly accepted.

The plaintiffs contend that since the irrigation system was installed to ensure the better husbandry of 200 acres of vegetables grown by the erstwhile Mankesim Co-operative Society, a sale of any portion of that land automatically carried with it pro tanto, the use of the irrigation facilities. The plaintiffs base their claim on a general understanding of this right by all the parties. The facts suggest otherwise especially in view of the defendants' agreement with N.I.B.

Turning again to the facts, it seems that when the plaintiffs' pressures yielded no results, they resorted to self-help to install a pump some fifteen feet away from the main pump to boost the pumping of water into the irrigation system. The defendants would have nothing of this surreptitious attempt at gaining some control of the system. They promptly undid whatever the plaintiffs did. In exasperation the plaintiffs sued. In a careful analytical judgment the court below dismissed the plaint, thus provoking a further dissatisfaction which has been expressed by this appeal.

In this court, the plaintiffs have categorically stated that their claim is not based on the principle of easement. Indeed, that aspect of the matter was extensively dealt with by the court below. The plaintiff's real complaint is that the court below paid scant regard to the negotiations preceding their contract of assignment, the understanding arrived at between the parties at the various meetings and discussions with the government and other bodies, the use to which the former society put the irrigation system, and their needs as sugar-cane growers for an irrigated field. The sum total of these matters, if considered, runs the argument, would demonstrate beyond doubt that the use of the irrigation facilities was in the contemplation of the parties and formed the basis of the plaintiffs' agreement with N.I.B.

(Continued)

(Continued)

The argument that the matrix of facts, events, surrounding circumstances and nuances should be taken into account in ascertaining the real intentions of parties to an agreement and in construing it, is sound as far as it goes: see Lord Wilberforce's opinion in *Prenn v. Simmonds* [1971] 3 All E.R. 237 at pp. 239–240, H.L.; but the fuller statement of the law, however, is that where parties have reduced into writing their intentions they are bound by their written word and the use of extraneous material as aids to interpretation can only be resorted to in extreme cases of genuine doubt.

Thus in *Bristol Tramways, etc., Carriage Co., Ltd. v. Fiat Motors Ltd.* [1910] 2 K.B. 831 at p. 838, C.A. Farwell L.J. said that where a formal document had been executed showing the terms of a contract no antecedent or subsequent negotiations are admissible to construe such a contract. See also *Bridges v. Hewitt; Bridges v. Bearsley* [1957] 2 All E.R. 281 and *Pritchard v. Arundale* [1971] 3 All E.R. 1011. As was stated by Lord Wilberforce in *Prenn v. Simmonds* (supra) at p. 240, H.L.: "It is only the final document which records a consensus." It is no function of the court to rewrite an agreement for the parties by inserting terms that would have been beneficial but were overlooked especially when such an interpolation would amount to an interference with a third party's bargain.

In this case the only suggestion that a rehabilitated irrigation system might be put to commercial use on hire, came from the government. There, an irrigation authority which had been newly formed, was to rehabilitate the irrigation system on the land and provide irrigation services for hire. That suggestion never got off the ground and the defendants had to rehabilitate the system at a cost of ¢40,000 borne solely by themselves. Exhibit B indeed was jettisoned by N.I.B., the plaintiffs' lessors, when they concluded an agreement with the defendants. Our attention has not been drawn to any document or statement emanating from N.I.B. giving credence to any suggestion that they would make available to the plaintiffs the irrigation facilities. If they had and failed to abide by their promise, they would have laid themselves open to legal action for breach. The fact that N.I.B. has not been sued is proof of the pudding. I am clearly of the view that exhibits 3 and 4 could not co-exist with the assumptions the plaintiffs are pressing on this court. To borrow the words of Godfrey Lane J. in *Ford Motor Co., Ltd. v. Amalgamated Union of Engineering and Foundry Workes* [1969] 2 All E.R. 481 at p. 496:

"Agreements such as these, composed largely of optimistic aspirations, presenting grave practical problems of enforcement and reached against a background of opinion adverse to enforceability, are, in my judgment, not contracts in the legal sense and are not enforceable at law. Without clear and express provisions making them amenable to legal action, they remain in the realm of undertakings binding in honour."

Here N.I.B. could not be bound even in honour, much less the defendants. Even the government which set in motion the idea of compromise could not be held responsible as it was not a contracting party. And as Megarry J. said in *Cordell v. Second Clanfield Properties Ltd.* [1968] 3 All E.R. 746 at p. 751:

(Continued)

(Continued)

"Where there are ill-drafted provisions in a conveyance there must always be a danger that each party at the time put his own disparate interpretation on them; and in such a case I would be slow, on motion to bind either party by more than is manifestly there, either expressly or by ineluctable implication."

Fine language from a great equity judge. The point, however, should not be forgotten that there is no contract, conveyance or specie of agreement whatsoever between the plaintiffs and the defendants. What each has, is a separate agreement with a common lessor, N.I.B. There is no easement to overreach the defendants' contract either.

In examining the plaintiffs' contentions further, it is apparent that long before their agreement with N.I.B., the plaintiffs were cultivating two other plots of land nearby. They never used the irrigation system. The plaintiffs also confessed that when they planted five acres of land they acquired from N.I.B. with nursery canes, they did not use the irrigation system but depended on domestic water supply "anticipating that it would meet the rains." The plaintiffs were consequently not using any irrigation system in July and part of August 1978. It was only in August, four months before the action was brought, that the plaintiffs made the first approaches to the defendants in any discussions about the system. If an understanding had been reached whereby the irrigation facilities were to be shared, the plaintiffs' conduct in not exacting their share of rights till a very late stage had been reached, seems incomprehensible to me. Another aspect of the plaintiffs' conduct which seems to contradict their stance is in their planting of five acres of the land with sugarcane in February—March and 20—25 acres of the land with maize in April—May. Maize does not require irrigation, so irrigation was not essential for the farming the plaintiffs actually engaged in. They had consequently not been utilising a facility which had ripened into a right in equity of which the defendants should take notice.

In this appeal, no claim by way of easement has been put forward by the plaintiffs. Tentative skirting around this area of the law was abandoned in the court below. Perhaps any argument on the application of easement can be buried by a quotation from Megarry and Wade on the *Law of Real Property* (1966, 3rd ed.) at p. 840 where the learned authors state:

"An easement or profit for life or for years, for example, may be expressly granted but cannot be acquired by prescription, for the theory of prescription presumes that a permanent right has been duly created at some unspecified time in the past. A claim by prescription must therefore fail if user can be proved only during a time when the servient land was occupied by a tenant for life or for years. But if it can be shown that user as of right began against the fee simple owner, it will not be less effective because the land was later settled or let."

In this case there was no covenant for use. No user was proved. Indeed, there was a clear concession that the co-operative society which installed the irrigation system could not have employed it for many years for a minute fraction of their 200 acres of land before the society went bankrupt, and that explains why the system had become "dysfunctional" as the Castle, the central government, aptly described its condition. Counsel for the plaintiffs has concentrated his fire power on the principle that the courts frown upon a derogation from a grant. The argument is put thus: A lessor is under an obligation not to interfere with the

(Continued)

(Continued)

reasonable use of the subject-matter of the letting for the purposes for which it was granted. This principle is formulated in a passage in *Gale on Easements* (1959) (13th ed.), p. 34 under the heading "Special immunities under the doctrine of non-derogation from grant":

"The same situation as if an easement had been created, although none has been, can arise from the principle that 'if a grant or demise be made for a particular purpose, the grantor or lessor comes under an obligation not to use the land retained by him in such a way as to render the land granted or demised unfit or materially less fit to be used for the particular purpose for which the grant or demise was made'."

An answer to the plaintiffs' argument is given by Plowman J. in *Woodhouse & Co., Ltd v. Kirkland (Derby) Ltd.* [1970] 1 W.L.R. 1185 at p. 1193 which I respectfully adopt:

"It may be, I think, that a purely negative right over the servient tenement or quasi-servient tenement such as a right of light can be acquired under the doctrine forbidding derogation from grant in a manner which is indistinguishable from an implied grant, but I am not satisfied that this is true of a positive right such as a right of way."

If the plaintiffs' deed of assignment did not positively grant them a right of user of the irrigation facilities, no grant can be implied, let alone a grant that by operation of law can give them a cause of action against the defendants who had positive and exclusive rights of user. Nothing prevents the plaintiffs from making use of the Otchi River to establish their own irrigation system with pumps, pipes and all. Nothing can prevent the plaintiffs from using the water in the river, but in my opinion, an irrigation system that was rehabilitated at great expense could not be provided free to the plaintiffs. The course of prudence and, I dare say also, the dictates of law, would counsel a commercial approach to the defendants for the use of the existing irrigation facilities at a price.

Judgment: *Held, dismissing the appeal:* (1) although the matrix of facts, events, surrounding circumstances and nuances should be taken into account in ascertaining the real intentions of parties to an agreement and in construing it, where parties had reduced into writing their intentions they were bound by their written word and the use of extraneous material as aids to interpretation could only be resorted to in extreme cases of genuine doubt. Thus where, as in the instant case, a formal document had been executed showing the terms of the contract, no antecedent or subsequent negotiations were admissible to construe such a contract. The suggestion that a rehabilitated irrigation system might be put to commercial use came from the government which was not a contracting party. The recommendation therefore had no legal viability. That recommendation was, moreover, rejected by the NIB, the lessors, when they concluded the agreement with GE Ltd. Consequently, neither NIB nor GE Ltd. were bound by that suggestion.

Ruling: I see no violation of the plaintiffs' rights in this matter. Consequently, I see no reason why the judgment of the High Court should be disturbed. I would dismiss the appeal.

Namibia Water Corporation Limited v AUSSENKEHR Farms (PTY) Ltd
High Court of Namibia

Case No. I 1286/2005, 09 January 2009

DAMASEB, JP

CONTRACT:

Parties had entered into written agreement containing a non-variation clause:

Defendant alleging that plaintiff vicariously guilty of breach of contract as a result of which defendant says it terminated contract. Court not finding such breach and that the defendant, even if there was such breach was required to communicate termination of contract which it failed to do. To be of any legal effect, termination of contract must be communicated to the guilty party: *Tsabalala v Minister of Health* 1987 (1) SA 513 at 520I.

Defendant alleging that the plaintiff's conduct amounting to repudiation of contract entitling it to cancel contract. Court finding no such conduct on plaintiff's part. In any event defendant failing to prove that it, acting on such repudiation, exercised its election to cancel contract.

Defendant relying on alleged oral agreement preceding written instrument. Defendant bearing *onus* to prove such oral agreement but failing to do so. Such claim difficult to prove and must be proved by facts "in the clearest and most satisfactory manner".

Judgment

Damaseb, JP: The plaintiff in this matter is Namibia's national water utility, created by Act of Parliament and registered as a public company under the Companies Act. In terms of s5 of Act 12 of 1997 its objects

"shall be to carry out efficiently, and in the interests of the Republic of Namibia"

(a) the primary business of bulk water supply to customers, in sufficient quantities, of a quality suitable for the customers' purposes and by cost-effective, environmentally sound and suitable means, and
(b) the secondary business of rendering water-related services, supplying facilities and granting rights to customers upon their request."

The defendant, Aussenkehr Farms (Pty) LTD, is a private company involved in grape production along the Orange River. In 2001, the defendant decided to embark upon a 2000 hectare irrigation scheme for the planting of vineyards for export purposes. The defendant is the owner of the land on which the vineyards were to be planted. To irrigate the vineyards it required 32.2 million cubic meters of water from the Orange River. The government of the day supported the initiative at the highest level; as did the plaintiff in whom the government of Namibia is the sole shareholder. On 15 March 2001, the Ministry of Agriculture, Water and Rural Development ("the Ministry") hosted a "Stakeholders' Conference" in collaboration with the grape growers to discuss the economic development potential along

(Continued)

(Continued)

the Orange River, including the development of the 2000 ha irrigation scheme at Aussenkehr farm. The objective of the Conference was stated as follows:

"to inform the general public on the development potential of the area; to give people in commerce an opportunity to state their interest in future developments; to address general developments of the area including settlement at Aussenkehr; to improve co-ordination amongst grape growers; and, to enhance collaboration amongst all stakeholders."

A minute of the conference deliberations attributes the following to Mr. Helge Habenicht, the then chief executive officer of the plaintiff:

"The CEO, Mr. H Habenicht, stated that the corporation does not operate along profit motives, but renders services at a cost. Namwater is involved in developing, managing as well as expanding and financing of water infrastructure. He indicated that <u>if invited, Namwater would be willing to provide, manage, as well as finance and maintain the supply of reasonable quality water to Aussenkehr</u> on condition that the contracting partner was a legal entity." (My underlining)

On 27 September 2007, the plaintiff, represented by its former chief executive officer, Helge Habenicht, and the defendant, represented by its managing director, Dusan Vasiljevic, entered into a written agreement in terms whereof the plaintiff was to render 'services' to the defendant as a precursor to the establishment of the 2000 ha irrigation scheme at Aussenkehr Farm. Clause 5 of the written agreement contains the following:

5. In the event of the Company requiring NamWater to proceed with the obtaining of tenders, detailed design and construction of the bulk water supply scheme, the company and Namwater will enter into a separate agreement for the obtaining of tenders, detailed design and construction of the bulk water supply scheme, as well as for the supply of water in bulk, in respect of the 2000 hectare irrigation project.
6. *The deliverables in terms of the Service are a planning and preliminary design report by NamWater of the complete bulk water supply scheme and a set of tender documents for the detailed design and construction of the bulk water supply scheme,* **to be supplied to the Company within the Project Period.** *The planning and preliminary design report to be compiled by NamWater of the complete bulk water supply scheme, shall include a detailed cost estimate pertaining to the complete bulk water supply scheme, which estimate shall be as close as possible to the actual costs to be incurred in respect of the design, construction and subsequent operation of the bulk water supply scheme."*

The agreement defines "the service" as:

"The planning, the preliminary design and the compilation of tender documentation for the provision and construction of a bulk water supply scheme capable of supplying 12500 cubic meters per hour of water for irrigation purposes to a 2000 hectare irrigation project at farm Aussenkehr, No 147, situated in the district of Karasburg, Namibia."

The plaintiff's case is that the agreement contemplated in clause 5 was never entered into. The defendant denies liability to pay the amount claimed on several grounds. The salient ones being: the intentional and deliberate refusal by the plaintiff to enter into the agreement

(Continued)

(Continued)

contemplated in clause 5; plaintiff's refusal to supply bulk water while in a position to do so and instead informing the defendant that the latter had to apply for a water abstraction permit; and the existence of an additional oral agreement which defeats the plaintiff's claim.

The plaintiff's claim

The plaintiff claims N$300 000 plus VAT of N$45,000 together with interest at the rate of 11.5% as from 21 May 2002 to 30 July 2003 and 16.75% from 1 August 2003 to date of judgment. It claims that on 26 September 2003 the defendant was indebted to it in the amount of N$422,272.68 which amount despite being due, the defendant refuses to pay.

The plaintiff's evidence

The first witness for the plaintiff was Mr. Schrueder Aldridge who, at the time the written agreement was concluded, was in the employ of the plaintiff in the capacity of "Manager: Capital Development." Before he became a NamWater employee, Aldridge had been employed by the Ministry and had been involved in the bulk water sector for close to twenty years. Aldridge testified that he was 'intimately involved with the compilation' of the document that ultimately became the written agreement on which the plaintiff's case is based. As interlocutor between NamWater and its lawyers, and with lawyers Diekman & Associates acting for the defendant, he acted in that capacity "until both parties were satisfied with the content of the agreement and then…obtained a signed agreement from the representatives of Aussenkehr Farms and submitted it to the chief executive officer of Namwater for signature."

Aldridge testified that Habenicht is no longer in the plaintiff's employ—and it is common cause that his separation with NamWater was not on amicable terms. According to Aldridge on or about 24 August 2001, and before the conclusion of the written agreement, the plaintiff in writing applied to the Ministry for a water abstraction permit from the Orange River for the purpose of supplying water in bulk to a proposed irrigation project. It is common cause that the proposed irrigation project is the subject matter of the written agreement.

Aldridge testified that the Ministry refused NamWater's application for a water abstraction permit on behalf of the defendant because NamWater was not the owner of the land in respect of which the permit was sought. He added that the preconditions set out in the policy document were those of the Ministry and not of NamWater.

Namwater has since been informed of the Ministry's policy and procedures pertaining to the allocation of water for irrigation purposes along the Orange River. The policy amongst other directs that a water abstraction permit for irrigation purposes is allocated to the owner of the land to be irrigated. In the case of the proposed development by the Aussenkehr Group of Companies the implication is thus that a water abstraction permit should not be issued to Namwater.

In all existing cases where Namwater is the bulk supplier of water to a customer, Namwater and not the bulk water customer is required to have a water abstraction permit. This situation pertains to all purposes of bulk water supply, whether it is to a town

(Continued)

(Continued)

(Noordoewer from the Orange River), a mine (Scorpion Mine from the Orange River), stock watering (in communal areas) and irrigation (at Hardap, Etunda and Naute).

It is clear from the above that from 23 November 2001 and certainly at the date of his letter above, Habenicht knew the defendant was required to apply for the permit and that not all the water required for the project was being considered by the Ministry. He was also aware by the date of that letter that the consultants appointed by NamWater to do the planning and preliminary design report were busy working and had recommended that 32.2 million cubic meters of water would be required for the project and not the 50 million cubic originally thought.

Aldridge testified that after the two deliverables were received, the defendant who had to bear the costs of the infrastructure construction had to decide whether to proceed with the project and that Namwater was not responsible for the capital amounts required for investment in bulk water supply. By reference to the deliverables, Aldridge testified that the consultants had established from the Ministry that in order for an irrigation permit to be considered favourably, the developer (i.e. the defendant) would have had to:

a) submit a full environmental impact assessment for the entire project;
b) fulfill the requirements of Namibia's Environmental Assessment Policy; and
c) submit a project feasibility study.

Aldridge testified that after delivery to the defendant of the deliverables and the meeting of 15 May 2002, the plaintiff never received any instruction from the defendant to proceed with the implementation of the 2000 ha irrigation scheme; and that by letter dated 20 May 2002 addressed to Vasiljevic, the plaintiff invoiced the defendant in the amount of N$345 000.00 (inclusive of VAT of 15%) for the "production and supply of the planning and preliminary design report, and a set of tender documents for the detailed design and construction of the scheme." Aldridge stated that the defendant was invoiced since, as per the agreement, a period of three months in which, at the behest of the defendant, the second agreement was to be concluded had lapsed, without such agreement being concluded.

The case for the defence

The first witness for the defence was Helge Habenicht who was the chief-executive officer of NamWater until he left its employ in July 2002. He concluded the written agreement with Vasiljevic. As NamWater's chief-executive officer at the time he had considered that Namwater should be made responsible for the abstraction and management of Namibia's share of the water from the Orange River. He had formally proposed as much to the Ministry. Habenicht considered that this would help bring the Orange River in line with the rest of the country as far as water abstraction and management was concerned in terms whereof NamWater holds the water abstraction permit for a particular water source and in turn supplies water out of this resource to a customer: an arrangement referred to in the evidence as the "umbrella permit". Under that arrangement, I was told, the end-user does not and would not apply for a water abstraction permit and the Ministry's officials would not be involved.

(Continued)

(Continued)

Habenicht testified that he met Vasiljevic for the first time in 1999. He confirmed that the latter was not satisfied with his dealings with the Ministry and was hoping that Namwater would supply him with water he required for Aussenkehr farm. Habenicht confirmed that the defendant did not have the financial resources to on its own finance any big water development on the farm. He testified that it was NamWater's mandate to (1) manage water infrastructure and (2) finance the establishment of water infrastructure. He confirmed that he had stated at the Stakeholder's conference that "if invited" NamWater would be willing to finance and maintain the supply of a reasonable quantity of water to Aussenkehr. He called that a vision of NamWater's as under the regime extant at the time only the Ministry could grant permits for the abstraction of water from the Orange River.

Habenicht testified that between the Stakeholders conference and the signing of the agreement on 27 September 2001, he had met Vasiljevic once or twice only. He agreed with defendant's allegation in the plea to the effect that it was agreed between the parties that the plaintiff would supply water to the defendant without defendant having to apply for a water permit to the Ministry and that the cost of the plaintiff's "service" (i.e. the consultants' report) envisaged in clause 4.1 of the written agreement would be incorporated in a cost per cubic meter of water supplied by plaintiff to defendant after the bulk water supply infrastructure had been built and became operational; and that if the plaintiff chose not to proceed with the construction of the bulk water supply infrastructure, it would itself bear the costs of the consultant's report and not pass that on to the defendant.

As regards NamWater's application to the Ministry for the water abstraction permit in furtherance of the 2000 ha irrigation project, Habenicht stated that at the time Namwater did not have the right to abstract the water which the project required. However, in the light of the Stakeholders conference, and the President's and the Minister's support for the project, he saw the application for the water permit "more as a formality rather than a cumbersome exercise".

THE DEFENCES CONSIDERED

The defendant relies on several defences to escape liability. It has relied a great deal on the notion, in different contexts, that there was "frustration" in the continuation of the 2000 ha irrigation scheme which defendant and others wanted to pursue: either because of the conduct of the plaintiff and its consultants, or that of the Ministry.

Consultants' failure to perform the service fully

In the first place it contends that the consultants rendered an incomplete service in that they failed in their duty to do a feasibility study and an environmental impact assessment and recommended to the plaintiff, who acted thereon, that the defendant be required to perform those functions. Vasiljevic testified that the consultants' failure to comply with the terms of reference under which they were appointed was vicariously attributable to the plaintiff. Mr. Barnard submitted that the plaintiff failed to prove that the plaintiff's consultants complied with their obligation as aforesaid. He submitted that since the plaintiff vicariously failed to perform this essential obligation resting on it, it is not entitled to enforce against the

(Continued)

(Continued)

defendant the obligation to pay for the work performed by the consultants. The plaintiff's vicarious breach, it is said, was material and effectively made it impossible for the defendant, in the short time it had available, to conclude the further agreement contemplated in clause 5, thus making it impossible for the defendant to implement the 2000 ha irrigation project.

This defence can be very briefly disposed of. Paragraph 7(c) of the plea is devoted to the issue of the *feasibility study* and the *environmental impact assessment* of the project. As I read that part of the plea, the complaint is that the conditions relating thereto were not the defendant's obligation and that, in any event, they were so vague as to make it impossible for the defendant to understand what was required and that compliance therewith would delay the project to such extent as to terminate the agreement between the parties. As I understand it, the plaintiff's response to this argument is that the requirement for the feasibility study and the environmental impact assessment was one imposed by the Ministry and not by the plaintiff.

The defence that the consultants, and the plaintiff vicariously, failed in their duty to do a feasibility study and an environmental impact assessment simply was not pleaded; and consequently, the plaintiff was not required to meet it. That defence therefore does not avail the defendant. In any event, at the meeting of 15 May 2002, the following is attributed to C Muir who attended as an advisor of Navico:

3.5 **Technical Status Quo of Project**

The obvious failure of the plaintiff to communicate with the defendant until 15 May 2002 about who was to apply for a water permit and that the Ministry intended to make available an insufficient quantity of water for the irrigation scheme—raises the question whether the plaintiff should not be non-suited. Should the plaintiff have stopped the work of the consultants when those facts were known? The duty to have informed the defendant could only arise if I should find that the defendant would have been at liberty at that stage to call off the performance of the service. It should be borne in mind that as at 23 November 2001, the consultants had already been appointed and had commenced with their work. They therefore had vested rights and could not simply be wished away. Venter's letter of 23 October 2001 confirms his oral evidence at the trial that time was of the essence in the performance of the obligations under the written agreement.

In that letter Vasiljevic was informed that as early as 16 November 2001, the consultants were expected to produce results under their mandate. The plaintiff would have been obliged to compensate the consultants for the performance of their mandate. In my view, therefore, nothing turns on the failure of the plaintiff to have informed the defendant at the time that the policy document became known. Good business practice would dictate that they should have, but I find no legal consequence in the omission. In any event, as at 15 May 2002, the defendant was aware of the requirement that it had to apply for the water permit.

No indication was given at that meeting or thereafter that it no longer felt bound to the performance of the service under the written agreement. Since it knew at that stage already that the consultants had completed their work one would have expected them, in view of the

(Continued)

(Continued)

posture they now take, to have told the plaintiff in unequivocal terms that the project had to come to an end.

Order

Accordingly, I have come to the conclusion that the defendant's claim to rectification must fail and that the plaintiff, having proved its case on a balance of probabilities, is entitled to judgment:

(i) In the amount of N$ 345, 000.00 plus interest thereon at the prime lending rate of First National Bank of Namibia from time to time, until payment thereof; with
(ii) Costs, occasioned by the employment of one instructing and two instructed counsel; including wasted costs occasioned by the abandonment of the defendant's counterclaim, and the wasted costs flowing from defendant's amendment of its plea at the end of the plaintiff's case.

Charliewell, Kakweni Chunga v City Council of Lusaka

High Court
P/928) (1981) Z.R. 54 (H.C.) (1973/H
SAKALA, E.L., J.
17TH SEPTEMBER, 1980

Facts: The plaintiff's claim is for a declaration that he is not entitled to pay any rates in respect of plot number 65 Buckley Township, Lusaka. In his oral evidence the plaintiff testified that he purchased subdivision 65 of Farm 1751, Buckley Estate, Lusaka, in 1970. At that time of the purchase the property was not within the city boundary of greater Lusaka. And thus he was not paying rates. But in 1972 after the boundary was extended to cover Buckley Estate the city of Lusaka started levying rates. The plaintiff further testified that he has his own water supply from his borehole; has no sewage disposal, but makes his own arrangements for this by digging pits in which it is buried; and that they have roads in Buckley but not maintained by the City Council but jointly maintained by the residents, and also that this applies to the cutting of the grass during the rainy season.

The learned counsel for the plaintiff submitted inter alia, that it would be legally and morally wrong to allow the defendant to levy rates on an area to which it does not provide services. On behalf of the defendant the learned counsel argued that rates must not be construed as a charge for services rendered but a tax on all property with value situated within the boundary of a council the purpose being to raise revenue for the city stands, lights and for the maintenance of cemeteries, libraries, things which serve the public as a whole.

(Continued)

(Continued)

The issue before the court was whether the Lusaka City Council is lawfully entitled to levy rates in terms of the Municipal Corporations Act, Cap. 470 on subdivision 65 of farm 1751 belonging to the plaintiff.

Opinion

SAKALA, J.: The plaintiff's claim is for a declaration that he is not entitled to pay any rates in respect of plot number 65 Buckley Township, Lusaka.

The statement of claim reveals that at all material time the plaintiff was the owner of all the property known as subdivision 65 of Farm 1751 near Lusaka while the defendant was the council for the City of Lusaka. By half-yearly rate demands dated 11th January, 1973, 4th April, 1973, 8th June, 1973, 1st August, 1973, 23rd November, 1973, and 28th February, 1974, the defendant levied rates on the plaintiff's property. The plaintiff, according to the statement of claim, contends that the defendant had no legal or moral right to levy the rates on his property. And thus he seeks a declaration of this court that the defendant is not entitled to demand payment of any rates in respect of his property.

The defendant in its defence admits that the plaintiff is the owner of the property in question and levied rates on it. Paragraphs 2, 3, 4 and 5 of the defence read as follows:

> "(2) The defendant council admits the contents of paragraph 2 of the statement of claim and adds that it was, and is, lawfully entitled to make and levy rates on the property described in paragraph 1 of the statement of claim in terms of sections 30 and 18 (1) of the Municipal Corporation Act, Chapter 470 of the Laws of Zambia;
> (3) The defendant council denies the contents of paragraph 3 of the statement of claim and puts the plaintiff to the strict proof thereof;
> (4) The defendant council maintains that, in terms of section 18 (1) of the Municipal Corporations Act, all land situated within the boundaries of the City of Lusaka is assessable properties within the meaning of the Act and it is for the plaintiff to prove that his above mentioned property which is situated within the City of Lusaka is specifically excluded or exempted as provided therein;
> (5) The defendant council has legal right to make and levy the rates upon the plaintiff's above mentioned property and to demands the payment of and to recover the rates from the plaintiff."

In his oral evidence, the plaintiff testified that he purchased subdivision 65 of Farm 1751, Buckley Estate, Lusaka, in 1970. At that time of the purchase the property was not within the city boundary of Greater Lusaka. And thus he was not paying rates. But in 1972 after the boundary was extended to cover Buckley Estate the City of Lusaka started asking for rates. As residents of Buckley, on receipt of the notices for rates, they made representations through an association which was formed within the area to the Mayor through the Town Clerk. The representations were subsequently forwarded to the Ministry of Local Government and Housing. Consequently each resident of Buckley including those of Makeni received letters in which the Ministry of Local Government and Housing approved 50 per cent remission in rates. According to the plaintiff this was done because they were not given services.

(Continued)

(Continued)

But after these letters the City Council continued to make half-yearly demands of rates without any omission at all. The witness stated that even after 1973 when they received the letter for 50 per cent remission for rates, they still got no services from the City Council. The plaintiff testified that he has his own water supply from his borehole. He has no sewage disposal; but makes his own arrangement for this by digging pits in which it is buried. He said they have roads in Buckley but not maintained by the City Council but jointly maintained by the residents. This applies to the cutting of the grass during the rainy season.

The plaintiff told the court that he feels he should not pay rates because he derives no benefit from the City Council. This he said applies equally to the other residents.

In cross-examination, the plaintiff told the court that he was not informed when Buckley Estates became part of Greater City of Lusaka. He also said he did not know that rates are payable to the Council irrespective of whether services are rendered or not. He agreed that residents of Buckley use a tarred road branching off from the Great North Road going to Hill Top Hotel. But he said nobody fills the pot-holes on that road. He explained that his property has a value. He has a house, a borehole, a chicken run and fruit trees. He would not sell his property at less than K43,000.00. The plaintiff also stated that his property has not been exempted from paying rates to the Council.

In re-examination the plaintiff testified that the road that branches off from Great North Road leading to Hill Top was built before the Federation. It was in existence before they were asked to pay rates.

DW1, the Chief Valuation Officer with Lusaka City Council, testified that he passed the final examination of the Royal Institute of Chartered Surveyors. He is a Fellow of Rating and Valuation Association of London and a member of the Surveyors Institute of Zambia. He is responsible for the preparation of valuation rolls of all types of property situated within the City Limits of Lusaka. He explained that the jurisdiction of Lusaka City Council extends up to Zanimuone Hotel on the Great North Road close to Chilanga Cement Factory on the South. On the Great East Road it extends to the turn-off to the International Airport while on the west it is a point on Mumbwa Road, three kilometres from the town centre.

The Chief Valuation Officer also testified that subdivision 65 of Farm 1751, Buckley Estates, is within the bounds of Lusaka City Council. He said this particular farm became part of Lusaka in July, 1970, when the Lusaka City boundary was extended. Following upon the extension a survey of the properties in 1971 was carried out by the City Council which included subdivision 65 of Farm 1751, which was also valued and included in the valuation roll. The City Council has since levied rates on all the properties in the extended area. The Chief Valuation Officer explained that rates are a tax levied on the owners of property situated within any local authority.

The basis of levying the rates is the value of property on the assumption it is sold. With regards to Lusaka City Council he said it can levy rates on all assessable property within its area. The Chief Valuation Officer also explained that rates, a form of tax, are not based on services or a charge for services rendered. He said that the City Council is empowered by the

(*Continued*)

(Continued)

Municipal Corporations Act, Cap. 470 of the Laws of Zambia to levy rates on all assessable property within its area. He said the property in dispute was valued in 1977 at about K35,000.00. This would be the figure the Council would take into account in levying rates on the property in question.

The Chief Valuation Officer also testified that the Council water and sewage charges are separate charges from rates. With regards to the property in question the witness informed the court that the amount of K85.40 by way of rates has not yet been paid.

In cross-examination the Chief Valuation Officer told the court that prior to 1970 the plaintiff was not paying rates. He agreed that because the property was not within the City boundary prior to 1970 no services were rendered by the Council to the area. But said that after the area came in the city boundary, services were rendered by the Council which included the grading of roads. The Chief Valuation Officer also told the court in cross-examination that the money raised for rates is used to improve the city on providing services to the people, in maintaining cemeteries, libraries and running the general affairs of the Council and on capital expenditure.

He said the money is not raised to provide services only but for other amenities like good roads, bus stops, bus stands, and lights and other things which will serve the public as a whole. He stated that he was aware that there are no water services provided in Buckley Township. But he was not aware that until 29th April, this year the roads were not being graded in Buckley Township. He was not aware that after the hearing of the case on 27th April, this year graders were seen on the roads the following day in Buckley.

The foregoing was the evidence in these proceedings. At the end of the defence evidence both learned counsel filed written submissions with the court. From the pleadings and the evidence the material and relevant facts are in my view not in dispute. These are—the plaintiff is the owner of property described as subdivision 65 of Farm 1751 Buckley Estates, Lusaka. He occupies this property and it has a value. He purchased it sometime in 1970. Before 1st July, 1970, the plaintiff did not pay any rates in respect of the property and the City Council did not demand any rates from him in respect of the same.

It is common cause that at the time the plaintiff paid no rates before 1st July, 1970. Although the evidence is not very clear as to the criterion used by Lusaka City Council in extending its boundaries, the point appears not to be in dispute that sometime in July, 1970, Lusaka City Council extended its boundaries covering the farm in issue. Following this extension the Council carried out a survey of the properties in 1971. The survey included subdivision 65 of Farm 1751.

On the evidence of the plaintiff which also appears not to be in dispute, I am satisfied that the plaintiff provides his own water and sewage disposal. It is conceded on behalf of the plaintiff that the defendant is under a mandatory obligation to value all assessable property situate within its boundaries. The plaintiff's contention is that the levying of rates is discretionary and the defendant must exercise the discretion properly. It was thus submitted on behalf of the plaintiff that it could be legally and morally wrong to allow the defendant to

(Continued)

(Continued)

levy rates on an area to which it does not provide any services. On this basis the plaintiff is asking this court to declare that the defendant is not entitled to demand payment of rates in respect of the said property.

The argument on behalf of the defendant is that rates are not a charge for services rendered but a tax on all property with value situate within a boundary of any council for purposes of raising revenue for the council. It was pointed out that the basis for levying the rates is the Municipal Corporations Act, Cap. 470 of the Laws of Zambia. It was submitted on behalf of the defendant that in terms of sections 18 (1) and 30 of Cap. 470 the defendant was and is lawfully entitled to make and levy rates on the plaintiff's property.

The remedy of declaration the plaintiff is seeking in this action is discretionary. This court has power to give a declaratory judgment particularly in cases where there is no adequate alternative remedy. The emphasis appears to be that the discretion must be exercised "with care and caution," and "judicially" (*Sithole v The State Lotteries Board*). I have considered the question of whether this is a fit and proper case in which to entertain a request for a declaration. In the light of the practical value of the declaration being sought and particularly that the issue raised is of public interest and importance, I take the view that I must deal with the matter on its merit.

The question for the determination of the court is this: Is the Lusaka City Council lawfully entitled to levy rates in terms of the Municipal Corporations Act, Cap. 470 on subdivision 65 of Farm 1751 belonging to the plaintiff? It must be observed that I have deliberately avoided the word "morally" because I do not consider that this is a proper forum to discuss the morality of the acts of the Lusaka City Council as opposed to the legality of those acts.

The objects of the Municipal Corporations Act, Cap. 470 as set out in the preamble read as follows:

"An Act to define certain functions of municipal councils relating to the control and care of streets and lands within municipalities, to make provision for the valuation of assessable property and the levying of rates; and to provide for matters incidental to or connected with the foregoing."

The Act defines functions of municipal councils relating to the control and care of streets and lands within municipalities. In addition it makes provision for the valuation of assessable property and the levying of rates. Section 18 (1) defines assessable property as follows:

"18 (1) All land within the Municipality, together with all improvements situated thereon, shall be assessable property within the meaning of this Act, save such property as the Minister may prescribe."

I have already observed that after 1st July, 1970, the property on Plot 65 of Farm 1751 came within the Municipality of the City of Lusaka. In terms of section 18 (1) that land together with all the improvements situated thereon became assessable property. The plaintiff concedes in his evidence that his property is not exempted. Thus by law the City Council has to cause a valuation of Plot 65 of Farm 1751 to be entered on the roll (section 19 (1)). For the purpose of this action, I find it unnecessary to deal with the provisions relating to the

(Continued)

(Continued)

method of valuation of assessable property. Section 30 (1) which empowers Council to levy rates reads as follows:

"30 (1) The Council may, with the consent of the Minister and subject to the provisions of this Act, from time to time make and levy an ordinary rate upon all assessable land or upon all assessable improvements or upon all assessable property."

The argument by Mr Lewanika on behalf of the plaintiff is that the levying of rates is discretionary and the discretion must be exercised properly. There is force in this argument and I certainly agree with it. Mr Lewanika goes further by submitting that it would be legally and morally wrong to allow the defendant to levy rates on an area to which it does not provide services. On behalf of the defendant, Mr Banda has argued that rates must not be construed as a charge for services rendered but a tax on all property with value situate within the boundary of a council the purpose being to raise revenue for the city which according to DW1 is used to improve amenities like good roads, bus stops and stands, lights and for the maintenance of cemeteries, libraries, things which again according to DW1 serve the public as a whole.

It would appear to me that at the end of the day the determination of this case will depend on the definition to be placed on the word *rate*. I must admit that after a very careful perusal of Cap. 470 I have been unable to find the word rate defined in the Act.

This court is greatly indebted to counsel for the defendant for the authorities on the point. After a perusal of the various authorities I have found that the clearest definition of the word rate is contained in Halsbury's laws of England, 3rd ed. Vol. 32, para. 11, para. 10 under the heading Meaning and Nature of rate which reads:

"10. The expression "rate" means a rate the proceeds of which are applicable to local purposes of a public nature and which is leviable on the basis of an assessment in respect of the yearly value of property, it includes any sum which, though obtained in the first instance by a precept, certificate, or other instrument requiring payment from some authority or officer, is or can be ultimately raised out of a rate, but does not include any drainage, church, commons, water, or garden rate."

The definition seems to me to conform to the evidence of the Chief Valuation Officer for the defendant. My understanding of this definition is that rate is a sum of money collected by the Council for purposes of services of a *public nature* as opposed to services to an individual. As correctly submitted by Mr Banda, therefore, rates are a tax on all property with value situate within the boundary of the Council for purposes of raising revenue for the maintenance of facilities offered to all the residents. The concept may perhaps sound "morally wrong" to a rate payer who perhaps provides his own water and electricity services etc. But rates are not charged on the basis of these services.

Judgment

While appreciating the plaintiff's sentiments in this matter, I cannot say that the City Council exercised its discretion improperly particularly considering that a 50 per cent remission was

(Continued)

(Continued)

made on the early rate demands. In the result I have come to the conclusion that the defendant is legally and perhaps morally entitled to levy rates on all assessable proper within its boundary. In coming to this conclusion I have no doubt that the City Council of Lusaka in arriving at the rateable value of property in different areas on which the rates are based takes into account the non-availability or lack of facilities of a public nature in different areas.

In the exercise of my discretion therefore I refuse to grant the declaration sought. The action is accordingly dismissed. The matter raised in this action is such that in the interest of justice, I make no order as to costs.

Notes

1. The volume of all water on earth is about 1,386,000,000 cubic kilometers (km^3). This includes all of the water in the oceans, ice caps, lakes, rivers, groundwater, atmospheric water, and even the water in you, your dog, and your tomato plant (U.S. Geological Survey, 2015). The measure for water is the cubic kilometer (km^3). In gallons, 1 km^3 is equal to $2.64172052 \times 10^{11}$ (in words, two hundred and sixty-four billion, one hundred and seventy-two million, fifty-two thousand).
2. Total freshwater withdrawal for municipal purposes is 18 km^3/year (15% of total available); 6 km^3/year (5% of total available) for industrial use; and 95 km^3/year (80% of total available) for agriculture use (FAO, 2005).
3. The rationale for charging fees for municipal water is supplied by the Arusha Urban Water Supply and Sewerage Authority (AUWSA) of Tanzania, "Since Tanzania is not in a position to meet the costs of maintaining and improving water supply and sanitation services from public revenues, this has led to the introduction of a commercial approach to the provision of these services on which they must be paid for, rather than a free right" (see Arusha Urban Water Supply and Sewerage Authority, 2013).
4. PURC in Ghana is to set tariffs taking into consideration, (a) consumer interest; (b) investor interest; (c) the cost of production of the service; and (d) assurance of the financial integrity of the public utility. PURC Act, 1997, Act 538 (sections 3a and 16) applies to urban water rate setting in Ghana (PURC, 2012). The Energy and Water Utilities Regulatory Authority (EWURA) of Tanzania (EWURA Act, Cap 414); The Water Services Regulatory Board (WASREB) (Water Act, 2002) of Kenya; The Gambia Public Utilities Authority Act of 2001 (The PURA Act); and the Zambia Water Supply and Sanitation Council (NWASCO) (Water Supply and Sanitation Act of 1997) perform similar functions as the PURC in Ghana. The African Forum for Utility Regulators (AFUR) has a list of several water regulatory agencies in sub-Saharan Africa (AFUR, n.d.).
5. See Boadu (1992). Also, Whittington et al. (2008) found that while water systems in communities were working, there were still major financial constraints, "another troublesome finding is that rural households in the sample villages are paying very little for the improved water services, and, as a result, the finances of many village water committees are in poor shape." On the use of nonmarket valuation methods to estimate households' willingness to pay for water, see Whittington (2002).
6. Almost all countries in SSA use some form of formula fee-setting (indexation) approach. For example, Uganda determines water tariffs taking into account level of local salaries, domestic retail prices, exchange rates, electricity costs, foreign costs and foreign inputs in water provision (see The Water Statute (General Rates) Instrument, 2004).
7. This discussion is based on Randall, pp. 1981, 81−85.
8. Enforcement of regulations at the local community levels is often not recorded. One effective way to document enforcement actions at the local and community levels is to rely on local and regional newspapers in the country of interest.

Questions

1. What governmental and nongovernmental institutions control water resources in your country?
2. How are the prices of urban and irrigation water determined? What is the role of private citizens in pricing urban and irrigation water?
3. In what ways are customary rules and norms important in protecting water resources in your country?
4. Expansion of agricultural production to meet the growing demand may entail an increase in pesticide and fertilizer use. What steps may government and private citizens take to prevent threats to water quality?

References

Arusha Urban Water Supply and Sewerage Authority (AUWSA), 2013. Status of water supply and waste water disposal Services in Arusha City, Arusha, Tanzania, cited in Mosha, H.D., 2004. "Effects of water pipe burst on water quality and non revenue water in arusha city: a case study of AUWSA." Dissertation, Masters of Science in Environmental Studies (Management) of the Open University of Tanzania, p. 4. Viewed at < http://repository.out.ac.tz/609/1/MOSHA_HORTENCIA_DOMINIC_-_JD.pdf >.

Banerjee, S., et al., 2008. Urban Water Supply in Sub-Saharan Africa, Africa Infrastructure Country Diagnostic Summary of Background Paper 12. World Bank, Washington, DC.

Boadu, F., 1992. Contingent valuation for household water in Rural Ghana. J. Agric. Econ. 43 (3), 458−465.

Food and Agricultural Organization of the United Nations (FAO), 2005. Water withdrawal by sector, around 2007. AQUASTAT. < http://www.fao.org/nr/water/aquastat/tables/WorldData-Withdrawal_eng.pdf >.

Randall, A., 1981. Research economics: An economic approach to natural resource and environmental policy. Grid Publication Inc., Columbus, Ohio.

U.S. Geological Survey, 2015. Water Science School: how much water is there? <http://water.usgs.gov/edu/gallery/global-water-volume.html> (accessed 13.07.15).

The Water Statute (General Rates) Instrument, 2004. <https://www.nwsc.co.ug/files/wateracts/The_Water_Statute_%28General_Rates%29_Instrument,_2004_SI_44.pdf>.

Whittington, D., 2002. Improving the performance of contingent valuation studies in developing countries. Environ. Resour. Econ., Eur. Assoc. Environ. Resour. Economists. 22 (1), 323−367.

Whittington, D., Davis, J., Prokopy, L., et al., 2008. How well is the demand-driven, community management model for rural water supply systems doing? Evidence from Bolivia, Peru, and Ghana. BWPI Working Paper 22. <http://hummedia.manchester.ac.uk/institutes/gdi/publications/workingpapers/bwpi/bwpi-wp-2208.pdf> (accessed 13.07.2015).

World Bank, (undated), The future of water in African cities: why waste water? (urban access to water supply and sanitation in sub-Saharan Africa: background report (Torres Carolina Dominguez, et al.) <http://water.worldbank.org/sites/water.worldbank.org/files/publication/water-Background-Report-Urban-Access-WSS-in-SSA-FINAL.pdf> (accessed 20.05.15).

World Bank/WRI: (undated), Water resources data, Earthtrends Database. <http://siteresources.worldbank.org/INTMENA/Resources/App-all-Scarcity.pdf> (accessed 14.07.15).

You, L.Z., 2008. Irrigation Investment Needs in Sub-Saharan Africa, World Bank: Africa Infrastructure Country Diagnostic (Summary of Background Paper 9). World Bank, Washington, DC.

CHAPTER 15

Environmental Law

Keywords: *Earth Summit*; externality; environmental economics; environmental and social impact analysis; legislative and regulatory scheme; market failure; Polluter-Pays Principle; sustainable development; unchecked population growth

15.1 Introduction

The *Earth Summit* (Rio) of 1992 marked an important milestone in the evolution of laws, policies, and guidelines to protect the global environment.[1] The deliberations and approaches to address environmental issues are important for countries in sub-Saharan Africa (SSA) because high population growth and the resulting demand for food, shelter, health and sanitation infrastructure, energy, and peace are exerting considerable pressure on environmental resources such as air, water, land, and forests. To achieve the vision of the *Earth Summit*, the United Nations Environmental Program (UNEP) developed a framework environmental legislation to guide countries in writing their environmental laws.[2] These laws are often found in constitutions, enactments by a Parliament, and Treaties. There are also several customary practices, norms, and community rules to protect the environment in SSA countries.

15.2 Environmental Law and Economics

Environmental law and economics refers to the use of economic tools in designing laws and regulations to study how humans impact the earth and its resources.[3] From a macroeconomics perspective, economic tools may be used to study how different tax and subsidy laws, regulations, and policies promote a healthy environment. At the microeconomic level, economic tools may be used to study how laws and regulations influence the behavior of firms and households to achieve a predictable environmental impact outcome. Environmental laws and regulations in both developed and developing countries vary in their emphases, complexity, and stringency given the diversity of the backgrounds of countries. A single generally accepted taxonomy of environmental laws and regulations is not possible given the complex environmental laws and regulations in different countries.

F.O. Boadu: Agricultural Law and Economics in Sub-Saharan Africa.
DOI: http://dx.doi.org/10.1016/B978-0-12-801771-5.00015-0

15.3 The Law and Regulatory Scheme

Environmental laws and regulations in SSA may be organized under three main categories: (1) pollution laws such as water, air, and noise control laws and regulations[4]; (2) laws protecting nature such as forest and wildlife laws[5]; and (3) product regulation laws such as pesticide and labeling laws and regulations.[6] There are common unifying themes in all three categories. For example, laws and regulations covering the three categories are found in both the national laws of countries, and also in the large number of multilateral, bilateral, and regional environmental treaties to which these countries are parties.[7] Participation in international treaties helps countries to acquire technical knowledge, expertise, and financial support for domestic programs to improve the environment. Another unifying theme is that the primary sources of environmental laws and regulations are the constitutions of countries.[8] Also, all countries have a designated agency responsible for the overall implementation of environmental laws and regulations.[9]

Another common theme in all environmental laws and regulations is the focus on sustainable development emphasized during the *Earth Summit* in 1992. Countries have also embraced decentralization of governmental functions as part of the democratization process in SSA. There has emerged a strong national–local interaction in overall governance that has filtered over to environmental management. One finds strong community participation in the design and implementation of environmental laws because land resources in SSA are often community-owned, so utilization of these resources must involve the community owners. In some countries, community participation in environmental decision-making is enshrined in the constitution of the country.[10] Also, enforcement of environmental laws in SSA is influenced by technical and science information. The laws establish scientific and technical committees to provide information necessary for effective enforcement. For example, Ghana's Food and Drug law states, "In any proceedings under this law, a certificate of analysis signed by a public analyst shall be accepted as prima facie evidence of the facts stated therein."[11]

15.4 Environmental and Social Impact Assessment

All countries require an Environmental Impact Assessment (EIA) which is intended to measure the overall impact of a project on the natural environment, humans, and the society at large. All multilateral agencies require an EIA for projects they fund and countries in SSA have included the requirement in various laws and regulations. The EIA framework found in countries in SSA reflects good practices followed in international and regional groupings and also reflect domestic conditions. By following this approach, countries are able to plan and implement policies that minimize the adverse impacts of projects. The type and location of project, available expertise and financial resources are important factors in performing an EIA. Generally, however, an EIA must provide a monetary value of impact using available prices. Where market prices are not available, for example, impact on a wetland, a nonmarket valuation approach may be used.[12] EIA requires identification and careful description of nonquantifiable impacts. A component of the EIA may address potential impacts on culture, norms, and values in the society.

15.5 Addressing Environmental Problems

The law and economics analysis of environmental issues centers on the concept of *market failure*, which has been described as a situation "when the market does not allocate scarce resources to generate the greatest social welfare." The concept of market failure applies to all three categories of environmental laws. In the context of pollution laws, economists are concerned about market failure because it may lead to the creation of an *externality*, which has been defined as "an unintended consequence of market decisions, which affects individuals other than the decision maker" (Tietenberg and Lewis, 2009). [13] Pollution, such as cyanide spillage into rivers by mining companies and the flaring of gas in countries with oil resources, are examples of externality. Firms profit from the mining or oil production activities but local residents may suffer adverse effects from the activities. The adverse effect may be the loss of the use of a village river, fish kill, and threat to health and well-being of local residents. In the context of laws protecting nature, market failure may lead to an overexploitation of forest and wildlife resources due to lack of clearly defined property rights, and in the context of product regulation, market failure due to information asymmetries between manufacturers and prevent consumers from making decisions regarding product safety and efficacy.

15.6 Regulatory Approaches

As a practical matter, two main approaches have been applied to pollution, nature and product regulation. The threshold question is whether an activity ought to be regulated in the first place. This initial inquiry is answered using benefits versus costs assessment. Once the determination is made to regulate then the next inquiry is what approach to follow, that is, whether to impose a tax per unit of pollutant on polluters so that they will bear the cost of pollution or set a standard for firms to comply with.[14] Figure 15.1 explains the economics argument in support of taxes or standards as a means to control pollution.[15] The basic question we seek to answer is: which policy tool, taxes or standards provides a given level of abatement (pollution cleanup) at the lowest economic cost? The left vertical axis (beginning 0 for no cleanup), represents the Supply of abatement and per unit tax, and the right vertical axis Q^0 represents total cleanup. The horizontal axis, Abatement, represents quantity of cleanup. Suppose there are three firms with abatement supply curves, S_1, S_2, and S_3. The horizontal line FF represents a straight line per unit emissions

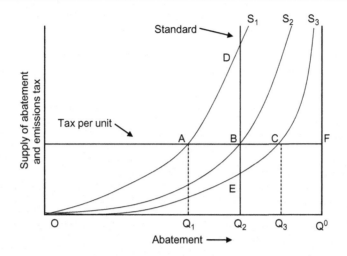

Figure 15.1
The Resource Cost of Abatement: A Comparison of Emissions Taxes and Standards.

tax, and Q_2Q is a pollution standard set by a regulatory agency. The per unit tax line intersects the supply curves at points A, B, and C, and the vertical standards line intersects the supply curves at E, B, and D. According to the figure, the quantities of cleanup by firms 1, 2, and 3 are OQ_1, OQ_2, and OQ_3 respectively.

To simplify the analysis,

$$Q_1 + Q_2 + Q_3 = 3\ Q_2$$

and

$$Q_3 - Q_2 = Q_2 - Q_1$$

These equalities mean that from an industry perspective the abatement under taxes or standards will be the same. The resource cost for abatement for each firm is the area under the firm's supply curve. The least cost of abatement between taxes and standards is obtained by subtracting the cost under taxes from the cost under standards, that is by summing the areas under firms' supply curves as follows:

$$
\begin{array}{lll}
\text{Standard: } OD\ Q_2 & + OB\ Q_2 + OE\ Q_2 \\
\text{minus tax } \underline{OA\ Q_1} & \underline{+ OB\ Q_2 + OC\ Q_3} \\
= DQ_2\ Q_1A & + 0 & - CQ_3\ Q_2E
\end{array}
$$

The results show that since $DQ_2\ Q_1A$ is greater than $CQ_3\ Q_2E$, for the same quantity of abatement, resource cost under tax is less than under a standard. This is explained as follows, "the emission tax encourages the most efficient supplier of abatement, whose supply curve is S_3 to do the lion's share of the abating; the least efficient abater, whose supply curve is S_1 does the least abating" (Randall, 1981).

There is a popular view that while the use of taxes, subsidies, and other economic mechanisms has been applied to regulation of pollution and nature (forest and wildlife), the same cannot be said when it comes to the regulation of environmental products such as pesticides. There is a strong aversion to using benefit and cost considerations in regulating environmental products. As one study on pesticide regulation put it in the context of pesticide regulation in the United States, "In fact, U.S. environmental policy could be termed schizophrenic with respect to the balancing of benefits and costs in standard setting" (Cropper et al., 1992).

15.7 Public Enforcement of Environmental Laws and Regulations

Governments use both civil and criminal actions to enforce environmental laws and regulations. Public enforcement of environmental laws and regulations is captured by the *Polluter-Pays Principle* (PPP), which means that the polluter should bear the cost of eliminating the pollution (OECD, 1972). The PPP has been argued to offer four main advantages: economically, it promotes efficiency; legally, it promotes justice; it promotes harmonization of international environmental policies; it defines how to allocate costs within a state (Bugge, 1996).

The PPP features prominently in several environmental laws and regulations in SSA countries. For example, Article 17 for *the Protocol for Sustainable Development of Lake Victoria Basin Preamble* states: "(1) the Partner States shall take necessary legal, social and economic measures to ensure that a polluter pays as near as possible the cost of the pollution resulting from their activities; and, (2) the costs recovered from the polluter shall be used for cleanup operations and restoration by that Partner State."[16] One of the "Guiding Principles" of Uganda's National Environmental Action Plan (NEAP) is the PPP. The Plan states, "The 'polluter pays' principle should be adopted whereby polluting industries and municipalities should pay a fee based on the location, nature, volume and chemical composition of the effluent which they discharge."[17] Lesotho and Kenya environmental laws contain similar provisions.[18]

15.8 Private Enforcement of Environmental Laws

High transaction cost of enforcement is one main reason for the poor environmental law enforcement record in SSA. The cost of enforcement includes filing the action, time involved in litigation, and attorney fees. Another reason may be cultural, that is, the use of community mediation versus formal complaint in resolving conflicts. Also, taboos, mores, and norms instead of formal complaint procedures are used extensively in resolving environmental conflicts. These costs must be compared with potential benefits from the enforcement action. One such benefit is the desire to have a clean environment. This benefit must be compared to the cost of enforcing the law to attain the benefit. A private party will institute enforcement actions if the net benefit is positive, that is, benefit minus cost is positive. The private party has an array of enforcement alternatives, and will pursue those for which the net benefit is greatest. This means the marginal benefit (MB) in pursuing enforcement activities will decline as enforcement increases. Thus, the MB curve will slope downwards. The marginal cost of enforcement increases with increased enforcement activities. Thus, the MC curve is positively sloped. A*, where MC = MB is the amount of enforcement activity that would be supplied by a private party (Figure 15.2).

The overlay of international, regional, domestic, and cultural practice poses unique challenges in enforcing environmental laws in SSA.[19] Private entities and the public, that is, government, are the primary enforcement agents. Private parties may enforce environmental laws and regulations in four main ways—(1) sue polluters for harms caused to the private entity; (2) complain to a public agency; (3) bring an action against a public agency to enforce the law and regulation within their jurisdiction; and (4) sue polluters to bring them in compliance with the laws and regulations (Tietenberg, 1996). A private party who has been injured by the actions of another party may bring a legal action based on one or a combination of applicable common law tort theories, including negligence, trespass, strict liability, and nuisance.

The cases that have been presented show how courts have interpreted and used the unifying themes in environmental law to address conflicts. The case of *M.K.O. Abiola v. Felix O. Ijoma* (Nigeria) presents a classic application of common law nuisance theory to resolve conflicts

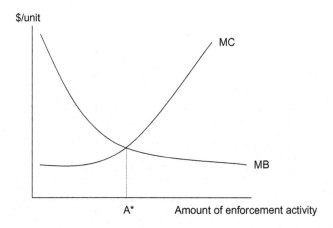

Figure 15.2
The Marginal Cost of Enforcement Increases with Increased Enforcement Activities.

between private parties. Note that the court granted both an injunction and money damages. In the case of *HTF Developers (PTY) Ltd. v The Minister of Environmental Affairs and Tourism and Ors.* (South Africa) the plaintiff challenged the authority of the government acting through the Minister to issue directives stopping land development that had been approved by a municipality. The court sustained the power of the Ministry to issue the directive and in doing so discussed the breadth of the Minister's powers to protect the environment following the principles of the EIA, public participation, and the precautionary principle. The plaintiffs in the case of *Mr. Felix Morka and The Social and Economic Action Rights Centre v Nigeria* (Nigeria) relies on a regional charter, the "African Charter on Human and Peoples' Rights" to press their claims against the Nigerian National Petroleum Company (NNPC), an agency of the Government of Nigeria and the Shell Petroleum Development Corporation (SPDC), a private oil company.

M.K.O Abiola v Felix O. Ijoma

High Court of Lagos, Nigeria
2nd December 1970
Suit. No. LD/422/70
Dosunmu, J.

DOSUNMU, J.: The plaintiff in this action is a Chartered Accountant, he lives with his family at 7 Shofidiya Close, Surulere. The defendant owns and occupies the adjoining property at 8, Shofidiya Close, Surulere. The two houses are situate in an area in the suburb of Lagos which zoned for residential purposes only. The defendant is a pharmacist by profession and he keeps poultry at the back of his house as a pastime.

It was in 1969 that he started the poultry business in a big way when he purchased some 400 day old chickens and had them delivered to his house. He keeps the chickens in pens which he erects on the boundary wall that separates his own building from that of the plaintiff. The pens, however, extend round until they nearly reach another adjoining plot of land owned by his wife. They do not, however, reach the back of this particular plot, and no reason has been given why they stop short. But I do not think there is any motive behind this. The boundary wall that separates the adjoining houses is said to be about 5ft. to 6ft. in height, and 8 ins. thick. It is about 5ft. distant to the building of the plaintiff and the pens rest on this wall.

When the defendant first introduced this large quantity of chicken into the house, the plaintiff said that he protested to him that it would cause him great offence; but the defendant assured him to the contrary. As time went on, he (the plaintiff) met the defendant to complain that his comfort is being disturbed as a result of the nuisance created by the keeping of the poultry so close to his dwelling house; and because the defendant took no action, he has to institute these proceedings, claim an injunction to restrain the defendant's acts of nuisance and damages.

(Continued)

(Continued)

The claim is broadly put on three bases: (1) Excessive noise made by the chickens in the early hours of the morning between 4.30a.m and 5a.m which prevents the plaintiff from having a good sleep. (2) Odious smells emanating from the same chicken pens as a result of the excreta or droppings in the poultry; and (3) Rats, flies and fleas escaping from the poultry into the house and disturbing his comfort and impairing his health. In the pleadings there is also an averment that the plaintiff's house has been rendered uninhabitable. It is sufficient, however, to say that there is no satisfactory evidence given in regard to this, and no claim for any loss in value has been advanced in respect of the property. In any case it is clear from the evidence that the plaintiff and his family still very well inhabiting the building with the new additions that were made thereto.

During the proceedings I was invited to say whether poultry keeping in this part of Surulere, and indeed, in other parts of Lagos, such as Apapa and Ikoyi is a statutory nuisance within the provisions of the Public Health Act. But I propose to deal with the facts of this case not on the basis as to whether there is a statutory nuisance or not; but to approach them from the principles which common law lays down for the protection of individuals in the exercise or enjoyment of their rights. There can be little doubt as to the law which applies to the facts of this case; and it is convenient to start by referring to the observations of Lord Lopreburn., L.C., in *Polsue and Affiery Ltd., v. Rushmer (1907) A.C at p. 123* when he said: "The law of nuisance undoubtedly is elastic, as was stated by Lord Halsbury in the case of *Colls. V. Hom & Colonial Stores Ltd. (1904) A.C. 185.* he said: what may be called the uncertainty if the test may also be described as its elasticity. A dweller in towns cannot expect to have as pure air, as free from smoke, smell, and noise as if he lived in the country, and distant from other dwellings, and yet an excess of smoke, smell, and noise may give a cause of action, but in each of such cases, it becomes a question of degree, and the question is in each case whether it amounts to a nuisance which give the right of action. This is a question of fact".

In the consideration of an alleged nuisance by noise Luxmoore, J., sets down in *Vanderpart v. Mayfair Hotel C. ltd., (1930)1 Ch.15* what seems to me to be a helpful approach to the matter. He said: "Apart from any right which may have been acquired against him by contract, grant or prescription, every person is entitled as against him by contract, grant or prescription, every person is entitled as against his neighbour to the comfortable and healthy enjoyment of the premise occupied by him, and in deciding whether, in any particular case, his right has been interfered with and a nuisance thereby caused, it is necessary to determine whether the act complained of is an inconvenience materially interfering with the ordinary physical comfort of human existence, not merely according to elegant or dainty modes and habits of living, but according to plain and sober and simple notions obtaining among English people; See *Walter v. Selfe (1851) 4 Deb and SM 315* and the remarks of Knight Bruse. V.C. It is also necessary to take into account the circumstances and character of the locality in which the complainant is living.

The making or causing of such a noise as materially interferes with the comfort constitutes an actionable nuisance, and it is not necessary to say that the best known means have taken to reduce or prevent the noise complained of, or that the cause of the nuisance is the exercise

(Continued)

(Continued)

of a business or trade in a reasonable and proper manner. Again, the question of the existence of a nuisance is one of degree and depends on the circumstances of the case". In any organized society everyone must put up with certain amount of discomfort and annoyance from the activities of his neighbours; and in this case, I have to strike a fair and reasonable balance between the defendant who likes to keep a poultry for his pleasure in his house and a neighbour who is entitled to the undisturbed enjoyment of his property. The standard in respect of the discomfort and inconvenience which I have to apply in this case is that of the ordinary reasonable and responsible person who lives in this particular area of Surelere. As Veale, J., puts it in *Halsey v. Esso Petroleum Co. Ltd.,(1961) 2 A.E.R at p. 151*: "This is not for himself. It is the standard of the ordinary man, and the ordinary man, who may well like peace and quite, will not complain for instance of the noise of traffic if he chooses to live in the main street of an urban centre, nor of the reasonable noises of industry if he chooses to live alongside a factory".

Bearing all these considerations in mind, I turn to the facts of this case and take the matter of noise first. The evidence of the plaintiff who alone testified on this aspect of the case is that in the early hours of every morning the chickens whose number he put at 800 make clickings or noise which disturbs his sleep. I have not heard satisfactory evidence as to the exact or actual number of chickens kept by the defendant. In the Statement of Claim which remained un-amended, it was pleaded that they were 300; but in the Statement of Defence the defendant was content with just pleading that he kept a reasonable number. In an earlier affidavit the defendant had deposed to keeping 300 chickens in his poultry. There is no dispute, however that the defendant started off with 400 chickens which he said the plaintiff helped him in obtaining. As there was no evidence of any pestilence which could have destroyed them, I am inclined to think that the defendant had some 400 chickens in his pens at the material time. The plaintiff's evidence continued that the noise increases as the chickens grew older. The defendant himself admitted that these chickens do make noise, but he said that it is not excessive and that they only make noise when they are hungry or being fed. I accept the evidence of the plaintiff that these chickens do make noise at the early hours of the morning, when some 400 chickens do join together to click or make noise about the same time and at this particular time of the night, it is bound to be excessive and to disturb the peace of a neighbour who is barely 5 ft. from their pens. After all, the main object of living in a house is to have a room with a bed in it where one can sleep at night. Night and up to the early hours of the morning is the time when the ordinary man takes his rest. No real complaint is made by the plaintiff of noise being made in the day time, although there was some evidence that the chicks also make noise in the day. It seems to me that noise made by the chickens at these hours of the night is more than triviality and the plaintiff is justified if he complains. I do not accept that the plaintiff is unduly sensitive for the defendant himself admitted that the portion of his house wherein he dwells is further away from the poultry than the additional building of the plaintiff wherein he once occupied.

I now deal with the question of smells. On this the plaintiff also testified that the smells coming out of the poultry are so nauseating that he has to feed outside at times. He called witnesses, not neighbours though, who called socially and otherwise at his house and sensed

(Continued)

(Continued)

the smells. Some of the witnesses went further to say that they had to stop visiting the plaintiff because of the smells, and as a result of this, some business deals had to be missed. The evidence of Dr. Daniel, a Medical Officer of the Lagos City Council is that on visiting the poultry of the defendant on the 5th May, 1970, he found dead fowls in it and they gave bad odour as well as the excreta of the chickens. This happened in the day time, and one can well imagine the intensity of the odour in the night depending on the direction of the winds. The witness continued by saying that he moved over to the plaintiff's house and from there he smelt the odour which he described as unbearable.

On the other hand the defendant testified that he never smells anything odious from his poultry. His brother and a brother-in-law also gave evidence that they never experienced any bad smells from the defendant's house and pens anytime they visited him. There can be no doubt, however, that droppings from chickens do smell when left for a while. Although the defendant claims to keep the poultry tidy, but not smell proof, it is weekly that the droppings are cleared by his labourers. These droppings or excreta will undoubtedly give out bad smells since they are not cleared up immediately and a person such as the plaintiff who is close to the poultry will sense it more than the defendant unless when the latter pays his regular visits to the poultry to satisfy his tastes. He has said that he loves to watch the chicken grow and lay eggs and in that circumstance he must be less sensitive to bad odour from the pens than an ordinary person. I do not believe that the plaintiff is being fanciful and all his complaints of excessive noise and smalls and they are, in my judgement, more than trifling inconvenience that an ordinary person living in that part of Surulere which is a residential area can be called upon to bear. I accept the plaintiff's evidence that bad smells came out of the defendant's poultry.

I now deal with the question of flies, rats and fleas. It is the case of plaintiff that the existence of the poultry near to his house attracts an unusual population of flies and they cross from the poultry into his house. One or two of his witnesses including a Medical officer testified to the great number of flies discovered in the plaintiff's house and some determined efforts were made to link the stomach complaints which the plaintiff and his family made to their Doctors as arising from the visitation of the flies and rats. Plaintiff's witness, Dr. Sogbetun testified that he treated the plaintiff for sleeplessness and family for dysentery, and this latter ailment is caused by eating or drinking anything contaminated by disease carrying agents, although he disagreed that bad smells can cause dysentery. The question here is whether it has been satisfactorily proved that they are the rats and flies from the defendant's poultry that infested them with dysentery. As the defendant's Counsel correctly pointed out, flies do abound everywhere, and unless they are tracked down, it is not easy to say that a particular group of flies originate from a particular source. I have received no evidence that flies located in the defendant's poultry eventually found their way into the plaintiff's house or that a group of flies moved particularly across the border into the plaintiff's room to disturb his sleep. I realize that the plaintiff said he saw rats creeping from the walls into his house but he could not say from where the rats started their journey. The evidence that there were no rats before the erection of the poultry nearby does not impress me. How large is the population of flies which the plaintiff spoke of, I do not know. What number of rats invaded him from the

(Continued)

(Continued)

defendant's poultry was not proved in evidence. I realize how difficult it is to prove all these things, but in the absence of satisfactory evidence on these points I find it difficult to say that nuisance has been established on this head. I do not say that the plaintiff and his children never suffered from the dysentery, but I can say that it has not been proved that they are the rats and flies that come from the defendant's poultry that give them this sickness. Surely, it has not been suggested that it is the noise and smells from the adjoining poultry that caused the dysentery. In my view, therefore, the plaintiff has made a good case under the heads of smells and noise only and the defendant is liable to him.

It is pleaded in paragraph 11 of the Defence that other neighbours keep poultry in their respective premises and that some of them started after the defendant. Apart from the fact that no evidence besides the defendant's own bare statement was led in support of this averment, it hardly affords a defence to the plaintiff's action. So, too, is the suggestion of the defence Counsel that some eminent personages in Lagos keep poultry in their respective premises. The editorial note to the case of *Leeman v Montague* (1936) 2 A.E.R 1677 seems relevant. The editor says, "Cases of nuisance usually raise a difficult question of degree, since practically everything that is held to be a nuisance is a trade or business that has to be carried on somewhere. The question, therefore, is as to what degree of nuisance is to be tolerated in particular circumstances and the present case defines with some precision that position with regard to poultry farm". The facts of the case are as follows:" The plaintiff purchased a house in a partly rural, but largely residential district. Adjoining this house was a poultry farm, and about 100 yds from the plaintiffs house was an orchard in which the poultry farmer kept a large number of cockerels.

The plaintiff complained of the noise made by the cockerels in the early morning and threatened proceedings unless they were removed. The cockerels were removed, but after some months numbers of cockerels reappeared (the figure was given as 200) and the farmer made no attempt to rearrange his farms so as to keep the cockerels further from the plaintiff's property. The plaintiff brought an action for an injunction. *Held*: A nuisance had been proved and an injunction should be granted.

So that whether it is true or not that others keep poultry in the neighbourhood or elsewhere in Lagos, what has to be appreciated is that there is no absolute standard in this matter of nuisance by noise or smell. It is always a question of degree whether the interference is so serious as to constitute a nuisance, and on the circumstances of each case.

The plaintiff also pleaded and gave it in evidence that he started to keep poultry over 5 years ago and occasionally. By this he explained that he kept a large stock for a straight period of 18 months and thereafter do away with them. After a lapse of 4 to 6 months he would bring new stock. It was not very clear from his evidence whether he meant that he started to keep poultry in the same house some 5 years ago. Although it does not matter much when he, in fact, started poultry; but I do not believe that it could be that far in the house because he himself testified that in July, 1969, in one of his conversations with the plaintiff when they were friendly, they both thought of what to do with the big gardens which they have on their hands and he decided to continue poultry. I suspect that the poultry was a recent venture.

(Continued)

(Continued)

The more important matter, however, is that if by suggestion that the poultry is being kept occasionally, and the nuisance, if there is one, therefore, temporary, it is my judgement that the discomfort which the neighbour has to bear for a period of one year or more is such that the Court must intervene.

I have reached the conclusion, therefore, that the plaintiff is entitled to damages.

As items of special damages the plaintiff claims as follows:

	£	s	d
a) To medical expenses re-treatment of children	500	0	0
b) To loss of business contacts	500	0	0
c) To bills for eating out at restaurants and hotels	26	0	0
d) To cost of insecticide to reduce flies	4	2	0

In her address the plaintiff's Counsel withdrew the claims for eating at restaurants but then, I can not allow the other items as well because I am not satisfied that it is the act of nuisance that the defendant is guilty of that leads to the complaints in the stomach in respect of which the plaintiff's doctor treated his children. As to the cost of insecticides, it was not proved that they were the flies from the poultry that the plaintiff was reducing rather than flies that abound all over. As for loss of business contacts the evidence of the plaintiff and his witnesses is so woolly that I have to reject it. The witness, Mr. Williams, said that as a result of his inability to contact the plaintiff in time for a particular business project, he estimated that the plaintiff lost £3,000 to £4,000, what a figure! Nevertheless, the plaintiff is entitled to damages and the fact that he suffers no ill health as a result of the nuisance is immaterial. *Crump v. Lambert (1867)15LT.600.* But this is sometimes not easy to assess in terms of money and I willingly do my best to award a sum in respect of the nuisances inflicted on him over the months.

On this head which is limited to noise and smells I will award £100. As to the future the evidence of the defendant is not very clear. At one stage I understood him to say that although he re-erected the pens after they were broken down by the Lagos City Council and in the same place, he did not put any chicken in them along the boundary walls of the plaintiff's house. And at another stage he seemed to be saying that he reduced the number of chickens to 100 following the institution of this action to appease the plaintiff. The principles on which the Court grants discretionary remedy of injunction are clear. As Vale, J., said in Halsey's case (*supra*) at page 160: "One, but only one, of these principles is that the Court is not a tribunal for legalizing wrongful acts by an award of damages". I take note also of the conduct of the defendant in not pulling down the pens resting on the divide wall when the plaintiff made a complaint to him. But I would have preferred to make a declaration that defendant is not entitled to commit the acts complained of instead of granting an injunction had I been satisfied that the defendant has stopped the acts of nuisance since the commencement of the action.

(Continued)

(Continued)

Having regard to all the circumstances, I will grant the injunction as sought in the writ. But I wish to add that I will not regard it as a breach of this injunction without much more evidence if the defendant removes the pens which he has erected close to the boundary wall to the far end of the property in the opposite side. The injunction will also be suspended for 2 weeks subject to the defendant taking active steps to reduce the nuisance. There will, therefore, be judgement for the plaintiff for an injunction as sought in the writ and £100 damages with cost fixed at 70 guineas cost. *Judgement for the Plaintiff: Injunction granted.*

HTF Developers (PTY) Ltd vs The Minister of Environmental Affairs and Tourism; The Member of the Executive Council of the Department of Agriculture Conservation and Environment; Dr S. T. Cornelius; (in his Capacity as Head of the Department Agriculture, Conservation and Environment); City of Tshwane Metropolitan Municipality

In The High Court of South Africa
(Transvaal Provincial Division)
Case No. 24371/05

JUDGEMENT

Murphy, J.

1. This case concerns the legality of a directive issued in terms of section 31A of the Environment Conservation Act 73 of 1989 ("ECA") by the third respondent, the Head of the Department of the Department Agriculture, Conservation and Environment for the Province of Gauteng.

2. The applicant is the registered owner of the property described as the remaining extent of Erf 232 Riveira, District of Pretoria. The property falls within the area of jurisdiction of the City of Tshwane Metropolitan Municipality, the fourth respondent and lies within an established township. The property is zoned in terms of the applicable Pretoria Town Planning Scheme as "special residential."

3. After the applicant purchased and took transfer of the property in March 2005, it applied to the fourth respondent for permission to divide the property into 12 subdivided portions. On 8 June 2005 the Department of Housing, City Planning and Environmental Management of the fourth respondent confirmed in writing that the fourth respondent had in terms of the provisions of section 92(2) of the Town Planning and Townships Ordinance, 1986 (Ordinance 15 of 1986) approved the application for subdivision subject to certain conditions set out in an annexure to the letter of approval. The conditions are extensive and relate to the provision of services, electricity, sanitation and the like. Clause 9.1 of the annexure records that the Environmental Management Division of the fourth respondent had no objection to the application.

4. The applicant's purpose in subdividing the property is to develop the subdivided portions into residential stands and eventually to market those stands to individual buyers for

(Continued)

(Continued)

residential purposes. In the final result the property of 18036 square meters is intended to be broken up into 12 distinct residential stands varying in size between 1018 and 3159 square meters.

5. Once it had received approval from the fourth respondent the applicant set about preparatory earthworks for the installation of pipelines and electrical infrastructure to service the subdivided portions with water, sewage and electricity services. It also proposes to develop access roads and needs to engage in site clearing for that purpose.

6. On 18 July 2005, in response to complaints received from members of the public, the third respondent addressed a letter to the applicant which was introduced by the heading:

Re: Notice of Intention to issue a directive in terms of section 31A of the Environment Conservation Act, Act 73 of 1989, in respect of the site clearing on remainder of Erf 232 Riveira.

7. The letter is lengthy and raises a number of issues which can be summarised as follows. Firstly, it notes that the Department was of the opinion that the applicant had undertaken an illegal activity in that it had begun clearing the property for the purposes of construction prior to receiving authorisation from the Department. In this regard the letter states:

Authorisation is required from this Department, in addition to any local authority approval, for the cultivation or any other use of virgin ground as set out in item 10 of Schedule 1 of Regulation 1182 (as amended) issued in terms of the Environment Conservation Act, Act 73 of 1989 ("the ECA").

8. The letter secondly informed the applicant that after a site inspection conducted by its officials, the Department had established that most of the site is located on an untransformed ridge, considered to be a sensitive environment, characterised by high biodiversity and that the earthworks and infrastructural development have resulted in the disturbance of the sensitive ecosystems and a loss of biological diversity. The Department emphasised that many "red data" species of plants and animals inhabit the ridge, which because they are threatened require priority conservation efforts in order to ensure their future survival. The letter goes on to say:

As ridges are viewed as naturally existing corridors that can functionally interconnect isolated natural areas, protecting these corridors promotes ecological processes and benefits regional and local biological diversity. The ridge systems in Gauteng represent particularly vital natural corridors as they function both as wildlife habitat providing resources needed for survival, reproduction and movement, and as biological corridors, providing for movement between habitat patches. The proposed development will have a significant impact on these corridors.

9. The letter further explains that the ridge in question is classified as a "class 3(A) ridge" in terms of the departmental ridges policy, meaning that no further subdivisions will be allowed and that only low impact development will be considered and then only after a full environmental impact assessment, involving a public participation exercise

(Continued)

(Continued)

and a full set of specialist reports including ecological, hydrological, geotechnical, pollution and social studies.

10. The Department concluded its commentary on the site development with the observation that in its view the applicant had not complied with key national environmental management principles enacted by the National Environmental Management Act 107 of 1998 ("NEMA"). (The principles contained in section 2 of NEMA apply to the actions of all organs of state that may significantly affect the environment; serve as the general framework within which environmental management and implementation plans must be formulated; serve as guidelines by reference to which any organ of state must exercise any function when taking any decision in terms of NEMA or other legislation concerning the protection of the environment; and guide the interpretation, administration and implementation of any environmental legislation). The principles not applied by the applicant during the planning of the development, according to the Department, were:
    (a) the disturbance of ecosystems and loss of biological diversity should be avoided, minimized or remedied;
    (b) a risk averse and cautious approach be applied, which takes into account the limits of current knowledge about the consequences of decisions and actions; and
    (c) environmental management must be integrated, acknowledging that all elements of the environment are linked and interrelated taking into account the effects of decisions and actions by pursuing the selection of the best practicable environmental option.
11. The Department accordingly afforded the applicant an opportunity to make written representations providing compelling reasons for it not to exercise its powers in terms of section 31A of ECA to issue a directive requiring it to cease all construction related activities until in possession of an authorisation in terms of the ECA.
12. The applicant replied to this letter in a letter dated 20 July 2005 contending that the ridges policy as a departmental policy had no statutory force and effect, and that unless the actions of the applicant amounted to a listed activity identified in terms of section 21 of ECA, there was no legal basis upon which the Department could insist that the applicant cease its activities on the land in question. In particular, it argued that the land is not "virgin ground" as contemplated in item 10 of schedule 1 of regulation 1182 and hence no authorisation was required for its development, because, so it says, the regulation governing the use of "virgin ground" was not intended to embrace land which is part of an erf in a proclaimed township. (I discuss these submissions more fully below).
13. On 12 August 2005 the third respondent issued a directive in terms of section 31A of ECA directing the applicant to immediately cease with the clearing of the site and its construction activities and to design and implement a plan for the land's rehabilitation. It reiterated its view that the land is "virgin ground" and expressed the opinion that the operation of the provisions of the ECA is not dependent on town planning legislation. It further justified its intervention on the basis that the applicant's activities on the land would result in serious damage to the environment for the reasons stated in its previous letter.

(Continued)

(Continued)

14. The applicant obeyed the directive and desisted in developing the land but on 17 October 2005 filed a notice of motion seeking relief in the following terms:

   1. An order declaring that the property described as remainder of Erf 232 Riveira Township is not virgin ground as defined in item 10 of Schedule 1 of Regulation 1182 promulgated in terms of the Environmental Conservation Act, No73 of 1989;

   2. An order declaring unlawful and setting aside the directive issued in terms of section 31A of Act 73 of 1989 by the third respondent in respect of remainder of Erf 232 Reveira Township, ...

15. A proper construction of the reach and ambit of item 10 of schedule 1 of regulation 1182 requires consideration of the purposes not only of the ECA, but also the environmental clause in section 24 of the Constitution as underpinned by the principles contained in section 2 of NEMA which are expressly required to be applied as a guide in the interpretation of any environmental legislation.

16. Section 24(a) of the Constitution guarantees the fundamental right of everyone to an environment that is not harmful to their health or well being. Section 24(b) imposes programmatic and positive obligations on the state to protect the environment through reasonable legislative and other measures that prevent pollution and ecological degradation; promote conservation; and secure ecologically sustainable development while promoting justifiable economic and social development.
   Prof. Jan Glazewski in his seminal work: *Environmental Law in South Africa* (Butterworths, 2000) makes the point that the contemporary international norm implicit to all environmental law is the notion of sustainable development, being development that meets the needs of the present without compromising the ability of future generations to meet their own needs. Such implies limitations imposed by the state of technology and social organisation on the environment's ability to meet present and future needs. Hence, the need to preserve natural systems for the benefit of future generations obliges environmental considerations to be incorporated into economic and other development plans, programmes and projects. The principle of environmental assessment as the means of ensuring intergenerational equity is the practical cornerstone of the principles of sustainable and equitable use of our natural resources and environment. Moreover, the principle of environmental assessment is premised upon and interrelated to a precautionary principle mandating a risk-averse and cautious approach. Where there is a risk of serious or irreversible damage, lack of full scientific certainty should not be used as a reason for postponing measures to prevent environmental degradation (see Glazewski pp 1–27). As I understand Prof Glazewski, this schemata of principles and obligations underpins the environmental right in section 24 of the Constitution.

17. Section 24 of the Constitution, as outlined above, contains two components. Section 24 (a) entrenches the fundamental right to an environment not harmful to health or well-being, whereas section 24(b) is more in the nature of a directive principle, having the character of a so-called second generation right imposing a constitutional imperative on the state to secure the environmental rights by reasonable legislation and other measures. Despite its aspirational form, or perhaps because of it, section 24(b) gives

(Continued)

(Continued)

content to the entrenched right envisaged by specifically identifying the objects of regulation, namely: the prevention of pollution and environmental degradation; the promotion of conservation; and the securing of ecologically sustainable development and use of natural resources while promoting justifiable economic and social development.

18. The scope of the right is therefore extensive. It does not confine itself to protection against conduct harmful to health but seeks also by, *inter alia*, the promotion of conservation and ecologically sustainable development, to ensure an environment beneficial to our "well-being." The term "well-being" is open-ended and manifestly is incapable of precise definition. Nevertheless it is critically important in that it defines for the environmental authorities the constitutional objectives of their task. Prof Glazewski (at pg 86) comments on the meaning of the expression "well-being" in the environmental law context as follows:

In the environmental context, the potential ambit of a right to "well-being" is exciting but potentially limitless. The words nevertheless encompass the essence of environmental concern, namely a sense of environmental integrity; a sense that we ought to utilize the environment in a morally responsible and ethical manner. If we abuse the environment we feel a sense of revulsion akin to the position where a beautiful and unique landscape is destroyed, or an animal is cruelly treated.

19. The attainment of this objective or imperative confers upon the authorities a stewardship, whereby the present generation is constituted as the custodian or trustee of the environment for future generations. From this it follows that owners of land no longer enjoy the absolute real rights known to earlier generations. An owner may not use his or her land in a way which may prejudice the community in which he or she lives, because to a degree he or she holds the land in trust for future generations — see *King v Dykes* 1971(3) SA 540 (RA) at 545.

20. The legislative measures contemplated in section 24(b) of the Constitution are principally those enacted in NEMA in 1998, which amended and repealed significant parts of ECA (which had been enacted in 1989 prior to the adoption of a fundamental constitution), but which at the same time kept intact the key provisions of ECA dealing with environmental assessments. Part V of ECA is concerned with the control of activities which may have a detrimental effect on the environment. Section 21(1)(a) confers upon the Minister the power to identify by notice in the Gazette those activities which in his or her opinion may have a substantial detrimental effect on the environment. Of particular relevance to the present application, section 21(2) of ECA includes land use and transformation as one of the categories of activity which the Minister may identify.

21. The first steps taken by the authorities after the adoption of the fundamental environmental right in the Constitution, before the enactment of NEMA, were the promulgation of Regulations 1182, 1183 and 1184 under section 21(1) of the ECA that listed the activities potentially detrimental to the environment and set out the rules regarding the compilation of environmental impact assessments relating to such activities. Once the Minister has declared activities as identified, no such activity may be undertaken unless a written authorisation has been obtained from the Minister or competent authority designated by the Minister. Section 22(2) of ECA provides that in granting

(Continued)

(Continued)

authorisation the competent authority may require reports concerning the impact of the proposed activity and of alternative proposed activities on the environment.

22. The environmental assessment regulations enacted in Regulations 1182, 1183 and 1184 are central to the present application. Regulation 1182 lists ten activities in general as activities which may have a substantial detrimental effect on the environment. They are extensive in their reach including for example the construction of facilities for energy generation and supply, road construction, intensive husbandary, the genetic modification of any organism and the disposal of waste. The identified activity of relevance to this application as appears from the correspondence between the parties, is item 10 of Regulation 1182 (inserted by GNR670 of 10 May 2002) being:

the cultivation or any other use of virgin ground.

Item 2 deals with the change of land use from agricultural or natural conservation use for other uses.

23. Regulation 1183, as I have said, contains the substantive body of rules regarding the conduct and content of environmental assessments required to be performed in terms of section 22 of ECA. They need not detain us, except to say that the third respondent apparently would expect the applicant to submit such reports should it seek authorisation to undertake the development in the event of it falling within item 10 of Regulation 1183. Broadly the assessment must be carried out by an independent consultant with expertise in the area of environmental concern as well as the ability to perform all relevant tasks including the ability to manage any public participation process. The regulations go on to set out fully the requirements of screening, scoping and carrying out of the environmental impact assessment as well as the authorisation process. Regulation 1184 is the regulation whereby the Minister designates the competent authority in each province as the authorised authority to issue written authorisations to undertake the listed activities. The second respondent is the competent authority for the province of Gauteng.

24. Section 31A of ECA, in terms of which the third respondent issued the directive, is part of the general regulatory scheme. It confers wide-reaching interdictory powers upon the Minister or competent authority. Section 31A(1) reads:

If, in the opinion of the Minister or the competent authority, local authority or government institution concerned, any person performs any activity or fails to perform as a result of which the environment is or may be seriously damaged, endangered or detrimentally affected, the Minister, competent authority, local authority or government institution as the case may be, may in writing direct such person -

    (a) to cease such activity; or

    (b) to take such steps as the Minister, competent authority, local authority or government institution, as the case may be, may deem fit within a period specified in the direction, with a view to eliminating, reducing or preventing the damage, danger or detrimental effect.

(Continued)

(Continued)

25. The other subsections of section 31A deal with the power of the Minister to order or perform rehabilitation and to recover expenditure incurred in that regard.

26. This then is the broad context and framework within which the third respondent's issuing of the section 31A directive and item 10 of Regulation 1182 are to be construed.

27. It may be recalled that the applicant seeks relief on two counts. Firstly it seeks an order declaring that Erf 232 Reveira Township is not virgin ground; and secondly it seeks an order (which it believes should necessarily follow) that the section 31A notice was unlawful because it was issued in respect of an activity not falling within item 10 of Regulation 1182. In other words, it maintains that the development does not involve "the cultivation or any other use of virgin ground", and hence the regulatory intervention is unlawful.

28. The concept of virgin ground is defined in Regulation 1182 to mean "land which has at no time during the preceding 10 years been cultivated." There is no definition of the concept "cultivate" in Regulation 1182. At first glance it conjures the image of preparing ground for the purpose of cultivating crops. The definition seems to have been borrowed, some might say inappropriately, from the Conservation of Agricultural Resources Act 43 of 1983, which contains a similar definition of the concept of "virgin soil." The primary meaning of the term is therefore an agricultural one. However, the term can be interpreted more extensively to mean "improve" or "increase." Considering the context in which it is used, that is in a statutory list of activities identified for environmental protection purposes as requiring authorisation from the regulatory authority, including the construction of roads, energy generating facilities, nuclear reactors, rail infrastructure, cableways, marinas, harbours, racing tracks and the like, a more extensive conception of the word "cultivate" to mean any improvement or variation of the land would seem legitimate. Such a construction is supported by the wording of the actual activity identified. It is not only cultivation of virgin ground that is targeted but also "any other use." On such a basis "virgin ground" can be construed purposively and generously, taking account of the constitutional imperative to promote conservation and ecologically sustainable development, to mean land that has not been used or developed in the last 10 years, such land being of obvious concern to the environmental authorities in the present age of accelerated environmental degradation. Interpreting the term in this way is compatible with the provisions of section 39(2) of the Constitution mandating the interpretation of legislation in a manner promoting the spirit and purport of the rights in the Bill of Rights, including the environmental right.

29. Mr Vorster, who appeared on behalf of the applicant, however raised a more challenging argument. He submitted that land within a proclaimed township could not fall within the scope and ambit of virgin ground for reasons beyond avoiding a strained description of the use of such land as "cultivation", but more compellingly because the proclamation of such land as residential invariably at some earlier stage in the process required environmental assessment. As mentioned above, the property in question is zoned in terms of the applicable legislation as special residential within the relevant town planning scheme. Erf 232 Riveira was originally a large erf in the township which had been subdivided prior to the applicant purchasing the remaining extent thereof. A township is

(Continued)

(Continued)

established by an owner of land by means of an application to the local authority in terms of section 69 of Ordinance 15 of 1986 (Transvaal). Regulation 18 of the regulations made in terms of Ordinance 15 of 1986 sets out the requirements for such an application, and Regulation 18(1)(b) in particular requires the submission of a detailed report with a comprehensive motivation relating to the need and *desirability* of the township. After the requirements of the application process have been met, section 68(6)(b)(iv) of the Ordinance permits the local authority to forward a copy of the application to any other department or division of the Transvaal Provincial Administration (read Gauteng Provincial Government) or any other state department which "in the opinion of the local authority, may be interested in the application." The question of desirability surely will embrace all social and environmental considerations which might render the establishment of a township undesirable in the location applied for. Such is borne out by other provisions of the Ordinance which identify the general purpose of a town planning scheme to be the co-ordinated and harmonious development of the area in such a way as will most effectively tend to promote *inter alia* the health and general welfare of the area in the process of such development. Accordingly, it was submitted, the application of the concept of "virgin ground" to land which forms part of a proclaimed erf in a township leads to the anomaly that the question of desirability is re-visited a second time as a prerequisite for the right of the owner to develop or improve its land. Hence, so the argument went, the concept of "virgin ground" should be narrowly construed to avoid the anomaly as applying only to land falling outside proclaimed townships.

30. As convincing as the argument might appear on the face of it, I do not accept it. Firstly, one naturally hesitates to rely upon a provincial ordinance enacted a decade before the enactment of a fundamental environmental right in order to set its parameters or give it content. A local authority's policy concerns in the proclaiming of a township will certainly be guided by the imperatives of the constitutional right, but that alone should not operate to shut out other competent authorities that may well have policy considerations and interests going beyond or different to those of the local authority. The ridges policy for instance is a very good example. Moreover, the fact that the local authority has a discretion to refer a township application to the provincial government should also not operate to exclude the provincial government from acting of its own accord in pursuance of provincial or national environmental interests. I see no anomaly or absurdity arising from the bestowal of a power upon the provincial authorities to revisit the environmental desirability of the establishment of a township previously approved by a local authority. In the end therefore I am not persuaded that "virgin ground" applies only to land falling outside proclaimed townships.

31. This brings me to the question of whether the remainder of Erf 252 Riveira is indeed virgin ground. The third respondent, on the basis of a site inspection conducted by its officials, says it is. In his view it is part of an untransformed ridge, characterised by high biodiversity, which is endangered. He contends, furthermore, that the applicant has failed to aver facts which show that the land has within the last 10 years been cultivated within the meaning of the regulation. The inspection report confirms that the property

(Continued)

(Continued)

is fenced to some extent and notes the existence of two old cement basins which resemble a duck pond or fish pond of sorts. The applicant avers that the installation of services has commenced, but that would seem to have taken place after 2002, the year in which item 10 was promulgated. There has also been some mention of a dwelling and garden, but it is not clear from the papers whether such were improvements upon the remainder of the Erf purchased by the applicant. The applicant's claim that the land is not virgin ground and the limited facts put up in support of that are accordingly trenchantly denied by the third respondent who has put up the inspection report in support of that denial. The applicant has not filed a replying affidavit. This gives rise to disputes of fact which cannot be resolved on the papers and the respondent's version should therefore prevail, precluding me from granting the applicant final relief in the form of a declarator.

32. But even if I am mistaken in that, and the property in question should be considered in fact and in law not to be virgin ground, it still seems to me that such would not inhibit the third respondent from issuing the section 31A directive. Mr Vorster has submitted to the contrary that a section 31A directive can be issued only in respect of activities that have been identified and promulgated under section 21. I disagree. Section 21 and section 31A fall in different chapters of the ECA. Section 21 is found in Part V of the ECA dealing with the identification of activities requiring authorisation by the competent authority after submission of environmental impact assessments. Section 31A, on the other hand, is found in Part VIII of the ECA, containing general provisions enacting general remedies and mechanisms of enforcement. The provision confers a general power upon the Minister or competent authority to direct *any* person to cease *any* activity which in his or its opinion may result in seriously damaging, endangering or detrimentally affecting the environment. The environment is defined widely in section 1 to mean the aggregate of surrounding objects, conditions and influences that influence the life and habits of man or any other organism or collection of organisms. Nothing in section 31A justifies limiting the power of the Minister or the competent authority to an authority to direct the cessation of damaging or degrading activity only in respect of those activities identified in regulations as activities requiring written authorisation supported by environmental impact assessments. The power conferred by section 31A is a necessary measure, contemplated in section 24(b) of the Constitution, to empower competent authorities to take steps to prevent ecological degradation and to secure ecologically sustainable development, and is intended also to enable the competent authority to deal expeditiously with harmful activities either not foreseen by the Minister when making regulations or not necessarily intended to be subjected to the principle of environmental assessment. In both his letter of 18 July 2005 and the eventual section 31A directive of 12 August 2005, the third respondent was mindful of the distinction. Beyond claiming that the property was virgin ground, the third respondent asserted the departmental ridges policy and his entitlement (indeed constitutional duty) to invoke the power under section 31A to prevent the development, which in his opinion may result in serious damage or detriment to the environment. Whether his opinion is reasonable, rational or justifiable is not in issue in the present application. The point is simply that the

(Continued)

(Continued)

directive would not be unlawful solely were it to be found that the property was not virgin ground.

33. It follows therefore that I do not accept the submission that the ridges policy is irrelevant to the dispute between the parties. The ridges policy is compatible with the objectives and values of the constitutional environmental right and the principles of sustainable development and environmental assessment embodied in the legislative framework. The third respondent is entitled to apply that policy, provided he does so reasonably and fairly, when acting to protect the environment from harm and degradation under section 31A.

34. In the premises I am of the view that the applicant is not entitled to the relief it seeks. Accordingly the application is dismissed with costs.

Mr Felix Morka and The Social and Economic Action Rights Centre v Nigeria

African Commission on Human & Peoples' Rights
Banjul, The Gambia
Ref: ACHPR/COMM/A044/1
27th May 2002

Dear Mr. Morka,

RE: COMMUNICATION 155/96L.

I have the honour to inform you that at its 30th Ordinary Session held in Banjul, The Gambia from 13th to 27th October 2001, the African Commission examined the above mentioned communication and found the **Federal Republic of Nigeria in violation of Articles 2, 4, 14, 16, 18(1), 21 and 24 of the African Charter on Human and Peoples' Rights.**

Please find attached herewith the said decision.

Yours sincerely,

Omari Holaki

Officer in Charge

Summary of Facts:

1. The Communication alleges that the military government of Nigeria has been directly involved in oil production through the State oil company, the Nigerian National Petroleum Company (NNPC), the majority shareholder in a consortium with Shell Petroleum Development Corporation (SPDC), and that these operations have caused environmental degradation and health problems resulting from the contamination of the environment among the Ogoni People.

(Continued)

(Continued)

2. The Communication alleges that the oil consortium has exploited oil reserves in Ogoniland with no regard for the health or environment of the local communities, disposing toxic wastes into the environment and local waterways in violation of applicable international environmental standards. The consortium also neglected and/or failed to maintain its facilities causing numerous avoidable spills in the proximity of villages. The resulting contamination of water, soil and air has had serious short- and long-term health impacts, including skin infections, gastrointestinal and respiratory ailments, and increased risk of cancers, and neurological and reproductive problems.

4. The Communication alleges that the Government has neither monitored operations of the oil companies nor required safety measures that are standard procedure within the industry. The Government has withheld from Ogoni Communities information on the dangers created by oil activities. Ogoni Communities have not been involved in the decisions affecting the development of Ogoniland.

5. The Government has not required oil companies or its own agencies to produce basic health and environmental impact studies regarding hazardous operations and materials relating to oil production, despite the obvious health and environmental crisis in Ogoniland. The government has even refused to permit scientists and environmental organisations from entering Ogoniland to undertake such studies. The government has also ignored the concerns of Ogoni Communities regarding oil development, and has responded to protests with massive violence and executions of Ogoni leaders.

6. The Communication alleges that the Nigerian government does not require oil companies to consult communities before beginning operations, even if the operations pose direct threats to community or individual lands.

9. The Communication alleges that the Nigerian government has destroyed and threatened Ogoni food sources through a variety of means. The government has participated in irresponsible oil development that has poisoned much of the soil and water upon which Ogoni farming and fishing depended. In their raids on villages, Nigerian security forces have destroyed crops and killed farm animals. The security forces have created a state of terror and insecurity that has made it impossible for many Ogoni villagers to return to their fields and animals. The destruction of farmlands, rivers, crops and animals has created malnutrition and starvation among certain Ogoni Communities.

Complaint:

10. The communication alleges violations of Articles 2, 4, 14, 16, 18(1), 21, and 24 of the African Charter.

LAW

Admissibility

35. Article 56 of the African Charter governs admissibility. All of the conditions of this Article are met by the present communication. Only the exhaustion of local remedies requires close scrutiny.

(Continued)

(Continued)

36. Article 56(5) requires that local remedies, if any, be exhausted, unless these are unduly prolonged.

After concluding that the complainants had satisfied the exhaustion requirement, the court continued...

Merits

43. The present Communication alleges a concerted violation of a wide range of rights guaranteed under the African Charter for Human and Peoples' Rights. Before we venture into the inquiry whether the Government of Nigeria has violated the said rights as alleged in the Complaint, it would be proper to establish what is generally expected of governments under the Charter and more specifically vis-à-vis the rights themselves.

44. Internationally accepted ideas of the various obligations engendered by human rights indicate that all rights — both civil and political rights and social and economic — generate at least four levels of duties for a State that undertakes to adhere to a rights regime, namely the duty to **respect, protect, promote, and fulfill these rights**. These obligations universally apply to all rights and entail a combination of negative and positive duties. As a human rights instrument, the African Charter is not alien to these concepts and the order in which they are dealt with here is chosen as a matter of convenience and in no way should it imply the priority accorded to them. Each layer of obligation is equally relevant to the rights in question.

45. At a primary level, the obligation to **respect** entails that the State should refrain from interfering in the enjoyment of all fundamental rights; it should respect right-holders, their freedoms, autonomy, resources, and liberty of their action. With respect to socioeconomic rights, this means that the State is obliged to respect the free use of resources owned or at the disposal of the individual alone or in any form of association with others, including the household or the family, for the purpose of rights-related needs. And with regard to a collective group, the resources belonging to it should be respected, as it has to use the same resources to satisfy its needs.

46. At a secondary level, the State is obliged to **protect** right-holders against other subjects by legislation and provision of effective remedies. This obligation requires the State to take measures to protect beneficiaries of the protected rights against political, economic and social interferences. Protection generally entails the creation and maintenance of an atmosphere or framework by an effective interplay of laws and regulations so that individuals will be able to freely realize their rights and freedoms. This is very much intertwined with the tertiary obligation of the State to **promote** the enjoyment of all human rights. The State should make sure that individuals are able to exercise their rights and freedoms, for example, by promoting tolerance, raising awareness, and even building infrastructures.

47. The last layer of obligation requires the State to **fulfil** the rights and freedoms it freely undertook under the various human rights regimes. It is more of a positive expectation on the part of the State to move its machinery towards the actual realisation of the rights. This is

(Continued)

(Continued)

also very much intertwined with the duty to promote mentioned in the preceding paragraph. It could consist in the direct provision of basic needs such as food or resources that can be used for food (direct food aid or social security).

48. Thus States are generally burdened with the above set of duties when they commit themselves under human rights instruments. Emphasizing the all-embracing nature of their obligations, the International Covenant on Economic, Social, and Cultural Rights, for instance, under Article 2(1), stipulates exemplarily that States *"undertake to take steps... by all appropriate means, including particularly the adoption of legislative measures."* Depending on the type of rights under consideration, the level of emphasis in the application of these duties varies. But sometimes, the need to meaningfully enjoy some of the rights demands a concerted action from the State in terms of more than one of the said duties. Whether the government of Nigeria has, by its conduct, violated the provisions of the African Charter as claimed by the Complainants is examined here below.

The Complainants allege that the Nigerian government violated the right to health and the right to clean environment as recognized under Articles 16 and 24 of the African Charter by failing to fulfill the minimum duties required by these rights. This, the Complainants allege, the government has done by:

— Directly participating in the contamination of air, water and soil and thereby harming the health of the Ogoni population,
— Failing to protect the Ogoni population from the harm caused by the NNPC Shell Consortium but instead using its security forces to facilitate the damage
— Failing to provide or permit studies of potential or actual environmental and health risks caused by the oil operations Article 16 of the African Charter reads:

(1) Every individual shall have the right to enjoy the best attainable state of physical and mental health.

(2) States Parties to the present Charter shall take the necessary measures to protect the health of their people and to ensure that they receive medical attention when they are sick.

Article 24 of the African Charter reads:

All peoples shall have the right to a general satisfactory environment favourable to their development.

51. These rights recognise the importance of a clean and safe environment that is closely linked to economic and social rights in so far as the environment affects the quality of life and safety of the individual. As has been rightly observed by Alexander Kiss, "an environment degraded by pollution and defaced by the destruction of all beauty and variety is as contrary to satisfactory living conditions and the development as the breakdown of the fundamental ecologic equilibria is harmful to physical and moral health."

52. The right to a general satisfactory environment, as guaranteed under Article 24 of the African Charter or the right to a healthy environment, as it is widely known, therefore imposes

(Continued)

(Continued)

clear obligations upon a government. It requires the State to take reasonable and other measures to prevent pollution and ecological degradation, to promote conservation, and to secure an ecologically sustainable development and use of natural resources. Article 12 of the International Covenant on Economic, Social and Cultural Rights (ICESCR), to which Nigeria is a party, requires governments to take necessary steps for the improvement of all aspects of environmental and industrial hygiene. The right to enjoy the best attainable state of physical and mental health enunciated in Article 16(1) of the African Charter and the right to a general satisfactory environment favourable to development (Article 16(3)) already noted obligate governments to desist from directly threatening the health and environment of their citizens. The State is under an obligation to respect the just noted rights and this entails largely non-interventionist conduct from the State for example, not from carrying out, sponsoring or tolerating any practice, policy or legal measures violating the integrity of the individual.

53. Government compliance with the spirit of Articles 16 and 24 of the African Charter must also include ordering or at least permitting independent scientific monitoring of threatened environments, requiring and publicising environmental and social impact studies prior to any major industrial development, undertaking appropriate monitoring and providing information to those communities exposed to hazardous materials and activities and providing meaningful opportunities for individuals to be heard and to participate in the development decisions affecting their communities.

54. We now examine the conduct of the government of Nigeria in relation to Articles 16 and 24 of the African Charter. Undoubtedly and admittedly, the government of Nigeria, through NNPC has the right to produce oil, the income from which will be used to fulfil the economic and social rights of Nigerians. But the care that should have been taken as outlined in the preceding paragraph and which would have protected the rights of the victims of the violations complained of was not taken. To exacerbate the situation, the security forces of the government engaged in conduct in violation of the rights of the Ogonis by attacking, burning and destroying several Ogoni villages and homes.

For the above reasons, the Commission,

Finds the Federal Republic of Nigeria in violation of Articles 2, 4, 14, 16, 18(1), 21 and 24 of the African Charter on Human and Peoples' Rights;

Appeals to the government of the Federal Republic of Nigeria to ensure protection of the environment, health and livelihood of the people of Ogoniland by:

— Ensuring that appropriate environmental and social impact assessments are prepared for any future oil development and that the safe operation of any further oil development is guaranteed through effective and independent oversight bodies for the petroleum industry; and
— Providing information on health and environmental risks and meaningful access to regulatory and decision-making bodies to communities likely to be affected by oil operations.

(Continued)

(Continued)

Urges the government of the Federal Republic of Nigeria to keep the African Commission informed of the outcome of the work of:

— The Federal Ministry of Environment which was established to address environmental and environment related issues prevalent in Nigeria and as a matter of priority, in the Niger Delta area including the Ogoni land;

— The Niger Delta Development Commission (NDDC) enacted into law to address the environmental and other social related problems in the Niger Delta area and other oil producing areas of Nigeria; and

— The Judicial Commission of Inquiry inaugurated to investigate the issues of human rights violations.

Done at the 30th Ordinary Session, held in Banjul, The Gambia from 13th to 27th October 2001

In another case of *Adediran and Anor v. Interland Transport Ltd,*[20] the appellants as residents of the Ire-Akari Housing Estate, Isolo, inter alia brought an action for nuisance due to noise, vibrations, dust and obstruction of the roads in the estate. *The Supreme Court dealt with the common law restrictions on the right of a private person to sue on a public nuisance. The Court held that in the light of section 6(6)(b) of the 1999 Constitution, a private person can commence an action on public nuisance without the consent of the Attorney-General, or without joining him as a party.*

The approach of the Supreme Court in the above case by abolishing the first problem of locus standi in Nigeria is commendable.

Notes

1. The word "environment" is used in the same sense as used by UNEP, that is, "the physical and social factors of the surroundings of human beings and includes land, water, atmosphere, climate, sound, odour, taste, energy, waste management, coastal and marine pollution, the biological factors of animals and plants, as well as cultural values, historical sites, and monuments and aesthetics" (United Nations Environmental Program, n.d.).
2. See United Nations Environmental Program, n.d.
3. Field (2008) described environmental economics as the application of economic tools to study resource management and use, and UNEP described environmental law as "the body of law that contains elements to control the human impact on the Earth and on public health" (UNEP, n.d.)
4. In Zambia, for example, air pollution has been identified as a major environmental problem in the copper belt, with about $300,000-700,000$ tons/year of sulfur dioxide (SO_2) into the air. SO_2 also contaminates the soil in the form of sulfuric acid (H_2SO_4) (World Bank, 2003).
5. For example, the Forest Act of 1988 makes it illegal to cut trees from forest parks. In convicting a party arrested for illegal logging under the Act, a District Tribunal Court referred to illegal logging as "barbaric". See Jawo (2014).

6. An example of a product regulation law is Ghana's *Pesticide Control and Management Act, 1996* (Act 528) which deals with the "manufacture, classification, labeling, importation, exportation, and use of pesticides in Ghana." The Act defines a pesticide as: "(a) a substance or mixture of substances intended for preventing, destroying, repelling or reducing the destructive effects of any pest; or (b) a substance or mixture of substances intended for use as a plant regulator, defoliant, desiccant or wood preservative." Pesticides in Kenya are regulated under the *Pest Control Products Act*, Cap 346, Laws of Kenya of 1982, "to regulate the importation and exportation, manufacture, distribution and use of pest control products." Nigeria's *Pest Control Production (Special Powers) Act*, CAP P9, LFN 2004 is concerned with export produce conditions and pest control. The Act provides an inspector authority to take emergency measures to control pest infestation of produce (Section 1).

7. An excellent source for environmental treaty resources is *Ecolex*: The Gateway to Environmental Law. This is a joint environmental reference sources project by FAO, IUCN, and the UNEP. See http://www.ecolex.org/start.php.

8. Section 20 of the 1999 Federal Republic of Nigeria Constitution empowers the State "to protect and improve the environment and safeguard the water, air and land, forest and wildlife of Nigeria." Chapter 5, Part 2, Article 69 (1) (a) of Kenya's new Constitution states "(1) The State shall (a) ensure sustainable exploitation, utilisation, management and conservation of the environment and natural resources, and ensure the equitable sharing of the accruing benefits." Environmental provisions in the constitution of the Republic of Gambia are found in *The principles of state policy*, which "shall not confer legal rights or be enforceable in any court." Articles 215 (d) and (e) of the Constitution exalt citizens and policy makers to work towards "(d) protecting the environment of the nation for posterity; and (e) co-operation with other nations and bodies to protect the global environment." Article 41 (k) of the 1992 Constitution places the protection of Ghana's environmental resources in the hands of the citizens of Ghana.

9. In Ghana, Parliament passed the *Environmental Protection Agency Act* 1994, and designated the Environmental Protection Agency (EPA) as the primary agency responsible for enforcing the environmental laws. The National Environmental Standards Regulation Agency (NESREA) Act 2007 designates NESREA administered by the Ministry of Environment as the agency responsible for the protection and development of the environment, biodiversity conservation and sustainable development of Nigeria's natural resources, environmental technology, including coordination and liaison with relevant stakeholders within and outside Nigeria on matters of enforcement of environmental standards, regulations, rules, laws, policies and guidelines. In Zambia the Environmental Management Act (EMA) No. 12 of 2011 established the Zambia Environmental Management Agency to provide for integrated environmental management and the protection and conservation of the environment and the sustainable management and use of natural resources.

10. Article 35 (5d) of the 1992 Constitution of Ghana directs the state "to take appropriate measures to ensure decentralisation in administrative and financial machinery of government and to give opportunities to people to participate in decision-making at every level in national life and government." The Constitution also established the District Assemblies Common Fund and provides that "not less than five per cent of the total revenues of Ghana" are paid into it for use in district assembly capital works. The Government also passed the *Local Government Act 1993* (Act 462) and the *District Assemblies Common Fund Act 1993* (Act 455). The passage of the *Local Government Act* (Act 462) shifted environmental planning and enforcement authority to the district and local levels since public health is a local issue.

11. Ghana's Food and Drug Law, Section 44 (a). Uganda's National Environment (Standards for Discharge of Effluent into Water or on Land) Regulations, S.I. No 5/1999 (Under section 26 and 107 of the National Environment Act, Cap 153) defines the role of a technical agency as follows:
(1) A lead agency applying the standards established under these Regulations shall, as required by Section 77 of the National Environment Act, Cap 153—(a) keep a record of the amount of waste generated by the activity and of the parameters of the discharges; (b) submit the record offered to in paragraph (a) to the Executive Director and to any other relevant lead agency, every 3 months from the commencement of the activity for which the permit was issued (National Environment, 1999).

12. One popular approach is the *Travel Cost Method*. The idea is to use the cost of travelling to enjoy the environmental amenity as the value of the amenity. For example, the cost of traveling to watch birds at the wetland is an estimate of the value of the wetland to the individual.
13. See Stavins (2009) for an excellent discussion of the theoretical and empirical issues associated with using benefit—cost analysis in environmental policy evaluation.
14. This is the famous "Pigouvian tax" advocated by Pigou (1920).
15. The discussion on the efficiency in using taxes and standards to control environmental pollution is based entirely on Randall (1981).
16. *Protocol for Sustainable Development of Lake Victoria Basin*, Article 17. "Application of the 'Polluter Pays' Principle." The Protocol was signed between Kenya, Uganda, and Tanzania for the management of the Victoria Basin. Date of text is 29 November 2003.
17. Uganda, National Environmental Action Plan (NEAP), "Control of Pollution and Management of Domestic and Industrial Waste and Hazardous Materials," Section 3.9.
18. See Kingdom of Lesotho, Environmental Act 2001 Part VII, "(4) In addition to any sentence that may be imposed upon a polluter under subsection (2), the court may require such person to—(a) to pay the full cost of cleaning up the environment and of removing the effects of the pollution; or (b) to clean up the environment and remove the effects of the pollution." The provisions under Kenya's law is identical, "In addition to any sentence that the Court may impose upon a polluter under subsection (1) of this Section, the Court may direct that person to—(a) pay the full cost of cleaning up the polluted environment and of removing the pollution; (b) clean up the polluted environment and remove the effects of pollution to the satisfaction of the Authority. See Kenya, *Environmental Management and coordinating Act*, 1999 (No. 8 of 1999) (entry into force 14 January 2000).
19. The term "enforcement" is used to mean formal enforcement of environmental law and not other enforcement mechanisms based on community norms, taboos, etc.
20. (1991) 9 NWLR (pt. 214) 155.

Questions

1. What governmental agencies are responsible for environmental protection in your country? How effective are these agencies?
2. In your opinion, have Environmental Impact Assessments (EIAs) in your country been effective?
3. How may the government encourage private participation in enforcing environmental laws in your country?
4. What are the economic and legal foundations of the "Polluter Pays Principle"?

References

Bugge, H.C., 1996. The principles of polluter pays in economics and law. In: Eide, E., van der Bergh, R. (Eds.), Law and Economics of the Environment. Juridisk Forlag, Oslo. In: Eide, E., van der Bergh, R. (Eds.), Law and Economics of the Environment. Juridisk Forlag, Oslo.

Cropper, M.L., et al., 1992. The determinants of pesticide regulation: a statistical analysis of EPA decision making. J. Pol. Econ. 100 (1), 175–197.

Field, B.C., 2008. Environmental Economics: An Introduction. fifth ed. The McGraw-Hill Companies, Inc, New York.

Jawo, L.S.M., 2014. Gambia: Niani district tribunal court fined men for logging. The Daily Observer (Banjul), 26 February. <http://allafrica.com/stories/201402261523.html> (viewed 09.10.15).

National Environment, 1999. Standards for Discharge of Effluent into Water or on Land Regulations. Available at: <http://www.nemaug.org/regulations/effluent_discharge_regulations.pdf>.

OECD, 1972. Recommendation of the Council on Guiding Principles Concerning International Economic Aspects of Environmental Policies. May. Council Document no. C(72)128. Organization of Economic Cooperation and Development, Paris.

Pigou, A.C., 1920. The Economics of Welfare. Macmillan, London.

Randall, A., 1981. Research Economics: An Economic Approach to Natural Resource and Environmental Policy. Grid Publication Inc., Columbus, Ohio.

Stavins, R., 2009. Is Benefit-Cost Analysis Helpful for Environmental Regulation?". Available at: <http://www.robertstavinsblog.org/2009/07/08/is-benefit-cost-analysis-helpful-for-environmental-regulation/>.

Tietenberg, T., 1996. Private Enforcement of Environmental Regulations in Latin America and the Caribbean: An Effective Instrument for Environmental Management? Inter-American Development Bank, Washington, DC, No. ENV 101.

Tietenberg, T., Lewis, L., 2009. Environmental and Natural Resource Economics. eighth ed. Pearson, Addison Wesley, Boston.

United Nations Environmental Program (UNEP) (n.d.), Training Manual on International Environmental Law, Chapter 2. The Role of National Environmental Law. <http://www.unep.org/environmentalgovernance/Portals/8/documents/training_Manual.pdf> (viewed 09.06.15).

World Bank, 2003. Project Appraisal Document: Copperbelt Environment Project. Report No. 25347-ZA, February 14.

CHAPTER 16

Transboundary Water Resources and Wetlands

Keywords: Transboundary water resources; climate change; ground water and surface water; River Basin Organization; development partners; Dublin partners; benefit sharing; relational treaty

16.1 Introduction

Transboundary water is water that crosses national boundaries (Lautze and Giordano, 2005).[1] The law and economics of transboundary water resources in sub-Saharan Africa (SSA) is important because Africa is home to 80 of the 200 water basins around the world; these 80 basins cover over 60% of the continent's total land area and several countries share the water as *co-riparian* owners (United Nations Economic Commission for Africa, 2000).[2] Table 16.1 shows that several common law SSA countries are co-riparians, and in countries such as Gambia (Gambia Basin), Nigeria (Niger Basin), Ghana (Volta Basin), Uganda (Nile Basin), and Zambia (Zambesi Basin) transboundary issues could be quite significant given the percentages of country area affected by basin water. The table also shows the uneven levels of rainfall that could be exacerbated by climatic changes accompanied by extreme conditions. Countries in SSA are currently not using large quantities of water for domestic, industrial, power, and irrigation purposes. However, over time population pressures and climate change could lead to conflicts as countries expand domestic, irrigation, and industrial water demand to meet food and agriculture and economic production needs.

Transboundary water resources are governed by different international institutional arrangements such as treaties, conventions, agreements, charters, declarations, and protocols depending on the objectives and vision of the co-riparians. All the institutional arrangements share some commonalities.[3] Some basin agreements contain provisions for *joint management* whereby countries agree to jointly manage the water resource together. Other arrangements contain specific provisions on how water will be *shared*. A third common theme is *environmental sustainability*, especially to support fragile ecosystems.

F.O. Boadu: Agricultural Law and Economics in Sub-Saharan Africa.
DOI: http://dx.doi.org/10.1016/B978-0-12-801771-5.00016-2

Table 16.1: SSA common law countries in transboundary water basin treaties[a]

Basin	Country	Area of Country (km²)	Area in Total Basin (%)	Area of Country (%)	Mean Rainfall in Basin (mm)
Gambia	Gambia	11300	14.5	100	
Lake Chad[b]	Nigeria	923770	7.5	19.4	670
Niger[c]	Nigeria	923770	25.7	63.2	1185
Okavango[d]	Botswana	581730	15.3	8.5	491
Volta[e]	Ghana	238540	38.6	63.7	1092.3
Nile[f]	Tanzania	945090	2.7	8.9	1015
	Kenya	580373	1.5	8	1245
	Uganda	235880	7.4	98.1	1140
Zambesi[g]	Botswana	581730	0.9	2.1	595
	Zambia	752610	42.5	76.4	955
	Zimbabwe	390760	15.8	54.5	710
	Tanzania	945090	2.1	2.9	1240
	Malawi	118480	8.0	91.5	990
West Coast[h]	Sierra Leone	71740	7.5	100	

[a]Only countries with complete information in FAO database are included in Table 16.1. Table 16.1 does not exhaust the large number of transboundary basins in Africa.
[b]http://www.fao.org/docrep/W4347E/w4347e0j.htm (viewed 16.09.15).
[c]http://www.fao.org/docrep/W4347E/w4347e0i.htm.
[d]http://www.fao.org/docrep/W4347E/w4347e0p.htm#the%20okavango%20basin.
[e]http://www.fao.org/docrep/W4347E/w4347e0u.htm.
[f]http://www.fao.org/docrep/W4347E/w4347e0k.htm.
[g]http://www.fao.org/docrep/W4347E/w4347e0o.htm.
[h]http://www.fao.org/docrep/W4347E/w4347e0v.htm#the%20west%20coast,%20excluding%20the%20gambia%20river%20and%20volta%20basins.

This theme gains special significance given concerns about climate change and predictions of dire consequences for countries in SSA. There are references to *equity* in some transboundary agreements, and in some cases, co-riparians have agreed to *data and information sharing*.

16.2 Law and Economics of Transboundary Water Resources

The structure of current arrangements for sharing water in SSA, and characteristics of water, shed light on the law and economics of the governance institutions to manage water resources in a transboundary context.[4] First, water is a *flow* resource, that is, it is mobile. For example, the Volta river flows through six countries and the quantity of water is difficult to ascertain due to physical and climatic conditions in each country. Even when the water is not flowing, such as a lake, there are losses due to evaporation and seepage. This mobile characteristic makes it difficult to establish exclusive property rights to the shared water resource. In the absence of exclusive rights, the water resource becomes a *commons* that must be collectively managed. The second characteristic of water is the variability in supply. Table 16.1 shows the uneven amounts of mean rainfall in the various transboundary water basins. Water availability is subject to the vagaries of nature and unpredictable. These characteristics have shaped the content of the major international laws governing transboundary water resources such as the 1997 UN Watercourses Convention on the Non-navigational Uses of Transboundary Waters.[5]

The basic rationale underlying the economics of transboundary water resources is that countries sharing the water resource are self-interested and seek to maximize the benefits from using the water to their national interest. Countries pursue this self-interest against the backdrop of the unique characteristics of water jointly owned by two or more countries in a basin. The tool of analysis used by economists is *game theory* which explicitly recognizes the interdependence of parties in a bargaining situation and attempts to derive outcomes based on strategies used by the parties.[6] One negotiation outcome in game theory is known as the *zero-sum* game where the gains to one party mean a loss to the other party. The commonalities found in transboundary water treaties support the proposition that the global community purposefully intended to avoid a zero-sum outcome in the implementation of transboundary agreements.[7] Box 16.1 uses a transaction cost economics framework to argue that even in those situations where one would suspect hegemony in transboundary water negotiations such as between the Republic of South Africa and the Kingdom of Lesotho, it is in the parties' interest to seek an outcome that promotes a *relation* and not a *contract*.[8]

16.3 River Basin Organizations

Despite the abundance of river basins in SSA, there is little research on the institutional arrangements governing the functioning of River Basin Organizations (RBOs).[9] RBOs are important in coordinating the interests of riparians in a river basin and may control significant resources in performing its defined responsibilities.[10] The role of RBOs will become more significant with increasing water scarcity that leads countries to lay strong claims to water. In a situation where there is coordinated regional planning of projects, such as irrigation, RBOs will play the important role of providing the information needed for efficient investment decision-making and pricing of water resources. RBOs essentially become vital institutions for achieving the broader vision of the African Union. An assessment of RBOs points to major technical and financial constraints facing these organizations. The assessment also suggests that the role of development partners is vital to the survival of the RBOs.[11]

BOX 16.1 Elements of Sustainable Transboundary Water-Sharing Treaty: The Lesotho Highlands Water Project

I. **The Treaty Vision**

   The treaty, the Lesotho Highlands Water Project (LHWP) will transfer water from the highlands of the Kingdom of Lesotho (KOL) to the Republic of South Africa (RSA). The Senqu River, a major river in KOL, originates from the highlands and joins the Orange River in RSA to become the Senqu-Orange River System. Water from the highlands in Lesotho constitutes 50 percent of the input into the Senqu-Orange River System. The direction of flow of the Senqu River does not favor RSA because the water flows south into the Orange River, when it is needed north of the Drakensberg Range in the Vaal River above the Vaal Dam. The Vaal Region, also called the "Pretoria-Witwatersand-Vereeniging (PWV)" region is critical to the economy of RSA because it accounts for approximately 40 percent of Gross Domestic Product (GDP) and about 50 percent of its total industrial output, with 31 percent of the total population living in the area.

II. **A Paradigm of Relational and Transactional Treaties**

   The theoretical and analytical approach used to analyze the KOL-RSA treaty draws from the transaction costs paradigm of institutional economics. Under the paradigm, contracting parties weigh the benefits and costs of entering into a treaty or agreement, and therefore would search for the appropriate organizational structure (governance regime) which minimizes the transaction costs, that is, the "information, contracting and policing costs (ICP)" of their participation in a treaty. Governance regimes can be looked at on a continuum, ranging from a single, "one-shot" interaction (transactional) to a long-term repeated interaction (relational). Parties may define their interaction to reflect a hybrid of these two extreme poles. The essence of the characterization of a contract as transactional or relational is "to categorize contract transactions and relations along some kind of behavioral lines." This means that by carefully examining the language, duties, and responsibilities in a treaty, one may gain an understanding of the parties' aspirations, hopes, and the choice of governance regime intended to govern the distribution of benefits between the present and the future. Where the language, duties, and responsibilities convey a sense of a "one-shot" deal, the parties intended a transactional treaty, and where there is a sense of continuity and conscious effort to jointly minimize costs by reducing risks.

III. **Application of the Transaction Cost Paradigm to the KOL-RSA Treaty**

   a. *Information Costs*

      In negotiating the treaty, KOL and RSA took joint action to reduce information costs, thus indicating a mutual desire to work towards a relational governance structure. They accomplished this in two ways: (1) by incorporating and building on the historical commonalities between the two countries rather than a costly search for new sources of trust and, (2) by a joint undertaking to share the information cost for all the technical and non-technical aspects of the treaty.

   b. *Bargaining Costs*

      A relational governance structure requires that parties avoid cost-increasing bargaining techniques such as hold-outs, risk-increasing techniques in the form of ambiguities in

(Continued)

> **BOX 16.1 Elements of Sustainable Transboundary Water-Sharing Treaty: The Lesotho Highlands Water Project (Continued)**
>
> language, and opportunism-promoting techniques like open-ended drafting of provisions. A basic strategy used by RSA and KOL to reduce bargaining costs was the reliance on independent, international experts. RSA and KOL also followed guidelines suggested by the international community of nations.
>
> c. *Policing Costs*
>
> The KOL-RSA treaty was given a life of its own to minimize policing costs and also protect it from potentially subversive domestic legislation. This was accomplished by setting up three new institutions specifically tailored to deal with the implementation and monitoring of the project. The internal structure and operation of these institutions encourage the use of risk-reducing strategies and the prevention of opportunism by contracting parties. Furthermore, the provisions governing the sharing of benefits (royalty payments) and for the settlement of disputes lend support to the relational objectives of the parties because they are structured to allow each party to easily determine gains under the treaty. This reduces policing costs.

16.4 Role of Development Partners

Several factors combine to make bilateral and multilateral organizations important partners in designing governance institutions to manage transboundary water resources. First is the very nature of transboundary water itself. This is water that crosses jurisdictions. Development partners help to develop those overarching institutions free from any particular country bias to oversee the use of the water resource. The partners help to prevent conflicts.[12] Second is the science. Laws and regulations governing water resources are based on scientific information about the characteristics of the water and its location. The development partners work with the science and technology community in several countries and also operate some research facilities that produce science information for use by developing countries. The development partners are also involved in institution building and organizational improvements, for example, support of extension systems, capacity-building in these institutions and the provision of infrastructure (computers, ICT, training aides, etc.). The partners were instrumental in the development of the *Dublin Principles* based on which several countries in SSA have developed their water sector policies.[13] Some of the major partners are the ECA, FAO, UNDP, WB, UNEP, IWMI, EU, and USAID.[14] The role played by these partners is acknowledged under the MDGs.[15]

16.5 Benefit Sharing

"Benefit sharing" from transboundary water resources means that the countries sharing the water basin (riparians) will cooperate and share the benefits and costs (associated with water use such as agriculture, fishing, recreation) from a basin rather than share the physical water, thereby encouraging each country to plan its water economy independent of the policies of other countries in the basin.

Joint management of transboundary water addresses the difficult problem of externalities in transboundary water resource use. The use of transboundary water by one riparian may have adverse consequences on another riparian. For example, a dam built by one riparian on a shared river system will have adverse consequences on another riparian. Joint management internalizes the costs and increases the benefits accruing to the riparians. Economists have used public goods and game theoretic models to explain the dimensions of cooperation when confronted with a common pool resource such as transboundary water. The general conclusion from these theories is that cooperation by riparians may not be possible due to self-interest, defection, and free riding. This conclusion justifies the use of River Management Organizations (RMOs) to oversee the management of a basin on behalf of the riparians. More recently researchers have found that where riparians recognize their long-term interdependence, they may cooperate to capture benefits (Axelrod, 2006).

Several principles and concepts are available to assist riparian countries in designing institutional arrangements to promote cooperation in sharing a common pool resource. Information and data sharing about the resource is important and the interest of all riparians must be counted. Parties may also purposefully link issues to make it costly for a riparian to abandon the agreement. A riparian who rejects the water agreement may suffer losses in some other water or non-water sector of the economy. Riparians must strive to accurately identify benefits and costs facing each member and the group as a whole. Counting benefits and costs is complicated because the measure must capture a diverse array of outputs including income generation, environmental, wetland improvement, improved institutional innovation (governance and security), and human capital improvements.[16] It has been suggested that measures associated with the attainment of the MDGs be included in the benefit count given the central role of water in achieving the goals (Axelrod, 2006).

16.6 Wetlands

Wetlands have been broadly described as "all lakes and rivers, underground aquifers, swamps and marshes, wet grasslands, peatlands, oases, estuaries, deltas and tidal flats, mangroves and other coastal areas, coral reefs, and all human-made sites such as fish ponds, rice paddies, reservoirs and salt pans" (RAMSAR, 2014). Wetlands provide both ecological and economic uses. Ecologically, wetlands serve as habitat for fish and wildlife species, biodiversity, and micro-organisms that support life. Wetlands also help purify water resources, contribute to flood control, and support such economic activities as fishing, hunting, and grazing areas. Wetlands also provide eco tourism, and recreational revenues to support a large number of communities in SSA. Fig. 16.1 shows the distribution of wetlands

Figure 16.1
Location of Wetlands in Africa. *Web source: https://rsis.ramsar.org/ (viewed on 20.09.15).*

in SSA. Most wetlands are located south of the Sahara. Even though wetlands cover less than 1% of the surface land area of Africa, it is known that the biodiversity richness of the wetlands is immense.[17] This view is supported by the distribution of wetlands in the common law countries in SSA (Table 16.2).

Table 16.2 is not an exhaustive presentation of the number of wetland sites in common law countries in SSA. However, the number of sites in countries such as Uganda, Nigeria, Zambia, and Zimbabwe points to the need for effective involvement of countries to protect wetlands and the biodiversity they provide. It is not only the number of wetland sites in a country that matters because even in a country with very few sites, the number of species unique to the sites becomes a critical element in determining the value of the wetland.

The policies, laws, and regulations governing wetlands in SSA are based on the Ramsar Convention of 1971.[18] The philosophical foundation of the Ramsar Convention is the principle of "wise use," defined as, "*the maintenance of their ecological character, achieved through the implementation of ecosystem approaches, within the context of sustainable development.*" The "wise use" principle requires that countries plan how best to utilize services from a wetland to the benefit of communities, and also offer research and training on how best to preserve the wetland for the enjoyment of future generations.

16.7 The Law and Economics of Wetlands

Wetland management is one subject that depends on a strong intersection between biology, economics, and law, because the objective is to determine how laws and regulations

Table 16.2: Number and characteristics of Ramsey sites in common law African countries

Country	Number of Sites	Location of Sites
Botswana	1	Okavango Delta
Gambia	3	Niumi National Park; Baobolon Wetland Reserve; Tanbi Wetland Complex.
Ghana	6	Owabi Wildlife Sanctuary; Sakumono Ramsar site; Densu Delta; Muni-Pomadze; Songor; Keta Lagoon
Kenya	6	Lake Bogoria; Lake Baringo; Tana River Delta; Lake Nakuru; Lake Naivasha; Lake Elmenteita
Malawi	1	Lake Chilwa
Nigeria	11	Lake Chad; Baturiya Wetland; Dagona Sanctuary Lake; Nguru Lake; Maladumba Lake; Pandam and Wase Lakes; Lower Kaduna-Middle Niger Floodplain; Foge Islands; Oguta Lake; Upper Orashi Forests; Apoi Creek Forests
Sierra Leone	1	Sierra Leone River Estuary
Uganda	12	Sierra Leone River Estuary; Lake Opeta Wetland System; Lake Bisina Wetland System; Lake Nakuwa Wetland System; Mabamba Bay Wetland System; Lutembe Bay Wetland System; Rwenzori Mountains Ramsar Site; Lake George; Lake Nabugabo Wetland System; Nabajjuzi Wetland System; Sango Bay-Musambwa Island-Kagera Wetland System; Lake Mburo-Nakivali Wetland System; Nabajjuzi Wetland System
Tanzania	4	Lake Natron Basin; Rufiji, Mafia and Kilwa Marine Ramsar site; Kilombero Valley Flood Plain; Malagarasi-Muyovosi Wetlands
Zambia	9	Mweru wa Ntipa; Tanganyika; Bangweulu Swamps; Luangwa Flood Plains; Busanga Swamps; Kafue Flats; Barotse Floodplain; Dambo; Lukanga Swamp
Zimbabwe	7	Mana Pools; Chinhoyi Caves; Victoria Falls National Park; Monavale Wetland; Lake Chivero and Manyame; Cleveland Dam; Driefontein Grassland

This table is a summary from Ramsar, *Country Profiles*, http://www.ramsar.org/country-profiles (viewed 20.09.15).

influence economizing decisions by individuals and firms and the impact on the physical environment. The economic analysis of wetlands is referred to as *ecological economics*, which deal with how humans interact with the physical environment. There are two ways to approach the economic issues associated with wetlands. First is the issue of the appropriate theoretical framework to use in modelling wetlands. The second is the tools used in measuring the economic value of wetlands.

The economic framework for modeling wetlands is based on a combination of biology and economics.[19] Management of fisheries is an example of the combination of biology and economics. Biophysical modelling may be applied to determine the optimal level of fish stocks. This information may be introduced into an economic model to determine the impacts on employment, revenues, and other socioeconomic impacts. The second economic issue is measuring the economic value of wetlands. Some of the benefits from a wetland, such as fish catch, may be captured using existing market prices. Other benefits from a wetland, such as flood control, are not captured in market prices because of the public good nature of the benefit. The mixture of private and public benefits from a wetland poses significant challenges when designing laws and regulations to promote sustainable and wise use of wetlands.

Nyakana v NEMA & Others (Uganda) introduces a layer of complexity in wetland litigation that several SSA countries will face as populations growand settlements expand to fragile land areas. The case also highlights the conflict between the right of private landowners to use their land as they wish versus the power of government to preserve wetlands for the benefit of the community at large.

Amooti Godfrey Nyakana (Petitioner) v NEMA & Others (Respondents)

In the Constitutional Court of Uganda at Kampala
Constitutional Petition No. 03/05
November 9, 2009

Judgment of Byamugisha, JA

Facts

The petitioner filed the instant petition under the provisions of **Article 137(3)** of the Constitution and **rule 3** of the Constitutional Court (Petitions and References) Rules S.I No. 91/05. The petition is challenging the constitutionality of sections 67, 68, and 70 of the National Environment Management Act (Cap 153) Laws of Uganda. He averred that the impugned sections contravene and are inconsistent with Articles 21, 24, 26, 27, 28, 42, 44, 237, and 259 of the Constitution and various international Human Rights Conventions and Instruments entrenched in the Constitution under Articles 20 and 45 of the Constitution. The petitioner sought one declaration and orders for redress. The petition was opposed by the first and second respondents who filed answers to the effect.

The facts which led to the filing of the petition are not in dispute. The petitioner is the proprietor of land comprised in LRV 3148 Folio 2 Plot 8 Plantation Road Bugolobi, a Kampala suburban. He obtained the title in 2004 to construct a residential house on the plot. He obtained the necessary approvals and commenced the work. In June 2004 the first respondent through its inspectors carried out an inspection of Nakivubo wetland located in Nakawa Division. The inspectors found that the petitioner was constructing a house within a wetland. The first respondent issued a restoration order which was served on the petitioner's foreman on the 20th July 2004. The order required the petitioner to comply with the conditions stated therein within a period of 21 days. He failed to do so and his unfinished building was demolished on 8th January 2005 — hence this petition.

Opinion

The parties agreed on one issue namely:

Whether sections 67, 68, and 70 of the NEMA Act are inconsistent or contravene Articles 21, 22, 24, 26, 27, 28, 43, 237, and 259 of the Constitution.

(Continued)

(Continued)

I shall first set out the articles of the Constitution and provisions of the Neema Act that require interpretation. **Article 21** of the Constitution provides as follows:

(1) All persons are equal before the law in all spheres of political, economic, social and cultural life and in every other respect and shall enjoy equal protection of the law.

(2) Without prejudice to clause (1) of this article, a person shall not be discriminated against on the ground of sex, race, colour, ethnic origin, tribe, birth, creed or religion, social or economic standing, political opinion or disability.

(3) For the purposes of this article "discriminate" means giving different treatment to different persons attributable only or mainly to their respective descriptions by sex, race, colour, ethnic origin, tribe, birth, creed or religion, social or economic standing, political opinion or disability.

(4). . . . .

Article 24 states that:

No person shall be subjected to any form of torture or cruel, inhuman or degrading treatment or punishment.

Article 26 is couched in the following terms:

(1) Every person has a right to own property either individually or in association with others.

(2) No person shall be compulsorily deprived of property or any interest in or right over property or any interest in or right over property of any description except where the following conditions are satisfied-

(a) the taking of possession or acquisition is necessary for public use or in the interest of defence, public safety, public order, public morality or public health; and

(b) the compulsory taking of possession or acquisition of property is made under a law which makes provision for-

(i) prompt payment of fair and adequate compensation, prior to the taking of possession or acquisition of the property; and

(ii) a right of access to court of law by any person who has an interest or right over the property".

Part of **Article 28** provides thus:

Right to a fair hearing:

(1) In the determination of civil rights and obligations or any criminal charge, a person is entitled to a fair, speedy and public hearing before an independent and impartial court or tribunal established by law.

Article 43 also provides that:

(1) In the enjoyment of the rights and freedoms prescribed in this Chapter, no person shall prejudice the fundamental or other human rights and freedoms of others or public interest.

(2) Public interest under this article shall not permit-

(Continued)

(Continued)

(a) political persecution;

(b) detention without trial;

(c) any limitation of the enjoyment of the rights and freedoms prescribed by this Chapter beyond what is acceptable and demonstrably justifiable in a free and democratic society, or what is provided in this Constitution.

The provisions of *section 67* under which the environment restoration order was made provides as follows:

(1) Subject to the provisions of this Part, the authority may issue to any person in respect of any matter relating to the management of the environment and natural resources an order in this Part referred to as an environmental restoration order.

(2) An environmental restoration order may be issued under subsection (1) for any of the following purposes-

(a) Requiring the person to restore the environment as near as it may be to the state in which it was before the taking of the action which is the subject of the order;

(b) Preventing the person from taking any action which would or is reasonably likely to do harm to the environment;

(c) Awarding compensation to be paid by that person to other persons whose environment or livelihood has been harmed by the action which is the subject matter of the order;

(d)............

(3)..............

(4)...............

(5) In exercising its powers under this section, the authority shall-

(a) have regard to the principles as set out in section 2;

(b) explain the rights of the person, against whom the order is issued, to appeal to the court against that decision.

Section 68 governs the service of the restoration order. It states:

(1) where it appears to the authority that harm has been done or is likely to be done to the environment by any activity by any person, it may serve on that person, an environmental restoration order requiring that person to take such action, in such time being not less than twenty one days from the date of the service of the order, to remedy the harm to the environment as may be specified in the order.

(2).............

(7) It shall not be necessary for the authority in exercising its powers under subsection (3) to give any person conducting or involved in the activity the subject of the inspection or residing or working on or developing land on which the activity which is the subject of the inspection is taking place, an opportunity of being heard by or making representations to the person conducting the inspection.

(Continued)

(Continued)

Section 69 governs reconsideration of an environmental restoration order. It provides as follows:

(1) At any time within twenty one days after service of the environmental restoration order, a person upon whom the order has been served may, by giving reasons in writing, request the authority to reconsider that order.

(2) Where a written request has been made as provided for under subsection (1), the order shall continue in effect until varied, suspended or withdrawn under subsection (3) and, if varied, shall continue in effect in accordance with the variation.

(3) Where a request has been made under subsection (1), the authority shall, within thirty days after receipt of the request, reconsider the environment restoration order and notify in writing the person who made the request of her or his decision on the order.

The authority may, after reconsidering the case, confirm, vary, suspend or withdraw the environmental restoration order.

(4) The authority shall give the person who had requested a reconsideration of an environmental restoration order the opportunity to be heard orally before a decision is made. (Emphasis added).

Counsel for all the parties addressed court orally and they also filed conferencing notes.

Chapter 4 of the Constitution deals with protection and promotion of fundamental and other human rights and freedoms. It is evident from these provisions that some rights and freedoms are absolute while others are subject to some limitations and qualifications. Before dealing with the issue which was framed for our determination it is imperative to remind myself of the principles of constitutional interpretation which have been laid down by this Court and the Supreme Court.

In the case of *Attorney General v Silvatori Abuki — Constitutional Appeal No. 1/98(SC)* Order JSC stated the principle thus:

The principle applicable is that in determining the constitutionality of legislation, its purpose and effect must be taken into consideration. Both purpose and effect are relevant in determining constitutionality of either an unconstitutional purpose or unconstitutional effect animated by an object the legislation intends to achieve. This object is realized through the impact produced by the operation and application of the legislation. Purpose and effect respectively, the sense of the legislation's object and ultimate impact are clearly linked if not indivisible. Intended and actual effect has been looked up for guidance in assessing the legislation's object and thus its validity. See The Queen v Big Drug Mark Ltd 1996 CLR 332.

In the case of *Ndyanabo v Attorney* [2001] EA 495 the Court of Appeal of Tanzania stated the principles when it stated that

In interpreting the Constitution the court is guided by the general principles that (i) the constitution was a living instrument with a soul and consciousness of its own, (ii) fundamental rights provisions had to be interpreted in a broad manner, (iii) there is a rebuttable presumption that legislation was constitutional, and (iv) the onus of rebutting the presumption rested on those who challenge the

(Continued)

(Continued)

legislation's status save that, where those who supported a restriction on a fundamental right relied on a claw back clause, the onus was on them to justify the restriction.

What these two decisions establish is that if the purpose of an Act of Parliament is inconsistent with a provision of the Constitution, the Act or the provision being challenged shall be declared unconstitutional. Similarly, if the effect of implementing a provision of the Act is inconsistent with a provision of the Constitution, that provision of the Act shall be declared unconstitutional. Mr. Mbabazi and Bakiiza represented the petitioner while Mr. Kakuru, Ms. Akello and Mr. Kalemera, State Attorney, represented the respondents.

In his submissions Mr. Mbabazi stated that the property of the petitioner is protected by Article 26 of the Constitution and the demolition of the house affected his rights. He referred to article 28 which provides for fair hearing in the determination of civil disputes and contended that the petitioner was not accorded a fair hearing as the owner of the house. He claimed that the petitioner was subjected to degrading and inhumane treatment and there was unequal application of the law in that the petitioner's neighbours have continued to develop their plots without any interference from the respondents.

He invited court to grant the orders sought together with orders for redress.

In reply, Mr. Kakuru opposed the petition and submitted that the petitioner was not deprived of his property and that ownership of property goes with duties and obligations. He pointed out that section 43 of the Land Act requires an owner of land to manage and utilize it in accordance with the Forest Act, the Mining Act, the National Environment Act, the Water Act, the Wildlife Act and any other law. He claimed that what was taken away from the petitioner was abuse of the land. On the impugned sections, counsel submitted that section 68 gives a person who has been served with a restoration order 21 days to lodge a complaint and request for reconsideration of NEMA's decision. The opportunity to be heard is embedded in section 69 which provides for oral hearing by a person who has been served with a restoration order.

He invited court to dismiss the petition.

Ms. Akello submitted on behalf of the first respondent. She stated that Article 39 of the Constitution guarantees a clean and healthy environment. She pointed out Article 237 (2)(b) of the Constitution and section 44 of the Land Act make wetlands a public resource which must be protected. On the restoration order learned counsel submitted that the 1st respondent carried out an inspection and found that the petitioner was erecting a structure on a wetland. She claimed that the petitioner knew about the restoration order and he was also called at a sensitization meeting. She, too, pointed out that section 69 provides for a hearing. She invited court to dismiss the petition.

Mr. Kalemera associated himself with the submissions of counsel for the respondents and added that the right to own property is not absolute. He invited court to find that the impugned sections fall under Article 43 of the Constitution. In order for the petitioner to succeed, he has to show prima facie that the impugned sections are inconsistent with or

(Continued)

(Continued)

contravene the articles of the Constitution which he cited. The purpose of the National Environment Act according to its preamble is:

> To provide for sustainable management of the environment; to establish an authority as a coordinating, monitoring and supervisory body for that purpose and for other matters incidental to or connected with the forgoing.

The functions of the first respondent with regard to environment are set out in section 6 of the NEMA Act. With regard to the wetlands **section 36** of the Act imposes restrictions on the use of wetlands and to carry out any activity on the wetlands requires written approval of the first respondent. The petitioner is not challenging the constitutionality of these restrictions. In my view, it is these restrictions which gave the first respondent power to carry out inspection on the petitioner's property to ascertain whether the activities he was carrying out on the land were in conformity with the provisions of the section — hence the service of the restoration order.

The restoration order is like a charge sheet that commences the prosecution of a person who is charged with a criminal offence. Normally a police officer does not give a hearing to a suspect before charging him or her. The purpose of the Act is to give the first respondent power to deal with and protect the environment for the benefit of all including the petitioner. The impugned sections in my view have in built mechanisms for fair hearing as is enshrined in Article 28.

On receipt of the restoration order, the petitioner had 21 days within which to make a presentation to the first respondent for a review or variation of its order. Procedures before any tribunal which is acting judicially should be fair and be seen to be so. The petitioner had to show that the procedures laid down in the sections are insufficient to achieve justice without frustrating the intention of the legislation. The petitioner failed to show that the safeguards contained in the impugned sections are insufficient to accord him or anyone else a fair hearing.

Ruling

I have not been persuaded that the petitioner's proprietary rights were infringed by the acts of the first respondent. What was taken away from him was misuse of the land and this was done to protect the environment. I am not satisfied on the evidence before us that the petitioner made out a case on which this court can grant the declarations he sought.

Consequently the petition is dismissed with costs to the respondents.

C.K. Byamugisha Justice of Appeal

Judgment of Hon Justice A.EN.MPAGI-BAHIGEINE, JA

I have read the judgment prepared by C.K. Byamugisha, JA. I entirely agree with her reasoning and would only add for emphasis that such wetlands could not be granted to private individuals/entities because the State holds such natural resources in trust for the citizenry and they must be preserved for the public benefit, in this case to protect the environment.

(Continued)

(Continued)

The petitioner would not be entitled to any redress.

Since my Lords A. Twinomujuni, C.N.B. Kitumba and S.B.K. Kavuma JJA all agree the petition stands dismissed with costs to the respondents as proposed in the lead judgment.

Dated at Kampala this …..09th …… day of ……November……2009.

Notes

1. Lautze and Giordano were citing the U.N. Educ. Scientific & Cultural Org. (UNESCO) (2003).
2. The eight basins are the Congo, the Niger, the Ogadugne (Gabon), the Zambezi, the Nile, the Sanga, the Chari-Lagone, and the Volta (UNECA, 2000, p. 1).
3. These commonalities are discussed in Lautze et al. (2005).
4. The discussion in this section is based on the excellent survey of the economics of water resources undertaken by Young and Haveman (1985). The authors discuss several more characteristics of water than the two discussed in this section.
5. (UN Water Convention of 21 May 1997). The characteristics of water as an economic commodity have also been discussed in Hanemann (2006).
6. "Game theory is the science of strategy. It attempts to determine mathematically and logically the actions that 'players' (countries, *mine*) should take to secure the best outcomes for themselves in a wide array of "games (water agreement negotiations, *mine*)." "… But the games all share the common feature of interdependence. That is, the outcome for each participant depends on the choices (strategies) of all. In so-called zero-sum games the interests of the players conflict totally, so that one person's gain always is another's loss. More typical are games with the potential for either mutual gain (positive sum) or mutual harm (negative sum), as well as some conflict." See Dixit and Nalebuff.
7. "The 1997 United Nations Convention on Non-Navigational Uses of International Watercourses is one international instrument that specifically focuses on shared water resources. It established two key principles to guide the conduct of nations regarding shared watercourses: 'equitable and reasonable use' and 'the obligation not to cause significant harm' to neighbours" (United Nations Department of Economic and Social Affairs (UNDESA), 2015).
8. The paradigm used in Box 16.1 is based on the transaction cost literature. The principal studies are Macneil (1974, 1978) and also Williamson (1979).
9. "Of the over 80 transboundary river/lake basins in Africa, less than 10% have any kind of inter country mechanism or agreement for coordination of their integrated development efforts" (United Nations Economic Commission for Africa, 2000).
10. For example, "NEPAD's *Comprehensive Africa Agriculture Development Program* (CAADP), calls for US $38 billion of new investment in the sector (water) by 2015, to rapidly expand the area under sustainable agricultural water management" (International Water Management Institute (IWMI), 2004). REBOs along with individual countries in SSA will be responsible for managing the committed investment resources.
11. Between the 1960s and 1980s many transboundary river basin organisations were created with external support and according to the AICD Report "…nearly three decades later, with few exceptions, these transboundary organisations are still in the emergent stages. Factors are: waning political commitment, poor cooperation, management and technical difficulties, armed conflict, political instability, poorly defined goals, insufficient capacity and dwindling donor support." Stockholm International Water Institute (SIWI) (2010).
12. The conflict-prevention role of the development partners is evident in their role in the Volta Basin, "In the mid-1990s, the World Bank took an active role in the water affairs of Ghana and Burkina Faso and invoked

its transboundary waters policy whereby a country proposing to execute any project which will regulate, abstract or otherwise change river flows must notify co-riparian states of its intentions so that each state may consider whether it wishes to lodge an objection." Also "In 1996, Burkina sought World Bank support to construct a dam at Ziga, which would alter the flow of water into Ghana. To satisfy the Bank, a Ghanaian delegation visited Burkina and signed a 'no-objection' document agreeing to the dam's construction" (Lautze et al., 2005, pp. 26–29).

13. Current efforts to manage water resources in an integrated fashion (IWRM) are based on the Dublin Principles that were adopted in 1992 as part of the United Nations Conference on Environment and Development (UNCED), Rio de Janeiro, 1992. They include: (1) water and land resources should be managed at the lowest appropriate level; (2) fresh water is a finite and vulnerable resource, which is essential to sustain life, development and the environment; (3) effective management should link land and water uses on an integrated catchment basis; and (4) water management and development should be based on a participatory approach, involving users, planners, and policy makers. See Note 5.

14. These partners are instrumental in addressing the underinvestment in (1) water information as an input to decision making; (2) water governance setting right policies to plan, allocate water and build institutions; and (3) water services, see Note 10.

15. Goal 8 of the Millennium Development Goals directs the global community to "develop partnership for development" (United Nations, 2015).

16. It is true that counting benefits and costs is challenging. However, the position that security considerations are "vague and distant notion" fails to account for the critical institutional issues that drive the negotiation and stability of negotiated outcomes. See, for example, "While recognising the widest possible range of potential benefits that cooperation could bring is of conceptual interest, it is argued here that vague and distant notions of, for example, 'security' are of a secondary order. The primary goal is to benefit regional populations, and specifically to tackle the key issue of poverty reduction through sustainable development. This overarching goal also makes the distinction between 'economic' and 'environmental' benefits perhaps unnecessary" (Qaddumi, 2008).

17. See, Kabii (1996).

18. Ramsar, History of the Ramsar Convention, "The Ramsar treaty was negotiated through the 1960s by countries and non-governmental organizations concerned about the increasing loss and degradation of wetland habitat for migratory waterbirds. It was adopted in the Iranian city of Ramsar in 1971 and came into force in 1975. As of 2015, 169 countries had joined the agreement which seeks to govern how over 2212 wetland sites are managed and protected. The agreement governs over 200 million hectares of wetlands around the world."

19. See, for example, Whitten and Bennett (2004).

Questions

1. Discuss a water conflict between two or more countries in sub-Saharan Africa and how the conflict was addressed.

2. How will water resources affect poverty alleviation efforts in sub-Saharan Africa?

3. Why are River Basin Organizations vital to sub-Saharan Africa?

4. What alternative institutional arrangements may countries sharing a river basin use to share water resources?

References

Axelrod, R., 2006. The Evolution of Cooperation. revised ed. Perseus Books Group.

Dixit, A., Nalebuff, B., Game Theory. In: Summers, L., Henderson, D.R. (Eds.), The Concise Encyclopedia of Economics. Library of Economics and Liberty, Indianapolis, Indiana <http://www.econlib.org/library/Enc/GameTheory.html> (viewed 22.09.15).

Hanemann, W.M., 2006. The economic conception of water. In: Rogers, P., Llamas, M., Martinez-Cortina, L. (Eds.), Water Crisis: Myth or Reality. Taylor & Francis, London.

International Water Management Institute (IWMI), 2004. Investment in Agricultural Water Management in Sub-Saharan Africa: Diagnosis of Trends and Opportunties. *Inception Report* Volume 1 − Main Report *submitted* to the African Development Bank, p. 4.

Kabii, T., 1996. An Overview of African Wetlands, Technical Officer for Africa, Ramsar Bureau, Switzerland. (viewed at: http://www.oceandocs.org/bitstream/handle/1834/457/Africa_Wetlands_1.pdf;jsessionid=BDFA3F1350864FD6027805F8F5EE1CD8?sequence=1).

Lautze, J., Giordano, M., 2005. Transboundary water law in Africa: development, nature, and geography. Nat. Resources J. 45, 1053.

Lautze, J., Giordano, M., Borghese, M., 2005. Driving forces behind African transboundary water law: internal and external, and implications. In: International Workshop on African Water Laws: Plural Legislative Frameworks for Rural Water Management in Africa, 26−28 January 2005, Johannesburg, South Africa, pp. 26−29.

Macneil, I., 1974. The many futures of contract 47 S. Cal. L. Rev. 691.

Macneil, I., 1978. Adjustments of long-term economic relations under classical, neoclassical and relational contract law 72 Nw. U. L. Rev. 854.

Qaddumi, H., 2008. Practical approaches to transboundary water benefit sharing. Working Paper 292. Overseas Development Institute.

Ramsar Convention Secretariat, 2014. Ramsar Convention and its Mission. <http://www.ramsar.org/about/the-ramsar-convention-and-its-mission> (viewed on 22.09.15).

Stockholm International Water Institute (SIWI), 2010. Challenges and Opportunities for Financing Transboundary Water Resources Management and Development in Africa: Concept Note. (Final). Prepared for the EUWI Finance Working Group by the Stockholm International Water Institute (SIWI), p. 5 (John Joyce and Jacob Granit of SIWI lead authors). Obtained from <http://www.euwi.net/files/EUWI_TB_Waters_Financing_Concept_FINAL_0.pdf> (viewed 20.11.10).

U.N. Educ. Scientific & Cultural Org. (UNESCO), 2003. World Water Assessment Programme, The U.N. Water Development Report: Water for People, Water for Life, at 300, U.N. Doc. FAOCV/18/61/FAO/LOWA/ Legislative Study 61 (2003).

United Nations Department of Economic and Social Affairs (UNDESA). Transboundary Waters, International Decade for Action 'Water for Life' 2005−2015. <http://www.un.org/waterforlifedecade/transboundary_waters.shtml> (viewed 20.09.15).

United Nations Economic Commission for Africa, 2000. Transboundary River/Lake Basin Water Development in Africa: Prospects, Problems, and Achievements. ECA/RCID/052/00. Addis Ababa, Ethiopia.

United Nations, 2015. We Can End Poverty. Millennium Development Goals. <http://www.un.org/millenniumgoals/global.shtml> (viewed 20.11.2010).

Whitten, S.M., Bennett, J., 2004. A bio-economic model of wetland protection on private lands. Paper Prepared for Presentation at the American Agricultural Economics Association Annual Meeting, Denver, Colorado. <http://ageconsearch.umn.edu/handle/20122> (viewed on 19.09.15).

Williamson, O., 1979. Transaction cost economics: the Governance of contractual relations. J. Law Econ. 22, 233.

Young, R.A., Haveman, R.H., 1985. Economics of water resources: a survey. In: Kneese, A.V., Sweeny, J.L. (Eds.), Handbook of Natural Resources and Energy Economics, vol. II. Elsevier Science Publishers.

CHAPTER 17

Climate Change

Keywords: Climate change; greenhouse effect; adaptation; mitigation; nonmarket evaluation; hedonic pricing; travel cost; stated preferences

17.1 The Science of Climate Change and Law

The United Nations Framework Convention on Climate Change (UNFCCC) defines climate change as "a change in climate which is attributed directly or indirectly to human activity that alters the composition of the global atmosphere and which is in addition to natural climate variability observed over comparable periods of time" (UNFCCC, 1992).

Fig. 17.1 presents a basic depiction of the climate change concept (greenhouse effect). Solar energy enters the earth's atmosphere and warms the planet's surface. Some of the sun's heat reflects back into the atmosphere and is scattered. The earth's atmosphere is often defined as the "gaseous envelope" surrounding the planet and consists of nitrogen (78%), oxygen (21%), and active greenhouse gases (GHGs). GHGs include water vapor (H_2O), carbon dioxide (CO_2), methane (CH), nitrous oxide, ozone, and other trace gases (Baede, n.d.). These gases represent about 1% of the earth's atmosphere but they act like a "blanket" wrapped around the earth (Baede, n.d.). This "blanket" allows some of the heat from the sun to pass through and scatter in the atmosphere, while trapping additional heat at a comfortable temperature. In the absence of a "blanket" to trap some of the heat, all heat would simply bounce back into the atmosphere and scatter—resulting in the earth's surface being too cold to support human life. However, if the GHGs increase, then the blanket will be too "thick" and will trap heat, making the earth warm. This is the "greenhouse" effect; it gets worse when more GHGs are released into the atmosphere.

17.2 Climate Change Impacts on SSA

The year 2014 was the warmest since records began in 1880. The temperature was 0.69°C (1.24°F) above the 20th century average. This is the 38th consecutive year that global temperature was above historic average and nine of the 10 warmest in the 135-year record occurred in the 21st century (Fig. 17.2).

F.O. Boadu: Agricultural Law and Economics in Sub-Saharan Africa.
DOI: http://dx.doi.org/10.1016/B978-0-12-801771-5.00017-4

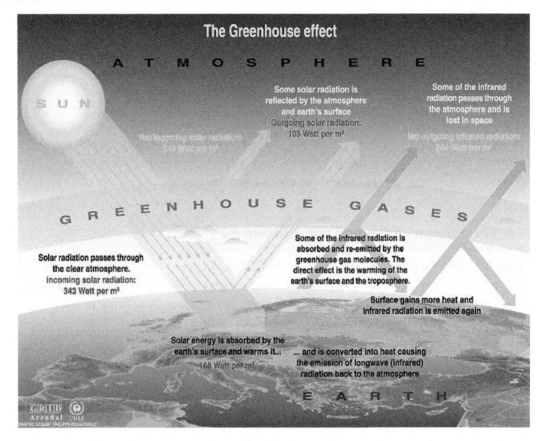

Figure 17.1

A Basic Depiction of the Climate Change Concept. *Source: Inter-Governmental Panel on Climate Change (IPCC) (n.d.). The earth's greenhouse - CO₂ and IPCC climate modeling. Global Warming Science.* *<http://appinsys.com/globalwarming/gw_part5_greenhousegas.htm>.*

Climate projections have concluded that for all regions in sub-Saharan Africa (SSA), "the median temperature increase lies between 3°C and 4°C, roughly 1.5 times the global mean response. Half of the models project warming within about 0.5°C of these median values." (Fig. 17.3) (IPCC, 2007).[1]

The IPCC defines climate impact as "the effects of climate change on natural and human systems" (IPCC, 2007). The hydrologic cycle (see Figs. 17.4 and 17.5) shows that countries in SSA will experience stress over time.

There are both market and nonmarket impacts. Market impacts are quantifiable in monetary terms, for example, changes in the price of agricultural outputs and inputs due to climate change effects (IPCC, 2007). Nonmarket impacts "affect ecosystems or human welfare, but that are not easily expressed in monetary terms, eg, an increased risk of

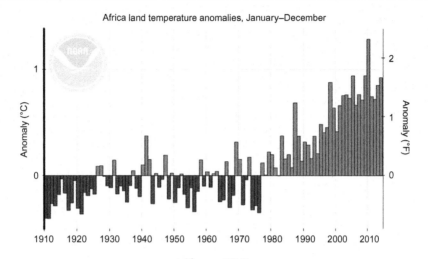

Figure 17.2

Climate Change to Date. *Source: From NOAA State of the Climate. http://www.ncdc.noaa.gov/cag/time-series/global/africa/land/ytd/12/1910-2015.*

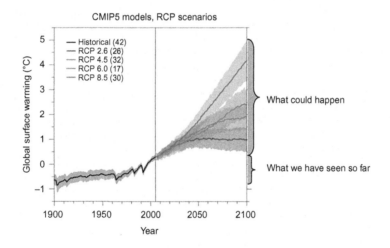

Figure 17.3

Climate Projections for all Regions in SSA. *Source: Knutti, Reto, and Jan Sedláček. Robustness and uncertainties in the new CMIP5 climate model projections.* Nature Climate Change 3.4 (2013): 369—373.

premature death, or increases in the number of people at risk of hunger" (IPCC, 2007). Several studies have discussed market and nonmarket impacts of climate change and concluded that the impact on the SSA region will be severe.[2] Projected climate change impacts on agriculture are especially dire. One study concluded, "by 2100, parts of the Sahara are likely to emerge as the most vulnerable, showing likely agricultural losses of between 2 and 7% of GDP. Western and central Africa are also vulnerable, with impacts

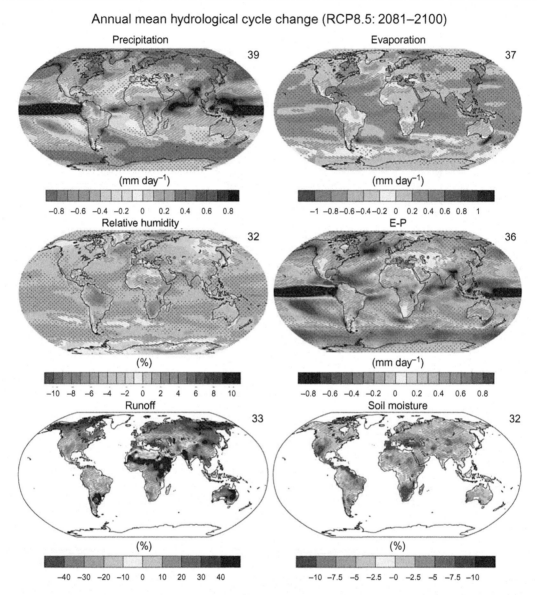

Figure 17.4
Annual Mean Hydrological Cycle Change.

ranging from 2 to 4%. Northern and southern Africa, however, are expected to have losses of 0.4 to 1.3%" (IPCC, 2007).[3] The report continues, "In other countries, additional risks that could be exacerbated by climate change include greater erosion, deficiencies in yields from rain-fed agriculture of up to 50% during the 2000–2020 period, and reductions in crop growth period" (IPCC, 2007).[4] Pressures on water and energy resources and food security have also been noted.

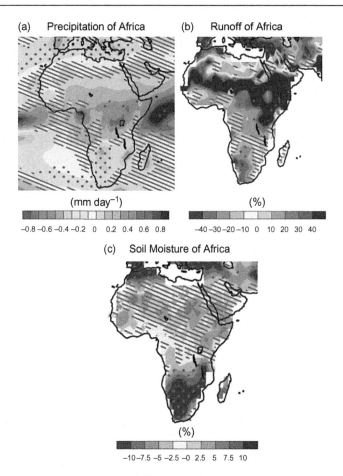

Figure 17.5
(a) Precipitation of Africa; (b) runoff of Africa; (c) soil moisture of Africa.

17.3 Law and Climate Change

There is a major relationship between law and science in the search for solutions to the problems created by climate change. Information from scientific research is used as input in making laws and regulations targeting patterns of behavior human behavior that contribute to climate change. It is generally accepted in the climate change literature that humans are at the center of the climate change problem. It is the activities by humans that lead to the release of the four major GHGs (carbon dioxide, methane, nitrous oxide, and the halocarbons) the primary cause of climate change.[5] For example, carbon dioxide is released through transportation and burning of fossil fuels for heating and cooling; methane is released in performing agriculture activities and natural gas distribution; nitrous oxide is released through fertilizer use; and the halocarbons are released through refrigeration and industrial processes (IPCC, 2007).[6]

Laws and regulations to curb climate change in SSA must target improvements in science and institutions. The role of law in addressing climate change problems may be viewed from two perspectives. First, law provides a forum for seeking redress for perceived injury caused by climate change. An injured party may use a court action, administrative processes, or negotiations to recover compensation for the injury or stop the offensive activity.[7] Second, law influences humans' relationship with the use of resources by promoting those human practices and behavior that lead to a lowering of GHGs, and sanctions practices that increase GHGs.

Agriculture contributes about 10–12% of total global GHGs and over 50% of the two significant noncarbon GHGs (nitrous oxide and methane) (Smith et al., 2007). Science plays an importation role in two responses (adaptation and mitigation) by households to counter negative climate change impacts. The role of law is to create an environment supportive of the production and distribution of scientific information. The role of law is quite expansive because it runs through the value chain. This means the adaptation and mitigation activities influence input use and prices, outputs and prices, the processing, transportation, and distribution of agricultural products. Law is also important in defining the acquisition of property rights to the resources that are used in adaptation and mitigation activities. Adaptation and mitigation opportunities within the transportation sector are also subject to the operation of efficient laws and regulations.

17.4 Science, Law, and Adaptation

"Adaptation" has been defined as "initiatives and measures to reduce the vulnerability of natural and human systems against actual or expected climate change effects" (Baede, n.d.) Humans have always adapted to changes in the environment throughout history. What is unique in the context of climate change is that science offers humans a good understanding of the climate change phenomenon and the opportunities to address the problem. Farmers engage in adaptation strategies in their private capacities.[8] Government may also be the source of an adaptation strategy by sponsoring research or by creating an environment that promotes adaptation. For example, the provision of early warning systems to inform farmers of climate changes. The role of law in all these adaptation strategies is to reduce the transaction cost of adopting a strategy by laying down the rules under which climate information would be provided to farmers for adaptation purposes.[9]

17.5 Science, Law, and Mitigation

The role of law is easily understood in the context of climate mitigation. The IPCC defines mitigation as "Technological change and substitution that reduce resource inputs and emissions per unit of output. Although several social, economic and technological policies would produce an emission reduction, with respect to Climate Change, mitigation means implementing policies to reduce greenhouse gas emissions and enhance sinks" (Baede, n.d.). In Tanzania, for example, mitigation options included efficient technologies for transportation, paper and pulp production, cement production, and fuel switch in the transportation sector. The adoption of technologies occurs within a supportive legal and regulatory regime.

17.6 Law and Benefits from Environmental Resources

People in SSA depend heavily on ecosystem resources for food, shelter, clothing, entertainment, security, and general well-being. The Millennium Ecosystem Assessment, defines "ecosystem services" (ES) as "the benefits people obtain from ecosystems, including provisioning services such as food, water, timber, and fiber; regulating services that affect climate, floods, disease, wastes, and water quality; cultural services that provide recreational, aesthetic, and spiritual benefits; and supporting services such as soil formation, photosynthesis, and nutrient cycling."[10] Humans can take advantage of the abundant ES only through careful planning and management. Planning entails the use of reliable data and information about the multitude of resources that provide the services so vital for human well-being.

One important piece of information needed for planning purposes is the money value of the contribution of the ES to societal welfare. The difficulty arises because some of the environmental resources are traded in organized markets and others are not traded in markets. For example, provisioning services such as food, fiber, fuel, and timber have organized markets and values are determined by the interaction between demand and supply for the provisioning service. On the other hand, the value of regulatory services affecting climate change, aesthetics, and spiritual beliefs do not have organized markets so it is difficult to value the benefits from the services. For planning purposes, however, society must be able to put a value on both the market and nonmarket resources. The total value of output from ecological resources in a society is:

1. Total economic value = direct-use value + indirect-use value + nonuse value + intrinsic value.[11]

The total value of ES will be underestimated if benefits from nonmarket services are excluded.

The contribution of law to the production of ES is an example of nonmarket benefit evaluation because the output of law (eg, the quantitative benefits from applying laws and regulations to climate control, desertification, water quality, bays and estuaries, floods, pest control, protected wetland, ecotourism destinations, etc.) is a public good that is not bought and sold in a regular market. This means the valuation of the legal and regulatory regime is subject to nonmarket valuation techniques. A coherent legal and regulatory regime to

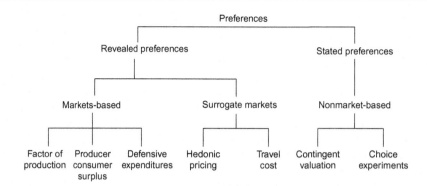

Figure 17.6

Summary of Environmental Valuation Methods. *Source: Adapted from: National Oceanic and Atmospheric Administration, "Environmental Valuation: Principles, Techniques, and Applications." http://www. csc.noaa.gov/coastal/economics/envvaluation.htm (viewed 29.11.10).*

manage environmental resources to maximize societal benefits demands that the values of the nonmarket resources be known.

Fig. 17.6 summarizes the various measures of ES that have been applied to environmental resources.

The determination and measurement of the value of a natural resource recognizes the centrality of the preferences and choices made by private individuals. The theoretical and statistical tools applied to evaluation are based on revealed and stated preference approaches. The techniques used under revealed preference theory may be market-based or based on a surrogate market. Where the measure is market-based, the services of that particular resource are bought and sold in a regular market so resource prices are available. One of the common examples of market-based evaluation is the use of benefit−cost (B/C) analysis.[12]

Where there is no identifiable market for an environmental service (ES), researchers have resorted to "surrogate markets" techniques to estimate environmental values. The two common surrogate market approaches are *hedonic pricing* and *travel cost* (TCM). TCM is used frequently for nature tourism and recreational site valuations. The assumption is that the amount of money and time an individual spends to visit a site is a useful proxy for the value the individual places on the services from the site. TCM measures direct use values of the site and does not account for future values. TCM has been applied to forest tourism (Mercer et al., 1995), park pricing in Namibia, and tourism to gorilla sites in Uganda (Krug et al., 2002; International Gorilla Conservation Programme (IGCP), n.d.).

The hedonic pricing method is another surrogate market approach to valuing environmental amenities. Suppose society seeks to determine the value of good air quality. One way to determine the value of good air quality would be to take property values (example home prices) from one location with a defined air quality and compare the values to another location where air quality is considered good. The difference in home prices from the two locations is an estimate of the willingness to pay for good air quality. Note in applying this method that the value of all other factors accounting for the variation in home prices have been accounted for so that the observed variation in home prices is due solely to the air quality. The approach can be applied to valuing ESs including scenery, security, ambience, culture, and historical integrity of neighborhoods.

Stated Preferences (SP)

The value of ES has been estimated using stated preferences approaches. The most popular stated preference approach is known as "contingent valuation" (CV). The CV is a "direct" approach to valuing ES because the information about a consumer's willingness-to-pay (WTP) for the ES is obtained from a survey administered to a respondent. The researcher describes the nature of the market for the ES being studied. The respondent is then asked a series of questions to elicit their valuation of the ES. The CV has been applied to several ES resources in SSA.[13] The approach does not require that the respondent actually uses the ES. This means unlike the TCM, the CV approach allows for the determination of what is known as *existence value*.[14]

How can Common Law Countries in Africa Benefit from Climate Change Projects under the Kyoto Protocol?

Countries in SSA could benefit from climate change policies and programs with effective and pragmatic public policy decisions. Countries could capture benefits from climate change policies and programs in two ways. First, countries may implement laws and regulations that encourage what is known in the literature as the "environmental goods" market. Second, countries may take advantage of the various flexibility mechanisms under the Kyoto Protocol.

a. *The Environmental Goods Market*

Various research institutions and international organizations have proposed definitions for what constitutes "environmental goods and services." One definition states that "environmental technologies advance sustainable development by reducing risk, enhancing cost-effectiveness, improving process efficiency, and creating products and processes that are environmentally beneficial or benign." (U.S. Department of Commerce/International Trade Administration, 2000). The OECD/EUROSTAT defines the environmental technology market as "all activities which produce goods and services to measure, prevent, limit, minimize, or correct environmental damage to water, air and soil, as well as problems related to waste, noise and ecosystems." (OECD/EUROSTAT, 1999). The Trade and Industry Outlook reports identify water supply and treatment, solid waste management, air pollution control, and environmental cleanup as the four main segments of the industry.

In contrast to the structural approach in defining the industry, the EU focuses on a functional approach, and considers three main categories of activities as defining the environmental technologies industry. These three activities are (1) pollution management of both a preventive or remediative nature (such as reducing emissions, reducing environmental risk, or clearing up environmental damage); (2) cleaner (integrated) technologies and products which are any activities that continuously improve, reduce, or eliminate the environmental impact of general technologies; (3) resource management (such as renewable energy and water supply (OECD/EUROSTAT, 1999, P. 11).

Various organizations and researchers have given different estimates of the size of the EGS market. The differences in measuring the size of the market are due to the fact that it is not easy to determine what constitutes the "product" or the "service" that must be counted as part of the environmental market. It is easy to consider a water filter as an environmental good but a screwdriver may or may not be considered an environmental good. The same may be said of consulting services; sometimes it is not easy to determine whether a service is an ES or not. The latest measure of the size of the global EGS market is US$782 billion (U.S. Department of Commerce/International Trade Administration/Manufacturing and Services, 2010). SSA countries are not competitive given the technology-driven nature of the environmental goods and service market. SSA accounts for less than 1% of the global trade in EGS but there is strong evidence that the demand for these goods will increase over time if historical trends hold.[15] Given the level of competition in the global market and entry barriers, SSA countries may want to focus on producing environmental goods and services that have positive implications for sustainable agriculture, and the achievement of the MDGs.[16] The global market is broken down as follows: services (47%), equipment (21%), and resources (32%).[17]

b. *Flexibility Mechanisms under the Kyoto Protocol*

The Kyoto Protocol introduced three interrelated flexibility mechanisms: (1) emissions trading that would allow an industrialized state to increase its emissions cap by purchasing part of another industrialized nation's Kyoto allocation; (2) joint implementation (JI) that encourages developed countries to meet their commitments by exploiting mitigation cost differentials between nations and jointly undertaking mitigating activities abroad to offset domestic GHG emissions; and (3) the clean development mechanism (CDM) that encourages a developed country party to invest in a host country (developing nation) and earn certified emission reduction (CER) credits to meet their Kyoto obligations while the host country gets cash as well as sustainable development benefits associated with the CDM project. Studies have shown that none of the industrialized nations will be able to honor this commitment within their borders. There is interest in exploring ways in which developing countries could generate incomes and technology from the CDM through their participation in the evolving carbon market.

17.7 What Is the Carbon Market?

A market is defined as an arena or forum where buyers and sellers meet to buy and sell goods and services. A market must have buyers, sellers, and a product or service to trade. The product in the carbon market is *carbon*, obtained from a CDM project, a joint implementation project, a voluntary market transaction, or a combination of the above sources.[18] The major buyers of carbon are the European countries with over 80% combined market share (World Bank, 2009). The private sector in European countries, especially the utilities are responsible for about 90% of all transactions (World Bank, 2009, p. 33). The United Kingdom tops all buyers with a 37% market share, followed by the Netherlands Ireland, France, Switzerland, Austria, and Greece (World Bank, 2010a) (22%). Germany, Sweden, Finland, Norway, Denmark, and Iceland (World Bank, 2010a) held 20% of the market, and other buyers and their market shares are Italy (7%) and Japan (13%) (World Bank, 2010a).

China is the major supplier with a 72% market share in 2009 (World Bank, 2010a, p. 40). Other notable suppliers are India (2%), Brazil (3%), rest of Asia (5%), rest of Latin America (4%), and rest of Africa (7%) (World Bank, 2010a, p. 40). The buyers and sellers interact in what is known as an *Exchange*. The well-known exchanges are the Chicago Climate Exchange (CCX), European Union Emission Trading Scheme (EU-ETS), the Regional Greenhouse Gas Initiative (RGGI), and the New South Wales Greenhouse Gas Abatement Scheme (NSW GGAS). It is the interaction of buyers and sellers in any of these markets that determines the prices and quantities of carbon credits traded at a particular time and at a particular place. Studies project a global average carbon price of between US\$80/tCO$_2$e and US\$120/tCO$_2$e in 2030 to achieve the goal of limiting the global warming to 2°C (World Bank, 2015).

Sub-Saharan Africa is not a major player in the global carbon market. As of 2010, the region is home to 122 projects out of 4884 global CDM programs (Table 17.1).

Table 17.1: Number and value (in Euros(€)/year) of CDM projects and CERs in common law SSA countries, 2007−2010

Country	2007	2008	2009	2010
Ghana	0	0	1	1 (2036)
Kenya	2	5	14	15 (788)
Liberia	0	0	1	1 (72)
Nigeria	2	4	7	8 (9325)
South Africa	21	24	30	32 (4261)
Tanzania	1	4	5	5 (458)
Uganda	2	8	11	12 (308)
Zambia	0	1	1	1 (130)
C'Law Total	28	46	70	75 (174)
SSA Total	30	55	91	97 (194)
Total Africa	42	75	116	122 (242)
Total Global	2205	3579	4696	4884

The quantity of CERs generated under these projects is shown in parentheses in the table. The current value of CDM projects in SSA is €194 million out of a global total value of over €4 billion. Common law countries, including South Africa, generated a value of over €174 million. Nigeria (€93 million), South Africa (€43 million), and Ghana (€20 million) are the major earners of value from the CDM market. Projections are that CDMs will increase to about €245 million in the near future. A total of about 35 million CERs have been projected, which at a CER price of 10 €/ton CO_2 would yield €350 million (UNEP Risoe CDM Pipeline, 2010). The distribution of projects shows that the contribution of agriculture is negligible.[19] There were no agriculture and land use projects even though SSA countries stand to benefit significantly from these projects.

There are several technical and institutional factors influencing increased implementation of CDM projects in SSA. One technical problem relates to how to measure the carbon that qualifies for CER credit. This problem is summarized in the concept of *additionality*. Under the Marrakesh Accord, a project activity is *additional* if anthropogenic emissions of GHGs by sources are reduced below those that would have occurred in the absence of the registered CDM project activity (Marrakesh Accords, 2001).[20] Accurate measures of rural development trends and the baseline based on which measurements are being made are necessary to properly measure *additionality*. Decisions regarding land use in a rural context and the opportunity to obtain credible commitments is consensus-driven and require the active participation of rural households. The challenge facing SSA countries is how to evolve effective institutions and protocols to address these technical constraints.

Another major constraint to increased CDM project activities is high *transaction costs*. In the context of CDM, consider the following scenario. Suppose a power plant from the United States wishes to enter into a contract with landowners in Ghana to obtain carbon offset credits through a land use, land-use change and forestry (LULUCF) program. The power plant purchases carbon credits in large quantities so investors interested in offsets generated through LULUCF require a minimum land area to capture economies of scale (McCarl et al., undated). By one estimate approximately a quarter of the ton of carbon is produced per acre tillage change. This means a 10,000 tonne annual lot of offsets would require 100 farmers each controlling 400 acres or 10,000 farmers in developing countries each controlling 4 acres (McCarl et al., undated). Since land is very fragmented in most SSA countries, including Ghana, a successful LULUCF program ought to consider the potentially prohibitive transaction costs associated with land consolidation to achieve the economically feasible land size.[21] While agents in developed countries have handled such land contracts, it is unlikely these agents would be successful in traditional societies where the institution of contract is tied more to trust than to "form" (Fafchamps, 1996). Thus, a credible land consolidation effort would have to be undertaken as joint action within a consensus-driven community decision-making regime.

There are also concerns about the uncertainties in government policies addressing various social, economic, and political issues. Some have pointed to a need to address stakeholder interests in planning carbon projects (World Bank, *Blog;* Greiner, 2000), the human dimensions of carbon sequestration (Tschakert, 2001), the linkage between climate change and sustainable development (World Bank, 2010b), climate change and equity (see Lind and Schule, 1998), the implications of uncertainty and contract design (Overseas Development Institute (ODI), 2006), the implications of poverty and food security concerns in the carbon debate (Food and Agricultural Organization (FAO), Intergovernmental Working Group on Climate Change, 2008), the need to safeguard the interests of indigenous people and property rights (Markelova and Meinzen-Dick (International Food Policy Research Institute (IFPRI)), 2009), and the implications of economic downturns on climate change policies (Bowen and Stern, 2010).

17.8 Climate Change Litigation

Climate change litigation has been described as "when claimants appeal to a court to enforce or clarify existing climate change laws—for example, if citizens believe government or a corporation is not meeting its legal requirements to reduce greenhouse gas emissions ('pro-climate' lawsuits) or where citizens, groups and companies go to court to challenge the legitimacy of climate change laws passed by government—in other words, 'anti-climate' lawsuits. For example, claimants may believe that climate-related laws undermine their other legal rights." (Climate and Development Knowledge Network (CDKN), undated). Climate change litigation is popular in developed economies such as the United States, the European Union, and Australia. No cases from sub-Saharan Africa have been reported.[22] Climate change interest groups and advocates, NGOs, and communities affected by what they consider as climate-induced harm are often the plaintiffs in climate change actions. Defendants are often governments for failing to enforce greenhouse emissions laws, private companies whose activities may lead to emissions of GHGs. Countries in sub-Saharan Africa will be confronted with the delicate issue of efforts to attract industry while protecting the human rights of communities and the integrity of the environment.

Notes

1. The IPCC has identified over 20 different models in the climate change literature. See Chapter 8, pp. 8–93 of IPCC, 2007.
2. "All of Africa is very likely to warm during this century. The warming is very likely to be larger than the global, annual mean warming throughout the continent and in all seasons, with drier subtropical regions warming more than the moister tropics" (IPCC, 2007). One market impact being monitored closely is the impact of climate change on household incomes. Negative impacts on income could threaten the attainment of the MDGs. A difficult non-market impact is population displacement, armed conflicts, and lawlessness.

3. In particular see Section 9.4.4—Agriculture of (IPCC, 2007).
4. In particular see Section 9.4.4—Agriculture of (IPCC, 2007).
5. The literature is emphatic on the issue of human influence on climate change, "Human activities contribute to climate change by causing changes in Earth's atmosphere in the amounts of greenhouse gases, aerosols (small particles), and cloudiness. The largest known contribution comes from the burning of fossil fuels, which releases carbon dioxide gas to the atmosphere." Also, "Since the start of the industrial era (about 1750), the overall effect of human activities on climate has been a warming influence. The human impact on climate during this era greatly exceeds that due to known changes in natural processes, such as solar changes and volcanic eruptions" (IPCC, 2007).
6. See also the IPCC Frequently Asked Questions 2.1, p. 100, available at <http://www.ipcc.ch/pdf/assessment-report/ar4/wg1/ar4-wg1-faqs.pdf>.
7. Climate change litigation is becoming popular in the United States. The majority of court actions have been based on the application and enforcement of current U.S. Law. For example, in the case of *Center for Biological Diversity v Kempthorne*, No. 3:07-CV-0141 (D. Alaska April 22, 2008), transferred from No. 07-CV-00894 (N.D. Cal. filed February 13, 2007), environmental groups challenge an exception to the Marine Mammal Protection Act (MMPA), (16 U.S.C. §§ 1361-1421h) which allowed "incidental taking" rule—authorizing the incidental take of polar bears and Pacific walrus for 5 years (2006–2011) resulting from oil and gas activities in the Beaufort Sea and adjacent coastal areas of the Alaska north slope. According to the Plaintiffs the exception violates the MMPA by permitting more than a "negligible" impact on the species, based on the *combined* impact of oil-and-gas activities and the weakened condition of polar bears due to *climate change*. In *Pacific Coast Federation of Fishermen's Associations/Institute for Fisheries Resources v Gutierrez*, No. 1:06-CV-00245, 2008 WL 2223070 (E.D.Cal. May 20, 2008), brought under the Endangered Species Act (ESA), 16 U.S.C. §§ 1531-1544, the plaintiffs successfully challenged the NMFS biological opinion prepared in connection with the same project for various salmon and trout species—based on its "total failure to address, adequately explain, and analyze the effects *of global climate change* on the species." Some plaintiffs have relied on common law tort theories to climate change actions. In *Native Village of Kivalina v Exxonmobil Corp.*, No. 08-cv-01138 (N.D. Cal. filed February 26, 2008), a native village on the northwest Alaska coast sued certain oil and energy companies, claiming that the large quantities of GHGs they emit collectively contribute to climate change. Climate change, the village contends "is destroying the village by melting Arctic sea ice that formerly protected it from winter storms, leading to massive coastal erosion." (p. 24). These cases and several other examples are borrowed from Meltz (2009).
8. Rural farmers have been practicing coping strategies and tactics, especially in places where droughts recur, and have developed their own ways of assessing the prospects for favourable household or village seasonal food production (Downing et al., 1989). In Senegal and Burkina Faso, locals have improved their adaptive capacity by using traditional pruning and fertilizing techniques to double tree densities in semi-arid areas. These help in holding soils together and reversing desertification. Similar community-initiated projects in Madagascar and Zimbabwe have been acclaimed successes. See Baede (n.d.).
9. The IPCC defines adaptation costs to include, "Costs of planning, preparing for, facilitating, and implementing *adaptation* measures, including transition costs." (Baede, n.d.).
10. Provisioning services are the products humans acquire from ecosystems. Regulating services are defined as "the benefits obtained from the regulation of ecosystem processes...." Cultural services are those "nonmaterial benefits people obtain from ecosystems through spiritual enrichment, cognitive development, reflection, recreation, and aesthetic experiences...." Supporting services are described as the necessary services for the production of all ecosystem services whose impact on human populations are indirect or long term. Quoted in Lugo (2008). See also UNECA.
11. Abbreviated from Tiwari (2006). Indirect-use values are not directly measured, for example, good water quality. Non-use values consist of option and existence values. The option value is the value an individual places on the potential future use of the resource, for example, visit Mount Kilimanjaro one day; existence values include bequest, stewardship, and benevolence motives, for example, bequest value is the satisfaction gained through the ability to endow a natural resource on future generations. The intrinsic value of nature reflects the belief that all living organisms are valuable regardless of the monetary value placed on them by society.

12. Benefit—cost analysis has been applied to evaluating adoption of improved variety, farm machinery (Ethiopia), IPM-Biological control (27 countries in SSA), integrated aquaculture (Malawi), and fallow systems (Zambia). See Maredia and Raitzer (2010).

13. Control of trypanosomiasis (Kamuanga, 2003) (Kenya); water quality and quantity (Farolfi et al., 2004) (Swaziland); wastewater irrigation (Weldesilassi et al., 2009) (Ethiopia); breeding and production services for goats (Bett et al., 2009) (Kenya).

14. The term "existence value," embodies the proposition that people attach utility to the existence of things such as unspoiled wilderness, and, crucially, that this utility can be translated into monetary terms by the measurement of willingness to pay. See Quiggin (1998).

15. EGS exports by the United States alone grew considerably for several SSA countries during the period 2004—2008. Countries and percent growth rates are Zambia (441%); Namibia (492%); Ghana (162%); Kenya (162%); Zimbabwe (109%); Botswana (73%); Malawi (57%); Nigeria (43%); and Uganda (28%). See U.S. Department of Commerce/International Trade Administration/Manufacturing and Services (2010) (Attachment B) PP. 36ff.

16. "While 99% of U.S. ET private sector companies fall under the small- and medium-sized enterprises (SMEs) category, they generate only 20% of the total U.S. ET revenue. Large ET companies, which represent only 1% of all private sector activity, account for 49% of total U.S. ET revenue. Public-sector municipalities and similar entities account the remaining 31% of revenue and dominate water utilities, wastewater treatment works, and solid waste management." (U.S. Department of Commerce/International Trade Administration/Manufacturing and Services (2010), p. 1.)

17. U.S. Department of Commerce/International Trade Administration/Manufacturing and Services (2010), p. 1.

18. The carbon being bought and sold in the carbon market is not the physical carbon. It is the right one holds in carbon stored in a sink. For example, suppose a firm from Canada establishes a forestry project in Uganda and sequesters 100 units of carbon. The firm receives "certified emission reduction" credits. These credits *are* transferable to a purchaser who needs extra credits to meet their obligations in their country.

19. Renewables (hydro, wind, solar, geothermal, biomass, and tidal) top the list of projects (44 projects, 36%), followed by landfill gas (23 projects, 19%), afforestation and reforestation (19 projects, 16%), methane avoidance (11 projects, 9%), fuel switch (10 projects, 8%), demand-side EE (6 projects, 5%), HFC & N_2O reduction (5 projects, 4%), and supply-side EE (4 projects, 3%). U.S. Department of Commerce/International Trade Administration/Manufacturing and Services (2010) p. 3.

20. "Almost naturally, the question on the simplification of the CDM leads to additionality. This key element of the CDM is considered to be the most important field in which simplification could have major impacts. As illustrated by IGES additionality is held responsible for 67% of all reviews conducted posterior to a Request for Registration" (Schröder, 2010). The Marrakesh Accords is a set of agreements reached by the Conference of the Parties (COP) of the United Nations Framework Convention on Climate Change (UNFCCC) on its seventh session, held at Marrakesh, Morocco from 29 October to 10 November 2001, <http://unfccc.int/essential_background/library/items/3598.php?rec=j&priref=600001855&data=&volltext=FCCC%252FCP%252F2001%252F13%252FAdd.1&anf=0&sorted=date_sort&dirc=DESC&seite=>.

21. "There are around 33 million small farms of less than 2 hectares, representing 80% of all farms in the continent." See FAO (2009).

22. This observation is based on a review of the extensive database maintained by the Columbia Law School, Center for Climate Change Law, <http://web.law.columbia.edu/sites/default/files/microsites/climate-change/non-u.s._litigation_chart_7.23.15.pdf> (viewed 27.9.15).

Questions

1. What are some of the sources for legal action due to climate change?
2. Climate change litigation is common in advanced countries such as the United States but not so in sub-Saharan African countries. Why?

3. What are some of the legal theories that one may rely on in an action for damages caused by climate change?
4. Compare and contrast the roles of public interest lawyers, especially focusing on climate change in the United States as opposed to Ghana.

References

Baede, APM, on behalf of IPCC. Glossary of Terms. Available at: <http://www.ipcc.ch/pdf/glossary/ar4-wg1.pdf>.

Bett, R.C., Bett, H.K., Kahi, A.K., Peters, K.J., 2009. (Kenya). Evaluation and effectiveness of breeding and production services for dairy goat farmers in Kenya. Ecol. Econ. 68 (2009), 8–9.

Bowen, A., Stern, N., 2010. Environmental policy and the economic downturn. Oxford Rev. Econ. Policy. 26 (2), 137–163.

Climate and Development Knowledge Network (CDKN), undated. FEATURE: climate change litigation—a rising tide? <http://cdkn.org/2012/05/postcard-from-london-rising-tide-of-climate-change-litigation/> (viewed 09.10.15).

Downing, T. E., Gitu, K. W., Kamau, C. M., 1989. Coping with Drought in Kenya: National and Local Strategies (Food in Africa Series). Lynne Rienner, Boulder, Colorado, USA.

Fafchamps, M., 1996. The enforcement of commercial contracts in ghana. World Development. 24 (3), 427–448, <http://www.sciencedirect.com/science/article/B6VC6-3VVVNJK-2/2/2222ab50a0285a049e654044035d4288>.

FAO, 2009. How to Feed the World 2050. High—Level Expert Forum, Rome 12–13 October. <http://www.fao.org/fileadmin/templates/wsfs/docs/Issues_papers/HLEF2050_Africa.pdf> (viewed on 17.12.10).

Farolfi, S., Mabugu, R.E., Ntshingila, S.N., 2004. Domestic water use and values in (water quantity and quality) Swaziland: a contingent valuation analysis. Agrekon. 46 (1), 157–170.

Food and Agricultural Organization (FAO), (Intergovernmental Working Group on Climate Change), 2008. Climate Change and Food Security: A Framework Document, Rome. <ftp://ftp.fao.org/docrep/fao/010/k2595e/k2595e00.pdf> (viewed 17.12.10).

Greiner, S., 2000. Flexible instruments and stakeholder interests: A public choice analysis. In: Michaelowa, A., Dutschke, M., editors., Climate Policy and Development, Cheltenham-Northampton, pp. 45–58.

International Gorilla Conservation Programme (IGCP) (n.d.), Analysis of the Significance of Gorilla Tourism in Uganda. Final Draft. Environmental Monitoring Associates, Kampala, Uganda.

IPCC, 2007. Climate Change 2007: The Physical Science Basis. In: Solomon, S., Qin, D., Manning, M., Chen, Z., Marquis, M., Averyt, K.B., Tignor M., Miller H.L., (Eds.), Contribution of Working Group I to the Fourth Assessment Report of the Intergovernmental Panel on Climate Change. Cambridge University Press, Cambridge and New York.

Kamuanga, M., 2003. Socio-economic and Cultural Factors in the Research and Control of Trypanosomiasis. FAO, PAAT Technical and Scientific Series 4, Nairobi, Kenya.

Krug, W., Suich, H., Haimbodi, N., 2002. Park Pricing and Economic Efficiency in Namibia. DEA Research Discussion Paper, Number 45.

Lind, R.C., Schule, R.E., 1998. Equity and discounting in climate change decisions. In: Nordhaus, W. (Ed.), Economics and Policy Issues in Climate Change. Resources for the Future Press, Washington, DC, pp. 59–89.

Lugo, E., 2008. Ecosystem services: the millennium ecosystem assessment and the conceptual difference between provided by ecosystems and benefits provided by people. J. Land Use Envtl. Law. 23, 243.

Maredia, M.K., Raitzer, D.A., 2010. Estimating overall returns to international agricultural research in Africa through benefit-cost analysis: a 'Best-evidence' approach. Agricul. Econ. 41 (2010), 81–100.

Markelova, H., Meinzen-Dick, Ruth (International Food Policy Research Institute (IFPRI), 2009. The Importance of Property Rights in Climate Change Mitigation. 2020 Focus 16 Brief 10.

McCarl, B., Butt, T., Kim, M.-K., undated. How Much Would Carbon Cost a Buyer? <http://agecon2.tamu.edu/people/faculty/mccarl-bruce/papers/1015.pdf> (viewed 16.12.10).

Meltz, R., 2009. Climate Change Litigation: A Survey. Congressional Research Report to Congress, CRS RL 32764.

Mercer, E., Kramer, R., Sharma, N., 1995. Rain forest tourism—estimating the benefits of tourism development in a new national park in madagascar. J. Forest Econ. 1, 2.

Organization for Economic Co-operation and Development (OECD)/ Statistical Office of the European Communities (EUROSTAT), 1999. The environmental goods and services industry: manual for data collection and analysis, p. 9. OECD Publication Service, 2, rue Andre-Pascal, Paris, France.

Overseas Development Institute (ODI), 2006. Can Payments for Avoided Deforestation to Tackle Climate Change also Benefit the Poor? ODI Forestry Briefing 12. <http://www.odi.org.uk/resources/download/25.pdf> (viewed 17.12.10).

Quiggin, J., 1998. Existence value and the contingent valuation method. Aust. Econ. Papers. 37 (3), 312–329, p. 4.

Schröder, M., 2010. CDM Reform—Essential AND Possible. KfW Carbon Fund.

Smith, P., Martino, D., Cai, Z., Gwary, D., Janzen, H., Kumar, P., et al., 2007. Agriculture. In: Metz, B., Davidson, O.R., Bosch, P.R., Dave, R., Meyer, L.A., (Eds.), Climate Change 2007: Mitigation. Contribution of Working Group III to the Fourth Assessment Report of the Intergovernmental Panel on Climate Change. Cambridge University Press, Cambridge, and New York, p. 499.

Tiwari, B.K., 2006. Environmental goods and services. In: Singh, O.P. (Ed.), Environment and Natural Resources Ecological and Economic Perspectives. Regency Publications, New Delhi, pp. 14–33.

Tschakert, P., 2001. Human dimensions of carbon sequestration: a political ecology approach to soil fertility management and desertification control in the old peanut basin of senegal. Arid Lands Newslett. 49, <http://ag.arizona.edu/oals/ALN/aln49/tschakert.html>. (viewed 14.12.10).

UNECA, Climate Change and Ecosystem Sustainability. Seventh African Development Forum, Issue Paper #9, Addis Ababa, Ethiopia.

UNEP Risoe CDM Pipeline, 2010. CDM Update for Africa Carbon Forum. <www.cdmpipeline.org> p. 4.

UNFCCC, 1992. Article 1. <http://unfccc.int/resource/docs/convkp/conveng.pdf>.

U.S. Department of Commerce/International Trade Administration/Manufacturing and Services, 2010. U.S. Environmental Technologies Export Markets, 2004–2008, Environmental Technologies Industries: FY2010 Industry Assessment. p. 1.

U.S. Department of Commerce/International Trade Administration, 2000. U.S. Industry and Trade Outlook, 2000, p. 20–1. Mcgraw-Hill, 38th ed. <http://www.amazon.com/s/ref=dp_byline_sr_book_2?ie=UTF8&text=U.S. + Department + of + Commerce%2FInternational + Trade + Administration&search-alias=books&field-author=U.S. + Department + of + Commerce%2FInternational + Trade + Administration&sort=relevancerank>.

Weldesilassi, B., Fror, O., Boelee, E., Dabbert, S., 2009. (Ethiopia) The economic value of improved wastewater irrigation: a contingent valuation study in addis ababa, ethiopia. J. Agricul. Resour. Econ. 34 (3), 428–449.

World Bank Blog, 2010. A Tool Kit for Climate Change with Stakeholders at the Core. Submitted by Jane Ebinger, September 27, <http://blogs.worldbank.org/climatechange/toolkit-climate-change-stakeholders-its-core> (viewed 17.12.10).

World Bank, 2009. State and Trends of the Carbon Market (Capoor, K., Ambrosi, P., Eds.). Washington, DC.

World Bank, 2010a. State and Trends of the Carbon Market (Kossoy, A., Ambrosi, P., Eds.). Washington, DC, p. 41.

World Bank, 2010b. Development and Climate Change: Stepping Up Support to Developing Countries. Report on Progress by the World Bank Group. <http://www-wds.worldbank.org/external/default/WDSContentServer/WDSP/IB/2010/07/16/000334955_20100716050525/Rendered/PDF/556890W10SFDCC1box0349464B01PUBLIC1.pdf> (viewed 17.12.10).

World Bank, 2015. State and Trends of Carbon Pricing (Kossoy, A., Peszko, G., Eds.). Washington, DC, p. 24.

CHAPTER 18

Food Safety Regulation

Keywords: Food safety; foodborne illness; African Biosciences Inititative (ABI); marginal benefit; marginal cost; externality; transaction cost; food standards; tort and regulatory approaches

18.1 Introduction

Food quantity and quality have emerged as major public policy issues in sub-Saharan Africa (SSA) in recent years. This chapter focuses on food safety in SSA. Food safety describes "the potential hazards associated with food that can cause ill-health in humans" (Henson, 2003). There are several reasons for this heightened concern about food safety in SSA. First, hazards associated with food are known to cause considerable human morbidity and mortality. Second, foodborne illnesses lead to loss of productive work-days, and could undermine a country's efforts to achieve its growth objectives. The prevalence of foodborne hazards also affects a country's opportunity to enter global markets due to sanitary and phytosanitary laws and regulations imposed by other countries (Josling et al., 2004). The foodborne disease impacts on the economies of SSA countries are complicated by problems of poor sanitation, lack of access to good water, and poor governance.[1] The foodborne disease impacts...problems of sanitation, poor education, lack of access to good water, and poor governance.

Food safety has been at the forefront of both global and regional efforts to promote economic growth. For example, the *Rome Declaration on World Food Security*, 1996, under the auspices of the Food and Agricultural Organization "reaffirmed the right of everyone to have access to safe and nutritious food, consistent with the right to adequate food and the fundamental right of everyone to be free from hunger" (FAO, 1996). The World Health Organization is another institution that is actively involved in food safety issues at the global level.[2]

At the regional level, both the FAO and WHO have regional committees for Africa. In 2007, the WHO regional committee for Africa published a strategy paper for food safety and health for Africa (World Health Organization (Africa), 2007). African governments have also launched their own initiatives under the African Biosciences Initiative (ABI). Under ABI, a network of experts engage in research on several biosafety initiatives

F.O. Boadu: Agricultural Law and Economics in Sub-Saharan Africa.
DOI: http://dx.doi.org/10.1016/B978-0-12-801771-5.00018-6

including food safety (NEPAD Planning and Coordinating Agency, Africa Biosciences Initiative (ABI), n.d.). Other subregional organizations, such as the West Africa Health Organisation (WAHO), a specialized agency of the Economic Community of West African States (ECOWAS), also have programs to address problems of food safety and nutrition (WAHO, 2009). Several African countries have established regulatory bodies to address problems associated with food safety and standards.[3]

18.2 Economics of Food Safety

Economists consider the demand for a product as a demand for the attributes of the product. Safety is one such attribute.[4] Safety is however not observable so the idea of demand and supply of safety poses some analytical challenges. Still, safety is subject to the economist's demand and supply framework that helps to determine the optimal amounts of a product that a consumer will consume and what a supplier will supply. Fig. 18.1 shows the demand and supply for safety. The demand curve D_s slopes downwards because the benefits derived from consuming a product decline as more of the product is consumed. The supply curve S_s slopes upwards because the additional cost of supplying a product increases as more of the product is supplied. The intersection of the D_s and S_s curves gives the equilibrium price P^* and equilibrium quantity Q^* for safety.

The achievement of equilibrium in the market as discussed above is subject to several assumptions. It is assumed that there are many buyers and sellers in the market so no single entity can influence market price. The buyers and sellers have full information about the product being traded in the market and the products are homogeneous. It is also assumed that there is free entry and exit from the market and the market is competitive. Any departure from these basic assumptions leads to what economists call "market failure."

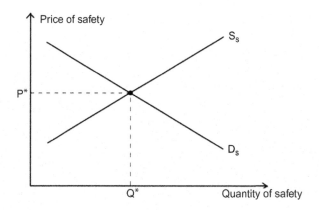

Figure 18.1
Demand and Supply of Food Safety.

There are several sources of "market failure." One source of market failure is termed *externalities*. Externalities occur where the benefits or costs associated with a product are not reflected in the price of the product. In the context of food safety, the consumption of some foods may lead to the incidence of disease. The cost of disease may be borne by the rest of society in the form of lost work days and loss of productivity. These costs may not be reflected in the price of the food, hence there is an externality (Henson, p. 23).

Another source of market failure is the supply of information. The efficient market requires that consumers have full information about the products they consume. This is not the case in most developing countries where product labeling laws are poorly enforced. This latter source is also reflected in what economists call *transaction costs*. Transaction costs must be low to promote efficient market outcomes. Consumers may incur significant transaction costs in searching for information about risks and product quality. It is also important for markets to be competitive to achieve maximum outcome in the market. Such competition may not be available in food markets in developing countries, thereby leading to market failure. The popular view is that governments enter markets to regulate in those circumstances where there is market failure.

18.3 Using Liability and Regulatory Approaches in Setting Food Standards

A standard is "something set up and established by authority as a rule for the measurement of quantity, weight, extent, value, or quality," (Merriam Webster, n.d.). Standards in food systems play a "signaling" role to indicate that the products from the system are safe, healthy, high quality, and trustworthy. There are two approaches in developing standards in food systems. One approach is a liability orientation, that is, a system based in tort. This approach is based in private law. The second approach is based in regulation, which is based on statute. This is based in public law. Table 18.1 summarizes the characteristics of the two approaches.

Table 18.1: Characteristics of statutory and regulatory approaches in food safety

	Liability (Tort) (Private Law)	Regulation (Public Law)
Who decides outcome	Judges and juries	Agency officials
Decision time	Based on individual cases	Makes general rules
Information used	Judicial procedure	Uses technocratic information
Procedures used	Ex post harm must occur	Ex ante without waiting for harm to occur
Scope of decision	Individual adjudication may lead to inconsistent and unequal coverage	Minimizes inconsistent and unequal coverage

Based on Susan Rose-Ackerman, 1991. Regulation and the law of torts. American Economic Review 81 (2), 54–58.

Table 18.2: Distinguishing the use of tort versus regulatory approaches in setting food standards—the Shavell scheme

Alternative Governance Regimes	Privately Initiated	State-Initiated
Ex post (backward-looking)	Tort liability	Fines for harm done
Ex ante (forward-looking)	Court injunctions	Command-and-control regulation or corrective taxes

Based on Steven Shavell, 1984. "Liability for Harm versus Regulation of Safety", The Journal of Legal Studies Vol. 13, No. 2, pp. 357–374.

One observation from the table is that the use of liability is generally an after the fact (ex post) option while the regulatory approach is a before the fact (ex ante) option. In countries such as the United States, both approaches feature prominently in their laws, that is, private parties sue for injuries quite regularly and regulatory agencies are also very busy introducing new regulations. This is not the case in SSA countries where food injury law suits are not common and even though there are several food safety agencies, enforcement of food regulations is weak due in part to budget and personnel constraints.

An alternative approach to explaining the distinction between tort and regulatory approaches is the scheme suggested by Shavell and shown in Table 18.2. The Shavell scheme makes the distinction between ex ante and ex post approaches and the responses in a tort versus regulatory contexts clearer.

A private person may bring a tort action for injuries suffered from using a food item. In this case, the injury has already occurred (ex post) so the court has to determine the damage award to the injured party. An example of such action is the *Michael Chilufya Sata MP and Zambia Bottlers Limited* where the plaintiff sued for mental anguish upon finding a cockroach in a bottled drink. The court rejected the plaintiff's claim because the drink was not actually consumed. Mental anguish upon seeing a cockroach in a drink is not a basis for damages. *The State of Montana v Steven Joseph Wilmer* case is an example of a state-initiated action for fines for harm done. In this case also the harm has already occurred (ex post). *The GEERTSON Seed Farms v Mike Johanns et al.* case is an example of an injunction rule whereby the plaintiffs brought an action to stop the U.S. Department of Agriculture, Animal Health and Inspection Service (APHIS) to deregulate a genetically engineered product without first conducting an environmental impact assessment. The court rejected the challenge to permit APHIS to deregulate the product because they found the injunction remedy to be drastic. Box 18.1 shows an example of command-and-control regulation approach from the Food and Drugs Board in Ghana.

Five factors determine the choice of private (ex post) and regulatory (ex ante) approaches to setting food standards.[5] First, if harm is widespread such that individuals have little incentive to sue on their own, or if the cost of organizing a group to sue is too high, then regulation (ex ante) is desirable. This is an example of private law failure and recommends the need for regulation. Second, if those causing harm are too poor to pay remedies for

---

BOX 18.1 FDB Destroys Large Consignment of Unwholesome Fish

The Ashanti Regional Office of the Food and Drugs Board (FDB) has destroyed a large consignment of unwholesome fish seized from the "Adom Mbroso" Cold Store at Asafo in Kumasi. It has also arrested a businesswoman at Apianim-Kokoben in the Atwima-Kwanwoma District.

Mrs. Nora Narkie Terlabi, the Regional Officer of the Board, told the Ghana News Agency (GNA) that, their action followed a tip off. She said the office received information that somebody was smoking a truck-load of rotten fish at Apianim-Kokoben for sale, and when officers moved in they found 44-year-old Gladys Mbeah smoking fish that emitted foul stench. Mrs. Terlabie said, they seized the entire stock and brought the woman to the Kumasi Central Police Station where she mentioned "Adom Mbroso" as the source.

Officials of the Board and the police proceeded to the Cold Store and seized 200 unlabeled cartons of the unwholesome fish and destroyed them at the Kaase dumping site. She pledged firm action against the culprits. The Manager of the Cold Store, Kofi Badu, confirmed that Madam Mbeah bought the fish from them but insisted that the fish were not in bad condition when they sold them to her.

Health News of Monday, 16 April 2012

Source: Ghana News Agency.

---

harm caused, then a system based on ex post liability will not deter them. This supports an ex ante regulatory system. One observes that in most countries in SSA, food safety agencies regulate the manner in which roadside food is sold to the public largely because vendors may not be able to pay for extensive harm caused to the consuming public. Third, ex ante regulation is recommended where harm can be determined on a statistical basis and not on an individual basis. Car seat belt regulation is an example. Fourth, a regulatory approach is recommended when several scenarios of harm are subject to the same cost and benefit assessment, and finally high costs of planning, implementing, and enforcing a food safety regulation will support a regulatory approach.

18.4 The Precautionary Principle

One of the key guiding principles in environment and food safety regulation is the "precautionary principle." The precautionary principle is driven by a realization that humans do not have complete information and knowledge about the consequences of actions taken to influence the environment or food safety. The principle suggests that humans take action to protect even if full information about consequences is not available. The principle is best stated in what is popularly known as the *Wingspread Statement*, "When an activity raises threats of harm to the environment or human health, precautionary measures should be taken even if some cause and effect relationships are not fully established scientifically" (see Science and Environmental Health Network (HESN), 1998). Several countries have defined the principle in different ways but the general thread is that caution is paramount when proposing and implementing new controls over environmental resources and food safety. Several countries in SSA have incorporated the principle in their sustainable development and biosafety regulations.

Michael Chilufya Sata (MP) v Zambia Bottlers Limited

Supreme Court
19th March, 2002 and 19th February, 2003
SCZ No. 1 OF 2003.

Lewanika, DCJ delivered the judgment of the court.

FACTS

This is an appeal against the decision of a Judge of the High Court dismissing the Appellant's claim for damages for personal injuries and consequential loss and damage caused by the negligence and/or breach of statutory duty by the Respondent in the manufacture and bottling of one bottle of sprite beverage and interest on the sums found to be due and costs.

The facts before the learned trial Judge are not in dispute and are common cause. The Appellant bought a case of sprite from an outlet known as Melissa Supermarket for K12,000.00 on 3rd June, 1998. The sprite is manufactured by the Respondent a company involved, inter alia, in the production of soft drinks like sprite. When the Appellant took the sprite at home, he drank some bottles with his children. When the bottle produced in the court below was taken to be opened it was found to contain a dead cockroach. Neither the Appellant nor any of his children opened the bottle or drunk its contents. On seeing the cockroach in the bottle the Appellant alleged that he and his children fell sick and went to see a private medical practitioner who treated them for nausea. The learned trial Judge took the view that as the Appellant and his children did not consume the adulterated drink and did not suffer injury there from; the claim could not succeed, hence this appeal.

JUDGMENT

Counsel for the appellant has filed three grounds of appeal namely:

the first being:

that the learned trial Judge misdirected himself in law when he held that to constitute negligence under the principal laid down in *Donoghue v Stevenson*, a Plaintiff must actually have consumed the adulterated drink or food wholly or partially, and in consequence of which the plaintiff must suffer injury.

In arguing this ground submitted that the case of *Donoghue v Stevenson* besides adding a new jurisprudence to the law of negligence in so far as liability of a manufacturer is concerned, set down the principles or ingredients to be proved in order that liability may exist. He said that

(Continued)

(Continued)

the principles of liability outlines in that case are that the party complained against should owe to the party complaining, a duty of care should show breach of that duty and that he has as a consequence suffered damage as a result of that breach. That neither Lord AFKIN nor the principles enumerated in the *Donoghue v Stevenson* case suggested that the Plaintiff must first have consumed the food/drink complained of in order to succeed in an action of this nature as the learned trial Judge found. He said that in the case of *Continental Restaurant and Casino Limited v Arida Chulu (Z)* this court found a duty of care was owed to the Plaintiff by the Defendant and had been breached on the strength of the provisions of Section 3(b) of the Food and Drugs Act, Cap 303 of the Laws of Zambia. That reference to the Donoghue case in Arida Chulu's case was on the necessity of medical evidence of the Plaintiff's illness and not the consumption of the adulterated food as suggested by the learned trial judge.

He said the court had made it clear in the Arida Chulu case that the issue before it was one for damages and not liability as the court below appears to have suggested. That the question whether one consumed the product or not only arises when considering the quantum of damages to be awarded. He said that the finding of the court below that liability only arises when the Plaintiff opens the drink and consumes it, neither wholly or partially is not only misguided but is also unsupported in law.

He said that there was evidence in this case to show that by reason of the Respondent's breach, the Appellant suffered mental injury resulting from nausea, discomfort and mental distress and had to receive medical treatment. That the evidence given on behalf of the Appellant by Dr. Kawimbe a medical practitioner was that nausea is an illness resulting from mental stress/injury. He said that the law has always recognized and awarded damages under the head non pecuniary damages for loss suffered as a result of physical or mental injury.

The second ground of appeal argued was:

That the learned trial Judge erred in law when he held that manufacturers of drinks and food will be inundated with law suits by money seeking people who will go around deliberately to look for adulterated food and drink to buy to bring law suits against manufacturers.

In arguing this ground, counsel submitted that the learned trial Judge erred by imposing a qualification on the principles of liability as yet unrecognized in law. The only safeguards which the law has this far recognized to avoid flood gates of actions for economic loss are inter alia, reasonably foreseeability and the relationship of proximity.

Counsel said that Section 3(b) of the Food and Drugs Act places a duty on the manufacturers to ensure that food manufactured by them is not adulterated. The Act goes on to state that contravention of this duty amounts to an offence. That it is not untrue therefore that Parliament sought to cure the evil of manufacture of unwholesome and adulterated food when it enacted this statute. This is because it is not common that food is manufactured with cockroaches or other foreign matters and where this is so, then the onus is on the manufacturer to show that he exercised reasonable care. He said that the legislature could not have had in mind prevention of lawsuits against manufacturers by people going round deliberately looking for adulterated drinks and food when it enacted this law.

(Continued)

(Continued)

That moreover such an argument ignores the fact that Judges by their training are capable of determining which cases are real and which ones are not.

He further said that it is a notorious fact that cockroaches are common sight in Zambia of which the court took judicial notice of, is different from it being a notorious fact that food is manufactured with cockroaches or filthy adulterated foreign substances, otherwise this would render obsolete the legislature's intention in enacting legislation such as the Food and Drugs Act which is meant to protect consumers against unwholesome or adulterated food manufactured below the standards of hygiene recognized by the law.

The third ground of appeal argued was:

That the learned trial Judge misdirected himself both in law and fact when he refused to find the Respondent liable for breach of statutory duty on the ground that the Appellant first needed to prove that he suffered injury as a result of such breach of statutory duty by the Respondent.

In arguing this ground, counsel, submitted that it cannot be disputed that Section 3(b) and (c) of the Food and Drugs Act places a duty on manufacturers not to manufacturer unwholesome or adulterated food.

He said that the general law is that a statutory duty frequently gives rise to a liability in civil action. He referred us to what Lord Wright said in the case of *London Passenger Transport Baord v Upson* [1949] AC. 155 where he said:-

> The statutory right has its origin in the statute but that particular remedy for an action for damages is given by that common law in order to make it effective, for the benefit of the injured Plaintiff, his right to the performer by the Defendant of the Defendant's statutory duty.....it is not a claim in negligence in the strict or ordinary sense.

He said that a statutory duty being placed on the Respondent and this duty having been breached in the manner envisaged by the Food and Drugs Act, the court below ought to have held the Respondent liable and should not have tried liability under breach of statutory duty to proof of injury. He said that the magnitude of injury is what determines that quantum of damages that should be awarded to the Appellant and has no bearing on the question of liability. That consideration of proof of injury should only have arisen after having settled the question of liability first and then proceed to determine the quantum of damages to be awarded to the Appellant. He said that where a statute creates a duty but gives no remedy or where liability at common law is affirmed by statute as in casu, the law is that an action for damages can be brought provided that the person suing is one of a class intended to be benefited by the duty.

In reply counsel for the Respondent submitted that with regard to the first ground of appeal, the learned trial Judge was right when he held that for the Plaintiff to succeed under the principle of *Donoghue v Stevenson*, he must actually consume the adulterated drink or food wholly or partially and in consequence of which the Plaintiff must suffer injury. He said that this action was launched in the lower court on the basis of negligence and breach of

(Continued)

(Continued)

statutory duty. That the case of *Donoghue v Stevenson* (1) clearly established the tort of negligence in relation to manufacturers as it sets out the principles that a manufacturer did owe a duty to the consumer. The said case is composed of specific facts upon which the principle was founded. Consequently in order for a Plaintiff to have a claim for "actionable" negligence or "a reasonable cause of action" in negligence against a manufacturer of drinks or food, he must bring himself on all fours within the facts of *Donoghue v Stevenson*. He said that the law makes a clear distinction between "actionable" negligence and negligence on which a "cause of action does not arise" as all the elements based on the facts of *Donoghue v Stevenson* must be present. He submitted that the Appellant failed to do so in this case as he did not consume the drink in issue at all or even open the bottle. That as the Appellant did not consume any part of the said drink, he does not have any cause of action against the Respondent in negligence. He referred us to paragraph 16 of the 6th edition of Charlesworth on negligence which reads:

> *Negligence is only actionable if actual damage is proved. There is no right of action for nominal damages. . ...Negligence alone does not give a cause of action, damage alone does not give a cause of action, the two must co-exist.*

He said that in essence the learned trial Judge was merely stating that the essential ingredients of actionable negligence had not been established by the Appellant. That the only legally recognized way at present by which the Appellant could have established his case was by him consuming the said drink and in consequence of which he should have suffered injury through credible evidence of illness.

As to the second ground of appeal counsel submitted that the learned trial Judge was correct when he held that the manufacturers of food and drink will be inundated with law suits from money seeking people who will go round deliberately to look for adulterated food and drink to buy in order to bring a law suit against the manufacturer. He said that the remarks by the learned trial Judge should not be taken out of context. That the correct context in which the remarks were made is that there was no tort of negligence that covers the facts established by the Appellant, facts which were completely outside the legal boundaries of the tort of negligence relating to manufacturer of drinks and food. He said that the learned trial Judge was merely stating that the likely consequences of not upholding the law is as it stands at present.

As to the third ground of appeal, Counsel submitted that the learned trial Judge was correct when he refused to find the Respondent liable for breach of statutory duty on the ground that the Appellant needed to prove that he suffered injury as a result of the breach of statutory duty by the Respondent. He said that the Respondent has not breached any statutory duty imposed on it by either the Food and Drugs Act or any other statute. That no evidence of this nature proving any breach was adduced in the court below. Further that there was no evidence adduced in the court below proving that the Respondent was convicted of any breaches or violations of the Food and Drugs Act.

He said that the Food and Drugs Act is silent as regards the availability of any remedy in civil law for damages arising out of any penalties imposed for breach of its provisions. That in the

(Continued)

(Continued)

circumstances, there is a presumption that the remedy prescribed by the criminal law (ie, penalty) is the only remedy available. He referred us to paragraph 1104 of Charlesworth on Negligence on the point. He further said that there is consequently no right available to the Appellant in these circumstances to bring a civil action on the basis of any breach of statutory duty by the Respondent. That further, if a civil action is brought by an Appellant, he has a legal burden to establish or prove that the breach of statutory duty caused or materially contributed to his damage. He said that as the learned trial Judge correctly observed and found, the Appellant failed to prove the injury or damage he suffered as a result of the alleged breach of statutory duty by the Respondent. He referred us to paragraph 1105 of Charlesworth on Negligence on the point.

We are indebted to both counsel for their submissions which have been of great assistance to us arriving at our decision.

As we have stated earlier; the facts in this case are not in dispute. It is common cause that the Appellant bought a case of sprite manufactured by the Respondent from a retailer. It is also common cause that one of the bottles of sprite contained a dead cockroach, this bottle was not opened and its contents were not consumed by the Appellant.

The first ground of appeal was that the learned trial Judge misdirected himself in law when he held that to constitute negligence under the principles held down in *Donoghue v Stevenson*, a Plaintiff must actually have consumed the adulterated drink or food wholly or partially and inconsequence of which the Plaintiff must suffer injury. In the case of *Donoghue v Stevenson* (1) Lord Atkin in enunciating the principles said as follows:

> *My Lords, if your Lordship accept the view that this pleading discloses a relevant cause of action you will be affirming the proposition that by Scots and English law alike a manufacturer of products, which he sells in such a form as to show that he intends them to reach the ultimate customer in the form in which they left him, with no reasonable possibility of intermediate examination, and with the knowledge that the absence of reasonable care in the preparation or putting up of the products will result in an injury to the consumer's life or property owes a duty to the consumer to take that reasonable care.*

It is important to point out that in that case, the Plaintiff had partially consumed the adulterated ginger beer and the sight of the dead snail caused her shock and she also had a bout of gastroenteritis which necessitated her being hospitalized. In the case of *Continental Restaurant and Casion Ltd v Arida Chulu* (2) the Plaintiff had partially consumed the contaminated soup before she saw the dead cockroach. Similarly in the case of *Zambian Breweries Plc v Reuben Mwanza* (3) the Plaintiff had partially consumed the adulterated beer before he saw the dead lizard in the bottle. The principles laid down in *Donoghue v Stevenson* were based on the fact that the Plaintiff consumed the adulterated drink and suffered injury as a consequence thereof. We do not believe that it is permissible to extend those principles to a case of this nature where there has been no ingestion of the adulterated food or drink. The learned trial Judge was on firm ground in holding as he did and his ground of appeal cannot succeed.

(Continued)

(Continued)

We shall deal with the second and third grounds of appeal together as we believe that they are interrelated. There is no dispute that the bottle of sprite produced in the court below was adulterated as it contained a dead cockroach. Section 3(b) of the Foods and Drugs Act makes it a criminal offence to sell any food or drink which is contaminated with any foreign matter. The penalties for a breach of this section are contained in Section 31(2) of the Act and these are, in the case of a first offence, a fine not exceeding one thousand penalty points or to imprisonment for a term not exceeding three months, or to both. Thus, it will be observed that the only remedies for a breach of Section 3(b) of the Food and Drugs Act are criminal sanctions and there is no provision for the recovery of damages in a civil suit. As the learned authors of Charlesworth on Negligence observed at paragraph 1104 *"it would seem that if the statute has imposed a penalty for its breach but was silent as regards any remedy in civil law for damages there may be a presumption initially that the remedy prescribed by the criminal law is the only remedy."* Further the learned authors go on to point out that unless the statute or regulations provide to the contrary, the burden rests on the Plaintiff to prove on a balance of probabilities that the breach of duty caused or materially contributed to his damage. In other words, negligence is only actionable if actual damage is proved, there is no right of action for nominal damages. As Lord Reading, C.J. said in the case of *E. Suffolk Rivers Catchment Board v Kent* [1941] A. C. 74 *"Negligence alone does give a cause of action, damage alone does not give a cause of action; the two must co-exist."* There was no injury or damage caused to the Appellant by the adulterated drink as he did not consume any part of it. Even Dr. Kawimbe the medical practitioner called by the Appellant in the court below admitted that no treatment was prescribed for the Appellant and his children for the *"nausea"* caused by the sight of a dead cockroach in an unopened bottle of sprite. Grounds 2 and 3 cannot also succeed and in the event we dismiss the appeal with costs, the costs are to be taxed in default of agreement.

Appeal dismissed

State of Montana (Plaintiff and Appellee) v Steven Joseph Wilmer (Defendant and Appellant)

DA 10-0159
Supreme Court of Montana
2011 MT 78; 360 Mont. 101; 252 P.3d 178; 2011 Mont. LEXIS 109
March 2, 2011, Submitted on Briefs
April 19, 2011, Decided

On January 27, 2009, Warden Michael Fegley (Fegley) received an anonymous tip from 1-800-TIP-MONT indicating Wilmer had a deer hanging on the side of his trailer since Thanksgiving. Fegley visited Wilmer's residence on January 28, 2009. Fegley observed a deer carcass that was dried out with frozen water in the chest cavity and mold growing on the

(Continued)

(Continued)

interior and exterior. The carcass was hanging on Wilmer's deck exposed to the elements. Based on Fegley's observations about the general appearance and texture of the carcass, he determined the meat was not fit for human consumption. After seeing the carcass and inquiring about the location of the animal tag, Fegley warned Wilmer that it was illegal to waste game, to kill an animal without a tag, and to fail to keep the tag attached to the animal at all times.

Fegley returned to Wilmer's residence on January 31, 2009. At that time, Wilmer presented Fegley with a deer tag marked for two different days, November 11, 2008 and November 19, 2008. When Fegley asked Wilmer what exact day the deer was shot, Wilmer responded that he didn't remember. Fegley explained to Wilmer that the standard for a violation of the law prohibiting waste of a game animal is whether the meat is fit for human consumption. According to Fegley, Wilmer's only response was "it's my deer, I can do with it what I want."

Fegley wrote Wilmer two tickets, Waste of a Game Animal and Failure to Tag the Carcass of a Game Animal. Fegley confiscated the carcass and put it in the back of his truck. For three days, the carcass remained uncovered in the bed of Fegley's truck. On February 3, 2009, Fegley photographed the carcass and disposed of it.

Wilmer was tried before a jury in the Mineral County Justice Court and convicted of both charges. Wilmer appealed to the District Court.

Prior to trial, Wilmer filed a motion in limine to exclude, among other things, the photographs Fegley took of the carcass and the testimony of Jerry Stroot (Stroot). Stroot is the owner and operator of Superior Meats. He has worked in meat processing for approximately thirty years and is certified by the United States Department of Agriculture in Hazardous Analysis of Critical Control Points in **food processing**. He also regularly attends Montana Meat Processors Association training. Stroot regularly inspects wild game to determine whether the meat is fit for human consumption. While Stroot had not personally inspected the deer carcass that Fegley seized from Wilmer's property, he had examined the photographs and was offered by the State to present expert testimony regarding the condition of the meat.

The District Court denied Wilmer's motion in limine and held a jury trial on December 30, 2009. Fegley, Wilmer, and Stroot all testified at trial. The photographs of the carcass were admitted over objection after Fegley testified that the carcass was in the same condition at the time of disposal as the day he confiscated it from Wilmer's property.

The jury found Wilmer guilty of both charges and the court sentenced him to twelve months in the county jail, all suspended, imposed the maximum **fine**, and suspended all of his hunting, fishing, and trapping privileges for twelve months. Wilmer now appeals.

Geertson Seed Farms, et al. (Plaintiffs) v Mike Johanns, et al. (Defendants)
No. C 06-01075 CRB

United States District Court for the Northern District of California

2011 U.S. Dist. LEXIS 129381

November 8, 2011, *Decided*

In 2006, Plaintiffs (alfalfa growers and environmental groups) brought suit challenging the decision of Defendant U.S. Department of Agriculture, Animal Health and Inspection Service ("APHIS") to deregulate RRA, alfalfa genetically engineered to resist the herbicide Roundup. Plaintiffs brought claims under the National Environmental Policy Act ("NEPA"), the Endangered Species Act ("ESA"), and the Plant Protection Act ("PPA"). Plaintiffs' claims related to APHIS having deregulated RRA without having first prepared an environmental impact statement ("EIS"). The Court granted summary judgment for Plaintiffs on their NEPA claim, finding that APHIS was required to prepare an EIS before deregulating RRA. The Court therefore held that it "need not address plaintiffs' claims under the ESA and PPA," and dismissed those claims without prejudice. The Court then invited the parties to meet and confer and to submit a proposed judgment to the Court. Defendants' proposed judgment "would have ... expressly [allowed] a continued planting of RRA subject to certain limited conditions."

The Court rejected Defendants' proposed judgment, and ultimately fashioned its own remedy, which consisted of: (1) vacating APHIS's June 2005 deregulation decision (the "vacatur"); (2) ordering the government to prepare an EIS before making a decision on the deregulation petition; (3) enjoining nationally the planting of any RRA pending the completion of the EIS and decision on the deregulation petition; and (4) imposing certain conditions on the handling and identification of already-planted RRA.

Defendants appealed, "challenging the scope of the relief granted but not disputing the existence of a NEPA violation." A divided panel of the Ninth Circuit affirmed. Defendants filed a petition for writ of certiorari, arguing that this Court had "imposed ... a permanent nationwide injunction against any further planting of a valuable genetically-engineered crop, despite overwhelming evidence that less restrictive measures proposed by an expert federal agency would eliminate any non-trivial risk of harm."

Third, it held that this Court had erred in enjoining APHIS from partially deregulating RRA until an EIS had been completed. The basis for this holding was that "[i]n our view, none of the traditional four factors governing the entry of permanent injunctive relief supports the District Court's injunction prohibiting partial deregulation." Finally, the Court held that this Court had erred in entering a nationwide injunction against planting RRA, both because (1) foreclosing any possibility of partial deregulation was wrong, then enjoining all parties from acting in accordance with such a decision was also wrong, and (2) the injunction had no "meaningful practical effect independent of [the] vacatur," and so the "drastic remedy" of an injunction was unwarranted.

Notes

1. The complexity in dealing with food safety in Sub-Saharan Africa was recognized during a high level meeting of African leaders to establish a Food Safety Authority. The African Union's Minister for Trade and Industry, Mr. Francois Kanimba stated, "In other parts of the world, such as European Union, there exists the "European Food Safety Authority and a Rapid Alert System for Food and Feed" (RASFF)....Our body could be along similar lines but *taking into consideration the several food safety, cultural, social, economic, political and even scientific peculiarities of our continent*" (Gretchen, 2012).
2. The Fifty-third World Health Assembly adopted WHA53.15 on Food Safety in May 2000. The resolution urges member countries among other efforts to "*to integrate food safety as one of their essential public health and public nutrition functions, and to provide adequate resources to establish and strengthen their food safety programmes in close collaboration with their applied nutrition and epidemiological surveillance programmes*" (World Health Organization, 2002).
3. For example, the Tanzania Food and Drugs Authority (TFDA) is "responsible for controlling the quality, safety and effectiveness of food, drugs, herbal drugs, cosmetics and medical devices." It was established under the Tanzania Food, Drugs and Cosmetics Act No. 1, 2003. See International Regulatory Affairs Updates (2009).
4. "Safety is only one of many attributes of food, and consumer preferences for safety are typically modeled using a multiattribute utility function that recognizes possible trade-offs among attributes". See Hoffman (2010).
5. This discussion is based on Ackerman (see Rose-Ackerman, 1991).

Questions

1. Some have suggested that climate change is a cause of foodborne hazards. What is your opinion, and why?
2. Why would one wish to search for information about product quality and risks?
3. Explain the difference between the private ex post and regulatory ex ante approaches.
4. In your own words, describe the *Wingspread Statement* and provide an example.

References

Gretchen, G., 2012. African Union Makes Plans for Food Safety Authority. Food Safety News. <http://www.foodsafetynews.com/2012/11/african-union-makes-plans-for-food-safety-authority/#.VtiuTuYYOB0>.

FAO, 1996. Rome Declaration on World Food. World Food Summit 1996, Rome, Italy, 13–17 November 1996. Available at: <http://www.fao.org/docrep/003/w3613e/w3613e00.htm>.

Henson, S., 2003. The Economics of Food Safety in Developing Countries. FAO, ESA Working Paper No. 03-19, p. 2.

Hoffman, S., 2010. Food Safety Policy and Economics: A Review of the Literature. Resources for the Future (RFF) Discussion Paper, RFF DP 10-36, p. 14 (viewed online at <http://www.rff.org/files/sharepoint/WorkImages/Download/RFF-DP-10-36.pdf> (14.08.15).

International Regulatory Affairs Updates, 2009. Regulatory Bodies in Africa. Available at: <http://www.iraup.com/results.php?page_name=regions_africa>.

Josling, T., Roberts, D., Orden, D., 2004. Food Regulation and Trade: Towards a Safe and Open Global System: An Overview and Synopsis. Selected Paper prepared for presentation at the American Agricultural Economics Association Annual Meeting, Denver, Colorado, August 1–4, 2004.

Merriam Webster's Collegiate Dictionary, 10th Edition. <http://www.merriam-webster.com/dictionary/standard>.

New Partnership for Africa's Development (NEPAD) (n.d.). Africa Biosciences Initiative (ABI). <http://www.nepad.org/foodsecurity/africa-biosciences-initiative-abi/about>.

Rose-Ackerman, S., 1991. Regulation and the Law of Torts, *The American Economic Review* Vol. 81, No. 2, Papers and Proceedings of the Hundred and Third Annual Meeting of the American Economic Association (May, 1991), pp. 54–58.

Science and Environmental Health Network (HESN), 1998. Wingspread Conference on the Precautionary Principle. <http://www.sehn.org/wing.html> (viewed 10.01.13).

WAHO (West Africa Health Organisation), 2009. Programs. Available at: <http://www.wahooas.org/spip.php?article305&lang = en>.

World Health Organization (WHO), 2002. Global Strategy for Food Safety, (see ANNEX: RESOLUTION WHA53.15 ON FOOD SAFETY ADOPTED BY THE FIFTY-THIRD WORLD HEALTH ASSEMBLY (MAY 2000). Viewed at <http://apps.who.int/iris/bitstream/10665/42559/1/9241545747.pdf>.

World Health Organization (Africa), Regional Committee for Africa, 2007. Food Safety and Health: A Strategy for the WHO African Region. Fifty-seventh session, Brazzaville Republic of Congo, 27–31 August 2007. AFR/RC57/4.

Index

Note: Page numbers followed by "*b*", "*f*" and "*t*" refer to boxes, figures and tables, respectively.

Printed in the United States
By Bookmasters